SEXUALITY COUNSELING

AN INTEGRATIVE APPROACH

W9-AUK-591

Lynn L. Long
Stetson University

Judith A. Burnett
Stetson University

R. Valorie Thomas

PEARSON

Merrill
Prentice Hall

Upper Saddle River, New Jersey
Columbus, Ohio

Library of Congress Cataloging-in-Publication Data

Long, Lynn L.
  Sexuality counseling : an integrative approach / Lynn L. Long, Judith
A. Burnett, R. Valorie Thomas.
     P. ; cm.
  Includes bibliographical references and index.
  ISBN 0-13-171052-4
  1. Sex counseling. 2. Couples–Counseling of.
  [DNLM: 1. Sex Counseling–methods.] I. Burnett, Judith A. II.
Thomas, R. Valorie. III. Title.
  HQ60.5.L65 2006
  613.9'071–dc22

                                          2005012188

Vice President and Executive Publisher: Jeffery W. Johnston
Publisher: Kevin M. Davis
Editorial Assistant: Sarah Kenoyer
Production Editor: Mary Harlan
Production Coordinator: Karen Ettinger, TechBooks/GTS, York, PA Campus
Design Coordinator: Diane C. Lorenzo
Text Design and Illustrations: TechBooks/GTS
Cover Design: Ali Mohrman
Cover Image: Corbis
Production Manager: Laura Messerly
Director of Marketing: Ann Castel Davis
Marketing Manager: Autumn Purdy
Marketing Coordinator: Brian Mounts

This book was set in Garamond by TechBooks/GTS, York, PA Campus. It was printed
and bound by Hamilton Printing Company. The cover was printed by Coral Graphic
Services, Inc.

Pearson Education Ltd.
Pearson Education Singapore Pte. Ltd.
Pearson Education Canada, Ltd.
Pearson Education–Japan

Pearson Education Australia Pty. Limited
Pearson Education North Asia Ltd.
Pearson Educación de Mexico, S.A. de C.V.
Pearson Education Malaysia Pte. Ltd.

10 9 8 7 6 5 4 3 2 1
ISBN: 0-13-171052-4

PREFACE

Sexuality is a strong life force that involves physiological and psychological processes. It is pervasive and integral for all human beings, a way of "being" that enables us to express what we think or feel about our gender, our bodies, our self-images, our sexual choices, and our sexual preferences. Sexual messages emerge from our culture, parental role models, and peer relationships. Although sexual scripts are rooted in the early stages of development, they evolve throughout the life span.

Sexuality counseling explores sexual experiences as a part of life experiences and focuses on identifying and resolving underlying problems and strengthening positive relational and sexual functioning. It includes the examination of sexual attitudes and beliefs, values clarification, sex education, cultural messages, gender role development, and relational patterns.

AN INTEGRATIVE COUPLES' MODEL

We believe that an integrative couples' model for sexuality counseling offers counselors an opportunity to draw on multiple theories and skills so that they may use the most progressive methods for implementing change in couples' sexual expression and functioning. The integrative couples' model that we propose incorporates developing a nonblaming, shared view of the problem so that couples can join together and mobilize their resources in order to address their sexual and relational concerns. By developing a shared definition of their problem, couples collaborate with sexuality counselors to establish cognitive, behavioral, and affective goals that emphasize their statement of the problem. Interventions are chosen according to specific issues that have been identified in counseling and are drawn from a variety of theories.

The model is based on the premise that couples want to achieve a more satisfying intimate relationship. In order to do so, they focus on their strengths, resiliencies, and resources to contribute to change, and they implement them creatively in order to identify and practice new behaviors. They use their persistence, tenacity, and loyalty to continue maintaining their changes. As they near their goals, they are able to celebrate a wide range of successes from their hard work and accomplishments.

This book is organized according to the following premises:

1. Sexuality counseling is a unique discipline that requires specialized knowledge and training.
2. It is essential to have a broad theoretical understanding before a model can be used.
3. Historical, sociocultural, and developmental factors all influence sexuality counseling.
4. An integrative couples' model provides a systematic framework that allows sexuality counselors a wide array of choices for treating couples with sexual issues.
5. Because of the intimate nature of sexual issues, ethical considerations must be examined throughout the course of sexuality counseling.
6. A wide range of knowledge of special topics is essential in order to assess and treat clients with a variety of sexual concerns.

With these concepts in mind, we have organized our book into three parts. Part I addresses the conceptual and theoretical implications. Chapter 1 introduces the discipline of sexuality counseling and explores the impact of cultural and developmental factors on sexuality. It also examines the connections of intimacy, love, and sexuality, and provides a foundation for thinking about the development of sexual concerns. Chapter 2 provides a theoretical framework that explains the use of an integrative couples' model for counseling couples with sexual concerns.

Part II offers information on the practical applications of treatment issues. Chapter 3 introduces the integrative couples' model by providing information on assessment and the initial tasks of sexuality counseling. The primary task of this stage of the model is to develop a shared view of the problem that couples present when they come to counseling. Chapter 4 focuses on goal setting, treatment planning, interventions, and the selection process for determining a course of action in treatment. Chapter 5 describes methods for maintaining new behaviors and validating the successes that have been accomplished during counseling. Chapters 6 and 7 discuss female issues and male issues while offering interventions to treat a wide array of sexual concerns. Chapter 8 describes the most common sexually transmitted infections and diseases as well as the relational impact of these problems on couples.

Part III highlights special issues in sexuality counseling. Chapter 9 discusses sexual minorities and some of the particular concerns of each population, particularly gay and lesbian couples. Chapters 10 and 11 address aging and health-related issues in sexuality counseling and provide examples of treatment for chronically ill clients, disabled clients, and older adults and their partners. Chapter 12 offers information and treatment options for couples who engage in variant and atypical forms of sexual expression. Chapter 13 provides a treatment perspective for working with survivors of rape and their partners and outlines specific information on how to address their unique issues. Chapter 14 offers information on assessment and treatment of survivors of sexual abuse and incest and how the trauma associated with these issues affects sexuality.

All of the chapters in this book are interrelated so that assessment and intervention strategies can be generalized for a varity of couples concerns. It is a truly comprehensive book, building on the notion of a systemic, integrative model for sexuality counseling with couples.

ACKNOWLEDGMENTS

The ideas for the integrative couples' model for sexuality counseling evolved over many years of counseling, teaching, and consulting. We first would like to thank Mark Young and Lynn Long, who developed this relational model based on their work with couples. We would also like to convey our appreciation to clients over the past twenty years who have challenged us and helped us refine our thinking about sexuality counseling. Our students at Stetson University also provided feedback and support for this project, especially Jane Updyke and Ximena Mejia, who continue to return each year to share their expertise in the sexuality counseling class.

The development of this manuscript was a result of the untiring efforts and dedication of Donna Schick at Stetson University; our graduate assistants Elisa Carter, Machelle Votra, H. Leveta Horne, and Jacqueline Williams; and our student assistant Sara Collins. We also thank Larry Rosen for his caring and for his big heart throughout the writing of this book. We are grateful to Philip Toal, who served as a consultant on aspects of this project, and Andrea Trolice and Stephanie Preston, who assisted with research.

We are indebted to our editor, Kevin Davis, and the following reviewers: Carolyn R. Brandon, Western Illinois University; Chris Brown, University of Missouri at Kansas City; Marsha Carolan, Michigan State University; Emery J. Cummins, San Diego State University; Stephen Fortson, Wright State University; Steven M. Harris, Texas Tech University; Robert E. Hayes, Ball State University; Philip Hemphill, Tulane University; Michael S. Kelly, Henderson State University; Frances A. Martin, South Dakota State University; Lin Myers, California State University at Stanislaus; D. Kim Openshaw, Utah State University; Anne Petrovich, California State University at Fresno; and William M. Walsh, University of Northern Colorado. All of these individuals offered feedback and provided continued support and ideas for strengthening and shaping the direction of this book. Thanks for staying the distance with us.

We also thank Bogusia Molina for offering suggestions for an ethical framework for this manuscript.

A very special thank you is extended to Richard H. Harris for his expert counsel, generosity, friendship, and encouragement.

It is with love and gratitude that we remember Lynn Long's late parents, Dr. Osborne and Mary Littleford, for inspiring her career path as a marriage and family therapist. We also acknowledge her sisters Candy and Heather, brother Ted, and in-laws J.C. and Cheryl for their witty anecdotes about family challenges and strengths and reaffirming what it means to be a family.

On a light note, we wish to thank Lynn Long's bridge group—Sharon Foster, Maureen Crowell, Gwynne Homan, Debi Crouch, Marsha Johnson, Jan Ariko, Pat Arcidiacono, Susan Dolan, and Linda Seay—for always keeping topics of sex and sexuality in the forefront throughout the duration of this project. In addition, we thank her women's tennis team at Fort Gatlin for their enthusiasm and the examples they provided. We offer a special thank you to Linda Coleman for the lingerie display.

We also wish to express our gratitude to Judith Burnett's parents, Frank and Gwendolyn Burnett, for their unconditional love, encouragement, prayers, and sacrifice, and to her brother, sister-in-law, and niece—John, Lydia, and Jordan Burnett—for their affection, humor, and ongoing support. In addition, we thank her parents-in-law, Monroe and Ruth Manning, for their kindness, faith, and generosity. Judith's extended family—William and Gail Seeney; Gloria Wagner; Robert Wagner Jr.; Terri Seeney; Joelle, Leo, and Robert Lynch; Joshua, Stephanie, and Jazmyne Seeney; Judith and Alison Case; and Charles, Denise, Miles, and Kyle Christian—served as our foundations of familial love. We offer special recognition and remembrance to earlier generations of Judith's family for their conviction, determination, and courage.

We express sincere gratitude to Valorie Thomas's mother, Ann Wasman, for her unending encouragement, love, faith, and countless hours of caring for John Michael; to her late father, Robert Wasman, for his guiding spirit and gentle reminder that "in God all things are possible"; to her sisters—Trisha, Maureen, Bernadette, Mary, and Ave Maria—and brothers—John, Tom, Timothy, and Bobby—for providing humor and inspiration throughout this project. A special thanks to Valorie's parents-in-law, Mae and Gene Thomas, for their support and positive outlook, and to Susan and Lorin Dupree who provided timely encouragement. We thank friends and colleagues Jennifer Castner, Liz Harvey, Barbara Jordan, and Meredith Neil for their pearls of wisdom, and Valorie's mom's group, especially Kathy Walker and Karen Tortorici, for encouraging balance, self-expression, and spiritual reflection.

Again, we thank our families, particularly our husbands—Stan Long, Kelvin Manning, and Donald Thomas—for their patience and support of our many deadlines, missed weekends, and stressful times as we prepared this book.

Finally, we salute each other for the passion, dedication, tenacity, education, and support we have given and received during this endeavor. We embrace the challenges and joys of womanhood that we have shared over the past three years. We celebrate our friendship and collegiality with hopes that we have made a contribution to the field of sexuality counseling.

RESEARCH NAVIGATOR: RESEARCH MADE SIMPLE!

www.ResearchNavigator.com

Merrill Education is pleased to introduce Research Navigator—a one-stop research solution for students that simplifies and streamlines the entire research process. At www.researchnavigator.com, students will find extensive resources to enhance their understanding of the research process so they can effectively complete research assignments. In addition, Research Navigator has three exclusive databases of credible and reliable source content to help students focus their research efforts and begin the research process.

HOW WILL RESEARCH NAVIGATOR ENHANCE YOUR COURSE?

- Extensive content helps students understand the research process, including writing, Internet research, and citing sources.
- Step-by-step tutorial guides students through the entire research process from selecting a topic to revising a rough draft.
- Research Writing in the Disciplines section details the differences in research across disciplines.
- Three exclusive databases—EBSCO's ContentSelect Academic Journal Database, *The New York Times* Search by Subject Archive, and "Best of the Web" Link Library—allow students to easily find journal articles and sources.

WHAT'S THE COST?

A subscription to Research Navigator is $7.50 but is **free** when ordered in conjunction with this textbook. To obtain free passcodes for your students, simply contact your local Merrill/Prentice Hall sales representative, and your representative will send you the Evaluating Online Resource Guide, which contains the code to access Research Navigator as well as tips on how to use Research Navigator and how to evaluate research. To preview the value of this website to your students, please go to www.educatorlearningcenter.com and use the Login Name "Research" and the password "Demo."

BRIEF CONTENTS

CONTENTS

INTRODUCTION TO SEXUALITY COUNSELING

KEY CONCEPTS

- An integrative approach to sexuality counseling provides a step-by-step model for conceptualization and treatment of sexual concerns.
- A shift in focus from individually oriented sexual dysfunctions to systemic couple-based treatment is a cornerstone of an integrative couples model for sexuality counseling.
- Sexuality is an integral part of self-expression that is informed by our physical and psychological views of self, sexual choices, and identification as male or female.
- The *Diagnostic and Statistical Manual of Mental Disorders IV-TR* is the recognized sourcebook for the diagnosis of psychosexual disorders.
- Sexual disorders are conceptualized as clinically significant behavioral or psychological syndromes or patterns that occur in an individual.
- Sexual dysfunction refers to disturbances in sexual needs and wants as well as physical and emotional changes that typify the sexual response cycle.
- Experts in the field often use the terms *disorders* and *dysfunctions* interchangeably.
- Persons of various ages, cultures, beliefs, and abilities benefit from sexuality counseling.
- Historical, social, and developmental factors all influence sexuality counseling.
- Counselors' understanding of their personal values and ethics regarding sexuality is an important first step for treating couples with sexual concerns.
- Cultural aspects of sexuality include cultural influences, gender role socialization, and communication patterns and gender in relationships.
- Sexuality and love are closely connected and include three key elements: passion, intimacy, and commitment.
- Intimacy is more than sexuality. It is at the core of loving relationships and occurs when people share meaning and achieve relatedness, attachment, and unity.
- Couples must explore and recognize sexual myths—the faulty explanations that most often lead to errors in judgment regarding sexual expectations in a relationship.
- Annon's P-LI-SS-IT model offers an ethical guideline for clinical decision making when treating sexual problems.

For many years counselors have recognized the diversity of styles and patterns of human sexual expression. However, most of the literature about human sexuality was found in medical textbooks where attention was focused on the biological and physiological aspects of sexual functioning. In recent years, sexuality has been thought about more broadly than just information about sexual organs and their functions. Sexuality is a strong life force involving physiological and psychological processes (L'Abate & Talmadge, 1987).

Sexuality is an integral part of self-expression that is informed by our views of self, our sexual choices, our identification as male or female, and our physical selves (L'Abate & Talmadge, 1987). Sexual scripts based on culture, parental role models, and peer relationships form during early childhood development. Our sexual scripts are deeply rooted in early stages of development but evolve throughout the lifespan (L'Abate & Talmadge, 1987, p. 24).

Sexuality counselors address a couple's desire to participate in sexual activity, improve self-image, and enrich their sexual lives. Couples may present with a sexuality-related issue, such as gender identity confusion, infertility, sexual abuse, or health issues that may also manifest in one or more sexual dysfunctions. Similarly, sexual dysfunctions (hypoactive sexual desire, vaginismus, erectile dysfunction, premature ejaculation) may result in a variety of sexuality-related problems and can be addressed in sexuality counseling as well.

These interacting influences contribute to an increasing need for sexuality counseling services. We believe that the field of sexuality counseling must address the interaction between sexual expression and interpersonal problems, as well as the interaction between sexual expression and physiological problems. Sexuality counseling must also pay close attention to a couple's relationship, the most important aspect of sexuality.

1988). Based on this premise, sexuality counseling is a dynamic interactional process between counselors and clients that facilitates exploration and understanding of connections between sexual desires, practices, attitudes, ideals, and duties (Rosen & Weinstein, 1988). Furthermore, sexuality counseling with couples helps them address the underlying relational problems that are influenced by each partner's sexual experiences.

Sexuality Counseling: An Integrative Approach focuses on couples' sexual issues, taking into account historical, sociocultural, and developmental factors. These influences have a broad impact on couples' sexual scripts and include their sexual interactions, behaviors, and choices. By focusing on these interrelated factors, we can begin to understand the complexity of couples' relational and sexual concerns.

We will also focus on female and male sexual functioning, the impact of sexually transmitted infections/diseases on couples, counseling sexual minorities, aging and health-related issues, sexual variations within couples' relationships, and survivors of rape and incest and the effects on their sexuality. Through the use of a step-by-step, integrative model for sexuality counseling, we will highlight the therapeutic process. Specific intervention strategies for each step and for specific populations will be emphasized. We propose a change in focus from working with individual sexual dysfunctions to a systemically oriented model focusing on couples' sexual well-being.

SEXUALITY COUNSELING DEFINED

Sexuality counseling is a process that addresses sex education, values clarification, exploration of sexual attitudes and beliefs, and exploration of self-image, sexual identity, gender role development, and relationship issues (Rosen & Weinstein, 1988a). The identification and examination of sexual beliefs and practices as a natural part of a person's life experiences is designed to strengthen positive sexual functioning, facilitate relational connectedness, and find solutions to sexual problems (Rosen & Weinstein, 1988a). The overall goal of sexuality counseling is to improve relational and sexual functioning.

It might be helpful to think of the word *sex* as biological maleness or femaleness and myriad styles of sexual activity and the word *sexuality* as a wide-ranging concept of the total person (Rosen & Weinstein, 1988). This definition of sexuality includes biological, psychological, and social attributes (Rosen & Weinstein,

THE EMERGING FIELD OF SEXUALITY COUNSELING

Over the past few decades, sex therapy and counseling has traditionally been defined as the assessment, diagnosis, and treatment of psychosexual disorders, as described in the *Diagnostic and Statistical Manual of Mental Disorders IV-TR* (American Psychiatric Association [APA], 2000). During this period, the focus was primarily on the individual who was diagnosed with a sexual dysfunction, with minimal attention paid to the relational aspects of sexuality problems.

Although there have been many attempts to clarify fundamental differences between sexuality counseling and sex therapy, this book will focus specifically on sexuality counseling with couples and will address issues regarding the training of the practitioner, type of treatment, the setting of treatment, and the degree of specificity of the problem. We will not debate the issues of sexuality counseling versus sex therapy, nor become involved in the impossible task of differentiating clearly between the two disciplines. We will instead offer Annon's P-LI-SS-IT model, described later in this chapter, as an ethical guideline for counselor determination of competency related to the treatment of sexual issues (Annon, 1974, 1975).

Typically, sexuality counseling with couples has included the behavioral and cognitive-behavioral approaches to the treatment or remediation of sexual disorders or sexual dysfunctions as developed by Masters and Johnson (1970) and Kaplan (1974). Sexual disorders are referred to by Masters and Johnson (1970) and Kaplan (1974) as clinically significant emotional, cognitive, or behavioral patterns that occur in individuals and are manifested in their relationships. Sexual dysfunction refers to disturbances "in sexual desire and in the psychophysiological changes that characterize the sexual response cycle" (APA, 2000, p. 535). We will be using the terms *disorder* and *dysfunction* interchangeably, which is similar to descriptions of psychosexual disorders and sexual dysfunctions found in the *DSM IV-TR* (APA, 2000). We believe, however, sexuality counseling encompasses a broader perspective which includes the historical, sociocultural, developmental, and relational aspects of sexual behavior. By defining sexuality counseling in broader terms, the totality of the individual along with the couple's system can be conceptualized systemically, providing multiple opportunities for intervention. Although treatment may address single or multiple diagnoses for each individual, partners are treated as a unit in the integrative model because their sexual scripts impact and are impacted by each other. In order to use the integrative couples model effectively, sexuality counselors must be trained in and understand assessment, diagnosis, and treatment of sexual disorders in addition to possessing the knowledge and skills to work with couples from a systemic framework.

TRAINING OF SEXUALITY COUNSELORS

Training requirements can vary from state to state, and national training standards—for example, through the American Association of Sex Educators, Counselors, and Therapists (AASECT)—are specific regarding membership and certification (see www.aasect.org for specific information on training standards). AASECT provides a national registry of certified sex educators,

sexuality counselors, and sex therapists. It also provides continuing education opportunities as well as a code of ethics for sexuality practice. Prior to treating clients, sexuality counselors must decide whether they possess the training, knowledge, and expertise required to counsel clients effectively through the use of the P-LI-SS-IT decision-making model described later in this chapter.

People at all life stages—children, adolescents, midlife and aging adults—as well as the physically and emotionally disabled may have myriad needs that can be served by sexuality counselors (Rosen & Weinstein, 1988a). Professionals holding a variety of degrees (MA, EdS, and PhD) and professional licenses (marriage and family therapist, mental health counselor, licensed professional counselor, social worker, psychologist, and psychiatrist) may be trained to provide sexuality counseling services in order to meet these needs.

PEOPLE WHO BENEFIT FROM SEXUALITY COUNSELING

There is no archetype for the person who needs and will benefit from sexuality counseling. Instead, sexuality counseling helps persons of various ages, cultural backgrounds, beliefs, and abilities. In addition, there are historical, social, and developmental factors that will have an impact on a person's sexual problems.

Historical Factors

The need for sexuality counseling is supported by a variety of historical factors, most notably the way that gender roles and sexual standards of right and wrong have changed over time. For example, during the 1950s, women served primarily as wives and mothers, whereas men served as breadwinners and heads of households. Characteristics such as warmth and empathy were seen as feminine, whereas strength and aggressiveness were identified as masculine (Rosen & Weinstein, 1988a). In more recent times, a wider range of behaviors and feelings have become common for both males and females.

Sexual standards of right and wrong have also changed over time. Once considered unacceptable, sexually assertive behavior and premarital sexual activity by women is now considered acceptable in many cultures (Rathus, Nevid, & Fichner-Rathus, 2000; Rosen & Weinstein, 1988a). Adaptation and adjustment issues related to these changing gender roles and sexual standards have impacted sexual and relational roles. For example, many women are involved in busy careers similar to their male partners. The demands of these careers can negatively impact time for sexual intimacy. Flexibility in role definitions and expectations is critical to the survival of intimate relationships (Young & Long, 1998). Contemporary couples must be willing to function outside of traditional male and female gender roles in order to negotiate multiple challenges such as child rearing and career responsibilities. Sexuality counselors can help couples negotiate and, when appropriate, cross over traditional boundaries to promote relational health and satisfaction.

Social Factors

Sexual Coercion

In addition to changing gender roles and sexual standards, allegations and incidents of rape, sexual abuse, and sexual harassment are increasingly prevalent. Historically, the incidence of rape has been seriously underreported (Schafran, 1995). High-profile cases, such as the Tailhook incident in which naval aviators sexually assaulted unsuspecting females, the rape allegations presented against William Kennedy Smith in 1991 and 2004 and Kobe Bryant in 2003–2004, and the sexual harassment allegations by Anita Hill during the 1991 Senate confirmation hearings of Supreme Court Justice Clarence Thomas, highlight the increased attention being paid to sexual aggressors and their victims (Rathus et al., 2000).

Many survivors are extremely distressed following sexual assault (Valentiner, Foa, Riggs, & Gershny, 1996). Sexuality counselors can provide treatment for the emotional, relational, and sexual aftermath of sexual coercion.

Childhood Sexual Abuse

The sexual abuse of children is currently a major social problem. Although it is not clear exactly how many children are sexually abused, the number is a significant one. Several researchers estimate that this number ranges from 4% to 16% of boys (e.g., Janus & Janus, 1993) and exceeds 20% of girls (Janus & Janus, 1993; Kohn, 1987).

Children who are sexually abused often experience significant emotional injury, including rage, self-destructive behavior, sexual promiscuity, fearfulness, low self-esteem, mistrust of others, somatic complaints, and sexual dysfunction (Beitchman et al., 1992; Green, 1993; Rathus et al., 2000; Thompson & Rudolph, 2000). The effects of childhood sexual abuse are often long-lasting. For example, female survivors of sexual abuse are more likely to feel depressed, experience low self-esteem, and have problems with sexuality (Hoagwood, 1990; Wincze & Carey, 2001).

Substance Abuse

The use of alcohol and drugs is often identified as an adjunct to sexual activity and connected with a liberated social role (Rathus et al., 2000). Alcoholism is a serious health problem in the United States. The occasional use of alcohol and other drugs can lead to sexual difficulties when people mistakenly attribute the sexually dampening effects of alcohol and drugs to causes within themselves. If they are unable to perform sexually after having several alcoholic drinks and do not recognize that alcohol can depress performance, they might believe that something else is wrong. This belief can create anxiety at the next sexual opportunity and prevent normal functioning. Continued anxiety at subsequent sexual opportunities might set off an unproductive cycle in which self-doubts prompt more anxiety, leading to repeated failure. Sexuality counselors can work with couples to understand and reverse this cycle. Although substance abuse may occur at any stage of the life cycle, it may be more pronounced during developmental crises in couples' lives.

Developmental Factors

Developmental factors also contribute to the need for sexuality counseling as sexual issues emerge at various stages in the life cycle. According to Carter and McGoldrick (1980), there are two key factors that impact couples' sexual development: vertical stressors and horizontal stressors. Vertical stressors include relational patterns that are transmitted from one generation to another. These patterns involve family attitudes, secrets, taboos, hopes, failures, expectations, and emotional struggles (Carter & McGoldrick, 1980). Horizontal stressors include predictable events that occur as families move from one life cycle stage to another. Those transitions that occur in the normal course of couple development include the birth of a child, parenting adolescent children, children leaving home, and the death of a parent

(Carter & McGoldrick, 1980; Young & Long, 1998). For example, parents with young children may struggle with finding time for sexual intimacy. Similarly, age-related physical changes such as menopause and health concerns raise sexuality issues. Society's emphasis on youthfulness as an important ingredient to sexual attractiveness creates considerable stress during middle adulthood. Changes in self-image—from graying and thinning hair to concerns about physical and sexual attractiveness—are factors that can influence sexuality. There are physical changes (e.g., changing waistlines, perimenopause, and menopause) as well as lifestyle considerations (e.g., a new family constellation that involves caring for aging parents) that impact sexual relationships. Other factors such as career shifts, workplace competition, and retirement also influence sexuality at various developmental stages. Horizontal stressors that affect sexuality also include unpredictable life events such as unexpected death, accident, loss of a job, loss of income, infidelity, infertility, and chronic illness (Carter & McGoldrick, 1980; Young & Long, 1998).

In addition to understanding the historical, social, and developmental factors influencing couples' sexual functioning, sexuality counselors must examine their own ethical standards and sexual histories and clearly formulate their values and beliefs about sexuality.

ETHICAL CONSIDERATIONS IN SEXUALITY COUNSELING

Counselors are ethically responsible for providing the best treatment possible while protecting their clients' well-being (Corey, Corey, & Callanan, 2003). Codes of ethics serve to guide practitioners toward responsible practice while holding them accountable for their professional behavior (Herlihy & Corey, 1996). Codes of ethics are available from a variety of professional organizations—the American Association for Marriage and Family Therapy (AAMFT), the American Psychological Association (APA), the American Counseling Association (ACA), the American Mental Health Counselors Association (AMHCA), and the National Association of Social Workers (NASW) to name a few. Although the content of their respective codes is similar, differences exist in their areas of emphasis and specialization (Corey et al., 2003).

Counselors who plan to work with individuals or couples with sexual problems or dysfunctions should be familiar with and adhere to ethical codes specifically created for sexuality practice. The *Code of Ethics* of AASECT provides guidelines for individuals interested in "promoting understanding of human sexuality and healthy sexual behavior" (AASECT, 2004, p. 1). These guidelines describe the "rules of ethical conduct for practice-related conditions, qualities, skills, and services" (AASECT, 2004, p. 1) encouraging self-regulation among its members and adherence to legal requirements.

Burlew and Capuzzi (2002) provide the following highlights of the five principles of AASECT ethical codes:*

Principle 1: Competence and Integrity Competence and **integrity** refers to your own ability to provide sexuality counseling in terms of your training, as well as your basic integrity as a human being and practitioner. It requires members to: have appropriate training in sex education, counseling, therapy, and supervision; recognize your limits of competence; help the [client] identify your **credentials** and training: participate in **continuing education**; demonstrate integrity in all interactions with the public (e.g., not paying for referrals); and refer when you are **emotionally, physically, or otherwise impaired**.

Principle 2: Moral, Ethical, and Legal Standards Moral, Ethical, and Legal Standards refers to your judgment as it relates to ethical practice in such situations as dual relationships and supervision. It requires members to: have some type of supervision, regardless of level of experience or training; avoid dual relationships; not violate any [client's] legal rights; not discriminate; be honest in advertising your services; act in accordance with AASECT ethics; follow the ethical guidelines of other professional affiliations; and report ethical violations within thirty (30) days to the Chair of the AASECT Ethics Committee.

Principle 3: Welfare of the Consumer [or Client] The *Code of Ethics* begins this section with: "The AASECT member shall accept that the [client] is in a unique position of **vulnerability** in respect to services related to sex education, counseling, therapy, and supervision, and shall constantly be mindful

---

*From *Sexuality Counseling* (pp. 11-12), by L. D. Burlew and D. Capuzzi, 2003. Hauppauge, NY: Nova Science Publishers. Copyright 2003 by Nova Science Publishers. Reprinted with permission.

of the responsibility for protection of the [client's] welfare, rights and best interests and for the rigorous maintenance of the trust implicit in the educational, counseling, or therapeutic alliance" (p. 15). This principle requires members to: make sure [clients] are clear about your abilities/training, nature of services, **limitations, personal values**, exceptions to confidentiality, and **financial** issues; keep all information from a [client] confidential; obtain legal determination for the **release of any information** about a [client]; divulge a [client's] information only under certain circumstances (e.g., [client] provides a **written and informed consent; clear and imminent danger** to the [client] or another); get written consent from any [client] to use his/her information in any **research or publication**; deal with records within the guidelines provided; . . . **use standard of practice** for **diagnosing, treatment planning, evaluation**; not engage in sexual behavior at any time because "the counseling or therapeutic relationship is deemed to continue in perpetuity" (p. 16); terminate when appropriate.

Principle 4: Welfare of Students, Trainees, and Others   The principle relates directly with and treating **students, trainees** and others in a professional and ethical manner. It is best described in the opening statement: "The [AASECT] member shall respect the rights and dignity of students, trainees, and others (such as employees), maintain high standards of scholarship, and preserve academic freedom and responsibility" (p. 16).

Principle 5: Welfare of Research Subjects   This principle requires that individuals involved as **subjects** in research must be treated professionally and appropriately. It begins with the statement: "The [AASECT] member shall conduct his/her investigations with respect for the dignity, rights, and welfare of the subjects. Research must be ethical and legal at its inception and not justified solely by its intended or achieved outcome" (p. 17). Seven guidelines are provided including concepts like informed consent, providing a clear purpose of the research, and a proposal for the research to be peer reviewed before beginning.

Professional codes such as this serve to guide practitioners when faced with complex ethical dilemmas. Knowledge of these codes, however, cannot ensure that practitioners will behave ethically. This responsibility lies with each individual practitioner and should be guided by thoughtfulness and consultation (Corey et al., 2003). Developing responsible ethical behavior begins with an awareness of personal values and beliefs about sexuality.

Examining Values and Beliefs

In order to provide services that promote client growth and development, sexuality counselors are ethically obligated to become "aware of their own values, beliefs, and behaviors and how these apply in a diverse society, and avoid imposing their values on clients" (American Counseling Association [ACA], 1995, sec. A.5.b.). This involves exploration of a counselor's personal feelings, attitudes, values, and beliefs about human sexuality and sexual behavior. It is well-documented that counselors' beliefs, attitudes, and values impact their therapeutic relationship with clients (Baruth & Manning, 2003; Corey et al., 2003; Young & Long, 1998). For example, sexuality counselors who believe that premarital sexual relations are immoral will need to understand and address how this belief impacts their ability to work with couples who are engaging in premarital sexual activity.

Values and beliefs influence ideas, feelings, thoughts, and behaviors about acceptable and unacceptable roles, communication styles, conduct, and practices in couples' relationships. Counselors must be able to help clients understand how these systems impact their sexual relationship and then help them to develop a common language and framework for addressing their problems and concerns.

A first step toward counselors' exploration of their values and beliefs is to become aware of their cultural and sexual beliefs, values, and attitudes about sexuality.

Counselor Self-awareness

There are several activities in which counselors can participate in order to develop their sexual self-awareness. They can engage mentors from sexual cultures different from their own who are willing to provide honest feedback regarding their sexual behaviors, attitudes, and beliefs. Other awareness activities focus on how, when, where, and what was learned about sexuality during childhood as well as personal comfort level with various sexual practices, orientations, and values. Figures 1.1 and 1.2 present awareness activities that might be used.

Counselor and Client Values

Both sexuality counselors and their clients are influenced by the values that guide them in making important life choices. Beliefs and preferences are at

Directions: Place an "X" in the corresponding box for each statement below.

	For Me			For Others		
SITUATION	*ACCEPTABLE*	*NEUTRAL*	*NOT ACCEPTABLE*	*ACCEPTABLE*	*NEUTRAL*	*NOT ACCEPTABLE*
Premarital genital touching						
Premarital intercourse						
Children masturbating in privacy of bedroom or bathroom						
Adolescents masturbating in privacy of bedroom or bathroom						
Adults masturbating in privacy of bedroom or bathroom						
Homo-sexuality						
Lesbianism						
Children's sex play (e.g., "doctor")						
Birth control for girls under age 18						
Anal intercourse						
Oral-genital stimulation						
Bisexuality						
Extramarital sexual relations						
Alternative forms of marriage						

FIGURE 1.1
Where I Stand on Sexuality

ASPECT OF HUMAN SEXUALITY	(1) AGE	(2) MAIN SOURCE	(3) POSITIVE (+) OR NEGATIVE (−) MESSAGES	(4) CHANGES
Human conception and birth				
Menstruation ("periods")				
Male erections				
Male ejaculations				
Female orgasm				
Sexual intercourse				
Birth control practice				
Masturbation				

FIGURE 1.2
Awareness Activity: Learning About Sexuality

(1) At what age did you learn about this particular aspect of human sexuality?

(2) Who and what were your main source(s) of information on that aspect of human sexuality? (In other words, how did you find out?) Examples would be mother, father, sibling, cousin, best friend, books, school, etc.

(3) As you were learning about this aspect of sexuality from your source of information (be it person or book), were the messages that you picked up about this subject positive (+) or negative (−)?

(4) If you could start over and change anything about the way in which you learned about this aspect of sexuality, what would you change?

the core of these values and are formed over years of experiences.

There is a wide range of definitions of values. Maslow (1971) describes values as instinctive drives toward health. Corey et al. (2003) define values as "beliefs and attitudes that provide direction to everyday living" (p. 11). When addressing issues of sexuality, counselors are required to be aware of personal values and how they influence interactions with clients. Awareness helps counselors recognize how these values influence their language, tone of voice, and body posture as well as all other forms of verbal and nonverbal communication with clients. For example, a client may state "I am feeling much better about masturbating myself since our last session." If the counselor responds with a nonjudgmental circular question (how is this helping you?) but with raised eyebrows or a facial grimace, the client may recognize the nonverbal cues and feel embarrassed about the self-disclosure. The client may then be reluctant to self-disclose in subsequent sessions.

Ethical codes have been created to ensure that counselors' values do not interfere with decisions that promote client welfare and emphasize positive growth (Corey et al., 2003; Kitchener, 1984).

Recognizing Counselors' Values

In order to facilitate a self-awareness of values, we suggest that sexuality counselors answer the following questions:

Should sex be reserved for married people only?

Is sex an expression of love and commitment?

What do you think about casual sex?

What do you think about group sex?

What do you think about extramarital sex?

What do you think about premarital sex?

What do you think about homosexuality? Bisexuality?

What do you think about teenage sex?

Examining their answers to these questions helps sexuality counselors gain awareness of their personal values and offers clarification in order to make more competent clinical decisions.

Perspective-taking

An important step in counselor self-awareness and values clarification is to engage in perspective-taking with clients—putting yourself in another person's position and understanding that person's viewpoint. Young and Long (1998) discuss the importance of perspective-taking while working with couples who want to improve sexual communication and interactions. Gaining an awareness of values and the impact they have on others increases the potential for positive outcomes of sexuality counseling.

Once sexuality counselors have successfully explored their values and beliefs and have gained a clearer perspective of their beliefs, they can assist couples as they undergo a similar process in learning how to understand each other regarding issues of sexuality. Sexuality counselors can guide couples as they learn about themselves and each other, perhaps by answering the following questions:

Who am I as a sexual being?

Who is my partner as a sexual being?

Who are we as sexual partners when we are together?

After couples have explored their values and beliefs they can make informed choices based on their shared values, rather than the implicit family or societal conditions each partner brings to the relationship.

The process of clarifying clients' values begins at intake, and continues throughout the counseling process. This assessment process will be examined in detail in Chapter 3. In addition to understanding sexuality counselors' and clients' values and beliefs and the impact they have on each other, we must be aware of the cultural aspects of sexuality.

CULTURAL ASPECTS OF SEXUALITY

Cultural factors have been connected with sexual dysfunctions and problems (Rathus et al., 2000). These factors include cultural influences, gender and gender roles, and communication patterns and gender in relationships.

Cultural Influences

Culture has been broadly defined by researchers as being group-oriented (a group being two or more individuals) and as having social structure, kinship systems, inclusion and exclusion criteria, historical and developmental contexts, and rules for inappropriate and appropriate behavior, attitudes, beliefs, and values (Axelson, 1999). Culture has also been described as "the ways a people have learned to respond to life's problems" (Diller, 2004, p. 59). Counselors can be members of multiple cultural groups and respond to life's difficulties in diverse ways. The interaction and integration of these cultural contexts can significantly impact their professional orientation. The *Operationalization of the Multicultural Counseling Competencies* (Arredondo et al., 1996) provides a framework that incorporates the personal dimensions of identity model (Arredondo & Glauner, 1992) and focuses on building the awareness, knowledge, and skills needed to be an effective counselor when working with multicultural and diverse populations. Arredondo et al. (1996) conclude that in order to be culturally competent, counselors must be aware of their own cultural values and biases. We would take their model one step further to include awareness of one's own sexual values and biases.

Assimilation and Acculturation

Culture is a powerful force in each person's sexual identity, although couples may not always recognize the role that culture plays in their sexual relationship. It is thus particularly challenging for sexuality counselors to help couples make the connection between culture and sexuality. Counselors must demonstrate respect and sensitivity for clients' culturally based sexual behavior and help them view whatever problems they have encountered as solvable ones. Counselors must also consider the impact of assimilation and acculturation status on a couple's sexual relationship.

Assimilation.   Cultural group members vary considerably in the extent of their assimilation with other cultures. This issue takes on particular relevance in the United States, given the considerable ethnic, racial, and cultural diversity found there. Assimilation means the convergence of "two distinct cultures to create a new and unique third cultural form" (Diller, 2004, p. 114). This assimilation process "consists of a shift toward the dominant culture coupled with a rejection of one's culture of origin" (Aponte & Johnson, 2000, p. 21). Assimilation occurs through disconnection from one's culture of origin while developing a new cultural identity based on identification and affiliation with the majority group (Aponte & Johnson, 2000; LaFromboise, Coleman, & Gerton, 1993).

The assimilation process has significant implications on individual, relational, and societal levels. Couples risk being rejected by their families, cultural communities, and the majority culture if they do not follow the family structure they have learned over generations (Phinney, Chavira, & Williamson, 1992). Rejection by family, community, or society often places considerable stress on a couple and results in decreased intimacy in the relationship. A culturally sensitive counselor will be responsive to the individual and the relational impact of this inclusion and absorption process as well as the societal ethnocentrism that often underlies assimilation (Helms & Cook, 1999). If one member of a couple is a first-generation immigrant from Latin America and the other is a fifth-generation immigrant, they may experience differences in level of assimilation as well as relational and societal pressure that may impact their sexual connectedness.

Acculturation.   Acculturation occurs when a person adopts the cultural way of life of another cultural group, primarily those of the majority group culture (Diller, 2004; Helms & Cook, 1999). It is the "product of culture learning that occurs as a result of contact between the members of two or more culturally distinct groups" that includes "attitudinal and behavior change" (Casas & Pytluk, 1995, p. 158). With prolonged contact, it is assumed that intercultural borrowing or adapting will occur between diverse peoples. As a result of this intercultural transformation, original cultural and behavioral patterns will be modified (Diller, 2004).

Acculturation can cause emotional strain for bicultural couples and have a negative impact on their intimate relationships. Let's consider the example of a newly arrived Chinese woman with her Irish American (immigrant descendant) spouse. The expectation that she should initiate sexual intercourse and behave in a sexually provocative manner may create stress for her. She may feel compelled to uphold traditional cultural customs that expect sexual passivity for females. Also, she may believe it is inappropriate to openly discuss sexual matters. The divergence of this couple's culturally based sexual traditions could have significant impact on their ability to develop a satisfying intimate relationship. A counselor working with this couple should help them find a common language with which to communicate, paying particular attention to specific gender differences in their communication patterns (see Figure 1.3).

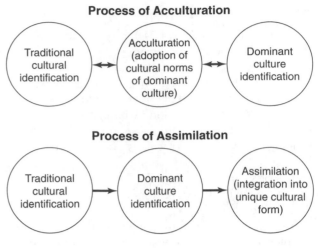

Process of Acculturation

Traditional cultural identification ⟷ Acculturation (adoption of cultural norms of dominant culture) ⟷ Dominant culture identification

Process of Assimilation

Traditional cultural identification → Dominant culture identification → Assimilation (integration into unique cultural form)

FIGURE 1.3
The Impact of Acculturation and Assimilation

Gender and Gender Roles

Gender

The term *gender* refers to cultural, social, and emotional features that are associated with maleness and femaleness (Gilbert & Scher, 1999). The term *sex* is used to designate biological identity as female or male (Andersen, 2003) and to describe the physiological aspects of human sexual behavior (Baumeister, 2000). Men and women often perceive different realities based on what they have consciously and unconsciously learned from family and society about gender. Because these beliefs about gender permeate our society, they can easily be overlooked. However, differences in attitudes about sexual expression can contribute to sexual problems in a relationship. For example, in the past men were shown to be more lenient in their values and attitudes about sex than were women (Snyder, Simpson, & Gangestad, 1986). Men were also more likely to participate in sex without intimacy (Whitley, 1988). More recent studies indicate that the so-called "double standard" is diminishing or has diminished entirely (Andersen, 2003; Sprecher & Hatfield, 1996). This may be partly due to changing gender roles in family structural systems.

Gender Roles

Gender roles play an important role in sexuality and cultural messages. Andersen (2003) describes gender roles as "the expectations for behavior and attitudes that the culture defines as appropriate for women and men" (p. 33). Children learn their gender roles from their parents through verbal mimicking and modeled behavior. Cognitive development theory asserts that once children understand the rules and roles inherent in their gender, they begin to act like "proper little girls" or "strong assertive boys." Once children come into contact with school personnel, friends, and media influences, their ideas about their gender are reinforced (Strong & DeVault, 1994).

As they approach adulthood, it is evident that there is a correlation between gender socialization and sexual expression. Sexual behavior is closely intertwined with gender roles and expectations, so much so that it is difficult to differentiate between them. The roles and expectations that we learn and internalize from our various cultures inform us as sexual beings. In some cultures, men are expected to be assertive or even aggressive, whereas women are expected to be compliant, passive, and subservient. It is often expected that men initiate sexual relations whereas women are expected to function as sentries guarding the sexual access gate (Gilbert & Scher, 1999). Although many men and women adhere to these roles, there are new possibilities to consider. Motherhood, career, and marital status have become options rather than rigid scripts for women. Men can take a more active role in parenting, even serving as the primary caregiver. Sexual scripts offer more equality of behavior. For example, more women are comfortable initiating sex and do not necessarily believe they are solely responsible for their partner's sexual pleasure.

Communication Patterns and Gender

Communication styles differ according to gender and gender roles, particularly in the use of verbal and nonverbal communication between men and women.

In verbal exchanges, women tend to communicate about emotions to maintain relationships whereas men tend to report facts (Tannen, 1994). Both verbal and nonverbal communication styles have cultural roots. For example, men and women have different cultural expectations regarding touch and personal space. Although women in general have a smaller personal space, in some cultures, such as African American culture, getting "too close" to a woman can be interpreted as negative aggression (Okun, Fried, & Okun, 1999).

How do these factors affect sexuality? Different communication agendas can often create confusion for couples. A woman may say "Turn off the television, I want to talk to you" although she may mean "I want to spend some time together and be close to you." His re-

sponse is likely to be "What do you want to talk about?" Another confusing style stems from the various uses of nonverbal communication around sexuality issues. Couples may use words to initiate or refuse sexual interaction, but nonverbal messages are used more frequently than verbal methods (Sprecher & McKinney, 1993). For example, one partner may avoid eye contact with the other and maintain a stiff posture rather than verbally reject sexual advances. Because nonverbal communication can be ambiguous, a couple's sexual relationship may be tinged with tension and embarrassment. When communication about sex is satisfactory, couples judge the sexual relationship and the relationship as a whole as satisfactory (Cupach & Comstock, 1990). Clear communication is one of the most important aspects for maintaining a healthy intimate relationship.

LOVE, INTIMACY, AND SEXUALITY

Definitions of intimacy have received considerable attention in the professional literature because intimacy has been identified as a fundamental factor in human relationships (Young & Long, 1998). "It is a relatively unique phenomenon within the animal kingdom—something we share with few other species (if any), and one that's singularly sophisticated in humans" (Schnarch, 1997, p. 101).

Intimacy is more than sexuality. It is at the heart of nurturing and emotionally nourishing relationships, and it is linked with maintaining positive relationships (Heller & Wood, 1998). Intimacy is described as occurring when people share meaning and achieve relatedness, attachment, and unity (Sternberg, 1986). Similarly, Weingarten (1991) also conceptualizes intimacy occurring when people share meaning or co-create meaning and are able to behave in ways that reflect their mutual interests. Waring (1988) describes intimacy as a complex interpersonal dimension that addresses a level of closeness in a relationship at a particular point or life stage.

Intimacy has also been described as an active process that involves attempts at closeness by exploring similarities and differences in emotions, cognitions, and patterns of behavior. Similarly, intimacy is referred to as self-understanding, including cognitive, emotional, and behavioral reactions as well as how partners disclose innermost feelings to each other. According to Hatfield (1988), intimate partners are open to sharing themselves through disclosure and revelation and to listening to each other's feelings, concerns, and secrets. Schaefer and Olson (as cited in Heller & Wood, 1998) describe intimacy as

> a process and an experience that is the outcome of the disclosure of intimate topics and sharing of intimate experiences, and an intimate relationship as two people who share intimate experiences over time and who expect continuity of the relationship and those experiences. (p. 273)

Schnarch (1997) cautions that intimacy includes much more than relational experiences. It is an "I-Thou" connection that involves awareness of separateness from one's partner with many aspects of self that remain to be shared. Separateness is maintained by keeping a clear and undistorted sense of self, managing personal anxieties, remaining unreactive to a partner's overreactions and tolerating discomfort in order to achieve personal and relational growth (Schnarch, 2002).

Why is intimacy such a difficult process to describe and why do most of us cite intimacy as one of the most important aspects of human relationships? Most people do not want to live their lives alone. However, the degree, intensity, and style of being intimate vary significantly from one person to another. Intimacy is culturally assumed to be a vital component of love, companionship, family connections, and sexuality (Sherman, Oresky, & Rountree, 1991). The intimacy experienced by a couple generally involves a gradual process of partners getting to know each other, a process that begins at the first encounter and continues throughout a couple's lifetime. Although intimacy is not essential for a successful marriage or relationship, it can be one of the most gratifying aspects of a close relationship and can provide stability and cohesiveness as couples face life challenges.

Couples who are able to hear each other's innermost thoughts satisfy a need to move beyond self to joining and becoming a part of another (Heitler, 1997). Because intimacy involves mutual sharing, it is assumed that bonding will occur between partners and that a safe haven will typically develop as well. Safety means that partners trust each other with all shared information and treat confidences with special care (Heitler, 1997). It also involves confidentiality, empathy, understanding, and acceptance without judgment or blame. When we talk intimately with someone, the desire for physical intimacy tends to arise as well (Heitler, 1997). Spiritual growth and development is also a benefit of relational intimacy (Heitler, 1997). For example, the more intimacy you have in a relationship, the more accepting you can be of both yourself and your partner.

There are also practical aspects of intimacy in relationships. Communicating candidly about emotions and perceptions enables couples to be more receptive and responsive to the wants and needs of each person (Heitler, 1997). Making shared decisions and resolving conflicts is usually more successful when couples experience a level of trust and understanding (Heitler, 1997).

Sexual Intimacy

When elements of trust, openness, love, affection, understanding, and emotional safety are present, couples are able to connect intimately and nourish their sexual relationship.

> Sexual expression, especially the act of intercourse, is one of the most vulnerable [and exciting acts] that a couple undertakes. The experience of lying nude with one's partner in the process of giving and receiving pleasure is a most vulnerable and dependent state. . . . The act of intercourse, of having a portion of another person's body inside another's body cavity [creates a physiological openness that provides emotional attachment and an intimate connection]. (L'Abate & Talmadge, 1987, p. 25)

However, sexual intercourse is not always an expression of intimacy and should not be offered as the primary ingredient for measuring a couple's level of intimacy in their relationship. It is easy at times to confuse sexual intercourse with sexual intimacy. Couples talk about the act of intercourse as their intimate time together. There are many types of sexual expression, all of which could be considered intimate if certain conditions exist. If the behavior also includes sharing of self and fostering feelings of closeness, then sexual intercourse is intimate. Rape is not intimacy. Depersonalizing a partner as an object to satisfy a physical need does not lead to intimacy.

Obstacles to intimacy can occur when there is misuse of power or control over another person, or when there is not mutual consent about acceptable and pleasurable sexual behaviors. Fear of performance, fear of subservience, and fear of losing oneself in the relationship all can create a sense of caution and can block intimacy (Sherman et al., 1991). Other obstacles are anger, fatigue, lack of attraction toward one's partner, differences in levels of sexual desire, fear of pregnancy or of infection, reminders of prior abuse or incest, or a partner's involvement in an extramarital relationship. Obstacles may appear in some instances, yet are absent at other times. These inconsistencies invite partners to be close and then push each other away when they are unable to tolerate or sustain closeness. Unfortunately, double messages exacerbate the obstacles and create mistrust in a relationship (Sherman et al., 1991).

Dimensions of Intimacy

It is useful to consider sexual intimacy within the context of other relational aspects of intimacy in order to understand a couple's interactions. Sexuality counselors assess couple's intimate qualities on physical, emotional, and spiritual levels. Waring (1988) has identified eight elements of intimacy:

1. *Conflict resolution*—the ease with which differences of opinion are resolved
2. *Affection*—the degree to which feelings of emotional closeness are expressed by the couple
3. *Cohesion*—a feeling of commitment to the relationship
4. *Sexuality*—the degree to which sexual needs are communicated and fulfilled by the [relationship]
5. *Identity*—the couple's level of confidence and self-esteem
6. *Compatibility*—the degree to which the couple is able to work and play together comfortably
7. *Autonomy*—the success to which the couple gains independence from their families of origin and their offspring
8. *Expressiveness*—the degree to which thoughts, beliefs, attitudes, and feelings are shared within the [relationship] (pp. 39–40)

Couples may be intimate in some aspects of their relationship, yet not in others. For example, they may be able to work and play together comfortably but be uncomfortable about their performance during sexual activities. Performance may be affected by fear of pregnancy, worry over infections, fatigue from chronic illness, stress from work or family, or any number of stressors or situations that impact sexual relationships. Sexuality counselors must be familiar with all aspects of intimate functioning in order to identify the presence of other factors that may influence couples' sexual expression.

Imbalances of Intimacy

Imbalances of physical and emotional closeness and distance occur when partners have different styles for establishing and maintaining intimacy in their relationship. Two typical patterns of imbalance are described by Roughan and Jenkins (1990):

1. Belongingness–separateness: This pattern involves one partner attempting to create and maintain a sense of closeness and belongingness in the relationship. This partner will tend to take most responsibility for planning and organizing[sic] activities which promote togetherness, sharing and emotional expression. The other partner . . . takes most responsibility for separateness and physical and emotional distance in the relationship . . . [either overtly or covertly through emotion and behavioral reactions]. Over time, the polarization of these roles produces feelings of frustration and anger in both partners. One partner will request more time together, while the other will try to establish boundaries and independence. As a result, hurt feelings lead to a breakdown in sexual intimacy.

2. Sexual intimacy–nonsexual intimacy: In this relationship pattern, one partner attempts to contribute to a sense of intimacy in the relationship mostly with sexual initiatives. This partner subscribes to a style whereby it is believed that sex is the correct and most appropriate medium for expressing love, affection, and caring. Sex is expected to lead to the creation of loving feelings and a fulfilling relationship. The other partner attempts to contribute to intimacy in the relationship by taking nonsexual initiatives. This partner subscribes to a sexual style whereby it is believed that certain nonsexual intimate behaviors (talking, emotional expression, nonsexual physical contact) are the most correct and most appropriate media for expressing love, affection, and caring. (pp. 133–134)

If these imbalances are not reconciled, a conflict can either escalate to become a crisis in the relationship or the couple can withdraw from each other physically and emotionally. Some couples remain stalled in this vicious cycle because they are unaware of their options or they are fearful of change in the relationship. Sexuality counselors help couples become aware of these patterns and intervene so that they create more productive ways of expressing and achieving intimacy in their relationship (Roughan & Jenkins, 1990).

Love and Intimacy

Two beliefs about intimate relationships are particularly widespread: the belief that they are based on love and the belief that they use skills to negotiate and accommodate each other. The first describes a romantic view of intimate relationships, and the second, a pragmatic one (Wile, 1993). Some experts believe that the sexual interactions of loving couples demonstrate the most intimate form of relating. Love drives them to emotional and physical closeness. Emotional closeness is satisfied through the acceptance and sharing of self, while the physical closeness is addressed through touch, affection, and sexual activity (Lowen, as cited in L'Abate & Talmadge, 1987). Couples who nurture their love tend to express more pleasure in their sexual relationship (L'Abate & Talmadge, 1987).

Most counselors reject the notion that people "fall in love." Rather, people grow to love one another, and love establishes itself in the relationship. Ideally, people love their partner and feel "in love" with that partner. Intimacy is the force that links "loving" someone with "being in love" with someone. "Love involves tenderness and compassion, as well as cuddling, stroking, and touching. . . . Sexual intimacy, at its highest level, is probably expressed best when physical sensations and emotions are fused with empathy and sensitivity" (McCary & McCary, 1984, p. 129). We believe that love and intimacy are understood most clearly when integrated with a couple's commitment to a physical and emotional relationship.

Sternberg's Triangular Theory of Love.   Sternberg's triangular theory of love emphasizes three elements: (a) passion, (b) intimacy, and (c) decision and commitment (Sternberg, 1986, 1988). This model, illustrated in Figure 1.4, proposes that love is based on the degree of intensity of the three elements. In addition, the style of love one experiences is relative to the connections of the dimensions (Young & Long, 1998). Sternberg (1986) describes stable, loving relationships as containing degrees of all three components of intimacy, passion, and commitment. Other definitions of intimacy have been described earlier in this chapter.

Passion may begin as sexual interest in another. "The drive that leads to romance, physical attraction, and sexual [feelings] can be described as passion" (Sperry & Carlson, 1991, p. 15). Passion may develop quickly but has a tendency to diminish in long-term relationships. Sometimes couples complain that their relationship has lost its "feeling" when in reality they are referring to a difference in the intensity of passion (Sperry & Carlson, 1991).

Loyalty in a relationship is maintained by a couple's decision to be with only one partner to the exclusion of all others. It includes an immediate decision to love one another and an enduring pledge to maintain and safeguard that love (Sperry & Carlson, 1991).

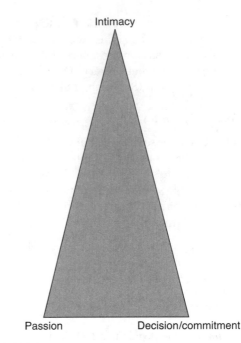

FIGURE 1.4
Sternberg's Triangular Theory of Love
Source: From "Triangulating Love" by R. J. Sternberg in *The Psychology of Love* (pp. 120–121), edited by R. J. Sternberg and M. L. Barnes, 1988, New Haven: Yale University Press. Copyright 1988 by Yale University. Reprinted with permission.

Intimacy and Sexuality Counseling.   Addressing emotional and physical intimacy must be a primary goal for sexuality counselors. Figure 1.5 presents some suggestions for helping couples develop intimacy in counseling. The interventions can be used with couples who express a variety of sexual concerns. Being able to achieve intimacy is an important variable in determining the health or pathology of a relationship. Messages about intimacy begin during early childhood and continue through adulthood. There are many methods to assess early childhood messages about intimacy. Chapter 3 provides additional information on assessment of familial and social influences through the use of a sexual genogram and sex history. Closeness and distance and other aspects of intimacy should be thoroughly explored in counseling in order to understand the impact of a couple's emotional intimacy on their sexual expression. Intimacy is a learned process and can be practiced in treatment if it has not been learned previously. Techniques to promote increased sexual pleasure can be prescribed for homework. Intimacy

1. Help partners assign good intentions to each other while they strengthen their intimate relationship.
2. Teach them active listening and how to paraphrase, summarize, and reflect feelings as they attempt to understand each other.
3. Explore gender myths and resentments.
4. Teach them to use "I" statements and to avoid blaming each other.
5. Help the couple understand that difference is a positive factor that keeps the relationship alive and interesting.
6. Help the couple create time to talk and problem-solve as well as time for play and relaxation.
7. Encourage expression of feeling as key ingredient in solution-focused discussions.
8. Eliminate unfair tactics from their conflicts such as blaming, diversions, silent treatment or negation, grocery-listing complaints, interruptions, humiliation tactics, and mixed messages.

FIGURE 1.5
Suggestions for Helping Couples Develop Intimacy in Counseling
Source: Copyright 1991 from *Solving Problems in Couples and Family Therapy* (pp. 179–187), by R. Sherman, P. Oresky, and Y. Rountree, 1991. Reproduced by permission of Routledge/Taylor & Francis Books, Inc.

is enhanced most frequently when partners are emotionally comfortable with each other and are engaging in a variety of pleasurable sexual activities (Russell, 1990).

Sexual Myths and Sexuality Counseling

Sexual myths play an important role in the maintenance of relationships. They may help people feel knowledgeable about sexuality and may become part of a person's belief system. At the same time myths may also have a negative impact, perhaps contributing to an avoidance of sex with beliefs such as "sex is for the young," or "menopause or a hysterectomy terminates a woman's sex life."

Myths are most dangerous when they are not recognized for what they are. Although some of us are content to believe that myths are what other people believe, many of us in fact understand that myths are faulty ideas or explanations without foundation that often lead to error and value judgments (Daines, 1990). However, we may be unaware of the effect myths have on our physical and emotional relationships. Zilbergeld (1999) has identified nine common myths with regard to male sexuality that should be explored in a counseling session when sexual issues are presented:

1. We're liberated folks who are very comfortable with sex.
2. A real man isn't into sissy stuff like feelings and communicating.
3. All touching is sexual or should lead to sex.
4. A man is always interested in and always ready for sex.
5. A real man performs in sex.
6. Sex is centered on a hard penis and what's done with it.
7. If your penis isn't up to snuff, we have a pill that will take care of everything.
8. Sex equals intercourse.
9. A man should make the earth move for his partner, or at the very least knock her socks off. (pp. 19–30)

Although these sexual myths continue to hold true for many adults, many women have begun to challenge the notion that males are responsible for a satisfying sexual relationship. Women more often communicate their sexual needs to their partners and initiate sexual activity.

We must continue to challenge myths because many of the values, beliefs, and attitudes that inform myths are imbedded in the socialization process. At times, myths guide sexual messages, beliefs, and behaviors and may play a role in couples' sexual problems.

THE DEVELOPMENT OF COUPLES' SEXUAL PROBLEMS

Relationship Problems

Each partner carries certain attitudes, feelings, ideals, dreams, and plans regarding the structure of a meaningful intimate relationship. These beliefs may or may not be explicitly understood by their partner (Roughan & Jenkins, 1990). We know from family therapy and family systems research that the various subsystems (couple, individual, family, extended family, biological, social, etc.) interact with and impact each other. Sexuality is an important part of a loving relationship and includes sexual self-image as well as the interactions of partners. In other words, couples' relationships have an impact on sexual problems and the sexual problems in turn have an impact on the relationship in a recursive manner. That is to say, they influence and are influenced by each other in a type of feedback response loop that shapes all aspects of their relationship.

Relationship problems typically evolve as couples expect their beliefs about a caring relationship to match that of their partners. These beliefs are often referred to as styles of loving. Each partner's style contains a prescription indicating how both partners should think, act, and feel in their relationship. This pattern can be further complicated as partners expect their styles to be the same in some instances and of a complementary nature in others (Roughan & Jenkins, 1990). Of course, these styles cannot be the same for any two individuals, and they are influenced by many factors such as family of origin messages, gender role expectations, and societal messages about love, intimacy, and sexuality. In many relationships, couples have rarely discussed these expectations in depth, but each partner acts as if they have and is often disappointed when the other partner does not respond as expected (Roughan & Jenkins, 1990).

A loving, intimate relationship is an integral part of a couple's sexual relationship. Sexuality counselors must thoroughly evaluate and understand relational dynamics and identify relationship-enhancing forces that will facilitate and support couples as well as relationship-diminishing forces that may inhibit the process of treatment (Hof, 1987). The following questions adapted from Hof (1987) will help sexuality counselors assess information about couples:

- What is the balance between the expression of thoughts, feelings, and behaviors in the relationship?
- How are intimacy issues and affection handled?
- How thoroughly have the partners explored their early family messages about love and sexuality?
- How have societal, cultural, and religious beliefs impacted their emotional and sexual relationship?
- How are gender concerns treated in the relationship?
- How is power and control negotiated?

- How successfully do partners communicate with each other?
- How successfully do partners manage conflict?
- What is the couple's problem-solving and decision-making process?

Once a clear picture of the relationship is provided, it is important to examine it within the context of the role that sex and sexuality play in the couple's life. If there is evidence of severe relational stress or abuse, relationship or sexuality counseling is contraindicated. Individual treatment may be required to explore sexual concerns until the relationship is stable.

Sexual Problems

Sexual and relationship problems are interrelated. Researchers have estimated that 80% of couples seeking treatment have sexual difficulties, and that 80% of couples seen in sex therapy have significant relational problems (Heiman, LoPiccolo, & LoPiccolo, 1981). Because the two are inextricably intertwined, sexuality counselors must fully understand the dynamics of relationship counseling and sexual dysfunction. Sexual problems often develop because of discrepancies in conflict styles or between partners' sexual styles (Roughan & Jenkins, 1990). Similar to the development of relational problems, couples hold beliefs, values, attributions, attitudes, and expectations about sexual behavior and experience. However, the meanings attributed to these are often discordant. For example, one partner may believe frequent sexual activity is the most important indicator of love and harmony in the relationship, whereas the other partner believes that nonsexual touching and communication is the most important. As they become frustrated with one another, arguments or accusations might follow:

> "You must not love me very much. We haven't had sexual intercourse for two weeks."

> "Why would I want to have sex with you, we haven't talked much or held hands during our walks for a long time."

Each partner has different ideas about how a loving, sexual relationship should take place, and judges their partner's style of loving based on those beliefs. Over time, as these misunderstandings intensify, significant sexual issues may emerge.

The types of sexual problems couples experience are also influenced by the developmental stages of their relationship. Early in the relationship (the "honeymoon" stage), couples most often have differences as they reconcile their expectations about their styles of sexual expression. During this anticipatory stage, couples do not typically experience sexual concerns, particularly desire problems (Roughan & Jenkins, 1990). Young and Long (1998) suggest that as relationships develop and the daily stressors such as work, children, and chores at home intrude, partners may be less physically available for each other. Lack of accessibility may create hurt feelings and lead one partner to seek other outlets such as work, extramarital affairs, hobbies, volunteer work, or children's activities in order to address sexual frustration.

This pattern often leads to sexual imbalances in relationships, and couples may become more polarized. One partner may blame the other until ultimately neither may initiate sexual intimacy. These problematic styles of relating can continue to increase until they reach a crisis or until there is a split in the relationship (Young & Long, 1998). Sometimes an impasse will develop when both partners fear a collapse or loss of control in the relationship (Young & Long, 1998). In many cases couples decide to maintain a status quo in their relationship until the children are older, their careers are stable, or they have addressed a particular crisis in their relationship.

Sometimes sexual problems develop due to a life crisis such as sudden illness, loss of a job, death of a parent or child, financial distress, or a catastrophic world event. Other times, sexual problems emerge as couples move from one stage of the life cycle to the next. It is not unusual to hear couples report in counseling that they have had difficulty since the birth of their child, or after one spouse returns to the workplace, or as they age and their children leave home.

Is It a Sexual Dysfunction or a Sexual Problem?

A couple's sexual problems may be presented to the clinician as part of the initial complaint or may emerge during or after other issues have been explored over the course of treatment. These complaints may be specifically identified as *sexual problems*, meaning that they encompass a broad spectrum of factors already mentioned in this chapter as related to sexuality issues. On the other hand, a diagnosed sexual dysfunction may be evident that can be treated with cognitive-behavioral techniques in counseling (Nichols, 1987).

Sexual dysfunctions, as noted earlier, are impairments, either physical or psychological, of one of the three phases of the sexual response cycle. These dysfunctions consist of conditions such as erectile disorder, premature ejaculation, male orgasmic disorder, and sexual aversion disorder in males; orgasmic disorders and vaginismus in females; and dyspareunia and hypoactive sexual desire in both males and females (APA, 2000).

Aside from these dysfunctions, people experience a wide range of other sexual difficulties—from dissatisfaction with sexual frequency and sexual boredom to incompatibility with respect to sexual activity and lack of sexual fulfillment. These are referred to as *sexual problems*. These more emotionally based problems also include exploration of the degree of passion that couples express sexually, the type of communication employed by each partner, and the level of commitment partners exhibit to work on the sexual aspect of their relationship (Goldsmith, 1988; Karpel, 1994; Young & Long, 1998).

We caution all professionals who work with sexual problems or sexual dysfunctions to be careful not to become too embroiled in a debate over the differences between a dysfunction and a problem. Likewise, subtleties regarding differences in disorders and dysfunctions should not be dwelled on, as they do not necessarily affect decisions about treatment. As sexuality counselors use integrative approaches to effectively address sexual problems, we expect to see increased overlap in treatment approaches. For example, sexuality counselors are equipped to treat issues of hypoactive sexual desire because it also relates to emotionally based issues in relationships stemming from career stress or family stressors. Similarly, sexuality counselors explore the relational development of dysfunctions as they are rooted in early childhood messages, sexual misinformation, or faulty communication patterns. Anxiety about sexual performance from any of these factors is usually the most immediate cause of sexual dysfunction (Dove & Wiederman, 2000). Finally, when sexuality counselors are cross-trained, they recognize a sexual dysfunction such as erectile dysfunction and can identify both biological and medical explanations and situational causes such as difficulties at work, fear of death after an illness, or coping with the aftermath of an extramarital relationship. Sexuality counselors must continually monitor themselves as professionals in order to determine which sexual issues they are competent to treat and which need to be referred to other trained professionals.

A counselor's understanding of a wide variety of treatment approaches and an openness to work through consultation with other professionals who possess expertise in these areas will continue to pave the way for more comprehensive and integrative treatment modalities (Young & Long, 1998).

Clinical Decision Making When Treating Sexual Problems

Accurate assessment of sexual concerns is crucial to effective treatment. Often, counselors are unsure about their level of competence when confronted with a sexual problem or dysfunction. Although sex histories and attitudinal and behavioral inventories about sexuality are helpful and often essential, many clinicians feel inadequate to offer specific sexuality counseling in the context of relationship therapy and would rather refer to a certified sex therapist. The dilemma lies in the decision-making process. Counselors must decide what level of intervention is appropriate for treating each sexual concern and determine whether or not they are adequately trained to treat each level of care (Heiman, LoPiccolo, & LoPiccolo, 1981).

One model that is currently used and has been effective for counselors and therapists for many years is Annon's (1974, 1975) P-LI-SS-IT model. Its components can be summarized as follows:†

> **P**—Permission to talk about sexual issues, reassurance and empathy, and the acknowledgement that we are sexual beings.
>
> **LI**—Limited information, including sex education, clarification of sexual myths and stereotypes, and bibliotherapy with suggested related books.
>
> **SS**—Specific suggestions such as Kegel exercises, the squeeze technique, or sensate focus.
>
> **IT**—Intensive sex therapy, individual or conjoint, including focus on relationship dynamics and psychological concerns and other complex sexual issues. (Annon, as cited in Mason, 1991, p. 499)

Annon suggests that as the intensity or stage of the intervention increases, additional education and skills training is needed (as cited in Mason, 1991). This model provides counselors with a decision-making tool to help them determine what they are therapeutically qualified to do. We believe that sexuality counseling as part of family therapy or mental health counseling training typically includes adequate training to intervene in the first two levels of the model. At the third and fourth levels, clinicians require specific training as determined by their state licensure board or by the AASECT, AAMFT, and ACA, or they may choose to refer couples to a sexuality counselor with more in-depth training.

Referring Couples for Other Types of Treatment

Sexuality counseling has been very promising for treating a wide variety of biopsychosocial problems and dysfunctions. However, these treatments are not appropriate for all couples. Several factors may contraindicate sexuality counseling, including (a) severe pathology, (b) severe relationship discord, (c) extreme crisis or stress from developmental or situational factors in the family, (d) severe depression, (e) substance abuse, or (f) a lack of commitment on the part of one partner to the other (Dove & Wiederman, 2000; Phillips, 2000; Young & Long, 1998).

Many of these factors are subject to clinical judgment based on the training and experience of the clinician. Medical experts must be sought whenever a condition exists that is influenced or influences physical functioning. Sexuality counselors should refer when it is not within the scope of their training or expertise. In situations in which there are historical, social, and developmental problems, and when couples counseling is not indicated, it is important that clinicians advise clients in a helpful direction—from individual counseling and group treatment to other appropriate methods of care. The principle to guide these decisions rests on each state's legal definition of the profession and on national legal, ethical, and professional standards of conduct that address counselors' competence to treat only those problems for which they are trained, licensed, or certified to practice within their areas of expertise. All sexuality counselors should be skilled in diagnosing and treating the emotional and sexual aspects of intimate relationships.

---

†Copyright 1991 from *Handbook of Family Therapy* by M.J. Mason in A. S. Gurman and D. P. Kniskern. Reproduced by permission of M.J. Mason.

SUMMARY

An integrative approach to sexuality counseling provides a step-by-step model for conceptualization and treatment of sexual concerns. We have proposed a shift from a focus on individual sexual dysfunctions to a systemic approach to working with couples and their sexual concerns. This change in focus requires a broader definition of sexuality counseling encompassing historical, social, and developmental perspectives.

Sexuality counseling refers to the process of interaction between professionals and clients that allows clients to explore and understand the interaction between their sexual feelings, values, responsibilities, needs, and behaviors.

Sexuality counseling includes the assessment, diagnosis, and treatment of psychosexual disorders described in the *Diagnostic and Statistical Manual of Mental Disorders IV-TR*, which is the sourcebook used to make appropriate diagnoses regarding psychosexual disorders.

In addition to understanding historical, social, and developmental aspects of couples' sexual functioning, sexuality counselors must examine their own ethical standards and sexual histories, which help to formulate their values and beliefs about sexuality.

Sexuality counselors must also be skilled in diagnosing and treating emotional and sexual aspects of intimate relationships, as most sexual problems are imbedded in couples' emotional struggles. Intimate relationships are part of a dynamic process involving feelings that promote relatedness, attachment, and unity. These feelings assist couples with knowing and understanding themselves, and with self-disclosing in the presence of their partners (Schnarch, 1991).

Sternberg describes a triangular theory of love based on components of passion, intimacy, and decision and commitment that further defines love, sexuality, and intimacy in couples' relationships. Components of passionate, intimate, and committed love are evaluated, along with criteria for sexual disorders and sexual dysfunctions, in order to provide interventions that address the complexity of couples' relationships.

Sexuality counselors may also use the P-LI-SS-IT model for clinical decision making to determine the level of intervention they are trained and competent to deliver when working with couples having sexual prolems.

THEORIES APPLIED TO SEXUALITY COUNSELING

KEY CONCEPTS

- Theoretical approaches to sexuality counseling have been developed from theories of individual, couple, and family therapy.
- An integrative couples' model for sexuality counseling blends theoretical perspectives primarily from cognitive-behavioral, systemic, and psychodynamic concepts.
- Multiple perspectives provide an increased range of treatment interventions appropriate for addressing couples' concerns.
- Cognitive-behavioral approaches have been useful in the treatment of both male and female sexual problems, including dyspareunia, erectile dysfunctions, and desire problems.
- Systems theories applied to the treatment of sexual dysfunctions include Bowen's intergenerational approach, brief problem-focused and solution-focused approaches, a narrative approach, and communication theory.
- Psychodynamic approaches, particularly object relations, have been useful in the treatment of sexual disorders, including desire disorders, anorgasmia, atypical sexual behavior, premature ejaculation, and vaginismus.
- Feminist theory emphasizes the exploration of gender and sex-role issues as they apply to a couple's sexual concerns.

WHY WE NEED THEORIES

Theories have been described "as a group of logically organized laws or relationships that constitutes explanation in a discipline" (Heinen, 1985, p. 414). They are composed of definitions that relate basic assumptions of the theory to observations in human behavior (Hall, Lindzey, & Campbell, 1998). Theories are methods of "learning something new, or relearning something one has forgotten, . . . unlearning . . . [or even] learning what one already knows" (Corsini & Wedding, 1995, p. 6). Theories influence people to change their thoughts, feelings, behaviors, and way of interpreting their world (Corsini & Wedding, 1995).

Most important, theories provide the background to offer sexuality counselors building blocks and other tools as they conceptualize and intervene in couples' sexual concerns. Without theories, counselors would simply be choosing random strategies to promote change with little regard for an organized cognitive plan for interventions. Many call this a "cookbook" approach, a little of this and a little of that. It is difficult to understand how to maintain change in relationships and how to celebrate success when counselors and clients have little information about what worked, what needs to happen to maintain change, and how to evaluate success. Thus the need for theories.

In this chapter we provide understandable language for thinking about and intervening in couples' sexual interactions. We introduce key terms, identify some important tenets, and describe interventions that can be used from several theoretical orientations. Specifically, we address behavioral and cognitive-behavioral approaches, Bowen's intergenerational approach, brief problem-focused (structural/strategic and systemic) and solution-focused approaches, narrative therapy, communication theory, psychoanalytic/object relations approaches, and a feminist perspective. It is important to remember that theories other than those addressed in this chapter may also be applicable to an integrative model for couples, and by no means are the theories we have outlined representative of the totality of counseling theories.

We conclude this chapter by providing a confluence of theoretical constructs, organized in such a way that they can be integrated into a systemic model used to counsel couples who experience sexual problems or dysfunctions. A first step includes thinking about commonalities of these theoretical concepts as they apply to sexuality counseling for couples.

COMMONALITIES IN THEORETICAL CONCEPTS

Integrative sexuality counselors incorporate a wide variety of concepts into their therapeutic styles. Grencavage and Norcross (1990) reviewed the literature and identified six concepts that most theories share. We have modified these similarities to focus on six of the most prevalent factors among theories as they apply to sexuality counseling:

- The development of a therapeutic relationship between sexuality counselors and couples is crucial.
- Couples have the opportunity for emotional expression and catharsis and are able to discuss their sexual concerns.
- Couples glean new behaviors and are able to practice them.
- Couples can expect that sexuality counselors will help them make positive changes toward a more mutually satisfying intimate relationship.
- Sexuality counselors have personal qualities that promote hope for couples in solving their sexual concerns.
- Sexuality counselors help couples understand their symptoms and create a plan for solving their sexual concerns.

In addition, postmodern theoretical approaches share commonalities that are present throughout social construction, contemporary theories, and narrative theories (Anderson, Carleton, & Swim, 1999). In a review of Anderson's earlier (1995, 1997) work, Anderson et al. (1999) identify the following concepts as parallel among postmodern theories:

- The meanings and understandings that we attribute to the events and experiences in our lives are communally, culturally, and historically embedded;
- Meanings and understandings, including knowledge, are socially created and shaped through language;
- What is created [has many authors] among a community of persons and relationships rather than [only one author];
- What is created is only one of multiple perspectives and possibilities;
- Language and knowledge are relational and generative;
- Transformation [takes place] in the inventive and creative aspects of language, dialogue, and the narrative; therefore,
- The potential for transformation and change is as infinite in variety and expression as the individuals who realize them. (p. 210)

An integrative couples model uses interventions, language, and perspectives from many theoretical orientations and combines them together in a systematic way (Young & Long, 1998).

THE USE OF AN INTEGRATIVE APPROACH

An integrative sexuality counselor uses a model that provides for a variety of theoretical perspectives in order to create change in a couple's system. We have expanded an integrative approach initially created by Young and Long (1998) to specifically address couples' sexual issues. According to this model, counselors select a theoretical viewpoint that is not only best for the couple but also useful (Young, 2001; Young & Long, 1998). Counselors also look at the couples' situation through many lenses and select the precise intervention to assist them with their specific sexual concern. In this way, sexuality counselors are able to draw from a multitude of theoretical approaches and select what works best for a particular couple (Young & Long, 1998).

In this chapter we unite the most useful concepts of several theories to present an integrative model for sexuality counseling. Our goal is to provide counselors with a step-by-step approach for conceptualization and treatment of couples' sexual

:rns from a systems perspective rather than focusing solely on individual concerns. A systemic model enables counselors to describe couples' sexual problems in interactive terms and to identify functional and dysfunctional patterns of behavior. This systemic conceptualization guides sexuality counselors in choosing the most appropriate theory and intervention.

Before we outline the integrative couples' model, we will review seven theoretical approaches that will be useful for an integrative approach to sexuality counseling. You should note your responses to each theory described. In fact, expect to feel pulled toward one or more different perspectives based on your personal values, beliefs, and assumptions about life and human nature. Our hope is that you will be able to unite theory and practice in an integrative and systemic way and apply your learning into practice with couples experiencing sexual concerns.

THEORETICAL APPROACHES

Behavioral and Cognitive-Behavioral Approaches

Several models for the treatment of sexual problems or dysfunctions have emerged from behavioral and cognitive-behavioral approaches. Based on the work of Pavlov (1928), Watson (1914, 1919), and Skinner (1953), behavioral theory proposes that problem behaviors are a result of the way in which persons react to their environment. It assumes that all behavior is learned and therefore can be unlearned. For example, sexual desire problems, often rooted in couples' unresolved relationship issues, can be treated by focusing on changing couples' interactional patterns and by relearning communication skills, enabling partners to explore issues that impact their sexual responses to each other. In addition, sexual problems stemming from past trauma in childhood may require behavioral techniques developed specifically for the identified sexual problem or dysfunction.

A variety of behavioral techniques were developed by Masters and Johnson (1970), Kaplan (1974, 1979, 1983), and LoPiccolo (1978) and have been used to treat sexual dysfunctions. For example, Masters and Johnson's (1970) *squeeze technique* as well as Kaplan's (1987) adapted *start-stop technique* have been widely accepted for the treatment of premature ejaculation. Likewise, Heiman, LoPiccolo, and LoPiccolo (1981)

employ behavioral approaches aimed at reduction of anxiety, sex education, communication skills training, and belief and attitude change.

Cognitive approaches are also used to address sexual problems and dysfunctions. Cognitive theory stresses the importance of belief systems in determining behavior and feelings (Beck, 1967, 1976). The basic premise is to understand faulty beliefs or "crooked thinking" and use techniques to change these maladaptive thoughts, while also incorporating affective and behavioral methods (Dattilio, Epstein, & Baucom, 1998). Sexuality counselors employing cognitive methods typically explore cognitions and beliefs about sexuality that partners bring into the relationship from their families of origin (Dattilio & Padesky, 1990; Dattilio et al., 1998). For example, a woman shares that she was taught by her mother and grandmother that being attractive was sinful because it caused men to have lustful thoughts. She argues with her partner that she should not try to enhance her looks with makeup because she could cause other men to sin. The couple explores how these beliefs impact their current relationship, particularly the ways in which they relate emotionally and sexually.

Counselors also explore faulty beliefs that may contribute to a couple's current sexual problem or dysfunction (Epstein, Baucom, & Daiuto, 1997). Cognitive interventions are used to help couples examine their thought processes and belief systems while recognizing the need for behavioral change.

Sexuality counselors who embrace a cognitive-behavioral approach use a variety of interventions, including communication skills training, problem-solving training, assertiveness training, and systematic desensitization to facilitate cognitive and behavioral change. Interventions are aimed at helping couples examine their thoughts, feelings, and beliefs and how each influences their sexual relationship. Couples are encouraged to engage in specific exercises to help them reduce negative feelings and anxiety related to sexual problems, thus allowing them to enjoy sexual experiences (Goldenberg & Goldenberg, 2000).

Some Premises of the Theory

The following are some premises of behavioral and cognitive-behavioral approaches as they apply to sexuality counseling with couples.

1. All behavior (adaptive and maladaptive) is maintained according to the principles of learning theory (Gladding, 1998).

2. Partners have sexual histories based on past behavior patterns that can be changed through behavior rehearsal and vicarious learning experiences (Young & Long, 1998).
3. According to Young and Long (1998), some sexual behavior is learned and "treatment normally involves education or a relearning process" (p. 23).
4. Reinforcement helps couples learn and maintain new sexual behaviors (Young & Long, 1998).
5. Cognitive, behavioral, and affective factors interact and influence couples' sexual relationships (Dattilio et al., 1998).
6. According to Gladding (1998), "cognitions are either rational or irrational. They can be modified and, as a result, bring about change in [partners' sexual] interactions" (p. 203).
7. According to Young and Long (1998), "behavior therapy has significantly contributed to understanding and treating couples' communication patterns and in [the treatment] of sexual problems [and dysfunctions]" (p. 23).

Some Key Terms

- *Positive reinforcement* refers to the use of a favorable consequence following a behavior that increases the likelihood that the behavior will be performed again (Goldenberg & Goldenberg, 2000). For example, one partner expresses to the other that caressing breasts is enjoyable and creates feelings of closeness. Expression of feelings about sexual touching is a positive reinforcer and increases the chance that a partner will do something like this again.
- *Negative reinforcement* refers to the removal of an adverse stimulus or event that increases the likelihood that the behavior will be performed again (Goldenberg & Goldenberg, 2000). For example, one partner stops complaining about the other partner's busy schedule, and as a next step there is more initiation of oral sex.
- *Shaping (behavior)* involves gradually reinforcing parts of a behavior to resemble more closely the desired target behavior (Bandura, 1969). For example, during sensate focus exercises, each time a woman feels pleasure, she expresses her enjoyment. Each touch reinforces her pleasure and encourages her partner. The activity continues and eventually leads to the targeted behavior, which is typically intercourse.

- *Cognitive distortions* are negative sexual thoughts or ideas originating in early childhood sexual meanings. For instance, a woman who was sexually abused in childhood enjoyed sexual activity prior to marriage; now married, she no longer wants to have sex with her partner whom she now considers "family." Her belief that "sex with a family member is wrong" takes on a new meaning and becomes a cognitive distortion.

Selected Interventions and Techniques

- *Caring days* refers to an exercise based on Stuart's (1980) approach to behavioral marital therapy that requires each partner to describe exact behaviors a partner can do to demonstrate caring. For example, partners fill in the blank "I feel loved when you . . . fix me a bubble bath." Behaviors requested by each partner should be specific, small, and positive, and practiced daily.
- *Assertion training* helps partners increase their behavioral repertoire so they can make choices and express their thoughts and feelings when they want to assert themselves. Such training is based on the assumption that we have basic rights as human beings. For example, a woman may say to her partner, "When you make love to me without kissing me, I feel angry and used, and I want to push you away."
- *Psychoeducational training* refers to educational resources and materials such as articles, books, and training tapes that assist people with increasing their knowledge and understanding of sexuality and of specific sexual issues. Such training may include understanding themselves as sexual beings, identifying the emotional aspects of sexuality, and understanding the physiology of male and female sexual response.
- *Cognitive restructuring* is aimed at teaching couples to identify, evaluate, and change self-defeating or irrational thoughts and beliefs about sexuality and helping them to associate positive feelings with their sexual behavior (Ellis, 1975). Cognitive restructuring techniques are discussed in more detail in Chapters 6 and 7. An example of an irrational belief may be the following: "My partner does not make love with me each night. I must not be sexually attractive."
- *Systematic desensitization* is "the process of unlearning the connection between anxiety and a particular situation" (Bourne, 2000, p. 143) by

constructing a hierarchy of situations that provokes increased anxiety (Wolpe, 1958). Partners learn to gradually approach the situation through a sequence of steps (Wolpe, 1969). For example, a woman fearful of masturbating may begin examining her genitalia, with a goal of becoming more familiar with her own body and learning to stimulate herself manually.

Bowen's Intergenerational Approach

Bowen's theory is based on individuals' ability to successfully differentiate their thoughts from their feelings and themselves from others (Kerr & Bowen, 1988). According to this theory, anxiety is the primary reason for all symptoms we experience, whether they are physical or emotional. The degree of anxiety we experience is related to the degree of differentiation we have from our families of origin. The more differentiated we are, the less anxiety and fewer symptoms we experience. The more fused (emotionally connected) we are, the more anxiety or symptoms we experience. Our reaction to this life anxiety in the present is based on how our family of origin passed the anxiety or symptoms down from one generation to another (Friedman, 1991).

Schnarch (1995) uses Bowen's concepts of self-differentiation and fusion (emotional connectedness) to address treatment of couples' sexual problems, suggesting that sexuality counselors should focus on couples' relationships when conceptualizing their sexual concerns rather than attend solely to symptoms of sexual dysfunction. By treating couples within the context of their relationships, partners develop more committed relationships, which foster greater autonomy and sexual intimacy. Thus, this approach is aimed at helping couples "to balance [their] needs for autonomy and togetherness" (Schnarch, 1995, p. 240). Schnarch proposes that partners with low differentiation experience more intimacy problems due to a greater dependence on the other for togetherness, thus losing their sense of self. This dependence places "responsibility for adequate functioning in the hands of the other person in the relationship" (Goldenberg & Goldenberg, 2000, p. 293). In contrast, partners with higher differentiation "can tolerate more intimate connection . . . before they feel controlled or lose themselves in their relationship" (Schnarch, 2000, p. 27). Therefore, they are less dependent on their partner for emotional closeness, allowing for more intimacy in the relationship.

Achieving differentiation is critical for committed relationships to endure life's challenges and maintain intimate connections (Schnarch, 1995).

Bowen (1978) identified eight basic concepts that are used to address chronic anxiety and understand emotional and intimate systems. Three of these are central to successful treatment in working with couples having sexual problems or dysfunctions: differentiation, emotional triangles, and multigenerational transmission.

Some Premises of the Theory

The following are some premises of Bowen's (1978) intergenerational theory as they apply to sexuality counseling with couples.

1. Couples repeat family sexual patterns from one generation to the next.
2. According to Schnarch (1995), "differentiation is fundamental for sustaining intimacy, eroticism, and sexual desire in long-term relationships" (p. 128).
3. People are attracted to partners who have the same level of differentiation as their own.
4. Uncontrolled anxiety can result in sexual problems or dysfunctions.
5. Uncontrolled anxiety is manifested in the formation of emotional triangles that later interfere with sexual activity. For example, by triangulating a child into the marital/relational bed, all sexual activity ceases.

Some Key Terms

- *Differentiation* is a lifelong process of becoming emotionally and intellectually separate from one's family of origin (Bowen, 1978). It involves being able to remain clear about one's goals and values in the midst of intense emotional systems, while at the same time being able to accept and respect the opinions of others. Differentiation is central for maintaining sex and intimacy in committed relationships (Schnarch, 1991, 1995). It requires "the ability to maintain one's sense of separate self in close proximity to a partner" (Schnarch, 1991, p. 114).
- *Emotional triangles* refer to "any three parts of [a relational] emotional system, either three individuals or two persons and an issue" (Friedman, 1991, p. 150). Bowen (1978) suggests that triangles occur as a result of anxiety between two people trying to maintain their sense of self and create stability in a relationship. One option for maintaining a relationship is to bring in a third party. For example, a

man presents in counseling with difficulty maintaining an erection when he is having intercourse with his partner. During counseling, he discusses his preoccupation with his aging mother who has recently come to live with them and how it contributes to his physical and emotional exhaustion. As the counseling sessions shift to focusing on how the couple can better take care of his mother (the third person), anxiety is diffused and the conflict is abated. The counselor continues to work with the couple to integrate his mother into their home, thus contributing to increased sexual response during lovemaking.

- *Multigenerational transmission* is a process in which emotional reactions are passed from one generation to the next (Friedman, 1991). Patterns of how people cope with stress in the past repeat themselves in the next generation. For example, a woman has multiple extra-relational affairs to deal with her stressors and also distances herself from her partner. This results in relational and sexual problems. Her father also dealt with the pressures of life by having multiple affairs, something that was observed but not discussed openly in the family.

Selected Interventions and Techniques

- *Genograms* involve the construction of a pictorial diagram that records pertinent information about couples and their relationships with their families over a minimum of three generations (McGoldrick & Gerson, 1985). *Sexual* genograms can provide important information regarding messages from family of origin and critical events in couples' sexual development (Hof & Berman, 1986). See Chapter 3 for more details on the use of genograms.
- *Person-to-person relationships* occur when two partners "relate personally to each other about each other; that is, they do not talk about others (triangulating) and do not talk about impersonal issues" (Piercy & Sprenkle, 1986, p. 11). This direct focus on one another can promote intimacy in relationships.
- *Detriangulation* is "the process whereby an individual keeps himself or herself (or someone else) outside the emotional field of two others" (Piercy & Sprenkle, 1986, p. 10). For example, when partners attempt to involve the sexuality counselor in a discussion about each other's lack of sexual desire, anxiety increases. If the counselor can remain objective and not align with one partner during the

discussion, couples learn to speak more directly to each other. Thus, their patterns of sexual communication change (Piercy & Sprenkle, 1986).

Problem-Focused Approaches

Problem-focused approaches that are useful in the treatment of sexual problems or dysfunctions include structural or strategic and systemic approaches that are usually brief (up to ten sessions) in duration. Problem-focused approaches draw on an individual's or a couple's combined resources to overcome sexual problems. These approaches are similar in theory but are different in many of the techniques they employ.

Structural therapy is a problem-focused approach based on the work of Minuchin (1974) and on the notion that an individual's symptom is best understood by examining the interactional patterns of the couple system. In other words, how, when, and to whom members in the system currently relate is a way of understanding the problem. In order for change to take place, a change in the organization of the couple structure must occur. For example, a man states that he has difficulty maintaining an erection during intercourse: "I feel like one of the kids in the family, my partner controls everything from the finances to what happens in our sex life." This example demonstrates the need for change in the structure of the couple's relational system.

Strategic and systemic therapy are also problem-focused approaches that have roots in the work of Erickson (1944, 1966, 1973). This therapy emphasizes the use of a particular approach or strategy for each specific problem while using the positive aspects of people in order to create change (Haley, 1963, 1973; Madanes, 1991). For example, Erickson used hypnotic techniques to help clients trust their own instincts as they received specific directives aimed at relieving their symptoms.

Contributors to strategic and systemic theory include Bateson (1951, 1978), Haley (1963, 1973), Madanes (1991), Watzlawick, Beavin, and Jackson (1967), and Weakland (1960), along with Selvini-Palazzoli, Boscolo, Cecchin, and Prata (1978). According to strategic theory, symptoms (problems) are forms of communication that serve a function in relationships, thus preventing couples from achieving their basic purpose. Symptoms often occur when couples are "stuck" at a particular stage in the life cycle. For example, a postmenopausal woman may experience a decrease in sexual functioning (e.g., decreased vaginal lubrication and orgasmic intensity) resulting in emotional distancing and withdrawal interfering with the goal of maintaining physical and emotional intimacy with her partner.

Some Premises of the Theory

The following premises are common to problem-focused approaches as they apply to sexuality counseling with couples.

1. Partners interact within a context. Therefore, sexual problems must be considered within the interactional context in which they occur (Stanton, 1981).
2. "The [couple] is a system" (Young & Long, 1998, p. 50). Change in one part of the system (one partner) will affect all other parts of the system. For example, if an inorgasmic woman learns how to have an orgasm, her new behavior will affect her partner.
3. Systems have a tendency to seek homeostasis (Stanton, 1981). Symptoms help keep couples balanced. For example, a symptom such as arguing over career choices may preoccupy couples, preventing them from addressing their lack of sexual desire in the relationship. This action maintains stability and can prevent change.
4. Methods used to restore balance (attempts of individuals to solve problems) can become problems themselves (Carlson, Sperry, & Lewis, 1997). For instance, partner-assisted masturbation to help a woman with inorgasmia may result in more frustration if she is not ready to work with her partner on her sexual behaviors.
5. Interruptions in a couple's developmental stage in the life cycle (e.g., birth of a child) can lead to sexual concerns.
6. Insight is less important than facilitating change in a couple's behavior and functioning (Stanton, 1981).
7. Sexuality counseling occurs in the here-and-now. The present is more important than what has happened in the past.

Some Key Terms

- *Homeostasis* is the tendency for couples to seek balance and resist change (Goldenberg & Goldenberg, 2000). For example, couples may repeat the same foreplay activities even though they both express a desire for a more "exciting and satisfying" sex life and have explored new techniques.

- *Structure* refers to the rules that have been developed by couples to determine how partners relate to each other (Minuchin, 1974). Every couple has structure and rules. For example, in one couple's relationship an implied rule may be that only the missionary position will be practiced during intercourse. This rule impacts how partners relate to each other sexually.
- *Boundaries* refer to invisible barriers that surround the couple system and separate them from other systems. They "range from 'rigid' (extreme separateness) to 'diffuse' (extreme togetherness). [Healthy] boundaries are 'clear'" (Piercy & Sprenkle, 1986, p. 31). For example, partners with rigid boundaries may experience difficulty being intimate with each other. This can result in sexual problems and dysfunctions because they have difficulty achieving the degree of vulnerability necessary for healthy sexual activity.
- *Power* refers to the person in the system who makes the decisions or guides the relationship (Haley, 1976). For example, a man might complain that his partner determines whether or not they are going to make love depending on her ovulation cycle and her desire to become pregnant.

Selected Interventions and Techniques

- *Joining* is the process through which sexuality counselors establish rapport with couples, which leads to them temporarily becoming part of the system (Minuchin, 1974). For example, sexuality counselors take time in the first session to form a bond with couples by talking about natural desires of couples to relate to each other sexually.
- *Enactment* refers to the acting out of problematic behavior sequences in the presence of the counselor as opposed to talking about the incident (Minuchin & Fishman, 1981). During counseling, couples may enact how they suggest to each other that they are interested in sexual intercourse.
- *Reframing* is the process of offering a different meaning to a situation enabling couples to think and behave differently (Watzlawick, Weakland, & Fisch, 1974). This is also referred to as "relabeling" and "positive connotation" (Minuchin & Fishman, 1981; Selvini-Palazzoli, 1986). For example, reframing a man's inability to sustain an erection as a way of protecting his partner from discomfort during intercourse may change his partner's response.

- *Intensity* refers to adjusting the degree of impact of a therapeutic message by the counselor's use of strong affect, repeating the same message to the couple, or increasing pressure within a relationship (Piercy & Sprenkle, 1986). For example, a sexuality counselor may repeat the message that "it is OK to enjoy sexual activity" to a woman who believes that sex is only for her partner's enjoyment.
- *Directives* are instructions given by sexuality counselors asking partners to interrupt their normal behavior patterns and behave differently. For example, assigning a sensate focus exercise to a couple for practice at home is a directive.
- *Rituals* are clearly marked events or prescribed actions (Imber-Black, Roberts, & Whiting, 1988) designed to help couples celebrate therapeutic success and to maintain desired sexual behavior through repetitive activities.

Solution-Focused Approaches

Solution-focused approaches used in the treatment of sexual problems and dysfunctions include the work of Berg and deShazer (1993), DeJong and Berg (1998), and deShazer (1985, 1988, 1991, 1994), along with O'Hanlon and Weiner-Davis (1989). Solution-focused or solution-oriented therapy is most concerned with the solutions to problems rather than how problems are formulated. Similar to problem-focused therapies, these approaches are brief in duration and require sexuality counselors to be active, directive, and goal-oriented when working with couples (Young & Long, 1998).

Based on postmodern constructivist thinking, solution-focused approaches support the idea that "language and [the] meaning [of] events take precedence for the [counselor] over attending to behavioral sequences or family interactive patterns" (Goldenberg & Goldenberg, 2000, p. 303). Truth is best understood by exploring each individual member's view of reality as it is tied to their experiences. Sexuality counselors from a constructivist point of view are interested in couples' conversations and the techniques used to empower them to reconstruct their stories and redirect their lives (Goldenberg & Goldenberg, 2000).

Solution-focused sexuality counselors concur with a constructivist notion that there are multiple perspectives of sexual problems and dysfunctions, not a single truth or reality. The emphasis is on change and listening to the language the couple uses to describe their sexual problem or dysfunction, with little interest in why the sexual problem has developed. A sexuality counselor helps couples construct possible solutions to problems based on goals they jointly identify in counseling. By engaging in solution-focused language, couples "come to believe in the truth or reality of what they are talking about" (Berg & deShazer, 1993, p. 9), thus discussing the solution they want to construct.

Solution-focused sexuality counselors believe their clients have the skills and resources to solve their own problems. The sexuality counselor's task is to help them construct new solutions, not previously considered, based on skills and knowledge they already have.

Some Premises of the Theory

The following solution-oriented premises are adapted from Selekman (1993, pp. 139–142). We have expanded on each concept as it applies to couples with sexual concerns.

1. "Resistance is not a useful concept." Couples want to change. Thus, resistance is nonexistent in the therapy process. Couples may need to relearn what they already know.
2. "Change is inevitable." Sexuality counselors stress that change will occur and that solutions to sexual problems or dysfunctions are possible.
3. "Only small changes are necessary." Once small changes take place, couples feel encouraged and build confidence to look forward to greater changes.
4. "People have the strengths and the resources to implement change." Sexuality counselors focus on strengths and de-emphasize pathology.
5. "Problems are unsuccessful attempts to resolve difficulties." Couples get "stuck" trying to resolve their problems (deShazer, 1985). Couples' repeated attempts at solving a sexual problem or dysfunction (their solutions) help maintain the problem. Couples can benefit from sexuality counseling to get "unstuck" from repeating the same solutions that have been unsuccessful in the past.
6. "You don't need to know a great deal about the problem in order to solve it." Identifying "exceptions" or times when sexual problems or symptoms are not present can help couples find ways to create more exceptions.
7. "Multiple perspectives." There are many different ways to view a sexual problem, thus there are many possible solutions.

Attributions

Key Terms

- *Exceptions* refer to times when the problem or dysfunction does not occur or is not as prevalent (deShazer, 1991). For example, a man might state that there are times when he has little or no difficulty maintaining an erection. A sexuality counselor might ask him how he created those times when he did not have difficulty with an erection and direct him to find more ways to create exceptions.
- *Skeleton keys* are interventions that have worked in the past and can be applied to many situations, based on deShazer's (1985) approach. For example, couples may be given the following directive by their sexuality counselor: "Between now and next time we meet, I would like you to observe what is happening in your sexual relationship that you want to continue to happen."
- *Second-order change* refers to changing the function or structure of the system resulting in new rules and changes in the system (Watzlawick, Beavin, & Jackson, 1967). For example, a woman may be the initiator of sexual activity in the relationship. A change in the structure of the couple system would require that her partner become the initiator.

1. 1st order

Selected Interventions and Techniques

- *Miracle questions* are used by sexuality counselors to help couples think about how things would be different if a miracle occurred and their sexual problem was solved (deShazer, 1985, 1988). For example, a sexuality counselor might ask, "Suppose that tonight there was a miracle and you no longer experienced pain during intercourse. What would be different in your life?"
- *Scaling* is used by sexuality counselors to help couples numerically rate their perceptions of a particular sexual problem or dysfunction (deShazer, 1988). A scale of 1 to 10 is used with "1" being the worst it could be and "10" the best it could be. If a man who presents with premature ejaculation rates himself as a "3" regarding his sexual performance, a sexuality counselor might ask him how he would act differently if he were a "6" (improvement). Scaling can help couples externalize and modify their behavior.
- *Past successes* in solving problems are highlighted by sexuality counselors to encourage couples and to keep them focused on solutions and strengths.

Skeptism

Narrative Approaches

A narrative approach (Epston & White, 1992; White & Epston, 1990) is based on constructivist theory and is focused on collaborative solutions to problems. Narrative therapy is used by sexuality counselors to help empower couples to re-author their life stories, enabling them to make changes not possible before. New stories are created by focusing on "unique outcomes" or times when solutions were found. Through conversation and the retelling of stories in a new way, oppressive sexual problems are "externalized" or separated from couples (Atwood & Dershowitz, 1992). The concept of externalizing requires that couples learn how to remove themselves from their problems by placing their problems out in front of themselves so to speak, so that they do not view themselves as part of the problem. By creating distance between themselves and their issues, couples can move to combine their resources and combat sexual issues, thus finding solutions to their problems.

Questions are used to help couples externalize a sexual problem as separate from their identity. Questioning can help couples create distance from sexual problems that have controlled their lives and impacted their personal perspectives. They can begin to construct new views of themselves. Chapter 9 provides other examples of a narrative approach as applied to sexuality counseling.

Some Premises of the Theory

The following premises are offered by narrative theorists:

1. Sexual problems or dysfunctions are viewed as external to couples.
2. Sexual problems should be confronted by combining and using couples' resources.
3. Couples can be empowered through emphasizing strengths and resiliencies in their stories.

Some Key Terms

- *Unique outcomes* refer to exceptional moments when the problem or symptom did not occur (Freeman, Epston, & Lobovits, 1997). A counselor using narrative interventions listens for these when couples tell their stories. By focusing on these outcomes, new stories are generated. For example, a woman might say that she used to enjoy sex. The sexuality counselor would ask her to talk more about the times she did enjoy sex: "What was different then? What were your thoughts about sex? Your feelings? What did you do differently that is not happening now?"

- *Constructivism* is a "relativistic point of view that emphasizes the subjective construction of reality. [It] implies that what we see in [couples] may be based as much on our preconditions as on what's actually going on" (Nichols & Schwartz, 1991, p. 589). Thus, couples' language and interactions construct their reality, and it is continuously influenced by their surroundings (Atwood & Dershowitz, 1992).

- *Multiple perspectives* refers to the notion that there can be many realities in a given situation based on individuals' past experiences. For example, one partner views lack of sexual desire in their relationship as a sign that her partner must be involved in an affair, while the other partner views the same problem as a lack of time and energy for intimacy. Both have different interpretations based on their personal history and past experiences.

Selected Techniques and Interventions

- *Externalizing the problem* is a process in which sexuality counselors strive to help couples separate sexual problems from themselves (White & Epston, 1990). They then have the opportunity to reconstruct a more empowering story. For example, sexual desire disorder can be defined as a problem couples must address rather than identifying the partners as being uninterested in sex.

- *Circular questions* are a technique used to help individuals or couples consider how the current *sexual* problem has affected their lives and how family members or others have influenced the problem (Nelson, Fleuridas, & Rosenthal, 1986). For example, a woman may be asked the following: How has your anorgasmia affected your life? Your partner's life? Your relationship? How has the problem affected you as sexual partners? How has it affected your view of yourself? Her partner may be asked the following: How have you influenced the problem? Circular questions can help couples realize that they are separate from the problem (externalization) and that they have power over the problem (White & Epston, 1990).

Communication Approaches

A number of professionals have significantly contributed to the development of communication theory. Among the most notable are works originating in 1959 at the Mental Research Institute (MRI) in Palo Alto, California.

Early researchers included Bateson, Jackson, Haley, & Weakland (1956), Jackson (1957, 1965), Satir (1964), and Watzlawick, Beavin, & Jackson, (1967). These individuals began studying the communication patterns of schizophrenic families and how these interactional patterns contributed to family dysfunction. In the 1980s, aspects of communication theory were refined into an approach focusing on communication or problem-solving training to be used with the intent of helping couples to negotiate, in nonblaming ways, resolutions to their conflicts (Hahleweg, Baucom, & Markman, 1988). Communication skills, the ability to talk, especially about problems, became the focus of creating good relationships and predicting marital satisfaction (Markman, 1981).

Traditional communication approaches propose that clear communication leads to healthy relationships and that distorted communication results in relationship problems. Healthy or functional individuals are able to talk openly about their vulnerabilities, hopes, and fears. They are flexible, express a wide range of emotions, and foster self-esteem and growth in each other (Satir, 1988). Effective communication involves the use of "I" statements or messages in which individuals express their own feelings as well as facial expressions, body position, and voice tone that match the message being delivered. When communication is clear and congruent, self-esteem and self-worth improve (Satir, 1972, 1988).

In dysfunctional or problematic relationships, communication can be rigid and superficial, causing couples to conceal their vulnerabilities. Emotional expression is restricted, thus preventing partners from feeling loved and accepted. Partners often speak indirectly and give unspecific messages (Satir, 1988). When communication is unclear and incongruent, self-esteem and self-worth are stifled. Satir (1972, 1988), who grew from the communication approaches to later becoming involved in aspects of humanistic and experiential approaches, identifies four communication patterns or stances that can be maladaptive because they suppress emotions: (a) placating, (b) blaming, (c) computing (being super-reasonable), and (d) distracting. These will be described in the section highlighting key terms.

Some Basic Premises of the Theory

The following are some premises of communication theory as they apply to sexuality counseling with couples.

1. All behavior is communication at some level (Watzlawick, Beavin, & Jackson, 1967).

2. All communication has a report (content) and a command (relationship) level: The report level refers to the verbal information (data) transmitted; the command level refers to the nonverbal aspects of the communication that defines the relationship (Watzlawick et al., 1967). For example, a woman who announces "I have been unable to have an orgasm" is offering information. She is also telling her partner that she expects him to do something about it by learning to stimulate her differently.

3. Communication takes place within a context and is more than the content of what is being said. It involves the unspoken language of facial expressions, voice tone and intensity, and gestures (Satir, 1983).

4. The expression of a wide range of emotions helps couples to feel loved and accepted. Unexpressed emotions can lead to sexual problems or dysfunctions.

5. Increasing self-awareness also encourages self-esteem and personal growth and contributes to healthier sexual relationships.

6. Open and clear communication fosters healthy sexual relationships.

Some Key Terms

- *Placating* is a communication stance that occurs when one partner sacrifices personal needs to please the other. For example, a woman who is having difficulty achieving orgasm may not express to her partner that she wants to spend more time engaging in sexual foreplay. She may fear being rejected or judged if she expresses her needs.

- *Blaming* is a communication stance that occurs when one partner undermines the other in order to maintain a personal sense of self and to avoid responsibility by blaming others. A man might say, "If you knew how to please me, I'd be able to have an erection."

- *Computing* is a communication stance that occurs when one partner becomes super-reasonable and strives to stay detached and avoid becoming emotional. For example, a man might say, "I'm OK if I never have another erection; it's just a part of the aging process."

- *Distracting* is a communication stance that occurs when partners display irrelevant behavior in an effort to avoid talking about the present issue. For example, a woman discusses how her partner's recent heart attack has affected her desire to engage in in-

tercourse. While she is speaking, her partner begins to program his newly acquired beeper intended to alert him to any physiological abnormalities.

- *Relationships* are patterns of interactions that are either symmetrical or complementary (Griffin & Greene, 1999).

- *Symmetrical relationships* are equally interactive. Each partner mirrors the other's behavior. For example, if one person brags, the other person brags more, causing the first person to brag even more.

- *Complementary relationships* are unequal and imply a superior or inferior position. In this case one person takes the "one up" position and the other the "one down" position.

Selected Techniques and Interventions

Although the following techniques are applicable to cognitive-behavioral-oriented sexuality counselors, they are also credited to communication strategies, particularly the work of Satir (1988).

- *"I" statements* involve the expression and owning of one's feelings (Satir, 1988). For example, a woman might say to her partner, "I feel ashamed when I talk about enjoying sex with you."

- *Communication skills training* teaches couples to listen to each other, express their thoughts and feelings clearly, and communicate in a constructive manner. It includes teaching couples to practice active listening, use "I" statements, paraphrase each others' thoughts and feelings, give and receive feedback, and use clarification and questions in order to check out nonverbal and verbal behaviors with a partner.

- *Problem-solving skills training* involves teaching couples to access their personal and relational strengths, communicating those strengths to each other, and then using their strengths to solve problems. Couples learn skills to specify what they want, negotiate for it, and make a specific plan to implement new solutions.

Psychodynamic and Object-Relations Approaches

Psychodynamic theory is derived from Freud's (1910) psychoanalytic model proposing that human behavior is driven by innate, instinctive drives, irrational forces, unconscious motivations, and early experiences. It maintains that early childhood development is critical to successful adjustment made during psychosexual stages of development (Rosen & Weinstein, 1988a). In the past, sexual dysfunctions were considered to be symptoms of serious pathology resulting from psychological conflict during certain developmental stages, and they were thus treated with a traditional psychoanalytic model (Kaplan, 1974). More recently, psychoanalytic theory has focused on how interpersonal and intrapersonal aspects of life affect each other. In other words, the way people relate to themselves impacts how they relate to those around them. One result has been the birth of object-relations theory (Kohut, 1977; Scharff, 1989; Slipp, 1988).

There are multiple models of object-relations theory (Fairbairn, 1954; Klein, 1957, 1975; Scharff & Scharff, 1987, 1991, 1997; Schnarch, 1991; Schwartz, 1994; Siegel, 1992). We will discuss some of their commonalities in this section.

Object-relations theory embraces the principles and techniques based on Freud's (1910) psychoanalytic theory. Scharff and de Varela (2000) explain this process as "following unconscious themes by listening to words, silence, and gestures; responding to unconscious material; developing insight; interpreting dreams and fantasies; and working with transference" (p. 81). According to object-relations theory, current sexual difficulties originate in early parent-child interactions (Scharff & Scharff, 1991). Male-female committed relationships mirror the early mother-infant relationship that provided "devotion, commitment, intimacy, and physicality" (Scharff & Scharff, 1997, p. 145). These relationships provide a framework for couples to express repressed parts of themselves. This can result in conflict and confusion because individuals are reacting unconsciously to images of their past rather than from current situations that create relationship distress (Kernberg, 1976; Kohut, 1971). Sexuality counselors help couples learn about transference of feelings that influence sexual functioning by exploring the source of their emotional response toward each other or toward the sexuality counselor (Scharff & Scharff, 1997). Through this process, couples mutually "attempt to heal and make reparation to the object refound in the spouse . . . and then to find . . . a new, more integrated self" (Sharff & Scharff, 1997, p. 145). Intimate sexual relationships can be threatened because couples "re-create a demand for meeting another's emotional needs" (Heiman, 2000, p. 129). Conflicts regarding closeness in the relationship result in anger and hostility as well as the inability to trust, all leading to the development of sexual problems or dysfunctions.

Central to object-relations theory is the concept of the "holding environment." This requires that sexuality counselors create a safe and nurturing environment for couples to explore repressed thoughts and feelings while being aware of and working with their transference issues (Sharf, 2000). Scharff and Scharff (1997) emphasize helping couples to be able to determine how their current interactions are affected by these holding relationships.

Some Premises of the Theory

The following are some premises of psychoanalytic and object-relations theory as they apply to sexuality counseling with couples.

1. Marital sexuality is the single greatest tool for human development (Schnarch, 1991).
2. Sexuality counselors who use an object-relations approach help partners develop a capacity for attachment, autonomy, and developmental progression (Scharff & Scharff, 1997).
3. Sexual problems may manifest themselves as both individual as well as relationship difficulties (Young & Long, 1998).
4. Intimate sexual relationships carry with them a risk of lost autonomy as well as dependency on another individual (Young & Long, 1998).
5. People often have expectations that their intimate relationships will somehow fulfill needs that were neglected by their parents during childhood (Young & Long, 1998).

Some Key Terms

- *Denial* is the process of refusing to acknowledge an unpleasant or traumatic event or situation. Denial operates at the unconscious or conscious level. For example, in the treatment of anorgasmia "denial [might] be expressed [by] the minimization of physical sensations" (Heiman, 2000, p. 129).
- *Repression* is a defense mechanism that allows individuals to unconsciously exclude painful or distressing thoughts or memories from their awareness in order to function. For example, a person with a history of early childhood sexual abuse may repress painful memories associated with the event in order to be able to engage in intercourse.
- *Projection* is the process of attributing unacceptable thoughts, feelings, or motives to someone else in an effort to deny that characteristic or emotion in oneself. For example, a woman struggling with

an issue of infertility may not believe that her part-ner wants to bear children when she herself is ex-periencing feelings of ambivalence.

- *Transference* is the process of transferring onto the counselor or partner one's pleasant and unpleasant feelings, or one's desires. Most often, a person is mirroring their early relationship with a family member (Griffin & Greene, 1999). For example, a husband reminds his wife of her father who was sexually abusive; she responds to her partner as though this is accurate and has difficulty expressing her needs sexually because she fears her husband.

Selected Interventions and Techniques

- *Interpretation* occurs when sexuality counselors offer meanings or motives behind couples' thoughts, feelings, or actions. One strategy used by sexuality counselors involves linking responses in the pres-ent to responses from the past (Griffin & Green, 1999). For example, a young couple having infre-quent sexual activity seeks counseling and shares that they both grew up in alcoholic families. The sexuality counselor interprets their lack of sexual intimacy as a possible reflection of their childhood reality (constant disappointment and rejection). Siegel (1992) believes that interpretations help clients to connect events from the past to present issues that are distressing.
- *Listening* is a process that creates a nonjudgmen-tal atmosphere that promotes analytic neutrality (Nichols & Schwartz, 1998).
- *Analytic neutrality* is maintained by listening to couples in order to understand them rather than focusing on trying to solve their problems (Nichols & Schwartz, 1998).
- *Examining the past* is a significant method used in object-relations psychodynamic therapy to ex-plore developmental history and early childhood experiences (Finkelstein, 1987; Young & Long, 1998). Examining the past can help couples gain insight into their own behaviors in the present. Sex-history interviews along with the use of a sexual genogram can reveal deeper relationship issues and secrets from the past, and it can demon-strate how sexual concerns can be related to unre-solved issues in childhood (Boszormenyi-Nagy & Spark, 1973; Kaplan, 1974; LoPiccolo & Heiman, 1978; Masters & Johnson, 1970).
- *Creating a holding environment* is a technique that devises a setting in which couples feel pro-tected and safe to explore repressed thoughts and

emotions (Scharff & Scharff, 1997) and to accept therapeutic interpretation. For example, through active listening and by encouraging verbal and nonverbal responses, a sexuality counselor creates a supportive atmosphere for a man to explore his interactions with his mother and to discover how these patterns of relating impact his current sexual relationship with his partner.

Feminist Theory

Unlike many other theories we have presented, fem-inist theory has a brief history that has evolved from the collective efforts of therapists, primarily women, who emphasize the central importance of gender and sex-role issues as it relates to counseling individuals, couples, and families. Beginning in the late 1970s and early 1980s, therapists began to challenge family ther-apy models for ignoring how gender and power dif-ferences in male-female relationships influenced the dynamics in families and couples. These early studies (Avis, 1985; Gilligan, 1982; Goldner, 1985; Hare-Mustin, 1978; Walters, Carter, Papp, & Silverstein, 1989) were unprecedented attempts to alter gender bias, and they began "to challenge the social, cultural, historical, economic, and political conditions that shaped not only the unique development and experiences of women but also their relationships with men" (Gold-enberg & Goldenberg, 2000, p. 46).

Feminist theory finds fault with systemic viewpoints suggesting that the concept of "circular-causality . . . implies that each partner has equal power and con-trol in a transaction" (Goldenberg & Goldenberg, 2000, p. 47). This notion is challenged, thus engaging in a never-ending, repetitive pattern of mutually rein-forcing behaviors. This type of thinking also implies that no one person is to blame. When applied to cer-tain situations involving men against women, such as physical abuse (rape, battering, and incest), a circular concept removes responsibility from the aggressor, which may infer coresponsibility for violence and abuse (Goldenberg & Goldenberg, 2000). In this con-text, this type of interaction is oppressive to women and promotes powerlessness.

Since those first studies, a strong feminist voice has emerged in the field of psychotherapy, including philosophies that endorse a belief that "gender is at the core of therapeutic practice, that understanding a client's problems requires adopting a sociocultural perspective, and that empowerment of the individual and societal changes are crucial goals in therapy" (Corey, 2001, p. 346).

Feminist-oriented sexuality counselors "work to help women and men recognize, claim, and embrace their personal power" enabling them to break free of gender-role socialization and increase their options for living (Corey, 2001, p. 353). Couples are assisted by sexuality counselors to examine the effects of society's unrealistic expectations about women and to create relationships that are egalitarian, interdependent, cooperative, and mutually supportive. Thus, Worell and Remer (2003) suggest a variety of goals for using a feminist orientation to counsel clients. These include helping them to (a) become aware of their own gender-role socialization process; (b) identify internalized messages and beliefs that are oppressive and stereotypical and replace them with more productive messages; (c) understand and identify how sexist and oppressive societal practices influence their personal experiences and affect their behavior in a negative way; (d) learn skills to make changes in their own environments such as restructuring organizations in which they are affiliated; and (e) develop behaviors that allow them to express their personal and social power (i.e., becoming more direct and assertive, making sexual decisions without coercion from others, expressing their sexual orientation).

In addition, goals related to promoting egalitarian relationships include helping clients to (a) gain the skills to become self-supporting and autonomous; (b) cultivate egalitarian relationships that reflect a balance of autonomy and interdependence; (c) enhance life skills, such as how to be assertive, manage anger constructively, and address interpersonal conflict; and (d) identify and use personal strengths and assets.

Worell and Remer (2003) also promote an emphasis on valuing women's perspectives and suggest goals that help women to (a) trust their individual experiences and instincts as valid information about themselves and the world around them, (b) appreciate female-related values and perspectives, (c) recognize their personal strengths and mobilize these strengths to make changes, (d) learn to recognize their personal needs and cultivate a nurturing relationship with themselves, (e) recognize the value of themselves and other relationships with women, (f) accept themselves and enjoy their bodies, and (g) recognize their own sexual needs and express themselves in accordance with these needs in lieu of focusing on someone else's needs.

The integrative model for sexuality counseling encourages a perspective that promotes the awareness of gender and power relations across theories by maintaining the idea that there is no one set of techniques to address couples' diverse sexuality issues. We recognize that the concept of circular-causality (sharing responsibility) is inappropriate in certain cases, including those involving rape, incest, sexual abuse, and domestic violence. However, it is important to examine the circular interactions in order to determine how partners influence each other and how one person may move out of the relationship in order to break the cycle. Chapters 12 and 13 will present more specific information on this topic. We encourage sexuality counselors to adopt a collaborative style that promotes equality for men and women and fosters sensitivity to gender, cultural, and socioeconomic factors.

CONCEPTUAL APPROACHES AND RATIONALE FOR AN INTEGRATIVE MODEL

According to Nichols and Schwartz (2004), there is no one approach that is universally adopted by sexuality counselors. The dominant trend is toward integration of multiple theories and treatment strategies. Integration refers to three approaches:

1. Eclecticism, which draws from a variety of models and methods.
2. Selective borrowing, which involves the occasional use of techniques from other approaches but grounded in one particular paradigm. Selective borrowing is most useful when it includes a conceptual focus. It cannot mean a mix and match hodgepodge of techniques.
3. Designed integrative models, which combines elements of complementary approaches.

These approaches can vary in form. Some include a whole range of approaches under one umbrella, while others simply combine elements of one approach with another forming an eclectic model. Unlike metaframeworks models, which synthesize key ideas from various schools of thought, integrative models link ideas together theoretically and do not attempt to revise existing models.

Jacobson and Christensen (1996) developed a model for integrative couples therapy after they determined that adding a humanistic element to their standard behavioral approaches helped their clients improve (Nichols & Schwartz, 2004). Other integrative models such as those developed by Andersen and Stewart (1983), Duhl and Duhl (1981), Feldman (1990), Gurman (1981), Liddle (1991), and Scharff (1989), use the most useful theoretical approaches and intervention strategies to promote a higher success rate for relationship counseling (Nichols & Schwartz, 2004).

Nichols and Schwartz (2004) have identified the following guidelines for creating effective integrative models:

1. Unify conceptual threads that tie together disparate ideas.
2. Add techniques from various models without eliminating focus.
3. Draw on existing theories in such a way that they can be practiced coherently within one consistent theoretical framework.
4. Create a balance between breadth and focus.
5. Provide clear direction in order to maximize the long-term usefulness of the approach. (p. 365)

Goldenberg and Goldenberg (2004) describe integration as a way to offer a more "holistic or comprehensive way of assessing and intervening" (p. 118) with couples.

The integrative couples model for sexuality counseling we have developed addresses each of the components identified by Nichols and Schwartz (2004):

1. The model offers a unified philosophy of change regardless of the theoretical framework or the selection of treatment strategies. Change is based on identifying the strengths of each partner and of the couple. These positive assets are the basis for formulating a plan for change. Throughout the model, change is also promoted by reducing blame, empowering couples to reduce relapse, and focusing on creativity to celebrate success. In addition to promoting change through the identification of positive assets, acceptance and creating a nonblaming atmosphere are fundamental to the success of our integrative model. Acceptance includes partners understanding each other's past in order to explain the present and the future, reducing blame by developing a shared view of the presenting problem, externalizing the problem, using personal strengths to collaborate on solutions, and validating each other to highlight the positive changes that have been made.
2. The model offers a comprehensive, holistic approach that includes strategies drawn from the cognitive, behavioral, and affective therapies. These components are evident in assessment, goal-setting, treatment planning, relapse prevention, and validation stages of the model.

3. The model draws from various schools of thought, particularly cognitive-behavioral, systemic, narrative, and solution-focused theories. Selection of appropriate interventions is based on the usefulness of one theory or intervention that may work best for a particular couple. For example, with gay and lesbian couples it is useful to consider narrative strategies such as restorying when looking at family-of-origin issues and relationship development. Similarly, when working with one partner's sexual dysfunction it is necessary to also focus on the feeling of the other partner as a significant component of treatment.
4. The model encompasses a comprehensive biopsychosocial perspective in which all "the biological, psychological, relational, community, and even societal processes are viewed as relevant to understanding people's problems" (Nichols & Schwartz, 2004, p. 365). Focus is evident in our circular model as couples move from "we have a problem" to "we have a solution."
5. The model offers clear direction through a five-stage circle. If couples become stuck, they can return to a previous stage without losing their sense of direction as they move toward solutions to their problems.

Conceptual Elements of the Integrative Model for Sexuality Counseling

Taking a Constructionist View of Sexuality Counseling

Constructionist sexuality counseling focuses on understanding and altering a couple's view of the problem, attempts to challenge the meaning of the problem, and questions the sexual script (Atwood & Dershowitz, 1992). One way this can be achieved is to ask couples about exceptions to their problem, to create a larger context for the problem, or to use techniques such as reframing, metaphors, or narrative storytelling. These techniques offer a positive approach and de-emphasize pathology and blame when addressing sexual problems and dysfunctions.

Using a Circular Model of Causation

An important element of an integrative couples model involves "a circular or recursive process of assessment, goal setting, treatment planning, and therapeutic intervention" (Young & Long, 1998, p. 67). *Circular* and *recursive* "means that the interactive patterns of relationships form a type of feedback-loop response system" (Landis & Young, 1994, p. 210). In contrast to linear thinking where A causes B, recursive thinking emphasizes "the reciprocal interaction and mutual causation of events" (Landis & Young, 1994, p. 210) where "A does not cause B, nor does B cause A; both cause each other" (Goldenberg & Goldenberg, 2000, p. 14). "Thus, each individual influences, and in turn is influenced by, [their partner] in a circular pattern" (Young & Long, 1998, p. 67). Like a wind chime that has been gently touched, each individual part of the chime affects the functioning of the whole and a pattern of sounds emerges. In relationships, an event affecting one partner affects the reaction of the other, thus the interaction is changed. For example, if partner A expresses low sexual desire, partner B may become hurt or angry and change her style of approaching her partner. In turn, partner A may not feel desired by her partner.

Predictable events in various stages of the life cycle, crises, social and environmental factors, health, and family members and/or friends also influence sexual meanings, behaviors, and interactions. Sexuality counseling focuses on patterns of sexual dysfunctions while keeping in mind other contributions to problems, which might include feelings, beliefs, and behaviors that interact as part of the problem and are taken into consideration when couples cocreate solutions to the negative pattern in which they have become "stuck."

Using Circular Questioning

Circular questions are based on the concept of circularity—a systemic pattern that has no beginning or end and where all information will impact a situation. Such questions are used to help couples view their problems in a larger context (Nelson et al., 1986). Sexuality counselors ask couples to think about each partner's contribution to the problem, and they then offer alternative solutions that may not yet have been considered. As the sexuality counselor questions one partner, the other is able to hear the answer. Because the questions are not blame-directed, couples are often able to open up to each other and reveal secrets or hidden emotions in a more solution-focused manner. For example, a nonblaming query, "How sexually compatible are the two of you right now?" may lead to an open discussion about pressures they both feel and how the pressures affect their sexual relationship.

Types of Circular Questions

There are four types of circular questions [...] selors can ask when addressing sexual [...] counseling:

- *Problem definition questions* are used to obtain information about both partners' perceptions of their present sexual functioning along with their current sexual concerns (Nelson et al., 1986). "When did you notice that you were not enjoying your sexual relationship as much as before?" is an example of a problem definition question (Nelson et al., 1986, p. 119). Such questions enable counselors to gain information about each person's view of the problem and the social, environmental, and developmental influences related to the problem (Young & Long, 1998). These factors may provide a historical glimpse of what was happening when the couple's lovemaking was more satisfying.

- *Sequence of interaction questions* provide a contextual view for events preceding, during, or after the onset of couples' sexual concern as well as taking into account their interactions (Nelson et al., 1986). This line of questioning directs the therapist to a more lucid view of each partner's role in the problem and how the problem is perpetuated by the reaction of each partner (Young & Long, 1998). Examples of this type of question include the following:

> "Does your partner agree or disagree with your idea about the lack of sexual contact the two of you experience?"
>
> "What reaction do you get from your partner when you do initiate sex?"
>
> "What happens when the two of you try to talk about your concerns?"

- *Comparison and classification questions* help couples define the intensity and duration of the problem (Young & Long, 1998). Relationships, beliefs, values, myths, thoughts, and feelings are explored through this type of question (Nelson et al., 1986). Questions might include the following:

> "How often do you think she would like to make love?"
>
> "Where did you get your ideas about how often you should have sex?"
>
> "When you felt satisfied, what was happening in your relationship that isn't happening now?"

- *Interventive questions* help reframe the problem in a more positive way and challenge couples' patterns of interacting by offering new information and opportunities for change (Nelson et al., 1986). For example, the counselor might ask the following questions:

> "If you were willing to explore new ways to relate to each other sexually, where would you begin?"
>
> "If you were able to help your partner with her worry about another pregnancy, what would you do?"

Getting Away from Blame

A notable premise in relational integrative models is that partners usually begin "with different, often contradictory, ideas about [their] problem in the relationship" (Young & Long, 1998, p. 68). These ideas frequently include pointing the finger at the other partner and taking little or no personal responsibility for the problem.

Typically, we blame others in order to protect our egos and to avoid guilt. Although blaming might superficially accomplish these goals, it also results in helplessness for the blamer (Young & Long, 1998). As a result, it may be difficult to feel competent to create effective solutions. "We believe a primary task [for sexuality counseling] is to define the problem 'interactionally' so that there is emphasis on the reciprocal or shared nature of the relationship" (Young & Long, 1998, p. 68).

Taking a Neutral Stance in Counseling

Neutrality is a key concept in couples sexuality counseling. Because a nonblaming and objective stance is critical to the outcome of counseling, counselors cannot align with one partner or view the problem in the same way only one partner views it. Instead, a shared definition of the problem weaves together both partners' views and eliminates a blaming, one-sided perspective by the couple and the counselor.

Taking a Stage Model Approach

Most systems models include a developmental approach that associates certain tasks and behaviors with a particular stage. In our integrative model, we take couples through five predictable stages: (a) obtaining a workable view of the problem, (b) setting goals, (c) making changes, (d) maintenance, and (e) termination. However, we are aware that couples progress through each stage of therapy at their own rate and are likely to return to a previous stage at some time during treatment. This is an expected part of counseling and should be used as a learning tool rather than viewed as "backsliding" or "failure."

SPECIFIC CONCEPTS FOR AN INTEGRATIVE COUPLES' MODEL

As documented in the literature, integrative approaches work well for relationship counseling (Nichols & Schwartz, 2004; Goldenberg & Goldenberg, 2004). They also work well for sexuality counseling. Our integrative couples' model of sexuality counseling is the process of blending concepts and methods from a variety of theoretical orientations with the idea that no one theory is the "truth" and that no one group of counseling interventions is effective for treating every problem and every couple (Kelly, 1991; Young & Long, 1998). For example, to treat erectile disorders, sexuality counselors might draw on cognitive, behavioral, communication, psychoeducational, and couples counseling approaches. These techniques require counselors to draw on multiple skills—from establishing a relationship with their clients to providing direction and support during the counseling process.

Norcross and Newman (1992) identify factors that have contributed to a general movement toward integration of theories in relationship counseling. We have adapted several of these factors to reflect a focus on couples' sexual concerns: (a) a proliferation of therapies that can be used to treat sexual problems; (b) the lack of a single theory that is useful to all clients and all sexual problems; (c) external socioeconomic contingencies, including managed mental health care and national health care pressures; (d) the increased use of brief, problem-focused and solution-focused therapies to treat sexual concerns; (e) increased opportunities to observe and experiment with the therapies used to treat sexual problems; (f) the paucity of differential effectiveness among therapies; (g) the recognition that therapeutic commonalities (i.e., the therapeutic relationship) play a major role in determining therapy outcomes; and (h) the development of professional organizations focused on the integration of psychotherapies.

The movement toward integration recognizes that one theory cannot accommodate the range of problems and treat diverse clients needs. The use of an integrative couples' model to deal with the wide array of sexuality issues prevalent today provides sexuality counselors with a variety of options to help couples with their sexual concerns.

Some Premises of an Integrative Couples' Model

Several theoretical orientations have been developed during the last 30 years in order to counsel couples experiencing an array of sexual dysfunctions or problems. Lebow (1997) identifies the benefits of integrative approaches, which include flexibility for practitioners to draw from a wider variety of treatment interventions; increased use of several domains of functioning including cognitive, affective, and behavioral components. These interventions are tailored to meet the specific needs of clients and offer a more promising outcome for both treatment acceptability and efficacy among clients.

The premise of our integrative approach allows the use "of the most progressive methods from a [variety] of theoretical positions" (Young & Long, 1998, p. 66), allowing sexuality counselors to determine which approach works best for couples experiencing sexual problems (Young, 1992). The integrative couples model for sexuality counseling that we propose incorporates a systemic focus by understanding problems from both partners' perspectives so that blaming is reduced and couples are able to view each other as allies. By taking steps to understand problems from each partner's perspective early in the counseling process, goals can be established and intervention strategies can be selected according to the specific needs of the couple (Young, 1992; Young & Long, 1998). Central to the integrative couples model is the attention given to cognitive, affective, and behavioral changes within the scope of couples' sexual patterns. Emphasis is placed on helping partners mobilize themselves to solve their struggles by heightening their strengths and resources.

Cognitive Change and Its Impact on Therapy

Challenging beliefs, thoughts, and ideas about sexual issues is key to the success of sexuality counseling. Effective counseling interventions are dependent on gaining a comprehensive view of couples' cognitions and then helping them think about the problem in a different way. As couples shift their thinking to a more useful, nonblaming, solution-focused stance, they are able to broaden their concept of the issue and interact in a more positive manner with each other.

Changing Both Feelings and Behaviors

In an integrative couples' model, we believe it is important to address feelings and behaviors because both are equally important in order to create and maintain change. Some individuals may respond more easily to feelings, while others respond to actions or behaviors. Learning styles vary from individual to individual. Connecting feelings to behaviors helps many couples gain a larger picture of their issues. One partner might state, "When we hug and kiss each other before we initiate intercourse, I feel more connected, and I want to be closer to you."

Creating Solutions to Problems

Creating solutions to problems is an important part of the work of Berg and deShazer (1993) as they observe patterns of interactions and focus on what patterns are most open to change. Two disparate perspectives of the same problem are not viewed as productive if couples cannot understand each other's point of view. We believe that couples have the ability to reshape and shift their individual perceptions and definitions of reality in an effort to find joint solutions to their problems. The counselor's task is to guide couples as they redefine the problem as one for which they both contribute information and can find many potential solutions. If couples are able to view the problem as external to themselves, they can attack it together. Couples can then set realistic, shared goals with help from their counselors and begin to view their issues as solvable.

This approach focuses on the positive assets of each partner and on their interactional assets as they join together to conquer their problems. In later stages, the model suggests they will need to continue to monitor success as they find creative solutions throughout their life span. The model challenges couples to focus on positive growth and change while emphasizing the need to adopt strategies to prevent reoccurrence of old patterns.

Emphasizing Strengths and Resilience in Therapy

The integrative couples' model is based on the notion that couples want to achieve a satisfying intimate relationship but do not know how. Each partner comes to the relationship with sexual messages and ideas from their families of origin, culture, and society. We believe that couples possess resiliencies and strengths that shape how they relate as sexual beings. As they identify these resources and gain confidence in selves and in each other, they will begin to relate positively (Young & Long, 1998). They will also feel more hopeful and will usually be able to view the problems without blaming each other, and they will discover multiple possibilities for resolving problems in the future (Young & Long, 1998, p. 75). For example, couples who are able to overcome anger with each other by increasing nonsexual playtime together should continually assess the degree of fun in their relationship. If they get "out of balance," they can use previously identified strategies to reverse the process.

The ability to identify strategies empowers couples to view their sexuality as a positive rather than a problematic part of their relationship.

AN INTEGRATIVE COUPLES' MODEL FOR SEXUALITY COUNSELING

Figures 2.1 and 2.2 are pictorial representations of a five-stage integrative couples' model used in sexuality counseling. Figure 2.2 was initially created by Young

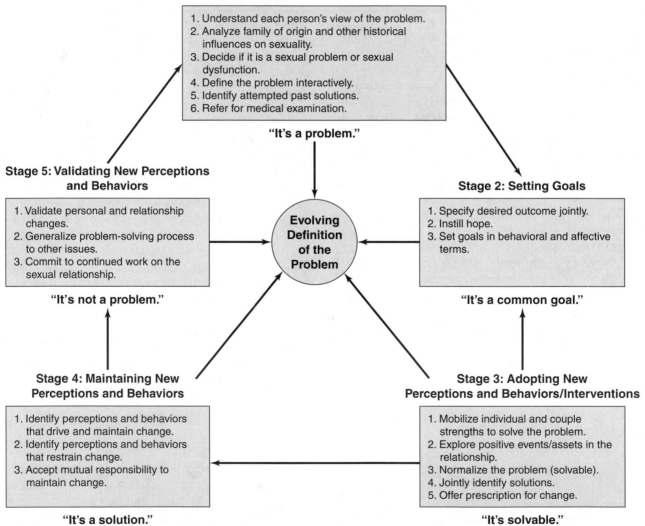

FIGURE 2.1
Integrative Couples' Model for Sexuality Counseling
Source: Adapted from *Counseling and Therapy for Couples,* 1st ed., by M. E. Young and L. L. Long. © 1998. Reprinted with permission of Wadsworth, a division of Thomson Learning: www.thomsonrights.com. Fax 800-730-2215.

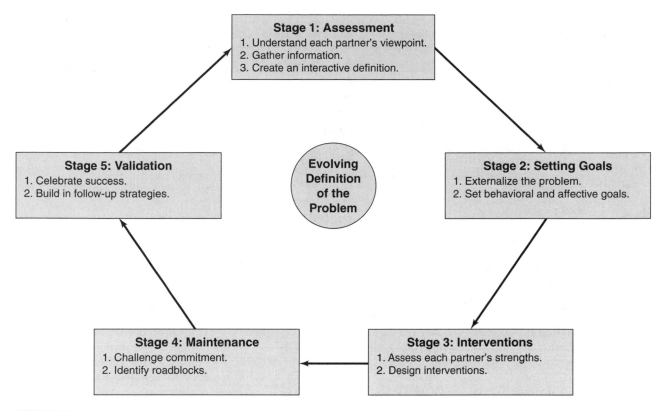

FIGURE 2.2
Integrative Model at a Glance
Source: From *Counseling and Therapy for Couples,* 1st ed., by M. E. Young and L. L. Long. © 1998. Reprinted with permission of Wadsworth, a division of Thomson Learning: www.thomsonrights.com. Fax 800-730-2215.

and Long (1998), and it has been expanded into Figure 2.1 to specifically address couples' sexual issues. Although in circular models we understand that assessment is also intervention, the model is sequential and proceeds from assessment to validation. Central to the model is the evolving definition of the problem, which begins as a problem and emerges as a solution. Couples' interactions with each other and with sexuality counselors help shape the changing view as they undergo the difficult process of enhancing and strengthening their sexual relationship.

THEORIES AND INTERVENTIONS INFLUENCING EACH STAGE OF THE INTEGRATIVE COUPLES' MODEL

We will now describe the tasks of each stage of the integrative couples' model and how different theoretical approaches can be used by sexuality counselors.

Table 2.1 provides a brief matrix of each of the five stages of the integrative model, listing theoretical concepts and major theories contributing to each stage. In-depth discussion of the stages of this model will be provided in Chapters 3, 4, and 5.

Case Example

Simon, age 35, and Mikala, age 32, have been married for six years. They have two children, ages 4 and 2. Simon has just completed a medical residency and is beginning private practice. Mikala has been an assistant professor in elementary education for two years. The couple present in counseling with complaints of low sexual desire since the birth of their second child.

Stage 1: Assessing the Problem
Stage 1 involves helping couples to describe each person's perspective of the problem, while

BLE 2.1

Concepts and Theories for Each Stage of the Integrative Model for Sexuality Counseling

	CONCEPTUAL FRAMEWORK	THEORETICAL CONTRIBUTION
Stage 1	Assessing the problem	
	• Joining with the individual or couple	Problem-focused (structural)
	• Gathering family of origin information (use of sexual genogram)	Bowenian
	• Exploring developmental history and childhood experiences	Psychodynamic/object relations
	• Identifying past and current behaviors and feelings about the identified problem (identifying cognitive distortions)	Cognitive-behavioral
	• Expressing feelings (use of "I" statements)	Communication theory
	• Identifying attempted past solutions	Brief/solution-focused
Stage 2	Setting goals	
	• Use of "miracle question"	Brief/solution-focused
	• Externalizing the sexual problem	Narrative/constructivist
	• Identifying specific goals	Cognitive-behavioral
	• Behavioral goals	
	• Affective goals	
Stage 3	Developing a treatment plan and a focus on strengths	
	• Identifying past and present strengths and successes	Brief/solution-focused
	• Constructing new stories about the problem based on positive attributes in the couple's sexual relations history	Problem-focused (strategic/systemic) Narrative/constructivist
	• Focusing on a "here and now" plan	Problem-focused (strategic/systemic) Brief/solution-focused
	• Exploring exceptions to the problem	Narrative
	• Use of "miracle question," unique outcomes	Brief/problem- and solution-focused
	• Designing interventions based on the couple's unique problem while utilizing their strengths and resources	Cognitive-behavioral Communication theory
Stage 4	Maintenance	
	• Continuing to focus on strengths and positive assets	Problem-solving (strategic/systemic)
	• Continuing to focus on solutions	Brief/solution-focused
	• Redefining goals based on gained information	Cognitive-behavioral
	• Setting realistic goals	Communication theory
	• Reinforcing positive communication skills	Cognitive behavioral
	• Maintaining changes in feelings, thoughts, and behaviors	
	• Identifying behaviors for healthy sexual patterns and planning for setbacks	Brief/solution-focused, problem-solving
	• Identifying specific techniques to prevent relapse	Brief/solution-focused, problem-solving
	• Use of questions (i.e., circular, exceptions, challenging)	Narrative brief/solution-focused
Stage 5	Validation	
	• Continuing to focus on strengths and resources	Brief/solution-focused
	• Listening to client stories about their therapeutic journey	Narrative/constructivist
	• Finding rituals to celebrate success and renewed relationship	Problem-focused (strategic/systemic)
	• Establishing follow-up strategies	Brief/solution-focused

gathering past and present influences that have contributed to the formation of the presenting issue. The goal of this stage is to co-create with the couple a shared definition of the presenting problem, including each partner's views and shared responsibility for the problem. Therapeutic

tasks to be accomplished at this stage include the following:

1. Join with Simon and Mikala.
2. Explore each person's perspective of the problem.

3. Gather current and historical information regarding the problem.
4. Identify current behaviors and feelings each person has about the problem.
5. Create a shared definition of the problem based on both partners' individual perspectives and other assessment instruments.

Stage 1 involves structural, Bowenian, psychodynamic, cognitive-behavioral, communication, narrative, and brief/solution-focused approaches. For example, from a structural approach, the assessment stage begins with establishing a relationship through joining. Sexuality counselors focus on establishing rapport by talking about the common desire people have to express and experience sexuality. In the case of Simon and Mikala, the counselor addresses the commonality of dual-career couples in struggling to maintain balance in their busy lives.

The sexuality counselor uses Bowenian and psychodynamic approaches to gather important current and past history. A sexual genogram helps Simon and Mikala recognize familial patterns related to sexual attitudes, beliefs, and cultural differences. In addition, examining developmental history and childhood experiences helps the couple gain insight into how behaviors from the past may be contributing to their sexual problem in the present.

Drawing from cognitive-behavioral theory, the counselor helps Simon and Mikala identify cognitive distortions or negative sexual thoughts or ideas stemming from early childhood or current experiences that may be forcing them to repeat the same unsuccessful pattern of behavior.

Using concepts from communication theory, Simon and Mikala learn to use "I" statements to express their feelings about their lack of sexual desire to each other. For example, Simon states, "Mikala, I feel resentful toward you when you take time to build relationships with your students by mentoring them and then say you have no energy left to have sex with me." Mikala offers her view of the situation: "Simon, I feel angry when you tell me that you have to devote your time and energy to your studies and that our relationship will have to come second in your life right now."

From a constructivist perspective, Simon and Mikala are asked to describe their reality or perception of the problem as they see it. By obtaining a clear picture of the presenting issue from both perspectives, the couple and the therapist can move to constructing a shared definition of the problem. For example, Simon sees the problem as Mikala spending too much time focusing on her career and, consequently, neglecting home life. Mikala states that Simon cares more about his residency and getting ahead than making love to her. Their shared definition of the problem is that neither of them has the time or the energy to devote to their relationship. The problem is now redefined as "a time and energy" problem. They benefit from a solution-focused approach by exploring ways they have been successful in the past and by creating time for each other in order to gain energy in their busy lives.

Stage 2: Setting Goals

During this stage, couples try to set realistic goals based on a shared definition of the problem they have jointly identified in Stage 1. By setting these goals, couples can chart their progress and feel successful. They can also learn to externalize or think about the problem as separate from themselves so that blaming is minimized. Finally, specific affective and behavioral goals are set to help couples get a picture of what they will be doing and how they will be feeling once they have attained success. The therapeutic tasks to be accomplished in this stage are as follows:

1. Help the couple to set realistic and specific goals addressing their sexual problem or dysfunction.
2. Externalize or separate the problem from the couple.
3. Set behavioral and affective goals based on a couple's shared definition of the problem.

Narrative, solution-focused, and cognitive-behavioral approaches may be utilized at this point. Drawing from a narrative approach, for example, Simon and Mikala externalize their "desire problem" as something that they can both work on as a team. After viewing this as a "time and energy" problem in Stage 1, they can focus on a cooperative problem-solving approach in Stage 2. They then create goals based on their shared definition of the problem.

To begin setting behavioral and affective goals, the sexuality counselor can draw from a solution-focused approach by using the "miracle question" to get Simon and Mikala to think specifically about what they will be doing differently and how they will be feeling once their goals are attained. For example, the counselor might ask, "If a miracle occurred tonight, and you woke up in the morning and had time to spend with each other nurturing your relationship and you both felt rested and energized, what would your relationship be like? What would you be doing? How would you feel?" Cognitive-behavioral theories aimed at changing thinking and behavior about the sexual problem are then used to help establish specific behavioral and affective goals based on a shared definition of the problem. For example, Simon and Mikala might set the following goals:

Goal 1: We would like to go out on dates once a week and plan fun activities (behavior) in order to feel more connected to each other (affect).

Goal 2: We would like to learn how to communicate our sexual needs and desires (behavior) so that we can feel mutually loved and understood (affect).

Stage 3: Interventions
Couples must identify their individual and relational strengths and resources during this stage. In addition, the sexuality counselor may ask them to focus on times when their problem did not exist or existed minimally. The overall goal of this stage is to help couples view their problems as solvable. Therapeutic tasks during this stage include the following:

1. Help couples change feelings, behaviors, and thoughts about their relationship.
2. Help couples identify and access their personal and relational strengths.
3. Help couples identify times when the sexual problem was not as evident (exceptions).
4. Help couples experience success by attaining their shared goals.
5. Provide feedback to the couple about their progress and observations of their success.

6. Design interventions that are specific to a couple's goals in counseling.

During this stage, solution-focused, narrative, strategic/systemic, cognitive-behavioral, and communication approaches can be used. In addition, medical and pharmacological treatment may be implemented when appropriate. For example, Simon and Mikala benefit by identifying their individual and relational strengths (solution-focused), by sharing stories about their relationship, and by exploring times when they had "sexual desire" for each other (solution-focused, narrative approaches). While focusing on individual and relational strengths and successes in this stage, Simon and Mikala gain a feeling of optimism about successfully solving their current and future problems.

Systemic interventions are then designed by sexuality counselors drawing from a multitude of theoretical approaches that involve changing the interaction and behavioral patterns of the couple. In this way Simon and Mikala work toward creating a mutually satisfying relationship in which the need for time and energy with each other is addressed. For instance, they benefit from cognitive-behavioral approaches such as psychoeducational and guided masturbation training along with sensate focus activities. Their sexuality counselor assigns psychoeducational reading encompassing literature about changes in males and in females and their sexual relationships after having children, the impact of career and home stress on sexual behavior, or ways to entice the other sex. The couple is asked to read the literature and share their reactions with each other. Questions such as "What did you learn about yourself?" or "How does this reading apply to our relationship?" stimulate Simon and Mikala to interact while exchanging their thoughts and feelings about sex. They even discover undisclosed stories from the past that help them to understand their present sexual behavior. This discovery can create the closeness they are looking for to rekindle their sexual relationship.

Likewise, the counselor assigns guided masturbation exercises for both Simon and Mikala in order to help them get to know their bodies more intimately. These assignments include self-exploration exercises to be practiced individually. The exercises can be explained to the couple together or individually based on their comfort level. If they are explained individually, they will later be shared in the presence of the partner. In the case of Simon and Mikala, each feels comfortable with an open discussion of sexual exercises. In addition, sensate focus activities aid Simon and Mikala in accomplishing their goals. (A more detailed description of sensate focus exercises is provided in Chapter 6.)

These exercises involve a series of sexual and nonsexual touching and can be used to help couples create sexual desire for each other, increase communication and pleasure, and create closeness. Simon and Mikala are first instructed to refrain from intercourse or genital caressing for two weeks and explore their bodies through kissing, hugging, touching, and massage. Next, they begin to engage in genital touching without emphasis on orgasm and intercourse. During this time, they communicate to each other what feels good sexually and what is enjoyable to them. Finally, they engage in intercourse.

It is important to recognize that when individual assignments such as self-exploration occur privately, the impact of the assignment on the couple system is discussed and brought into focus in a subsequent counseling session. Simon and Mikala have the opportunity to communicate how their new self-discoveries affect their interactions and behaviors toward each other.

In addition, drawing from communication theory, communication skill-building experiences may be helpful. These include teaching Simon and Mikala to be more attentive to each other by making them aware of their eye contact, body language, voice tone, facial expressions, and physical touch when communicating. For example, Simon complains that when discussing the issue of not having enough time and energy for their sex life, Mikala gets very emotional about her point of view and seldom sits down, often raising her voice as if shouting. He states, "I feel paralyzed when you behave this way. I'm afraid to say anything because you might get more

emotional. You look so upset." Mikala states that Simon has little eye contact with her when conversing about sex and often responds to her by agreeing that they need to make changes. She states, "You look bored and uninterested in what I have to say. I feel frustrated!"

Becoming aware of nonverbal communication and working to become more attentive increases Simon and Mikala's ability to be heard. In addition, they learn how to summarize what each partner has said using their own words. For instance, Mikala responds to Simon's complaint by summarizing: "It is difficult for you to hear and understand my point of view when I hover over you and raise my voice. You choose not to respond because you feel overwhelmed." Likewise, Simon summarizes Mikala's complaint: "I look uninterested in listening to your concerns about making changes in our sex life although I often agree with you."

Simon and Mikala learn to express and communicate their feelings along with their sexual needs by the use of "I" statements. Simon states, "I feel intimidated and crippled when you stand over me and raise your voice when we are trying to talk about our sexual problems. I want to learn how to please you sexually; however, I find talking about sex difficult." Mikala retorts, "I feel angry and neglected when you look away while I'm talking to you about specific ways you can stimulate me sexually while we are making love. I want to learn new ways of being able to feel more pleasure in our sexual relationship." By learning specific communication skills such as those discussed above, Simon and Mikala work to become more attentive to each other and increase their ability to feel listened to while communicating clearly and effectively. In this way, they are better able to communicate their specific sexual desires and needs.

Stage 4: Maintenance
During this stage, couples must maintain the changes they have already made in their sexual and intimate relationship. This involves a continued focus on realistic goals and on the development of a healthy, satisfying sexual relationship. Barriers to healthy sexual functioning are identified and plans to address these barriers are outlined. The goal is to prevent relapse. The

therapeutic tasks to be accomplished are as follows:

1. Help couples to identify barriers and plan for setbacks.
2. Help couples to recommit to sexual intimacy and satisfaction.

Sexuality counselors can continue to draw upon strategic/systemic, solution-focused, cognitive-behavioral, communication, narrative, and solution-focused approaches to help couples solidify healthy sexual behavior. By maintaining changes in feelings, thoughts, and behaviors, couples reduce the chance for relapse. For example, to help couples recommit to their revised goals, circular questions (drawn from a narrative approach) and exception and challenging questions can be utilized (solution-focused, narrative approaches). In the case of Simon and Mikala, the sexuality counselor says, "What will you do when you realize that your hectic schedules are intruding upon the time you have created for yourselves as a couple?"

Stage 5: Validation

During this stage, couples celebrate their success in overcoming their sexual problem. They have become more accepting of themselves and of each other and have learned to appreciate their unique way of relating sexually. They are also less apt to blame one another for their sexual problems as they focus on the role sexuality plays in shared pleasure, creation of intimacy, and reducing tension in their lives. Couples learn, with the help of their sexuality counselor, to continue to identify strengths and offer feedback in the form of compliments.

Through the use of narrative techniques, they tell their original story from a different perspective, one that highlights strengths and resources and moves them into thinking about their present and future expectations for their sexual relationship. Finally, a ritual is often designed as a symbol of celebration and success and a plan to maintain their desired sexual behavior is discussed. For example, Simon and Mikala decide to write love letters to each other on a monthly basis, sharing three things they appreciate about each other. They plan to exchange the letters by candlelight prior to a hot-tub bath. The overall goal of Stage 5 is the celebration of both individual and relationship successes. Therapeutic tasks to be accomplished in this stage include the following:

1. Help couples recognize strengths and resources they used in conquering their sexual problems.
2. Help couples celebrate their individual and relational successes.
3. Devise a maintenance program to ensure continued success.

This stage draws upon solution-focused, narrative, strategic/systemic, and communication approaches. Through a continued focus on strengths, a solution-focused approach helps couples continue to highlight successes and identify resources for future problem solving. Their "new story," based on a narrative approach, allows them to recognize the resources they used and see themselves as successful partners who have overcome their sexual problems.

SUMMARY

Theories provide the background to offer us building blocks and other tools as we conceptualize and intervene in couples' sexual relationships. This chapter briefly reviewed theoretical approaches from cognitive-behavioral, systemic, and psychoanalytic sources. We presented key terms and major tenets, and described techniques used by each theory for the treatment of sexuality issues. We also attempted to unite the "best of several theories" to present an integrative couples' model with the goal of providing counselors with a structured way of thinking about sexual problems from a systemic viewpoint rather than focusing solely on the individual. A paradigm shift to a systemic focus enables sexuality counselors to describe couples' relationships in interactive terms and to choose the most appropriate theory and intervention.

An integrative couples' model for sexuality counseling is a synthesis of concepts and methods from a variety of theoretical perspectives drawn from various schools of thought. The central idea of this model is that no one theory is the "truth" and that no one set of counseling techniques is effective for treating every problem and every client. The model provides a map for counselors to identify steps to move couples from "she is the problem" or "he is the problem" to "there is not a problem." The constructivist philosophy behind this model presumes that, as couples make behavioral and affec-

tive changes, their thinking about the problem also changes.

The integrative couples' model and the theories discussed in each stage of the model offer guidelines for practice. Sexuality counselors may employ a variety of methods and strategies from other theoretical perspectives not mentioned in this chapter based on their personal theory of counseling as well as the needs of their clients.

ASSESSMENT IN SEXUALITY COUNSELING

KEY CONCEPTS

- Assessment is a continuous process in sexuality counseling. It begins at the first contact with couples and continues throughout treatment.
- Assessment and treatment are inextricably bound. The process of assessment is also an intervention as it has therapeutic effects throughout all stages of treatment.
- Assessment involves gathering a wide variety of data and synthesizing this information into a description of problems, dysfunctions, or disorders that can be integrated to understand and treat sexual concerns more effectively.
- The initial interview is a critical assessment activity that is also an intervention.
- Determining whether a couple has a sexual problem or sexual dysfunction has important implications for treatment.
- Assessment of past and present sexual beliefs and practices is an important precursor to sexuality counseling.
- A sexual genogram is a useful assessment and intervention tool that provides meaningful historical information about sexual, cultural, and family messages and practices, as well as about the structure of relationships.
- There are a number of assessment instruments (standardized and nonstandardized) available to aid sexuality counselors in evaluating and treating couples' sexual concerns.
- Interventions utilized during the assessment stage include creating a shared language, assigning homework tasks, providing a shared view of the problem, setting specific solvable goals, constructing a time line, collapsing time, and planning the next session.

DEFINING ASSESSMENT

Assessment is the process by which sexuality counselors seek out unique information about individuals, couples, and families so that they are able to apply meaningful and appropriate counseling interventions (Young & Long, 1998). It is a critical and continuous part of "helping" and begins at the first contact with potential clients. Simply stated, assessment involves collecting and organizing information about clients and their reported concerns (Young, 2001). The purpose of this chapter is to analyze this information-gathering process in a thorough, concise, and systematic manner.

Why is this information important? It allows counselors to adapt the prescribed treatment to the client, rather than the client to the treatment. Effective sexuality counselors must "know their clients." Taking the time needed and using appropriate counseling tools and interventions to know clients enables them to develop more helpful and effective treatment goals and strategies.

Adapting counseling approaches to meet the unique needs of clients is consistent with the tenets of our integrative couples' model. The model incorporates several theoretical approaches, which were discussed in Chapter 2, and supports the modification of counseling to couples' specialized sexual issues and concerns.

How do sexuality counselors obtain information about couples? There are a number of ways. For example, counselors usually start by observing partners' behavior and listening to their stories. Informal assessment methods, such as observing and listening, may be used in conjunction with formal assessment methods, such as surveys or questionnaires to elicit important client information. In addition, obtaining medical information about each partner is an important part of assessment as it informs referral and treatment. This is of particular importance in sexuality counseling as medical causes for sexual problems must be ruled out. This chapter will describe many of the informal and formal assessment interventions used to gather client information in sexuality counseling.

INTERTWINING ASSESSMENT AND TREATMENT

It is important to keep in mind that assessment is a continuous process—that assessment and treatment are not separate entities. Although we will describe them as distinct, they are, in fact, inextricably bound together. There is not a precise amount of time spent assessing couples' problems and concerns, nor is there a beginning and an end regarding treatment. Formal assessment may take place at a particular time in counseling, but informal assessment continues throughout the counseling process (Drummond, 2000; Young, 2001).

Counseling interventions have been described as actions by counselors helping clients accomplish their goals and objectives (O'Leary, Heyman, & Jongsma, 1998). They have also been identified as therapeutic activities having a positive effect on overall client functioning. Simply stated, the process of assessment is a type of counseling intervention. The very nature of gathering information, forming problem statements, and completing the other tasks of assessment is a counseling intervention because couples can gain awareness through the exploration process. The integrative couples' model requires that couples, with the assistance of their sexuality counselors, continually evaluate and assess their goals and progress and incorporate their findings into their treatment plan.

Assessment is an important first activity for sexuality counselors working with couples having sexual concerns. Counselors help couples describe their current situation, identify historical and family trends and messages, highlight personal and relational strengths, and increase awareness about the relational and sexual aspects of their presenting problems. Assessment informs sexuality counselors so that they may make sound clinical decisions.

In this chapter we provide an overview of assessment in sexuality counseling for couples. We outline assessment and the initial contact, specifically detailing the activities of the initial session. We also provide information on interventions for assessing sexual issues in counseling. Examples of clinically useful inventories and a discussion on sharing assessment results with couples are included. Finally, we describe Stage 1 of our integrative couples' model using a continuing case example to illustrate the role and purpose of assessment in sexuality counseling.

ASSESSMENT IN SEXUALITY COUNSELING

Assessment is an integral part of any therapy. It is the way in which sexuality counselors begin to understand what is unique about each couple. Figure 3.1

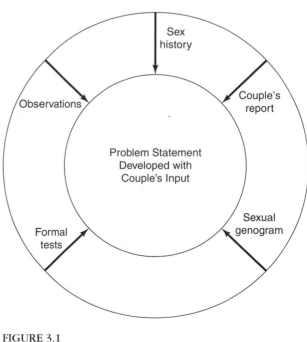

FIGURE 3.1
Wheel of Assessment

illustrates an information wheel with data flowing from various sources that sexuality counselors must evaluate when assessing couples' sexual concerns. It is important that sexuality counselors are accepting and maintain a nonjudgmental attitude to all information received while working to obtain a comprehensive representation of a couples' sexual functioning (Young & Long, 1998).

There are unique issues to consider when obtaining information about couples' sexual concerns. When sexuality counselors focus on the counselor/couple relationship first and foremost and invite couples to share their stories, couples feel a greater sense of connection to their counselor rather than feeling analyzed by questions and tests, and they believe in the usefulness of treatment (Young, 2001).

Assessment and the Initial Contact

Assessment begins with the first contact a sexuality counselor has with a couple. This contact includes the initial telephone contact and the first visual impression, and in-person contact. We recommend that the initial session take approximately one and one-half to two hours. This extended session allows counselors to conduct sexual genograms, take sex histories, and listen to the couple's stories about their problem. Given the intimate nature of sexuality counseling, counselors must be aware of and sensitive to couples' possible hesitancy or reluctance to initially discuss their sexual concerns. Counselors should tailor their questions about sexual intimacy sensitively, as well as understand that sexual genograms and sex histories may take more time than the initial session allows. It is also important for sexuality counselors to help couples feel comfortable in the setting, establish rapport, and view their problems as solvable ones (Young & Long, 1998).

During the initial session, sexuality counselors develop an understanding of the relationship on several dimensions. Information gathered from each partner during this session helps couples develop a joint formulation of their sexual concerns that can lead to collaborative goal setting (Gilbert & Shmukler, 1996). Gathering information through brief questions— Why now? What is expected? Why me/us?—provides counselors with an avenue to begin to assess couples' current emotional and relational status (Gilbert & Shmukler, 1996).

The following questions adapted from Gilbert and Shmukler (1996) will help sexuality counselors gain a systemic view of the issues:

1. Why now? What precipitated the request for counseling? The response to these questions provides information about expectations and the current issues involved. For example, a crisis such as termination of a pregnancy may have motivated a couple to seek sexuality counseling.

2. What perceptions and expectations does each partner have about the process and outcome of counseling? Often, couples have specific, detailed, and realistic expectations of the counseling process while others may expect a "magic" cure.

3. Why me/us or why this particular context? It is helpful to know why couples seek to contact you for counseling. The response to this question reveals much about couples' hopes, fears, and regrets regarding sexuality counseling and provides counselors the opportunity to address these feelings at the outset of sexuality counseling.

There is additional information gathered during the initial session that is integral to the assessment process. One important step is to obtain pertinent medical information so that a referral for medical intervention can be made if necessary (Young & Long, 1998). It is also critical to rule out serious problems such as substance abuse and physical violence in the relationship. The answers to questions about substance abuse and violence may indicate needs for specialized treatment and may contraindicate couples' sexual counseling (Young & Long, 1998). The initial screening provides data that enable sexuality counselors to determine a preliminary course of action for additional information gathering, treatment or, if indicated, referral.

The initial interview is also important because it determines whether or not couples return to sexuality counseling. As noted earlier, because the nature of sexuality counseling includes discussing very personal and intimate details of couples' lives, they may be embarrassed, or hesitant to offer information. In the first session, sexuality counselors must be able to offer hope and encouragement to couples and help them view their problem as a solvable one (Young & Long, 1998).

Goals of the Initial Session

There is much to do in the initial interview. In addition to offering hope, counselors describe the process of counseling, organize the paperwork, assess current and historical sexual problems including a detailed sex history, create a language for talking about sexual issues, and make plans for future sessions (Young & Long, 1998). The goals of the session can be organized by the sexuality counselor into twelve tasks:*

1. Join with the couple.
2. Describe the process of sexuality counseling.
3. Complete all paperwork, including informed consent and confidentiality contracts.
4. Obtain all pertinent medical information or make a referral for a medical examination.
5. Assess current sexual functioning and current relationship dynamics.
6. Create a sexual genogram in order to gather historical information about early family messages, gender roles, and rules in couples' family of origin of early sexual information.
7. Take a detailed sex history.
8. Create a useful sexual language in order to discuss issues in counseling.
9. Begin to help couples state a solvable, shared view of the problem.
10. Discuss the need to set specific, solvable goals together that address both behavioral and affective domains.
11. Offer a homework task and form an allegiance with the couple for the next session.
12. Make concrete plans for the next session.

Sexuality counselors' completion of the tasks of the initial session with couples helps create a working alliance that is essential for the continuation of treatment.

Joining

The most important task of the initial session is joining—the sexuality counselor's attempt to put couples at ease and form an allegiance with them. The first session is almost always characterized by an intensity of feeling, whether it is expressed or not. Couples often feel shame, guilt, frustration, embarrassment, or anger about revealing personal sexual information to a total stranger (Karpel, 1994).

*From *Counseling and Therapy for Couples,* 1st ed. (pp. 97–98), by M. E. Young and L. L. Long. © 1998. Reprinted with permission of Wadsworth, a division of Thomson Learning: www.thomsonrights. com. Fax 800-730-2215

Telephone Contact

The goal of the initial telephone contact is to exchange information about counseling and to make an appointment for the first meeting. Basic information about fees, working hours, mode of therapy, insurance reimbursement, counselor accessibility after hours, and directions to the office should be offered at that time. It can also be helpful to ask couples to describe what is bringing them into counseling at this particular time.

Couples are typically seeking confidence and trust in the counselor, while counselors attempt to establish rapport and convey support regarding the couples' resourcefulness demonstrated by seeking treatment (Young & Long, 1998). As early as the initial telephone contact, helping couples view themselves as "stuck" rather than "sick" will convey a sense of hope and empowerment to tackle their problems (Karpel, 1994; Nichols, 1987).

If the legal system or other community agencies are involved, it may also be necessary to briefly discuss confidentiality, including the limits and parameters during the telephone contact (Young & Long, 1998). Creating this type of frank atmosphere on the telephone conveys respect, trustworthiness, and professionalism to the couple prior to a face-to-face meeting (Karpel, 1994).

Greeting

The sexuality counselor should walk into the waiting room to greet couples (Young & Long, 1998). It is important to shake hands and make contact with both partners, typically first with the caller because telephone contact has been made prior to the initial session. Couples are invited to sit wherever they prefer for the first interview. It is useful to have portable furniture as some couples prefer to sit close together, while others choose separate seating and may move their chairs apart from each other (Young & Long, 1998). Observing their seating can offer some preliminary information about the relationship.

Social Period

A brief social period helps couples feel less threatened and will put them at ease (Young & Long, 1998). It is important that everyone feels comfortable prior to beginning more difficult stages of assessment and treatment (Haley, 1973). As a necessary part of the therapeutic process, this period enables couples to adjust to the new surroundings and then to begin to focus on the presenting problem. It is an important part of bonding with couples and helps them talk about issues that are less threatening before they begin to discuss more intense issues that led them to make an appointment for sexuality counseling (Young & Long, 1998).

Orienting Couples to the Process of Sexuality Counseling

An important step during the information period of counseling is for the sexuality counselor to describe his or her philosophy of counseling. Counselors describe in simple language their beliefs about how people change and what types of expectations they have to help them make the necessary changes. This information can also be provided in a handout attached to a contract for counseling.

It is also useful if counselors provide information about their training and formal education and answer any questions that couples might have about professional licenses and credentials. Couples should be informed about the method or modality of treatment, specifically whether there will be conjoint, individual, or group sessions, how frequently the sessions will occur, and an approximate time frame for each session. Customarily, couples are seen once a week for fifty minutes. Sometimes early in sexuality counseling, it is necessary to be seen more than once a week until the crisis has diminished. It is not unusual to extend early sessions to one and one-half to two hours. Couples may also want to know how many sessions are typical for others who have had similar problems.

Fees should be clearly outlined along with the policy on late arrivals and missed appointments. If there is a charge for appointments not cancelled twenty-four hours in advance, couples should be made aware of that policy. Likewise, if there is a separate fee for court appearances, meetings with other agencies, or evaluative reports, this should be stated in the first session. Couples should also be informed of emergency policies so that they know whether the counselor will be available or what agency to contact should a crisis arise. It is helpful to put this policy in writing in the therapeutic contract.

Discussing Informed Consent and Confidentiality

Because legal and ethical issues are of major concern to sexuality counselors, informed consent and confidentiality policies should be clearly defined at the outset. Informed consent means signing an agreement for treatment that indicates the possible benefits

and hazards (Young & Long, 1998). Duty to protect or duty to warn clients who may harm themselves or others should also be stated, and legal policies on child sexual abuse should be outlined in writing, as it may reduce the risk of accusations of counselor wrongdoing. When audio or other electronic recording is used, it is necessary to obtain the written consent of both partners. The counselor must inform couples that they are being taped, explain the purpose of the taping, and make it clear that they have the right to rescind the consent for taping at any time (Young & Long, 1998).

It is also important for sexuality counselors to comply with the Health Insurance Portability and Accountability Act (HIPAA) of 1996. This is a comprehensive law that calls for "standards governing transactions and code sets, unique identifiers, security and privacy of health care information" (Wheeler, 2003, p. 1), as well as privacy rules for health care providers who engage in electronic claims transactions ("covered entities"). Those sexuality counselors who do not submit claims electronically nevertheless "should realize that the current standards regarding privacy, confidentiality, client access to records and rights to amend records will likely be influenced by HIPAA requirements" (Wheeler, 2003, p. 1). Careful attention by sexuality counselors to the limits and parameters of privacy and confidentiality serves to foster increased trust in the counseling relationship.

Finally, if couples are to be seen separately or partners are permitted to call the counselor on the telephone individually, a policy regarding "secrets" should be discussed. We believe that keeping secrets about current relationship and sexual issues is not conducive to effective sexual counseling because it can create blocks for intimacy. However, past sexual behaviors that no longer impact their current relationship may do more harm than good if they are brought to light at a time when couples' confidence and trust in each other is low and when they are frustrated about their ability to solve their sexual problem.

Substance Abuse and Suicidal Behavior

Information about partners' use of drugs or alcohol is necessary for determining the appropriate course of treatment for couples. If there is problematic and untreated substance use, it is important to make a referral for substance abuse counseling. Abuse of drugs or alcohol may be causal factors in sexual problems and dysfunctions, and such use could obstruct the goals of sexuality counseling.

In addition, it is necessary to obtain information about partners' history of suicidal ideation and behavior as well as their current status regarding suicidal thoughts and plans. Active suicidal ideation or a suicidal plan must be treated immediately and takes precedence over sexuality counseling. Referral to a psychiatrist or other mental health professional may be appropriate to help clients address suicidal feelings.

Referral for Medical Examination

It is also important to ask couples in the first session about their most recent medical examination and to get a complete account of all medications they are currently taking. Frequently, medications can be a contributing factor in impaired sexual functioning of one or both partners and may need to be reviewed by a physician. If a physician has seen neither partner in the past six months, or if there has been a recent change in their physical condition, they should be referred for an examination at once. It should be clear that you will require them to sign a written release form or receive information form so that you may consult with their physician.

Assessing and Evaluating Couples' Current Sexual Functioning and Relationship Dynamics

Assessing

When couples experience "cycles of imbalance" in their styles of demonstrating love or outside stresses that negatively impact their relationships, the results are often sexual problems (Roughan & Jenkins, 1990). During the early stages of the relationship, it is uncommon for couples to have sexual desire concerns. Over time, however, factors such as work demands, children, civic responsibilities, and extended family concerns may intrude (Young & Long, 1998). If one partner becomes less physically available, the other might feel hurt or resentful and may begin to blame the first for a lack of sexual or emotional intimacy in the relationship. A pattern of blaming and retreating from hurt or disappointment may escalate until a crisis occurs or until there is a significant breakdown of the relationship (Young & Long, 1998).

Observing Interactions

As each partner begins to describe his or her present concerns, it is important for sexuality counselors to take note of the nonverbal messages (e.g., body language) of the partner who is speaking, in addition to observing how the other partner is responding (Young & Long, 1998). Two styles of relating that are often observed during the initial session include those pertaining to the way couples communicate and how they pursue or distance themselves from each other.

Communication Styles

Physical characteristics such as grooming, voice tone, posture, and facial expressions are easy to observe. However, it is equally useful to notice the interacting verbal and nonverbal messages that couples convey (Young & Long, 1998). Does she look away when he is describing her behavior toward him sexually? Does he interrupt her when she speaks about his lack of interest in sex? Do they sit closely or touch each other when discussing sensitive topics, or does she fold her arms or fidget with her purse as he describes their lack of intimacy? These verbal and nonverbal cues provide a great deal of information about a couple's sexual communication style and offer ideas about where counselor intervention may be able to break a negative cycle of communication (Young & Long, 1998).

Pursuer-Distancer Style

The pursuer-distancer style may appear in a couple's sexual relationship or in other aspects of their relationship. It begins when one partner avoids expressions of intimacy, quietly and politely withdrawing by reading or watching television, or by just saying "I need more space." Another partner might withdraw by focusing primarily on the children or on work, or by having an extramarital affair.

As one partner withdraws, the other often feels left out, hurt, or abandoned and may begin to complain about lack of time for loving and intimacy, or about being ignored or unloved. If the pursuer-distancer sequence continues over a period of time, both partners are wary of initiating sexual contact because the fear of their partner's response is so painful. Once the pattern of withdrawal/blaming or aggression is identified and the role of each partner is examined, he cycle can be interrupted and replaced with more positive interactions (Young & Long, 1998).

Sexual Problem or Sexual Dysfunction

It is important for a sexuality counselor to determine whether a couple has a sexual problem or dysfunction because of the significant implications this involves (Young & Long, 1998). When no problems are reported by either partner in any phase of the sexual response cycle, they probably do not have a sexual dysfunction (Heiman, LoPiccolo, & LoPiccolo, 1976). It is important for the sexuality counselor to then explore other factors such as unresolved relationship issues or the presence of a sexual problem.

Evaluating Levels of Intimacy in the Relationship

There are specific questions that sexuality counselors must answer in order to assess the intimacy levels in relationships and begin to develop a possible diagnosis or hypothesis for treatment (Hof, 1987; Leiblum & Rosen, 1984; Young & Long, 1998). These would include the following questions:

1. How are affection and physical closeness handled in the relationship?
2. What is the degree of intimacy experienced between the partners and to what extent are they each satisfied with it?
3. What is each partner's perception of the quality and quantity of physical expressions of intimacy in the relationship?
4. In what ways are couples intimate and how satisfied are they with their sexual interactions?
5. What family of origin messages did each partner receive regarding sexuality? (A sexual genogram would provide an answer to this.)
6. What significant events in the relationship (divorce, separation, affairs, pregnancies, miscarriages, death, and so on) might influence sexual functioning?
7. What effect does illness or the aging process have on each partner's sexuality?
8. How do couples manage conflict and problem solving in other areas of their relationship?

These questions inform the problem definition process and assist sexuality counselors in determining specific interventions to be used in the assessment phase of counseling.

INTERVENTION STRATEGIES FOR THE ASSESSMENT STAGE IN SEXUALITY COUNSELING

There are a number of helpful intervention strategies for use during the assessment stage in sexuality counseling with couples. Keep in mind that the process of assessment is joined with treatment. In other words, all assessment activities are interventions in couples' systems. The tools and methods of assessment are also referred to as intervention strategies.

Use of a Sexual Genogram

A sexual genogram is an assessment tool useful for gathering information by visually representing partners' family of origin messages, transgenerational patterns of sexual behavior, and significant events in their sexual development (Hof & Berman, 1986; Sherman, 2000; Young & Long, 1998). It combines information derived from the sex history combined with the family history to gain an understanding of the influence of partners' family taboos, allegiances, secrets, and expectations on sexual behavior and functioning (Hof & Berman, 1986). The genogram, introduced by Murray Bowen (1978; 1980) and further described by McGoldrick and Gerson (1985), is a graphic representation of each partner's family tree. This pictorial view of the larger system typically reaches as far back as the couple's parents and grandparents. Most counselors believe that sexuality can be best understood in the broader context of family patterns involving issues related to gender, intimacy, and sexuality. Sexual genograms are perhaps most useful when completed with both partners present. This method allows couples to hear first-hand their partner's sexual messages, and they can understand more clearly the origin of some of their own and their partner's current sexual behaviors. If there is reticence by one partner to complete the genogram conjointly, sexuality counselors may separate the couple, conduct each genogram separately, and then reunite them to discuss the results of each partner's sexual history.

The genogram uses geometric figures, lines, words, and colors to represent the family tree and interactions among the generations (McGoldrick & Gerson, 1985). Figure 3.2 illustrates the sample genogram symbols that provide the necessary sexual information that will enable sexuality counselors to draw inferences to be used during the goal-setting stage. The use of a pictorial representation helps

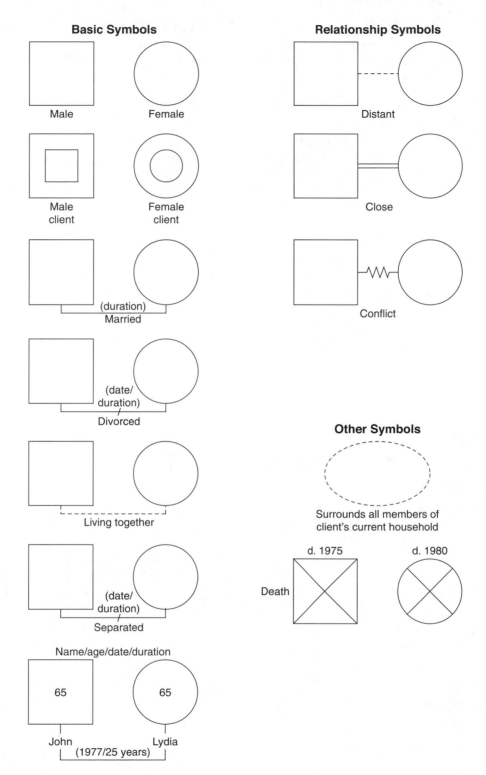

FIGURE 3.2
Genogram Symbols

Source: From *Counseling Methods and Techniques: An Eclectic Approach* (fig. 4.2), by M. E. Young, © 1992. Adapted by permission of Pearson Education, Inc., Upper Saddle River, NJ.

sexuality counselors and couples understand sexuality from "each partner's respective family-of-origin perspective and helps counselors normalize family-of-origin differences [in sexuality]" (Sherman, 2000, p. 84).

The sexual genogram consists of five components: (a) introduction; (b) creation and exploration of a genogram; (c) creation and exploration of a sexual genogram; (d) exploration and discussion of information generated from the genogram; (e) review of process and integration with the treatment plan (Hof & Berman, 1986).

Introduction

Sexuality counselors introduce the process of constructing a genogram to couples by presenting it as a representation of early family learning about sexuality and how this learning influences their current ideas, beliefs, and behaviors about sexuality and intimacy. This usually piques their interest to at least explore some of their transgenerational messages. As they continue to consider the impact of family of origin on their current sexual relationship, there is motivation to learn more about the process (Hof & Berman, 1986).

Creation and Exploration of a Genogram

After the genogram is defined as a visual family tree representing a minimum of three generations (Hof & Berman, 1986), the sexuality counselor begins to draw basic symbols while couples provide basic information to complete it. Sometimes family albums, Bibles, and photographs can help fill in gaps about the family tree.

Creation and Exploration of a Sexual Genogram

After the genogram is drawn, both partners are asked to comment on their observations about the transmission of sexual information from one generation to another. Hof and Berman offer couples specific questions to consider:*

1. What are the overt/covert messages . . . regarding sexuality/intimacy? Regarding masculinity? Regarding femininity?
2. Who [did not discuss areas of] sexuality/intimacy?

3. Who was the most open sexually? Intimately? In what ways?
4. How was sexuality/intimacy encouraged? Discouraged? Controlled? Within a generation? Between generations?
5. [What information about sexuality was offered?]
6. What were the [family secrets] regarding sexuality/intimacy? (e.g., incest, unwanted pregnancies, extramarital affairs, [sexual orientation])?
7. [Where did you first learn about sexuality in your family?]
8. [What would you like to change in your present family about messages and experiences of sexuality/intimacy?]

Exploration and Discussion

Once couples' perceptions about their transgenerational messages and experiences are explored, partners have an opportunity to reflect on each other's information (Hof & Berman, 1986). Inferences can then be made about how family of origin affects the couple in their current relationship, and they can identify obstacles that may have been repeated over several generations. It is important for sexuality counselors to encourage partners to be respectful and nonjudgmental about each other's sexual histories, and to help them to use this information for understanding and creating new possibilities for positive interaction in their present lives (Hof & Berman, 1986).

Review of Process and Integration with Treatment Plan

As the sexuality counselor and couple review what they have learned, partners gain valuable insights and new perspectives, and as a result, approach each other with increased empathy and objectivity (Hof & Berman, 1986). There is a decreased tendency to blame, and instead a movement toward increased understanding of how deep-seated some of the issues may be. Subsequently, couples are usually more ready to direct their new perceptions or discoveries toward concrete goals for their own relationships and for sexuality counseling (Hof & Berman, 1986).

A sample sexual genogram for Simon and Mikala is provided in Figure 3.3. Each generation is illustrated vertically, while horizontal lines connect couples at each end with their children. The counselor's notes are included to clarify the nature of the various relationships. Questions that were asked to obtain the information for this genogram included "What were

---

*From "The Sexual Genogram," by L. Hof and E. Berman, 1986, *Journal of Marital and Family Therapy, 12,* pp. 41–42. Copyright 1986 by American Association for Marriage and Family Therapy. Reprinted with permission.

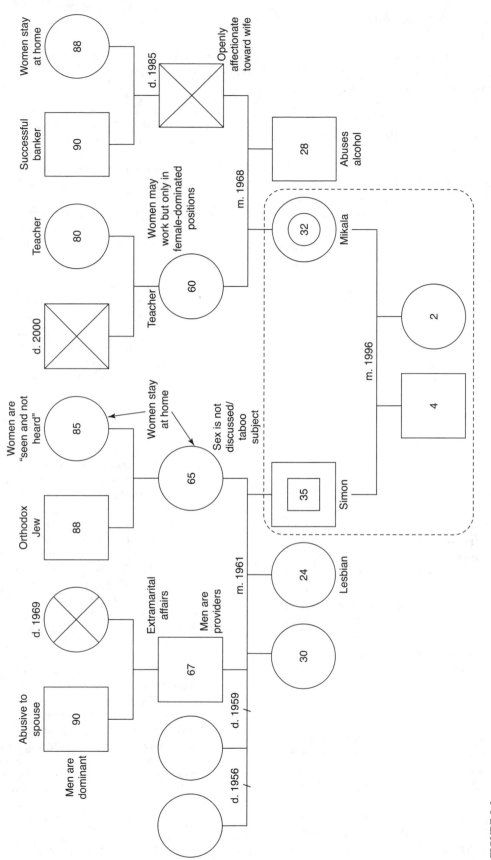

FIGURE 3.3
Sample Sexual Genogram

some of the subtle and obvious messages in this family regarding sexual intimacy? Regarding gender roles?" Based on the information gathered from this genogram, their sexuality counselor was able to help Simon and Mikala discover the ways in which Simon's history of "male privilege" and Mikala's fairy tale messages about romance were affecting their current sexual relationship.

The sexual genogram is a highly adaptable and versatile assessment tool. Sexuality counselors can therefore be flexible with how it is used. For example, notes may be written next to the symbols to highlight future areas of exploration or questioning (Young & Long, 1998). In addition, an abbreviated sexual genogram may be used as a component of a routine sex history as a way of identifying possible problem areas (Hof & Berman, 1986, p. 46).

Taking a Sex History

The sexual genogram is an integral component of the assessment and counseling process, its graphic representations clearly showing the effects of family of origin on the sexual history of clients. However, a detailed verbal account of the current historical information about the sexual relationship of partners must also be gathered. As previously discussed, it is most useful to conduct a sex history with both partners present, but there are times when it is more appropriate to separate them and then reunite them to discuss the results of the sex histories.

A detailed sex history encourages couples to look at their sexuality in relational terms and to begin to develop a language to openly discuss sexual issues with each other. As sexual health and adjustment is closely interwoven with physical health and emotional well-being, the role of the sexuality counselor is to help couples develop clear communication about their sexuality (Leiblum & Rosen, 1984).

Sample Sex History

There are few individuals in our society who do not experience concern about their sexuality at some point in their lives. Despite the growing acceptance of open discussion of sexual matters, many people have never had the opportunity to openly discuss their sexual concerns with an informed professional. Sexuality counselors should be aware of a number of stylistic recommendations that help to build rapport and encourage honest reporting. Leiblum and Rosen (1982)

have offered the following strategies for interviewing couples about sexual issues:*

A. Interviewing Styles:
(i) A general *nonjudgmental* stance should characterize the sexuality counselor's manner throughout the interview. If the couple perceives either verbal or nonverbal signs of disapproval, surprise, disgust, or embarrassment as reactions from the counselor, they are likely to censor sensitive material.
(ii) *Language* used during the interview should be neither overly colloquial nor overly technical. Words like "fuck," "cunt," and "cock," when expressed by the sexuality counselor can interfere with the appropriate couple-counselor relationship. On the other hand, "copulation," "coitus," and "fornication" are words that distance the counselor from the couple and may prevent adequate comprehension. Similarly, some words carry moral connotations and should be avoided in the interest of being nonjudgmental. These words include words such as "promiscuity," "nymphomania," "adultery," and "perversion." Finally, very general or euphemistic terms such as "getting it on" or "making love" may obscure important details of sexual behavior.
(iii) *Open-ended* questions are generally preferable for opening an area of discussion. For example, the question: "How did you first learn about masturbation?" is much better than, "Did you masturbate as a teenager?" A related point is the counselor's assumption of experience with common sexual behaviors. This assumption leads to the use of "ubiquity" questions such as: "Most people experience sexual concerns at one time or another. What issues have troubled you?"
(iv) A good interviewing style generally involves moving gradually from the *least sensitive* material to areas of greater sensitivity. Especially, topics that are likely to elicit anxiety or embarrassment should be reserved for the latter part of the interview when better rapport and greater comfort have been established.
(v) *Privacy* and *confidentiality* are obvious but important aspects of conducting a successful sexual interview. Closed doors, no interruptions, and verbal assurances of confidentiality all serve to demonstrate to the couple the counselor's respect and interest. Listening

---

*From *Guidelines for Taking a Sex History* (pp. 26–31), by S. R. Leiblum and R. C. Rosen, 1982. Copyright 1982 by S. R. Leiblum and R. C. Rosen. Reprinted with permission.

attentively and providing verbal and nonverbal feedback are also essential.

B. Content of Sexual History: General Information

The following content areas are appropriate for initial history taking with *all* couples:

(i) *Current sexual function and satisfaction:* Are both partners able to perform satisfactorily in current sexual relationship(s)? Included here would be the ability to obtain erection, control ejaculation, and reach orgasm without pain or discomfort. Are both partners satisfied with current sexual frequency and quality of the sexual relationship?

(ii) *Partner function and satisfaction:* Is each partner able to stimulate and satisfy the partner and vice versa? Do they each experience sexual and social compatibility?

(iii) *Brief relationship/marital history:* Duration, satisfaction, and major events in the relationship should be covered. Divorce, separation, pregnancies, etc., are all relevant.

(iv) *Effects of contraception, pregnancy, illness, medication, and aging on sexual response:* For example, has a recent hospitalization or trauma interfered with interest or sexual performance? Special attention should be paid to incidences of sexually transmitted infections, rape, molestation, abortion, miscarriage, and so forth, and the counselor should inquire (with sensitivity) about the impact of such experiences.

(v) *Current sexual concerns and difficulties:* Brief history should conclude with an invitation to couples to ask the counselor questions about any aspect of sexuality, including, for example, anatomy, physiology, normality. In the event that the above brief history suggests significant sexual difficulties, a more detailed evaluation should be undertaken along the following lines.

C. Detailed History

(i) History of the presenting problem, including onset, duration, and severity; contributing factors and couples' explanation of problem; previous attempts at overcoming problem and outcome.

(ii) Early sexual development—parental, religious, and peer influences on sexual beliefs, attitudes, and behaviors. Puberty milestones and subjective responses, including masturbation and menstruation. Adolescent social and sexual development, homosexual experiences, and dating behavior. Pre-marital and post-marital sexual history, including extra-marital relationships.

(iii) Goals and expectations of couples with respect to the problem: How do they expect to deal with the difficulty—do they expect it to be re-solved without treatment? Evaluation of the couple's interest and appropriateness for counseling and consideration of referral options.

In conclusion, partners' current level of sexual function and satisfaction should always be seen in the context of an overall level of physical and emotional health. Sexual problems can represent "the tip of the iceberg" and the counselor's judgment in interpreting the significance of sexual symptoms is always important.

The sexual history form is another tool designed to provide specific information for the counselor (see Figure 3.4).

Creating a Language for Sexuality Counseling

After a couple has spent some time openly discussing historical information and current sexual concerns, the sexuality counselor progresses with them to the more difficult tasks of setting goals, communicating openly about their sexual interactions, and trying out new behaviors, thoughts, and feelings. In order to do this, the couple must be able to agree on sexual terminology that is specific but not demeaning. As mentioned earlier in the section on taking a sex history, overly clinical terms like "copulation" or "fornication" may be too academic, whereas overly colloquial expressions like "dick" or "boob" may be disrespectful. Words such as "adultery" or "promiscuity" that are of a judgmental nature should be eliminated. Sometimes agreeing on what words couples use for body parts or sexual activities can foster a therapeutic conversation and make room to air long-held grievances about their sexual communication and behaviors (Leiblum & Rosen, 1984).

Using Tests and Formal Tools

The use of standardized instruments to assess sexual and intimacy issues is also illustrative of the assessment and counseling relationship. Standardized evaluation instruments are often viewed as sterile measures aimed at highlighting sexual pathology. We believe that standardized instruments can be an important adjunct to the assessment and counseling process. If these instruments are introduced and used with the goal of helping couples to identify sexual and relational strengths and resiliency as well as problem areas, then their value to assessment and sexuality counseling is considerable.

Given the considerable number of clinically useful tests for sexuality counseling that are available, it would be an impossible task to describe all of them.

Please find the most appropriate response for each question.

1. How frequently do you and your partner have sexual intercourse or activity?
   (a) more than once a day
   (b) once a day
   (c) 3 or 4 times a week
   (d) twice a week
   (e) once a week
   (f) once every 2 weeks
   (g) once a month
   (h) less than once a month
   (i) not at all

2. How frequently would you like to have sexual intercourse or activity?
   (a) more than once a day
   (b) once a day
   (c) 3 or 4 times a week
   (d) twice a week
   (e) once a week
   (f) once every 2 weeks
   (g) once a month
   (h) less than once a month
   (i) not at all

3. Who usually initiates sexual intercourse or other sexual activities?
   (a) I always do
   (b) I usually do
   (c) my partner and I initiate equally
   (d) my partner usually does
   (e) my partner always does

4. Who would you like to have initiate sexual intercourse or activity?
   (a) myself, always
   (b) myself, usually
   (c) my partner and I equally often
   (d) my partner, usually
   (e) my partner, always

5. How often do you masturbate?
   (a) more than once a day
   (b) once a day
   (c) 3 or 4 times a week
   (d) twice a week
   (e) once a week
   (f) once every 2 weeks
   (g) once a month
   (h) less than once a month
   (i) not at all

6. How frequently do you feel sexual *desire*? This feeling may include wanting to have sex, planning to have sex, feeling frustrated due to a lack of sex, etc.
   (a) more than once a day
   (b) once a day
   (c) 3 or 4 times a week
   (d) twice a week
   (e) once a week
   (f) once every 2 weeks
   (g) once a month
   (h) less than once a month
   (i) not at all

7. How many years have you and your partner been having sexual intercourse?
   (a) less than 6 months
   (b) less than 1 year
   (c) 1 to 3 years
   (d) 4 to 6 years
   (e) 7 to 10 years
   (f) more than 10 years

8. How long do you and your partner usually engage in sexual foreplay (kissing, petting, etc.) before having intercourse?
   (a) less than 1 minute
   (b) 1 to 3 minutes
   (c) 4 to 6 minutes
   (d) 7 to 10 minutes
   (e) 11 to 15 minutes
   (f) 16 to 30 minutes
   (g) 30 minutes to 1 hour

9. How long does intercourse usually last, from entry of the penis until the male reaches orgasm (climax)?
   (a) less than 1 minute
   (b) 1 to 2 minutes
   (c) 2 to 4 minutes
   (d) 4 to 7 minutes
   (e) 7 to 10 minutes
   (f) 11 to 15 minutes
   (g) 15 to 20 minutes
   (h) 20 to 30 minutes
   (i) more than 30 minutes

FIGURE 3.4
Sexual History Form

10. Does the male ever reach orgasm while he is trying to enter the woman's vagina with his penis?
    (a) never
    (b) rarely, less than 10% of the time
    (c) seldom, less than 25% of the time
    (d) sometimes, 50% of the time
    (e) usually, 75% of the time
    (f) nearly always, more than 90% of the time

11. Overall, how satisfactory to you is your sexual relationship with your partner?
    (a) extremely unsatisfactory
    (b) moderately unsatisfactory
    (c) slightly unsatisfactory
    (d) slightly satisfactory
    (e) moderately satisfactory
    (f) extremely satisfactory

12. Overall, how satisfactory do you think your sexual relationship is to your partner?
    (a) extremely unsatisfactory
    (b) moderately unsatisfactory
    (c) slightly unsatisfactory
    (d) slightly satisfactory
    (e) moderately satisfactory
    (f) extremely satisfactory

13. When your partner makes sexual advances, how do you usually respond?
    (a) usually accept with pleasure
    (b) accept reluctantly
    (c) often refuse
    (d) usually refuse

14. When you have sex with your partner, do you feel sexually aroused (i.e. feeling "turned on," pleasure, excitement)?
    (a) nearly always, over 90% of the time
    (b) usually, about 75% of the time
    (c) sometimes, about 50% of the time
    (d) seldom, about 25% of the time
    (e) never

15. When you have sex with your partner, do you have negative emotional reactions, such as fear, disgust, shame or guilt?
    (a) never
    (b) rarely, less than 10% of the time
    (c) seldom, less than 25% of the time
    (d) sometimes, 50% of the time
    (e) usually, 75% of the time
    (f) nearly always, over 90% of the time

16. If you try, is it possible for you to reach orgasm through masturbation?
    (a) nearly always, over 90% of the time
    (b) usually, about 75% of the time
    (c) sometimes, about 50% of the time
    (d) seldom, about 25% of the time
    (e) never

17. If you try, is it possible for you to reach orgasm through having your genitals caressed by your partner?
    (a) nearly always, over 90% of the time
    (b) usually, about 75% of the time
    (c) sometimes, about 50% of the time
    (d) seldom, about 25% of the time
    (e) never
    (f) have never tried to

18. If you try, is it possible for you to reach orgasm through sexual intercourse?
    (a) nearly always, over 90% of the time
    (b) usually, about 75% of the time
    (c) sometimes, about 50% of the time
    (d) seldom, about 25% of the time
    (e) never
    (f) have never tried to

19. What is your usual reaction to erotic or pornographic materials (photographs, movies, books)?
    (a) greatly aroused
    (b) somewhat aroused
    (c) not aroused
    (d) negative—disgusted, repulsed, etc.

20. Does the male have any trouble in getting an erection, before intercourse begins?
    (a) never
    (b) rarely, less than 10% of the time
    (c) seldom, less than 25% of the time
    (d) sometimes, 50% of the time
    (e) usually, 75% of the time

21. Does the male have any trouble keeping an erection, once intercourse has begun?
    (a) never
    (b) rarely, less than 10% of the time
    (c) seldom, less than 25% of the time
    (d) sometimes, 50% of the time
    (e) usually, 75% of the time
    (f) nearly always, over 90% of the time

FIGURE 3.4
(*Continued*)

22. Does the male ejaculate (climax) without having a full, hard erection?
   (a) never
   (b) rarely, less than 10% of the time
   (c) seldom, less than 25% of the time
   (d) sometimes, 50% of the time
   (e) usually, 75% of the time
   (f) nearly always, over 90% of the time

23. Is the female's vagina so "dry" or "tight" that intercourse cannot occur?
   (a) never
   (b) rarely, less than 10% of the time
   (c) seldom, less than 25% of the time
   (d) sometimes, 50% of the time
   (e) usually, 75% of the time
   (f) nearly always, over 90% of the time

24. Do you feel pain in your genitals during sexual intercourse?
   (a) never
   (b) rarely, less than 10% of the time
   (c) seldom, less than 25% of the time
   (d) sometimes, 50% of the time
   (e) usually, 75% of the time
   (f) nearly always, over 90% of the time

25. (WOMEN ONLY, MEN GO ON TO QUESTION 28). Can you reach orgasm through stimulation of your genitals by an electric vibrator or any other means such as running water, rubbing with some object, etc.?
   (a) nearly always, over 90% of the time
   (b) usually, about 75% of the time
   (c) sometimes, about 50% of the time
   (d) seldom, about 25% of the time
   (e) never
   (f) have never tried to

26. (WOMEN ONLY). Can you reach orgasm during sexual intercourse if at the same time your genitals are being caressed (by yourself or your partner or with a vibrator, etc.)?
   (a) nearly always, over 90% of the time
   (b) usually, about 75% of the time
   (c) sometimes, about 50% of the time
   (d) seldom, about 25% of the time
   (e) never
   (f) have never tried to

27. (WOMEN ONLY). When you have sex with your partner, including foreplay and intercourse, do you notice some of these things happening: your breathing and pulse speeding up, wetness in your vagina, pleasurable sensations in your breasts and genitals?
   (a) nearly always, over 90% of the time
   (b) usually, about 75% of the time
   (c) sometimes, about 50% of the time
   (d) seldom, about 25% of the time
   (e) never

28. (MEN ONLY). Do you ever ejaculate (climax) without any pleasurable sensation in your penis?
   (a) never
   (b) rarely, less than 10% of the time
   (c) seldom, less than 25% of the time
   (d) sometimes, 50% of the time
   (e) usually, 75% of the time
   (f) nearly always, over 90% of the time

FIGURE 3.4
(Continued)

We have therefore chosen to list those that are psychometrically sound (see Figure 3.5). As with all assessment techniques, however, there are several factors that must be considered to help in determining appropriateness for use. Young and Long (1998) modified the work of Beavers and Hampson (1990), Grotevant and Carlson (1989), and Corso (1993) to develop a list of activities for choosing appropriate assessment methods:*

_____

*From *Counseling and Therapy for Couples,* 1st ed. (p. 89), by M. E. Young and L. L. Long. © 1998. Reprinted with permission of Wadsworth, a division of Thomson Learning: www.thomsonrights.com. Fax 800-730-2215

1. Examine the couple's [sexual] needs being served and fit the assessment device to the kinds of problems the couple is experiencing.
2. Information gained during assessment should provide useful information about what areas to examine in therapy, rather than labeling the couple.
3. Choose instruments that are easy to administer, understanding that shorter is not always better.
4. Timing of the assessment is important. Use assessment instruments (especially tests and questionnaires) as early in therapy as possible while the couple is becoming oriented to the process. This allows assessment information to be used when planning treatment.

- *Marital Intimacy Needs Questionnaire* (Bagarozzi, 1997): Evaluates the degree to which partners are meeting each other's intimacy needs
- *The Pinney Sexual Satisfaction Inventory* (Pinney, Gerrard, & Denney, 1987): Assesses general sexual satisfaction and satisfaction with partner.
- *Brief Index of Sexual Functioning for Women* (Taylor, Rosen, & Leiblum, 1994): A 22-item self-report measure that assesses female sexual desire, arousal, orgasm, and sexual satisfaction. Additional items address body image, partner satisfaction, and sexual anxiety.
- *Sexual Desire Inventory* (Spector, Carey, & Stein, 1996): Assesses dyadic sexual and solitary sexual desire.
- *Inventory of Dyadic Heterosexual Preference* (Purnine, Carey, & Jorgensen, 1996): Assesses individuals' sexual behavior preferences.
- *Personal Assessment of Intimacy in Relationships* (*PAIR*) (Schaefer & Olson, 1981): Measures the ideal versus the realized level of intimacy in a relationship.
- *PREPARE-ENRICH* (Olson, Fournier, & Druckman, 1986; Olson, 1986): Marriage preparation and enrichment inventories that identify areas of strength and growth.
- *Sexual Interaction Inventory* (LoPiccolo & Steger, 1974): Assesses level of sexual functioning and satisfaction
- *Golombok-Rust Inventory of Sexual Satisfaction* (Golombok, Rust, & Pickard, 1984). Measures global sexual functioning, impotence, premature ejaculation, anorgasmia, and vaginismus.

- *Dyadic Adjustment Scale* (Spanier & Filsinger, 1983): Measures overall marital adjustment, cohesion, and affectional expression.
- *The Multidimensional Sexual Approach Questionnaire* (Snell, 1998): Assesses several different ways in which people can approach their sexual relationships.
- *Dyadic Sexual Communication Scale* (Catania, 1998): Assesses perceptions of the communication process encompassing sexual relationships.
- *The Derogatis Sexual Functioning Inventory* (Derogatis & Melisaratos, 1979): Measures constructs believed to be fundamental to successful sexual functioning (e.g., drive, body image, sexual satisfaction); in addition, it measures several basic indicators of general well-being.
- *Scale of Marital Problems* (Swenson & Fiore, 1982): Assesses problem solving, decision making, goal setting, child rearing, and home labor, relatives and in-laws, personal care and appearance, money arrangements, affection, and relationships with people outside of marriage.
- *The Family of Origin Scale* (Hovestadt, Anderson, Piercy, Cochran, & Fine, 1985): Clients rate their family of origin on ten scales: trust, empathy, conflict resolution, positive tone, ability to express feelings, willingness to deal with separation and loss, openness of family boundaries, respect, personal responsibility, and clarity of expression.

FIGURE 3.5

Some Clinically Useful Tests for Sexuality Counseling

Source: Adapted from Davis, Yarber, Bauserman, Schreer, & Davis (1998), Mason (1991), and Young & Long (1998).

5. Use a combination of measures in order to be thorough. Use screening tests that measure a wide array of potential problems.
6. Be particularly aware of ethnic variations among clients and differences in social class, gender, and disabilities. All of these factors affect therapy, but they also influence differences from the norms that testing is based on.

Sexual-marital adjustment inventories can be useful in helping couples determine what they want and how to ask for it. As early as the 1970s, the *Journal of Sex and Marital Therapy* devoted their Fall 1979 issue

to the subject, describing approximately fifty instruments. For example, the Sexual Interaction Inventory (LoPiccolo & Steger, 1974) appraises sexual satisfaction and functioning and helps couples describe their level of sexual enjoyment as well as the frequency of particular sexual behaviors. It can also aid couples in values clarification "when couples can discuss nondefensively in a supportive environment what behaviors fit with their personal and shared value systems" (Mason, 1991, p. 501). Another instrument, the Golombok-Rust Inventory of Sexual Satisfaction (Golombok, Rust, & Pickard, 1984), assesses overall sexual functioning, impotence, premature ejaculation, anorgasmia, and vaginismus.

More recently, the *Handbook of Sexuality-Related Measures* (Davis, Yarber, Bauserman, Schreer, & Davis, 1998) describes a wide variety of instruments useful to measuring sexuality-related constructs. This handbook provides information on measures that address areas such as sexual motivation, sexual risk, sexual arousability, sexual attitudes, body image, and sexual desire.

Sharing Assessment Results with Couples

It is important for sexuality counselors to share with couples the major issues and concerns as well as the strengths derived from the assessment data. Boen (1988) recommends that couples receive a copy of the written assessment findings in addition to a verbal explanation of the testing findings. We believe that not sharing this information can be detrimental to the counselor-couple relationship. When couples understand the reason for testing, the test selection process, and the meaning of the results, it is likely to help them set meaningful and realistic goals and to increase their awareness so that they can begin to recognize areas for growth.

Providing a Solvable Shared View of the Problem

The evolving definition of the problem is central to our integrative couples' model for sexuality counseling. There are three basic steps that enable this definition to begin as a problem and emerge as a solution.

Step 1: Understanding Each Partner's View of the Problem

The initial stage of most relational models is to obtain information about the relationship, which includes current functioning and historical information. Sexuality counselors ask each partner to define the problem and then explore with each of them the origin of some of their ideas and ways in which they act on these ideas in their current relationship (Young & Long, 1998).

Step 2: Gathering Historical Information

In addition, sexuality counselors assess whether the sexual issue is relatively recent, situational (new child, job, health-related), or chronic (physical disability,

effects of medication). In healthy sexual functioning, couples are in a positive feedback loop of anticipation and a regular rhythm of sexual contact. Chronic sexual problems stem from increased anxiety when thinking about sexual encounters, experiencing inadequate sexual performances, or avoiding sexual relations entirely (McCarthy, 1994).

Several factors contribute to chronic sexual problems and must be understood fully by sexuality counselors during the assessment stage, well before goals are set. According to McCarthy (1994), these factors include the following:

1. Amount of time the problem has existed;
2. Lack of hope that the problem can be overcome;
3. Pattern of inhibited sexual desire and sexual avoidance;
4. A full-blown relapse that has lasted over six months;
5. Couple caught in blame/guilt trap, not motivated to work as an intimate team;
6. Cessation of affectionate and/or sensual contact;
7. Conflict over whether to try again, have an affair, or end the [relationship]. (p. 52)

Examine Motivation for Change. Sexuality counselors should also examine the couple's motivation to change and to address the intensity of the disappointment in the relationship. This is an important step in providing a solvable shared view of the problem. Sometimes partners act out their frustrations by shutting down sexually, feeling depressed, or avoiding sexual contact with each other. Others express themselves by having an affair or threatening divorce, while some retreat into self-pleasuring, their work, or their children (McCarthy, 1994). It is important to identify problematic coping styles and to ascertain how strongly embedded they are in a couple's interactions.

Review Past Attempts to Solve Problem. The final exploration before formulating a workable therapeutic definition of the problem is to assess what has been tried in the past, what has been successful, and what has failed. It is also important to determine what was identified as useful, yet not tried due to fear, apathy, or lack of knowledge.

Step 3: Creating an Interactional View of the Problem

Sexuality counselors cocreate with couples a shared definition of the problem that takes into account both partners' presenting views but expands the ideas to include a resolvable statement with shared responsibility implied for both parties. This concept is illustrated in the relationship of Simon and Mikala. Simon believes that Mikala is unavailable to him because of the amount of time she spends with her students and her career at the university. Mikala complains that Simon is unwilling to take time from his busy medical training to spend time with her. A shared definition is that neither of them have the time to devote to their relationship. Time and energy, rather than their relationship, can become the focus of their disappointment.

This nonblaming definition takes into account both of their complaints but frames the problem in such a way that they are more willing to find ways to be together in a more loving relationship and join together to conquer their time and energy problem.

In summary, the next steps should be followed:

- *Step 1:* Obtain each partner's definition of the problem.
- *Step 2:* Gather historical information, assess chronicity of the problem, and identify current behaviors and feelings.
- *Step 3:* Create a shared, interactive definition of the problem based on the information the partners have provided from their personal points of view and from other assessment procedures such as the sexual genogram or sexual history.

Setting Specific Solvable Goals

Following the creation of a shared, interactive definition of the problem, it is important to discuss with couples the goals of treatment. The information gathered as a result of the assessment thus far will help sexuality counselors facilitate a discussion with couples about the short-term and long-term goals. It is important to help each partner identify the desired outcome of counseling (Young & Long, 1998). Detailed information about goal setting and treatment planning will be provided in Chapter 4.

Constructing a Time Line

The concept of time is another important aspect of sexuality counseling (Atwood & Dershowitz, 1992). Drawing and developing an actual representation of a time line will give couples information about the origin and duration of problems and how the trends developed over time. This helps dispel beliefs that people are "born that way," or are "just like their parents." Sexual-

ity counselors help couples understand their sexual concerns as situated in time instead of in themselves. This alterative way of framing the problem allows its facets to be observed and evaluated in a less defensive manner (Atwood & Dershowitz, 1992). It is useful to include positive dimensions of sexual functioning on the time line as well, thus avoiding an overemphasis on the negative aspects of the relationship or conveying the impression that it is too difficult to conquer.

The sexuality counselor needs to remind couples that although the relationship is depicted from a linear perspective, in actuality there are more circular, interactive patterns.

Collapsing Time—The Rubber Band

Another strategy to help couples understand the contained time frame of the problem is to ask the "rubber band" question: "If I were to take a rubber band and stretch it back to when the sexual problem was not there, what was your relationship like?" (Atwood & Dershowitz, 1992, p. 201). Other questions that may be useful include, "How long have you been experiencing this concern?" and "At what point did you initially notice this problem?" This manner of questioning provides a developmental perspective for the sexual problem (Atwood & Dershowitz, 1992). It is implied that there was a period in a couple's relationship that the sexual problem was not present and also that at some time in the future it will not be present, when sexuality counselors ask "What was your life like before the problem?" (Atwood & Dershowitz, 1992, p. 201).

Assigning Homework Tasks

Assigning homework is a useful tool in sexuality counseling. It allows couples to work on skills acquired during counseling and facilitates small changes that may ultimately lead to larger changes (Dattilio & Bevilacqua, 2000). Homework also helps provide direction and a specific method of working toward identified goals as well as giving a reason for couples to return to counseling and report on their progress (Young & Long, 1998).

Homework assignments are designed to address the unique needs of couples and should be specific in their focus. In addition, the emphasis of tasks and assignments are on positive development and do not underscore negative feelings, attitudes, or behaviors. In order to promote positive development, homework assignments are collaboratively designed with couples so that they are invested in the results of the tasks.

Two types of homework assignments that are helpful in sexuality counseling are "observational assignments" and "experimental learning tasks" (Dattilio & Bevilacqua, 2000, p. 154). Observational assignments include noticing and recording thoughts, beliefs, and feelings about sexuality. Experimental learning tasks are more diverse and tailored more specifically to couples' needs. For example, these tasks may include trying out new sexual communication methods and noting the result (Dattilio & Bevilacqua, 2000).

Couples may not always complete homework assignments in spite of the fact that homework is appropriately and collaboratively designed. If that occurs, sexuality counselors work with couples to identify what may be hindering their completion of assignments and address these issues directly during the session. Important therapeutic information can be gathered when thoughts and feelings about incomplete homework tasks are processed during sessions (Dattilio & Bevilacqua, 2000).

Planning the Next Session

A discussion of "what happens next" in treatment completes the initial session. Couples unfamiliar with the process of sexuality counseling benefit from having additional information about what to expect. Sexuality counselors discuss plans for the next session—for example, by saying "We will review your progress on your homework." Additional opportunities will be provided for questions, comments, or concerns regarding counseling, and the counseling schedule will be finalized. It is also helpful for sexuality counselors to provide couples with information on additional assessment tools, instruments, or techniques they may employ. Finally, this may be the right time for counselors to make a referral for specialized treatment if it is indicated.

In addition to the interventions previously described, Box 3.1 provides a brief list of suggested assessment interventions that sexuality counselors can use with couples.

BOX 3.1
Assessment Interventions at a Glance

- Assess the frequency of sexual interactions across the history of the relationship.
- Assess the partners' enjoyment of sexual interactions across the history of the relationship.
- Identify sexual expectations in the relationship and how they have changed across time.
- Describe any past traumatic experience that now may be impacting the sexual interaction.
- Identify any religious [or cultural] beliefs or training that may be interfering with experiencing pleasure from sexual activity.
- Discuss the development of sexual attitudes in family of origin, identifying those experiences which enhance and those that deter one or both partners from currently experiencing sexual pleasure.
- Ask partners to describe the perceived causes of decline in sexual activity and enjoyment thereof.
- Ask partners to describe the positive nonsexual aspects of the beginning of their relationship.
- Verbalize feelings regarding body image and how it relates to sexual functioning.
- Assess role of any known or possible existing physical condition that could interfere with sexual functioning (e.g., diabetes, substance abuse, depression, anxiety disorders).
- Assess role of any medication that could interfere with sexual functioning (e.g., antihypertensive medication, antidepressant medication).
- Explore whether the decrease in the frequency and range of sexual activities is related to a decline in body image (e.g., [loss of hair], increased body weight, lack of muscle tone, or the residual effects of surgery).
- Probe feelings that relate to perceived or actual extramarital affairs, and make certain that such relationships have stopped.

Source: From *The Couples Psychotherapy Treatment Planner* (pp. 231–234), by K. D. O'Leary, R. E. Heyman, and A. E. Jongsma, Jr. © 1998 by K. Daniel O'Leary, Richard E. Heyman, Arthur E. Jongsma, Jr. This material is used by permission of John Wiley & Sons, Inc.

Case Example

We will look again at the case example of Simon and Mikala to highlight how assessment is used in the integrative couples' model. The presenting issues of Simon and Mikala can be briefly summarized as follows: They have been married for six years and complain of low sexual desire since the birth of their second child two years ago. Both also have very busy careers.

Stage 1: Assessment

During this stage, the primary tasks of the sexuality counselor are as follows: join with the couple, obtain each person's definition of the problem, gather historical information, assess chronicity of the problem, identify current behaviors and feelings, and create a shared, interactive definition of the problem based on the information the partners have provided from their personal points of view and from other assessment procedures, such as the sexual genogram or sex history.

At the outset of the counseling relationship with Simon and Mikala, their sexuality counselor focuses on establishing rapport with the couple. The sexuality counselor relates the commonality of dual-career couples who struggle to maintain balance in their busy lives. This helps create a nonthreatening environment by connecting with the unique dilemma this couple faces.

The sexuality counselor takes time to describe the process of treatment while also making note of Simon and Mikala's interactions, specifically noting the body language and other interacting nonverbal communication. For example, the counselor notices that while Mikala is speaking, Simon tends to look away or look down and that the couple sits quite distantly from each other. In addition to joining with the couple, establishing a framework for treatment, and observing the couple's interactions, the sexuality counselor gathers other important information during the assessment interview.

It is critical that the counselor also gather information about potential for violence, substance abuse, mental status (when a mental disorder is suspected), personal health, and family history. Such data are helpful in establishing the framework for treatment or making a treatment referral. For example, when Mikala reports that sexual in-tercourse is painful for her and she has not had a medical examination since the birth of her last child two years ago, a referral is made to rule out medical causes for her pain. Often sexuality counselors work in conjunction with medical professionals who may be treating medical causes for sexual problems.

In order to gather relevant sexual and relationship information, the sexuality counselor takes a thorough sex history. This includes obtaining information about current sexual concerns and difficulties, partner function and satisfaction, history of the presenting problem, early sexual development, and other details of the couple's life experiences. The counselor also uses a sexual genogram as a means of obtaining relevant sexual and relationship information. The sexuality counselor actually draws the genogram during the time that the couple provides information. The sexual history reveals that Mikala believes that men "should" initiate sexual contact, while the genogram shows that one of the messages and rules in Simon's family is that women are "supposed" to focus on home life, not their careers.

The counselor also works with Simon and Mikala to create a language that is comfortable for both to use when discussing sexual matters. For example, Mikala prefers to call sexual intercourse "making love," while Simon refers to this particular sexual behavior as "doing it." The counselor works with them to find and use terms that are agreeable to both.

As a result of the information gathered thus far, the sexuality counselor begins to formulate problem definition questions in order to obtain information. The counselor asks, "Simon, when did you first notice that you and Mikala did not have sexual intercourse as often?" Simon's response indicates that he sees the problem as Mikala's emphasis on her career as well as the work demands of his medical residency as the start of the decrease in their sexual intimacy. The counselor then asks, "Mikala, did you notice the lack of time for sexual intimacy at the same time that Simon did?"

At this point in sexuality counseling, couples are asked to describe their perception of the problem as they see it. The picture painted by the couple aids them as they coconstruct a shared definition of the problem. In this case, the shared definition is as follows: As a result of the many changes in your professional and family life, you have not found the time or energy for your intimate time and your sexual relationship. This definition provides an explanation that is not blaming and is something that the couple can regain. It presupposes that they have temporarily lost the "time and energy" and can find it again.

During this stage of assessment, Young & Long (1998) identify the following sources that can be used to gather client information:*

1. Observations the [counselor] makes based on the couple's spontaneous [responses to the counselor's suggestions].
2. Questionnaires [or intake forms] completed by the couple outside of the session.
3. The couple's reports regarding their behavior outside of the session.
4. Historical data from the genogram or from [partner's sex] histories.
5. Reports from other sources, such as family members, the courts, or police reports.
6. [Information from medical examinations].
7. The results of paper-and-pencil testing.

The sexuality counselor also uses the Sexual Interaction Inventory (LoPiccolo & Steger, 1974), a useful assessment instrument that provides valuable feedback about Simon and Mikala's sexual functioning and satisfaction.

At the conclusion of the initial interview, the sexuality counselor provides an overview of the major problems and issues identified during the assessment stage. The results of all assessment instruments are shared with the couple. In addition to outlining the specific issues identified, the sexuality counselor summarizes the content and feelings brought forth during the session, while providing a hopeful statement in order to help the couple remain motivated for treatment. The counselor says to Simon and Mikala, "We discussed several important issues today. We discussed your careers and the birth of your second child and how these have impacted your sexual relationship. I feel optimistic that the

*From *Counseling and Therapy for Couples*, 1st ed. (p. 85), by M. E. Young and L. L. Long. © 1998. Reprinted with permission of Wadsworth, a division of Thomson Learning: www.thomsonrights.com. Fax 800-730-2215

two of you will be able to resolve your concerns. You're committed to working together and once new ways of managing time and energy are dealt with, I believe your sexual relationship will improve."

The sexuality counselor also decides to assign a homework task in order to help Simon and Mikala begin to change their patterns prior to returning to treatment. The counselor suggests, "Write out some playful things you would like to do together between now and the next time we meet." This task has a positive emphasis on togetherness and helps this couple focus on positive rather than negative aspects of their relationship. Box 3.2 presents the assessment interventions used with Simon and Mikala as they move from individual views to a shared definition of their sexual concern.

BOX 3.2

Assessment Interventions for Case Example: Simon and Mikala

His View "Mikala never wants to 'do it' anymore. Her career is more important to her than I am."

Her View "Simon doesn't want to be with me anymore. He spends all of his time in his residency program and tries to avoid me."

Shared View We can't seem to make time for nor do we have the energy for sexual intimacy since our career demands have increased and since the birth of our child.

Interventions Used for Assessing Simon and Mikala

Sexual genogram

Sexual history

Creating a shared language

Providing a solvable shared view of the problem

Developing solvable goals

Sexual Interaction Inventory

Assigning homework

Planning the next session

SUMMARY

When couples come to counseling with sexual concerns, they are usually frustrated yet embarrassed to air such personal information with a stranger. Sexuality counselors join with couples in order to help them feel secure and hopeful for the resolution of their problems while obtaining from each of them their definition of the current problem. Sexuality counselors also educate couples about the course of treatment and the process of counseling.

Assessment is an important part of the first session. Interventions in the assessment stage include a thorough sexual history of a couple's families of origin. A sexual genogram is one useful tool for gathering this information, as is a sex history and other paper-and-pencil assessment instruments. Interventions may also include creating a shared language, assigning homework tasks, providing a shared view of the problem, setting specific solvable goals, constructing a time line, collapsing time, and planning the next session.

The primary reason for assessment is to help sexuality counselors and their clients create solvable shared goals and develop a meaningful treatment plan.

GOAL SETTING, TREATMENT PLANNING, AND INTERVENTIONS IN SEXUALITY COUNSELING

KEY CONCEPTS

- Goal setting and treatment planning are based on information gathered during the assessment stage.
- Goal setting and treatment planning are also forms of therapeutic treatment interventions that can help couples achieve clarity and optimism.
- Goal setting in sexuality counseling involves helping couples identify what they would like to achieve as a result of treatment.
- Identified goals must be realistic and achievable, leading to overall improvement of sexual intimacy.
- Treatment plans are based on collaborative goals and provide the therapeutic structure for sexuality counseling.
- Treatment planning involves deciding which goals should be addressed first, keeping in mind that crises should be tackled as they arise.
- Counseling interventions are based on the goals of treatment and are specific strategies developed by counselors to help couples reach their identified goals.
- The integrative couples' model includes individual definitions of problems evolving into an interactive shared view of the problem.
- An interactive definition of the problem is an important component for the development of treatment goals in sexuality counseling.
- A sexuality counselor's role is to help couples transform identified problems into goals focused on how they would like their sexual relationship to develop.
- Sexuality counselors help couples externalize problems and create behavioral and affective goals stated in a solvable form.
- Interventions used in sexuality counseling are based on individual and relational strengths.
- Sexuality counselors select activities (e.g., communication training) that help clients reach their goals—specifically, to help couples realize concrete behavioral change and experience positive feelings about their sexual relationship.

In Chapter 3, we introduced the first stage of the integrative couples' model for sexuality counseling by describing various methods of assessment—an ongoing process in which counselors gather pertinent information about their clients' problems. During the assessment stage, sexuality counselors obtain information about couples' sexual concerns, obtain each partner's view of the problem, and construct an interactive definition of the problem. Assessment is a type of treatment intervention that has therapeutic effects in all stages of treatment.

In this chapter, which focuses on the next two stages of the integrative couples' model, goal setting, treatment planning, and intervention strategies will be introduced. Goal setting and treatment planning, like assessment, also have therapeutic effects and can be considered forms of treatment interventions. The process of constructing goals and developing and implementing an action plan helps couples achieve "clarity of purpose" and experience hopefulness (Young, 2001, p. 209). Goal setting and treatment planning are critical components in sexuality counseling as they provide a therapeutic framework for couples and counselors.

THE ROLE OF GOAL SETTING AND TREATMENT PLANNING

Goal setting and treatment planning are the building blocks of treatment. Goal setting is a primary component of treatment planning. Goals identify what couples want to achieve in their sexual lives. The development of goals plays an important role in counseling, driving the counselor's decisions regarding the best course of action to help couples. With adequate goal setting and subsequent treatment planning, the likelihood of successful treatment increases (O'Leary, Heyman, & Jongsma, 1998). Detailed, measurable treatment plans benefit not only couples but also counselors because treatment plans are guides that structure the focus of sexuality counseling.

THE LINK BETWEEN ASSESSMENT, GOAL SETTING, AND TREATMENT PLANNING

Assessment, goal setting, and treatment planning are linked in important ways. Goal setting and treatment planning are based on information gathered during the assessment stage. Without this information, goal setting and treatment planning are not meaningful.

Goal setting in sexuality counseling involves helping couples identify what they would like to achieve as a result of treatment—specifically, what changes they would like to create in their sexual relationship. Couples often come to counseling with vague hopes: "I want to have a better sexual relationship with my partner," or "We don't seem to be as intimate as we used to be and I miss that." The role of the sexuality counselor is to help them go beyond such generalizations and describe their hopes in concrete terms that will culminate in specific goals (Brown & Brown, 2002). Unrealistic or problematic goal setting will result in unsuccessful and frustrating treatment outcomes for both couples and counselors.

Treatment plans are based on collaborative goals set by couples with the guidance of their sexuality counselor. The action or treatment plan provides a template for interventions designed to address couples' sexual concerns.

THE RELATIONSHIP BETWEEN GOAL SETTING, TREATMENT PLANNING, AND INTERVENTIONS

Treatment planning involves developing treatment interventions, strategies, and methods that best help couples make positive changes in their sexual relationship. Interventions, which are part of the larger treatment plan, are based on couples' goals.

Counseling interventions—specific strategies developed by counselors to help couples reach their identified goals—are based on the goals of treatment. Although we describe them separately, we believe that the development of goals and treatment plans are also interventions.

THE GOAL-SETTING PROCESS

Goals are series of steps that, when completed, result in the attainment of successful treatment (O'Leary, Heyman, & Jongsma, 1998). The attainment of treatment goals is also the best measure for determining when treatment should be terminated (Young, 2001). Realistic, shared goals developed during the early part of treatment increase the likelihood that both counselors and couples will have a shared vision throughout treatment and will know when it is time to terminate counseling. Goal setting can make the difference between success and failure in sexuality counseling, and poor goal setting can demoralize both counselors and couples (Young, 2001).

Developing Goals

Goal specificity is an important ingredient in the counseling process. When clients are able to develop specific goals, they are more likely to achieve their goals over time (Borelli & Mermelstein, 1994). Individual problems evolve into a statement of a joint problem that we call the "shared view of the problem." This view drives the development of goals and also helps to modify and shape couples' expectations about what can realistically be achieved. Young (1998) outlines six favorable outcomes that result from a joint process of counselor/couple negotiation of goal statements:*

1. When based on [couples'] goals, . . . the counseling process is more likely to be aimed at [couples'] needs rather than derived from the [counselor's] theoretical orientation alone.
2. When goals are clearly understood by [couples] and [their counselor], the [counselor] can determine whether he or she possesses the requisite skills to continue with the counseling or whether a referral is needed.
3. Many [couples] have problems imagining or envisioning success. Visualizing a positive outcome has the tendency to focus [couples'] resources and energies and increase hope.
4. Goals provide a rational basis for selecting treatment [interventions] in [counseling].
5. Goals enable [counselors] to determine how successful [counseling] has been for [couples]. Goal statements also provide feedback to [couples], who can be asked to evaluate the outcome based on the degree to which goals have been achieved.
6. Setting goals can be therapeutic. [Couples] feel less "stuck." [Couples] who [are] clear about [their] goals will be able to work on these goals in and out of [counseling] sessions. The setting of goals also motivates [couples] to work harder.

It is also important that goals are realistic and constructive. Realistic goals are achievable and pragmatic. Because of their clarity, practicality, and attainability, they ensure that couples are more likely to have success. Constructive goals are clear, simple, concise, and specific. They address crises first and are geared toward improvement in couples' sexual lives (Young, 2001).

Goals represent couples' visions of the future. Frequently, such goals are the opposite of their problem statements. Counselors move couples from vague descriptions of problems to clearly defined goals. In order to help delineate couples' goals, Bertolino and O'Hanlon (2002) suggest the following questions:

1. How will you know when things are better?
2. How will you know when the problem is no longer a problem?
3. What will indicate to you that therapy has been successful?
4. How will you know when you no longer need to come to therapy?
5. What will be happening that will indicate to you that you can manage things on your own? (p. 91).

With the guidance of their counselor, these questions help couples focus on their desired outcomes and enable them to work in a collaborative, realistic, and solution-oriented manner.

Developing Common Goals

Setting Interactional Goals

When a shared definition of the problem has been clearly identified, realistic goals are set that can be measured in both behavioral and affective terms. In other words, what will the couple *do* and how will they *feel* once they have accomplished their goals? Each partner is asked to imagine life if the problem never existed and identify what they would be *doing* differently and how they would be *feeling* if the problem ceased.

Defining goals in realistic terms while also identifying behavioral and emotional changes are important elements of the integrative couples' model. At this stage of the model, couples begin to transform problem statements into goals. The resulting goals are tailored to their unique needs. To help couples transform problem statements into goals, sexuality counselors work with couples to separate problems from their individual and relational selves. As a result, placing blame is reduced and couples work with increased effectiveness and unity to state their goals clearly and concretely (Young & Long, 1998). Placing the problem outside the relationship as a force they must both conquer is a useful strategy for establishing a cooperative, problem-solving approach to the problem.

Externalizing the Problem

Pioneered by White (1989), externalizing is a narrative approach used by sexuality counselors to help couples work cooperatively. It involves helping partners to conceptualize sexual and relational problems as separate or disconnected from their self-identification (Young & Long, 1998). It does not imply avoidance of the problem and instead offers a way of conceptualizing that includes both partners' definitions of the problem in solution-focused language. It is a process of challenging a dominant discourse in a couple's life story. Initially, sexuality counselors talk about the couples' sexual problem as existing outside the relationship. Soon, couples imagine and redefine their sexual problems as "the time problem," "the orgasm problem," "the erection problem," or "the masturbation problem."

Couples begin to see themselves not as "having" a sexual problem, but rather as having an outside force that negatively affects their sexual relationship. Examples of statements or thoughts that are destructive to

---

*From *Learning the Art of Helping: Building Blocks and Techniques* (pp. 124–125), by M. E. Young, © 1998. Reprinted by permission of Pearson Education, Inc. Upper Saddle River, NJ.

the goal-setting process include: "We aren't compatible because we don't have sex frequently," "She doesn't love me because she's always too tired to have sex," "He never gets excited when we are together, so intercourse or penetration is impossible," or "He doesn't want me, so he must have someone else." Once a problem is located as being external, the couple can view it differently or consider alternate meanings. For example, "lack of frequency of sexual play" is viewed as "the time problem" that couples must solve by putting their heads together to find an effective solution for more intimate time together. "He doesn't get excited sexually when we are together" can be viewed as "the passion problem" and can initiate dialogue to facilitate a new understanding (physiologically, psychologically, situationally, or interactionally). When partners are able to separate problems from themselves and join forces to overcome them, the relative importance of the problem in the relationship can decline (Young & Long, 1998). However, this process does not occur quickly or easily, nor does the problem remain externalized permanently. The couples' history and their social influences are usually more accepting of their traditional dominant narrative and will press to have couples return to their more comfortable explanation or story about their problem. Then, realistic goals can be set.

Realistic Goals

Changing sexual attitudes, behaviors, and emotions is a complex task. This complexity is increased when facing sexual problems or chronic sexual dysfunction, particularly inhibited sexual desire. Sexuality counselors must ensure they do not become overwhelmed by the chronicity, complexity, or emotional intensity involved in the problem (McCarthy, 1997).

If sexuality counselors help couples describe their goals in terms of sexual functioning that is comfortable but not perfect for them, there is greater likelihood of a positive outcome. Counselors should stress a general point here: We do not behave perfectly in any other aspect of our lives, and it is doubtful that any of us can behave or act "perfectly" in our sexual relationships. This pragmatic yet optimistic approach is integral to treatment because it helps couples define more clearly and reasonably the changes they want to make in their sexual relationship (McCarthy, 1997).

Creating Goals Tailored to the Unique Problems of Couples

First and foremost, goals must be relevant. Sexuality counselors must simply help couples clarify what they want to accomplish in interactional, nonblaming language and make certain they are not setting themselves up to fail by describing goals of perfection that cannot be attained or sustained over time. For example, a couple tells their counselor that they would like to set a goal of increasing the frequency of sexual intercourse so that they both achieve orgasm at least four times per week. They believe that accomplishing this goal would help them feel successful in their sexual relationship. The counselor, who understands that one partner has not achieved orgasm in eight years, knows that they will most likely be unsuccessful in meeting this goal. With the counselor's assistance, this couple can begin to set more realistic goals that take into consideration their current sexual functioning. This intervention allows them to ultimately feel successful in achieving their goal.

Describing Goals in Interactional Terms

As we defined the problem in interactional terms (a shared view of the problem) during the assessment stage, we must now set goals in the same way. When partners initially describe goals they would like to achieve in sexuality counseling, they typically make statements indicating that their partner is the one who needs to make changes. One partner states, "Our problem is that my partner hurts me when we have sex, so I don't want to try it anymore." When comments such as this are made, sexuality counselors can return to the interactive definition they have jointly created during the assessment stage and restate it as a shared problem. For example, their problem could be viewed as "we need to identify some comfortable ways to express ourselves sexually with each other and feel more connected to each other." Then they can design goals specific to the stated shared definition of the problem. Realistic goals such as the following can be set in interactional terms:

Goal 1: We would like to learn how to please each other sexually so that we can feel more positive and connected to each other.

Goal 2: We would like to explore some sexual techniques in order to help us relax, feel less pressure, and emphasize more fun in our relationship.

Setting Behavioral and Affective Goals

Couples often get stuck on "what is wrong" rather than "what can be," causing their relationship to take on a negative tone (Young & Long, 1998). The emphasis in the integrative couples' model is on creating goals that reawaken interest in what their relationship "can be" and de-emphasize "the same old problem."

The approach of the integrative couples' model is to help partners identify both *behavioral* and *affective* changes they would like to make in their sexual interactions, and then to state them concretely and specifically. When goals include both of these dimensions, partners have a clearer notion of what they are trying to achieve (Young & Long, 1998), including what they will do and how they will feel when they achieve it. This process helps negate the desperation, disappointment, and helplessness they have been feeling in their relationship (Young & Long, 1998). Couples can use behavioral and affective language to describe their problems as goals:

Shared Problem 1: We would like to spend more intimate time together.

Shared Goal 1: We will begin to set the mood for our intimate time together by using music and candles, so that we feel more relaxed and loving with each other.

Shared Problem 2: We have gotten "stuck" in our sexual relationship and have not found new ways to pleasure each other.

Shared Goal 2: We will try the sensate focus program so that we will gradually feel more comfortable with mutual masturbation and sexual play with each other.

Most counselors believe that enduring change occurs when modifications are made in all three domains of human functioning: the affective (emotional), the behavioral (doing), and the cognitive (thinking) (Young & Long, 1998). According to the integrative couples' model, changed perceptions (thinking) occur with reliable changes in actions and emotions (Young & Long, 1998). When the couple in the example above sets the stage for sexual intimacy, they are able to be more relaxed and creative about their sexual options and feel more positive about the expected outcome. Thus, they will think more positively about their relationship.

The integrative couples' model also focuses on cognitive and perceptual changes by constantly challenging couples to view problems and goals differently at each stage of the counseling process (Young & Long, 1998). By the close of the goal-setting stage, partners have made a short-term shift from "we have a problem" to "we have a goal" (Young & Long, 1998, p. 74). This cognitive shift helps couples maintain a shared view of the problem. To accomplish this shift,

couples and their counselors move through the following series of steps:

Step 1: Setting realistic goals.

Step 2: Creating goals tailored specifically to the couple.

Step 3: Externalizing the problem.

Step 4: Stating goals in interactional terms.

Step 5: Setting behavioral and affective goals.

THE TREATMENT-PLANNING PROCESS

Goals set the foundation for the development of treatment planning—a systematic way of reviewing client problems and developing a set of strategies, techniques, or interventions to address these sexual problems. Treatment planning is a process that involves sequential, interdependent steps (O'Leary, Heyman, & Jongsma, 1998). O'Leary, Heyman, and Jongsma (1998) outline the following six steps in the development of meaningful treatment plans:*

1. *Problem selection.* In choosing which problems to focus on, it is important to note both those problems that are most acute or disruptive to [couples' sexual] functioning and those concerns that are personally most important to the clients.
2. *Problem definition.* Each problem selected for treatment focus requires a definition specific to the particular [couple].
3. *Goal development.* [It is important] to set broad [or long-term] goals for the resolution of target problem. These statements need not be crafted in measurable terms but instead should focus on the long-term global outcomes of treatment.
4. *Objective construction* [short-term goals]. Objectives are stated [clearly] in behaviorally measurable language. It [is] clear when couples have achieved the established objectives [or short-term goals]. Each objective [is] developed as a step toward attaining the broad treatment goal. In essence, objectives [are] thought of as a series of steps that, when completed, . . . result in the achievement of the long-term goal.
5. *Intervention creation.* Interventions are [created and selected] to help [couples] achieve the objectives. If [couples] do not accomplish the objective

---

*From *The Couples Psychotherapy Treatment Planner* (pp. 3–5), by K. D. O'Leary, R. E. Heyman, and A. E. Jongsma, Jr.: Copyright 1998 by K. Daniel O'Leary, Richard E. Heyman, Arthur E. Jongsma, Jr. This material is used by permission of John Wiley & Sons, Inc.

after the initial intervention, new interventions [are] added to the plan.

6. *Diagnosis determination.* The determination of an appropriate diagnosis is based on an evaluation of [each partner's] complete clinical presentation. The [counselor] compares behavioral, cognitive, emotional, interpersonal, [and sexual] symptoms presented by the clients to the criteria for diagnosis of a [sexual disorder] as described by [DSM-IV-TR (2000)].

Most sexuality counselors are familiar with formalized treatment planning based on a diagnostic or medical planning model. The goal of such is to arrive at a diagnosis that is the basis for determining the treatment that clients receive. Although diagnosis provides important information and is an integral (and often required) component of counseling, the integrative couples' model is goal-oriented, not driven solely by a particular sexual diagnosis. Diagnosis is considered as a piece of information to be integrated into the overall process. For example, a female diagnosed with severe vaginal pain (possibly vaginismus) is first referred for a medical evaluation to rule out medical causes. She may learn specific sexual techniques to address her "pain problem" (e.g., the use of vaginal dilators, Kegel exercises). Sexuality counselors help the couple to address issues around sexual communication, sexual messages, and other relational considerations affecting their sexual intimacy as well as helping them define their sexual partnership as they make progress with the dilator and Kegel exercises. Chapters 6 and 7 will outline specific diagnostic categories and treatment techniques for female and male sexual dysfunctions. An understanding of sexual diagnosis enables sexuality counselors to make informed treatment-planning decisions and to devise comprehensive case formulations.

Case Formulation in Treatment Planning

Weeks and Treat (2001) propose a case formulation method for couples in treatment that incorporates diagnostic as well as intersystem assessment. Their intersystem assessment framework includes obtaining information about individual, interactional, and intergenerational system issues. Individual systems include intrapsychic components, such as cognitive distortions and irrational thinking, defense mechanisms, definitions, predictions, and interpretations. *DSM-IV-TR* (APA, 2000) diagnoses are also included. Interactional systems include emotional contracts, styles of communication, patterns of dyadic interaction, and conflict resolution

skills. Intergenerational systems include "anniversary reactions, scripts, boundaries, [emotional] cutoffs, triangles, and [issues of] closeness and distance" (Weeks & Treat, 2001, p. 11). Figure 4.1 presents an example of a case formulation form.

DESIGNING AND IMPLEMENTING INTERVENTIONS

Interventions Defined

Interventions are counseling strategies or techniques designed to help couples accomplish their goals. They are the "actions" of the treatment plan. They have often been described as "what the [counselor] does" in treatment (Smith, 2001, p. 46). Interventions are based on couples' needs and the counselor's full treatment repertoire. When designing interventions, sexuality counselors employ advanced skills and techniques to encourage couples to be proactive in working toward their goals (Young, 2001). The integrative couples' model uses a solution-oriented, strength-based approach when designing interventions.

Developing a Conceptual Model for Intervention

A conceptual model is important to the intervention development process. The ability to conceptualize or "see the big picture" when choosing interventions moves counseling in the direction agreed upon by the sexuality counselor and the couple. A theoretical framework, such as cognitive-behavioral or strategic therapy, provides a structure for conceptualization of the larger picture. Chapter 2 details specific theories and practice related to intervention design. Remember that an integrative model provides a conceptual framework that integrates a variety of theoretical approaches (Young & Long, 1998).

The conceptual framework and subsequent treatment intervention are based on couples' problems and goals. For example, if couples describe sexual problems with roots in an inability to communicate effectively about sexual needs and desires, sexuality counselors may use interventions based on structural or strategic thinking or narrative or communication theory. In this case, the understanding of symmetrical and complementary communication is helpful in choosing an appropriate intervention. For example, in order to provide increased equality in a relationship, couples can identify times in their relationship

Case Formulation Form

Family name: _____ Date of 1st interview: _____

Partner's name: _____ Age: _____ Occupation: _____

Partner's name: _____ Age: _____ Occupation: _____

Children and other family in home:

_____   _____   _____

_____   _____   _____

Ethnic group: _____ Years married/in relationship: _____

Referred by: _____ Reason for referral: _____

1. Initial impressions and reactions:

_____

_____

2. Presenting problem(s)—Give a concrete description, including the who, where, what, how. What is each member's view of the problem? How is the problem maintained in the system?

_____

_____

3. History of the problem—abbreviated form of No. 2 above:

_____

_____

4. Solutions attempted, including previous therapy:

_____

_____

5. Changes sought by client(s):

_____

_____

6. Recent significant changes—stressors and life-cycle changes (e.g., new job, move, death, divorce, child leaving home):

_____

_____

Intersystem Assessment Questions

7. *Individual system(s)* (Intrapsychic components; i.e., cognitive distortions and irrational thinking, defense mechanisms such as denial, projection; definitions, predictions, and interpretations; also include Axis I, II, III DSM-IV diagnoses):

_____

_____

8. *Interactional system* (e.g., emotional contacts, styles of communication, patterns of dyadic interaction, linear attributional strategies such as debilitation, justification, vilification, rationalization, conflict–resolution skills):

_____

_____

9. *Intergenerational system* (e.g., anniversary reactions, scripts, boundaries, cutoffs, triangles, closeness–distance issues):

_____

_____

FIGURE 4.1

Source: Copyright 2001 from *Couples in Treatment: Techniques and Approaches for Effective Practice,* 2nd ed. (pp. 9–12) by G. Weeks and S. Treat. Reproduced by permission of Routledge/Taylor & Francis Books, Inc.

Treatment Plan Questions

10. Hypothesis regarding the client(s):

_____

_____

11. Treatment plan and strategies (individual, interactional, intergenerational)

_____

_____

Individual Problems   Change Strategy or Techniques

_____   _____

_____   _____

Couple Problems   Change Strategy or Techniques

_____   _____

_____   _____

Family-of-Origin Problems   Change Strategy or Techniques

_____   _____

_____   _____

12. Prognosis and expected length of therapy (provisional):

_____

13. What are your strengths and weaknesses in dealing with this client system?

_____

_____

FIGURE 4.1
(*Continued*)

when they try to "one up" each other for power. By identifying this pattern, an intervention is designed to help couples relate in a more equal manner.

Once an intervention is chosen based on a conceptualization of the couples' problems and goals, the next step is to design the intervention.

Designing Interventions

Designing interventions are activities that draw on the sexuality counselor's expertise to select methods and strategies that help solve couples' sexual problems or dysfunctions. This is often a complex task. How do counselors choose certain interventions? The first thing to remember is that interventions are based on couples' problem statements and goals. Specifically, the intervention needs to provide an avenue to address the current problems, thus moving couples toward their goals. For example, if each person in a relationship has identified a problem related to meeting a partner's sexual needs—for example, difficulty knowing how to provide sexual pleasure—then an intervention is chosen that helps them work toward their goal of achieving mutual sexual satisfaction. However, how can sexuality counselors be certain that they have designed interventions that are appropriate for the identified problems and goals? Given the considerable number of interventions available, the decision of what intervention works best for identified problems and goals is complicated.

Interventions involve "doing." Couples are asked to *do* something to begin solving their problem. For example, in order to address a problem about lack of sexual satisfaction with a goal of achieving mutual sexual pleasure, a sexuality counselor suggests to a couple that they obtain information through books and videos on sexual techniques. They also identify sexual activities that interest each of them and discuss these preferences with each other. Throughout this "doing" process, the sexuality counselor checks on the couple's progress. Perhaps the first step for this couple is increasing knowledge about sexuality and sexual pleasuring techniques. This goal is accomplished once the couple is able to share possible sexual activities of interest to them. Additional interventions are designed to complement their increased sexual knowledge and move them closer to their goal of mutual sexual satisfaction. One simple way of addressing the question "how do we make sure the interventions designed are appropriate for the identified problems and goals" is to assume that if couples do not accomplish their goals after the initial intervention(s), new interventions should be implemented (O'Leary, Heyman, & Jongsma, 1998).

Implementing Interventions

Successful interventions depend on being able to engage couples in the treatment process by initiating interventions that engender a sense of trust and hopefulness and facilitate engagement in the therapeutic process (Sperry, 2001). Information gathered during the assessment and goal-setting stages helps counselors implement effective interventions. For example, a sexual genogram is used to uncover expectations about gender roles, communication patterns, and sexual rules in families of origin. After these messages and patterns have been identified, an intervention is created that focuses on effective sexual communication and role rehearsal techniques.

The purpose of interventions is to address the problematic sexual patterns of behavior in a different, positive frame of reference or context so that partners can view each other differently (Young & Long, 1998). This positive emphasis moves couples from a sense of failure to success.

Creating a Cooperative, Blame-Free Context

A critical component necessary for cooperation is a blame-free context. Too often, partners project and blame others to avoid addressing their own culpability or responsibility. This pattern of relating leads to feelings of frustration and helplessness, and it fails to establish a sense of responsibility for finding a solution (Young & Long, 1998). The belief that "it is not my fault, it is my partner's fault" creates a blaming environment that is not conducive to mutual problem solving and renders the blaming partner helpless to participate in a solution. Sexuality counselors help couples recognize the futility of the blaming pattern by moving them toward a sense of support and connection.

A blame-free context allows couples to move in the right direction—away from asking "Who caused this problem?" to "How can we work this out together?" The aim of sexuality counselors is to help couples recognize the shared nature and responsibility of the relationship and to eliminate feelings of helplessness (Young & Long, 1998).

Cooperation is necessary for success in any counseling situation, not only between the couple and the counselor but also within the partner relationship. Couples often start with conflictual and contradictory ideas about the problems in their relationship, and they blame their partner in the way that they demonstrate their conflict (Kottler, 1994). Getting rid of blame and moving toward cooperation is a key element to resolve their conflict.

Externalizing Strategies

Just as externalization is effective in goal setting, it can be useful as an intervention as well. The following examples illustrate interventions that sexuality counselors can use to help couples externalize problems and set achievable goals. We refer again to the case example of Simon and Mikala to illustrate these externalization strategies.

EXAMPLE 1:   It seems that the two of you demonstrate a pattern whereby Mikala gets frustrated when Simon does not make sexual overtures. Simon's reaction is to distance himself further. The result is a cycle of resentment and frustration. What might you do to work together to attack this problem?

EXAMPLE 2:   Your "hectic work schedules" create little time for sexual intimacy. What are some ways that you can use the time you do have together to increase sexual intimacy?

Focusing on Strengths

Couples often come into sexuality counseling after having struggled with repeated failures and a sense of helplessness about how to successfully manage their sexual problems. They may be unaware of or have become distanced from their individual and relational strengths. Identifying and using individual and relational strengths in counseling helps couples view each other and the situation more positively (Young & Long, 1998).

Counselors initiate the exploration of strengths by having the couple tell stories about their intimate relationships from past and present events (Young & Long, 1998). Couples are able to incorporate the positive features from their narratives in order to create constructive opportunities and achieve different results (Young & Long, 1998). Interventions are then designed to use the individual and relational strengths of couples. Sexuality counselors explore couples' intimacy by having each partner relate stories about their relationship.

EXAMPLE 1:   What were your first impressions of each other?

EXAMPLE 2:   Describe some of the most sexually satisfying times of your relationship.

This type of intervention serves to strengthen hope. As a result, couples are able to identify possibilities for growth in their relationship as they shift from reminiscing and cocreating stories about their relationship to a specific plan for change in the present.

Solving Problems Through Strength-Based Interventions

The discovery of individual and relational strengths and the development of treatment interventions are activities completed in tandem (Young & Long, 1998). By helping couples to identify the positive assets of each partner and to provide feedback for each other on how they have solved similar problems in the past, partners are able to experience each other in a more positive light (Young & Long, 1998). We believe that despite life's struggles and setbacks, all persons possess strengths that can be identified and directed to improve the quality of their relationships and their lives. An emphasis on personal and relational strengths helps empower couples and can provide them with the courage to mobilize their resources to solve their sexual and intimate problems. Discovering these strengths requires a process of cooperative exploration between the couple and the counselor and provides a creative environment for developing appropriate solutions to their problems (DeJong & Berg, 1998).

Exploring Exceptions

Exploring exceptions to sexual and intimacy problems helps identify current and past successes couples have experienced when they have been satisfied with their relationship (DeJong & Miller, 1995). Counselors ask couples to focus on exceptions by directing statements or asking questions that emphasize times they were successful.

EXAMPLE 1:   Tell me about a time in your relationship when you were intimate and close with each other. How did you get that to happen?

EXAMPLE 2:   When you were enjoying intercourse with your partner, what type of foreplay was most satisfying? How was it initiated?

EXAMPLE 3:   Let's discuss the time during the weekend when you feel more relaxed and would like to initiate sexual play with your partner. What do you do to make your time together more romantic?

Individual and couple strengths are highlighted when couples are able to describe what they did to make a situation work well. Counselors compliment these positive behaviors as they are identified and encourage further thinking about exceptions to the problems. In short, asking couples to describe exceptions to the problem and identifying the skills (strengths) used is central to creating a positive view of their sexual relationship. Couples feel optimistic they will be able to solve similar problems in the future.

After identifying couples' strengths and interventions, couples will have taken several key steps:

Step 1: Made shifts in feelings, behaviors, and perceptions about their sexual relationship.

Step 2: Identified individual and relational strengths.

Step 3: Explored exceptions to the sexual problems and understand the role they play in creating a plan for change.

Step 4: Experienced success based on the outcome of the interventions.

Step 5: Provided feedback to each other and to the counselor regarding changes that have positively

BOX 4.1

Goal Setting and Treatment Planning Interventions at a Glance

- Ask partners to describe the positive sexual aspects of their current relationship.
- [Ask partners to identify positive self attributes and identify ways these strengths can be used to help address their sexual concerns.]
- Ask partners to communicate with each other about a nonsexual matter. Listener should allow partner to speak without interruption and, to demonstrate understanding, should paraphrase speaker's intent.
- Ask [partners] to communicate with each other about a sexual matter. Listener should allow partner to speak without interruption and, to demonstrate understanding, should paraphrase speaker's intent.
- Ask each [partner] to describe initial expectations about his/her sexual life.
- Suggest that couples read book on sexual behavior and sexual functioning such as *Sex for Dummies* (Westheimer, 2005), *The New Male Sexuality* (Zilbergeld, 1992), *The New Joy of Sex* (Comfort, 1991), *The Gift of Sex* (Penner & Penner, 1981), and *When a Woman's Body Says No to Sex* (Valins, 1992).
- Instruct [couples] in use of sensate focus [or mutual masturbation] to learn how to touch each other.
- Obtain feedback from clients about the sensate focus [or mutual masturbation] exercises, and assist in minimizing any behaviors that affect either partner negatively.
- Request that [partners identify] sexual fantasies that increase sexual desire toward partner.
- [Ask couples to describe the ways that family/career/other demands impact with sexual intimacy.]
- [Assist partners to brainstorm ways of reallocating time to provide mutual support and enhance sexual intimacy.]

Source: From *The Couples Psychotherapy Treatment Planner* (pp. 232–236), by K. D. O'Leary, R. E. Heyman, and A. E. Jongsma, Jr.. Copyright © 1998 by K. Daniel O'Leary, Richard E. Heyman, Arthur E. Jongsma, Jr. This material is used by permission of John Wiley & Sons, Inc.

impacted their sexual relationship and identified those they may not wish to try again, or try at a later time.

During Stage 3 of the integrative couples' model, sexuality counselors actively choose interventions that help couples focus on identifying their resources to reach their goals (Young & Long, 1998). Box 4.1 presents some common interventions to address these problems. In subsequent chapters, a number of strategies designed for specific sexual concerns are described in detail.

We will continue the case example of Simon and Mikala used in Chapters 2 and 3 to illustrate how goal setting, treatment planning, and interventions are used in the integrative couples model.

Case Example

Simon and Mikala have been married six years and complain of low sexual desire since the birth of their two-year-old child. Both also have very busy careers.

The following tasks were completed during the assessment stage. The sexuality counselor noted the commonality of dual-career couples struggling to maintain balance in their busy lives. The process of treatment was outlined, and communication patterns were identified. Critical information about their mental status, potential for violence, and personal health was collected. A comprehensive sexual history was also taken, and data were gathered about current sexual concerns. A sexual genogram was used to obtain more detailed interactional and family information. A language was created that helped Simon and Mikala discuss their sexual relationship more effectively. Based on the information gathered, the sexuality counselor helped Simon and Mikala develop a shared, solvable definition of the problem, which has been identified as follows: The changes in their busy lives (i.e., busy careers, a young child) have resulted in a lack of time and energy for a sexual relationship. They want to create a better balance in their lives and reestablish their sexual intimacy. Following the development of this shared problem definition, the sexuality counselor begins to work with Simon and Mikala on goal setting.

Stage 2: Goal Setting

During this stage, the sexuality counselor must focus on the following tasks: help set realistic goals, create goals tailored specifically to the couple, externalize the problem, state goals in interactional terms, and set behavioral and affective goals.

Simon and Mikala have initially focused on what is "wrong" (the problem), with their relationship. The emphasis of sexuality counseling now moves to "what we could have" (a goal) in their sexual relationship. The sexuality counselor must encourage Simon and Mikala to describe the desired outcome of counseling and to develop the problem statement into realistic goals by identifying what they would like to change in their relationship, keeping in mind the increased demands in their lives. This allows Simon and Mikala to begin to think realistically about their time issues while considering what would make their sexual relationship more gratifying. Maintaining a realistic focus allows Simon and Mikala to develop goals that are solvable and achievable. The counselor helps them understand that flawless sexual behavior is not a realistic goal.

The sexuality counselor works with Simon and Mikala to tailor goals specific to their sexual concerns. Although the couple has identified several problems, their counselor chooses to focus on the problem of "limited time and energy for sexual intimacy"—the problem that is most troubling and that they are most willing, able, and ready to address.

The goal designed for Simon and Mikala focuses directly on the lack of sexual satisfaction in their relationship as a result of their busy lifestyles. It would not make sense to develop a goal that addressed communication if that had not been identified as their problem.

Externalizing the problem is also an important step in goal setting. The sexuality counselor helps Simon and Mikala view the problem as one that is separate from them— "the busy lifestyle dilemma," "the sexual divider," or "the time and energy struggle."

Characterizing the problem in this manner helps this couple to separate the problem from themselves and join together to defeat it. The counselor says to Simon and Mikala, "We have found that much of your time is spent on work, child care, and other responsibilities. Can you tell me some ways that managing these responsibilities interferes with your goal of having a satisfying sexual relationship?"

Once the couple is able to externalize the problem and think of it as a force to be reckoned with together, they can begin to set goals in interactional terms. Just as problems are defined in interactional terms, so are goals. Simon states, "Our problem is that Mikala is so busy with her career and our children, that she no longer has time or energy for me. She doesn't even want to make love anymore. I've stopped trying to make things happen between us." The sexuality counselor redirects the couple to focus on an interactive definition they have jointly created. The goal may then be stated as "We would like to find ways to spend quality time together so that we can feel more positive and sexually connected to each other."

The sexuality counselor helps Simon and Mikala describe in concrete terms behavioral and affective changes they would like to see. They are soon able to transform their problem into the behavioral and affective components of the following goals:

> *Goal 1:* We will get a babysitter and go out on a date—maybe dinner and a movie or concert—once a week (behavioral). This will help us feel closer to each other (affective).
>
> Goal 2: We will set aside time to communicate with each other about our sexual needs and desires (behavioral), so we can feel loved and understood (affective).

In order for change in perceptions to occur, there must be changes in behaviors and feelings. When Simon and Mikala set the stage for more time together, they are able to reconnect and feel closer to each other sexually. At the close of Stage 2, they have moved from "we have a problem" to "we have a goal."

Following the goal-setting stage, the sexuality counselor develops interventions to help Simon and Mikala recognize that they have a "solvable problem" as they undergo shifts in feelings, behaviors, and perceptions, and are able to identify individual and relational strengths. In addition, they explore exceptions to the sexual problems, experience success based on the outcome of the interventions, and provide feedback to each other and the counselor regarding positive changes. Finally, they identify those activities or tasks they may not wish to try again.

It is useful at this point to identify and implement strength-based interventions—finding the strengths and positive assets of each partner. The counselor asks Simon and Mikala to list their strengths as a couple and to describe some of their most romantic and sexually gratifying times. This helps them consider the past positive characteristics of their intimate and sexual relationship and enables them to consider future positive outcomes (Young & Long, 1998). Focusing on strengths instead of perceived weaknesses instills hope and empowers Simon and Mikala to begin to solve their sexual problems. This technique also helps identify who will be responsible for which changes (Young & Long, 1998). For example, Simon and Mikala move from their story about their past sexual relationship and romantic times to describing what they expect from each other based on their identified strengths. They decide how they will set aside the time in their schedules, who will arrange child care, and how they will make specific plans for the time they spend together. The development of a here-and-now plan will help them to begin exploring exceptions to the problems.

Exploring exceptions to problems involves asking couples to focus on past and present successes (DeJong & Miller, 1995). Simon and Mikala's counselor asks them to discuss a time in their relationship when they had time for sexual intimacy and how they enabled that to happen. This process highlights their ability to make positive things happen in their sexual relationship. The emphasis changes from "what is wrong" to "what we did or can do well." This also serves to instill hope and optimism.

The sexuality counselor designs interventions geared toward Simon and Mikala's problem statements and goals. They are asked to do

something to work toward their goals and subsequently solve their problems. The counselor suggests they use relaxation techniques and mutual massage to help them rekindle some of their lost intimacy. Their counselor also uses reframing techniques—a process that helps couples reinterpret situations or problems in a more positive manner. Simon and Mikala's counselor believes that if the appropriate interventions are selected and successfully implemented, it is more likely that the couple will experience success.

An important step during and following the implementation of interventions is the provision of feedback—a necessary process that can ascertain what has changed in the sexual relationship and the effects of the interventions. Without sharing feedback with each other and the counselor, there is no measurement of success. It is important to know what did and did not help. This will enable both couple and counselor to make adjustments as needed in the overall treatment plan. Box 4.2 lists the interventions used in Stages 2 and 3 with Simon and Mikala.

BOX 4.2

Interventions Used in Goal Setting and Treatment Planning with Simon and Mikala

Goal Setting

Describe desired outcome of counseling.

Set realistic goals.

Focus and design specific goals.

Externalize the problem.

Set interactional goals (behavioral and affective).

Treatment Planning

Identify individual strengths.

Identify relational strengths.

Explore exceptions to problems.

Use relaxation techniques and mutual massage.

Use reframing techniques to reinterpret problems in positive manner.

Solicit feedback.

SUMMARY

Goal setting, treatment planning, and interventions are based on the information collected during the assessment stage. Sexuality counselors use this information to help couples set interactional goals that are realistic and designed to address the couple's unique problems. Externalizing helps couples perceive a problem as something separate from themselves that interferes with their lives. This moves them to a united stance to address the problem together.

Setting behavioral and affective goals is an integral part of the goal-setting process. Counselors must help clients identify what they can do and how they would like to feel in specific ways so that they have a distinct idea of what they are trying to accomplish.

Interventions are designed to accommodate individual and relational strengths. Focusing on the strengths and positive attributes of a relationship helps couples develop a cooperative, blame-free environment for change and allows them to better explore exceptions to the problems and focus on success. An endless number of interventions exists to address sexual problems and to focus on what the couple will do to begin solving the problem. Counselors use their expertise to select and design interventions to enable couples to do something concrete to address their problem. Finally, communication about progress is ongoing to help both clients and counselors determine the effectiveness of interventions.

MAINTAINING AND VALIDATING NEW PERCEPTIONS AND BEHAVIORS IN SEXUALITY COUNSELING

KEY CONCEPTS

- Maintenance strategies in sexuality counseling involve helping couples recommit to the change process by continuing to practice behaviors that foster forward movement in their sexual relationship.
- Specific maintenance interventions can be used early in sexuality counseling, throughout the treatment process, and prior to termination of counseling.
- Minor lapses are a natural and expected part of the sexuality counseling process and can serve as learning opportunities for couples.
- Relapse or lapse can be remedied by identifying a plan to remediate behavior that has "slipped" and then progressing toward a prevention plan to minimize further backsliding. In this way, couples learn to interrupt this cycle by self-intervention.
- Factors such as couples' personal resources, external support, life events, biochemical events, and cognitive distortions influence the relapse process.
- By focusing on continued commitment and growth in couples' sexual relationships and by identifying barriers that impede growth, couples can maintain changes in their sexual interactions.
- Validating individual and relational success helps couples to maintain goals they have achieved and gains they have made in sexuality counseling.
- Couples compare goals they set at Stage 2 (goal setting) of counseling, reconfirm their long-term commitment in Stage 4 (maintenance), and validate the current state of their sexual relationship in Stage 5.
- Sexuality counselors help couples to reevaluate goals, develop new narratives, design and use rituals to validate and celebrate their successes. The use of feedback and therapeutic compliments are also useful interventions for helping couples validate new perceptions and behaviors.
- Follow-up strategies, including fading, booster sessions, and use of external support systems, are integral parts to continued sexuality counseling success.

In Chapters 3 and 4, assessment, goal setting, treatment planning, and interventions have been described within the framework of an integrative couples' model for sexuality counseling. During the first three stages of the model, sexuality counselors carefully assessed couples' problems, developed a shared definition of the problem, identified goals, and created appropriate intervention strategies for treating couples' sexual concerns. Couples have practiced new behaviors throughout their counseling sessions and have completed homework assignments. Now, in Stage 4, sexuality counselors offer intervention strategies that will help couples develop the skill set required to continue to progress in their relationships and to cultivate the evolving changes that have started (Young & Long, 1998). We will describe Stage 4 of the integrative couples' model with an emphasis on ways to maintain positive movement toward couples' goals. In addition, we will identify roadblocks to progress in the context of a relapse cycle. We have chosen to focus on the work of John Ludgate (1995) who has written extensively about relapse prevention and maximizing therapeutic progress. We will then present maintenance interventions designed to improve couples' sexual relationships and to reinforce the new skills they have acquired. Finally, in Stage 5, we focus on validation, including interventions such as goal reevaluation, therapeutic and relational compliments, celebrations of success, and the use of rituals for celebrating success. We also look at follow-up interventions such as the identification of external support systems.

MAINTAINING NEW PERCEPTIONS AND BEHAVIORS

Defining Maintenance in Sexuality Counseling

Maintenance in sexuality counseling involves helping couples recommit to the change process by continuing to practice behaviors that foster forward movement in their sexual relationship. Maintaining consistency in newly acquired behaviors and skills helps couples gain confidence in their ability to create and sustain a satisfying intimate relationship. This process includes helping couples identify what is going well and how they will continue their current positive behaviors. Couples also become aware of barriers that impede further intimacy and satisfaction.

Maintenance Strategies and Interventions

Ludgate (1995) outlines several interventions that can be used throughout sexuality counseling in order to promote maintenance of positive sexual behaviors:*

- Fade frequency of sessions later in counseling.
- Use booster/refresher sessions.

---

*From *Maximizing Psychotherapeutic Gains and Preventing Relapse in Emotionally Distressed Clients* (pp. 17–18), by J. W. Ludgate, 1995, Sarasota, FL: Professional Resource Press. Copyright 1995 by Professional Resource Exchange, Inc. Reprinted with permission.

- Increase couples' responsibility for their change and growth.
- Place greater emphasis on between-session activities/homework as [counseling] proceeds.
- Promote internal [awareness of sexual needs].
- Educate regarding relapse and create realistic expectations regarding [their future sexual and intimate relationship].
- Discuss the need for and the benefits of efforts in counseling.
- Help [couples] to develop a self-therapy program to be used after termination.
- Identify barriers to change or problems stemming from changes.
- Anticipate and plan for high-risk situations.
- Modify the environment, where possible, to support new behaviors or responses.

Other interventions used by sexuality counselors include focusing on a variety of behavioral changes in order to achieve couples' goals, training couples in specific skills for more positive sexual expression (discussions, videotapes, books), and enlisting each partner to help the other maintain change.

Such interventions offer sexuality counselors a quick reference of general strategies that will foster the maintenance of new behaviors and prevent or lessen the effects of setbacks. One intervention used to diminish setbacks is identifying "barriers" or roadblocks to success.

Identifying Barriers to Success

Because change is not naturally maintained, identifying barriers to success is an important part of sexuality counseling. Counselors monitor these barriers by asking couples questions that address potential pitfalls in their sexual relationship:

"Simon, how committed are you to creating intimate time for you and Mikala?"

"How will the two of you continue to stay motivated to increase your sexual repertoire?"

"What ways can you promote touching in and outside of the bedroom?"

In addition, sexuality counselors address barriers for change through these types of questions:

"What do you think would get in the way of your new sexual playfulness with each other?"

"What will happen when your hectic life begins to take over your relationship?"

"How will you react to your partner when you think there has been a 'lapse'?"

"Mikala, when you feel frustrated with Simon, what can you do instead of withdrawing?"

Questions such as these allow couples to plan maintenance tasks that help them avoid and minimize setbacks. Box 5.1 identifies additional maintenance interventions sexuality counselors can use to help couples sustain their improved sexual relationship.

During this stage of the model, sexuality counselors help couples foresee and normalize recurrences of problematic patterns of behavior, thus enabling them to use their new skills in order to maintain positive progress.

Although we have identified Stage 4 as the period during which couples can continue to develop newly acquired changes in their sexual relationships, there are specific maintenance interventions that can be followed throughout the sexuality counseling process.

BOX 5.1

Maintenance Interventions at a Glance

- Acknowledge couple's efforts and improvement.
- Assess each partner's commitment to the change process.
- Ask couple to evaluate their own performance, helping them to use realistic sexual standards.
- Predict relapses and "slippages" in couple's sexual growth.
- Ask partners to identify specific roadblocks that could sabotage change in their relationship.
- Have partners design solutions to address barriers to change.
- Concentrate on couple's present capacities, possibilities, and conditions rather than on perceived failures.
- Confront discouraging beliefs.
- Lend enthusiasm and ask for commitment toward goals.
- Demonstrate faith in couple's competency and capabilities.

Source: Adapted from O'Leary, Heyman, and Jongsma (1998) and Young (2001).

BOX 5.2

Maintenance Strategies and Interventions

Early Counseling Interventions

- Assessing setback risk
- Graphing progress
- Anticipatory closure
- Emphasizing a collaborative focus

Throughout Counseling Interventions

- Reviewing skills
- Teaching and learning skills with broad application
- Responding to negative thoughts
- Predicting thoughts about setbacks

Near Termination Interventions

- Readdressing closure
- Recognizing early warning signs of setbacks
- Encouraging early help seeking
- Rehearing setbacks
- Planning self-monitoring
- Specifying steps in setback prevention
- Examining lifestyle shifts or events

Source: From *Maximizing Psychotherapeutic Gains and Preventing Relapse in Emotionally Distressed Clients* (pp. 19–39), by J. W. Ludgate, 1995, Sarasota, FL: Professional Resource Press. Copyright 1995 by Professional Resource Exchange, Inc. Adapted with permission.

Ludgate (1995) identifies these as three distinct phases of counseling: (a) early counseling interventions, (b) throughout counseling interventions, and (c) near termination counseling interventions. Box 5.2 presents the maintenance strategies and interventions related to each phase.

Early Counseling Interventions

Assessing Setback Risk. During initial assessment as well as the beginning stages of treatment, sexuality counselors identify risk factors for potential setbacks (Ludgate, 1995). Once risk factors have been identified, counseling interventions can then be created. The assessment phase includes identifying the capacity for self-monitoring for progress as well as the factors that influence how couples relate to each other.

Graphing Progress.   When sexuality counselors discuss expectations with couples, they can help clarify the possible duration and scope of treatment through the use of a graph showing trends toward general improvement as well as fluctuations and diversions that are a normal part of the process (Ludgate, 1995). Although this type of graph is a linear description of progress, it should be noted that couples do in fact change in a more systemic manner. For example, a couple describes their sexual satisfaction as a 3 on a scale where 10 describes the optimal sexual relationship. Using this information, their sexuality counselor helps them identify issues that have gotten in the way of their optimal sexual satisfaction. Together with their counselor, they then devise homework interventions to increase their sexual satisfaction. When the couple next returns to counseling, they report their satisfaction has increased to a 5. As the normal ebb and flow of therapeutic progress continues and the couple returns for a third session, they indicate that their satisfaction has decreased to a 4. They also identify situational events that have impacted their life in the last couple of weeks that may have contributed to this fluctuation. Again, the counselor reminds the couple of this natural process and emphasizes their long-term commitment to change.

Anticipating Closure.   Sexuality counselors stress that closure—the end of counseling—will be based not on a function of time spent in treatment but rather on attainment of goals (Ludgate, 1995). By discussing the close of treatment throughout counseling, sexuality counselors are able to emphasize the significance of maintaining therapeutic gains and to help couples develop self-monitoring methods that are applied at each stage of counseling.

Emphasizing a Collaborative Focus.   Successful couples have been able to keep an open, collaborative focus on making changes in their sexual functioning. A team approach is essential for determining their personal counseling goals, responding to interventions, and codesigning homework tasks (Ludgate, 1995).

Throughout Counseling Interventions

Reviewing Skills.   Couples must learn reviewing skills in order to reach their goals during counseling. According to Ludgate (1995), sexuality counselors can review these steps intermittently by asking questions such as the following:

> What tools or skills do you have at this point to deal with your problems?

> What have you learned in [counseling] so far?

> What is different now from before, and what are you doing to make this happen? (Ludgate, 1995, pp. 20–21).

This review is part of self-monitoring skills that couples master in the early stage of sexuality counseling. These skills help them nurture their sexual and relational growth.

Skills with Broad Application.   Couples learn problem-solving skills that can be applied to other situations in their sexual relationship (Ludgate, 1995). Role reversals and imagery techniques are particularly useful for addressing a wide array of relationship problems.

Responding to Negative Thoughts.   Sexuality counselors work with couples to address negative thoughts and beliefs about themselves and to challenge and change aspects of such internal dialogues (Gilbert & Shmukler, 1996). Ludgate (1995) identifies some of these techniques:

> Identifying and testing negative thoughts.

> Recognizing distorted thinking patterns.

> Rationally responding to automatic thoughts.

> Identifying and revising underlying beliefs. (p. 23)

As couples challenge negative thinking, they are urged to consider the situation in a more positive way. They can normalize the process by refusing to "awfulize" with statements such as "we are back to square one" or "we can never change."

Predicting Thoughts About Setbacks.   Sexuality counselors help couples imagine experiencing a setback and predict what they would do, think, or feel when setbacks occur (Ludgate, 1995). This form of self-monitoring promotes a couple's sense of relational efficacy.

Near Termination Counseling Interventions

Readdressing Closure.   Sexuality counselors readdress couples' feelings about closure and begin to make plans to continue self-therapy after counseling has been completed (Ludgate, 1995). Anticipating and addressing potential negative feelings and thoughts about closure provides couples with opportunities to prepare for eventual termination and rehearse self-therapy interventions.

Recognizing Early Warning Signs of Setbacks.   Recognizing early warning signs can short-circuit the setback process if the signs are addressed prior to a recurrence of old behaviors. Self-monitoring regarding reactions that might trigger a setback is a key to the success of this strategy (Ludgate, 1995).

Encouraging Early Help-Seeking.   When rehearsed strategies have failed, it is important that couples seek additional help from their identified supporters. Together they can determine at what point it is necessary to seek outside help (Ludgate, 1995).

Rehearsing Setbacks.   The sexuality counselor can confront the couple with a range of setback situations that will enable them to rehearse ways to address the dilemmas and practice their responses to difficult situations (Ludgate, 1995).

Planning Self-Monitoring.   Couples are encouraged by their sexuality counselors to develop a plan and to continue to focus on the changes they have made in their intimate relationship after counseling ends (Ludgate, 1995). They may periodically ask each other questions related to their continued progress:

> "How are we doing with the changes we have made?"
>
> "Are we both comfortable with the changes we have made?"
>
> "What seem to be the problems we have encountered as we make changes?"
>
> "What can we do to follow up on the new behaviors we are using in our sexual relationship?"

Specifying Steps in Preventing Setback.   According to Ludgate (1995), couples should be encouraged to engage in the following behaviors when they experience an impasse:

> 1. Stop whatever they are [currently] doing.
> 2. Examine the situation that is [affecting the shift to old patterns].
> 3. Identify the automatic thoughts that are [linked to a return to old patterns and interrupt those thoughts]. (p. 36)

Examining Lifestyle.   Couples are encouraged to examine their current lifestyle—related to career, social life, personal time, and extended family interactions—in order to determine what is getting in the way of their intimate time together (Ludgate, 1995).

Setbacks as a Component of the Maintenance Process

In order to maintain new behaviors, it is important for couples to realize that there will be times when they revert to old patterns of behavior. Regardless of their progress in sexuality counseling, couples will encounter these "roadblocks" as a natural and expected part of the sexuality counseling process. In fact, it is through these setbacks that couples are able to evaluate and relearn new skills. Sexual relationships are not perfect, and couples should not expect to function without reverting back to old behaviors.

Defining Setbacks

Webster's New Collegiate Dictionary (2002) offers two distinct definitions of *relapse*. The first defines the word as "a recurrence of symptoms . . . after a period of improvement." This definition focuses on a specific outcome and implies dichotomous categories of dysfunctional and functional (Marlatt & George, 1998). The second defines the word as an "act or instance of backsliding, worsening, or subsiding." This refers to a process rather than an outcome and implies that something less serious—perhaps a slip, a mistake, or a regression—has occurred, which may or may not lead to a setback (Marlatt & George, 1998).

The definition of relapse as a "slip" or "backslide" has implications for the conceptualization, treatment, and prevention of further impasses (Ludgate, 1995) and is one that fits with the strength-based focus of the integrative couples' model. In addition, this definition implies that there are choices that can be made during the treatment process and further implies that a relapse or setback may be a reemergence of a previous habit or behavior that is not productive for couples and can be corrected.

Factors Associated with Setbacks

It is helpful to consider certain key factors when determining the potential and the severity of setback behaviors early in Stage 4 of the integrative couples' model. In this way, counselors can identify behaviors that are most likely to inhibit a couple's progress in counseling sessions. The following factors have been identified by Ludgate (1995) as being important influences on the setback process:*

> [Couples'] personal resources and skills [in addition to their] perceptions of these [skills]

---

*From *Maximizing Psychotherapeutic Gains and Preventing Relapse in Emotionally Distressed Clients* (p. 8), by J. W. Ludgate, 1995, Sarasota, FL: Professional Resource Press. Copyright 1995 by Professional Resource Exchange, Inc. Reprinted with permission.

External resources including support systems such as family, friends, community, professional help, [and spiritual advisor] and [their] perceptions of these resources

Life events/stressors and the [couples'] perceptions of these events

[Physiological events such as physical changes or medical conditions]

Residual symptomatology at the end of [counseling]

Residual or continuing cognitive deficits or distortions such as dysfunctional beliefs or biased information processing after [counseling]

Consider the following situation. Chan and Su Li are increasingly disinterested in sexual relations and both partners are exhibiting symptoms consistent with inhibited sexual desire. Both have demanding careers and their children's needs require most of their time in the evening. Su Li complains that there is not enough time for sexual interaction. Chan rebuffs all sexual advances and thinks "I wish she would leave me alone. If she would help more with the kids, I might be more interested." Su Li commits to playing team tennis on Wednesday evenings without discussing the effects this will have on the relationship. This triggered event provides less time for them to spend with each other and has created feelings of anger and resentment on the part of Chan. Currently, they are at an impasse and are hoping to find a way to reevaluate their behavior and reestablish their prior sexual balance. This scenario describes a typical situation that may take place after a couple has made changes in their sexual relationship and is attempting to maintain those changes over time.

These setbacks are normal and necessary parts of the sexuality counseling process and cannot be ignored. Couples who end counseling prematurely (after they feel better, usually during the intervention stage) typically find themselves disappointed because they have not prepared for the inevitable setbacks that are a normal part of the counseling process. Once couples have recognized these normal fluctuations, the sexuality counselor can help them validate and celebrate their successes in counseling.

VALIDATING NEW PERCEPTIONS AND BEHAVIORS

Validating Relational Success

Validation is a key factor in the success of Stage 5 of sexuality counseling. Couples compare the goals they set at Stage 2 (goal setting), reconfirm their long-term

commitment in Stage 4 (maintenance), and validate the current state of their sexual relationship in Stage 5. Partners validate themselves and each other for their success in conquering their sexual problems as a team and for enacting new behaviors. Generalizing the maintenance strategies they learned during Stage 4 to other issues that arise will ensure progress (Young & Long, 1998).

Throughout the course of counseling, couples have developed their unique style of initiation of sexual activities, have learned multiple stimulation techniques, and have practiced a variety of foreplay and afterplay behaviors (McCarthy, 1993). As their sexual style becomes more flexible, there is greater acceptance of a variety of sexual activities in their relationship. Couples learn not to overreact to negative experiences and challenge themselves to reframe their experiences in a positive, growth-enhancing manner (McCarthy, 1993).

By the validation stage of sexuality counseling (Stage 5), couples have increased self-acceptance and acceptance of their relationship and no longer want to "blame" or "prove something" to themselves or to their partners. They are able to focus on sexual quality and intimate connection, rather than solely on the frequency of intercourse. They do not compare themselves with a romantic movie ideal, or expect the intense sexual "high" experienced by a new couple. They are able to value the quality of their relationship and to focus on the present. They do not dwell on past mistakes, nor do they worry unnecessarily about the future. Sexuality plays a vital role in their relationship as a shared pleasure, a means of reinforcing intimacy and as a tension reducer for the stresses of life.

Interventions for Validating Success in Sexuality Counseling

Reevaluating Goals

Part of the validation process includes reevaluating goals as a means of measuring and assessing changes couples have made. Couples then compare the goals they set during Stage 2 (goal setting) with those in their current sexual relationship. How couples assess the achievement of their goals and define success versus failure is an integral part of the validation and celebration process. In order to maintain success and continue new perceptions and behaviors, couples develop a realistic, flexible, and multidimensional system to continue to self-evaluate their progress. One way that sexuality counselors can facilitate goal success is to help couples develop and use multiple sources of feedback.

Feedback

...e sources of feedback assist clients in shaping their perceptions of goal accomplishment, reevaluation of self-image, and performance-related outcomes (London & Smither, 1995). For couples working to maintain and validate new sexual perceptions and behaviors, developing varied sources of information and measures of success regarding their goals may be a helpful part of the validation process. For example, sexuality counselors work with couples to develop a long-term plan that includes periodic visits to their counselor in addition to working with them to determine ways to use information and measure their own success.

To validate or confirm that there is no longer a problem, couples strive to maintain cohesion through consistent empathy and reflection about themselves with each other. Without such continued self-monitoring and intervention, fragmentation and lack of unity may occur (Loring, Clark, & Frost, 1994). Another way couples can continue to validate themselves and their achievements is through the use of compliments.

Delivering Therapeutic Compliments

Through all stages of sexuality counseling, but particularly in Stage 5, counselors help couples identify and validate their strengths and offer them feedback in the form of therapeutic compliments. Individuals and couples possess personal qualities and past experiences, that, if drawn upon, are of great use in resolving problems and in creating more satisfying sexual relationships.

Therapeutic compliments focus on either past or present behavior, such as a sense of humor, fun-loving spirit, caring attitude toward each other, dedication to hard work, flexibility, or good organizational skills. These behaviors are labeled by sexuality counselors as "client strengths" and have been identified and mobilized in Stage 3 (interventions) in order to help find solutions to the identified problem. In Stage 5, these qualities are highlighted to assist couples so that they visualize and sustain their goals after terminating counseling.

Therapeutic compliments can also increase couples' confidence and inspire them to continue to prioritize their intimate and sexual needs. Couples are challenged to notice positive changes, strengths, and resources so they can feel positive about accomplishments they have achieved together (DeJong and

Berg, 2002). The following counselor responses underscore a positive perspective:

EXAMPLE 1: Simon, it sounds like you are very pleased with Mikala's new sexual playfulness. Can you tell her how important that is for you?

EXAMPLE 2: The two of you have been willing to explore together lovemaking techniques other than intercourse. Your flexibility seems to have created many options for you.

Narrative Therapy

Borrowing from narrative therapy, couples recount how and which resources they mobilized as they generated solutions to their sexual problems. White and Epston (1990) promote the idea of counselors asking couples to recount their transition from a problematic story about their relationship to a resolved one. This process of using questions as interventions underscores the achievements a couple has made.

EXAMPLE 1: What new meaning do you hold about your sexual expression?

EXAMPLE 2: How do you view yourselves in the future as you respond to each other sexually?

EXAMPLE 3: What is the most valuable part of your new sexual intimacy?

Schwartz (1999) discusses the significance of listening and then working with couples to find ways to change their relationships and their relational worlds and to become aware of the negative influences of cultural narratives on their self-concepts. Sexuality counselors often help couples develop new narratives in order to facilitate long-term success. These narratives should include ways to maintain positive individual and relational perceptions (Stage 4) and behaviors and to emphasize those strengths with each other.

If narrative therapy is to succeed, couples must cocreate a narrative or story about their journey through the process of sexuality counseling and focus on their current sexual relationship as well as their expectations for the future. One way for couples to create this narrative is to continue to emphasize their strengths and resources, to generate and try new solutions, and to celebrate their successes. An intervention that enables couples to celebrate and mark success is the development of rituals.

Using Rituals to Celebrate Successful Personal and Relational Changes

Rituals are customarily defined as repetitive symbolic or ceremonial acts designed to recognize a life event in a meaningful way (Imber-Black & Roberts, 1998; Young & Long, 1998). In a social or cultural context, rituals enable us to reaffirm traditions, behavior, ideologies, values, and norms. Rituals also serve to maintain social structure and to clarify the connections between individuals and their culture and "help people resist chaos and empower them to act appropriately" (Bewley, 1995, p. 203).

Using Rituals in Counseling

Rituals are powerful interventions that help couples effect change and find alternatives to life situations. Sexuality counselors use rituals to help people master life transitions, alter relationships, and construct more meaningful self-definitions (Laird & Hartman, 1988).

Rituals are important aspects of relational life. They encourage individual and relational identity, shield against hurt and tension, smooth the progression of change through transitional times, and create historical connections (Coale, 1994). Rituals also serve to help couples understand myriad roles and rules, heal emotional and relational pain, and connect with their sociocultural contexts (Coale, 1994).

The use of rituals in a therapeutic context helps couples maintain and validate their goals and successes. Rituals include plans cocreated between sexuality counselors and couples to change existing patterns or future emerging patterns.

Young and Long (1998) describe the following items to consider when creating a ritual:*

1. Understand the context for the event that requires a ritual. . . .
2. Explore in detail with . . . couple[s] the old sexual behaviors associated with the event and meanings ascribed to it.
3. Identify with . . . couple[s] the new context or manner in which they want to commemorate the passage of an event.
4. Identify the meaning . . . couple[s] would like to attach to the event.
5. Create a new behavior or way to commemorate the event that would ascribe new meaning to the event.
6. Explore with [couples] the barriers or "blockers" for the completion of the task or ritual.
7. Evaluate the effectiveness of the new behavior and meaning of the behavior for . . . couple[s] in the past, present, or future, modifying the ritual accordingly.

These steps enable sexuality counselors and couples to develop rituals that have meaning, provide alternatives for sexual behaviors, promote long-term sexual success, and help couples better manage life transitions.

For example, as sexuality counseling terminates, a ritual recognizing a "fresh start" or a "celebration of success" can be very effective. A couple may choose to celebrate their newly enhanced sexual relationship through a special ceremony or holiday depending on their culture and family heritage, or a series of written or oral strategies to describe their future template for a loving relationship. Fun and humor can be a part of planning and implementing rituals as couples continue to rekindle positive emotional and sexual feelings for each other. Sexuality counselors can pose questions that are designed to help couples reflect on rituals and celebration:

> "What type of celebration could the two of you plan to best describe your sexual intimacy?"
>
> "What type of romantic getaway could you create to reaffirm your positive feelings for each other?"
>
> "What kind of playful activity could you design together to demonstrate success in conquering sexual boredom?"

After couples have celebrated their successes, it is important to consider the closure process by examining ways to monitor success over time.

Building in Follow-Up Interventions

During Stage 5, couples may feel some trepidation about their ability to manage on their own. Some couples may feel anxious because the problem is not completely solved or fear that it may reemerge. Incorporating maintenance interventions and strategies in Stage 4 decreases client anxiety, as do rituals and celebrations of success in Stage 5. Other interventions in Stage 5 are designed around the counseling

---

*From *Counseling and Therapy for Couples,* 1st ed. (p. 219), by M. E. Young and L. L. Long. © 1998. Reprinted with permission of Wadsworth, a division of Thomson Learning: www.thomsonrights.com. Fax 800-730-2215.

process and frequency of therapeutic contact. One of these interventions is the process of fading.

Fading

Fading is the progressive extension of the amount of time between counseling sessions (Eyberg, Edwards, Boggs, & Foote, 1998). More emphasis is placed on couples' skills to anticipate and cope with circumstances that may increase the risk of setbacks (Eyberg et al., 1998). Without weekly counseling sessions, couples rely more on relational skills to identify challenges and implement changes. Between sessions, couples are encouraged to practice sexual skills and utilize new coping strategies to effectively manage sexual and relational issues that may arise. Information from couples about their progress between sessions is integrated in the next session.

Sexuality counselors challenge couples to validate their own achievements and revisit their progress when they return to counseling for a follow-up session (Young and Long, 1998).

EXAMPLE 1:   It sounds like the two of you have learned many new ways to achieve closeness. How do you let your partner know you are pleased with the results?

EXAMPLE 2:   Simon, tell Mikala the most exciting aspect of learning sexual playfulness together. How did she contribute to the fun?

It is important for sexuality counselors to show couples how their present achievements can be used to solve sexual issues that may arise in the future. A booster session is one method used to generalize skills over time.

Booster Sessions

The term *booster session* as it relates to posttreatment interventions can be defined as structured follow-up contacts with the sexuality counselor aimed at helping couples maintain sexual and relational goals. Such sessions have been viewed as a useful and cost-effective way of sustaining therapeutic improvement (Furey & Basili, 1988).

A long-term maintenance plan *can* and *should* include follow-up visits to the sexuality counselor at three- and six-month intervals. Brief, periodic contacts between sexuality counselors and couples after

counseling has formally terminated helps couples sustain the motivation and behavioral changes needed for long-term success (Eyberg et al., 1998). These contacts require minimal effort by sexuality counselors and are helpful in maintaining treatment progress (Perri, Sears, & Clark, 1993).

Sexuality counselors can work with couples to develop a plan for booster sessions, including face-to-face counseling as well as contacts by e-mail and telephone. These contacts serve to remind couples of their sexual and relational goals, encourage them to continue using the new skills they have developed, and reinforce their changes in sexual attitudes and behaviors.

Ludgate (1995) outlines a number of ways in which booster sessions can be set up:

1. They can be on a regular schedule for a prescribed period of time (e.g., every month or 3 months for 2 years).
2. They can be on a faded schedule (e.g., monthly, then tri-monthly, then twice a year).
3. They can be scheduled on an "as-needed" (in which case they may be crisis-driven and scheduled after other strategies have been tried and failed). (p. 42)

Booster sessions should be structured to achieve maximum benefit (Ludgate, 1995). When couples are given some guidelines prior to the end of active counseling in order to maximize the value of these sessions, the results are more effective. For example, couples may be encouraged to develop a plan for the follow-up session and "bring items for the agenda, writing down material so they will not forget in the longer intervals between these sessions" (Ludgate, 1995, p. 42–43). Ludgate (1995) suggests that couples ask the following questions to generate items to discuss in counseling sessions:

1. What has gone well for [us] since [our] last booster session?
2. What [sexual issues] have arisen recently and how did [we] handle them?
3. How could [we] have [handled our issues] better?
4. What [sexual issues] could arise in the near future or before [our] next session?
5. What have [we] done to maintain [our] progress after counseling?
6. What gets in the way of [us] maintaining [our] skills?
7. What else might [we] do?
8. What issues do [we] want to discuss with [our counselor] over and above the problems [we] have identified here? (p. 43)

Group Refresher Sessions.   An alternative type of booster session that is a useful follow-up intervention and aids in preventing setbacks is the group refresher session (Ludgate, 1995). Such sessions are similar to psychoeducational groups because of their emphasis on "education or skill-consolidation" (Ludgate, 1995, p. 43). Sexuality counselors may offer refresher sessions for groups of former clients, where the discussion focuses on methods for preventing setbacks as well as maintaining and celebrating success, not on focusing on the participants' problems. This strategy is also a means of receiving external support.

Identifying External Support and Community Networks

External support plays an important role for encouraging couples to remain proactive and positive in order to maintain and validate their new sexual perceptions and behaviors. Community networks also encourage and support new attitudes and skills, serving as powerful reinforcers that can assist couples trying to maintain sexual intimacy. Such networks of supporters (family, social, recreational) can directly or indirectly help couples maintain their goals.

For example, a couple who has struggled with finding time to be together in a social context may become members of a social or recreational group that meets weekly. This network of support provides a structure allowing couples to better cope with internal and external triggers potentially impacting their success. Having a community of support also aids couples in continuing to maintain, validate, and celebrate their successes. (Box 5.3 provides a list of validation interventions used by sexuality counselors.)

Returning to a Prior Stage of Counseling

If at any time during the sexuality counseling process couples get "stuck" or lack clarity about the focus or direction of counseling or their intimate relationship, it is important to return to an earlier stage of counseling in order to evaluate what is not working or what needs to be revisited (Young & Long, 1998). In fact, this occurs more often than not. Frequently, during counseling a more significant problem is revealed as a contributor to the problem. In this case, it is necessary to return to Stage 1 to reidentify a shared view of the problem and then to set appropriate goals for the problem that has been identified (Young & Long, 1998).

BOX 5.3
Validation Interventions at a Glance

- Ask couples to reevaluate their goals so that they can assess the changes they have made.
- Help partners practice giving feedback about their successes.
- Ask partners to compliment each other on their willingness to progress toward their goals.
- Help couples recount how and which relationship resources they have mobilized in order to conquer their problem.
- Ask partners to acknowledge sexual growth as a result of their teamwork.
- Help partners to design and implement specific activities (e.g., rituals) to celebrate success.
- Design a follow-up plan that provides periodic counseling to validate a couple's hard work.
- Develop an external support network to help couples maintain their goals.
- Help couples continue their work when issues arise by returning to a clearer relational definition if they feel stuck. They can then evaluate goals and make an action plan for changes.

Source: Adapted from Ludgate (1995) and Young & Long (1998).

Figure 5.1 illustrates the process of returning to a prior stage of the integrative couples' model. This return to a prior stage should not be viewed negatively or as backsliding. It should instead be looked upon as a means of gathering more information or gaining more knowledge in order to reevaluate a problem or a goal. The couple's evolving definition of the problem at the center of the model defines the need for more problem-specific goals. For example, a couple who has reached Stage 3 (interventions) may be unable to identify a partner's positive attributes. They may be harboring resentment and anger, both of which are more illustrative of Stage 1 of the model. Counselors must shift gears and return to Stage 1 (assessment) (Young & Long, 1998). By obtaining

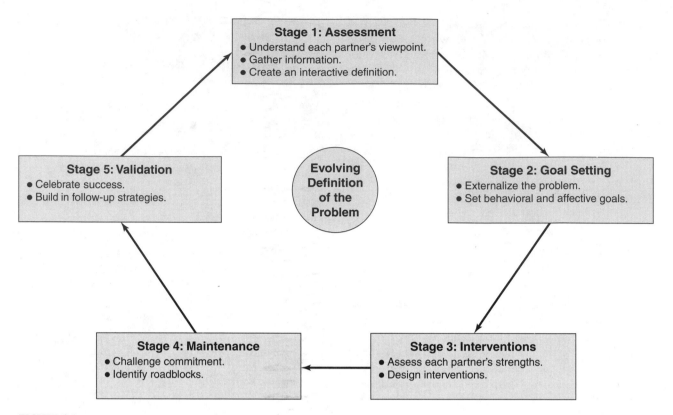

FIGURE 5.1

Returning to a Prior Stage of Counseling

Source: Adapted from *Counseling and Therapy for Couples,* 1st ed. (p. 78), by M. E. Young and L. L. Long. © 1998. Reprinted with permission of Wadsworth, a division of Thomson Learning: www.thomsonrights.com. Fax 800-730-2215.

more history of the sexual issues and revisiting transgenerational messages through the use of a genogram, couples may be able to understand and sort out their resentments before moving on to Stage 2 (goal setting). This directional change is shown in Figure 5.1 by the arrows that travel between Stages 1 and 3 in a circular path (Young & Long, 1998). This process is expected and should be normalized for couples by the counselor so they do not feel discouraged. Once they have returned to Stage 3, the sequence of treatment resumes its course around the perimeter of the entire circle. Young and Long (1998) have identified some important clues for counselors to consider when clients return to a prior stage:

1. The couple's view of the problem has not matured enough to initiate [intervention] activities.
2. Couples resist tasks or assignments and exhibit angry behavior. . . .
3. Couples seem confused about what they want for themselves or for their sexual relationship and

become immobilized in attempts to solve their sexual problems. (p. 79)

The process of "downshifting" or moving to an earlier stage of treatment is thus not a failure, and it can help couples learn more about themselves and accept their imperfections in their sexual relationships (Young & Long, 1998). If sexuality counselors remain optimistic and flexible about downshifting and convey this message to couples, they model a useful problem-solving approach for couples to emulate. In other words, when a solution to a problem is not working, it is time to find another solution. The pace at which couples progress toward goal attainment varies and is influenced by the nature and scope of their sexual issues as well as the individual and relational qualities they bring to counseling (Young & Long, 1998).

To illustrate Stages 4 and 5 of the integrative couples' model, we return to our case example of Simon and Mikala.

Case Example

At the end of Stages 2 and 3, Simon and Mikala set the following goals to address their "time and energy problem":

1. We will get a babysitter and go out on a date once a week. We will plan fun activities, so we can feel closer to each other.
2. We will make time to communicate with each other about our sexual needs and desires, so that we can feel loved and understood.

These goals were then codesigned with their sexuality counselor, who was able to help them recognize that they have a "solvable problem." Their counselor suggested the use of relaxation techniques and mutual massage as a first step to help them rekindle some of their lost intimacy.

At the conclusion of their sexuality counseling sessions, Simon and Mikala are able to implement a schedule that allows them to spend more time together and achieve improved communication that has resulted in increased sexual intimacy. However, they have experienced impasses and periods of uncertainty and frustration in their improvement process. The counselor works with them to plan long-term strategies to maintain the positive gains they have made. These include helping them identify potential pitfalls and roadblocks, developing a monitoring plan of successful and unsuccessful intimacy experiences, and maintaining positive, realistic sexual expectations so they can better manage frustration and setbacks. The counselor asks Simon and Mikala, "How will each of you stay focused on your intimacy goals?" and "How will you respond when your hectic lives interfere with your relationship?" Such questions will help them reiterate their commitment to the goals they established during counseling.

In order to maintain their renewed commitment to their sexual intimacy, Simon and Mikala work with their counselor to find ways to validate and celebrate their successes. They identify their problem as a solution and develop new ways of problem solving that aids them in future challenges. Their sexuality counselor makes use of compliments to help them validate their success: "Mikala, it sounds as if you are very pleased with Simon's new sexual initiative. Can you tell him how important that is for you?" Because rituals can play an important role in the success of their relationship, Simon and Mikala design a candlelight ceremony to reaffirm their love and commitment to each other.

To help Simon and Mikala become increasingly independent and resourceful in the maintenance of their goals, their sexuality counselor suggests a follow-up schedule of brief therapeutic contacts at three-month intervals to review their progress. They develop a network of support through community and family to help them with childcare needs and recreational activities.

SUMMARY

The integrative couples' model for sexuality counseling is a synthesis of theoretical perspectives drawn from various schools of thought regarding sexual problems and sexual functioning. The model identifies the steps needed to move couples from "she is the problem" or "he is the problem" to "there is not a problem." The systemic philosophy behind this model presumes that as couples make behavioral and affective changes, their thinking about the problem also changes. Stage 4 (maintenance) highlights the aftereffects of changes made in their relationship.

By focusing on continued commitment and growth in their sexual relationship and by identifying barriers that may impede growth, couples recommit and maintain changes in their sexual interactions. Sexuality counselors normalize setbacks to help the couple refocus and renew their relationship.

Techniques that focus on distorted perceptions and creating a new repertoire of behaviors are helpful during this stage.

During Stage 5 (validation), couples celebrate their sexual and relational successes. They compare the goals developed during Stage 2 with their current progress and validate themselves individually and relationally for their ability to work as a team to conquer their sexual issues. In addition, couples work with their sexuality counselor to implement follow-up strategies to ensure continued validation of their achievements. By the end of Stage 5, couples have completed four steps:

1. Identified the problem as a solution.
2. Congratulated themselves and each other on their successful experience.
3. Created a ritual as a way of celebrating success.
4. Generalized the step-by-step integrative approach for solving sexual issues that may arise (Young & Long, 1998).

Now that we have outlined the five stages of the integrative couples' model, we will focus on the course of sexuality counseling for specific populations and circumstances in the chapters that follow.

FEMALE SEXUALITY: DIAGNOSIS AND TREATMENT INTERVENTIONS

KEY CONCEPTS

- Women have unique issues that contribute to female sexual problems or dysfunctions.
- Sociocultural, developmental, aging, and family-of-origin issues contribute to female sexual problems and dysfunctions.
- Sexuality counselors must be familiar with the process of diagnosing all aspects of psychosexual disorders as described in the fourth edition of the American Psychiatric Association's *Diagnostic and Statistical Manual of Mental Disorders (DSM-IV-TR)*.
- Common presenting issues in women include sexual desire, arousal, and orgasmic and pain disorders.
- Treatment for female sexual dysfunctions include a variety of interventions appropriate for each stage of the sexual response cycle along with interventions for disorders associated with pain during intercourse.
- Understanding the systemic nature of diagnosis, assessment, and treatment of female sexual problems and dysfunctions is central to the development of appropriate interventions.
- Each partner's sexual issues must be understood within the context of a couple's relationship in order to formulate an interactive definition of sexual problems.
- Infertility affects all aspects of a couple's life and is associated with physical, psychological, and environmental factors.

Thus far we have presented the integrative couples' model with the goal of providing a structured way of thinking about sexual problems from a systemic rather than an individual viewpoint. In the next two chapters we will provide information related to female and male individual sexual problems within the context of couples' relationships. We believe that an understanding of individual sexual dysfunctions as described in the *DSM-IV-TR* (American Psychiatric Association, 2000) is important for formulating an interactive definition of sexual problems. By describing couples' relationships in interactive rather than individual terms, sexuality counselors are guided in all phases of assessment, treatment, and intervention. This systemic focus allows sexuality counselors to help individuals with their sexual problems while keeping in mind the effect these changes will have on the couple system.

In this chapter, we specifically address female sexual dysfunctions as presented in the *DSM-IV-TR*. We recognize that the Working Group on a New View of Women's Sexual Problems (2000) has recently proposed a classification system for conceptualizing women's sexual problems and dysfunctions, suggesting that they have roots in relational and cultural issues. Although this classification may be "more useful [for understanding] women's sexual problems" (Working Group on a New View of Women's Sexual Problems, 2000, p. 1), we have chosen to use the *DSM-IV-TR* for describing female sexual dysfunctions because it is the most commonly used classification system that sexuality counselors will encounter in clinical practice.

In this chapter we also address sociocultural and developmental influences specific to females in context with the process of sexuality counseling for women. We then describe commonly presented female dysfunctions along with factors that contribute to each of them. Diagnostic criteria are provided for each dysfunction as well as appropriate treatment interventions. We conclude the chapter with a case example highlighting a female sexual problem and apply the integrative couples' model for sexuality counseling.

SOCIOCULTURAL AND DEVELOPMENTAL INFLUENCES IN FEMALE SEXUALITY

Social Issues and Female Sexuality

There are myriad social issues that impact women and their sexuality. Women's roles have changed significantly in recent decades, and, as a result, so have their attitudes, beliefs, and practices. The women's liberation movement of the 1960s impacted traditional social ideology and pushed for more egalitarian roles and rules for women. This empowerment of women impacted their social and sexual attitudes and behaviors. Bra burning and "love-ins" became ways that some women rebelled against restrictive social and sexual traditions.

There have also been changes in women's traditional roles in the home and in the workplace. In earliest times, women fulfilled the role of "gatherer" in the male-female relationship. Males were the aggressors who hunted for the family, while females gathered fruit and vegetables and were responsible for nurturing the family. Today, many men and women share childcare and household responsibilities, while women hold highly demanding professional positions. These dual career issues have led to role overload, role ambiguity, and little time to spend with a partner. Unfortunately, these stressors foster anger, resentment, jealousy, and feelings of low self-esteem that result in decreased closeness and sexual intimacy for couples.

Women struggling with multiple roles often have decreased interest in sex. In fact, environmental influences, such as career and family, stress, and economic worries, interfere with sexual functioning (Wincze & Carey, 2001), and in some instances, women are diagnosed with low sexual desire as a result of these influences.

In addition to changing family and professional roles, there has been increased attention on women as sexual beings. Women are being encouraged to take responsibility for their sexual selves through self-exploration and learning how to create a sexually satisfying relationship through healthy communication with their partner (Barbach, 2000, 2001). It is no longer taboo for women to talk about sex, to ask for what they want sexually, or to display their bodies in a sexual manner. The popularity of Eve Ensler's *The Vagina Monologues*—a painfully authentic play that gives voice to female sexuality—clearly represents this yearning for sexual expression and validation and the continued struggle of women to defy traditional societal expectations. In the entertainment world, scores of popular performers—from Madonna to Christina Aguilera to Britney Spears—routinely dress and behave in sexually provocative ways, displaying their sexuality without shame or guilt. Female rap artists Salt-N-Pepa offer songs such as "Let's Talk About Sex, Baby." Although it is evident that women are more open to expressing themselves sexually, many women continue to remain embedded in traditional cultural beliefs and practices that prevent them from experiencing sexual pleasure and satisfaction (Barbach, 2001).

Cultural Issues

Cultural issues continue to have an impact on female sexuality, as sexual norms, attitudes, values, and practices are held up to a societal measuring stick. For example, some cultures in Africa and the Middle East perform clitoridectomies in late childhood or early adolescence. This procedure involves removal of the entire clitoris, not just the clitoral hood, and is considered a rite of initiation into womanhood. The clitoris stimulates feelings of sexual pleasure in females, and its removal represents an attempt to ensure a girl's chastity (Rathus, Nevid, & Fichner-Rathus, 2000). A woman who has had her clitoris removed may experience medical problems such as "infections, bleeding, tissue scarring, painful menstruation, and obstructed labor" (Rathus et al., 2000, p. 66). Certainly, sexual problems and dysfunctions may result from this culturally based ritual.

Developmental Issues

Until recent years, female development was defined in terms of male development models that emphasized differentiation and autonomy as primary values—for men only. The female's role was restricted to her place within the family life cycle (McGoldrick, Anderson, & Walsh, 1989). Male theorists such as Freud (1917), Erikson (1963), and Piaget (1932) tended to ignore female development. More recent theorists have, however, recognized the evolution of women in their own distinct place in the study of human development. Theorists who discuss female development focus on the importance of attachment, nurturing, and interdependence in the developmental process (Gilligan, 1982).

Female sexual development begins with the developmental stage of puberty and the factors concomitant to that stage. First menstruation is the most obvious sign of the onset of puberty in female adolescents. During this time, the sexual drive is heightened by sex hormones, and there is increased body fat, growth of internal and external reproductive organs, appearance of pubic hair, and breast development (Feldman, 2003). This period has also been perhaps transformed by female sexual independence. The result has been a rise in sexual exploration, teenage pregnancy, and sexually transmitted infections in young women (Rathus et al., 2000; Santrock, 1999).

As women mature, their ability to self-pleasure and receive mutual pleasure has become an integral part of the sexual response cycle. Communicating about sexual needs and actively participating in sexual relations has become an essential dynamic in female sexual culture throughout adult stages of the life cycle.

Age-Related Physical Issues

Age-related issues that impact women's sexual functioning include physical changes that occur during the aging process. A normal part of the aging process, many of these physical changes stem from a decline in the production of estrogen around the time of and after menopause. Women produce less vaginal lubrication, which can result in painful intercourse (Rathus et al., 2000; Santrock, 1999).

Other age-related physical changes include decreases in breast swelling during sexual excitement and a decrease in the intensity of the orgasm (Frishman, 1996; Rathus et al., 2000).

Situational Life Events

Situational events that impact female sexuality include the loss of a loved one, a change in living arrangements due to aging, or retirement. These events can lead to depression, reevaluation of one's life and priorities, and fatigue.

Other examples of situational life events include infertility, family illness, and infidelity. Infertility may create feelings of low self-esteem, mechanical sex, and reevaluation of the relationship. Family illness brings with it the juggling of many family members' schedules to include doctor's appointments and additional caregiving responsibilities, leaving little time for self-care and intimate relationships. Infidelity by one's partner can instigate anger, resentment, jealousy, and feelings of low self-esteem, resulting in anxiety and depression.

Family-of-Origin Influences

As we discussed in Chapter 3, family-of-origin influences in the form of sexual messages, values, beliefs, and behaviors are transmitted from one generation to the next and are central to understanding the relationship patterns of couples. Specific family events in one generation may dramatically alter the shape of future generations. Seldom transmitted directly, sexual information is usually conveyed through stories about family members whose sexual behavior was or was not acceptable to the family or who have been cut off due to strains in family interactions (Berman & Hof, 1987).

For example, one woman reported that her mother had married three physically abusive men over a period of thirteen years, with children born from each of these marriages. As a result, the mother believed men to be temporary and untrustworthy, and she passed on to her daughter negative messages such as "men will use you and leave you" and "men want sex and babies, but they don't want to take care of them." These messages were translated into the belief that women should not trust men or have sex with them because it might destroy the relationship. Currently, the woman finds herself in love with her partner but unable to express herself sexually due to her mistrust of men. She reports that her partner is frustrated and perplexed by her behavior.

It is important, however, to note that positive messages are also handed down from generation to generation. Family stories and legacies explain current ideas about sexuality but should not be viewed as causes or excuses for current negative sexual behaviors or patterns. The sexual genogram, a common method for recording family messages, was discussed in Chapter 3.

THE DIAGNOSTIC PROCESS FOR FEMALE SEXUAL ISSUES

Dysfunction or Problem?

As we discussed in Chapter 1, the factors that contribute to the development of sexual problems are difficult and complex to identify. The first step is to determine whether a woman is experiencing a sexual problem or a dysfunction, a critical point for accurate diagnosis and treatment.

Women typically present their sexual concerns to their gynecologist or family physician, hoping to find reassurance and intervention. Although some female sexual dysfunctions are managed through the use of medication, intervention by a sexuality counselor consisting of cognitive-behavioral as well as relational/couples counseling along with medication management is not uncommon. If a woman reports no problems in any phase of the sexual response cycle, she probably does not have a sexual dysfunction. Once this is determined, it is important for sexuality counselors to explore other factors such as unresolved relationship issues or the presence of a sexual problem (Heiman, LoPiccolo, & LoPiccolo, 1976; Kaplan, 1983). If a sexual problem is present, there must be further investigation to determine whether the problem is a result of internal or relational conflicts manifesting in the sexual relationship, or whether the problem is a result of external stressors. For example, one woman presents with little desire to have sexual intercourse with her partner. She states that in the past she wanted more sexual intimacy, but for the past two years she has been less interested. She reports that she is overwhelmed with balancing care for her 1-year-old son, a full-time job, and spending time with her partner. In order to help this woman, the sexuality counselor must first determine if she is experiencing a sexual problem or a sexual dysfunction.

Diagnosing Sexual Dysfunctions

Diagnosing and understanding a sexual dysfunction is an integral part of the clinical decision-making process for treating any woman or couple with a sexual problem or dysfunction. Implementation of treatment strategies is based on the counselor's personal skill and training level, as described in Chapter 1 in the P-LI-SS-IT model.

In order to be diagnosed with a sexual dysfunction, a client must exhibit those criteria for the dysfunction defined by the *Diagnostic and Statistical Manual of Mental Disorders IV-TR* (APA, 2000). In other words, the client must be experiencing distinct symptoms. The *DSM-IV-TR* states the following with regard to guiding sexuality counselors in making an accurate diagnosis:

> The specific diagnostic criteria included in the *DSM-IV* are meant to serve as guidelines to be informed by clinical judgement and are not meant to be used in a cookbook fashion. For example, the exercise of clinical judgment may justify giving a certain diagnosis to an individual even though the clinical presentation falls just short of meeting the full criteria for the diagnosis as long as the symptoms that are present are persistent and severe. (p. xxxii)

Sexuality counselors must be able to listen carefully to their clients' concerns and to determine whether their identified problems are sufficient to meet the criteria listed in the *DSM*. If clients' identified problems do not appear to meet the indicated criteria, the sexuality counselor's clinical judgement will become an integral part of the decision-making process. As noted above, if symptoms are significant and lasting, the sexuality counselor may decide it is appropriate to diagnose a particular disorder. It is important to realize that even if the decision is made not to give a client a *DSM* diagnosis, it does not mean that there are no issues that can be addressed in sexuality counseling. Knowledge about all aspects of the diagnostic process as suggested by the *DSM* is critical information for sexuality counselors.

According to the *DSM-IV-TR,* "sexual dysfunctions are characterized by disturbance in sexual desire and in the psychophysiological changes that characterize the sexual response cycle and cause marked distress and interpersonal difficulty" (APA, 2000, p. 535). For example, if a woman states that she is satisfied with her sexual relationship, although she admits she has never experienced an orgasm, she does not have an orgasmic disorder. However, if she states that she is upset because she is unable to have an orgasm and the sexuality counselor has ruled out any medical, drug, or psychiatric problems, she can be diagnosed as experiencing female orgasmic disorder.

The *DSM-IV-TR* identifies the following sexual dysfunctions specific to females: "Sexual Desire Disorders (i.e., Hypoactive Sexual Desire Disorder, Sexual Aversion Disorder), Sexual Arousal Disorders (i.e., Female Sexual Arousal Disorder . . .) Orgasmic Disorders (i.e., Female Orgasmic Disorder . . . [formerly Inhibited Female Orgasm]), Sexual Pain Disorders (i.e., Dyspareunia, Vaginismus)" (APA, 2000, p. 535). In order to complete a diagnostic formulation for these dysfunctions, certain key questions must be considered.

Questions to Consider

The sexuality counselor must ask specific questions regarding female sexuality in order to determine an accurate diagnosis. Leiblum and Rosen (as cited in Young & Long, 1998) suggest that the following topic areas be included:

1. Current sexual function and satisfaction [of women].
2. Family of origin messages and sexual practices for [the woman].
3. Relationship history that includes major events in the relationship such as divorce, separation, pregnancies, [miscarriages], [infertility], death and [other individual crises].
4. Effects of contraception, pregnancy, [miscarriages], [infertility], illness, medication, and the aging process.
5. Current [female] sexual concerns and relationship concerns. (p. 169)

The sexuality counselor should also complete a sexual history that includes information concerning past or present sexual or emotional abuse and/or domestic violence; see Chapter 3 for specific sexual history taking and interview techniques.

In addition, sexuality counselors can help couples understand how symptoms affect them at both the individual and relational level (Leiblum & Rosen, 2000). One method sexuality counselors may use to assist couples in understanding these dynamics is to pose the following questions devised by Leiblum and Rosen (2000):

What does having a [sexual dysfunction or problem] mean to the woman? To her partner?

What solution does the problem provide for the couple?

Does the woman have a sense of ownership over her body?

Does she want to achieve orgasm to satisfy her partner or herself?

Can [she] communicate directly [with her partner] about [her] sexual preferences? (p. 119)

These questions inform an individual and relational conceptualization of couples' identified problems as well as providing important information about commonly described female sexual dysfunctions.

COMMONLY DESCRIBED FEMALE DYSFUNCTIONS

This section will focus on the most commonly diagnosed female sexual dysfunctions and the factors that contribute to them. Diagnostic criteria will be presented here as well as the appropriate treatment interventions. It is important to keep in mind that the development of sexual dysfunctions is a complex process, and the defining features may vary. What is presented in this chapter will thus reflect the evolving nature of what is currently known about sexual dysfunctions and what new knowledge will be generated by future research and clinical experience. Sexuality counselors must have a solid working knowledge of the sexual diagnoses, presented in the *DSM-IV-TR,* and of the appropriate resources available to those experiencing sexual dysfunctions.

The *DSM-IV-TR* classification of sexual disorders is derived from the Masters and Johnson's (1966) four-phase sexual response cycle, which was later modified by Kaplan (1979) to include the sexual desire phase (see Figure 6.1).

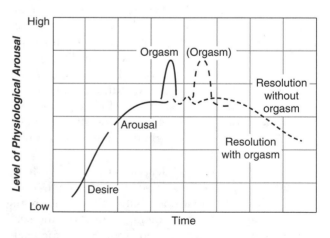

FIGURE 6.1

The Four Phases of the Female Sexual Response Cycle. Sometimes, women do not experience orgasm; in that case the resolution phase is less abrupt. In addition, some women may experience two or more orgasms in succession before the resolution phase.

Source: From *Abnormal Psychology,* 3rd ed., by R. J. Comer, 1998. New York: W. H. Freeman. Adapted with permission.

The sexual response cycle presented in the *DSM* is divided into four phases (APA, 2000):

1. *Desire*: This phase consists of fantasies about sexual activity and the desire to have sexual activity.
2. *Excitement*: This phase consists of a subjective sense of sexual pleasure and accompanying physiological changes. . . . The major changes in the female consist of vasocongestion in the pelvis, vaginal lubrication and expansion, and swelling of the external genitalia.
3. *Orgasm*: This phase consists of a peaking of sexual pleasure, with release of sexual tension and rhythmic contraction of the perineal muscles and reproductive organs. . . . In the female, there are contractions (not always subjectively experienced as such) of the wall of the outer third of the vagina. In [addition], the anal sphincter rhythmically contracts.
4. *Resolution*: This phase consists of a sense of muscular relaxation and general well-being . . . females may be able to respond to additional stimulation [such as genital stimulation] almost immediately. (p. 536)

Sexual problems may take place during any one or more of the sexual response cycle stages (APA, 2000). Sexuality counselors should consider a number of features that influence sexual functioning when diagnosing disorders based on the sexual response cycle. The *DSM* suggests that "such factors as the age and experience of the individual, frequency and chronicity of the symptom, subjective distress, and effect on other areas of functioning" influence clinical judgments regarding sexual response cycle diagnostic formulations (APA, 2000, p. 536). In addition, sociocultural factors (e.g., ethnicity, spirituality) also help define couples' sexual values and behaviors and may affect beliefs, attitudes, and feelings about sexual functioning (APA, 2000).

The next section of this chapter describes female sexual dysfunctions based on the *DSM-IV-TR* along with factors that contribute to these disorders and the ways to diagnose them. In addition, the section will present intervention approaches for each phase of the female sexual response cycle along with interventions for disorders associated with pain during intercourse. A list of interventions at a glance is provided in Box 6.1. Because many treatment strategies overlap for a variety of disorders, we describe the interventions commonly associated with each sexual disorder.

Desire Disorders

Hypoactive Sexual Desire Disorder/DSM-IV-TR Diagnosis 302.71

The *DSM-IV-TR* describes hypoactive sexual desire as follows:

Hypoactive sexual desire disorder (HSD) is a deficiency or absence of sexual fantasies and desire for sexual activity (Criterion A). The disturbance must cause marked distress or interpersonal difficulty (Criterion B). The dysfunction is not better accounted for by another Axis I disorder (except another Sexual Dysfunction) and is not due exclusively to the direct physiological effects of a substance (including medications) or a general medical condition (Criterion C). (APA, 2000, p. 539)

Diminished desire for sexual activity in some women may be related to their concerns in significant intimate relationships and the quality of these interactions. For example, a woman with a partner who uses rough or forceful arousal techniques can negatively impact sexual responsiveness.

In fact, the *DSM-IV-TR* describes the issue of low sexual desire as it relates to the relational aspects of female sexual functioning:

Low sexual desire may be global and encompass all forms of sexual expression or may be situational and limited to one partner or to a specific sexual activity (e.g., intercourse but not masturbation). There is little motivation to seek stimuli and diminished frustration when deprived of the opportunity for sexual expression. The individual usually does not initiate sexual activity or may engage in it reluctantly when it is initiated by the partner. . . . The [sexuality counselor] may need to assess both partners when discrepancies in sexual desire prompt the call for professional attention. (p. 539)

Sexuality counselors can help women and their partners discern factors that contribute to desire concerns and affect their relationship.

Contributing Factors. *Physical factors* that may contribute to low sexual desire include general medical conditions that "may have a nonspecific deleterious effect on sexual desire due to weakness, pain, problems with body image, or concerns about survival" (APA, 2000, p. 539). Likewise, "medical conditions such as neurological, hormonal, and metabolic abnormalities may specifically impair the physiological substrates of sexual desire" (APA, 2000, p. 540). In other words, there are medical conditions—from hormonal imbalance to obesity and negative body image—that

BOX 6.1

Treatment Interventions at a Glance

Desire Phase Disorders in Women

DYSFUNCTION	INTERVENTIONS
Female hypoactive sexual desire disorder	Hormone therapy
	Medication adjustment
	Relationship counseling
	Sensate focus
	Couples' communication skill building (active listening, paraphrasing, "I" messages)
	Psychoeducational training (bibliotherapy, educational information)
	Desensitization
	Sexual fantasy
Sexual aversion disorder	Medical/surgical
	Relationship counseling
	Couples' communication skill building
	Sensate focus
	Psychoeducational training
	Masturbation training
	Desensitization
	Cognitive restructuring
	Sensate focus

Arousal Disorders in Women

DYSFUNCTION	INTERVENTIONS
Female sexual arousal disorder	Hormone therapy
	Medical
	Use of lubricants
	Relationship counseling
	Couples' communication skill building
	Psychoeducational training
	Masturbation training
	Sensate focus
	Desensitization
	Sexual fantasy

Orgasm Disorders in Women

DYSFUNCTION	INTERVENTIONS
Female orgasmic disorder (formerly inhibited female orgasm)	Medical
	Sensate focus
	Relationship counseling
	Couples' communication skill building
	Psychoeducational training
	Masturbation training
	Desensitization
	Cognitive skills training

(continued)

BOX 6.1

Treatment Interventions at a Glance (Continued)

Pain Disorders in Women

DYSFUNCTION	INTERVENTIONS
Dyspareunia	Medical/surgical
	Hormone therapy
	Use of lubricants
	Relationship counseling
	Couples' communication skill building
	Psychoeducational
	Desensitization
	Cognitive skills training
	Relaxation (general/deep muscle)
	Kegel exercises
	Sensate focus
	Vaginal dilation
Vaginismus	Medical/surgical
	Relationship counseling
	Couples' communication skill building
	Psychoeducational
	Desensitization
	Cognitive skills training
	Relaxation training
	Sensate focus
	Kegel exercises
	Vaginal dilation

---

directly and indirectly affect sexual desire. Low sexual desire has also been related to clinical depression (LoPiccolo & Friedman, 1988).

Psychological factors can stem from negative conditioning related to incest or rape, domestic violence, emotional abuse, family messages from parents regarding masturbation, oral sex, and other sexual practices, and sexual anxiety stemming from ignorance, unrealistic expectations about sexual functioning, performance, or guilt (Crooks & Baur, 2002; LoPiccolo & Friedman, 1988).

Relational factors such as former successful sexual experiences, a compatible partner, and an overall successful relationship with a sexual partner can influence sexual desire in a positive way (Rosen & Leiblum, 1989). Extra relational affairs that have not been resolved can lead to unsatisfactory sexual functioning, creating desire problems due to feelings of anger, shame, fear, or anxiety (Crooks & Baur, 2002; Kaplan, 1979; Young & Long, 1998).

Diagnosis. The following *DSM-IV-TR* criteria are used in making this diagnosis:*

**Diagnostic Criteria for
302.71 Hypoactive Sexual Desire Disorder**

A. Persistently or recurrently deficient (or absent) sexual fantasies and desire for sexual activity. The judgment of deficiency or absence is made by the clinician, taking into account factors that affect sexual functioning, such as age and the context of the person's life.

B. The disturbance causes marked distress or interpersonal difficulty.

C. The sexual dysfunction is not better accounted for by another Axis I disorder (except another Sexual Dysfunction) and is not due exclusively to the

---

*Reprinted with permission from the *Diagnostic and Statistical Manual of Mental Disorders,* Text Revision (p. xxx), Copyright 2000, American Psychiatric Association.

direct physiological effects of a substance (e.g., a drug of abuse, a medication) or a general medical condition.

Specify type:

Lifelong Type

Acquired Type

Specify type:

Generalized Type

Situational Type

Specify:

Due to Psychological Factors

Due to Combined Factors

Assessing hypoactive sexual desire disorder is a crucial step for developing appropriate treatment. Diagnosing sexual dysfunction continues to be based on Kaplan's triphasic model (1979) of the sexual response cycle that includes, as its first step, the desire phase.

A thorough assessment should include ruling out medical factors. This process can begin by asking questions such as "Do you take any medicines to help you sleep, wake up, concentrate, feel less nervous, or deal with pain?" followed by "How long have you taken these?" (See Chapter 10 for more information on how medications affect sexual functioning.) In addition, information about substances such as street drugs and alcohol should be obtained, including the type of substance used, the frequency, and the amount. Depression can be assessed by use of depression inventories. Common symptoms of depression may be reported as sleeplessness, irritability, isolation, fatigue, alcohol use or overuse, or withdrawal from sexual interactions. These issues relate to women's overall health and their perception of health.

Age-related issues must also be taken into consideration. Fear of death and dying may be sexual inhibitors, particularly with middle-aged women who may have experienced the death of their parents or are concerned about care for aging parents. Other age-related issues may relate to myths surrounding loss of vitality and sexual excitement after the age of 40. In addition, symptoms related to menopause (e.g., depression, hot flashes, and irritability) should be explored with women who are between the ages of 35 and 50 (Klein, 1997). It is important to ascertain if a woman is under the medical care of her physician for any of these symptoms.

Treatment.   Sexual desire problems are considered by many counselors to be the most difficult to treat of all the sexual problems and dysfunctions (Pridal & LoPiccolo, 2000) and require an array of interventions to help couples resolve their issues. In some cases hormonal therapy or medication adjustments are necessary although general treatment strategies common to many sexual dysfunctions (e.g., psychoeducational training, desensitization) are also used. In addition, the use of sexual fantasy can elicit sexual desire and enhance sexual arousal for some women (Byrne & Osland, 2000; Pridal & LoPiccolo, 2000). Women's fantasies most often include themes of romance and passion focusing on the emotional content of the relationship (Byrne & Osland, 2000). We will focus on sexual fantasy as an intervention in Chapter 7.

Sexual desire disorder is often the result of unresolved relational issues, including imbalances in power, fears about being vulnerable, or inadequate sexual skills (LoPiccolo & Friedman, 1988). In addition, past or current issues related to intimate time together, finances, children, or work contribute to lack of sexual desire (Young & Long, 1998). In these situations, relationship counseling is required. Relational treatment strategies enhance couples' communication and include exploring and understanding underlying motivations. These strategies focus on interactions within the couple's relationship that contribute to lack of sexual desire.

In some situations, a lack of sexual desire serves the purpose of establishing distance in a couple's relationship. For example, Forrest and Rita have been married for one year. Rita is from a large family of twelve children. She has just received her bachelor's degree in elementary education and is feeling insecure about pursuing her new profession, as she is the first female in her family to obtain a college degree. She sometimes states she "should have babies" and abandon her career. When Rita thinks of this option, she "feels secure" that Forrest will take care of her and protect her. Forrest states, "Rita is a lot like my mom; she meets my every need and is my emotional rock." Both partners complain of feeling smothered by each other and needing more independence. They also report a lack of interest in foreplay and sexual intercourse. Because they are worried about their lack of sexual desire and confused about their need for intense closeness, they have decided to seek help from a sexuality counselor. Rita and Forrest hope to establish independence from each other in order to regain a healthy balance in their relationship and then restore their interest and desire for sex.

The most commonly used interventions that help couples improve sexual communication are sensate focus activities and communication skill building (LoPiccolo & Friedman, 1988). Some communication skills that are used include active listening, paraphrasing, and "I" statements. These skills help couples better understand each other's sexual needs.

Interventions for Treating Female Hypoactive Sexual Desire Disorder

Sensate Focus.   Sensate focus exercises and general nonsexual touching activities are positive ways to help couples create sexual desire. Eventually, more erotic touching is initiated, leading to intercourse and other forms of sexual pleasuring (Young & Long, 1998). Sensate focus is a series of touching exercises developed by Masters and Johnson (1970) that can be used in the treatment of a variety of sexual disorders. Such activities help couples reduce anxiety, increase communication, and create feelings of intimacy. This intervention requires that couples refrain from intercourse or genital caressing for approximately two weeks and that they explore their bodies through kissing, hugging, touching, and massaging. The goal is to reawaken natural sensuality, improve sexual skills, and remove anxiety as they move through four phases:

Phase 1—Nongenital Pleasuring: This phase is designed to increase and enhance physical activity. Couples are instructed to choose a time when both partners agree to initiate sensate focus exercises. The partner who is identified as the most hesitant about sexual activity (Partner A) makes the request. As long as Partner B is neutral or positive regarding the session, the session begins. Partner B lies down on a flat surface in a comfortable position with Partner A sitting comfortably next to Partner B. This session can occur with clothes on, underwear on, or without clothing. Once both partners are comfortable, Partner A begins to touch Partner B's body for Partner A's pleasure for as long as they agree. This excludes touching of the genitals, and may include kissing, hugging, touching, and massaging. If Partner B experiences any discomfort, Partner A must be informed at once. When Partner A has completed the touching exercise, it is Partner B's turn to touch Partner A's body for Partner B's pleasure. Partner A follows the same instructions as above. It is recommended that couples participate in two sensate focus sessions each week for approximately two weeks and until their next visit with their sexuality counselor.

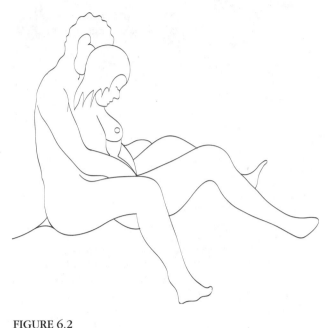

FIGURE 6.2
Genital Pleasuring

Source: From *Sex Therapy Manual* (p. 268), by P. Gillan, 1987, Oxford, England: Blackwell Publishing. Year Book Medical Publishers. Copyright 1987 by Blackwell Publishing. Reprinted with permission.

Phase 2—Genital Pleasuring Without Emphasis on Intercourse and Orgasm: In this phase, couples are instructed to follow the steps for Phase 1 but introduce genital touching into the session (see Figure 6.2). For example, Partner A massages Partner B's breasts and nipples. Some couples enjoy using a lightly scented lotion. Partner A then moves on to include stimulation of Partner B's genitals. It is suggested that a water-soluble vaginal lubricant be used at this stage if desired (information about a variety of such lubricants is available at http://www.wdxcyber.com/rx/lub.htm). For women, this includes having her partner touch the clitoral shaft and glands and entrance into her vagina. The woman next assumes a comfortable position while her partner leans against pillows or another type of support. Then, using her hand, she guides her partner according to her own pleasure. Her partner may stimulate her outer vagina and clitoris very gently at first and then increase the speed of stimulation. This activity may lead to orgasm, but it is not part of the plan at this phase. The speed of the stimulation can be varied. This may also lead to a manual orgasm, but it is not necessary. The important point is for both partners to enjoy the touching session.

Phase 3—Intercourse in Stages: For heterosexual couples this phase introduces the penis into the vagina. Following a period of touching as described above, the male introduces his penis into the vagina. This is accomplished by stuffing the penis into the vagina in a flaccid state. No movement is to occur at this time. Depending on the couple and their comfort level, movement of the penis in the vagina may occur, or it can be reserved for another session.

Phase 4—Continued Intercourse in Stages: During this phase, the couple follows the above instructions and then moves into Phase 3 with the male partner introducing his penis into the vagina and thrusting. Depending on the phase of sexuality counseling and the progress of treatment, the couple may achieve orgasm through vaginal intercourse (Crooks & Baur, 2002; Gillan, 1987; Masters & Johnson, 1970; Masters, Johnson, & Kolodny, 1986, 1995).

It is important to remember that movement from one phase to another occurs only when both partners are relaxed and ready to take the next step together (Masters et al., 1995). Sometimes, however, couples are unsuccessful when they attempt to progress to the next phase of sensate focus. In these cases, the sexuality counselor can help them reassess what may not be working and explore with them what they can do differently. Often a minor change such as modifying the time of day to engage in this activity or encouraging the couple to return to an earlier phase of the exercise may be all that is needed for them to achieve success.

Couples' Communication Skill Building. Many couples find it difficult to talk about the sexual aspects of their relationship, but such a failure to communicate needs and expectations hinders solutions to sexual problems and contributes to relationship difficulties (McCabe & Delaney, 1992). In order to help couples communicate more effectively, sexuality counselors teach couples basic communication skills such as the following (Young & Long, 1998):

Listening Skills: Being an active listener requires that partners are both listening and interested in what the other person has to say. This can be communicated through eye contact, body language, voice tone, facial expressions, physical distance, and touching. These skills enhance the probability that each partner is heard (Young, 1998).

Paraphrasing Techniques: One way of increasing the probability that couples listen to each other more

effectively involves the use of paraphrasing, a technique that asks a person to listen and then summarize in his or her own words what a speaker has said (Young, 1998). Here's an example:

WOMAN: While I enjoy our lovemaking very much, I wish we could explore new and different types of sexual expression.

MAN: You find pleasure in our sexual activity, but you would like us to explore other lovemaking techniques.

WOMAN: Yes, I think that sometimes we tend to resort to our same pattern of sexual activity, and I would like to increase our use of oral sex.

MAN: That's really exciting. The thought of your desire for more oral contact is a real turn-on for me.

If the paraphrase does not accurately reflect what the speaker says, the listener attempts to reflect the message again in different words until the speaker feels heard. This basic communication process helps couples to feel heard, to establish trust, and to become more aware of their sexual feelings, wants, and needs.

"I" Statements: Partners who communicate their desires and are willing to take responsibility for their own pleasure can create fulfilling sexual relationships. In order to do this, couples must learn to express their needs in a clear and concise manner. The use of "I" statements helps couples express their needs to their partners in a nonblaming manner. The following example illustrates a couple scenario with and without the use of "I" statements:

Without "I" Statements

WOMAN: Would you like to practice our sensate focus exercises tonight?

MAN: Oh, I don't know. Would you?

WOMAN: Well, I thought we should practice since we have a counseling appointment next week.

MAN: I guess we can if you want to.

With "I" Statement

WOMAN: I feel like staying home tonight and having some intimate time just touching each other.

MAN: I was looking forward to going to bed early. I'm exhausted from the week. I'd love to be intimate with you when I'm more rested.

WOMAN: I'm disappointed but maybe we can cuddle awhile.

MAN: I'd like that. Let's find time to be close this weekend.

Sexual Aversion Disorder/DSM-IV-TR Diagnosis 302.79

The *DSM-IV-TR* describes sexual aversion disorder as follows:

> Sexual Aversion Disorder is the aversion to and active avoidance of genital sexual contact with a sexual partner (Criterion A). The disturbance must cause marked distress or interpersonal difficulty (Criterion B). The dysfunction is not better accounted for by another Axis I disorder (except another Sexual Dysfunction) (Criterion C). (APA, 2000, p. 541)

This disorder is the most severe form of sexual desire disorder (Kaplan, 1979).

Persons with sexual aversion disorders often state that they experience anxiety, fearfulness, or even physical symptoms if they are faced with the possibility of a sexual encounter. In other words, they phobically avoid sexual activity. The most common specific sexual experiences that individuals with sexual aversion avoid include "penetration, oral sex, anal sex, masturbation, kissing, caressing, looking at genitals, semen, vaginal secretions, pubic hair, getting undressed, etc." (Kaplan, 1979, p. 22).

Some persons experience a reaction to all feelings, thoughts, and images suggesting sexuality. Videotapes or sexual language may be upsetting to more severely impaired people. Other responses as a result of extreme distress may include sweating, rapid heart rate, nausea, dizziness, trembling, and/or diarrhea at the thought or sight of anything sexual (Kaplan, 1979; Masters et al., 1995). In severe cases, people may experience panic attacks. They also may use covert behavior to avoid sexual encounters (APA, 2000). One woman reports neglecting to take a bath or attending to her personal hygiene for several days. Another states that she has no time for sex in her busy schedule attending to family needs. Both women have thus created positions that allow them to avoid sexual situations. All of these reactions create disturbances in significant relationships.

Contributing Factors.
Sexual aversion disorders are often related to sexual traumas in early childhood (e.g., sexual abuse, rape, incest, parental sexual attitudes), anxieties about a person's sexual performance, unresolved sexual identity issues, relationship problems, the transmission of sexually transmitted infections, and a fear of becoming pregnant (Everaerd, Laan, Both, & Van Der Velde, 2000; Kaplan, 1995; Masters et al., 1995). All of these factors can disrupt a person's sexual desire for years to come.

Diagnosis.
The following *DSM-IV-TR* criteria are used in making this diagnosis:*

Diagnostic Criteria for 302.79 Sexual Aversion Disorder

A. Persistent or recurrent extreme aversion to, and avoidance of, all (or almost all) genital sexual contact with a sexual partner.
B. The disturbance causes marked distress or interpersonal difficulty.
C. The sexual dysfunction is not better accounted for by another Axis I disorder (except another Sexual Dysfunction).

Specify type:
Lifelong Type
Acquired Type

Specify type:
Situational Type
Generalized Type

Specify:
Due to Psychological Factors
Due to Combined Factors

When diagnosing an individual with sexual aversion disorder, sexuality counselors explore any form of past or present physical, sexual, or emotional abuse; their clients' comfort with their own sexuality; and any past history of problematic sexual experiences (Gold & Gold, 1993; Masters et al., 1995; Pridal & LoPiccolo, 2000).

Treatment.
Treatment for sexual aversion disorder involves helping women to reduce fear and anxiety that has led to the avoidance of sexual situations (Kaplan, 1979). The use of cognitive restructuring techniques to address issues such as rape, abuse, and incest is recommended. Couples' communication and relationship counseling is also helpful in creating a desired change. In addition, bibliotherapy, masturbation training techniques, desensitization, and sensate focus techniques are used. Bibliotherapy and masturbation training are discussed in this section. Sensate focus has already been discussed under treatment for hypoactive sexual desire disorder.

---

*Reprinted with permission from the *Diagnostic and Statistical Manual of Mental Disorders,* Text Revision (p. xxx), Copyright 2000, American Psychiatric Association.

Interventions for Treating Sexual Aversion Disorder

Bibliotherapy.   Bibliotherapy is a form of psychoeducational training that involves the use of reading materials including articles, books, or pamphlets addressing sexuality and specific sexual problems or dysfunctions. Bibliotherapy is very effective for clients who like to read and is used for discussion in counseling couples. A list of suggested resources is provided in Box 6.2.

Masturbation Training for Women.   Masturbation training involves helping women get to know their bodies through emotional and physical responses, relaxation, and both manual and vibrator-assisted stimulation. The process is gradual and is performed alone until women teach their partners what they find pleasurable. Then they guide their partner through specific behaviors and sexual positions selected to enhance orgasmic responsiveness. LoPiccolo developed a nine-step directed masturbation program that is often used to teach women the "art" of self-pleasuring (Heiman, LoPiccolo, & LoPiccolo, 1976, 1988; LoPiccolo & Lobitz, 1972). Barbach's *For Yourself: The Fulfillment of Female Sexuality* (2000) offers a step-by-step guide for women who desire to learn self-satisfying techniques. Masturbation training is the most frequently utilized intervention strategy for women who experience sexual aversion and primary anorgasmia disorder (LoPiccolo & Stock, 1986). Following this intervention, many women have reported feeling increased self-esteem, improved sexual activities, and more relaxed attitudes about sex (Fisher, Swingen, & O'Donohue, 1997).

BOX 6.2

Recommended Reading for Couples

Barbach, L. (2000). *For yourself: The fulfillment of female sexuality.* New York: Signet.

Barbach, L. (2001). *For each other: Sharing sexual intimacy.* New York: Signet.

Berzon, B. (1990). *Permanent partners: Building gay and lesbian relationships that last.* New York: Dutton/Plum.

Dodson, B. (1995). *Sex for one: The joy of self-loving.* New York: Random House.

Gottman, J., Notarius, C., Gonso, J., & Markman, H. (1979). *A couple's guide to communication.* Champaign, IL: Research Press.

Gray, J. (1992). *Men are from Mars, Women are from Venus: A practical guide for improving communication and getting what you want in your relationships.* New York: Holt.

Heiman, J. R., LoPiccolo, J., & Palladini, D. (1992). *Becoming orgasmic: A sexual and personal growth program for women.* New York: Simon & Schuster.

Kaplan, H. S. (1989). *How to overcome premature ejaculation.* New York: Brunner/Mazel.

Kilmann, P. R., & Mills, K. H. (1983), *All about sex therapy.* New York: Plenum.

Love, P., & Robinson, J. (1989). *Hot monogamy: Essential steps to more passionate, intimate lovemaking.* New York: Penguin.

McCarthy, B., & McCarthy, E. (1993). *Sexual awareness: Enhancing sexual pleasure.* New York: Carroll & Graf.

McCarthy, B. (1998). *Male sexual awareness: Increasing sexual satisfaction* (rev. and undated ed.). New York: Carroll & Graf.

McCarthy, B., & McCarthy, E. (1998). *Couple sexual awareness.* New York: Carroll & Graf.

Milsten, R., & Slowinski, J. (1999). *The sexual male: Problems and solutions.* New York: Norton.

Ogden, G. (1999). *Women who love sex: An inquiry into the expanding spirit of women's erotic experience.* Cambridge, MA: Womanspirit Press.

Rosenthal, S. H. (1999). *The new sex after 40.* New York: Putnam.

Schnarch, D. M. (1998). *Passionate marriage: Love, sex, and intimacy in emotionally committed relationships.* New York: Holt.

Sheehy, G. (1998). *The silent passage: Menopause.* New York: Simon & Schuster.

Tannen, D. (1990). *You just don't understand: Women and men in conversation.* New York: Morrow.

Wincze, J. P., & Barlow, D. H. (1997). *Enhancing sexuality: A problem-solving approach.* San Antonio, TX: Psychological Corp.

Zilbergeld, B. (1999). *The new male sexuality* (rev. ed.). New York: Random House.

Zilbergeld, B., & Ullman, J. (1984). *Male sexuality: A guide to sexual fullfillment.* New York: Bantam Books.

Sexuality counselors can use the following format to instruct women on how to masturbate:*

1. Look at your genitalia in the mirror. Try to locate the sensitive parts of your genitalia by touching yourself and looking at that area.
2. Concentrate on stimulating that area. Vary the stimulation you use. Try making circular or up and down movements of your finger on your clitoris. Vary the speed of movement and pressure. You can lubricate yourself by placing the tip of your finger in your vagina, but if this is not yet moist enough, try a little KY jelly on your finger.
3. Try to imagine some of the fantasies you like and stimulate yourself with your finger until something happens or you feel sensation or you get tired. If you do not climax, you may choose to use a hand-held vibrator. If you climax, immediately switch to the image of your partner.
4. As you practice the self-stimulation exercise, try to make the switch to the image of your partner earlier on, before you climax.
5. Lastly, try a couple of sessions stimulating yourself in front of your partner. If it's difficult, try again the next day and do not worry. Remember, there is no 'set way' of masturbation; the idea is to have fun and *please yourself*. (p. 265)

Be mindful that the use of masturbation training should be considered as a technique within the context of a woman's cultural and religious beliefs and values (Kelley, 2004). For example, masturbation has been viewed as a "sinful act" in the Catholic religion and it is therefore discouraged. Feelings of guilt may influence a woman's ability to enjoy self-pleasuring (Kelley, 2004). Sexuality counselors should help women and their partners explore their values and beliefs related to the use of masturbation when discerning an appropriate avenue for intervention.

Arousal Disorders

Female Sexual Arousal Disorder/DSM-IV-TR Diagnosis 302.72

The *DSM-IV-TR* describes female sexual arousal disorder as follows:

Female Sexual Arousal Disorder is a persistent or recurrent inability to attain, or to maintain until the completion of sexual activity, an adequate lubrication-swelling response of sexual excitement (Criterion A). The arousal response consists of vasocongestion in the pelvis, vaginal lubrication and expansion, and swelling of the external genitalia. This disturbance must cause marked distress or interpersonal difficulty (Criterion B). The disturbance is not better accounted for by another Axis I disorder (except another Sexual Dysfunction), and is not due exclusively to the direct physiological effects of a substance (including medications) or a general medical condition (Criterion C). (APA, 2000, p. 543)

Contributing Factors. General medical conditions may produce physiological effects that contribute to sexual arousal disorder. These include conditions such as "menopausal or postmenopausal reductions in estrogen levels, atrophic vaginitis, diabetes mellitus, [and] radiotherapy of the pelvis. Reduced lubrication has also been reported in association with lactation" (APA, 2000, p. 543).

Sexual arousal problems may also be due to sexual myths (e.g., a larger penis provides more stimulation), lack of knowledge about one's body, interpersonal as well as relational conflict between partners, anger, fear, and guilt (Bartlik & Goldberg, 2000; Everaerd et al., 2000; Masters et al., 1986). In addition, lack of adequate sexual stimulation contributes to arousal problems (Everaerd et al., 2000).

Diagnosis. The following *DSM-IV-TR* criteria are used in making this diagnosis:*

**Diagnostic Criteria for
302.72 Female Sexual Arousal Disorder**

A. Persistent or recurrent inability to attain, or to maintain until completion of the sexual activity, an adequate lubrication-swelling response of sexual excitement.
B. The disturbance causes marked distress or interpersonal difficulty.
C. The sexual dysfunction is not better accounted for by another Axis I disorder (except another Sexual Dysfunction) and is not due exclusively to the direct physiological effects of a substance (e.g., a drug of abuse, a medication) or a general medical condition.

---

*From *Sex Therapy Manual* (p. 265), by P. Gillan, 1987. Oxford, England: Blackwell Publishing. Copyright 1987 by Blackwell Publishing. Reprinted with permission.

*Reprinted with permission from the *Diagnostic and Statistical Manual of Mental Disorders,* Text Revision (p. xxx), Copyright 2000, American Psychiatric Association.

Specify type:

Lifelong Type

Acquired Type

Specify type:

Generalized Type

Situational Type

Specify:

Due to Psychological Factors

Due to Combined Factors

Treatment.   Treatment may include hormonal therapy and the use of lubricants (Bartlick & Goldberg, 2000). In addition, couples' counseling, which incorporates communication skills training, psychoeducational training, masturbation training (with an emphasis on becoming self-focused and assertive), sensate focus activities, desensitization, and the use of sexual fantasy may be utilized. Psychoeducational training will be discussed in this section. (See the section on hypoactive sexuality disorder for communication skills training and the section on sexual aversion disorder for masturbation training techniques.)

Interventions for Treating Arousal Disorders
Psychoeducational Training.   Psychoeducational training is a primary curative factor in working with couples with a variety of sexual problems or dysfunctions. Psychoeducational training refers to the integration of educational resources and materials such as articles, books, training tapes, and interaction with sexuality counselors as they assist couples with increasing their knowledge and understanding of sexuality and specific sexual problems and dysfunctions. Providing educational information helps to correct sexual myths and to reverse misunderstandings that may adversely affect sexual interactions between partners.

For women, goals of psychoeducational training include (a) understanding themselves as sexual beings, (b) the sexual response cycle, (c) education related to female functioning due to aging, and (d) education related to the origin and treatment of their sexual dysfunction. In addition, understanding how a couple's relationship dynamics can contribute to the sexual disorder is addressed. Barbach's *For Each Other: Sharing Sexual Intimacy* (2001) provides a helpful guide on how to educate women about their sexuality in order to experience greater sexual satisfaction and sexual awareness.

Orgasmic Disorders

Female Orgasmic Disorder / DSM-IV-TR Diagnosis 302.73

The following *DSM-IV-TR* criteria are used in making this diagnosis:

> Female Orgasmic Disorder [formerly Inhibited Female Orgasm] is a persistent or recurrent delay in, or absence of, orgasm following a normal sexual excitement phase (Criterion A) . . . . The disturbance must cause marked distress or interpersonal difficulty (Criterion B). The dysfunction is not better accounted for by another Axis I disorder (except another Sexual Dysfunction) and is not due exclusively to the direct physiological effects of a substance (including medications) or a general medical condition (Criterion C). (APA, 2000, p. 547)

Orgasmic disorder is a common sexual complaint among women of all ages. Women experiencing this dysfunction often feel "deficient, deprived, and sometimes depressed" (Leiblum & Rosen, 2000, p. 118). Consequently, a woman's sexual relationship may suffer. In addition, there is no definitive measure for an orgasm. Each woman's experience of orgasm is different: "There is no clear agreement on the subjective or objective criteria for an orgasm. . . . a variety of orgasmic difficulties exist ranging from a complete lack of orgasm to intermittent or absent orgasm during intercourse" (Leiblum & Rosen, 2000, p. 118).

Contributing Factors.   Physical factors that may contribute to orgasmic disorder include damage to the central nervous system, multiple sclerosis, and genital changes that occur after menopause (Comer, 1998; Everaerd et al., 2000). Some medications can also lead to orgasm difficulties (Comer, 1998).

Psychological factors such as fear and anxiety related to past sexual traumas, depression, anger, and relationship issues can also inhibit orgasm (Comer, 1998). "Spectatoring," a term coined by Masters and Johnson (1970) in which a woman is more an observer than a participant in her own sexual pleasure, has been associated with performance anxiety and orgasmic dysfunction (McCabe & Delaney, 1992).

Diagnosis.   There are two significant categories of female orgasmic disorders. Primary (lifelong) orgasmic disorder occurs when a woman has never reached an orgasm, and secondary (situational) orgasmic disorder when a woman may be able to experience an orgasm from time to time (through masturbation or partner assistance) (Everaerd et al., 2000; Masters et al., 1995).

To make this diagnosis, the following *DSM-IV-TR* criteria should be met:*

Diagnostic Criteria for
302.73 Female Orgasmic Disorder

A. Persistent or recurrent delay in, or absence of, orgasm following a normal sexual excitement phase. Women exhibit wide variability in the type or intensity of stimulation that triggers orgasm. The diagnosis of Female Orgasmic Disorder should be based on the clinician's judgment that the woman's orgasmic capacity is less than would be reasonable for her age, sexual experience, and the adequacy of sexual stimulation she receives.

B. The disturbance causes marked distress or interpersonal difficulty.

C. The orgasmic dysfunction is not better accounted for by another Axis I disorder (except another Sexual Dysfunction) and is not due exclusively to the direct physiological effects of a substance (e.g., a drug of abuse, a medication) or a general medical condition.

Specify type:

Lifelong Type

Acquired Type

Specify type:

Generalized Type

Situational Type

Specify:

Due to Psychological Factors

Due to Combined Factors

It is important to recognize that some women are content without experiencing orgasms or are unconcerned about how they reach orgasm. For other women, the experience of being anorgasmic or experiencing periodic orgasms creates strain in their relationships and leads to feelings of depression, inadequacy, or low self-esteem. For example, a woman might present in counseling stating that she does not feel close to her partner and has been unable to achieve an orgasm during sexual intercourse. Although she reports that she is able to reach orgasm through self-stimulation, she feels inadequate during lovemaking. She states she feels depressed and she is fearful that she may never find fulfillment in her sexual relationship.

Treatment.   Treatment for orgasmic dysfunction depends on the category of the dysfunction. For instance, different approaches are used for women who have never reached orgasm than for women who are able to achieve orgasm situationally. Similarly, depending on the origin of anorgasmia, treatment strategies will vary. For some women, medical intervention is necessary due to general medical conditions. Others, who have been incapable of communicating sexual desires to their partners, are taught assertiveness skills.

Common techniques used in treating anorgasmia include masturbation training, desensitization, communication skill building, and some combination of education and sexual technique development, which were already described as techniques relevant for treatment of desire and arousal disorders. Cognitive skills training is also used in the treatment of this disorder.

Interventions for Treating Female Orgasmic Disorder

Cognitive Skills Training.   Cognitive skills training is useful for treating a variety of sexual dysfunctions (Heiman & Meston, 1997). The goals of this technique include assisting clients to "promote cognitive change, [create] attitude shifts, [reduce] anxiety, [increase] orgasmic frequency, and [increase] connections between positive feelings and sexual behavior" (Heiman, 2000, p. 130). Couples learn to associate positive feelings about their sexuality with their sexual behavior (Ellis, 1975). This entails assisting them to identify, evaluate, and change irrational thoughts and behaviors that interfere with enjoyable sexual experiences. In the case of orgasmic difficulties, anxiety inhibits a person's ability to experience an orgasm (Heiman, 2000).

Cognitive skills training is acquired by educating clients about sexuality and sexual functioning and helping them to develop a belief that sex is a normal part of daily living and a healthy experience. Once couples are educated regarding this belief, identifying and deprogramming irrational beliefs can be initiated. In this way, couples learn to challenge illogical beliefs and attitudes, which may intrude on their sexual functioning (Fisher et al., 1997).

Cognitive skills training addresses specific elements related to sexual dysfunctions and partners' belief systems. The following guidelines, modified from Bourne (2000), can be used to address couples' irrational beliefs about their sexuality or sexual dysfunction.

---

*Reprinted with permission from the *Diagnostic and Statistical Manual of Mental Disorders,* Text Revision (p. xxx), Copyright 2000, American Psychiatric Association.

Sexuality counselors help clients to identify irrational beliefs and assumptions they have about sexuality and the problems they are experiencing. This information may be generated when taking a sexual history in the assessment phase or when discussing the couple's presenting problem. An example of an irrational belief in a case of anorgasmia would be "I believe that women are not supposed to enjoy sex. If they do, they are sluts."

Bourne (2000) suggests that sexuality counselors ask the following questions to challenge a client's thinking:

1. What is the evidence for this belief? Looking objectively at all of my life experiences, what is the evidence that this is true?
2. Does this belief *invariably* or *always* hold true for me?
3. Does this belief look at the whole picture? Does it take into account both positive and negative ramifications?
4. Does this belief promote well-being and/or peace of mind?
5. Did I choose this belief on my own or did it develop out of my experience of growing up in my family? (p. 221)

Beliefs that have little evidence to support them, are rarely true, or those that do not encourage a client's well-being are probably irrational. Many of our beliefs about our sexuality originate in our families of origin and are related to cultural practices.

Once clients have identified their irrational beliefs, they are ready to counter each one of them through positive affirmations—statements used to change thinking and replace irrational self-talk. Affirmations "should be short, simple, and direct," constructed in the "present tense," and believable to the client (Bourne, 2000, p. 225). For example, a client experiencing anorgasmia might express the following affirmation: "My sexuality is beautiful and expressing it is healthy and fun."

Sexual Pain Disorders

Dyspareunia/DSM-IV-TR Diagnosis 302.76

The *DSM-IV-TR* describes dyspareunia as follows:

> Dyspareunia is genital pain that is associated with sexual intercourse (Criterion A). . . . The disturbance must cause marked distress or interpersonal difficulty (Criterion B). The disturbance is not caused exclusively by Vaginismus or lack of lubrication, is not better accounted for by another Axis I disorder (except another Sexual Dysfunction), and is not due

exclusively to the direct physiological effects of a substance (e.g., a drug of abuse, a medication) or a general medical condition (Criterion C). (p. 554)

Dyspareunia can occur at any age, prior to intercourse, during sexual activity, or after intercourse (Everaerd et al., 2000; Masters et al., 1995). In women, the pain has been described as "burning, sharp, searing, or cramping; it can be external, within the vagina, or deep within the pelvic region or abdomen" (Masters et al., 1986, p. 474). It can range in "intensity and duration" (Everaerd et al., 2000, p. 131).

Contributing Factors.   Female dyspareunia has been associated with physical factors stemming from any condition leading to painful intercourse. Many medications such as antidepressants and antihistamines can contribute to vaginal dryness (Masters et al., 1986, 1995). Medical disorders such as diabetes and estrogen deficiencies can also contribute to this disorder. Most commonly, however, dyspareunia is caused by physical "injuries to the vagina, cervix, uterus, or pelvic ligaments during childbirth" (Comer, 1998, p. 457).

General psychosocial factors associated with dyspareunia include developmental factors such as a traumatic first sexual experience, childhood abuse, psychological traits including anxiety and fears, and interpersonal issues such as poor communication, power struggles, distrust, and gender role conflicts (Everaerd et al., 2000; Lazarus, 1989).

Diagnosis.   The following *DSM-IV-TR* criteria are used in making this diagnosis:*

Diagnostic Criteria for 302.76 Dyspareunia

A. Recurrent or persistent genital pain associated with sexual intercourse in either a male or a female.
B. The disturbance causes marked distress or interpersonal difficulty.
C. The disturbance is not caused exclusively by Vaginismus or lack of lubrication, is not better accounted for by another Axis I disorder (except another Sexual Dysfunction), and is not due exclusively to the direct physiological effects of a substance (e.g., a drug of abuse, a medication) or a general medical condition.

Specify type:

Lifelong Type

Acquired Type

---

*Reprinted with permission from the *Diagnostic and Statistical Manual of Mental Disorders,* Text Revision (p. xxx), Copyright 2000, American Psychiatric Association.

Specify type:

Generalized Type

Situational Type

Specify:

Due to Psychological Factors

Due to Combined Factors

Dyspareunia can cause stress and detract from sexual enjoyment, arousal, and orgasm. Women who experience dyspareunia often avoid all sexual activity.

Treatment. Treatment for dyspareunia consists of a variety of approaches, including cognitive-behavioral and medical as well as surgical interventions (Binik, Bergeron, & Khalife, 2000). It is important that sexuality counselors refer couples for a medical evaluation prior to initiating psychological treatment, as this disorder is commonly associated with physical problems that require medical intervention. Cognitive behavioral interventions including psychoeducational training, systematic desensitization techniques, relaxation, Kegel exercises, and vaginal dilation. In addition, couples' counseling and sensate focus activities previously described as treatment strategies for hypoactive desire disorder can be utilized.

Interventions for Treating Female Pain Disorders
Cognitive-Behavioral Techniques. Cognitive-behavioral techniques are designed to help women reduce or control the pain they experience during intercourse. Treatment begins with learning about how a pain disorder such as dyspareunia influences desire, arousal, orgasm, sexual anatomy, and pain. Systematic desensitization, relaxation techniques, Kegel exercises, and vaginal dilation are used. Finally, cognitive restructuring exercises are effective and are described as effective treatment (Binik et al., 2000, p. 166).

Medical and Surgical Treatment. Medical and surgical treatments typically involve the use of medication as well as surgical correction of the anatomy of the vestibulovaginal areas. Sometimes with early endometriosis or endocrine imbalances, hormonal therapy is necessary (Binik et al., 2000; Meana & Binik, 1994).

Vaginismus/DSM-IV-TR Diagnosis 306.51

The *DSM-IV-TR* describes vaginismus as follows:

Vaginismus is the recurrent or persistent involuntary contraction of the perineal muscles surrounding the outer third of the vagina when vaginal penetration

with a penis, finger, tampon, or speculum is attempted (Condition A). The disturbance must cause marked distress or interpersonal difficulty (Criterion B). The disturbance is not better accounted for by another Axis I disorder (except another Sexual Dysfunction) and is not due exclusively to the direct physiological effects of a general medical condition (Criterion C). (APA, 2000, p. 556)

Women experiencing vaginismus have little or no difficulty in becoming sexually aroused, lubricating, or experiencing sexual desire. This condition can occur at any age and range from a tightly closed vagina to less severe conditions where vaginal penetration results in pelvic pain (Masters et al., 1995).

Contributing Factors. Vaginismus has been described as a psychosomatic condition that results from the contraction of the outer muscles of the vagina and is caused by a fear of penetration (LoPiccolo & Stock, 1986; Masters & Johnson, 1970).

Factors that may contribute to this disorder include rape, incest, and other sexual traumas such as being "caught" masturbating at an early age or a traumatic first sexual experience. It has also been linked to women's response to their partner's sexual dysfunction (Leiblum, 2000; Masters & Johnson, 1970). Women experiencing vaginismus struggle with depression, anxiety, and low self-esteem.

For example, Wiona and Bill report that they were "virgins" when they married two years ago. Both come from a "religious" upbringing and are eager to start a family. Wiona states that she began masturbating at an early age but was caught by her mother. She states that she feels "dirty" having sex with Bill, becomes tense, and has trouble relaxing during intercourse. She states, "I feel like someone might walk in on us and catch me doing the dirty deed." Wiona and Bill have never had successful intercourse, and Wiona fears that she will never be successful. She reports feeling depressed and inadequate in her relationship with her partner.

Diagnosis. The following *DSM-IV-TR* criteria are used in making this diagnosis:*

Diagnostic Criteria for 306.51 Vaginismus

A. Recurrent or persistent involuntary spasm of the musculature of the outer third of the vagina that interferes with sexual intercourse.

---

*Reprinted with permission from the *Diagnostic and Statistical Manual of Mental Disorders,* Text Revision (p. xxx), Copyright 2000, American Psychiatric Association.

B. The disturbance causes marked distress or interpersonal difficulty.

C. The disturbance is not better accounted for by another Axis I disorder (e.g., Somatization Disorder) and is not due exclusively to the direct physiological effects of a general medical condition.

Specify type:

Lifelong Type

Acquired Type

Specify type:

Generalized Type

Situational Type

Specify:

Due to Psychological Factors

Due to Combined Factors

For couples who desire to have children, the condition of vaginismus can be disconcerting (Masters et al., 1995). Confusion and frustration often occurs in couples' relationships as a result of the male misperception that the female partner is purposefully avoiding intercourse. In addition, a male partner's belief that he is hurting his partner may result in tentativeness and passivity in the couple's sexual relations. Overall, vaginismus can have damaging effects on women's sexual relationships, resulting in disappointment, emotional pain, and frustration.

Treatment. Common treatment approaches for vaginismus include the use of psychoeducational materials, desensitization techniques, cognitive skills training, relaxation training, sensate focus, Kegel exercises, and the use of vaginal dilators. In addition, couples' communication building offers skills for a healthy exchange of sexual information.

Interventions for Treating Vaginismus

Cognitive Skills Training.   Cognitive skills training helps women overcome illogical beliefs and attitudes that stem from family background and religious or cultural beliefs. By understanding the disorder, couples can be supportive of treatment methods that initially require private time for female partners who must later learn how to incorporate their partner's participation.

General Relaxation Techniques.   General relaxation techniques result in physiological changes, including decreased heart rate, respiration rate, blood pressure, and skeletal muscle tension.

Box 6.3 presents general relaxation instructions that can be used by couples.

Progressive muscle relaxation, developed by Jacobson (1974), is often used to accomplish a deeper state of relaxation. It involves a sequential succession of tensing and relaxing of the muscles. Each muscle group is tensed for 10 seconds and then relaxed for 15 to 20 seconds. The purpose of this exercise is to help women learn the difference between tense and relaxed feelings and learn how to elicit a relaxed response.

Box 6.4 presents guidelines for practicing progressive muscle relaxation based on Jacobson's (1974) methods.

Systematic Desensitization.   Systematic desensitization is a technique first devised by Wolpe (1958) and later used by Masters and Johnson (1970) in the treatment of sexual anxiety. Desensitization is defined as "the process of unlearning the connection between anxiety and a particular situation" (Bourne, 2000, p. 143). For example, a woman with vaginismus must unlearn the connection between vaginal penetration and muscle contraction and begin to relate tranquility and ease with penetration. This task is accomplished by constructing a hierarchy of situations that provokes a progressive increase in anxiety and learning to gradually approach sexual situations through a sequence of steps (Wolpe, 1958, 1969). Sexuality counselors assist clients in constructing their hierarchy based on the client's unique experiences. Bourne (2000) suggests the following steps when constructing a hierarchy:*

1. Choose a particular sexual problem (fear of penetration/vaginismus).
2. Imagine having to deal with this situation in a most limited way (penile-vaginal contact without penetration). Select a way that bothers you very little. In addition, you can visualize a supportive person encouraging you at your side (such as your sexual partner).
3. Now imagine what might be the most challenging scene related to your sexual fear; for example, penetration of your vagina by your partner's penis. Then, identify parameters of your fear that make you more or less anxious and use them to develop scenes of varying intensity—for example, inserting a tampon into your vagina.
4. Take time to imagine a total of six scenes of gradual intensity related to your sexual fear and rank-order their anxiety-provoking potential. Then, write them down.

---

*From *The Anxiety and Phobia Workbook,* 3rd ed. (p. 145), by E. J. Bourne, 2000, Oakland, CA: New Harbinger Publications. Reprinted with permission.

BOX 6.3

General Relaxation Instructions

Relaxation is a useful technique whenever you feel tense.

Preparation: Sit in a comfortable chair or, better still, lie down. Choose a quiet, warm room, when you are not too tired and where you will not be interrupted.

If you are sitting, take off your shoes, uncross your legs, and rest your arms along the arms of the chair.

If you are lying down, lie on your back, with your arms at your sides.

Close your eyes, and be aware of your body: notice how you are breathing, and where the muscular tensions in your body are. Make sure you are comfortable.

Breathing: Start to breathe slowly and deeply, expanding your abdomen as you breathe IN, then raising your rib cage to let more air in, till your lungs are filled right to the top. Hold your breath for a couple of seconds and then breathe OUT slowly, allowing your rib cage and stomach to relax, and empty your lungs completely.

Do not strain; with practice it will become much easier.

Keep this slow, deep rhythmic breathing going throughout your relaxation session.

Relaxation: After you have your breathing pattern established, start the following sequence:

1. Curl your toes hard and press your feet down: Tense up on an IN breath, hold your breath for 10 seconds while your muscles tense, then relax and breathe OUT at the same time.
2. Now press your heels down and bend your feet up: Tense up on an IN breath; hold your breath for 10 seconds; relax on the OUT breath.
3. Now tense your calf muscles: Tense up on an IN breath; hold 10 seconds; relax on an OUT breath.
4. Now tense your thigh muscles, straightening your knees and making your legs stiff: Tense up on an IN breath; hold for 10 seconds; relax on an OUT breath.
5. Now make your buttocks tight: Tense up on an IN breath; hold for 10 seconds; relax on an OUT breath.
6. Now tense your stomach as if to receive a punch: Tense up on an IN breath; hold for 10 seconds; relax on an OUT breath.
7. Now bend your elbows and tense the muscles in your arms: Tense up on an IN breath; hold for 10 seconds; relax on an OUT breath.
8. Now hunch your shoulders and press your head back into the cushion: Tense up on an IN breath; hold it for 10 seconds; relax on an OUT breath.
9. Now clench your jaws, frown, and screw up [sic] your eyes real tight: Tense up on an IN breath; hold for 10 seconds; relax on an OUT breath.
10. Now tense all your muscles together: Tense up on an IN breath; hold for 10 seconds; relax on an OUT breath.

Remember to breathe deeply, and be aware when you relax of the feeling of physical well being and heaviness spreading through your body.

After you have done the whole sequence from 1-10, still breathing slowly and deeply, imagine a white rose on a black background.

Try to "see" the rose as clearly as possible, concentrating your attention on it for 30 seconds. Do *not* hold your breath during this time, continue to breathe as you have been doing.

After this, go on to visualise [sic] anything else your counselor may have suggested, or give yourself the instruction that when you open your eyes you will be perfectly relaxed but alert.

Count to 3 and then open your eyes.

When you have become familiar with this technique, if you want to relax at any time when you have a few minutes, do the sequence in a shortened form, leaving out some muscle groups, but always working from your feet upwards. For example, you might do [number] 1, 4, 6, 8, and 10 if you do not have time to do the complete sequence.

Source: From *Sex Therapy Manual* (pp. 260–261), by P. Gillan, 1987, Oxford, England: Blackwell Publishing. Copyright 1987 by Blackwell Publishing. Reprinted with permission.

BOX 6.4

Progressive Muscle Relaxation

Progressive muscle relaxation involves the tensing and relaxing, in succession, sixteen different muscle groups of the body. The idea is to tense each muscle group hard (not so hard that you can strain however) for about 10 seconds, and then let go of it suddenly. You then give yourself 15–20 seconds to relax noticing how the muscle group feels when relaxed in contrast to when it was tense, before going to the next group of muscles. You might also say to yourself "I am relaxing," "Let go," "Let the tension flow away," or any other relaxing phrase during each relaxation period between muscle groups. Throughout the exercise, maintain your focus on your muscles. When your attention wanders, bring it back to the particular muscle group you're working on. The guidelines below describe progressive muscle relaxation in detail.

Once you are comfortably supported in a quiet place, follow the detailed instructions below:

1. To begin, take three deep abdominal breaths, exhaling slowly each time. As you exhale, imagine that tension throughout your body begins to flow away.
2. Clench your fists. Hold for 7–10 seconds and then release for 15–20 seconds. *Use these same time intervals for all other muscle groups*.
3. Tighten your biceps by drawing your forearms up toward your shoulders and "making a muscle" with both arms. Hold . . . and then relax.
4. Tighten your *triceps*—the muscles on the undersides of your upper arms—by extending your arms out straight and locking your elbows. Hold . . . and then relax.
5. Tense the muscles in your forehead by raising your eyebrows as far as you can. Hold . . . and then relax. Imagine your forehead muscles becoming smooth and limp as they relax.
6. Tense the muscles around your eyes by clenching your eyelids tightly shut. Hold . . . and then relax. Imagine sensations of deep relaxation spreading all around the area of your eyes.
7. Tighten your jaws by opening your mouth so widely that you stretch the muscles around the hinges of your jaw. Hold . . . and then relax. Let your lips part and allow your jaw to hang loose.
8. Tighten the muscles in the back of your neck by pulling your head way back (be gentle with this muscle group to avoid injury) as if you were going to touch your head to your back. Focus only on tensing the muscles in your neck. Hold . . . and then relax. Since this area is often especially tight, it's good to do the tense-relax cycle twice.
9. Take a few deep breaths and tune in to the weight of your head sinking into whatever surface it is resting on.
10. Tighten your shoulders by raising them up as if you were going to touch your ears. Hold . . . and then relax.
11. Tighten the muscles around your shoulder blades by pushing your shoulder blades back as if you were going to touch them together. Hold the tension in your shoulder blades . . . and then relax. Since this area is often especially tense, you might repeat the tense-relax sequence twice.
12. Tighten the muscles of your chest by taking a deep breath. Hold for up to 10 seconds . . . and then release slowly. Imagine any excess tension in your chest flowing away with the exhalation.
13. Tighten your stomach muscles by sucking your stomach in. Hold . . . and then release. Imagine a wave of relaxation spreading throughout your abdomen.
14. Tighten your lower back by arching it up. (You can omit this exercise if you have lower back pain.) Hold . . . and then relax.
15. Tighten your buttocks by pulling them together. Hold . . . and then relax. Imagine the muscles in your hips loose and limp.

(continued)

BOX 6.4
Progressive Muscle Relaxation (continued)

16. Squeeze the muscles in your thighs all the way down to your knees. You will probably have to tighten your hips along with your thighs, since the thigh muscles attach at the pelvis. Hold . . . and then relax. Feel your thigh muscles smoothing out and relaxing completely.
17. Tighten your calf muscles by pulling your toes toward you (flex carefully to avoid cramps). Hold . . . and then relax.
18. Tighten your feet by curling your toes downward. Hold . . . and then relax.
19. Mentally scan your body for any residual tension. If a particular area remains tense, repeat one or two tense-relax cycles for that group of muscles.
20. Now image a wave of relaxation slowly spreading throughout your body, starting at your head and gradually penetrating every muscle group all the way down to your toes.

The entire progressive muscle relaxation sequence should take you 20–30 minutes the first time. With practice, you can decrease the time needed to 15–20 minutes.

Source: From *The Anxiety and Phobia Workbook*, 3rd ed. (pp. 81–82), by E. J. Bourne, 2000, Oakland, CA: New Harbinger Publications. www.newharbinger.com. Copyright 2000 by New Harbinger Publications, Inc. Reprinted with permission.

Clients take adequate time to become relaxed by practicing deep muscle relaxation (described in an earlier section). Then they progress through the hierarchy, beginning with fifteen minutes of deep relaxation and progressing to their first scene. Once clients report managing their anxiety effectively in the first scene, they can continue progressing up the hierarchy. This technique is used and modified with a variety of sexual disorders involving anxiety. It is most effective in women who may have experienced a trauma.

Kegel Exercises.   Kegel exercises were developed by Arnold Kegel in 1952 to help women with problems controlling urination. They are aimed at strengthening and restoring muscle tone and have been shown to increase sexual awareness. The exercises teach women to control the muscles around their vagina (Crooks & Baur, 2002).

The following steps are suggested by Ono (as cited in Crooks & Baur, 2002) to instruct women in the use of Kegel exercises:

1. Locate the muscles around the vagina. This is done by stopping the flow of urine to feel which muscles contract. An even more effective way of contracting the pelvic floor muscles is to contract the anal sphincter as if to hold back gas.
2. Insert a finger into the opening of your vagina and contract the muscles you located in step 1. Feel them squeeze your finger.
3. Squeeze the same muscles for 10 seconds. Relax. Repeat 10 times.
4. Squeeze and release as rapidly as possible, 10 to 25 times. Repeat.
5. Imagine trying to suck something into your vagina. Hold for 3 seconds.
6. This exercise series should be done three times a day. (p. 90)

Dilation Techniques.   Dilation techniques are the most common method of treatment for vaginismus. This technique involves the use of various-sized plastic dilators. The smallest dilator is the size of a pencil and the largest, the size of an erect penis. Women are instructed to use sterile lubrication before inserting a dilator and to keep the dilator in place for ten to fifteen minutes at a time (Masters et al., 1995). Once women become comfortable with this technique, they can include their partners in the sessions by asking them to insert the dilators. It is important that sufficient time is taken in order to feel in control of the exercise. A woman may need to practice general and vaginal relaxation before, during, or after the sexual encounters. Once she feels comfortable with the largest dilator, she can guide her partner's penis into her vagina at her own pace, working up to complete insertion of the penis (Masters et al., 1995). As a result, the transition to successful intercourse is generally easier.

INFERTILITY AND ITS EFFECTS ON SEXUAL DYSFUNCTIONS AND PROBLEMS

Infertility is the inability to conceive during one year of sexual intercourse without the use of contraception or the inability to carry a pregnancy to live birth (Cook, 1987; Speroff, Glass, & Kase, 1994). Infertility is described in two different ways based on whether a couple has previous children. "*Primary* infertility occurs in couples who have never had a child, and *secondary* infertility with those who experience the inability to conceive or to achieve a live birth after previously bearing one or more children" (Diamond, Kezur, Meyers, Scharf, & Weinshel, 1999, p. 8).

Infertility is a heartfelt crisis for couples, interrupting their normal developmental transition on both an individual and relational level. It has been referred to as "a life crisis, an identity crisis, a chronic illness, a trauma, a cause of grief and mourning, and an existential experience, as well as a combination of all of these" (Diamond et al., 1999, p. 9). Infertility often leads to profound distress for women and may affect sexual functioning in couples' relationships.

Infertility in women is associated with a wide range of physical, psychological, and environmental factors. Physical factors are attributed to hormonal, anatomical, genetic, and immune system problems (Metzger, 1998; Harrison, O'Moore, & O'Moore, 1986). In addition, problems with women's eggs and blocked fallopian tubes can also pose a threat to becoming pregnant (Gibson & Meyers, 2000; Meyers et al., 1995; Robinson & Stewart, 1995; Trantham, 1996). Psychological factors include denial, grief, helplessness, anger, anxiety, and guilt (Cooper-Hilbert, 1998). Environmental factors include work-related stress, family issues, and gender role expectations.

Counseling focuses on ways to help women to explore their beliefs about creating a family, to identify and explore their feelings and reactions to infertility, to create a support system, and to provide educational material related to their medical procedures (Cooper-Hilbert, 1998; Diamond et al., 1999; Leiblum, 1997a). In addition, sexuality counselors can assist women and their partners to communicate about their sexual relationship. Issues such as pressures to perform sexually, timing, feelings of inadequacy, and learning how to enjoy sex during the process of treatment can be addressed. It is important to help couples define their infertility problem jointly so that blaming does not occur. In this way, couples move toward identifying a solution to their family issues. This process of counseling follows an inte-grative couples' model, which is helpful for addressing a variety of sexual problems and dysfunctions.

ABORTION AND ITS EFFECTS ON SEXUAL DYSFUNCTIONS AND PROBLEMS

The word "abortion" is a medical term that refers to "any pregnancy loss, spontaneous or induced, that occurs within the first 20 weeks of gestation" (Kohn & Moffitt, 1992, p. 81). Spontaneous abortions (also termed miscarriages) occur in one out of four pregnancies (Marrs, Bloch, & Silverman, 1997). The number of women who undergo intended abortions each year in the United States is estimated to be 1.4 million (Alan Guttmacher Institute, 2003).

Sexuality counselors may encounter women who are seeking guidance to determine whether or not to pursue an induced abortion. In these cases, it is most important to assist women in exploring their values and beliefs in order to help them make a decision (Schweibert, 2002). Although the reasons for abortions vary, the loss associated with early pregnancy demise is most often significant (Glazer, 1997). Sexuality counselors should be familiar with the complexity of an abortion experience on a woman and her partner and how this impacts their sexual relationship and functioning.

In the same way that couples are affected by infertility, those who experience pregnancy loss resulting in abortion will be affected in all aspects of life. On a physical level, the woman must confront the aftermath of a medical procedure such as a D&C (dilation and curettage) or a spontaneous abortion, which includes adjusting to fluctuating hormone levels as well as physical discomfort. Psychological symptoms may include self-blame, anger, guilt, anxiety, shame, denial, depression, feelings of loss, and helplessness (Cooper-Hilbert, 1998; Glazer, 1997; Schwiebert, 2002). These reactions may vary based on a woman's values, beliefs, and circumstances surrounding the experience (Schwiebert, 2002). On a social level a woman is confronted with friends and family who may or may not agree with the circumstances that led to the abortion. Some women find themselves alone and isolated and begin to withdraw from gaining social support that is most needed (Glazer, 1997).

It is also important to recognize the effect of an abortion experience on a couple's relationship. In the aftermath of an early pregnancy loss, couples may tend to engage in blaming each other for the loss, experience feelings of depression, or disconnect from their partner due to differing reactions to their experience (Kohn & Moffit, 1992; Glazer, 1997). These varied responses affect a couple's relationship and can lead to sexual problems and dysfunctions.

For example, Jenny reports she had an induced abortion after much ambivalence and agonizing over her decision. She states that since her pregnancy loss she has been experiencing pain during intercourse with her partner. She admits feeling regretful and angry, and she is experiencing feelings of depression. She states that she is angry with her partner for not talking her out of the procedure; her partner states that he feels guilty and disheartened and admits to having difficulty attaining an erection since the incident.

Another woman undergoing infertility treatment states that after her third pregnancy loss she began to "tense up" during sexual intercourse. She states, "I'm so afraid I'll get pregnant again. I can't cope with another loss." Both she and her partner express reluctance to continue any further infertility treatment.

Sexuality counselors assist women and their partners during the aftermath of an intended or unintended pregnancy loss by helping them to recognize and identify their own as well as their partner's feelings, validate the significance of the loss to each partner, and recognize their differing coping styles (Scharf & Weinshel, 2000). They can also explore the impact of the event on their relationship and facilitate communication about sexual concerns, such as when to resume sexual intimacy. In addition, counselors provide ongoing support for couples who may have difficulty resolving feelings of intense loss and find themselves "stuck" and unable to move on in their lives (Kohn & Moffit, 1992). This is especially common in couples who have experienced multiple spontaneous or induced abortions. An integrative couples' model assists couples to address issues and concerns related to an abortion experience and find solutions to moving forward in their relationship.

Case Example

George, aged 51, and Dharma, aged 47, have been living together for six years but have recently reported being frustrated with sexual intercourse. Dharma has been unable to achieve an orgasm through intercourse and, instead, has often begun to masturbate after they complete their sexual encounter. George complains that he cannot satisfy her and feels frustrated that he does not know how to please her. Dharma assures George that it is not his fault but that she's "just a little bored with the same sexual routine after so many years." George is hurt and blames himself for their problem. For the last three weeks, he has stopped approaching Dharma sexually and instead masturbates in the shower three or four mornings per week.

Application of the Five Stages of the Integrative Couples' Model
Stage 1: Assessing and Obtaining an Interactional View of the Problem
Dharma believes that their sexual relationship has become boring and that George is not imaginative or creative during their lovemaking. George, on the other hand, blames Dharma for closing the door on their sexual relationship and just "carrying on without him." After obtaining a historical view of the problem through a sexual and relational history, the sexuality counselor determines that Dharma can be diagnosed with Hypoactive Sexual Desire Disorder (*DSM-IV-TR* 302.71). The counselor defines the problem for the couple in interactional terms: "It sounds as if the two of you are disappointed about the way things are going in your sexual relationship and would like to learn different ways of relating sexually so that you feel more connected with each other." This nonblaming explanation offers them an opportunity to learn together about sexual pleasuring.

Stage 2: Goal Setting
With the assistance of their sexuality counselor, three goals are set in both behavioral and affective terms:

1. We would like to learn to express our sexual desires openly and attempt to try new techniques like sensate focus, so that we can feel playful again.
2. We want to include each other in our sexual activities, even if the activity is mutual masturbation in order to feel more connected with each other.
3. We would like to make more "sexual dates" with each other to try to recapture some of the passion we used to feel with each other.

Stage 3: Adapting New Perceptions and Behaviors
In this stage, Dharma's fun-loving spirit is emphasized as well as her ability to find humor in most situations. George's imagination as an

artist is also identified, along with his persistence at seeking solutions to problems. They recall how in their earlier years together they would do spontaneous things such as going to a midnight poetry reading, driving to the beach for sunrise, or just getting in the car and figuring out where to go next.

The sexuality counselor next devises interventions that mobilize these positive assets and helps them begin to change their relational system.

1. They will spend an hour twice a week in bed hugging and touching each other, without intercourse (modified sensate focus activity).
2. They will locate books, videos, and other available materials on sexual techniques to explore new possibilities (bibliotherapy).
3. Each partner will take a turn planning a fun date night.
4. Masturbation may be as frequent as they like but must include the other person in some manner (masturbation training

techniques). The counselor reminds them that a change in one dimension of their relationship will affect all other dimensions.

Stage 4: Maintaining Perceptions and Behaviors
Dharma and George both realize that the success of their efforts depends greatly on their ability to keep up with the changes they have made and acknowledge them each week.

They know that their busy schedule could interfere with their creativity, so they have determined to set aside time at the beginning of each week to ensure that they make their relationship a priority.

Stage 5: Validating New Perceptions and Behaviors
George reminds Dharma that they need to celebrate their new passion for each other often and find pleasure in all of the time they have together (sexual and nonsexual). They also agree to continue to find ways to infuse joy and laughter in everyday life.

SUMMARY

Social issues have impacted women's roles as have the attitudes, beliefs, and practices that surround female sexuality. Women's new roles have led to conflict, anger, and resentment resulting in decreased closeness and intimacy in their relationships with their partners. Both biological and environmental factors lead to sexual distress in relationships. In addition, sociocultural, developmental, aging, situational life events, and family-of-origin issues all play a critical part in determining whether women experience a sexual problem or sexual dysfunction.

When evaluating women's sexual concerns, it is important for sexuality counselors to explore their sexual history—from beliefs and attitudes to cultural issues that contribute to sexual difficulties. A thorough medical examination is part of this process. In addition to taking a sex history and obtaining medical information, sexuality counselors need to be familiar with common female sexual dysfunctions and their treatment in order to help resolve their problems. Sexuality counselors treat women's sexual issues based on their level of training and expertise. According to

AASECT standards, however, they must obtain advanced information and training on all *DSM-IV-TR* diagnoses of psychosexual disorders prior to treating couples.

Common psychosexual disorders fall into four major categories: (a) desire disorders (hypoactive, aversion), (b) arousal disorders (female sexual arousal disorder), (c) orgasm disorders (female orgasmic disorder), and (d) pain disorders (dyspareunia, vaginismus). Treatment strategies include communication skill building, sensate focus training, masturbation techniques, psychoeducational training about the specific disorder, cognitive skills training, relaxation exercises, Kegel exercises, and dilation techniques.

The integrative model allows couples to establish a nonblaming interactional view of the problem, set behavioral and affective goals, adapt new perceptions about each other based on carefully chosen treatment strategies mentioned earlier, work to maintain new behaviors that promote healthy interactions, and generalize their changes in sexual behaviors to other aspects of their relationship.

MALE SEXUALITY: DIAGNOSIS AND TREATMENT INTERVENTIONS

KEY CONCEPTS

- Men have unique issues that contribute to sexual problems and dysfunctions.
- Sociocultural factors, developmental concerns, aging, and family-of-origin issues contribute to male sexual problems and dysfunctions.
- Sexuality counselors must be familiar with the process of diagnosing all aspects of psychosexual disorders as described in the fourth edition of the American Psychiatric Association's *Diagnostic and Statistical Manual of Mental Disorders (DSM-IV-TR).*
- Common presenting issues for men include desire disorders, erectile disorders, and premature ejaculation.
- Treatment for male sexual dysfunctions include a variety of interventions appropriate for each stage of the sexual response cycle along with interventions for disorders associated with pain during intercourse.
- Understanding the systemic nature of assessment, treatment, and diagnosis of male sexual problems and dysfunctions is central to the development of appropriate interventions.
- Each partner's sexual issues must be understood within the context of couples' relationships in order to formulate an interactive definition of sexual problems.
- Infertility affects all aspects of a couple's life and is associated with physical, psychological, and environmental factors.

I n the previous chapter, we provided information specific to individual female sexual problems within the context of couples' relationships. In this chapter, we address within this same context male sexual dysfunctions as presented in the *DSM-IV-TR* (American Psychiatric Association, 2000). We include sociocultural and developmental influences specific to males in addition to describing the process of sexuality counseling for men. We then describe commonly presented male dysfunctions along with factors that contribute to each of them. Diagnostic criteria are provided for each dysfunction as well as appropriate treatment interventions. We conclude the chapter with a case example that demonstrates the application of the integrative couples' model highlighting a male sexual problem.

SOCIOCULTURAL AND DEVELOPMENTAL INFLUENCES IN MALE SEXUALITY

Social Issues and Male Sexuality

Although women have clearly been impacted by social injustice and discrimination, as confirmed by the women's movement of the 1960s, we cannot overlook the fact that men have also been cast in specific roles and subject to stereotypes. As men's roles have continued to change, so have the attitudes, beliefs, and practices surrounding male sexuality. Similar to women "being treated as sex objects, men sometimes have suffered from being success objects, expected to provide status and security to their partners" (Kelly, 1996, p. 139). Societal pressures of this kind have resulted in men feeling helpless as they struggle to be successful in the workplace. Kelly (1996) suggests that men often feel distressed because of the expectations associated with traditional male roles, such as viewing men as responsible for the sexual pursuit of women and being resourceful providers as well as keeping control of their emotions.

However, over the last two decades, a focus on men's issues has permeated our society. The men's movement brought to light that men are confronted with a constant struggle to successfully communicate their thoughts, feelings, concerns, and dilemmas in a changing world. Traditional expectations of men's roles no longer fit for most men. For example, it is not unusual to find men who are "stay-at-home-dads" whose female partners have assumed the role of the breadwinner. Likewise, men are reaching out to each other and establishing lasting friendships. Sam Keen (a leader of the men's movement and author of *Fire in the Belly—On Being a Man*) comments that the men's movement "made men understand that they were living friendlessly and that they needed male friends with whom they could talk" (Keen, 2002). Certainly, men have made major shifts in their beliefs about themselves.

Although the men's movement has helped some men to become more self-aware and connected with their true values, many men continue to struggle as they find themselves lacking time and energy to spend with their families. Thus, they have become distant participators in family functions. The demands of "keeping up with the Joneses" and providing for their families require many men to work harder and longer, spending less quality time with their children and significant other.

The stereotypes of the past that portrayed men as aggressors, hunters, healers, and warriors have been replaced with new roles that have left men feeling lost and disconnected from their families and from other men. Competition to climb the corporate ladder and to achieve success and power in our society has contributed to this feeling of detachment. As a result, some men are preoccupied with a "need to perform" in their work, play, and personal world. This creates tremendous stress and takes a significant toll on some men. It affects their mental health as well as their relationships, both of which can contribute to sexual difficulties.

For example, a man who is having difficulty climbing the corporate ladder because he does not meet his company's expectations may have sexual difficulty that is manifested as an erectile problem. It is not uncommon for erectile dysfunction to occur as a result of job stress. Young and Long (1998) note that many sexual problems that men experience "are not necessarily [a result of] internal conflicts . . . [or] physical dysfunctions" (pp. 167–168). Instead, as in this case, environmental influences such as job stress, family pressures, or financial strain can impact a couple's emotional system and contribute to sexual problems (Wincze & Carey, 2001; Young & Long, 1998). Often, men's sexuality is tied to who they are in the professional and social world, and as a result, experiencing sexual difficulty can be devastating to both their personal and public selves.

Cultural Issues

Culture also impacts male sexuality. Sexual norms, values, and practices influence how individuals view themselves sexually. For example, in certain cultures there are "strong beliefs about altering male genitalia" (Kelly, 1996, p. 125). One form of genital alteration, circumcision, involves removal of the foreskin of the penis. This practice supports "social, religious, or historical imperatives" that influence genital altering (Lightfoot-Klein, Chase, Hammond, & Goldman, 2000, p. 459). In contrast, castration—the removal of the male's testicles—involves "a more extreme male genital mutilation . . . [and] has been justified [in some cultures]: to prevent sexual activity . . ., to render war captives docile; to preserve the soprano voices of European choirboys . . ., and as part of religious ceremonies (in ancient Egypt)" (Crooks & Baur, 2002, p. 120).

Circumcised men may experience decreased penile sensitivity while men who have been castrated no longer experience a strong sexual drive. Both culturally based rituals can contribute to sexual problems and dysfunctions.

Developmental Issues

Freud (1917), Erikson (1963), and Piaget (1932) discuss male development and emphasize differentiation and autonomy as primary values in male culture. At a young age, boys learn to play games that develop independence and organizational skills (Lever, 1976).

In addition, they learn to manage competition and receive social acceptance for playing by the rules of the game despite the relationships they may have with their friends (Lever, 1976). As a result, boys arrive at puberty with a different range of social experiences than girls, having had opportunities to develop skills that fit the requirements for modern corporate success (Lever, 1976).

At the onset of puberty, the hormone testosterone accounts for many changes in male growth that determines sexual differentiation (Everaerd, Laan, & Spiering, 2000). Around the age of 13, "the testes increase in size, the penis grows thicker and longer, pubic hair and body hair begin to appear, and lowering of the voice begins" (Everaerd et al., 2000, p. 71). It is soon after puberty that a boy may experience his first ejaculation. Fantasies about sexual acts and an increase in interest in sexual behavior are often present. For males, sex hormones are in higher concentration. During this time, men identify strongly with the "power of the penis," which carries over into adult development in the form of being stereotyped as a "success object." Pressure to perform and possess power both sexually and in the marketplace often contributes to male sexual dysfunctions.

Age-Related Physical Issues

Age-related physical issues impact men's sexual functioning and occur as part of the normal aging process. For example, physical changes such as decreased testosterone output steadily but slowly declines with age (Rathus, Nevid, & Fichner-Rathus, 2000). In addition, men may notice a decrease in the size and firmness of their testicles along with reduced sperm production.

Changes in orgasmic and erectile functioning may also occur during the male aging process. Men typically require more time to reach orgasm; however, their partners may view delayed ejaculation as a positive part of sexual relations. After about the age of 50, men take progressively longer to have an erection, which may require direct stimulation of the penis (Crooks & Baur, 2002; Rathus et al., 2000).

Aging men may also confront prostate difficulties such as prostate cancer or excessive development of the prostate (Stone, 1987). Prostatitis (inflammation of the prostate) can result in pain in the pelvic area, backaches, urinary complications, and occasionally a cloudy discharge from the penis (Crooks & Baur, 2002). In addition, as men age, they often develop benign prostatic hyperplasic, an increase in the size of the prostate gland which can result in decreased urine flow (Crooks & Baur, 2002). These age-related problems and their treatments contribute to a variety of problems in sexual functioning (Litwin et al., 1995). For example, hormone treatments may result in erectile dysfunction, and surgical removal of the prostate can damage the neck of the bladder, which can result in retrograde ejaculation or ejaculate draining into the bladder (Crooks & Baur, 2002).

Family-of-Origin Influences

As we discussed in Chapter 3, sexual messages, values, beliefs, and behaviors are passed from one generation to the next and are often conveyed through the use of stories depicting sexually acceptable and unacceptable behaviors (Berman & Hof, 1987). These stories contain vital information that may be utilized to determine current sexual practices, beliefs, and behaviors.

For example, Cornelius reports that his father was absent for much of his upbringing due to the nature of his job as a traveling sales representative. Cornelius's father was the oldest and only son of five children. He describes both his mother and grandmother as domineering and smothering. As a result of messages they relayed, his father believed that women were controlling and demanding and required more than he could offer. His father passed his ideas about women to Cornelius, creating a message that "women are controlling and it is impossible to please them." In addition, he learned to "protect his personal independence by maintaining emotional distance from women." Cornelius learned to develop superficial and nonemotional relationships with women so that he did not compromise his personal goals and dreams. He has thus received negative messages about females regarding their intent to control men. As an adult, he and his sexual partner seek counseling due to his inability to become emotionally and sexually intimate in their relationship.

Positive messages are also passed from generation to generation, as in the case of Jonathan. Jonathan's father reported that his mother was a woman of great faith. He shared stories with Jonathan that were passed down by his mother about surviving during the Great Depression. His mother instilled in him an ability to believe he could accomplish anything if he put his mind to it. Jonathan was told by his mother that women are strong and breed independence in others. Jonathan grew up believing that women are warm, nurturing, and supportive. He received positive messages about women and their encouraging nature.

The sexual genogram illustrated in Chapter 3 is a tool used by counselors to help couples explore sexual messages, beliefs, and values passed from one generation to another, as happened with Cornelius and Jonathan.

THE DIAGNOSTIC PROCESS FOR MALE SEXUAL ISSUES

Dysfunction or Problem?

As we discussed in previous chapters, contributing factors in the development of sexual problems are complex, making it crucial that sexuality counselors accurately diagnose these problems and provide effective treatment plans to address them. Therefore, defining whether or not a man is experiencing a sexual problem or dysfunction determines a sexuality counselor's course of treatment.

Men are often reluctant to share their sexual concerns with others due to societal messages about performance or feelings of shame or inadequacy. When they do disclose intimate information, they often confide in their physician, hoping to find a physiological solution for their sexual problem. Some male dysfunctions such as erectile dysfunction are managed through the use of medication. Most often, however, a combination of medication, cognitive-behavioral strategies, and couple/relational counseling is the treatment of choice. As is the case with women, if men report no problems in any phase of the sexual response cycle, they probably do not have a sexual dysfunction. It is important for sexuality counselors to then explore other factors, such as unresolved relationship issues or the presence of a sexual problem (Heiman, LoPiccolo, & LoPiccolo, 1976; Kaplan, 1983). In these cases, sexuality counselors determine if the problem is a result of an internal conflict, an unresolved relational conflict manifested in their sexual relationship, or stressors in lifestyle. For example, Matt admits that he is having difficulty maintaining an erection and, as a result, is unable to have consistent intercourse with his partner. He states that he has had this difficulty "off and on" in their relationship of two years and is fearful that he

is losing his virility. To combat the problem and heighten his arousal, he has invited his partner, Mona, to view pornographic videos during their sexual foreplay. He states, however, that Mona has become very critical of his "new technique" and refuses to participate. Mona has recently been passed over for a promotion at work and blames Matt because of his unwillingness to relocate for her new position. Matt offers that Mona is demanding and critical, similar to his mother, and is unrealistic regarding her expectations of him. In order to help this couple, a sexuality counselor must first determine if Matt is experiencing a sexual problem or a sexual dysfunction.

Diagnosing Sexual Dysfunctions

Diagnosing and understanding sexual dysfunctions is an integral part of the clinical decision-making process for treatment. In Chapter 6 we discussed how to diagnose a sexual dysfunction by using specific criteria listed in the *DSM-IV-TR*. It was also pointed out that "sexual dysfunctions are characterized by disturbances in sexual desire and in the psychophysiological changes that characterize the sexual response cycle" (APA, 2000, p. 535). It is important to keep in mind that in order for a problem to qualify as a diagnosable sexual disorder, it must "cause marked distress and interpersonal difficulty" (APA, 2000, p. 535). For example, if a man states that he has no problem attaining and maintaining an erection but he does not always ejaculate and is quite satisfied with his sexual relationship, he does not have a diagnosable orgasmic disorder. If, however, he states that he is distressed because he is unable to ejaculate each time he has intercourse and the sexuality counselor has ruled out any medical, drug, or psychiatric problems, he can be diagnosed as experiencing Male Orgasmic Disorder. Sexual dysfunctions categorized specific to males encompass "Sexual Desire Disorders (i.e., Hypoactive Sexual Desire Disorder, Sexual Aversion Disorder), Sexual Arousal Disorders (i.e., . . . Male Erectile Disorder), Orgasmic Disorders (i.e., . . . Male Orgasmic Disorder [formerly Inhibited Male Orgasm], Premature Ejaculation), [and] Sexual Pain Disorders (i.e., Dyspareunia . . .)" (APA, 2000, p. 535).

Making a *DSM-IV* diagnosis is an important and necessary step in a comprehensive sexual evaluation. Chapter 3 addressed specific questions that assist sexuality counselors in making a dynamic formulation of the presenting problem.

Questions to Consider

Sexuality counselors must ask specific questions regarding male sexuality in order to determine an accurate diagnosis. (Refer to Chapter 3 for specific sexual history and interview techniques.) The following sample questions are based on topic areas suggested by Young and Long (1998):

1. How often do you engage in sexual intercourse? Other sexual activities? Are you satisfied with your sexual life?
2. Tell me about your family of origin. Was sex ever discussed? How do men in your family relate to women? What did your family teach you about men's roles in a relationship regarding having sex? Who told you about "the birds and the bees"? What does your culture or religion believe about sexual intercourse and sexual activities?
3. Have any major events such as divorce, separation, death of a loved one, infertility, or any other individual crisis affected your sexual life? In what ways?
4. Has illness, medication, or the process of aging affected your sexual life? In what ways?
5. What sexual concerns do you have at this time? How have these concerns affected your relationship with your partner?

Sexuality counselors also need to consider past or present sexual abuse and domestic violence when completing a comprehensive sexual history (Rosen & Leiblum, 1989).

In addition, sexuality counselors help couples understand how symptoms affect them at both individual and relational levels (Leiblum & Rosen, 2000). One way of assisting them is to explore the following questions, suggested by Leiblum and Rosen (2000):

> What does having a [sexual dysfunction or problem] mean to the [man]? To [his] partner?
>
> What solution does the problem provide for the couple?
>
> Does he want to [resolve his sexual problem or dysfunction] to satisfy [his] partner or [himself]?
>
> Can [he] communicate directly [with his partner] about [his] sexual preferences? (p. 119)

These questions provide essential information that is helpful in conceptualizing a couple's sexuality problems from both an individual and a relational level. Furthermore, the sexuality counselor is able to obtain the information needed to identify specific features of commonly described male sexual dysfunctions.

COMMONLY DESCRIBED MALE DYSFUNCTIONS

This section will focus on the most commonly diagnosed male sexual dysfunctions and discuss contributing factors and methods for treatment and intervention. Knowledge of these diagnoses is required by the American Association of Sex Educators, Counselors, and Therapists (AASECT), and treatment parameters should be based on the clinician's use of the P-LI-SS-IT model, which was discussed in Chapter 1.

The *DSM-IV-TR* classification of sexual disorders is derived from Masters and Johnson's (1966) four-phase sexual response cycle, later modified by H. S. Kaplan (1979) to include the sexual desire phase (see Figure 7.1).

The *DSM* divides the sexual response cycle into the following phases (APA, 2000):

1. *Desire:* This phase consists of fantasies about sexual activity and the desire to have sexual activity.
2. *Excitement:* This phase consists of a subjective sense of sexual pleasure and accompanying physiological changes. The major changes in the male consist of penile tumescence [the amount of swelling of the penis] and erection.

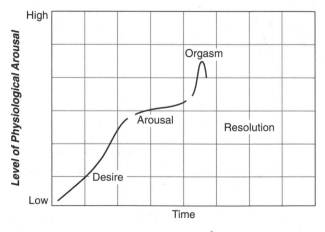

FIGURE 7.1

The Four Phases of the Male Sexual Response Cycle

Source: From *Abnormal Psychology,* 3rd ed., by R. J. Comer, 1998. New York: W. H. Freeman. Adapted with permission.

3. *Orgasm:* This phase consists of a peaking of sexual pleasure, with release of sexual tension and rhythmic contraction of the perineal muscles and reproductive organs. In males, there is the sensation of ejaculatory inevitability, which is followed by the ejaculation of semen. . . . In both genders, the anal sphincter rhythmically contracts.

4. *Resolution:* This phase consists of a sense of muscular relaxation and general well-being. During this phase, males are physiologically refractory to further erection and orgasm for a variable period of time. (p. 536)

Although most male sexual problems occur during the excitement phase of the sexual response cycle, sexual disorders may occur at any one or more of these phases (APA, 2000). In order for sexuality counselors to make an accurate diagnosis, they must consider "such factors as the age and experience of the individual, frequency and chronicity of the symptom, subjective distress, and effect on other areas of functioning" (APA, 2000, p. 536). It is also important for counselors to determine the effect a sexual problem is having on a couple's daily life and to remember that what is considered "normal" for some men and their partners may be considered "abnormal" for others. This is dictated by sociocultural factors (e.g., ethnicity, spirituality) and can "influence sexual desire, expectations, and attitudes about [sexual] performance" (APA, 2000, p. 537).

The next section of this chapter describes male sexual dysfunctions based on the *DSM-IV-TR*, along with factors that contribute to the disorders and ways to diagnose them. Box 7.1 will present treatment interventions at a glance for each phase of the male sexual response cycle as well as interventions for treating pain disorders. It should be noted that both desire and pain disorders (Hypoactive Sexual Desire Disorder, Aversion Disorder, and Dyspareunia) are present in both men and women. They share common characteristics, some contributing factors, and similar treatment interventions for both genders and have been discussed in detail in Chapter 6. The two sections that follow here address additional information pertaining specifically to men.

Desire Disorders

Hypoactive Sexual Desire Disorder/DSM-IV-TR Diagnosis 302.71

The *DSM-IV-TR* describes hypoactive sexual desire disorder as follows:

Hypoactive sexual desire disorder (HSD) is a deficiency or absence of sexual fantasies and desire for sexual activity (Criterion A). The disturbance must cause marked distress or interpersonal difficulty (Criterion B). The dysfunction is not better accounted for by any other Axis I disorder (except another Sexual Dysfunction) and is not due exclusively to the direct physiological effects of a substance (including medications) or general medical condition (Criterion C). (APA, 2000, p. 539)

Although hypoactive desire disorder is common in both men and women, some sexuality counselors consider this disorder to be the primary complaint of men over the age of 50 who seek treatment (Botwin, 1979; Strong & DeVault, 1994).

Let's look at the case of Adam, a retired 55-year-old former CEO of a pharmaceutical company. He complains that since his retirement three months ago he has experienced a significant decrease in his interest in sex and claims that it is impacting his relationship with his wife. According to Adam, she is angry and disappointed and states that he has no time for her and she is feeling distant from him. She tries to explain her situation to Adam: "I thought it would be different when you retired, that we would take trips and spend time together. I thought you would want to be close to me like we were when we were first married." Adam feels guilty and inadequate that he does not seem to have a desire to have sexual intercourse with his wife. In order to help Adam and to make an accurate diagnosis, a sexuality counselor may want to talk to both partners to identify any discrepancies in the couple's sexual desire.

Contributing Factors. Common contributing factors to low sexual desire disorders in both genders are addressed in Chapter 6. Medical conditions such as abnormalities in testosterone and prolactin in men may indicate physiological causes for loss of sexual desire as well (LoPiccolo & Friedman, 1988). It should be noted, however, that low interest in sexual activity in men is often experienced after exhibiting another sexual dysfunction (such as erectile disorder). According to Kolodny, Masters, and Johnson (1979), this may occur as a coping mechanism that protects the individual from the aftermath of unpleasant feelings associated with the diagnosis of a sexual problem. Some men attribute low sexual desire to their aging partners, indicating that if their partner were more youthful, their sex drive would be stronger (LoPiccolo & Friedman, 1988).

BOX 7.1

Treatment Interventions at a Glance

Desire Phase Disorders in Men

DYSFUNCTION	INTERVENTIONS
Male hypoactive sexual desire disorder	Medication adjustment
	Hormonal therapy
	Relationship counseling
	Sensate focus
	Couples' communication skill building (active listening, paraphrasing, "I" messages)
	Psychoeducational training (bibliotherapy, educational information)
	Desensitization
	Masturbation training
	Sexual fantasy
Sexual aversion disorder	Medical/surgical
	Relationship counseling
	Couples' communication skill building
	Sensate focus
	Psychoeducational training
	Masturbation training
	Desensitization
	Cognitive restructuring
	Sensate focus

Arousal Disorders in Men

DYSFUNCTION	INTERVENTIONS
Male erectile disorder	Hormone therapy
	Oral medication
	Relationship counseling
	Couples' communication skill building
	Psychoeducational training
	Relaxation training
	Injection therapy
	Vacuum erection device
	Penile prosthesis
	Vascular surgery
	Sensate focus
	Desensitization
	Sexual fantasy

Orgasm Disorders in Men

DYSFUNCTION	INTERVENTIONS
Male orgasmic disorder (formerly inhibited male orgasm)	Medication adjustment
	Sensate focus
	Relationship counseling
	Couples' communication skill building
	Psychoeducational training
	Relaxation training
	Masturbation training
	Desensitization
	Cognitive skills training

BOX 7.1

Treatment Interventions at a Glance (Continued)

Orgasm Disorders in Men

DYSFUNCTION	*INTERVENTIONS*
Premature ejaculation	Oral medication
	Relationship counseling
	Couples' communication skills training
	Sensate focus
	Psychoeducational training
	Relaxation training
	Desensitization
	Start-stop technique
	Squeeze technique

Pain Disorders in Men

DYSFUNCTION	*INTERVENTIONS*
Dyspareunia	Oral medication
	Surgical
	Use of lubricants
	Relationship counseling
	Couples' communication skill building

Diagnosis. The following *DSM-IV-TR* criteria are used in making this diagnosis:*

**Diagnostic Criteria for
302.71 Hypoactive Sexual Desire Disorder**

A. Persistently or recurrently deficient (or absent) sexual fantasies and desire for sexual activity. The judgment of deficiency or absence is made by the clinician, taking into account factors that affect sexual functioning, such as age and the context of the person's life.

B. The disturbance causes marked distress or interpersonal difficulty.

C. The sexual dysfunction is not better accounted for by another Axis I disorder (except another Sexual Dysfunction) and is not due exclusively to the direct physiological effects of a substance (e.g., a drug of abuse, a medication) or a general medical condition.

Specify type:

Lifelong Type

Acquired Type

Specify type:

Generalized Type

Situational Type

Specify:

Due to Psychological Factors

Due to Combined Factors

A thorough assessment includes ruling out medical factors and taking a complete sexual history. (See Chapter 6 for a more in-depth discussion.)

Treatment. Sexual desire problems in both men and women are considered by many counselors to be the most difficult to treat of all the sexual problems and dysfunctions (Pridal & LoPiccolo, 2000). They require an array of interventions to help couples resolve their issues. Medication adjustments or hormonal therapy may be indicated in some cases, and in others general counseling intervention strategies may be used, including relationship counseling, reducing anxieties with sensate focus activities, improving communication to enhance sexual experiences, and expanding a couple's repertoire of sensual and sexual activities (LoPiccolo & Friedman, 1988). In addition, psychoeducational training, desensitization, self-stimulation

---

*Reprinted with permission from the *Diagnostic and Statistical Manual of Mental Disorders,* Text Revision (p. xxx), Copyright 2000, American Psychiatric Association.

(masturbation training), and the use of sexual fantasy are helpful.

Interventions for Treating Male Hypoactive Sexual Desire Disorder

Masturbation Training.   Masturbation training involves helping a man get to know his body through emotional and physical responses, relaxation, and manual stimulation. As with women, this process is performed alone until a man teaches his partner what he finds pleasurable. Again, it is important for sexuality counselors to be aware that cultural or religious beliefs and values may influence the outcome of this technique and thoughtful exploration of these issues may offer opportunities for success (Kelley, 2004).

Gillan (1987) offers the following guidelines on masturbating techniques:*

1. Using a hand mirror, sit in a comfortable position on the floor or bed that will allow for maximum viewing of your genitalia. Try touching your scrotum gently. Then run your hand up and down your penile shaft. Touch your frenulum.
2. Explore the sensations you find most pleasurable. If you are uncircumcised, try drawing back your foreskin very slightly and then pull it up again to cover your glans. Your glans can be very sensitive, but explore this area [paying attention] to your sensations. If you are circumcised, move the skin covering your penis, squeezing and releasing it to induce accumulated tensions in your glans.
3. Vary the pressure of your touch. You may enjoy grasping yourself firmly, but you may also enjoy stroking areas of your penis very gently. Vary the speed of your movements. Some men like a slow downward movement and a rapid upward movement, others like it the other way around. It is up to you to choose what you personally like.
4. At this stage try to imagine some sexual fantasies as vividly as possible.
5. As you get more excited, stimulate your penis more quickly to a point where you feel you are going to "come" or climax. Then, switch to a mental or actual picture of your partner in the nude and imagine you are making love at the same time you have your orgasm.
6. The next time you try this technique you will be familiar with which areas to stimulate. You may then want to switch to the image or fantasies of your partner at earlier points in time.

7. The last step is to invite your partner to watch you stimulate yourself.
8. If you are not achieving an orgasm or if you are not getting excited, you may want to use a handheld vibrator to assist you. If you feel anxious about these sessions, you may wish to use relaxation techniques to help you overcome your anxiety.

Sexual Fantasy.   The term *sexual fantasy* refers to "*any* mental representation of *any kind* of sexual activity" (Zilbergeld, 1999, p. 79). Such fantasies may be used as interventions to elicit sexual desire and generate sexual arousal (Byrne & Osland, 2000; Pridal & LoPiccolo, 2000). Fantasy is thought of as a precursor to desire serving to arouse interest "about the object [or person desired]" (Everaerd et al., 2000, p. 90). Because many desire problems coexist with arousal disorders, sexual fantasy is encouraged for women and men to prompt both desire and arousal (Byrne & Osland, 2000; Everaerd, Laan, Both, & Van Der Velde, 2000; Pridal & LoPiccolo, 2000).

Common sexual fantasies include having sex with a different partner, same gendered partner, or multiple partners; having sex in an unusual place (e.g., the beach, an elevator, an airplane); or exploring new sexual positions (Kelley, 2004). Romantic or sexually explicit scenarios, erotic literature or movies, books with romantic themes, erotic scenes and pictures, and stories can be used to encourage sexual fantasy (Byrne & Osland, 2000; Zilbergeld, 1999).

For men, sexual fantasies are often impersonal, visual, and active, and they focus on physical characteristics with the purpose of sexual contact (Byrne & Osland, 2000; Kelley, 2004). Women's fantasies tend to be more passive and to focus on romance and sensual touch (Byrne & Osland, 2000).

Sexual Aversion Disorder/DSM-IV-TR Diagnosis 302.79

The *DSM-IV-TR* describes sexual aversion disorder as follows:

> Sexual aversion disorder is the aversion to and active avoidance of genital sexual contact with a sexual partner (Criterion A). The disturbance must cause marked distress or interpersonal difficulty (Criterion B). The dysfunction is not better accounted for by another Axis I disorder (except another Sexual Dysfunction) (Criterion C). (APA, 2000, p. 541).

Sexual aversion disorder involves a fear of sexual intercourse and an intense desire to avoid sexual

---

*From *Sex Therapy Manual* (pp. 260–261), by P. Gillan, 1987, Oxford, England: Blackwell Publishing. Copyright 1987 by Blackwell Publishing. Reprinted with permission.

situations (Masters, Johnson, & Kolodny, 1995). Sexual aversion disorder ranges from significant feelings of discomfort and disgust to extreme irrational fear of sexual activities. Symptoms may include sweating, increased heart rate, nausea, dizziness, trembling, and diarrhea at the thought or sight of anything sexual (Kaplan, 1979; Masters et al., 1995).

Contributing Factors.   Sexual aversion disorders are attributed to a wide variety of factors common to both men and women, as discussed in Chapter 6. In men, this disorder is often related to an aversion to a woman's vagina or genitals (LoPiccolo & Friedman, 1988). For example, a man may avoid sexual contact with his partner because he is repulsed by the outward looks or smell of her vagina. In other cases, he may avoid sex because he experienced a trauma (such as getting blood on his penis during intercourse) that has created a fear of sexual contact (LoPiccolo & Friedman, 1988). His reaction to his partner's body and sexuality can greatly impact the quality of their relationship.

Diagnosis.   The following *DSM-IV-TR* criteria are used in making this diagnosis:*

**Diagnostic Criteria for
302.79 Sexual Aversion Disorder**

A. Persistent or recurrent extreme aversion to, and avoidance of, all (or almost all) genital sexual contact with a sexual partner.
B. The disturbance causes marked distress or interpersonal difficulty.
C. The sexual dysfunction is not better accounted for by another Axis I disorder (except another Sexual Dysfunction).

Specify type:

Lifelong Type

Acquired Type

Specify type:

Situational Type

Generalized Type

Specify:

Due to Psychological Factors

Due to Combined Factors

Before making a diagnosis of sexual aversion disorder, sexuality counselors should pay particular attention to any form of past or present physical, sexual, or emotional abuse; their clients' comfort with their own sexuality; and past problems in sexual experiences (Gold & Gold, 1993; Masters et al., 1995; Pridal & LoPiccolo, 2000).

Treatment.   Treatment for sexual aversion disorder is focused largely on the reduction of fear and anxiety (Gold & Gold, 1993). The use of cognitive restructuring techniques to address issues such as rape, abuse, incest, and sexual myths is recommended (Pridal & LoPiccolo, 2000). Couples' communication and relationship counseling can also be helpful for creating desired changes. In addition, bibliotherapy, masturbation training techniques, desensitization, and sensate focus techniques can be used. Masturbation training was discussed in the previous section under hypoactive sexual desire disorder.

Interventions for Treating Sexual Aversion Disorder

Cognitive Skills Training.   Cognitive skills training helps men overcome illogical beliefs and attitudes that may stem from family background, religious, or cultural beliefs and helps them to develop the belief that sex is a normal part of daily living and is a healthy experience (Fisher, Swingen, & O'Donohue, 1997). An example of an irrational belief in a case of sexual aversion disorder might be as follows: "Sex is a nonemotional and immoral act that degrades women." The sexuality counselor challenges such thinking by asking the client to answer the following questions (Bourne, 2000):

1. What is the evidence for this belief? Looking objectively at all of my life experiences, what is the evidence that this is true?
2. Does this belief *invariably* or *always* hold true for me?
3. Does this belief look at the whole picture? Does it take into account both positive and negative ramifications?
4. Does this belief promote my well-being and/or peace of mind?
5. Did I choose this belief on my own or did it develop out of my experience growing up in my family? (p. 221)

At this point, the client should be ready to replace irrational thinking with a positive affirmation such as the following: "Sex is a healthy, pleasant experience that is shared by two people who care about each other."

---

*Reprinted with permission from the *Diagnostic and Statistical Manual of Mental Disorders*, Text Revision (p. xxx), Copyright 2000, American Psychiatric Association.

Arousal Disorders

Male Erectile Disorder/DSM-IV-TR 302.72

The *DSM-IV-TR* describes male erectile disorder as follows:

> Male Erectile Disorder [previously known as "impotence"] is a persistent or recurrent inability to attain, or to maintain until completion of the sexual activity, an adequate erection (Criterion A). The disturbance must cause marked distress or interpersonal difficulty (Criterion B). The dysfunction is not better accounted for by another Axis I disorder (except another Sexual Dysfunction), and is not due exclusively to the direct physiological effects of a substance (including medications) or a general medical condition (Criterion C). (APA, 2000, p. 545)

Male erectile disorder occurs in the excitement phase of the sexual response cycle and is present in some form in "20 to 30 million men in the United States" (Epperly & Moore, 2000, p. 3,662). It can be divided into two categories: *primary* and *secondary* erectile disorder. The first category refers to men who have never attained an erection sufficiently for intercourse; the second refers to men who have had an erection sufficient for intercourse in the past but are now unable to have an erection (Masters et al., 1995). For example, some men report they have never *attained* an erection. Others have experienced partial erections; however, they lose them or their erection weakens prior to penetration (Masters et al., 1995). Still others are only able to achieve and maintain an erection in certain circumstances. For instance, John states that he oftentimes awakens in the morning with an erection and has no problem maintaining one while masturbating alone. He complains, however, that he is unable to attain and keep his erection when he initiates sexual play with his partner. Carl, on the other hand, reports being able to attain and maintain an erection only while having sexual intercourse outside his committed relationship. These examples demonstrate situational circumstances that influence some men's ability to achieve orgasm.

It should be noted that many men occasionally experience difficulties in having or maintaining an erection. However, when difficulty persists (failure at intercourse occurs 25 percent of the time or more), erectile dysfunction should be considered (Masters & Johnson, 1970). Secondary erectile dysfunctions are more common (Kolodny, Masters, & Johnson, 1979) and less complex to treat. They are usually related to

situational factors such as loss of a job, birth of a child, death of a family member, lack of privacy, work pressures, financial or family stressors, and physical stress (Masters et al., 1995; Young & Long, 1998). For example, Miguel states that he and his wife, Marta, have had serious financial strain since the birth of their second child, at which point Marta decided to stay home to care for their children. He complains that he feels powerless over their financial burdens. Miguel reports that over half of the time he engages in sexual play he is frustrated and fails to maintain an erection sufficiently to please his wife. He is embarrassed about his problem and feels inadequate as a sexual partner.

Contributing Factors. Physical factors that may contribute to erectile dysfunctions include endocrine deficiencies (i.e., low testosterone levels), vascular diseases (i.e., arteriosclerosis), and neurological diseases (i.e., multiple sclerosis, spinal cord injuries, diabetes, renal failure) (Coleman, 1998; Kaplan, 1974; Wincze & Carey, 2001). In addition, the physiological effects of stress and fatigue, medications, alcohol, and narcotics can cause male erectile disorder (Coleman, 1998; Kaplan, 1974; Masters & Johnson, 1970).

Psychological factors can also impact erectile problems. Feelings of guilt, anxiety, shame, fear, depression, resentment, hostility, and doubt evoked during sexual arousal can affect a man's ability to achieve sexual satisfaction (LoPiccolo, 1978). For many men, the sexual act is viewed as an evaluation of performance. This evaluation places men in the position of succeeding or failing, which means that a responsibility to perform can become unmanageable (Masters & Johnson, 1970).

Men may also experience and maintain erectile problems due to "interfering thoughts that precede and/or occur during sexual relations" (Wincze & Carey, 2001, p. 144). These may include being "preoccupied with worries about firmness of his erection; images of his partner being disappointed, angry, or even ridiculing; and distinct feelings of anxiety, embarrassment, and depression" (Wincze & Carey, 2001, p. 144). In the case of Miguel and Marta, Miguel has persistent thoughts that he is an inadequate provider and sexual partner. Such thinking interferes with his ability to maintain an erection.

Erectile dysfunction can also have its roots in a couple's relationship. According to this perspective, interactions between partners affect men's ability to attain or maintain an erection (Kaplan, 1974). For example, if a man is feeling humiliated or critiqued by his partner and the couple has been caught in a cycle of putting each other down verbally while arguing, erectile problems may result.

Finally, sexual arousal problems may be due to "inadequate stimulation, myths, and misinformation" (Charlton & Brigel, 1997, p. 239). Regardless of the origin of this difficulty, erectile difficulties deeply affect a man's self-image.

Diagnosis.   The following *DSM-IV-TR* criteria are used in making this diagnosis:*

Diagnostic Criteria for 302.72 Male Erectile Disorder

A. Persistent or recurrent inability to attain, or to maintain until completion of the sexual activity, an adequate erection.
B. The disturbance causes marked distress or interpersonal difficulty.
C. The erectile dysfunction is not better accounted for by another Axis I disorder (other than a Sexual Dysfunction) and is not due exclusively to the direct physiological effects of a substance (e.g., a drug of abuse, a medication) or a general medical condition.

Specify type:

Lifelong Type

Acquired Type

Specify type:

Generalized Type

Situational Type

Specify:

Due to Psychological Factors

Due to Combined Factors

When sexuality counselors are making a diagnosis of male erectile disorder, it is important that they rule out physical and psychological contributing factors by referring clients to their physician for a complete medical or urological examination. After the physician gathers a detailed medical history, a course of treatment will be determined. In addition, obtaining a thorough sexual history will help the sexuality counselor "differentiate between [a] true erectile [disorder], changes in sexual desire, and orgasmic and ejaculatory [problems]" (Gill, 1997, p. 115). It is imperative that sexuality counselors and physicians

work together to achieve success when treating erectile disorders.

Treatment.   Treatment for erectile dysfunctions may involve a variety of techniques, including cognitive skills training and sensate focus (Gagnon, Rosen, & Leiblum, 1982; Masters & Johnson, 1970). Cognitive skills training focuses on helping men to replace interfering beliefs about being able to achieve an erection with more functional thoughts. Likewise, the goal of sensate focus is to assist the man in altering his belief about the possibility of losing his erection and his erection not returning (Masters et al., 1995).

Treatment may also include couples' counseling, which incorporates communication skills training, psychoeducational training, and relaxation techniques. In addition, behavioral techniques such as desensitization training may be used for prolonged erection problems (Althof, 2000). Medical interventions include the use of oral medication, hormone therapy (due to low testosterone levels), injection therapy, a vacuum erection device, and a penile prosthesis (Coleman, 1998). The use of sexual fantasy may also be used to increase sexual arousal. Sensate focus techniques specific to male erectile disorders, systematic desensitization, and medical interventions are discussed in the next section.

Interventions for Treating Erectile Dysfunction

Sensate Focus.   According to Masters and Johnson (1970), there are three goals for treating erectile dysfunction: "First, to remove the [man's] fears for sexual performance; second, to reorient his involuntary behavioral patterning so that he becomes an active participant, far removed from his accustomed spectator's role; and third, to relieve [the woman's] fears for her [partner's] sexual performance" (p. 196). In other words, men need to learn to worry less about their sexual performance and allow themselves to become part of a broader sexual experience. Their partners must in turn become less apprehensive about their mates' ability to achieve an erection. These goals focus on eliminating men's anxieties and creating experiences for men to achieve some success in attaining an erection. This helps to build confidence and reduce fear of performance. One way of helping couples achieve these goals is to teach them sensate focus.

According to Kaplan (1974) treatment begins by instructing couples to abstain from sexual intercourse. Several days later they may begin to engage in nondemanding caressing through the use of sensate

---

*Reprinted with permission from the *Diagnostic and Statistical Manual of Mental Disorders,* Text Revision (p. xxx), Copyright 2000, American Psychiatric Association.

focus techniques. Couples learn to give and receive pleasure in a relaxed atmosphere away from the demands of performance. While it is important to focus on what is pleasurable to each partner and to spend time touching each other, Kaplan (1974) emphasizes that the man keep his focus on his own erotic pleasures, free from worries about his partner's experience. Although erection is not the goal of this activity (LoPiccolo, 1978; Masters & Johnson, 1970), this nondemanding pleasing often produces a spontaneous erection in men (Kaplan, 1974). In other words, sensate focus activities serve to alleviate anxiety and obsessive thoughts that may have interfered with a man's ability to perform.

When anxiety has subsided and both partners are comfortable with exploring and giving pleasure to each other, the next step can be initiated. In this phase, couples focus on genital stimulation (Kaplan, 1974). This involves oral or manual pleasuring, or both. Once an erection is achieved, all stimulation should subside, returning the penis to its flaccid state. It is important to remember that one of the goals of the sensate focus activity in treating erectile dysfunction is to help alter a man's belief about his erection being lost and not returning (Masters et al., 1995). When his erection has completely subsided, his partner can begin the process again.

The final phase of sensate focus involves penile penetration into the vagina (Kaplan, 1974). For this step, couples begin with sensate focus and genital stimulation. Once an erection has occurred, the woman assumes a female-superior position and guides the man's penis into her vagina. She lowers herself onto his penis slowly moving up and down to continue stimulation. Prior to ejaculation the couple disengages (Kaplan, 1974). Eventually, the man may continue to thrust until he reaches orgasm (Kaplan, 1974; LoPiccolo, 1978; Masters & Johnson, 1970).

Systematic Desensitization. Systematic desensitization is the most common behavioral treatment for erectile dysfunction (Althof, 2000). This technique is used to help men decrease their anxiety and fear about being able to attain and maintain an erection. This is accomplished by assisting clients to construct a hierarchy of sexual situations that provoke a progressive increase in anxiety and helping them learn to gradually approach these situations through a sequence of steps. (See Chapter 6, which discusses the steps in constructing a hierarchy.) Once clients are able to manage their anxiety effectively in the first

scene, they can continue up through the hierarchy. In this way, clients learn to pair pleasurable feelings with anxiety-provoking sexual situations (Althof, 2000). The sexuality counselor might suggest the following progression up through a hierarchy:

1. Imagine yourself in a situation where you desire to have an erection (with your partner or by self-stimulation).
2. View sexually stimulating material such as a Victoria's Secret catalog or the swimsuit edition of *Sports Illustrated* magazine.
3. Have a conversation with your sexual partner about being sexually intimate.
4. View sexually stimulating material (magazines or videos) with your partner.
5. Engage in masturbation alone while viewing sexually stimulating material. It is important that you place no expectation on yourself to have an erection.
6. Engage in masturbation alone, but this time allow yourself to attain an erection.
7. Engage in sensate focus exercises (see Chapter 6) with your partner with no expectation of having an erection.
8. Engage in sensate focus activities again, allowing your partner to stimulate your penis with a lubricant with the desired goal of attaining an erection.
9. Engage in intercourse with your partner, allowing yourself to attain and maintain a full erection.

Medical Interventions. When behavioral and cognitive strategies fail to restore potency, the sexuality counselor may suggest that the client consider one of the following solutions (Coleman, 1998):

1. *Oral medication:* Oral medications include yohimbine, apomorphine, phentolamine, trazodone, and most recently the use of Viagra (sildenafil citrate), Levitra (vardenafil), and Cialis (tadalafil) (Strong, DeVault, Sayad, & Yarber, 2005). These medications are used to increase blood flow to the penis. It is important to encourage men to explore the effect of medication intervention on their relationship with their partner. Some partners may be unsupportive of such interventions or feel pressured themselves to respond to their partners revitalized sexual desires furthering relational problems. Ideally, medication interventions should be considered in conjunction with counseling (Strong et al., 2005).

2. *Injection therapy:* Injections of one or more drugs such as papaverine, phentolamine, and prostaglandin-E1 can be self-administered into the penis to increase blood flow. This takes place prior to the sexual encounter and works by opening up the arteriolar spaces, allowing blood to flow into the penis. This treatment option is the most successful with men who experience organic erectile disorder.

3. *Vacuum erection device:* This treatment option involves slipping a hollow, plastic cylinder over a flaccid penis. The man then attaches a hand pump to draw air out of the cylinder, creating a vacuum that draws blood into his penis. When his penis becomes erect, he slips an elastic ring over the cylinder on to the base of his penis and removes the cylinder. The ring keeps blood flowing outward, allowing intercourse.

4. *Penile implants (prosthesis):* If other treatments are not successful, penile implants, which are inserted surgically and are composed of malleable rods and inflatable cylinders, can be used.

5. *Vascular surgery:* This treatment option is offered to men who experience erectile disorder as a result of vascular trauma or arteriosclerosis. Surgical procedures eliminate the need for injections, penile implants, or the use of a vacuum device.

Couples' counseling is also beneficial in treating erectile disorders. Discussing anxieties with a partner and receiving support can greatly enhance relationships. Also, such counseling helps couples resolve issues related to the dysfunction, such as power and control struggles between partners, unresolved anger, and communication difficulties stemming from situational factors.

Orgasmic Disorders

Male Orgasmic Disorder (Formerly Inhibited Male Orgasm)/DSM-IV-TR Diagnosis 302.73

The *DSM-IV-TR* describes male orgasmic disorder as follows:

> Male Orgasmic Disorder [formerly Inhibited Male Orgasm] is a persistent or recurrent delay in, or absence of, orgasm following a normal sexual excitement phase. In judging whether the orgasm is delayed, the [sexuality counselor] should take into account the person's age, and whether the stimulation provided is adequate in focus, intensity, and duration (Criterion A). The disturbance must cause marked distress or interpersonal difficulty (Criterion B). The orgasmic dysfunction is not better accounted for by another Axis I disorder (except another Sexual Dysfunction) and is not due exclusively to the direct physiological effects of a substance (including medications) or a general medical condition (Criterion C) (p. 550).

Male orgasmic disorder encompasses men who have never been able to ejaculate intravaginally during intercourse as well as men who have been able to ejaculate in the vagina while engaged in intercourse but are now unable to do so (Masters et al., 1995). In both of these cases, men typically are able to ejaculate by partner stimulation or by masturbating alone (Masters et al., 1995). There are few documented cases of men who have been unable to reach orgasm, even through masturbation (Kaplan, 1974). In addition, a more common form of male orgasmic disorder occurs when a man is able to ejaculate only by prolonged stimulation (Masters et al., 1995). For example, Jacob is 35 years old and in his second year in medical school. He has just begun a new relationship with Gina, but he is frustrated because it takes him a long time to reach orgasm and ejaculate. He reports that as a young boy of seven he was burned on both of his thighs, an incident that left him significantly scarred and makes him uncomfortable showing his body to Gina. Jacob states that he is able to become erect every time they have intercourse, but it takes him a long time to have an orgasm. Frustrated and angry, he says that his body "doesn't work right." He also offers that Gina has shared that she feels less fulfilled because she cannot bring him to orgasm earlier in their lovemaking.

Contributing Factors. Although rare, physical conditions involving "central nervous system damage from a stroke, brain tumor, or spinal cord injury or [a] neurological disease such as multiple sclerosis [can] actually prevent men from reaching an orgasm" (Schover, 2000, p. 406). In addition, a variety of drugs, including psychotropic medications, have been related to this disorder (Schover, 2000; Wincze & Carey, 2001). Diabetes, uremia, Parkinson's disease, and alcoholism can also interfere with orgasm (Kelly, 1996; Schover, 2000).

Psychological factors that contribute to male orgasmic disorder stem from guilt about sexual activities, conflict with a partner, ambivalence about commitment to a relationship, fear of a partner getting pregnant, or dislike of one's partner (Wincze & Carey, 2001). In addition, resentment, anger, and mistrust of one's partner can create ejaculatory problems (Masters & Johnson, 1970). Feelings of anxiety related to sexual performance about ejaculating can also contribute to this disorder (Masters & Johnson, 1970).

One theory about men who experience this orgasmic disorder is that they are "so focused on their partner's pleasure, or have so many conflicting feelings about sexual pleasure, they have what we might call a 'numb' erection" (Kelly, 1996, p. 566). In other words, they do not experience sexual arousal associated with orgasm, even though they are able to maintain an erection (Garippa, 1994). In these cases, a man's delay in orgasm has to do with his increased focus on his partner and away from his own excitement (Wincze & Carey, 2001).

Infertility may also be related to orgasmic problems when partners want to try to conceive a child (Schover, 2000). This disorder can thus prevent men from engaging intimately with their partners.

Diagnosis. The following *DSM-IV-TR* criteria are used in making this diagnosis:*

**Diagnostic Criteria for
302.74 Male Orgasmic Disorder**

A. Persistent or recurrent delay in, or absence of, orgasm following a normal sexual excitement phase during sexual activity that the clinician, taking into account the person's age, judges to be adequate in focus, intensity, and duration.

B. The disturbance causes marked distress or interpersonal difficulty.

C. The orgasmic dysfunction is not better accounted for by another Axis I disorder (except another Sexual Dysfunction) and is not due exclusively to the direct physiological effects of a substance (e.g., a drug of abuse, a medication) or a general medical condition.

Specify type:

Lifelong Type

Acquired Type

Specify type:

Generalized Type

Situational Type

Specify:

Due to Psychological Factors

Due to Combined Factors

Treatment. A behavioral approach using sensate focus is generally used in the treatment of male orgasmic disorder with the goal of intervaginal ejaculation (Masters & Johnson, 1970). Other interventions include medication adjustments, relaxation, educational and sexual technique development, masturbation training, desensitization, and cognitive skills training to reduce anxiety (Masters & Johnson, 1970; Fisher et al., 1997). In addition, couples' counseling with emphasis on communication skill building can be helpful in building trust and reducing anger toward one's partner when the relationship contributes to ejaculatory control (Masters & Johnson, 1970).

Premature Ejaculation/DSM-IV-TR Diagnosis 302.75

The *DSM-IV-TR* describes premature ejaculation as follows:

Premature ejaculation is the persistent or recurrent onset of orgasm and ejaculation with minimal sexual stimulation before, on, or shortly after penetration and before the person wishes it (Criterion A). . . . The majority of males with this disorder can delay orgasm during self-masturbation for a considerably longer time than during coitus. . . . The disturbance must cause marked distress or interpersonal difficulty (Criterion B). The premature ejaculation is not due exclusively to the direct effects of a substance (e.g., withdrawal from opioids) (Criterion C). (p. 552)

This disorder is the most common male sexual disorder; however, it is often of most concern to women (Kaplan, 1974; Masters & Johnson, 1970; Masters et al., 1986; Polonsky, 2000). In these instances, women become highly frustrated due to sexual tensions elevated by foreplay that result in an unfulfilled orgasm (Masters & Johnson, 1970).

Contributing Factors. Premature ejaculation is rarely caused by organic factors (Masters & Johnson, 1970). Most often, "past experiences are likely to contribute to a pattern of rapid ejaculation stemming from striving to reach orgasm too quickly to alleviate anxiety or to demonstrate sexual prowess" (Crooks & Baur, 1990, p. 566). Power struggles, sexual performance anxiety, depression, unresolved anger, or low self-esteem may also affect ejaculatory control (McCarthy, 1989; Masters & Johnson, 1970; Polonsky, 2000). In some cases,

---

*Reprinted with permission from the *Diagnostic and Statistical Manual of Mental Disorders,* Text Revision (p. xxx), Copyright 2000, American Psychiatric Association.

premature ejaculation is situational, influenced by external stressors such as family pressures, life crises, or work stress (Polonsky, 2000).

Diagnosis. The following *DSM-IV-TR* criteria are used in making this diagnosis:*

Diagnostic Criteria for 302.75 Premature Ejaculation

A. Persistent or recurrent ejaculation with minimal sexual stimulation before, on, or shortly after penetration and before the person wishes it. The clinician must take into account factors that affect duration of the excitement phase, such as age, novelty of the sexual partner or situation, and recent frequency of sexual activity.
B. The disturbance causes marked distress or interpersonal difficulty.
C. The premature ejaculation is not due exclusively to the direct effects of a substance (e.g., withdrawal from opioids).

Specify type:

Lifelong Type

Acquired Type

Specify type:

Generalized Type

Situational Type

Specify:

Due to Psychological Factors

Due to Combined Factors

It is important to recognize that rapid ejaculation is not a distressing problem for all men. For some men, however, lack of ejaculatory control is intensified by a fear of sexual performance and can eventually manifest itself as an erectile dysfunction (Masters et al., 1995).

Treatment. Treatment for premature ejaculation may involve a variety of techniques aimed at helping a man learn ejaculatory control (Polonsky, 2000). This may be attained with or without a partner involved. Treatment may include the use of education and support, cognitive skills training, practicing relaxation, sensate focus exercises, increasing the effectiveness of couples' communication by skill building techniques, and in some cases the use of medication

(Kaplan, 1974; Masters et al., 1986, 1995; Masters & Johnson, 1970; Polonsky, 2000). Systematic desensitization techniques are also helpful for men who experience ejaculatory problems due to performance anxiety or fear associated with loss of control (Hogan, 1978; Wolpe, 1958). In addition, simple ejaculatory control exercises such as the start-stop technique and the squeeze technique are commonly used to assist men and their partners to increase sexual pleasure (Masters & Johnson, 1970; Semans, 1956).

Interventions for Treating Premature Ejaculation
The Start-Stop Technique. The start-stop technique was developed by urologist James Semans in 1956 as a way for men to sustain pre-ejaculatory sensations. Semans believed that "premature ejaculation stemmed from a man's lack of awareness of the neuromuscular sensations that precede orgasm and ejaculation" and that men who ejaculated rapidly had not learned to recognize this sensation and bring it under control (Crooks & Baur, 1996, p. 460). According to Semans (1956), couples wanting to practice this exercise should engage in mutual manual and/or oral stimulation of the penis and clitoris. Once a man begins to feel that he is about to have an orgasm, he tells his partner to stop stimulating him until he feels the climax subside. After a short delay, couples repeat this method of interrupting the man's ejaculatory response. Once a couple feels comfortable with this technique, they are instructed to lubricate the penis and repeat the procedure. Semans (1956) suggests that "ejaculation can eventually be postponed indefinitely" (p. 354). Each time the couple practices this technique, they follow the same start-stop sequence eventually allowing for ejaculation to occur.

The Squeeze Technique. Masters and Johnson (1970) modified the start-stop technique into what they called the "squeeze technique" (see Figure 7.2). Instead of simply stopping stimulation prior to ejaculation, a man's partner squeezes his penis with her thumb and forefinger "just above and below the coronal ridge" for 3 to 4 seconds and then releases the pressure, causing him to lose the urge to ejaculate (Masters et al., 1986, p. 493). After 15 to 30 seconds of inactivity, his partner begins to stimulate him again, and just before he ejaculates, squeezes him again. After the couple uses this technique for 15 to 20 minutes, the man ejaculates. Once he gains confidence in his ability to control himself, his partner assumes the top position and inserts his penis making slow movements (Masters & Johnson, 1970; Masters et al., 1986, 1995).

---

*Reprinted with permission from the *Diagnostic and Statistical Manual of Mental Disorders,* Text Revision (p. xxx), Copyright 2000, American Psychiatric Association.

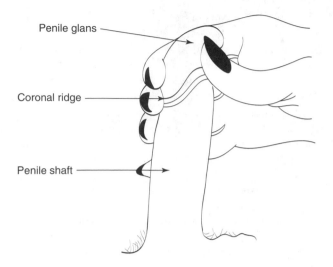

Penile glans

Coronal ridge

Penile shaft

FIGURE 7.2

Premature Ejaculation and the Squeeze Technique

Source: From *Sex Therapy Manual* (p. 286), by P. Gillan, 1987, Oxford, England: Blackwell Publishing. Copyright 1987 by Blackwell Publishing. Reprinted with permission.

Sexuality counselors can suggest the following step-by-step instructions to couples who are learning this technique (adapted from Gillan, 1987):*

1. Begin by general relaxation and follow the sensate focus technique up to phase 2. (See sensate focus in Chapter 6.)
2. Relax and enjoy your partner touching and playing with your penis manually until it becomes erect. Your partner can then use the *squeeze* technique by holding your penis firmly between her thumb and two fingers. Some women find that they cannot exert enough pressure with one hand and have to use both hands (thumb on top of thumb and fingers on top of fingers). The thumb should be placed on the frenulum, and the two fingers on either side of the ridge where the glans meet the shaft of the penis, opposite the thumb. Then, have your partner squeeze really hard for 3 to 4 seconds. Do not be afraid that this will cause pain. The squeeze will make you lose the urge to ejaculate and lose part of your erection. Then after 15 to 30 seconds, have your partner stimulate your penis again, and once again apply the squeeze technique. You can repeat this procedure

several times, and enjoy 15 to 20 minutes of sex play after which you can ejaculate. Your partner can vary the squeeze technique by stimulating your penis orally, using the fingers and the thumb to squeeze as before.

3. Once you and your partner are successful, try getting into another position. Use the following as a guideline:
   A. *Woman:* Kneel or sit astride your partner and mount him in this kneeling position, with your knees placed approximately in line with his nipples and parallel to his trunk.
   B. *Man:* Lie flat on your back and allow your partner to come down on you and insert your penis inside her; she will do this for you, so you won't have to fumble around looking for her vagina.

Neither of you should move after penetration. You should let her know when you think you are going to have an orgasm and then she can raise herself, slowly and gently, and apply the "squeeze technique" and then remount. This can be repeated several times. This stage is often quite tricky, as ejaculation can occur when the female partner raises herself. The secret is practice and good communication.

4. Now that you and your partner are beginning to experience success in a new position (by learning to control your sexual excitement when you are inside your partner), proceed with the following guidelines:
   A. *Man:* Begin to thrust slowly and while maintaining your erection. If you feel you might lose control at any time, you can ask your partner to squeeze you.
   B. *Woman:* When your partner is gently thrusting, be prepared to pull out gently and squeeze hard. Then try making some slow pelvic thrusts yourself, still being alert for signs of his becoming overaroused; if he does, apply the squeeze technique.
5. Practice the squeeze technique each time you have intercourse, at least two or three times before penetration. Once you have finished treatment, continue to enjoy the squeeze technique at least once a week for six months following treatment. During menstruation, if you do not want to have intercourse, take advantage of having a session of 15 to 20 minutes devoted specifically to manual stimulation of the male with the squeeze technique applied several times.

*Adapted from *Sex Therapy Manual* (pp. 286–287), by P. Gillan, 1987, Oxford, England: Blackwell Publishing. Copyright 1987 by Blackwell Publishing. Reprinted with permission.

It is important to keep in mind that some men may prefer to practice ejaculatory control methods alone. In this way they can experience mastery before involving their partner. This may help lessen their anxiety about performance. In these instances, the squeeze and the start-stop techniques are easily modified by performing the technique in private. Once he has mastered the techniques with a dry hand, he can add the use of a lubricant to simulate the vagina. Polonsky (2000) offers a series of exercises for clients wanting to learn ejaculatory control with or without a partner involved.

Medication. The use of selective serotonin reuptake inhibitors (SSRIs) have been reported effective in helping men to increase ejaculatory control (Polonsky, 2000). In addition, Viagra has provided some promising results in limited clinical reports; however, no conclusive evidence can be drawn. Clients considering the use of medication should consult their physician.

Sexual Pain Disorders

Dyspareunia/DSM-IV-TR *302.76*

The *DSM-IV-TR* describes dyspareunia as follows:

> Dyspareunia is genital pain that is associated with sexual intercourse (Criterion A). . . . The disorder can occur in both males and females. . . . The intensity of symptoms range from mild discomfort to sharp pain. The disturbance must cause marked distress or interpersonal difficulty (Criterion B). The disturbance is not caused exclusively . . . by lack of lubrication, is not better accounted for by another Axis I disorder (except for another Sexual Dysfunction), and is not due exclusively to the direct physiological effects of a substance (e.g., a drug of abuse, a medication) or a general medical condition (Criterion C). (p. 554)

For men, discomfort can occur in the penis and testes as well as internally (Masters & Johnson, 1970). Individuals with this disorder have significant pain during or after intercourse, making the experience extremely unpleasant (Kaplan, 1983; Masters & Johnson, 1970).

Contributing Factors. Dyspareunia in men is less common than in women, but it does occur (Masters & Johnson, 1970). It is often attributed to "inflammation or infection of the penis, the foreskin, the testes, the urethra, or the prostate" (Masters et al., 1995, p. 589). In addition, Peyronie's disease (a condition that distorts the shape of the penis) and some dermatological lesions can contribute to pain during intercourse (Masters & Johnson, 1970; Reckler, 1983).

Occasionally, if the foreskin of an uncircumcised penis is too tight, continual infections are likely to occur, resulting in discomfort (Masters & Johnson, 1970). If proper hygiene (washing the penis with soap and water) does not alleviate a man's symptoms, circumcision may be indicated (Masters & Johnson, 1970).

In gay couples, pain "may be caused by improper lubrication of the anal meatus or because of anal sphincter contractions (similar to vaginismus in women)" (Everaerd et al., 2000, pp. 90–91). Contractions of this kind often indicate "anxiety or fear of pain" and should be addressed by the sexuality counselor (Everaerd et al., 2000, p. 91).

Diagnosis. The following *DSM-IV-TR* criteria are used in making this diagnosis:*

Diagnostic Criteria for 302.76 Dyspareunia

A. Recurrent or persistent genital pain associated with sexual intercourse in either a male or a female.
B. The disturbance causes marked distress or interpersonal difficulty.
C. The disturbance is not caused exclusively by Vaginismus or lack of lubrication, is not better accounted for by another Axis I disorder (except another Sexual Dysfunction), and is not due exclusively to the direct physiological effects of a substance (e.g., a drug of abuse, a medication) or a general medical condition.

Specify type:

Lifelong Type
Acquired Type

Specify type:

Generalized Type
Situational Type

Specify:

Due to Psychological Factors
Due to Combined Factors

Treatment. For men, treating dyspareunia can involve oral medication, minor surgery, proper care and cleaning of the penis, sufficient lubrication, couples' communication, and proper medical attention (Masters & Johnson, 1970). It is important that sexuality counselors refer clients for a medical evaluation before beginning treatment for this disorder as it is often associated with problems requiring medical intervention.

---

*Reprinted with permission from the *Diagnostic and Statistical Manual of Mental Disorders,* Text Revision (p. xxx), Copyright 2000, American Psychiatric Association.

INFERTILITY AND ITS EFFECTS ON SEXUAL DYSFUNCTIONS AND PROBLEMS

The crisis of infertility has been referred to as a "silent sorrow" because it is often an isolating and misunderstood experience affecting all aspects of a couple's life. Although couples experience similar reactions to this crisis, it has been found that gender plays a role in the way individuals cope (Abbey, Andrews, & Halman, 1991; Daniluk, 1997; Gibson & Meyers, 2000). For example, many men withdraw from their partners, friends, and family, unable to express their concerns and fears throughout the infertility process (Cooper-Hilbert, 1998). They may become so focused on their partner's pain and distress that denial and distancing become a way of coping through this crisis (Abbey et al., 1991). These unexpressed feelings can become barriers to the couple's relationship, leading to feelings of resentment, guilt, anger, depression, or sexual problems. For these men, the experience of infertility can be an isolating and lonely process.

As discussed in Chapter 6, infertility is associated with a wide range of physical, psychological, and environmental factors. In men, physical causes may include low sperm count as well as anatomical, genetic, and immune system problems (Metzger, 1998). Psychological reactions to infertility in men mirror those of women and include denial, grief, helplessness, anger, anxiety, and guilt (Cooper-Hilbert, 1998). What is different, however, is the frequency, intensity, and duration of these feelings and the fact that they may fluctuate (Cooper-Hilbert, 1998; Daniluk, 1997). Finally, environmental stressors such as work, family pressures, and gender role expectations all contribute to creating sexual pressures for men.

Sexuality counselors can help men to address the complex issues surrounding the infertility process as well as communicate their sexual concerns to their partner. The integrative couples' model allows couples to explore solutions to their sexual problems while taking into account the myriad issues that can affect their relationship.

Case Example

Jason, aged 27, and Mariah, aged 25, have been married for two years. They seek counseling due to recent frustrations during sexual intercourse. Mariah reports feeling upset with Jason because he rushes their sexual lovemaking. She states

she wants to spend more time slowing down and enjoying sex. She is hurt and blames Jason for being self-centered. In addition, she complains that Jason does not have time for her and is "married to his job." Jason reports that he is unable to "hold out" for Mariah, and he is feeling pressured by her expression of frustration for him to perform. Feeling anxious, he states that he can please her in other ways by stimulating her to orgasm. He also states that he is baffled by his recent difficulty of ejaculating too quickly. Unfortunately, the more he tries to "hold out," the worse the problem gets. Jason offers that he has recently changed jobs and has accepted a position as head nurse in a critical care unit. He reports feeling anxiety over his new responsibilities and unsure of his ability to perform them. In addition, he is often "on-call" for emergencies at work and is tired and stressed.

Application of the Five Stages of the Integrative Couples' Model

Stage 1: Assessing and Obtaining an Interactional View of the Problem

Jason believes that his inability to "hold out" has to do with Mariah's pressuring him in their lovemaking, but he believes he is able to please her in other ways. He feels anxious about not being able to perform sexually and is angry that Mariah is so critical of him. Mariah blames Jason for "coming too soon," stating that he is only interested in pleasing himself and does not care about her feelings and sexual satisfaction.

After obtaining a historical view of the problem and taking a sexual and relational history, the sexuality counselor makes a *DSM-IV-TR* diagnosis of Premature Ejaculation (302.75) for Jason. Their problem is redefined in interactional terms by stating, "It sounds like the two of you want to feel more connected to each other and would like to explore different ways of being able to spend more time pleasing each other sexually so that you enjoy intimate time together."

Stage 2: Goal Setting

With the assistance of their counselor, Jason and Mariah set three goals in both behavioral and affective terms:

1. We would like to learn how to communicate positive sexual feelings and clear sexual

needs in order to feel more connected to each other.

2. We want to help each other feel less pressured to perform sexually and feel more relaxed with each other, then we will take more time for foreplay and we will learn new sexual techniques.

3. We want to spend more time together going out on dates and planning fun activities together in order to feel some renewed excitement in our relationship.

Stage 3: Adapting New Perceptions and Behaviors
During this stage, Jason's ability to connect with his patients at work through the use of humor and creative play are brought to light. Mariah's compassion for others as a social worker, along with her ability to exhibit patience with others, is emphasized. They are able to identify prior times in their relationship when they felt carefree and spent more time giving each other body massages and caressing each other before sexual intercourse. They also recall having "play time" together in the evenings and on the weekends when they would go to a movie, go to dinner, or just "kick back" and take a nap together.

The sexuality counselor devises interventions that mobilize these assets and begins to change the relational system.

1. They will write love letters to each other twice a week to practice communicating their feelings and intimate concerns in order to feel more emotionally connected.

2. They will massage each other once a week with no expectation of intercourse. This activity will create more relaxed feelings for their intimate time together.

3. They will participate in a sensate focus program and learn the squeeze technique. They will practice this technique while communicating to each other what feels good and is pleasurable to them.

4. They will take turns each week planning dates that include carefree relaxation time as a way of creating emotional connectedness.

Stage 4: Maintaining Perceptions and Behaviors
Jason and Mariah acknowledge that in order to maintain success, they must make time for their lovemaking and communicate with each other regularly. They are aware of how easily they can slip back into old patterns by not taking time for sexual play and keeping feelings to themselves. They recognize that failing to practice the squeeze technique and sensate focus activities can be a roadblock to their progress. In order to remedy this, they have made a plan to continue writing love letters once a week and will also request a weekly massage from each other. In addition, they have agreed to dispense with beepers and turn off the phone while having "sexual/intimate couple time together." They have also decided to continue taking turns with "date planning" each week.

Stage 5: Validating New Perceptions and Behaviors
Jason reminds Mariah of how much he loves her and wants to feel close to her. The couple agrees to continue to find ways to be playful in their relationship, find time for sexual intimacy, and communicate about events in their daily lives. They agree to plan one long weekend every six weeks to "get away" by themselves and enjoy each other's company. Jason and Mariah have new ideas about themselves as a couple. They now see themselves as caring and playful, and they are more attuned to each other's needs. They remind each other of their individual strengths and their strengths as a couple as reflected in their love letters.

SUMMARY

As men's roles continue to change, so have the attitudes, beliefs, and practices that surround male sexuality. The traditional male role defined men as competent workers and providers, emotionally controlled and stoic, and sexual aggressors and educators of the female. This tra-ditional role has been replaced over the last two decades by the men's movement. Many men are struggling to communicate their thoughts, feelings, issues, and dilemmas in a changing world, and they are longing for more intimate relationships with their partners.

Emerging roles and relational needs have led to conflict and anger with traditional male stereotypes often imparting sexual difficulties with one's partner. Both biological and environmental factors lead to distress in a relationship. These may include alcohol and drug usage, diseases, medications, and anatomical or genetic problems. Also, job stress, death of a loved one, family illness, birth of a child, economic worries, and gender role expectations create distress. In addition, cultural and developmental issues as well as family-of-origin influences all play a critical part in determining whether a man is experiencing a sexual problem or dysfunction.

When evaluating men's sexual concerns, it is important for sexuality counselors to take a thorough sexual history, including beliefs, attitudes, and cultural issues that can contribute to sexual problems. A medical examination should be a part of this process. In addition, sexuality counselors need to be familiar with male sexual dysfunctions and their treatment in order to help resolve problems. Sexuality counselors treat male sexual problems based on their level of training and expertise. According to AASECT standards, counselors are required to obtain advanced information and training on all *DSM-IV-TR* diagnoses of psychosexual disorders in order to provide effective and ethical treatment.

Psychosexual disorders fall into four major categories: (a) desire disorders (hypoactive, aversion), (b) arousal disorders (male erectile disorder), (c) orgasm disorders (male orgasmic disorder, premature ejaculation), and (d) sexual pain disorders (dyspareunia). Treatment strategies encompass a wide variety of interventions common to both genders as well as specific interventions appropriate for each stage of the male sexual response cycle.

Infertility is also a significant problem for many couples and can contribute to sexual problems. The complexity of issues that surround this crisis impact men and women differently, affecting their emotional states and hindering sexual functioning.

An integrative couples' model assists men and their partners to work together, to establish a nonblaming interactional view of the problem, to set realistic goals, to adapt to new perceptions about each other and their sexual issues, and to work to maintain behaviors that promote healthy coping strategies and effective communication skills for future problem solving.

SEXUALLY TRANSMITTED INFECTIONS AND DISEASES

KEY CONCEPTS

- Sexually transmitted infections and diseases (STIs and STDs) are increasing in epidemic proportions and affect approximately 15 million people each year.
- Individuals and their partners are often hesitant to seek medical attention or ask for counseling due to stigmas attached to STIs.
- Sexuality counselors should be familiar with the transmission and symptoms of common STIs and their medical and relational treatment interventions.
- Commonly described sexually transmitted infections/disease include but are not limited to bacterial vaginosis (BV), chlamydial infections, gonorrhea, syphilis, genital warts (HPV), herpes, viral hepatitis, HIV infection and AIDS, and trichomoniasis.
- Assessment of STIs is performed by a medical doctor and involves a physical examination and screening for STIs.
- Sexuality counselors help couples address sexual and relational problems that often result following an STI diagnosis.
- Treatment interventions for counseling couples affected by STIs include a variety of strategies aimed at assisting couples to create healthy sexual relationships.
- Preventive measures can be taken to reduce the risk of acquiring and transmitting STIs.
- An integrative couples' model for sexuality counseling offers a variety of intervention strategies to help couples who have STIs.

Sexually transmitted infections and diseases (STIs and STDs) affect approximately 19 million people in the United States each year (Centers for Disease Control and Prevention [CDC], 2004) and are the most common infections occurring in our society (Marr, 1998). STIs have formerly been described as "venereal diseases" associated with gonorrhea and syphilis (Rosen & Weinstein, 1988b) and more recently have been termed "sexually transmitted diseases" (STDs). In this chapter we will primarily use the term "sexually transmitted infections" (STIs) because it conveys a more accurate understanding that an infection may or may not lead to the development of a disease or illness (Strong, DeVault, Sayad, & Yarber, 2005). STIs have earned a stigma often associated with persons engaging in promiscuous behaviors or being unfaithful to their partner. Because of this stigma, STIs are difficult for many couples to talk about.

There are more than twenty STIs identified that can be transmitted by sexual contact as well as by nonsexual means (Marr, 1998; Rosen & Weinstein, 1988b). These include bacterial, viral, and protozoan infections. Many of these infections are at epidemic levels in our country and around the world and range from mild to life-threatening in their impact (Way, Schwartlander, & Piot, 1999). STIs are not selective with regard to culture, race, sexual orientation, or socioeconomic level (Marr, 1998). Because they influence a person's sexuality and sexual practices, sexuality counselors should be familiar with common STIs and be able to address the sexual, emotional, and relational concerns of couples who are affected by these.

In this chapter we describe some of the most common STIs and their symptoms, how they are transmitted, and how they are treated. In addition, we provide information on assessment of STIs along with medical treatment and counseling intervention strategies. Safer sexual practices and prevention of STIs are also discussed. We conclude the chapter with a case example demonstrating the use of the integrative couples' model for counseling partners affected by STI issues. It is important to remember that the information contained in this chapter provides a general overview of the current situation regarding STIs. The information must be updated as new advances are made in the treatment of STIs.

SOCIETAL IMPLICATIONS OF STIs

The discussion of STIs has been tainted by cultural meanings and prejudices throughout history (Brandt & Jones, 1999). For example, syphilis has been recognized since antiquity and significantly related to sex workers or prostitution (Plummer, Coutinho, Ngugi, & Moses, 1999; Sparling, 1999). STIs are cited in the writings of the philosophers of ancient Greece as well as in the Old Testament where gonorrhea and syphilis were considered punishments for blasphemy (Sparling, 1999). Cold sores (oral herpes) were described as early as A.D. 100 and genital herpes in 1754 (Corey & Wald, 1999). During World Wars I and II, soldiers were cautioned about engaging in sexual relations with indiscriminant women for fear of contracting socially unacceptable diseases (Marr, 1998). As such, STIs have emerged not only as medical concerns but also have influenced social and political problems.

STIs are most often associated with engaging in promiscuous behavior or being unfaithful to one's partner. These stigmas along with increased fears and denial about the reality of contracting STIs (especially the AIDS virus) combine to make many individuals and their partners apprehensive about asking for information they need and to seek the medical attention necessary to treat their often curable infections. For example, a woman admits that while on a business trip she had sexual relations with her boss, six years her junior. She is aware that he has had numerous sexual partners and is concerned that she should be tested for STIs. She is afraid to call her gynecologist because she fears her physician will give her a lecture, breach confidentiality, and tell her husband, or think less of her if she is diagnosed with an STI. She feels uncomfortable talking with her close friends because they might think she is unfaithful or promiscuous. At the same time she is worried because she has noticed several small bumps in her genital area. Eight months pass and she reluctantly calls an STI hotline. This is a common scenario.

Although the AIDS epidemic has begun to change people's attitudes and behaviors about the open discussion of STIs, conversations about STIs remain a major challenge in the twenty-first century (Brandt & Jones, 1999). Until society is able to view STIs as something other than a penalty for engaging in "casual" sexual relations, these infections remain difficult to eradicate and a distressing topic to discuss (Burke & Ratelle, 1998; Crowe & Norsigian, 1992).

COMMONLY DESCRIBED STIs

In this section, we describe bacterial, viral, and protozoan sexually transmitted infections. These infections vary in their mode of transmission, symptomatology, and treatment. Table 8.1 presents the modes of transmission, symptoms, and treatment of STIs. Although information about these diseases can be found in a number of sources, we have chosen to obtain information from three primary resources: *Sexually Transmitted Diseases* (Marr, 1998); *Sexually Transmitted Diseases* (Holmes et al., 1999), and *Sexually Transmitted Diseases Treatment Guidelines* (CDC, 2002). The most recent updates on advances for the treatment of STIs can be found in the *Morbidity and Mortality Weekly Report* (*MMWR*).*

Bacterial Infections

Bacterial Vaginosis

What is bacterial vaginosis?   Bacterial vaginosis (BV) is a common vaginal infection in women of childbearing age, associated with an imbalance of normally

---

*The *MMWR* is published weekly by the Epidemiology Program Office, Centers for Disease Control and Prevention, U.S. Department of Health and Human Services in Atlanta, Georgia (www.cdc.gov/std/).

TABLE 8.1

Common Sexually Transmitted Infections (STIs): Modes of Transmission, Symptoms, and Treatment

STI	TRANSMISSION	SYMPTOMS	TREATMENT
Bacterial vaginosis (BV)	The most common causative agent, the *Gardnerella vaginalis* bacterium, is sometimes transmitted through coitus.	Women will have a fishy- or musty-smelling thin discharge. Most men are asymptomatic.	Orally by metronidazole or clindamycin or intravaginally by application of topical metronidazole gel or clindamycin cream.
Chlamydia	The *Chlamydia trachomatis* bacterium is transmitted primarily through sexual contact.	In women, pelvic inflammatory disease (PID) caused by chlamydia may include lower abdominal pain, nausea, fever, dyspareunia (pain during intercourse) and abnormal bleeding, infertility, and ectopic pregnancy. In men, chlamydia infection of the urethra may cause discharge and burning during urination. Chlamydia-caused epididymitis may cause painful swelling in the testicles.	Azithromycin, doxycycline, ofloxacin, levofloxacin, or erythromycin.
Gonorrhea ("clap")	The *Neisseria gonorrhoeae* bacterium is spread through genital, oral-genital, or oral-anal contact.	The most common symptoms in men are a cloudy discharge from the penis and burning sensations during urination. If disease is untreated, complications may include inflammation of scrotal skin and swelling at base of the testicle. In women, some green or yellowish discharge is produced but commonly remains undetected. PID may later develop.	Dual therapy of a single dose of cefixime, ceftriaxone, ciprofloxacin, ofloxacin, or levofloxacin, plus arithromycin or doxycycline for one week.
Syphilis	The *Treponema pallidum* bacterium is transmitted from open lesions during genital, oral-genital, or genital-anal contact.	*Primary stage:* A painless chancre appears at site where the bacterium entered the body. *Secondary stage:* The chancre disappears and a generalized skin rash develops. *Latent stage:* There may be no visible symptoms. *Tertiary stage:* Internal organ damage may occur, causing heart failure, blindness, and many other symptoms. Death may result.	Benzathine penicillin G, doxycycline, tetracycline, or ceftriaxone.

(continued)

TABLE 8.1   *(continued)*

STI	TRANSMISSION	SYMPTOMS	TREATMENT
Genital warts	The virus is spread primarily through vaginal, anal, or oral-genital contact.	Hard and yellow-gray warts on dry skin areas; pinkish-red and cauliflower-like on moist areas.	Freezing, application of topical agents such as trichloroacetic acid or podofilox, electrosurgery, surgical removal, or laser surgery. Podofilox solution or imiquimod cream applied by the individual.
Herpes	The genital herpes virus (HSV-2) appears to be transmitted primarily through oral, anal, penile, or vaginal contact. The oral herpes virus (HSV-1) is transmitted primarily by kissing.	Small, painful pimplelike bumps appear in the genital region (genital herpes) or mouth (oral herpes). The bumps become painful blisters that eventually rupture to form wet open sores.	No known cure. A variety of treatments may reduce symptoms. Antiviral medications such as acyclovir, valacyclovir, and famciclovir can promote healing and shorten recurrent outbreaks.
Viral hepatitis	Hepatitis B may be transmitted by blood, semen, vaginal secretions, and saliva. Hepatitis A seems to be primarily spread by fecal-oral contact (usually by oral-anal sexual practices).	Vary from mild flulike symptoms to severe illness characterized by high fever, vomiting, and acute abdominal pain.	No specific therapy; treatment generally consists of bed rest and adequate fluid intake.
Acquired immunodeficiency syndrome (AIDS)	Blood and semen are the major vehicles for transmitting the human immunodeficiency virus (HIV), which attacks the immune system. It appears to be passed primarily through sexual contact or by needle-sharing among intravenous drug users.	Vary with the type of cancer or opportunistic infections that afflict an infected person. Common symptoms include fevers, muscle aches, skin rashes, night sweats, sore throat, gastrointestinal and central nervous system problems, swollen lymph glands among others.	Some antiretroviral drugs or a combination of three or more used in highly active anti-retroviral therapy (HAART).
Trichomoniasis	The protozoan parasite *Trichomonas vaginalis* is usually passed through sexual contact.	Yellowish-green vaginal discharge with an unpleasant odor; vulva is sore and irritated.	Metronidazole for both women and men.

Source: Adapted from *Our Sexuality,* 8th ed. (pp. 476–477), by R. Crooks and K. Baur. © 2002. Reprinted with permission of Wadsworth, a division of Thomson Learning: www.thomsonrights.com. Fax 800-730-2215.

occurring "good" and "harmful" bacteria in the vagina (Marr, 1998). It is caused by an overgrowth of "harmful" bacteria typically known as *Gardnerella vaginalis,* which develops when there is a change in the environment of the vagina (Hillier & Holmes, 1999).

How do women get bacterial vaginosis? There is mixed support about the development of BV in women

(Hillier & Holmes, 1999). We do know that it occurs more commonly in women who have a new sex partner or who have multiple sex partners, and it rarely occurs in women who are not sexually active. Although there is no evidence that the bacteria are transmitted from men to women, it can be transmitted during woman-to-woman sex (Marr, 1998). Circumstances such as sexual activity, genital infections, douching, and the use of an IUD make it more likely that BV will develop (Hillier & Holmes, 1999).

What are the symptoms? Women with BV often have mild symptoms including a thin gray discharge from the vagina that produces a "fishy" or "musty" odor, usually more intense after sexual intercourse (Marr, 1998). They may also experience burning during urination, itching around the outside of the vagina, or a combination of both. For some women the psychological effects of the infection lead to symptoms of depression and social withdrawal (Hillier & Holmes, 1999). Some women with BV report no symptoms at all and are diagnosed during an annual gynecological exam. Men with BV are most often asymptomatic (Crooks & Baur, 2002).

How is it treated? BV can be treated with a topical cream or gel or by oral medication (Centers for Disease Control and Prevention, 2002). Topical treatment includes metronidazole gel or clindamycin cream that is applied intervaginally. Oral medication includes the use of antibiotics such as metronidazole and clindamycin.

Chlamydia

What is chlamydia? Chlamydia is a common STI caused by the *Chlamydia trachomatis* bacterium (Schachter, 1999; Marr, 1998). This infection can lead to infertility because of irreversible damage in women's reproductive organs and result in pelvic inflammatory disease (PID).

How do people get chlamydia? Chlamydia is transmitted through sexual contact with an infected person through oral, vaginal, or anal sex, as well as by sex toys inserted in the vagina (Marr, 1998; Schachter, 1999). In addition, chlamydia can be transmitted during childbirth from a mother to her infant passing through an infected birth canal.

What are the symptoms? Three-quarters of the women and half of the men with chlamydia infections are asymptomatic and therefore are not diagnosed or treated until complications arise (Marr, 1998).

In women, the bacteria initially infects the cervix (the opening to the uterus) and the urethra (the urine canal) (Marr, 1998; W. E. Stamm, 1999). This results in symptoms such as vaginal discharge or a burning sensation with urination. If the infection spreads to the uterus, fallopian tubes, or ovaries, pelvic inflammatory disease may result. In these cases women experience lower abdominal pain, nausea, fever, dyspareunia, and abnormal bleeding (Crooks & Baur, 2002; Marr, 1998). Once the infection spreads into the upper reproductive system, a woman may be faced with irreversible damage that can lead to infertility or an ectopic pregnancy—a pregnancy outside the uterus, usually in the fallopian tubes (Schachter, 1999).

Infections in men occur in the urethra (urethritis), epididymus (epididymitis), and the prostate (prostatitis) (W. E. Stamm, 1999). Men with chlamydia might experience discharge from the penis, an itching or irritated feeling at the opening of the penis, a burning sensation with urination, or pain and swelling in the testicles (Marr, 1998).

How is it treated? Chlamydia is easily treated and cured with antibiotics (CDC, 2002). The most common antibiotic used for both men and women is a single oral dose of azithromycin. Other antibiotics such as doxycycline, ofloxacin, levofloxacin, and erythromycin can be taken over a period of one week. It is important that any sex partner of an infected person be treated as well.

Gonorrhea

What is gonorrhea? Gonorrhea (also commonly known as the "clap") is a sexually transmitted infection/disease caused by the bacterium *Neisseria gonorrhoeae* (Hook & Handsfield, 1999). This bacterium thrives in warm mucous membrane tissues such as in the cervix, uterus, and fallopian tubes in women and in the urethra (urine canal) in both men and women. It can also cause infections in the throat, anus, and mouth.

How do people get gonorrhea? Gonorrhea is transmitted by sexual contact with an infected person through the vagina, mouth (throat), or anus (Hook & Handsfield, 1999). This includes oral-to-genital, genital-to-anal, and genital-to-genital contact. Gonorrhea cannot be contracted through inanimate objects or nonsexual contact (Hook & Handsfield, 1999; Marr, 1998).

What are the symptoms? Early symptoms of gonorrhea are typically more pronounced in men than in women (Crooks & Baur, 2002). However, some people are symptom-free although they are still infectious. The majority of men contracting gonorrhea have symptoms including a burning sensation during urination and a foul-smelling cloudy (yellowish-white) discharge from the penis (Marr, 1998). In some cases, the penis can become swollen, and lymph glands in the groin area may become tender. If left untreated, gonorrhea may cause complications such as prostate infection (prostatitis) resulting in urinary discomfort. Untreated gonorrhea can also cause a swelling of the testicles due to the gonococcal bacterium. This may result in scarring inside the testicle, blocking the flow of sperm, and lead to fertility problems.

Symptoms of gonorrhea in women are usually mild and are often overlooked due to similar symptoms from a variety of infections (Hook & Handsfield, 1999). The primary site for infection is the cervix. Symptoms include a yellowish vaginal discharge and spotting between periods or after intercourse. Untreated, gonorrhea can lead to PID (discussed in more detail under chlamydia infections) and cause chronic pelvic pain due to scarring (Hook & Handsfield, 1999; Marr, 1998). This disease is often more severe when it occurs as a result of gonorrhea and can lead to a risk of infertility and ectopic pregnancy (Hook & Handsfield, 1999).

In both men and women, gonorrhea can enter the bloodstream and spread throughout the body, causing symptoms such as chills, skin lesions, and pain in the joints (Marr, 1998). In rare cases, the bacterium may settle in the heart, liver, and lining of the brain and spinal cord, causing *meningitis.*

In addition, gonorrheal infection for both genders can occur in the anal opening (Hook & Hansfield, 1999). Although symptoms in this area occur infrequently, they may include rectal itching, pain, discharge, bleeding, and bowel disorders (Hook & Hansfield, 1999). Oral sex with a partner who is infected can result in transmission of the bacterium to the throat. This can cause a sore throat or tonsillitis, or no symptoms at all.

Women who are pregnant run the risk of infecting their infant (causing blindness) as the baby passes through the birth canal (Hook & Handsfield, 1999). Genital gonorrhea also places the pregnant mother at risk for a spontaneous abortion or premature delivery.

How is it treated?   A person infected with gonorrhea bacterium is also often treated for chlamydial infections because many people have both infections (Hook & Handsfield, 1999). Treatment for both infections is usually given together and involves a single dose of antibiotics such as cefixime, ceftriaxone, ciprofloxacin ofloxacin, and levofloxacin, along with arithromycin or doxycycline for one week (CDC, 2002). It is important to finish all medication even if

symptoms subside. Persons treated for gonorrhea can be reinfected if they have sexual contact with another infected person.

Syphilis

What is syphilis?   Syphilis is a complex sexually transmitted infection/disease caused by a bacterium called *Treponema pallidum* (Sparling, 1999). It is acquired through sexual contact or from mother to infant during pregnancy.

How do people get syphilis?   Syphilis is transmitted person to person from open lesions of an infected person to mucous membranes or skin abrasions of sexual partners (Marr, 1998; Sparling, 1999). These lesions are most often located on the external genitalia, vagina, anus, or in the rectum. Oral, anal, or genital sexual contact with these areas can result in transmission of the infection. A mother can also pass the disease to her unborn child through the placental blood system.

What are the symptoms?   Syphilis can progress through four stages of development: primary, secondary, latent, and tertiary (Sparling, 1999). The length of time the infection has been present and the nature of the symptoms determine which phase of the infection is present.

- *Primary stage:* Symptoms can take between 10 and 90 days to appear (the average is 21 days) and are generally manifested by a chancre—a painless sore that occurs at the site where the infection takes place (Sparling, 1999). Chancres are most often found on the inner vaginal walls or the cervix of women and on the penis of men (Musher, 1999). The chancre usually lasts from 3 to 6 weeks and heals without treatment. If untreated, the infection progresses to the secondary stage.
- *Secondary stage:* A variety of symptoms appear at this stage, including a nonitching skin rash on the palms of the hands, the bottoms of the feet, or on other parts of the body (Marr, 1998; Sparling, 1999; L. V. Stamm, 1999). Many times the rash is faint and not noticeable. Other symptoms that may occur in this stage include fever, sore throat, joint and muscle aches, headaches, patchy hair loss, weight loss, and fatigue. The symptoms often subside within a few weeks; however, this does not mean the infection has gone away. People are infectious during this time and left untreated may enter the latent stage.

- *Latent stage:* There may be no symptoms of the infection during this stage (Sparling, 1999). Beginning when secondary symptoms subside, this stage can last for several years. During this time, the syphilis-causing bacteria remain in the body and increase in number.
- *Tertiary stage:* Syphilis-causing bacteria begin to infect internal organs such as the central nervous system; blood vessels; the cardiovascular system; the eyes, liver, bones, skin, joints; and the brain (L. V. Stamm, 1999). These final manifestations may be serious enough to cause death.

How is it treated?   Syphilis occurring in the primary, secondary, and latent phases for less than one year can be treated and cured with one dose of benzathine penicillin G which is injected intramuscularly (CDC, 2002). If a person has allergies to penicillin, other antibiotics such as doxycycline and tetracycline may be used. Although penicillin cannot reverse the outcome of the disease, it can prevent additional damage to the body (Marr, 1998). All sex partners of the infected person should be treated. Follow-up tests are essential to ensure a successful outcome.

Viral Infections

Genital Warts

What is HPV infection?   This common STI is caused by the human papillomavirus (HPV) (Koutsky & Kiviat, 1999). There are more than 100 strains of this virus, including more than 35 that cause genital infections. Some types can contribute to abnormal Pap smears and cancer of the cervix, vagina, vulva, penis, and anus. Others may cause mild Pap smear abnormalities and genital warts.

How do people get HPV?   HPV is passed from one person to the other primarily through sexual contact (Koutsky & Kiviat, 1999). Most warts occur in the genital area such as the scrotum and penis for men and on the cervix, vagina, or vulva in women. They can also occur on the anus and in the mouth (CDC, 2002). Although uncommon, it is possible for an infected pregnant woman with visible warts to pass the virus to her newborn during delivery.

What are the symptoms?   Most people who have HPV infection are asymptomatic and therefore unaware that they are infected (Marr, 1998). For this reason they may unknowingly pass the infection to another person. Those who do have symptoms de-

velop visible genital warts, usually soft and moist pink or flesh-colored swellings. If they are located on dry skin areas, they may be hard and yellowish-gray in color (Crooks & Baur, 2002). They may be flat or raised and occur singly or in clusters, forming a cauliflower-like shape. They typically appear on the vulva; in or around the vagina or anus; on the cervix; or on the penis, scrotum, groin, or thigh (Marr, 1998).

How is it treated?   There is no effective treatment to eliminate HPV (Koutsky & Kiviat, 1999). Most often, the goal of treatment focuses on removing visible warts, with the understanding that the warts may reoccur (CDC, 2002; Marr, 1998). The most common treatments include podofilox solution or gel or imiquimod cream that can be applied by the individual (CDC, 2002). Other treatments that can be administered only by a health care provider include cryotherapy (freezing warts with liquid nitrogen) and topical treatments (podophyllin or trichloroacetic acid painted on the warts). For larger or more persistent warts, electrosurgery (cutting out the wart with an electrified wire), surgical removal (performed with local anesthetic and a scalpel), and laser surgery (a high-intensity beam of light) may be used. The latter procedures are often costly and can cause severe side effects. Follow-up evaluations are recommended for some people.

Herpes

What is herpes?   Herpes is an infection/disease that is caused by the herpes simplex virus (HSV) (Corey & Wald, 1999; Marr, 1998). There are two classifications of this virus: herpes simplex virus type 1 (HSV-1), which usually occurs around the mouth causing cold sores or fever blisters, and herpes simplex virus type 2 (HSV-2), which usually occurs in the genital or anal area causing sores.

How do people get herpes?   Herpes simplex viruses (types 1 and 2) are transmitted through direct (skin-to-skin) contact at mucosal skin surfaces (such as the mouth, genitals, or eye) by genital or oral secretions (Corey & Wald, 1999; Marr, 1998). This can occur during oral, anal, penile, or vaginal sexual contact with an infected partner or may involve transmission immediately after the use of a shared sex toy. In addition, herpes can be transmitted to any area of the body that comes in contact with a sore, rash, or open wound of an infected person. This can occur even when a person is asymptomatic.

What are the symptoms? Most people who become infected with genital herpes experience no symptoms or only mild ones (Corey & Wald, 1999; Marr, 1998). Many are unaware that they contracted the infection. If symptoms occur, they usually begin with tingling or itching in the genital area 2 to 20 days after infection (Marr, 1998). Small painful pimplelike bumps then appear, and within 3 to 4 days they develop into painful blisters that rupture and form open sores that may weep or bleed (Corey & Wald, 1999; Marr, 1998). In men, blisters often appear on the penis and scrotum; in women, the infection site is usually the cervix or outer labia. Blisters may appear on the buttocks, pubic area, or anus in both men and women. During an outbreak of herpes, a person may experience symptoms such as vaginal or urethral discharge, swollen lymph nodes in the groin, pain, headaches, sore throat, flu-like symptoms, or burning while urinating (Corey & Wald, 1999; Marr, 1998).

Herpes is a recu....ent virus that does dissipate. It is believed to remain dormant but can later be triggered by emotional or physical stress such as depression, anxiety, poor nutrition, fatigue, particular foods, exposure to sunlight, or menstruation (Crooks & Baur, 2002; Marr, 1998). Some people experience relapses several years after being infected. Because of recurrent outbreaks and lack of an effective cure (see next section), many people who experience recurrent herpes encounter psychological distress ranging in intensity (Crook & Baur, 2002).

How is it treated? There is no effective medical cure for herpes; however, antiviral medications such as acyclovir, valacyclovir, and famciclovir can prevent and shorten outbreaks during the time that the drug is taken (CDC, 2002; Corey & Wald, 1999). In addition, the following alternative approaches to herpes management may help provide relief from symptoms:

1. Keep herpes blisters as dry as possible; this will speed healing and prevent further blistering. Drying agents such as cornstarch and alcohol can be applied directly to the lesions; however, alcohol may burn. It can be helpful to wear loose-fitting cotton underwear, which permits the lesions to dry.
2. Apply topical anesthetic creams such as lidocaine gel to reduce soreness until the antiviral medication begins to provide relief.
3. Applying ice directly to the area of outbreak will provide relief. Place the ice in a plastic bag and then wrap it in a thin towel to avoid wetting the lesion.

4. Some people have found that putting a small amount of black or green tea into a warm bath and soaking in it provides relief. It can also be especially helpful to urinate while sitting in a bathtub of warm water so that the acid in urine does not create a burning sensation as it comes into contact with an open lesion.
5. Become aware of your reaction to certain foods that might trigger an outbreak. Limit your intake of those foods, and keep in mind that some people have outbreaks associated with caffeine and alcohol consumption as well as smoking.
6. Try to reduce stress by relaxation, regular exercise, meditation practices such as yoga and tai chi, counseling, guided imagery, and cognitive stress management.
7. Keep track of triggers in your environment that occur prior to the outbreak (i.e., stress, fatigue, or specific foods) so you can avoid them in the future. (Adapted from Crooks & Baur, 2002, pp. 491–492; Marr, 1998, pp. 226–228)

Viral Hepatitis

What is viral hepatitis? Hepatitis is an infection and inflammation of the liver caused by a virus (Lemon & Alter, 1999). Although there are five known types of hepatitis, not all are associated with STIs. There are three types of viral hepatitis that can be transmitted through sexual contact as well as other ways: hepatitis A (HAV) (formerly infectious hepatitis), hepatitis B (HBV) (formerly serum hepatitis), hepatitis C (HCV) (Lemon & Alter, 1999). Hepatitis A and B are the most common types of the virus that are transmitted sexually and are therefore included in Table 8.1.

How do people get hepatitis? Hepatitis A is primarily transmitted sexually through fecal-oral contact (usually by oral-anal sexual practices) (Lemon & Alter, 1999). It can also be transmitted by eating improperly cooked shellfish that have ingested contaminated food sources. In addition, it can be transmitted during food preparation if an infected person contaminates his or her hands with stool (feces) and fails to wash them thoroughly after using the bathroom (Marr, 1998).

Hepatitis B is transmitted by blood, semen, vaginal secretions, and saliva (Lemon & Alter, 1999). Hepatitis B can be passed through anal, vaginal, and oral sex; sharing needles or "works" when "shooting" drugs; through needlesticks or sharps exposures on the job; or from an infected mother to her baby during birth

(Lemon & Alter, 1999; Marr, 1998). Hepatitis B is transmitted more often by sexual contact than hepatitis A.

Hepatitis C occurs when blood from an infected person enters the body of a person who is not infected (Lemon & Alter, 1999). This infection is most commonly transmitted by people who are intravenous drug users (particularly those who share drug paraphernalia) (Lemon & Alter, 1999). Likewise, persons who obtained blood transfusions prior to 1990 (when blood was not screened for the virus) carry an increased risk of infection (Marr, 1998). Hepatitis C transmission has also been correlated with people who have a history of hospitalizations, STIs, and tattoos (Lemon & Alter, 1999). Research is unclear about the role hepatitis C plays in the transmission of sexually transmitted diseases; however, recent reports associate the transmission of the virus with some sexual activities (e.g., activities involving sexual trauma, multiple sex partners, sex with an infected person, or failure to use condoms) (CDC, 2002).

What are the symptoms? Symptoms of viral hepatitis range from mild symptoms (such as fatigue, loss of appetite, joint aches, nausea, and diarrhea) to more severe symptoms (acute abdominal pains, vomiting, and high fever) (Lemon & Alter, 1999; Marr, 1998). In the more severe state, a person may develop a condition called jaundice, which causes a yellowish color in the skin and eyes and may darken urine. In the most severe cases, viral hepatitis B may cause hepatic failure that requires a liver transplant (Lemon & Alter, 1999). Hepatitis B has also been associated with causing liver cancer. Some people do not manifest any symptoms; for others, the virus can be fatal.

How is it treated? Although no treatment protocol is completely effective, bed rest, increased fluids, and medications to prevent nausea can be helpful while the infection runs its course (Marr, 1998). Most people recover within 6 weeks to several months (if symptoms persist). In more severe cases, hospitalization is required.

At the present time, vaccines are available to prevent hepatitis A and B (CDC, 2002). These vaccines are recommended for persons in high-risk categories (e.g., health-care workers, injection drug users, and persons who have been exposed to the virus) (Lemon & Alter, 1999). There is no effective vaccine available for immunization against hepatitis C (CDC, 2002).

Acquired Immunodeficiency Syndrome (AIDS)

What is acquired immunodeficiency syndrome? Acquired immunodeficiency syndrome (AIDS) is a common viral infection caused by the human immunodeficiency virus (HIV) (Marr, 1998). HIV belongs to a family of viruses known as retroviruses. There are two types of HIV that are recognized: HIV-1 and HIV-2. HIV-1 is the most common strain of the virus and causes the greatest number of AIDS cases seen in the world (Marr, 1998). HIV-1 can also be present in multiple strains. HIV-2 is less prevalent except in West Africa, where it predominates.

How do people get acquired immunodefiency syndrome (AIDS)? The human immunodeficiency virus can be transmitted by sexual contact, exchange of blood or other body fluids, or an exchange of fluids from a mother to her child (Ambroziak & Levy, 1999; Marr, 1998). It has been identified in seminal and vaginal fluids, blood, urine, saliva, tears, amniotic fluid, placental tissue, and breast milk of infected persons (Ambroziak & Levy, 1999). Sexual contact is the most common way HIV enters the body. This occurs by infected genital fluid exchanged during unprotected oral, anal, or vaginal sexual contact. Blood and other body fluids can also transmit HIV in the following ways (Marr, 1998):

> Through a transfusion with infected blood or an infected blood product
>
> Through a stick with a needle with blood on it
>
> Through a splash of infected body fluids onto a mucous membrane or a break in the skin
>
> Through exchanging needles or other works for injection drug use. (p. 237)

The virus can be passed from an infected mother to her infant while in the womb (through the placenta), during delivery (by contact with fluids in the vaginal canal), or after the infant is born (through breast milk) (Ambroziak & Levy, 1999; Marr, 1998). HIV infection cannot be transmitted by touching objects such as doorknobs, toilet seats, or telephones, nor can it be acquired through nonsexual contact with another person (such as hugging or shaking hands) (Masters, Johnson, & Kolodny, 1995).

What are the symptoms? About one-half of the people infected with HIV exhibit flu-like symptoms within several weeks after becoming infected (Ambroziak & Levy, 1999; Marr, 1998). Symptoms may include fevers, muscle aches, skin rashes, night sweats, sore throat, gastrointestinal and central nervous system problems (i.e., diarrhea, dementia), and swollen lymph glands throughout the body (i.e., in the neck, under the arms, and in the groin). Others exhibit no symptoms at all. Persons may remain symptom-free for a few months or for up to 17 years (with an average of about 10 years) (CDC, 2002). Infections have been reported as high as 18 years (Ambroziak & Levy, 1999). During this period of time, lymph node enlargement throughout the body is not uncommon (Marr, 1998).

As HIV continues to exhaust the immune system, it invades healthy cells in a person's body, and the immune system becomes unable to protect itself against infection. Symptoms such as headaches, fever, night sweats, loss of weight, blood in the stools, or exhaustion can occur (Crooks & Baur, 2002). Finally, the disease progresses to full-blown AIDS indicated by a drop in helper cells below 200 (a healthy person has a count of 500 or more), producing a vulnerability to outside infections such as bacterial pneumonia, pulmonary tuberculosis, shingles, encephalitis, lymphomas, and oral candida (yeast) infections, among other diseases (Marr, 1998).

How is it treated? Although there is no cure for AIDS, two classes of medications are used to treat it. The first is composed of five antiretroviral medications— zidovudine (AZT), didanosine (ddI), zalcitabine (ddC), stavudine (D4T), and lamivudine (3TC)—that block HIV's ability to replicate itself (Eron & Hirsch, 1999). The second group—saquinavir, indinavir, retonavir, nelfinavir, and amprenavir—is composed of protease inhibitors, which also inhibit the replication of HIV, although they affect a different step in the process (Eron & Hirsch, 1999).

The most recent development in the treatment of HIV is highly active antiretroviral therapy (HAART), which combines three or more antiretrovial drugs (Crooks & Baur, 2002). This treatment has been shown to inhibit the progression of the disease to improve immune functioning (Aral & Holmes, 1999). Although results have been promising, patient compliance (due to side effects) along with the cost of the drug (more than $10,000 per year) may indicate less-than-optimistic results in the future (Crooks & Baur, 2002). New drugs continue to be tested and will soon add to available treatment choices. For the most current information on treatment of HIV/AIDS, refer to the *Fact Sheet: HIV Infection and Aids: An Overview,* provided by the National Institute of Allergy and Infectious Diseases (2003), which can be accessed at www.niaid.nih.gov/factsheets/hivinf.

Protozoan Infections

Trichomoniasis

What is trichomoniasis? Trichomoniasis is a common sexually transmitted infection that occurs in both women and men. It is caused by *Trichomonas vaginalis,* a single-celled protozoan (Krieger & Alderete, 1999). The most common site of infection for women is the vagina, whereas for men it is the urethra.

How do people get trichomoniasis? Trichomoniasis is acquired primarily through sexual contact with an infected partner (Krieger & Alderete, 1999). It can be spread from penis-to-vagina intercourse or vulva-to-vulva contact. It can also be spread from the use of shared sex toys and has been known to live for under one minute on toilet seats, articles of clothing, bath water, and washcloths (Krieger & Alderete, 1999).

What are the symptoms? In women, trichomoniasis causes a yellowish-green vaginal discharge, itching, and irritation, and there is also redness of the female genital area and a strong fishy odor from the vagina (Krieger & Alderete, 1999; Marr, 1998). It may also cause discomfort during intercourse and urination. In severe cases, lower abdominal pain can occur. Some women are asymptomatic.

Most men with the infection typically do not have signs or symptoms (Krieger & Alderete, 1999; Marr, 1998). Those who do may experience symptoms of urethritis (urethral infection) causing discharge, burning, or irritation within the penis (Krieger & Alderete, 1999; Marr, 1998). Untreated trichomoniasis can lead to the blockage of urinal flow. In some cases, it has been associated with prostatitis (inflammation of the prostate), erectile dysfunction, and premature ejaculation, among other conditions. However, evidence in these areas is unclear (Krieger & Alderete, 1999).

How is it treated? Trichomoniasis is usually treated and cured with metronidazole, an oral antibiotic that is given over the course of one week and is effective in the treatment of both men and women (Krieger & Alderete, 1999). Persons having this infection should avoid sexual intercourse until treatment is completed and they have no symptoms (Marr, 1998).

THE PROCESS OF SEXUALITY COUNSELING FOR COUPLES AFFECTED BY STIs

Treatment for issues related to sexuality can be complex. Most people present their sexual concerns to their physician or gynecologist hoping to find reassurance or a solution to their problem. However, when couples are faced with the possibility of an STI, the process becomes multifaceted and systemic in nature. In other words, STIs affect both partners, and each partner is influenced by the STI. Many people with health concerns related to STIs are fearful and embarrassed and delay seeking medical attention because they are reluctant to find out if they are infected. Others who know they are infected may experience psychological effects that lead to sexual and relational problems (Masters et al., 1995). Some people feel uncomfortable talking to their health-care provider and seek counseling to discuss their concerns prior to seeking medical attention. Sexuality counselors should refer couples for a medical evaluation if they have not yet been evaluated and discuss with them what to expect during an exam (i.e., a thorough physical, lab tests, and confidentiality). In addition, counselors gather information from their clients to help them assess their risk for an STI. They explore with them their understanding of symptoms of STIs along with how STIs are transmitted and prevented. Sexuality counselors also help couples address the emotional and relational concerns brought about by a positive diagnosis of an STI.

Diagnosing STIs

Diagnosis of STIs takes place with a health-care provider and includes a physical examination and a screening for STIs. A full screening includes evaluation for a variety of infections including gonorrhea, syphilis, chlamydia, and HIV/AIDS (CDC, 2002). In addition, screening procedures may vary based on a person's situation or sexual practices. For example, a woman who is pregnant is typically screened for bacterial vaginosis, genital warts, and genital herpes, among other infections. A man who reports he has sexual relations with other men may be tested for specific bacterial STIs (CDC, 2002). More details about screening recommendations for specific populations can be found in the *Sexually Transmitted Diseases Treatment Guidelines* (CDC, 2002).

Persons being tested for STIs need to be informed about reporting procedures as they pertain to some STIs. For example, every state requires health-care providers to report syphilis, gonorrhea, chlamydia, and AIDS to both local and state health departments (CDC, 2002). The specifics for reporting other infections vary from state to state (CDC, 2002). Counselors should refer to federal and state statutes when discerning when to report or disclose an STI. (See www.hhs.gov/ocr/hippa/Title 45, Code of Federal Regulations [CFR] 164.512.) STI results are highly confidential and in most states statute protected from subpoena (CDC, 2002). This does not mean, however, that confidentiality is absolute. Confidentiality limitations should be discussed with clients as they pertain to reporting procedures as well as partner notification for specific STIs. Many people opt for anonymous testing to protect their identity.

Confidentiality of record keeping should also be addressed in sexuality counseling. Clients should be informed that their records can be released only by their request and with written permission. They must be made aware, however, of the limitations to confidentiality involved in the handling of their records by office staff as well as their insurance company. What is most important is that people be informed about confidentiality and its limitations within the health-care system in which they are involved. In this way, they have a choice as to how they wish to proceed with their testing and treatment.

It is incumbent for health-care providers as well as sexuality counselors to stay informed of their respective state laws governing the reporting and management of partner notification of STIs in order to help those who require testing for STIs.

Questions to Consider

In addition to medical tests, there are specific questions that assist health-care providers to assess people at risk for STIs and to make an accurate medical diagnosis. These questions are presented in detail by Marr (1998) and include gathering information about a client's most recent sexual contact, sexual practices (e.g., oral, anal, genital contact), partner preferences (male, female, or both), and current preventive methods (use of condoms, spermicides). Present symptoms of the individual and their current sexual partner is also explored. A thorough history of previous STIs or use of injection drugs by either sexual partner must also be evaluated (Marr, 1998).

Once a health-care provider makes a diagnosis, a sexuality counselor can help individuals and their partners to explore the impact of the diagnosis. Asking the following questions will facilitate this process:

1. What is your greatest concern about having an STI?
2. How has the STI affected you? Your partner? Your relationship with your partner?
3. How has the STI affected your sexual relationship?
4. Have you adapted your sexual relationship to accommodate for the STI? If so, in what ways?

Sexuality counselors also help couples understand feelings related to engaging in high-risk sexual behaviors. These include exploring feelings related to a client's need to be loved and cared for, feelings of insecurity and low self-esteem, as well as feelings related to loss (Dwyer & Niemann, 2002).

In addition, because of the increased prevalence and deadly consequences of HIV infection, the following questions have been suggested by Bor, Miller, and Goldman (1993) for assessing HIV risk:

> What was it that helped you decide to come for testing at this stage?
>
> Who else knows that you have come for testing today?
>
> Whose idea was it that you should be tested?
>
> Can you tell me the ways that you know HIV is transmitted?
>
> How do you think that you might have been infected with HIV?
>
> What do you mean by having sex? What do you mean by cuddling, kissing, and anal or vaginal intercourse? I need to have an understanding of the activity that you think was risky in order for us to assess your risk. (p. 65)

These questions are used most often by sexuality counselors specifically trained to assist individuals and their partners who are undergoing HIV testing.

The Development of Sexual and Relational Problems

Sexual problems/dysfunctions

Sexually transmitted infections/diseases (with the exception of AIDS) that are detected early and treated properly have minimal physical effects except during acute phases when intercourse can be painful (Masters et al., 1995). For the most part, these infections are not likely to interfere with a person's sexual desire or physical components of sexual functioning. They can, however, lead to sexual problems or dysfunctions due to the psychological effects they have on individuals and couples who become infected (Masters et al., 1995; Ross, 1999). For example, when people learn they are infected with an STI, they are often overwhelmed with an array of feelings ranging from disbelief and skepticism to feelings of shame and guilt for their sexual practices (Dwyer & Niemann, 2002). Relentless feelings of shame and guilt may be more pronounced if the STI affects a person's ability to bear children or if it becomes a continual occurrence (Dwyer & Niemann, 2002; Lindemann, 1988). Likewise, they may feel depressed and blame themselves, thinking that they are in some way being "punished" for their unsafe or immoral sexual practices (Dwyer & Niemann, 2002; Masters et al., 1995; Ross, 1999). These feelings may lead to the development of sexual problems in their current intimate relationship (Masters et al., 1995; Ross, 1999).

Other individuals may have unreasonable reactions to their diagnosis and become obsessive or preoccupied with concerns about cleanliness or bodily functions and the possibility of contracting another STI (Masters et al., 1995; Ross, 1999). They may even decide to alter their sexual practices with their partner (Dwyer & Niemann, 2002). These psychological effects may lead to sexual problems or dysfunctions or exacerbate existing ones. For example, fear of contracting or transmitting an STI may increase the likelihood of premature ejaculation, low sexual desire, erectile failure, vaginismus, and orgasmic disorder (Ross, 1999). In some couples it may lead to the avoidance of sexual activity altogether (Hedge, 1996).

Relational Problems

The diagnosis of a sexually transmitted infection in one or both partners in an intimate relationship creates havoc in a couple's life. Although some STIs can be transmitted by nonsexual means, the diagnosis of one partner has implications that the infected person has stepped out of the relationship and has had sexual contact with an infected person (Masters et al., 1995). However, it can also imply that the infected person contracted the STI in a previous relationship and failed to communicate this information to their current partner. Mistrust often results from both situations and may be compounded by more intense feelings of confusion, anger, and resentment in cases where one partner contracts the infection from the other (Masters et al., 1995). This may result in relationship problems that focus on issues of trust, commitment, resolving feelings of resentment by an uninfected partner, and physical and emotional withdrawal (distancing) of both partners (Dwyer & Niemann, 2002). For example, Lyle has been married for 10 years and is very much in love with his wife, Sonya. He attends his twentieth high school reunion alone and reconnects with his high school sweetheart. They have "a couple of drinks" and decide to go back to his room to reminisce about "old times." They engage in unprotected sex, and he contracts gonorrhea. Several weeks later he begins to notice a burning sensation when he urinates. He seeks medical advice, attributing it to a possible bladder infection. After a medical examination, he is told that he has contracted gonorrhea. He is embarrassed and ashamed as he tells his wife that he has contracted an STI, and she may have contracted the disease from him. Hurt and confused, she withdraws emotionally and refuses any sexual activity with him. She informs him that she is unsure of her future with him.

In this case, Lyle and Sonya are faced with the aftermath of a devastating confession. They need to identify and express their feelings to each other regarding Lyle's disclosure and gradually work toward reestablishing trust in the relationship. For this couple, the reality of an infectious sexual disease becomes a point of contention in their once caring relationship.

Counseling Couples Affected by STIs

Because of the systemic nature of STIs, couples affected with these diseases benefit from counseling (Bor et al., 1993; Dwyer & Nieman, 2002). Couples discuss symptoms and treatment of the disease and explore ways it will affect their relationship. Issues in counseling include concerns over disclosure, modifying sexual practices, fear of infection, safe sex practices, fears of sexual expression, along with sexual and relationship problems (Dwyer & Neiman, 2002; Hedge, 1996; Huber, 1996; Masters et al., 1995; Ross, 1999; Serovich, 2000). Issues of shame, guilt, embarrassment, anger, anxiety, or "feeling dirty" may also emerge and require attention (Dwyer & Niemann, 2002; Masters et al., 1995; Ross, 1999). Sexual problems such as premature ejaculation, erectile disorder, desire disorders, vaginismus, and orgasmic disorder may stem from these unresolved feelings (Ross, 1999). Sexuality counselors teach couples effective communication skills in order to help them discuss their issues and create solutions. Counselors must keep in mind that preexisting sexual and relational problems can be exacerbated by an STI diagnosis.

The following behavioral and affective goals may be used when working with couples from a systemic perspective:

1. Increase couples' knowledge and accurate understanding of the transmission and treatment of the diagnosed STI in order to decrease fears related to transmission or re-infection (affect) and to modify the couples' sexual practices (behavior).
2. Identify and communicate feelings (explore emotions) about a diagnosis and treatment of the STI and its impact on the couples' relationship (behavior) in order to feel validated and enjoy sex with each other again (affect).
3. Reestablish relationship parameters such as those related to fidelity issues (behavior) in order to feel emotionally safe and secure with one's partner (affect).
4. Identify the long-term impact of the STI on couples' lives (e.g., possible infertility, management of future outbreaks, caregiving issues, and medical, financial, and job-related concerns) in order to make decisions about issues (behavior) as they arise and feel hopeful about the future (affect).
5. Increase communication between partners about the diagnosis and its effects (behavior) in order to increase feelings of trust and intimacy (affect).
6. Enhance couples' coping skills related to the psychological and physical management of the STI (behavior) in order to feel in control and less overwhelmed by the infection (affect).

Counseling Couples with HIV

When one or both partners are diagnosed with HIV, interventions should be specific to the stage of the disease and the individual needs of the couple (Vaughan & Kinnier, 1996). For example, a person who has just been diagnosed with HIV will have different counseling needs than a person who is looking for ways to cope with a diagnosis of full-blown AIDS. Initially, counseling may include helping couples to identify and explore their reactions to the diagnosis and to learn how to mobilize themselves to receive appropriate help—from medical treatment or group support (Hoffman, 1991). A counselor may assist the individual in exploring how, when, and whom to tell about the diagnosis (Huber, 1996; Serovich, 2000). Intense emotional reactions such as anxiety, helplessness, hopelessness, depression, guilt, anger, and a loss of self-esteem commonly occur in one or both partners (Hedge, 1996). A person may even contemplate suicide.

Hedge (1996) suggested that sexuality counseling should focus on helping couples examine their current lifestyle and sexual practices and make adjustments to living with the reality of the AIDS virus. This includes informing couples on how to practice safer sex to prevent the transmission of the virus. Sexuality counseling is focused on helping couples address the difficulties of living with the uncertainty of the future, explore active coping skills for living with this uncertainty, and explore ways to maximize the quality of their life together while coming to accept the disease (Hedge, 1996).

In the next section we describe some useful interventions for counseling couples who are diagnosed with STIs. Specific interventions are also provided in Box 8.1.

INTERVENTIONS FOR TREATING COUPLES WITH STIs

Telling a Partner

Disclosing a diagnosis of an STI to a partner is difficult because it implies that one partner may have also transmitted the infection to the other (Masters et al., 1995). Disclosure may bring up issues related to infidelity in the relationship, which threatens mutual trust. Failure to disclose, however, places a partner at risk if the infection goes untreated. This can result in serious complications.

Sexuality counselors can expect to encounter individuals experiencing an array of emotions when it comes to disclosing an STI diagnosis. Difficulty disclosing is often related to the infected person's own reaction to their diagnosis, which can vary from experiencing little to no anxiety to feeling distraught and humiliated (Dwyer & Niemann, 2002; Lindemann, 1988). These differences are often influenced by a person's cultural and religious values and beliefs,

---

BOX 8.1
Interventions at a Glance

- Ask partners to communicate with each other about feelings and concerns related to discussing STIs.
- Ask partners to communicate with each other about how the STI has impacted their relationship.
- Ask partners to read pamphlets containing information on their diagnosed STI, including how it is transmitted and how it is treated.
- Suggest that couples contact the CDC National STD and AIDS hotline at 800-227-8922 to obtain information about their diagnosed infection. Spanish speaking couples can call 800-344-7432; TTY services for the Deaf and Hearing Impaired are available at 800-243-7889.
- Instruct couples on how to use condoms in order to protect themselves against the spread of STIs and reinfection.
- Instruct couples in the use of couples' massage to create intimacy and modify their sexual practices.
- Show partners how to brainstorm ways they can modify their sexual practices during "critical times."
- Ask couples to identify ways they can help each other to manage stress in order to help prevent outbreaks or infections.
- Ask partners to identify emotions and events that "trigger" the onset of a herpes or genital warts breakout.
- Ask partners to identify how each can reestablish trust in their relationship.
- Brainstorm with couples about how they can re-create emotional closeness.
- Ask couples to describe ways that the diagnosed STI has affected their reproductive decisions.
- Ask couples to identify religious or cultural beliefs related to STIs that may be interfering with their ability to express themselves sexually.
- Ask each partner to describe any sexual problem they are experiencing related to their diagnosed STI.

along with societal messages they may have received about STIs. For example, a young woman offers this explanation: "My strong Catholic upbringing taught me to keep my virginity until I was married. I should have known that I might be punished by contracting a disease if I had sex before that time. I feel so ashamed and unclean. No one will ever want to be with me if they know about the disease. I will never let anyone know about this."

Some people may hesitate to disclose because they fear their partner's reaction (Lindemann, 1988). They may worry about "hurting a partner physically or emotionally" (Lindemann, 1988, p. 65) or they may fear being rejected themselves (Dwyer & Niemann, 2002). For example, another woman described her situation as follows: "I was so upset about my diagnosis of herpes that I could not eat or sleep. I felt humiliated and paralyzed to talk about it with anyone. I cared deeply for my partner and knew I needed to tell him so he could seek treatment. I felt so guilty that I would ruin his life. I did not want to hurt him. I was afraid he would think less of me. I was afraid he would be angry and reject me. I feared he would never want to see me again."

Ho (as cited in Lindemann, 1988) suggests that sexuality counselors can assist individuals with disclosing by using a variety of approaches, including role-plays, rehearsal, modeling, and the "empty chair" technique. (See Lindemann, 1988, for details on these techniques.) Keep in mind that even those people who desire to tell their partner about an STI are often reluctant and uneasy because they are "worried about what to say" as well as "*how* [italics added] to tell their [partner]" (Lindemann, 1988, p. 59).

The suggestions presented in Figure 8.1 offer some general guidelines for telling a partner about an STI. Sexuality counselors can provide these guidelines to individuals or use them as guides to facilitate disclosure of an STI from one partner to another. It is important to remember that disclosure of an STI is often a difficult and emotional process. Therefore, interventions should be carefully planned and well thought out.

Education as an Intervention

Education about STIs is vital for helping couples to understand and cope with a diagnosed infection.

1. Be honest. There is nothing to be gained by downplaying the potential risks associated with STIs. If you tell your partner, "I have this little drip, but it is probably nothing," you may regret it. Be sure your partner understands the importance of obtaining a medical evaluation.
2. Even if you suspect that your partner may have been the source of your infection, there is little to be gained by blaming him or her. Instead, you may wish simply to acknowledge that you have the infection and are concerned that your partner gets proper medical attention.
3. Your attitude may have considerable impact on how your partner receives the news. If you display high levels of anxiety, guilt, fear, or disgust, your partner may reflect these feelings in his or her response. Try to present the facts in as clear and calm a fashion as you can manage.
4. Be sensitive to your partner's feelings. Be prepared for reactions of anger or resentment. These are understandable initial responses. Being supportive and demonstrating a willingness to listen without becoming defensive may be the best tactics for diffusing a negative response.
5. Engaging in sexual intimacies after you become aware of your condition and before you obtain medical assurances that you are no longer contagious is clearly inappropriate.
6. Medical examinations and treatments for STIs, when necessary, can be a financial burden. Offering to pay for some or all of these expenses may help to maintain (or reestablish) goodwill in your relationship.
7. In the case of herpes, where recurrences are unpredictable and the possibility of infecting a new partner is an ongoing concern, it is a good idea to discuss your herpes before sexual intimacies take place. You may wish to preface your first sexual interaction by saying, "There is something we should talk over first."

FIGURE 8.1
Telling a Partner
Source: From *Our Sexuality,* 8th ed. (p. 475), by R. Crooks and K. Baur. © 2002. Reprinted with permission of Wadsworth, a division of Thomson Learning: www.thomsonrights.com. Fax 800-730-2215.

Educational information from articles, books, educational tapes, and pamphlets along with interaction with sexuality counselors assist couples with increasing their knowledge and understanding of the transmission and treatment of a diagnosed infection. Providing educational information helps normalize couples' fears about engaging in sexual activities and living a normal sexual life. It can also help to correct sexual myths about STIs and reverse misunderstandings that may affect sexual interactions between partners.

Couples diagnosed with an STI can benefit from the following educational goals: (a) education related to the diagnosed STI, (b) education related to the transmission or reinfection of the STI, (c) education related to the treatment of the STI, and (d) education related to modifications in a couple's sexual practices due to the STI. It is also important for sexuality counselors to assist couples in understanding the systemic nature of an STI diagnosis as well as exploring the impact of the diagnosis on their relationship. In cases of HIV-related infections, this involves expanding the discussion to include significant others, particularly within both immediate families (Miller, Goldman, & Bor, 1994).

Modifying Sexual Practices

When an STI has been diagnosed, couples want to know if sex will ever be the same, if they will be able to enjoy sex despite the diagnosed infection. Sexuality counselors can clarify the situation for couples by helping them to modify their sexual practices while also exploring their feelings about these changes. This includes helping to identify "critical" times (such as a herpes outbreak) that may deter sexual contact. Couples may choose to remain abstinent during these times or experiment with other forms of sexual expression (e.g., kissing, caressing, massaging) in order to create intimacy. Other modifications may include the use of condoms or dental dams and other safe sex practices.

Managing Outbreaks

Sexuality counselors can help couples explore ways to manage outbreaks of long-term STIs (e.g., herpes and genital warts) while continuing to nurture their intimacy. Couples identify potential stressors that may trigger an outbreak and discuss ways to conquer them. They also communicate their anxieties and patterns about outbreaks. Some couples decide to modify their sexual practices during these times; others abstain from sexual activities altogether.

Identifying and Exploring Feelings

Couples experiencing STIs need an opportunity to explore their emotional reactions to a positive diagnosis along with discussing the impact of the STI on their relationship. Sexuality counselors help couples identify and share those feelings often related to anxiety, depression, guilt, shame, anger, embarrassment, and fear (Dwyer & Niemann, 2002; Masters et al., 1995; Ross, 1999). By expressing their emotions to each other, couples are able to normalize their experience and feel validated so that they can enjoy sex again and feel in control of their lives.

Addressing Infidelity Issues

Infidelity is often implied when one partner in an intimate relationship is diagnosed with an STI (Masters et al., 1995). Sexuality counselors help couples explore and reestablish relationship parameters in order to feel emotionally safe and secure with their partner. In addition, issues related to infidelity, including trust, commitment, resentment, and physical and emotional withdrawal (distancing) of one or both partners, should be addressed (Dwyer & Niemann, 2002).

Identifying the Long-Term Impact of an STI

Couples need to be able to identify and discuss the long-term impact of a diagnosed STI in order to feel less fearful and in control of their future (Dwyer & Niemann, 2002). Sexuality counselors can help facilitate communication about issues related to infidelity; infertility; managing future outbreaks; caregiving decisions; and medical, financial, and job-related concerns. Clear communication practices will enable couples to make decisions as these issues arise and to feel hopeful about their future.

Challenging Myths

Challenging myths related to STIs promotes changes in attitudes and beliefs and can help couples make well-informed decisions about their sexual health (Marr, 1998). In some cases, it reduces anxiety and helps couples to be less fearful about transmission or reinfection of an STI and better able to enjoy sex. In other cases, it can prevent the spread of infections or encourage couples to seek medical help. Some common myths make the following assumptions:

- Wearing a condom guarantees protection against contracting and spreading STIs.

- All STIs exhibit symptoms. Therefore, a person without symptoms must not have an STI.
- STIs cannot be contracted by using sex toys.
- People who get STIs are promiscuous and often unfaithful to their partner.
- A pregnant woman cannot contract an STI.
- A person diagnosed with an STI can no longer engage in or enjoy sexual intercourse.
- A pregnant woman with herpes cannot have a vaginal delivery.
- A person cannot contract an STI by engaging in oral sex.

These myths can lead to irrational beliefs, preventing couples from being able to experience sex and intimacy. For example, a couple with herpes might have the following irrational belief: "Because there is not a cure for herpes, we can no longer have sex." Such a belief might be devastating to them without the help of a sexuality counselor challenging their sexual myths, restructuring their beliefs, and helping them to create positive affirmations. For example, the couple holding the belief that they can no longer have sex can remedy their situation with the following affirmation: "Although there is no long-term cure for herpes, we can have a fulfilling sexual relationship and enjoy intimacy by using barrier methods or by choosing to engage in nongenital sexual activities."

Specific Interventions for Diagnosed Sexual Dysfunctions

Sexual dysfunctions (e.g., sexual desire disorder, vaginismus, orgasm disorder, premature ejaculation, or erectile dysfunction) may arise as a result of a diagnosed STI (Ross, 1999). In these cases interventions are specific to the phase of the sexual response cycle that is affected. (See Chapters 6 and 7 for specific intervention strategies for these issues.)

SAFER SEX AND STI PREVENTION

The AIDS epidemic has raised global awareness about the importance of practicing safer sex to avoid contracting a virus for which there is no cure (Stone, Timyan, & Thomas, 1999). It has also influenced an awareness of preventing other STIs that may facilitate the spread of HIV. However, despite this awareness and the attempts to diminish their spread, STIs continue at an alarming rate, affecting 15 million people

annually (CDC, 2003; Crooks & Baur, 2002). The epidemic is primarily attributed to risky sexual behavior involving unsafe sexual practices. It is therefore important that individuals and couples understand what "safer sex" entails.

Sexuality counselors provide couples with specific suggestions for minimizing their chances of contracting or spreading a sexually transmitted disease as well as helping them to better understand safer sex practices. The following guidelines are preventive measures to reduce the spread of STIs:*

- Consider abstinence. Although social pressures exist to become sexually involved, each individual must discern the risks and consequences of unprotected sexual contact. Abstaining from sexual activity is a viable alternative and rational choice.
- Obtain accurate information and know when to seek treatment. Having accurate information about STIs, how they are transmitted, what the symptoms are, and what to do to prevent infection can help protect you from exposing yourself to the risks of infection.
- Communicate with your sexual partner about sex and STIs. Although this may require that you take an assertive position, it is part of being responsible for your sexual behavior. Ask your partner about the possibility of any current symptoms of STIs or previous infections. In addition, talk about the use of barrier methods (such as condoms, vaginal pouches, spermicides, or dental dams). By communicating with your partner, you can assess your risks of becoming infected and decide together how you want to express yourselves sexually.
- Avoid sexual activity with multiple partners. Having numerous partners increases your risk of STIs and having casual sex with an anonymous partner is even riskier. Being selective in your choice of a sex partner will improve your chances of avoiding STIs.
- Inspect your partner's genitals. Looking is the best way of discovering if you or your partner has a rash, wart, sore, genital discharge, or other sign of sexual infection. If you observe something suspicious (a sore or blister), refrain from sexual contact and insist that a medical doctor examine your partner.
- Wash your genitals and your partner's genitals before and after sexual activity when the transmission

---

*Adapted from *Sexuality Today: The Human Perspective* (pp. 508–509), 5th ed., by G. Kelly. Copyright 1996 by The McGraw-Hill Companies. Reprinted with permission.

of an infection is a possibility. This can occur in the form of foreplay by taking a bath or shower together. After sexual intercourse, prompt washing is suggested.

- Use condoms, vaginal spermicides, sponges, diaphragms, or dental dams. If used consistently and correctly, a male condom will significantly lower chances of contracting or spreading an STI (CDC, 2002). Likewise, spermicidal foams and creams, especially nonoxynol-9, have been shown to reduce the risks of some infectious organisms. However, they have not been proved effective for all STIs (CDC, 2002). For protection during oral sex, a condom or dental dam is recommended.

- Obtain prompt testing and medical treatment. If you *suspect* you have been exposed to an STI, consult your physician for advice. If you are *sure* you have been exposed, get medical attention promptly and abstain from further sexual activity. A diagnosis and effective course of treatment will help to prevent the serious complications of STIs. Treatment can be obtained from a physician, hospital, or public health agency. It is important to be examined to be sure the disease has been eradicated. Sexual partners should be urged to be tested (and treated if necessary) as well.

- Inform your sexual partner if you have or suspect you have an STI. By doing so, you can avoid spreading the infection and alert your partner to watch for his or her own symptoms or to initiate medical intervention. It is important to remember that many STIs do not exhibit symptoms in the early stages but require prompt treatment to prevent complications.

In addition to the above guidelines, couples can explore alternative sexual practices. These may include mutual masturbation rather than intercourse, sensual massage, sharing sexual fantasies, hugging and dry kissing, and the use of sex toys that are not shared (Marr, 1998). These options provide sexual pleasure without the risk of STIs.

Case Example

Monroe, aged 30, and Annie, aged 34, have been married for eight years. Monroe is a law enforcement detective who works sexual assault cases and homicide; Annie is a dental hygienist in a large group practice. During the last year, Monroe and Annie have tried to conceive a

child with no success. Recently, they began infertility testing that required Annie to undergo a procedure to determine if she had blockage in her fallopian tubes. At the conclusion of the testing, the couple met with Annie's physician to discuss the test results. The physician indicated that Annie's fallopian tubes had irreversible scarring due to an untreated infection of chlamydia. She was informed that she should receive treatment for the infection and that the incurred damage to her fallopian tubes was beyond repair. The couple was told that their chance of conceiving a child through intercourse was not likely. Monroe and Annie were shocked and devastated.

Application of the Five Stages of the Integrative Couples' Model
Stage 1: Assessing and Obtaining an Interactional View of the Problem
Annie states that she seldom sees Monroe because of his schedule, which requires him to participate in "stakeouts" for days. She reports that she has been feeling distant from him since they began trying to conceive a child and has started to wonder if he wants to have children at all. Annie explains that after Monroe had an affair lasting several months in the third year of their marriage, they postponed having children because of her feelings of anger and mistrust toward him. She offers that she has never completely resolved her feelings of mistrust toward her husband and that since his affair, she has experienced a loss of sexual desire for him. Monroe recently told her that he believes he may be responsible for the chlamydia infection. Annie reports feeling betrayed, angry, hurt, depressed, and resentful. "I've lost my chance to have my own biological child because of this infection," she exclaims. "My body is damaged, it will never heal and be normal. I love Monroe, I just don't know if I can forgive him. We'll just have to wait and see." Annie is unsure how she will cope with the consequences of her infection but states she remains committed to her relationship.

Monroe, on the other hand, states that Annie is too caught up in "becoming a mom" and spends no time or effort on their relationship. He feels that she does not understand the enormous pressure he is under in his job.

He admits to the affair and is remorseful; however, he states that Annie rarely makes him a priority in her life and that her neglect contributed to him stepping out of the marriage. He recently told Annie that the woman he had the affair with contacted him months later telling him that she had been diagnosed with chlamydia. Since he had no symptoms at the time, he chose to ignore the information and received no treatment. He admits he never told Annie because he had already caused her too much pain. He is feeling guilty, ashamed, and angry that he may be responsible for their infertility problems. "I feel so responsible and humiliated," he states. "I never thought the infection would affect me or my relationship with Annie. I was afraid to tell Annie the truth. I feared she might leave me."

The sexuality counselor obtains a historical view of the problem in addition to a sexual and relational history that includes an exploration of STIs. Both Monroe and Annie indicate that they are receiving medical treatment for the chlamydia infection. After obtaining their permission, the counselor consults with their physician to understand any specific physiological concerns regarding their case. The couple is provided with symptom and treatment information on chlamydia. The counselor then focuses on the emotional impact of the STI as well as the sexual and existing relational issues that have been brought about by the STI diagnosis. Annie admits to strong feelings of anger toward Monroe for the affair and its consequences. Her emotions are complicated by the fact that she is experiencing her own loss of identity as a sexually productive female. The sexuality counselor validates the intensity of emotion that surrounds Annie's feelings of betrayal and loss along with Monroe's deep feelings of regret and remorse for his action. The counselor then helps the couple create a collaborative view of the problem based on their definition of the problem and states the problem in interactive terms: "Both of you are experiencing a lot of anger and hurt toward each other and are managing it by pushing each other away. It sounds like the two of you want to reestablish trust in your relationship in order to feel more intimate and connected."

Stage 2: Goal Setting
With the assistance of the sexuality counselor, Monroe and Annie set five goals outlined in both behavioral and affective terms:

1. We would like to increase our knowledge about chlamydia and determine if we need to modify our sexual practices in order to feel more positive about safety needs in our relationship.
2. We would like to communicate our feelings about having a diagnosed STI and its effect on our relationship in order to enjoy sex with each other and feel connected.
3. We would like to reestablish trust in our relationship in order to feel more committed and loving toward each other.
4. We would like to explore the long-term effects of chlamydia as it relates to having a family in order to feel more hopeful about the future.
5. We would like to learn ways to cope with our anger and resentment related to the consequences of the STI and our subsequent infertility in order to feel more in control.

Stage 3: Adapting New Perceptions and Behaviors
Monroe's strengths—being calm and persistent in the face of danger as well as his ability to solve difficult criminal cases—are emphasized. Annie's knowledge of the medical field and her communication skills are identified along with her commitment to her husband. As a couple, they discuss their willingness to face their diagnosis and its consequences on their family planning. They recognize their desire to have a more trusting and intimate relationship.

The counselor next devises interventions that mobilize their assets and begin to change the relational system.

1. They will read recommended books and pamphlets about STIs and specifically about chlamydia and its common occurrence, transmission, symptoms, and prevention.
2. They will learn to communicate their feelings and discuss the effects of their diagnosis by practicing clearer communication and assertiveness skills. By exploring their feelings, they have an opportunity to express their fears and concerns and move on to enjoying sex with each other again.

3. They will establish trust by following through on commitments they make to each other, including fidelity commitments, time frames, social engagements, and household activities. In addition, each will support the other's need for a degree of independence within the context of the relationship that will allow them to follow individual pursuits.
4. They will schedule an appointment with their physician and explore options for family planning.
5. They will attend a weekly support group for couples experiencing infertility problems.

Stage 4: Maintaining New Perceptions and Behaviors

Monroe and Annie realize that they need to move very slowly in resolving their issues related to trusting each other again and moving on to planning for a family of their own. They acknowledge that they could easily fall into old behavior patterns by blaming their partner for the transmitted STI, emotionally and physically withdrawing from each other, failing to communicate their concerns and feelings, creating mistrust by not following through on their commitments, and failing to plan their weekly dates and "care days." At this point, the sexuality counselor might ask, "Monroe and Annie, what will you do when you realize that you are managing your trust issues by withdrawing from each other?" In addition, the counselor might suggest that Monroe and Annie keep a personal log of their contributions to increasing trust in their relationship and communicate their success to each other on a weekly basis.

Stage 5: Validating New Perceptions and Behaviors

Monroe and Annie are encouraged by their commitment to each other and yet anxious about their ability to reestablish a loving and stable foundation to their relationship. They struggle with trusting each other as new issues arise in their relationship. Both commit to supporting and encouraging each other in an effort to build trust; however, they are apprehensive about their ability to feel intimate and connected again. Recognizing their success through intermittent feelings of hope, they are encouraged and see themselves as committed and determined people who have grown closer by confronting their difficult issues.

SUMMARY

Sexually transmitted infections (STIs) affect millions of people in our society each year. Sexuality counselors need to be familiar with the most common STIs, in addition to being able to address the emotional and relational concerns resulting from these infections. This chapter provides information on the transmission, symptoms, and treatment of some of the most commonly occurring STIs, including bacterial vaginosis, chlamydia, gonorrhea, syphilis, genital warts, herpes, viral hepatitis (A, B, and C), acquired immunodeficiency syndrome (AIDS), and trichomoniasis. Sexuality counselors provide couples with specific suggestions for minimizing their chances of contracting or spreading sexually transmitted infections as well as helping them to better understand safer sex practices.

When assessing an individual or couple for a sexually transmitted infection, a physician performs a physical examination, including a screening for STIs. Once a diagnosis is determined, sexuality counselors help couples address the resulting psychological effects, such as the development of sexual problems or dysfunctions along with relational issues that may emerge. Sexual problems and dysfunctions include premature ejaculation, low sexual desire, erectile dysfunction, vaginismus, orgasmic disorder, or complete withdrawal from sexual activity. Relationship problems often focus on issues of trust, commitment, anger, and resentment as well as the physical and emotional withdrawal by one or both partners.

An integrative couples' model for sexuality counseling offers a variety of options to meet these goals by providing couples with the ability to revisit issues throughout the counseling process. The model identifies those interventions that will help couples to move toward creating healthy sexual relationships. These interventions include telling a partner about a diagnosed STI, reviewing psychoeducational materials, modifying sexual practices, and managing outbreaks. Other interventions include addressing issues of infidelity, discussing long-term effects of STIs, challenging sexual myths, and designing specific interventions for diagnosed sexual dysfunctions.

COUNSELING SEXUAL MINORITY COUPLES

KEY CONCEPTS

- Sexual orientation is a complex concept influenced by myriad cultural, biological, and genetic components.
- Sexual minority couples include gay males, lesbians, bisexuals, and transgendered persons.
- Bisexual couples consider themselves part of the gay community.
- Transgendered people are included in social descriptions of the gay and lesbian community.
- There are multiple perspectives and definitions of gay and lesbian sexual orientation and lifestyle.
- Although the sexual revolution influenced greater acceptance for sexual minority cultures, homophobia and discrimination remain widespread.
- The attitudes, bias, and cultural competencies of sexuality counselors must be examined prior to working with members of sexual minority cultures.
- Internal factors such as identity development, identity management, aging issues, and socialization messages such as fusion challenge gay men and lesbians.
- External factors such as family of origin, social pressure, legal issues, career choices, and economic factors influence gay and lesbian culture.
- Both gay and lesbian sexual culture includes a wide diversity of sexual practices.
- Gay male sexual complaints include issues related to monogamy, performance anxiety, fear of AIDS, and maintaining sexual interest and arousal in long-term relationships.
- Abated sexual activity in long-term relationships is a frequent presenting issue for lesbians.
- An integrative couples' model offers a wide array of theories and intervention strategies to provide sexual minorities with up-to-date treatment options.

Human sexual orientation is a complex concept that is influenced by the interaction of cultural, biological, and genetic components. All of these factors contribute to characteristic patterns of sexual identity and orientation for most men and women. For example, the adages describing little boys—"snakes and snails and puppy dog tails"— and little girls—"sugar and spice and everything nice"—embodies how our society conceptualizes males and females. Most often in our society, males are sexually attracted to females and females are sexually attracted to males. What happens when we defy mainstream societal definitions? Today, intragender variations in sexual orientation such as homosexuality and bisexuality are increasingly being addressed in human sexuality research (Pattatucci, 1998) and must also be addressed by sexuality counselors and other experts. In this chapter, sexual minority couples include gay males, lesbians, bisexuals, and transgendered persons. We describe men who engage in same sex practices as gay, and women who engage in same sex practices as lesbian. Bisexuals and transgendered persons are included in our descriptions of gay and lesbian culture.

HISTORICAL DEVELOPMENT

The "Stonewall Rebellion" in 1969, a protest that took place in Greenwich Village, marked the beginning of the Gay Liberation Movement in the United States (Nichols, 2000). Some researchers suggest that a journal for gay males, *The Mattachine,* predated the Stonewall Rebellion by several years. Prior to these landmark events, the prevalent belief among Americans was that homosexuality was an illness, a sin, or both. Gay people themselves also shared this belief (Nichols, 2000). They attempted to pass for straight and did not come out of the closet to their family members or their coworkers. In fact, gay men were often jailed and branded sexual perverts or they were committed to psychiatric institutions. Police raided gay bars and treated gays as criminals.

Changes in beliefs and attitudes regarding sexual orientation began to emerge after these significant social events and thus provided gays and lesbians with a different perspective of themselves. During the 1970s, more gay men and lesbians "came out," or began to identify themselves as gay or lesbian to others (Nichols, 2000). Most Americans began to have exposure to gays and lesbians—a family member, someone they knew, or a public figure who was featured in the media.

Unfortunately, just as there was increased awareness and acceptance for gays and lesbians in the 1980s, acquired immunodeficiency syndrome (AIDS) first appeared in the gay male community. Initially, many gay men resisted the idea that the disease was communicated sexually, and they believed that there was a political plot to undermine the gay community. Gay bars and bathhouses were sources of concern and created fear for gay men regarding their personal safety. As the death toll increased, gay men became alarmed and the community reverted to more conservative views regarding sexual activities. Within a short time, sexual activity that seemed to be gaining acceptance in the community became a stigma and even a death sentence in the eyes of society. As a result, the incidence of casual or anonymous sex among gay men decreased significantly. Sexual prac-

tices changed: anal sex diminished in practice, oral sex was performed with caution or with condoms, and mutual masturbation became the practice of choice (Nichols, 2000). The heterosexual community blamed gay men for AIDS and reverted to prior beliefs that gay sex was sinful or sick.

Meanwhile, lesbians became more vocal about sex and sexual orientation. During the 1980s, the lesbian community initiated a sexual revolution of their own that moved beyond traditional female sex to activities that may have previously been described as masculine: "rough sex, 'dirty' sex, role-polarized sex, 'promiscuity,' sex without love, anonymous sex, and sadomasochistic sex" (Nichols, 2000, p. 343).

In the 1990s a "bisexual pride" movement began within the gay and lesbian community (Nichols, 2000). Many had viewed bisexuals as gays or lesbians who were afraid to "come out." Although bisexuality remains stigmatized to some extent, most bisexuals now consider themselves part of the gay community.

In the late 1990s transgendered people—males and females who physically change gender through surgical means—were identified with the sexual movement and are now included in social descriptions of the gay and lesbian community.

The gay, lesbian, bisexual, and transgendered community has enjoyed great strides in social acceptance, increased diversity of lifestyle, and more inclusive sexual attitudes of men and women (Nichols, 2000). Clearly, the baby boom generation has experienced profound changes regarding the acculturation of homosexuals in a heterosexual community.

Descriptions of Sexual Minorities

We use the following terms to describe relationships of sexual minorities:

- **Gay males:** Men who have intimate and sexual relations with men. This is generally the preferred term; homosexual carries a more clinical connotation.
- **Lesbians:** Women who have intimate and sexual relations with women. This is the preferred term, although some prefer *gay female*. Lesbian female is redundant.
- **Bisexuals:** Persons who "experience sexual attraction to either sex, although not necessarily in equal degrees" (Carl, 1990, p. 2).
- **Transgendered:** Men and women who "describe themselves as having been born in the wrong body; that is, they feel that emotionally they are

one sex while their bodies are another. For the most part, they do not consider themselves homosexual" (Carl, 1990, p. 3).

Descriptions of sexual minority couples extend beyond their sexual practices, however, and encompass aspects of sexuality that include cultural, emotional, and psychological factors, as well as sexual behaviors (Imber-Black, 1989).

CULTURAL ASPECTS OF GAY AND LESBIAN SEXUAL ORIENTATION

Cultural Factors

Most definitions of gay and lesbian culture reflect the countries or geographical regions in which they live. In fact, gay cultures in each community are different from each other. Similarly, various gay and lesbian subcultures have emerged, each defined by a variety of shared experiences and interests (Drescher, 1998).

Lesbians and gays from African American and African Caribbean communities often report their communities to be extremely heterosexist (Greene & Boyd-Franklin, 1996). In some ethnic groups, the male gender role is even more restrictive than the white male gender role, and the consequences for violating the gender role are severe. Many African Americans and Native Americans who have faced racist genocidal practices place more importance on reproduction as a means of ensuring the survival of their group and may be less tolerant of sexual practices that do not have procreation as a main goal.

Asian and Pacific Islander communities in the United States also emphasize the obligation of men to marry in order to carry on the family name. In these communities, homosexuality is often viewed as a rejection of cultural values or as a form of social deviance that brings shame to the family (Fukuyama & Ferguson, 2000). Thus, in African American, Native American, Asian American, and Pacific Islander groups in the United States, gay men and lesbians may be under pressure to adopt a heterosexual role and to marry and bear children based on fears of future representation of their culture (Greene & Boyd-Franklin, 1996).

Many African American lesbians and gay men are involved in interracial relationships. This can be attributed in part to a limited number of partner choices in the African American communities. Similar explanations are found in reports that most gay Asian Americans have partners from a different race: "Within the gay White male community, the term 'rice queen' refers to White men who prefer Asian men who presumably play out female roles" (Fukuyama & Ferguson, 2000, p. 95). Family values and responsibility to perpetuate the family placed on first-born sons in Asian American cultures are incompatible with the notion of gay and lesbian relationships. In fact, terms have been created in order to describe these relationships.

There are cultural differences designating what constitutes sexual relations between two gay men or lesbians. Among some gay men in Mexico, men who play an anal receptive role are stigmatized, but those who play an anal insertive role are not. For these men, homosexuality is a label only for those who play the female role (Fukuyama & Ferguson, 2000). Among Mexicans, Nicaraguans, and Brazilians, oral sex and masturbation are viewed as foreplay. If such activities do not include anal sex, the action is not considered "sex" (Fukuyama & Ferguson, 2000).

Some Latino, African American, and Asian men engage in same-gender sexual relations, but view themselves as heterosexual. For example, Latino men who play the insertive role in anal and oral sex with other Latino men consider themselves heterosexual. Men in the Latino culture who identify themselves as gay are more versatile, engaging in both receptive and insertive oral and anal sex. Latino men who identify themselves as "drag queens" mainly practice receptive oral and anal sex. These explanations offer more acceptable descriptions of gender identity (Fukuyama & Ferguson, 2000). However, in most cultures, fear of a sexual identity other than traditional heterosexuality creates stress for men and women.

Cultural Influences and Homophobia

Although there have certainly been great strides as a result of the sexual revolution in the United States, there remains a degree of homophobia and prejudice that cannot be ignored. Widespread discrimination continues to occur in the workplace, in schools, in places of worship, and in society at large. Society has not yet established terms to describe marriage and committed relationships for gays and lesbians. Although "partner" is probably the most widely used term to express a committed relationship, it does not adequately express the love and intimate attachment involved in these relationships. For example, in business we use the word "partner" to signify an associate or close affiliate, not someone we love and care about deeply.

Although there have been strides toward acceptance of gays and lesbians, there continue to be many faulty assumptions about being gay or lesbian in a heterosexual society.

Models for same-sex relationships are not the same or parallel to models of development for heterosexual couples. For example, it is not true that in gay relationships one man must play the "effeminate" role while his partner is more traditionally identified as a "macho male." Nor is it accurate to assume that in a lesbian relationship one woman exhibits masculine traits while the other is more passive and "feminine" (Young & Long, 1998).

There has also been some discussion in the literature that gay men are afraid of women (Brown & Zimmer, 1986) and therefore feel more comfortable in relationships with men. There is no evidence that fear of women is a characteristic of gay men. Neither is there any evidence that lesbians dislike men.

People are often judgmental about issues that they do not understand. Homophobia is born from lack of understanding and pervades every aspect of family and social life for gay men and lesbians. Brown and Zimmer (1986) define homophobia as "the fear and hatred of same-sex intimacy, love, sexuality, and relationships, and of those individuals and institutions that participate in, affirm, and support same-sex relating" (p. 452). Leslie (1995) further explains the problem:

> Although homophobia is an external reality that is imposed upon the lives of gay men and lesbians, most homosexuals have internalized these beliefs to some extent. Thus, lesbians and gay men must wrestle with their own feelings of self-hatred, shame, and inadequacy at the same time they are attempting to function as family members, partners, and parents. (p. 362)

As a result of both cultural and internalized homophobia, gay men and lesbians and their families constantly face rejection and consequently address issues of how open to be about their personal relationships. In many cases, sexual orientation is a factor in being cut off from family members, losing custody of children, suffering social isolation and rejection, and losing one's employment. Thus, normal family issues can be much more complicated for gay and lesbian couples and families than for heterosexual ones (Leslie, 1995). Diminished sexual desire, an effect of

homophobia, may be downplayed or ignored by counselors, or branded as a physiological impairment. Their tendency may be to address homophobia rather than to examine the sexual effects of isolation and rejection in a larger social context.

BIOLOGICAL ASPECTS OF SEXUAL ORIENTATION

There is considerable ambiguity about the development of gay and lesbian individuals. "The most fervent academic and research debate focuses on whether sexual orientation is the result of factors over which the individual has no control—essentialism—or is a choice made by the individual—social constructionism" (Ellis & Mitchell, 2000, p. 205). Researchers have long debated the dichotomous form—nature versus nurture—of the roots of sexual orientation. These explanations have generated a moderate stance asserting that genetic predisposition is influenced by social environment (Ellis & Mitchell, 2000). However, for some, a biogenetic explanation helps foster social acceptance and tolerance for gay and lesbian lifestyles. According to Ellis and Mitchell (2000), "there is a popular belief that research demonstrating a biogenetic explanation of sexual orientation offers a protection or 'moral shield' for gay [and lesbian] people" (p. 205). Interestingly, Marmor (1998) asserts that counselors' views on the etiology of sexual orientation influence how they work with gays and lesbians. In other words, an "etiology that [supports] a biogenetic component for sexual orientation is likely to lead [counselors] to treat [clients] with same-sex sexual desire in a manner that facilitates acceptance and respect" (Marmor, as cited in Ellis & Mitchell, 2000, p. 206).

Evidence regarding a genetic etiology certainly has important implications for treating sexual problems for gays and lesbians. Supporters of biological theory have recently reported that there are some differences in hormonal patterns that also affect sexual orientation (Ellis & Mitchell, 2000). Research provided by Hamer, Hu, Magnuson, Hu, and Pattatucci (1993) has linked instances of male homosexuality to DNA on the X chromosome, specifically the chromosomal region Xq28. Pattatucci (1998) offers this explanation:

> Linkage results on DNA at Xq28 for females were notably different than those for males. . . The finding of genetic linkage of Xq28 in gay men, but [absent] in lesbians, suggests that the mechanisms underlying

male and female sexual orientation are at least partially distinct. Family studies have generally shown that gay men have more gay brothers than they do lesbian sisters and that lesbians have more lesbian sisters than they do gay brothers, indicating some degree of etiological independence between male and female sexual orientation. (p. 377)

Pattatucci and Hamer (1995) also conducted research on biological and genetic components of sexual orientation but warned that there are sociocultural differences that must be addressed along with biological evidence. A significant factor to be considered when studying females is the influence of strong environmental, cultural, and political elements on lesbian and bisexual identities that are nonexistent for males.

There are other experts who support societal influences and disagree with the results of genetic research (McConaghy, 1993). Supporters of "environmental theory" claim that genetic research lacks validity. Social researchers believe that the basis of sexual orientation rests with environmental factors such as social and legal sanctions (McConaghy, 1993). The debate is ongoing, with supporters for both theories. However, whether one adheres to a theory of biology or a theory of social constructivism to explain sexual orientation, it is clear that there are emotional implications about sexuality and sexual orientation regardless of belief.

COUNSELOR ATTITUDE, BIAS, AND CULTURAL COMPETENCY WHEN WORKING WITH SEXUAL MINORITY COUPLES

Counselor Attitude

Sexuality counselors who feel comfortable with gay and lesbian clients talking about general issues—money problems, communication problems, or phase of life problems—may find their comfort level and confidence dissolving when gay or lesbian clients bring up the subject of sex (Markowitz, 1993). Gay and lesbian couples view their committed relationships as seriously as their heterosexual counterparts. Although they are deprived of the legal right to marry, lesbian and gay couples have a right to expect that their couple relationship will be validated when they seek sexuality counseling (Bepko & Johnson, 2000). They also have the right to know that their sexual issues will be treated with respect and will be treated as equally valid to heterosexual issues surrounding sex-

uality. Furthermore, they have a right to expect that their counselor will be knowledgeable about gay and lesbian culture and will be sensitive to their struggles.

Counselor Attitude Inventory

The following attitude inventory, adapted from Bernstein (2000, p. 456), will help sexuality counselors examine their attitudes toward working with sexual minority couples:

1. What are your values and beliefs about family life and a gay and lesbian culture?
2. Do you accept the notion that a "healthy and happy" normal sexual life is compatible with being gay or lesbian?
3. Will you let couples determine the focus of counseling, rather than make inaccurate assumptions about their sexual issues?
4. Do you believe that gay and lesbian parents are "good enough"?
5. Are you willing to be a client of a gay or lesbian sexuality counselor?

Counselor Bias

Sexuality counselors who work with members of the gay and lesbian community must first confront stereotypes and biases often based on misinformation about gay and lesbian sexual behavior. Sexuality counselors may rely on certain behavioral evidence to categorize a person as homosexual. These characteristic features can lead counselors to ascribe roles for gay men to behave in an effeminate manner and for lesbians to behave in stereotypical masculine ways. Gender-inconsistent role information also often leads to assumptions about sexual behavior and sex role expectations. It is essential that sexuality counselors educate themselves by reading literature on homosexuality and by attending lectures on specific sexual issues and treatment of these issues for gays and lesbians (Yarhouse, 1999). In addition, Bernstein (2000) suggests that counselors can become informed about aspects of gay life by reading trade books and gay fiction, or viewing films on gay themes. However, "developing personal friendships and becoming professional colleagues of gays and lesbians is the best source of education of all, although it cannot substitute for personal exploration" (Bernstein, 2000, p. 447).

Sexuality counselors must be sufficiently informed so that they focus on the specific issues raised by their clients in counseling—not on "why" clients are gay or lesbian. Counselors should also be careful not to identify pathology as intrinsic to gay and lesbian sexual orientation, which is not a diagnosable disorder. In addition, they must become familiar with social issues surrounding the gay and lesbian cultures and understand the bias that society perpetuates on them, particularly regarding behaviors such as holding hands or kissing in public that can invite rejection or even possible retaliation by opponents.

Sexuality counselors should ask themselves questions before treating gay and lesbian clients:

> Am I making assumptions about a client's sexual orientation? If I am, Why, and on what basis?

> What cues am I responding to when I make these assumptions?

> Am I treating my clients' sexual concerns as equal to those of heterosexual couples?

> Am I understanding the issues surrounding sexuality in a gay and lesbian culture?

> Am I being sensitive to the needs and problems my clients face in a heterosexual world?

Counselor Competency

Bernstein (2000) proposes a way to address a cultural competency model by sensitizing heterosexual sexuality counselors who work with gays, lesbians, and their families and asking them "to examine themselves, their own privilege as heterosexuals, and their attitudes, feelings, and beliefs about gay, lesbian, bisexual, and transgendered people" (p. 443).

Ethical issues are an important part of a counselor competency model. The Association for Gay, Lesbian, and Bisexual Issues in Counseling (AGLBIC), a division of the American Counseling Association (ACA) identifies guidelines for working with gay, lesbian, and bisexual persons. Gays and lesbians voice strong objections to having a counselor who "overtly or covertly disapproves of their sexual orientation and lifestyle" (Bernstein, 2000, p. 444). Sexuality counselors are also faced with the ethical dilemma of practicing within their level of expertise and competence. It is not ethical to deny counseling services because of a couple's sexual orientation, but if counselors are unable or unwilling to counsel gay or lesbian clients, they must refer them to a counselor having the appropriate expertise. Sexuality counselors can use the P-LI-SS-IT model presented in Chapter 1 to guide them in their decision making when treating sexual minority couples.

Although many gays and lesbians seek help from a counselor of the same sexual orientation, there are practical reasons why some do not, including the fact that small communities may not have gay or lesbian counselors practicing there. In addition, some gays and lesbians choose a heterosexual counselor in order to keep their therapy and social lives separate (Bernstein, 2000).

The last decade has witnessed a shift in attitude of many counselors toward a more affirmative view of gay and lesbian lifestyles. Sexuality counselors are more able, as a result of self-education, to acknowledge the courage and resilience of their clients who have broken with perceived social norms and who have created a different lifestyle. A willingness by gay and lesbian clients to raise issues in counseling outside mainstream sexual practices is itself an act of courage. Those professionals who are aware of their personal attitudes, bias, and competencies about gay and lesbian sexuality will be more prepared to take the next step toward helping minority couples with their sexual concerns and practices, and to provide appropriate methods of treatment.

THE PROCESS OF SEXUALITY COUNSELING FOR GAY AND LESBIAN COUPLES

Reasons for Seeking Sexuality Counseling

Same-sex couples seek sexuality counseling for many of the same reasons that heterosexual couples seek treatment. These reasons include difficulties in communicating, conflicts about money, developmental concerns, health problems, balancing career and family responsibilities, and sexual issues (Ossana, 2000). Sexual issues are usually related to time, attraction, intimacy, and physical considerations (Ossana 2000).

Although many gay and lesbian couples do not seek counseling specifically related to issues of sexual orientation, sexuality is a significant part of couples' relationships and it will usually emerge as an issue for consideration during a later stage of counseling. For example, couples may seek counseling because they do not feel close to each other anymore and have been unable to communicate effectively with each other. As counseling progresses, other issues of intimacy and sexual interactions surface. These issues relate to individual identity development, homophobia, age-related factors, difficulties related to lack of role models for the gay and lesbian community, and internal and external socialization is-sues such as fusion, family of origin, societal pres-sures, legal issues, career, economic concerns, and coparenting.

For the most part, gays and lesbians come to counseling with much caution. Much like heterosex-ual couples, they will usually wait until they feel safe enough to bring up the topic of sex. Even when they have selected a sexuality counselor whose expertise is in sexual problems or dysfunctions, they will pre-sent with relational issues or family issues prior to ini-tiating conversations about sex. Markowitz (1993) describes the situation:

> Sex is [typically] a risky subject of conversation for any client, unmasking vulnerabilities, [self-doubts], [inadequacy], and hidden shame. For gays and les-bians, whose sexuality so often marks them as targets of scorn and rejection in mainstream society, there has been a communal defensiveness about an open discussion of sexual dissatisfaction out of fear that it might be [used against them]. For these reasons, sex-uality counselors must remain aware that the risk of suicide is higher for these individuals and couples. (p. 52)

Establishing Counselor and Client Trust

Trust is a critical issue for gay and lesbian couples when they decide to seek the services of a sexuality counselor. Bernstein (2000, p. 448) refers to two dis-tinctions for choosing a counselor: "Lavender pages" referrals, which indicate that "clients have been as-sured by trusted sources that [counselors] are sensi-tive to and informed about [gay and lesbian] concerns" and "yellow pages" referrals, which indicate that "prospective clients have minimal information about the [sexuality counselor's] attitudes, values, and ex-perience and practice when it comes to gay and les-bian issues."

An initial issue for sexuality counselors is when or if to disclose their own sexual orientation. Some straight counselors believe that a first step toward cre-ating trust is to raise the issue of sexual orientation in the first session. A counselor might say "You have been referred to me. I am a heterosexual [counselor]. Would you prefer to see a gay [or lesbian] counselor, or do you want to come in and see how that goes for you?" (Bernstein, 2000, p. 450). Some clients feel strongly about openness as a prelude to trust. Other clients, however, do not believe that it is their place to ask about sexual orientation. Sometimes issues of

power and powerlessness dominate the first stages of counseling. Of course, as in any counseling, there is a period of testing to determine trust. Depending on their personal politics about a gay or lesbian lifestyle, clients may confront and challenge the counselor on personal bias and prejudice (Bernstein, 2000). Estab-lishing trust between gay and lesbian clients and their counselors is helping clients express anger and rage about society's homophobic attitude toward them.

Gay and lesbian sexuality counselors must also come to terms with their own philosophy about per-sonal disclosure to clients about their sexual orienta-tion. Some want to disclose their sexual orientation to their clients as a style of "coming out" and to model openness. Others believe that it is an issue of counselor privacy. All gay and lesbian professional counselors are not able to professionally "come out." Still others think that if clients are talking about gay or lesbian lifestyle and the client does not know that the counselor's re-sponse is based on a similar experience, the counselor may feel "secretive" until such information is disclosed. Decisions about choosing a straight or a gay or lesbian counselor, implications regarding the trust level of the client, and the counselor's personal reaction to their client's sexual orientation are all important issues to consider before and during the counseling process. These decisions may have to be revisited more than once during the course of treatment.

Understanding Gay and Lesbian Sexual Culture

Gays and lesbians have very distinct sexual cultures. A striking difference is that gay men tend to communi-cate more directly about the sexual practices they desire. Lesbian clients, on the other hand, express that they want a warm and loving sexual relationship but are often not clear on what that means. Some of these differences reflect the disparate ways men and women are socialized to view and express their sex-uality. Gay men continue to have many more porno-graphic films and magazines from which to choose. Lesbians tend to be portrayed in magazines such as *Playboy* according to the image that straight men have of them. Classified ads in local newspapers con-tinue to be specific regarding gay male expressions of sexuality by advertising whether they are "top" or "bottom," and whether they like to penetrate or be penetrated. Personal ads from lesbians focus more on the romantic relationship and companionship rather than the actual sexual practice.

Gay men have created an entire vocabulary to specify what they do sexually. For example, "shrimping" is the term for sucking on their lover's toes. Gay male sex is articulate, while lesbian sex is less articulable. There are not as many terms used to describe lesbian sexual acts. Some gay men, however, think that gays focus too much on sexual language, and envy lesbians who discuss their feelings in an intimate encounter. Internalized homophobia also interferes with sexuality when lesbians and gays uncritically accept limiting stereotypes of themselves. For example, a lesbian came to counseling feeling upset because she enjoyed penetrating her partner with a dildo and feared that she secretly wanted to be a man. A gay man reported that he didn't feel like a "real" gay man because he did not enjoy initiating oral sex, and another had similar feelings because he did not like anal penetration.

Similar to heterosexual culture, gay and lesbian sexual culture includes a wide diversity of sexual practices. Gay male practices include anal and oral sex, although there is more emphasis on safe sex when engaging in these practices. Other common sexual practices include "mutual masturbation, frottage (rubbing together), manipulation of nipples, kissing, caressing, rimming (tongue in anus), massage, and simultaneous masturbation" (Carl, 1990, p. 4).

Lesbians generally seem more private about their sexual practices. "They practice cunnilingus, mutual masturbation, manipulation of breasts and nipples, sensual massage, kissing, [and] caressing. . . they [also] use dildos, as do gay men and straight couples" (Carl, 1990, p. 6). Some lesbians believe that the political feminist rhetoric of the 1970s that described certain sexual acts as "patriarchal" was repressive and squelched lesbian sexuality. Younger lesbians may be more inclined to produce a strawberry flavored dental dam, used for safety reasons when performing oral sex, and discuss with each other the partners with whom they had sex over the weekend. This does not imply that they are more sexually active, but rather that they have more freedom to express themselves sexually than lesbians who came out twenty years ago (Markowitz, 1993). Both gays and lesbians report that sex is used at times as a way to avoid intimacy and to dissociate from feelings, similar to their heterosexual counterparts.

Lesbian Couple Sexual Issues

Many lesbians come to sexuality counseling complaining of abated sexual activity. This is a particular issue for those in long-term relationships. While diminished sexual activity is common for many couples regardless of their sexual orientation, lesbians feel an extra pressure because society does not view them as a couple and sex is the symbol that affirms that they are more than just friends. Lesbian clients may ask, "If we are not having sex, what is the difference between her and my best friend?" Sexuality counselors help lesbian clients define sex as more than genital contact and orgasms, thus opening options for a more satisfying sexual relationship. Diminished sexual activity may have to do with how women function sexually. Lesbian sex usually begins with a "willingness" rather than a "desire" to have sex, which does not require being sexually aroused to initiate. Also, because there are few role models for lesbian sexuality, women who come to counseling have basic questions about their sexuality and sexual practices. Issues include which partner initiates sex, whether sex has to be reciprocal, or if it is okay not to make love or have intense sexual desire. Performance concerns about orgasm are also raised in counseling, as well as differences in couples' desire regarding frequency, duration, and style. Lesbians may raise issues of fantasy dreams, sometimes about sex with a man, and are concerned about what this means about their sexuality and about their relationship with their partner (Bepko & Johnson, 2000).

Closeness and distance issues may also surface for lesbians. A phenomenon noted as "lesbian bed death" refers to the notion that both partners "may become so protective of one another's feelings that the growing loss of genuineness and true intimacy is expressed through sexual shut down and lack of desire" (Bepko & Johnson, 2000, p. 415). Other issues faced by lesbian clients that impact sexuality include an "imbalance in financial status and power, conflicts that were not discussed directly, fears about being too vulnerable and dependent, and the tendency to reach out to other women for connection when the primary relationship becomes too tense" (Bepko & Johnson, 2000, p. 414). These behaviors take on an added sexualized meaning for both partners in a lesbian relationship.

Gay Couple Sexual Issues

One characteristic of gay relationships is the complexity of negotiations around sex, particularly whether a relationship is to be monogamous. Typically, one partner may desire more or less openness in the relationship, therefore creating stress in the relationship.

Straight counselors must not pathologize infidelity in the same terms as they might for a straight couple because the secrecy of the culture has not encouraged monogamy in the same way it does in heterosexual relationships. Many sexuality experts believe that there is a higher frequency of nonmonogamy among gay men than in heterosexual or lesbian couples (Bepko & Johnson, 2000).

The AIDS virus continues to create concern for gay men, and it is an issue that many bring to counseling. AIDS is one of the most difficult issues many gays have had to face, bringing with it issues of multiple loss as they have watched their friends, lovers, and ex-lovers die. This can have a profound impact on their sexual desire, and limit their freedom during lovemaking.

Performance anxiety is another issue brought to counseling by gay men. A number of clients report that they are intimidated by the "body beautiful" gay men who spend much of their time in gyms and in exercise regimes, and are worried about how they will measure up to their partner (Markowitz, 1993).

Despite the oppressive effects of gender bias, gay men also must contend with the effects of male power and privilege in their couples functioning. Money is often an issue in gay male relationships as it is in heterosexual ones. The partner who earns the most money often has the most power in the relationship.

Many gay men report difficulty maintaining sexual interest and arousal in long-term and sexually monogamous relationships (Brown, 1995). In the past, gay culture valued sexual attractiveness and freedom. This changed with the prevalence of HIV and AIDS, both of which may have influenced gay males' development of the emotional skills necessary for long-term intimacy and commitment. Fear of HIV and AIDS has prevented some gay men from pursuing relationships as well as the traditional developmental models of gay relationships. Gay couples "may [also] lack knowledge about the developmental changes [typically] experienced by gay male couples in long lasting relationships" (Ossana, 2000, p. 490).

Bisexual Couple Issues

One of the most significant areas of concern for bisexual couples is the issue of fidelity in the relationship. It is important that they communicate clearly about their expectations of the relationship and the level of commitment of each partner. If one partner is bisexual, it should be agreed upon in advance whether the relationship will be monogamous or will allow for additional sexual partners.

Transgendered Couple Issues

Issues for transgendered couples can be quite complex. Like everyone else, they grew up in families with societal pressures to pursue traditional goals, including the desire to be loved and valued through intimate relationships. In many cases, they entered into relationships in their quest for tradition, although they did not seem appropriate, given their gender conflicts. Transgendered persons live and work as the opposite gender, although they typically have not undergone surgical genital reassignment. Transsexuals who have had such surgery also desire to live their lives as members of the other gender. They are most likely to experience "a profound lack of congruence between mind (gender identity) and body (biological sex) and are most uncomfortable with the gender role that society expects them to play based on their biological sex" (Gainor, 2000, p. 140). Many transsexual couples have had prior committed relationships before their biological and emotional sex change. Consequently, after a sex change has been completed and they have entered a satisfying relationship, there are residual factors they must address. Their family history and memorabilia have included a characterization of them as the opposite sex. Families and friends may not have made the shift in thinking about their gender change at the same pace as the transgendered couple. Thus, they may continue to be viewed as they were prior to surgery and the related biological and emotional changes they have made regarding their sexuality. Transgendered persons believe their emotional and biological descriptions of self are congruent, although they must continually adapt to confusing roles, rules, and family and societal pressures regarding their change in gender.

Because the term *transgender* is still in dispute, there is a broad definition that includes transsexuals, transvestites, crossdressers, persons with ambiguous genitals, and those who do not identify any gender. Transgenderism has been identified as a classification of individuals since it was investigated by Magnus Hirschfield in 1910. Currently, the American Psychiatric Association continues to classify gender identity disorder in the *DSM-IV-TR* (APA, 2000) as a mental illness. However, the work of Harry Benjamin and his book *Transsexual Phenomenon* (1966) "marked a movement toward a humane and sympathetic approach to addressing the stress experienced by many transsexuals" (Gainor, 2000, p. 132). In fact, prior to the 1960s, few countries offered safe medical procedures for transsexuals and many viewed cross-gender activities as criminal or insane. Consequently, the Standards of Care for Gender Identity Disorders were developed by Benjamin in order to ensure each individual's personal comfort with a gendered self and to maximize emotional health. The latest revision of this document was in February 2001. It has become the most widespread standard of care for counselors who work with transgendered persons. Referred to as HBIGDA-SOC (Harry Benjamin International Gender Dysphoria Association—Standards of Care), the standards are described by the *Free Dictionary* (2004):

> HBIGDA-SOC sections ten through twelve (of thirteen) specifically cover the surgical treatment of transsexuals. Section Twelve, titled "Genital Surgery," deals directly with all concerns about sexual reassignment surgery. It includes six "Eligibility Criteria" and two "Readiness Criteria," which are intended to be used by professionals for both diagnosis and guidance. . . . (p. 1)

Commonalities Between Same-Sex and Heterosexual Couples

Same-sex and heterosexual couples are faced with a variety of common issues (Bepko & Johnson, 2000). These include concerns about children, sex, money, communication, family of origin, conflict resolution, substance abuse, and balancing work with personal and couple commitments. Other issues include conflicts around distance regulation, power, differentiation, triangles, and other relational concerns that affect sexuality. In addition, there are similar developmental stage models that couples follow that are comparable to heterosexual relationships. These stages include the romantic love (honeymoon) stage, followed by conflict and negotiation, and the progression to resolution and integration (Bepko & Johnson, 2000). Although norms and sexual meanings may be different, the quality of lesbian and gay male relationships is in fact generally reported to be comparable to that of heterosexual relationships.

Issues Unique to Same-Sex Couples

Several issues are identified as unique to same-sex couples, including both internal and external factors that contribute to stress couples as they struggle to maintain healthy relationships.

Internal Factors

Identity Development. "Coming out" has been defined as the process whereby a person comes to identify himself or herself as gay, lesbian, bisexual, or transgendered, and recognizes that identity as part of a hidden, oppressed subculture. The development of this process begins early in life, however. Because of fear and lack of information about sexuality and sexual orientation, there may be feelings of confusion, shame, and guilt. By coming out, a person is adopting a nontraditional identity that involves restructuring one's self-concept, personal sense of history, and altering relations with others.

Cass (1979) has developed a six-stage model from a psychosocial perspective (Levine, 1997) that is based on interpersonal congruence theory. Individuals progress through each stage of the model or remain at a particular stage which prevents forward movement in the homosexual identity formation process." According to Degges-White et al. (2000), this is a model that integrates lesbian and gay identity into self-concept and encompasses cognitive, behavioral, and affective components:*

1. Identity confusion: During this stage one realizes that one's behavior or feelings could be defined as homosexual, which raises the question of whether or not one is gay, lesbian, or bisexual. Feelings of alienation and inner distress mark the characteristics of this stage.
2. Identity comparison: During this stage there is a tentative commitment to a gay or lesbian self. The primary task is to address the alienation that results as a gay or lesbian identity becomes clearer. Some people attempt to change their identity to heterosexual because they find their homosexual identity intolerable or unacceptable. If they are able to come to terms with their gay/lesbian identity, they then move from "I might be gay" to "I am probably gay."
3. Identity tolerance: A critical component of the success of this stage is characterized by the development of a support system with other gay, lesbian, or bisexual people.

---

* From "Revisiting Cass' Theory of Sexual Identity Formation: A Study of Lesbian Development," by S. Degges-White, B. Rice, and J. E. Myers, 2000. *Journal of Mental Health Counseling, 22*(4), pp. 318–320. Adapted with permission.

4. Identity acceptance: This stage involves selective identity disclosure to others and increased contact with other homosexuals. Other sexual minorities are viewed more positively and the gay subculture becomes more important in one's life.
5. Identity pride: This stage is characterized by a nearly complete acceptance of one's sexual identity and an immersion into gay/lesbian culture. This may lead to activism and purposeful confrontation with the establishment when intolerance is perceived.
6. Identity synthesis: During this stage, the gay and lesbian identity becomes one aspect of the self rather than an overriding independent identity. Being gay or lesbian is no longer viewed as one's sole identity. There may be increased interaction with heterosexuals and an integrated lifestyle with family, friends, and social structures. (pp. 318–320)

Coleman (1982) proposes a similar five-stage model for coming out: (a) pre-coming out, (b) coming out, (c) exploration, (d) first relationships, and (e) integration. As in Cass's model (1979), some people become stuck in a particular stage and must return to the previous one, and some never progress. The last stage, integration, is a lifelong process that is characterized by trust, acceptance, and freedom. To arrive at this stage, Coleman (1982) suggests that it will take from ten to fourteen years after the pre-coming out awareness experienced in the first stage.

Identity Management. Identity management is a fluid, developmental process through which a person explores, defines, and redefines what it means to be gay or lesbian (Young & Long, 1998). Most experts believe that a supportive gay and lesbian environment fosters a more positive self-identity. Coming out to friends and family also contributes to greater self-acceptance and self-esteem and shapes the overall identity of an individual. Family acceptance is a critical variable for a positive integration of identity. Unfortunately, parents often do not respond favorably and view their own identity as being threatened if they admit they have a gay or lesbian child. They may believe they have failed as parents. They may also go through many of the same feelings of shame, isolation, and fear as their gay and lesbian children (Young & Long, 1998).

Age-related Factors. According to Young and Long (1998), "The notion that gay and lesbian couples can be happy and grow old together is a relatively new concept in our society" (p. 306). A widely recognized barrier that continues to exist for same-sex couples is a lack of social and legal support. Issues such as legal restrictions regarding wills and next of kin, health and medical concerns are addressed with more frequency as we age. "Older same-sex couples fear they will not receive adequate care in institutions and senior-services centers because of discrimination. Older gay men and lesbians may have 'come out' at a time when their sexual orientation was considered sinful or sick" (Young & Long, 1998, p. 306). Many have challenged their religious beliefs due to discrimination in traditional churches, such as the case of Gene Robinson, the Episcopal priest who has openly admitted to being gay and has been consecrated a bishop in the Episcopal Church. Without spiritual guidance or connection with a church or religion, many gays and lesbians may be fearful of death and the afterlife. Unfortunately, most gays and lesbians continue to feel unwelcome in mainstream churches.

Internal Socialization Process and Fusion. Internal socialization refers to a process that focuses women toward their homes and family when they are under stress. Men, on the other hand, tend to create distance under stress, staying away from home, involving themselves in other activities, including sexual ones (Carl, 1990). These differences are not surprising given that traditionally women have been the ones to hold the family together and maintain the emotional well-being of the home and family. Although men and women both work outside the home, lesbian couples report that it is particularly necessary for both partners to do this, because salaries remain lower for women than for men in our society (Young & Long, 1998).

External Factors

Family of Origin. Too often, there is a lack of emotional and economic support from their families of origin when gay men and lesbians come out. The emotional strain can be quite painful to a gay or lesbian person who is already feeling different and isolated from society. LaSala (2000) supports the need for gay men and lesbians to come out specifically in the family of origin. Bepko and Johnson (2000) describe two reasons for this need: "(1) basic family systems ideas about secrecy and (2) the Bowen framework regarding differentiation. The [premise] is that couple relationships suffer, as does the gay or lesbian individual, when part of his or her life is hidden, secret, or compartmentalized from family of origin" (p. 411). Although openness may certainly be the goal, some families may not be able to tolerate or accept the information and may withdraw all support for their gay or lesbian children. When a person does "come out" to the family of origin, it is important to understand that the family's response will often be a long-term process, much like their own identity process and their acceptance of being gay or lesbian (Bepko & Johnson, 2000).

There may also be legal consequences related to family of origin responses for gay or lesbian couples if family members exclude them from their wills in an attempt to make certain that their partners (someone outside of the family) will not inherit any money. Fear or misinformation about AIDS may inhibit some families from participating in social functions with gays or lesbians, and cause them to be ostracized at these functions or holiday gatherings. If family members cannot accept their gay or lesbian children or relatives but do not want to be emotionally cut off from them, they may deny to themselves and others that their child or relative is gay or lesbian.

Social Pressure.   Prejudice is apparent in most social settings, including schools, courts, businesses, medical settings, and places of worship. As discussed earlier in this chapter, homophobia and heterosexism are widespread and often threaten positive self-identity for gays and lesbians. The threat of violence against gays and lesbians often inhibits any display of affection or togetherness in public. Lesbian or gay couples are often anxious about harassment and the threat of physical or sexual assault if their identity becomes visible.

Legal Issues.   Although there has been ongoing emotional debate over the rights of gays and lesbians to marry, they continue to face a glaring absence of legal privileges. Same-sex marriage is not recognized by most states in this country. Massachusetts became the first state to legalize marriage between members of the same sex in May 2004. The Supreme Judicial Court found that denying gay and lesbian couples the right to marry violated the state's constitution. Since this ruling, "more than 35 states have introduced legislation preserving the traditional definition of marriage as a union between a man and a woman" (Peterson, 2004, p. 1). Sixteen states have debated statutory legislation that supports bans on same-sex marriage. Recently, Alabama and Virginia have adopted nonbinding resolutions for Congress to pass a federal constitutional amendment to ban same-sex marriages. Nine other states have pending resolutions,

and thirty-nine states already prohibit gay and lesbian couples from marriage based on laws modeled after the Defense of Marriage Act passed by Congress in 1996. This act allows states to deny the marriages of gays and lesbians performed in other states. Vermont created civil unions in 2000 to provide lesbian and gay couples with the same state rights regarding benefits, but the state legislature has also attempted to ban same-sex marriages (Peterson, 2004, p. 6). Most gay rights activists do not view civil unions as equal under the law because they do not recognize the emotional bond inherent in a marital union. Civil unions are a business partnership, but stop short of defining partners as loving couples.

A lack of legal rights for gays and lesbians has additional implications:

1. Lack of automatic inheritance under probate laws
2. No paid bereavement for family illness or death
3. Inability to file joint tax returns
4. Reduced family insurance rates
5. No immediate access to each other in an emergency
6. Lack of decision-making rights for an incompetent partner
7. No right to claim a partner's body after death
8. Lack of shared parental rights

If gays or lesbians have children from a previous heterosexual relationship, their ability to gain custody may be in jeopardy if judged "unfit" because of sexual orientation. According to Pope and Barrett (2002), "Laws prohibiting discrimination against lesbians and gay men in employment and housing exist at local, state, and federal levels; they have been instituted through legislative statute and executive order" (p. 158). Although some institutions now offer paid leave and insurance benefits for partners of gays and lesbians as an attempt to comply with these laws, there remains a tremendous gap between benefits for heterosexual and homosexual couples.

It appears that the next decade will witness significant controversy and legislation regarding gay and lesbian marriages and the rights inherent in a marital union. Gay rights groups are constantly quoted by the news media, and political debates have brought the issues to the forefront. States will continue to debate and challenge the Defense of Marriage Act while the gay and heterosexual community looks on. Activists will continue to be involved in the struggles of each state and they will test the strength of the laws allowing gay and lesbian marriages as they did in California and

Massachusetts. Clearly, this issue will be the source of important social, political, and ethical discussions for some time.

Career. Career choice has important considerations for gay and lesbian couples. "A lesbian may realize at an early age that she will not [be able to] depend on a man's salary and may, therefore, choose a traditionally male-dominated profession in order to maximize her earning potential" (Young & Long, 1998, p. 304). Lesbians who choose these fields may be targets of discrimination in a male-dominated profession. "Similarly, gay men may choose careers that are not traditionally male in order to escape discrimination. Many gay men express the belief that heterosexual women are more supportive of their lifestyles than are heterosexual males" (Young & Long, 1998, p. 304). Gays and lesbians may be more wary of some careers than of others and may not choose to come out in the workplace. For example, many gays and lesbians remain "in the closet" in fields such as teaching, childcare, and child psychology because of the widespread erroneous belief that gay men and lesbians may recruit children to a same-sex lifestyle or may be more prone to molest children (Young & Long, 1998). Many same-sex couples choose to live in large metropolitan areas because of a wider variety of career opportunities and a more extensive support system.

Economic Factors and Career Choice. Career choice for lesbians is often limited and does not offer salary equal to that of a male counterpart. Economic disadvantage is widespread among two-women wage earners, and financial support from extended families may be nonexistent. For example, if lesbians choose a predominately male-populated career in order to maximize earning potential, they may not be supported by their families.

Coparenting. The last decade has experienced a sharp rise in the number of gay and lesbian couples who want to have children. They are primarily forming new families through adoption, artificial insemination, foster care, and surrogacy.

Some researchers estimate that there are between 1 million and 9 million children in the United States who have one lesbian or gay parent (Perrin, 2002). However, two states—Florida and New Hampshire—have laws that bar lesbians and gays from adopting children. Empirical evidence suggests that gay fathers demonstrate no difference than heterosexual fathers

in dealing with typical issues of parenting. Similarly, lesbian mothers compare with their heterosexual counterparts in self-esteem, psychological adjustment, and ideas about childrearing (Perrin, 2002).

Many gay and lesbian couples achieve parenthood by inseminated pregnancy or by bringing a child to a relationship from a heterosexual one. Stepparent adoptions allow gay and lesbian couples to have equal rights. Donor insemination also allows same-sex couples to bear children. Lesbian couples must determine which partner will become impregnated and then carefully choose a sperm donor to initiate the process. Surrogacy is an option for a couple who is unable to bear a child. A surrogate mother might use her own eggs or the eggs of the prospective lesbian mother and have them implanted in her womb. Gay couples can use this option with either man fertilizing the egg with his sperm. Although this option holds promise for same-sex couples, many surrogate agencies are less than eager to help. In fact, agencies in the United Kingdom will not help gay couples (Cooper, 2004).

As a result of misconceptions and bias about gay and lesbian couples' ability to parent, there are limited resources and support services available to them. Counselors often help couples sort through their options and identify their feelings about adoption, insemination, surrogacy, or foster care. If infertility is an issue, it may be overlooked in same-sex relationships and viewed by others as irrelevant. Counselors also help couples make decisions about the best method for bringing a baby into the relationship and help them explore their feelings about the choices they make. They can also help identify support systems in their families and in their communities. It is often helpful for sexuality counselors to refer these couples for legal advice prior to any decision. Disclosure issues related to the nature of conception and sexual orientation are necessary legal concerns. Attorneys can also assist with legal documents that outline coparenting structures, possible separation or divorce (if any of the new state legislations on same-sex marriage hold), or death.

Questions to Consider

Sexuality counselors must ask same-sex couples questions that are not typically asked of heterosexual couples. These include questions about acceptance of sexual orientation and gender that may be egodystonic—feelings related to inadequacy concerning body habitus, size and shape of sex organs, sexual performance, or other traits related to self-imposed standards of masculinity or femininity (APA, 2000). The following questions may be used by sexuality counselors to address gay and lesbian sexual issues:

1. How do you feel about your body?
2. When did you realize that you were gay (or lesbian)?
3. Tell me about your coming out process.
4. What have your sexual relationships been like since you came out?
5. How have your families adapted to your sexual orientation?
6. How have you negotiated traditional gender roles within your relationship?
7. How do you and your partner deal with societal pressures regarding your sexual orientation?

Gay and lesbian couples seek assistance clarifying the meaning of commitment and how it defines sexual practices in the relationship. They also address specific sexual problems or dysfunctions that are present.

Addressing Sexual Dysfunctions or Problems

Specific sexual dysfunctions presented by gays and lesbians in sexuality couples counseling are often different, or are presented with less or more frequency than by their heterosexual counterparts.

Lesbians do not typically present complaints of vaginismus and dyspareunia because they engage in other forms of sexual activities and tend to avoid penetrative sex. Similarly, gay men do not often have concerns of delayed ejaculation as do straight men. Gay sexual practices include in their repertoires the notion that masturbation is a way to "end" a sexual encounter, rather than as foreplay. Because HIV has negatively impacted anal sex for many gay males, oral sex is as important a part of sexual expression for gay men and lesbians as is vaginal penetration for heterosexuals (Nichols, 2000).

Garippa and Sanders (1997) describe one gay male's sexual concern defined by his sexuality counselor as

> excessive self-observation, obsessive thoughts, performance anxiety, and fear of failure, as well as his vigorous stimulation and high frequency of masturbation. Contributing factors included his inability to get lost in the moment sexually, his fear of losing his partner, and his unrealistically high expectations of

himself. The deeper causes seemed related to his feelings of guilt about and anger with his parents for nonacceptance of his homosexuality . . . Treatment goals were [developed to help] achieve consistent erections with his partner and to have orgasms through partner stimulation. . . [He learned how to] experience greater variety and pleasure in his sexual experiences and [how to enjoy] erotic sensations. . . Task assignments offered by the [counselor included learning] various behavioral techniques. [He was required] to reduce the number of times he masturbated. . . [and increase stimulation] of other parts of his body. . . [He focused on] sexual fantasies and slowed himself down through relaxation exercises. [In addition, through sensate focus activities he was able] to focus on his sensations, rather than on [his] orgasms, thus reducing the pressure about sexual performance. . . Finally, as his erections were firmer and more consistent, . . . [he learned to enjoy mutual stimulation with his partner] and achieve orgasm with his partner's stimulation. (pp. 128–129)

Lesbians also present unique sexual issues in counseling in addition to the common complaints considered for all couples (e.g., history of sexual abuse, communication problems, avoidance of sex due to unresolved anger and conflict). Unlike women in heterosexual relationships who have female friends in addition to their male partners, women in lesbian relationships sometimes find it more difficult to spend time with female friends due to jealousy. In order to keep peace in their relationships, they may spend almost all of their free time with their partners. Infrequent sexual contact may be a means for creating distance or separateness in couples for whom there is too much emotional intimacy and togetherness. Sexuality counselors must understand the concept of "fusion" and its manifestations in lesbian relationships as described earlier in this chapter so that treatment can focus on appropriate boundary-setting in the relationship (Ossana, 2000).

INTERVENTIONS FOR SEXUALITY COUNSELING

Narrative Storytelling

Narrative interventions are designed to emphasize the re-storying of sexual identity and sexual partnerships and promote the desire to "invent" or "create" a history, present and future, that focuses on sexual realities.

This way of thinking about sexuality counseling offers multiple alternatives and options for gay and lesbian couples who have not followed a traditional path in their sexual relationships. The premise of narrative therapy is that individual's lives and relationships are shaped by the stories that their communities support and engage in to provide meaning to their experiences. Addelston (2000) offers this explanation:

> Narrative ideas are situated in a context that (a) privileges the person's lived experience, (b) encourages a perception that change is always possible, . . . (c) encourages multiple perspectives [and can act to] deconstruct stories [from the past that have created shame, guilt, and negativity], (d) encourages [a hopeful future] through reconstruction and re-remembering alternative stories, . . . (e) acknowledges that stories are co-produced, (f) emphasizes clients' authorship of their own stories, and (g) believes that persons are multi-storied. (p. 5)

Narrative therapy interventions are particularly useful when counseling gay and lesbian couples. These interventions provide an alternative to internalizing all of the negativity and shame-based messages couples may have received from society and their families about being gay or lesbian. Couples are then able to separate their lives and relationships from stories they judge to be impoverishing, and they are challenged to re-author their future lives by creating preferred stories of identity, sexual orientation, and a same-sex relationship that has meaning and integrity in a heterosexual world. Narrative therapy helps gay and lesbian couples and their families retell the story of the family in a more healthy and integrated "before" and "after." Such therapy is particularly useful for sexuality counselors helping gay and lesbian clients who are shifting identities or addressing socially constructed political issues. The approach allows couples to reconstruct their lives interpersonally, intrapersonally, and on a social level and to incorporate their new selves into the larger community (Addelston, 2000).

Hall (2001) has created a mnemonic for a narrative approach for sexuality counseling based on the letters forming the word *lesbian:**

L: Long Lasting Love—Alternatives to the "forever-after" love story may include positive views of impermanent partnerships. They may also be described as "passages" or "present-oriented" relationships.

E: Equality—Lesbians often prize relationships that do not parallel heterosexual hierarchies and inequalities. However, regarding sexuality, it is unlikely that each partner will be equally as desirous of sexual activity. It is helpful for sexuality counselors to include stories that normalize asymmetrical desires or sexual roles. One partner may be the initiator most of the time, while another is more passive.

S: Sex—Love, sex, and ecstasy are typically associated and may prove problematic if passion and sex are fused. Lesbians may begin to develop new sexual stories that describe sex as a diversion and as a way to relax, rather than to make it a statement about their romantic capabilities.

B: Balance—Sex is a key element in life. However, so are recreation and other enjoyable activities. Alternative stories might feature weekend getaways or weekly dates. In other words, sexual rituals replace the notion of spontaneous erotic combustion.

I: Intimacy—Lesbians often tell stories about "us against them." Sex is a significant part of intimacy. Because lesbian couples are frequently connected and intimate without sex, it may be necessary to role-play or fantasize about becoming strangers to each other through distancing activities.

A: Achievement—In healthy relationships, partners resolve power struggles and come to understandings with each other. The fairy tale includes continual progress along gratifying paths. Unfortunately, there is no pot of gold at the end of the rainbow and lesbians must be realistic about their ability to create a healthy relationship. They may need to invent and reinvent their sexual relationship over the course of years.

N: Never Again—This aspect of lesbian sexuality counseling focuses on the tendency to repeat old patterns (relationships with parents or former partners who may have been abusive or exploitative).

Rituals of Commitment

Rituals have been well-established as important markers of life experiences and for resolving major life events (Imber-Black, 1989). Rituals also validate cultural messages and provide a sense of legitimacy and external support. "The lack of legal and social validation for some same-sex couples often enables invalidating responses from others, such as excluding partners from family and job functions and treating the relationship as nonexistent" (Ossana, 2000, p. 286).

Sexuality counselors provide a safe place for creating meaningful rituals that can be carefully planned and codesigned with couples based on their needs and desires. One important ritual is a ceremony to

---

* From M. Hall, "Beyond Forever After: Narrative Therapy with Lesbian Couples," in *New Directions in Sex Therapy* (pp. 282–284), by P. Kleinplatz. Copyright 2001. Reproduced by permission of Routledge/Taylor & Francis Books, Inc.

memorialize joining as partners. A ceremony is planned to include spoken vows, traditional toasts, and good wishes from friends, family, and other significant supporters (Young & Long, 1998). Other rituals may be designed to celebrate children, career success, anniversaries, or special holidays much like those of heterosexual couples. Rituals should reflect the couples' lifestyles and can address any important event they wish to memorialize.

Genogram of Family of Creation

In order to create a genogram for same-sex couples, the same steps of a traditional genogram are followed. However, the content of the genogram "differs in the definitions of family and the chronology of significant love relationships, rather than legal or biological unions. To accomplish this task, [couples may need] to create appropriate symbols for the genogram [that reflect both of their family histories]" (Young & Long, 1998, p. 314). Chapter 3 describes the specific steps for creating a genogram.

Identifying Role Models

Sexuality counselors provide a setting for same-sex couples to discuss the inequities they face, and to establish meaningful expectations regarding their relationship roles, equality, and lifestyle. Through directed tasks, they may seek community support services or identify important literature that helps them conceptualize healthy relationship functioning.

Role Reversals

Role reversals help each partner be more empathic of the other's position in the relationship and challenge couples to respond differently. Sexuality counselors ask each partner to "reverse roles" and think, act, and respond like their partner. As partners observe each other and reflect their behavior, they are able to empathize more successfully and understand what issues their partner faces. Later, as they assume their own role, they are able to discuss what it was like to pretend to be their partner and identify what they learned about their position, their partner, and their relationship from the experience.

Creating Dialogues About Children and Parent Issues

Sexuality counselors help facilitate dialogue that addresses the reality that many gay and lesbian couples are parents or would like to be parents. Counselors assist partners to clarify feelings and values regarding parenting and discuss needs to seek legal resources and procedures that can provide some protection for retaining custody of children from a prior relationship and can help with bearing children or adopting them, depending on the wishes of the couple.

Emphasizing Positive Assets Beyond Sexual Orientation

Counselors help gay and lesbian couples identify and celebrate their positive attributes and strengths as individuals and how those strengths impact their couple relationship. They identify how they have coped over the years with their sexual orientation issues and how they have found solutions to move forward in their lives. Validation for the strengths they have demonstrated in a largely heterosexual world is important for helping them review their strengths as a couple.

Sensual and Sexual Exercises

Often, while couples are exploring their sexual relationship, the sexuality counselor may place a "ban" on sexual intercourse, and instead suggest sensation-oriented, pleasurable exercises designed to increase physical awareness and dispel inhibitions. Open communication is encouraged during these activities and partners are directed to talk with each other about their needs and desires. For example, are vibrators to be used? Is a dildo important? Because gay and lesbian couples do not engage in sexual practices in the more traditional sense, they can be encouraged to explore and be playful in creating sexual scenarios with each other. (See Chapters 6 and 7, which discuss activities designed for couples.

Confrontational, Playful, and Creative Skills from Gestalt and Psychodrama

Gestalt counseling brings experiences into the "here and now." This task can be accomplished by focusing on the body's responses to verbal material so that conflicts blocking change can be worked through at a physical level. When focusing on sexuality, couples might be asked to become aware of genital sensations, or to have a conversation between the head (often the inhibitor of sexual sensation) and the genitals. This method helps inner conflicts emerge allowing the possibility for change through increased awareness. Values and societal taboos for gays and lesbians can be addressed using this intervention.

Psychodrama encourages couples to act out situations rather than talk about them. Partners might be encouraged to enact difficulties with their sexuality counselors by using symbols. Massaging each other's shoulders may be used as a symbol for sexual interaction. Couples may then view their sexual interaction from a broader perspective and may move beyond inhibitors or blocks they have self-imposed.

Clarifying Commitment and Monogamy

Couples (in particular those who are gay and bisexual) may need assistance clarifying the meaning of commitment. Couples who choose to be monogamous often need therapeutic support and assistance to clarify their choice of monogamy if it is unsupported in their gay community.

Other couples may want to create a contract that outlines their monogamous or nonmonogamous relationship. This method allows each partner to be clear on the details of the arrangement. Sexuality counselors are urged to leave their ideas about monogamy versus nonmonogamy at the office door and remain open to multiple possibilities for arrangements between partners (Ossana, 2000).

Interpersonal Skill Development

It is important for gay and lesbian couples to understand their comfort level for a repertoire of sexual behaviors and then identify potential pitfalls based on traditional models that have not worked for them. For example, two women who may have been raised in traditional households with specific ideas about how women behave may require skill practice in risk taking, assertiveness training, or learning skills about initiating activities.

Communication About Sex

Communication interventions for heterosexual couples are also especially useful for gay and lesbian couples. Partners must take responsibility for what they need and ask for it. Intimacy is based on mutual responsibility for understanding each other. Traditional listener-speaker activities, use of metaphor, and positive reframing are interventions that facilitate more experiences, acceptance, and responsibilities for a healthy sexual relationship.

BOX 9.1
Interventions at a Glance

- Help couples clarify where they stand in the coming out process.
- Help couples identify significant role models of successful gay and lesbian couples.
- Explore family of origin reactions to their sexual orientation.
- Facilitate a discussion on safe sex practices and transmission of STIs.
- Explore legal implications of gay and lesbian relationships and refer them to an attorney for specific legal advice.
- Identify meaningful rituals and support persons who may be present in their lives.
- Cocreate new narratives about their relationship that fit with a past, present, and future as a gay or lesbian couple.
- Clarify issues surrounding monogamy and commitment related to the gay and lesbian culture.
- Facilitate effective communication skills in order to address issues related to identity development and social and cultural stressors on their sexual relationship.

Psychoeducational Interventions

Similar to heterosexual couples, gay and lesbian couples benefit from knowledge acquired through books, lectures, classes, and stories from others.

In the next section, we will describe an intervention based on narrative therapy using the framework of an integrative couples' model. This intervention is a way to help couples restory their lives and create future relationships with hope and promise. Other interventions are found in Box 9.1.

Case Example

Peter and Leonardo have been together for three years. Peter came out in his late teens and has been accepted by his family, particularly his sister, Doria. Leonardo, on the other hand, has recently come out to his family. The family feels hurt and embarrassed by his disclosure, but they do not want to lose the relationship they have with their son. Leonardo's brother is having a difficult time with new information about Leonardo's sexual orientation and has essentially refused to see his brother. Leonardo is upset and has tried to bridge the relationship with his brother. Peter is becoming less tolerant of the situation and recently has been coming home from work late and arriving somewhat intoxicated. He is not initiating sex, and when approached by Leonardo says that he "just does not feel like it." Leonardo is feeling rejected and thinks that Peter does not want a sexual relationship with him because Peter is angry about his family problems. Leonardo is also angry with his family and is beginning to feel angry with Peter. They have both come to sexuality counseling expressing anger and frustration. Both acknowledge a problem with sexual desire and do not know what to do about it.

Application of the Integrative Couples' Model
Stage 1: Assessing and Obtaining an Interactive View of the Problem
Peter and Leonardo each have a different view of the problem. Peter states that he just does not feel close to Leonardo because he seems so depressed about his family and he brings them constantly into their conversation. Leonardo feels upset about his family, but when he attempts to get support from Peter he feels rejected and unsupported. The sexuality counselor helps them create a collaborative view of the problem and states the problem in interactive terms. "You have a lot of external family stress in your relationship and neither of you is sure how to continue to love and be loved by the other with all the interference." This shared view allows them to agree about the problem and reduces some of the blame they have targeted against each other.

Stage 2: Goal Setting
The couple, with the sexuality counselor, creates the following affective and behavioral goals:

1. We will develop a plan to have intimate time together during the week so that we can reestablish closeness in our relationship.
2. We will discuss ways to address Leonardo's family problems, but we will not let the problems interfere with our relationship. By doing

this, we can stay connected to each other and not let his family come between us.
3. We will present ourselves as a couple to both of our families in order to feel united in our attempt to gain acceptance for our relationship.

Stage 3: Adopting New Perceptions and Behaviors
Peter and Leonardo work with the sexuality counselor to access their positive contributions to the relationship. Leonardo has been the creative one who keeps the relationship alive and interesting, while Peter has been the nurturing, stable one. By employing techniques from narrative interventions, Peter and Leonardo restory their relationship and include a positive description about their weekends together, the house they are saving money to buy, and the supportive relationships they have with their friends. In this scenario, Peter is the nurturer and Leonardo plans exciting dates and intimate time together. Because they spend more time together, Peter feels more connected and part of Leonardo's life and does not feel left out. Consequently, he does not stay at work late and is in fact taking off early once in a while to participate in the plans made by Leonardo. Peter is initiating sex more frequently and feels more relaxed in their lovemaking. Feeling some of the old fun and excitement they shared, he can see a picture of a future with Leonardo. In this situation, inhibited sexual desire was a consequence of severe relational stress and could be addressed through restructuring the relationship and the stories about the relationship in the present and in the future.

Stage 4: Maintaining New Perceptions and Behaviors
During this stage, Peter and Leonardo both agree that it would be very easy to fall into the same old negative pattern. For example, Leonardo feels stressed, Peter feels left out, Peter distances from Leonardo, Leonardo does not prioritize couple time, Peter does not initiate sexual activity, Leonardo feels hurt and angry and lashes out, Peter stays away from the house, and so on. With the help of their sexuality counselor, they are able to see the pattern and interrupt it at any place in the cycle, and they can express their concerns to each other when they identify old negative patterns creeping back into their relationship. They emphasize

their commitment to each other and vow to maintain closeness and intimacy, regardless of outside interference. They recognize the importance of their physical relationship and commit to protect it by talking out their conflicts and feelings, rather than distancing and rejecting each other.

Stage 5: Validating New Perceptions and Behaviors
Peter and Leonardo compliment each other on their ability to problem-solve and stick together, even when their families and society in general were unsupportive. They celebrate their success by planning to commit one weekend each month to themselves. They can go to the beach, take a mini-vacation, or just stay home and be with each other without their friends around or without family obligations. They agree to celebrate all future holidays together and not leave the other out because their families may be disapproving of their relationship or supportive of it. They also agree that it is difficult to be a gay couple in a straight world and congratulate themselves on their hard work.

SUMMARY

Sexual orientation is influenced by the interaction of many factors, primarily cultural, biological, and genetic in nature. As a result of the sexual revolution and the Gay Liberation Movement, gay and lesbian lifestyles are recognized as legitimate rather than "sinful" or "sick." However, there continues to be widespread discrimination in the workplace, in schools, in places of worship, and in society at large.

Exploring the attitudes, biases, and cultural competencies of sexuality counselors is vital to client success in counseling. Misinformation must be confronted and awareness of sexual practices and relational issues should be identified. Sexuality counselors should also be aware of the differences between gay and lesbian sexual cultures and should not make assumptions that they are the same. Gay men tend to communicate more clearly about the sexual practices they desire, while lesbians express that they want a warm, loving relationship.

Regardless of the etiology of sexual orientation, there are significant stressors in the lives of gay and lesbian couples. Some stressors are similar to those of their heterosexual counterparts, but others are related to the unique issues of being gay or lesbian in our society. Internal factors most often center on identity development and coming out. This process can be identified in distinct stages and requires management of the definitions and redefinitions of what it means to be gay or lesbian. External factors include influences from family of origin, social pressures, and legal issues pertaining to marriage, career, and economics.

The narrative approach is an intervention that works well for reshaping the lives of gay and lesbian clients. Narrative ideas encourage the perception that change is always possible and that encouraging multiple perspectives can help clients deconstruct stories from the past that have produced shame and guilt and reconstruct and re-remember stories that are more positive. Interventions include rituals of commitment, genograms of family of creation, the identification of role models, role reversals, the creation of dialogues about children and parent issues, an emphasis on positive assets beyond sexual orientation, and sensual and sexual exercises. In addition, couples can practice confrontational, playful, and creative skills from Gestalt and psychodrama. Clarifying commitment and monogamy, interpersonal skill development, communication about sex, and psychoeducational interventions are also helpful. Through a flexible stage model such as the integrative couples' model, sexuality counselors can help gay and lesbian clients as they shift identities and address the socially constructed political issues they face. By doing so, they can reconstruct their lives interpersonally and socially as they integrate a new self into their communities. An integrative couples' model can offer a broader range of options for counselors and can provide a supportive, nonblaming environment in which to challenge sexual issues. This model uses interventions that promote growth and change and help couples join together to confront the prejudice and discrimination of their social community.

AGING AND SEXUALITY

KEY CONCEPTS

- Regardless of age, many couples experience sexual problems or dysfunctions, sexual communication difficulties, and other relational problems that suggest a need for sexuality counseling.
- The aging process creates changes in mental and physical functioning that can impact sexual functioning for both males and females.
- There are unique psychosocial factors that sexuality counselors must consider when working with aging couples.
- There are multiple sexual myths and negative stereotypes about older persons.
- Sexuality counselors should be aware of their own values, attitudes, and beliefs about aging and sexuality.
- There are unique physical changes that influence sexuality and aging.
- Sexuality counselors working with aging couples incorporate biological, psychosocial, and developmental elements in their assessment process (e.g., age-related changes, physical functioning).
- Concerns about sexuality often emerge in the context of counseling about phase of life and other issues in the aging process.
- An integrative couples' model offers a wide variety of intervention strategies for addressing the sexual concerns of aging couples.

The impact of aging on sexuality is a topic that is receiving increased attention in our society. The "Viagratization" of America has generated interest into the sexuality of people often assumed to have limited desire or need for sexual intimacy (Kingsberg, 2000). In addition, the baby boom generation is now middle-aged and senior citizens are the fastest-growing segment of the U.S. population (Rathus, Nevid, & Fichner-Rathus, 2000). For example, it is expected that women will live approximately one-third of their lives post-menopausally (U.S. Census Bureau, 1996). This trend has created heightened attention to issues such as menopause and the recent controversy surrounding hormone replacement therapy. In addition, as people live longer, there are myriad physical changes that accompany aging. Sexuality counselors should understand the context of the relationships of aging couples and the unique issues affecting their sexual lives (Kingsberg, 2000).

Regardless of age, couples experience sexual dysfunction, sexual communication difficulties, and other relational problems that suggest the need for sexuality counseling. Sexuality counselors offer hope to couples who may otherwise believe that their sexual relationships have ceased. In fact, the sexual concerns of our aging population are not qualitatively different from those in younger age groups (Stone, 1987). However, in spite of the many similarities between older and younger persons, there are unique age-related issues sexuality counselors must consider in order to be most effective in treating the sexual problems of this population. In addition, it is important to understand that aging persons do not necessarily have chronic health problems and people with chronic health problems are not necessarily old. However, as couples age, they may have more trouble coping with health issues because of the stereotypes and other social and psychological issues related to aging. As they struggle to make adjustments in sexual attitudes, values, and beliefs about their sexuality in connection with aging, they may feel strained and find it difficult to adapt to sexual variations.

This chapter defines aging and describes the psychosocial factors associated with aging. It also addresses sexual myths, double standards, and sexual attitudes and practices associated with aging couples. In addition, issues regarding physical implications of aging on sexuality, information on assessment techniques, and counseling interventions are addressed. A case example illustrates how the integrative couples' model is used with an aging couple.

A DEFINITION OF AGING

Traditionally, when words like "aged" or "aging" are used, they are assumed to mean an elderly population. Some definitions of the word "elderly" focus on individuals who are fifty-five years of age and older while others target people over sixty or over sixty-five. In addition, there are specific categories that define elderly as young-old (65 to 74 years of age), old-old (75 years and older) (Santrock, 1999) and oldest-old (85 years and older) (Pearlin, 1994; Santrock, 1999). Social markers that define aging are often based on age of retirement or the start of Social Security benefits, often age 62 (Weinstein & Rosen, 1988). We have chosen to focus on persons over 50 for this chapter because of the increasing population of Americans who fall into this age group (the "baby boomers").

A Statistical Profile of Aging

People over 50 are the fastest growing segment of the U.S. population. Likewise, the "percentage of Americans 65 years and older has more than tripled during [the] past century" (Leiblum & Segraves, 2000, p. 424), and it is estimated that by 2030, there will be more than 50 million retirees, more than double the current number of persons over age 65 (Weinstein & Rosen, 1988).

These data are a sign that our population is growing older. Over the years, life expectancies for men

and women have increased to 76 years of age and 82 years of age respectively (Leiblum & Segraves, 2000), and increased attention is being given to "successful aging" by the media and special interest groups like the American Association for Retired Persons (AARP). Older adults, many of whom have been reared in a less restrictive society, are active "movers and shakers" different from past generations of older persons (Weinstein & Rosen, 1988).

As the number of aging persons continues to increase, so does the need to understand physical differences that result from advancing years. These physiological differences often impact changes in health status, which in turn impact sexual functioning.

PSYCHOSOCIAL ASPECTS OF AGING

There are various psychosocial factors that are important to consider in order to assess and treat older persons appropriately. For both men and women, positive attitudes toward sexuality, greater sexual knowledge, satisfaction with a long-term relationship or a current intimate relationship, good social networks, general emotional well-being, and good self-esteem are associated with increased sexual activity, satisfaction, and interest in older adults (Hodson & Skeen, 1994; Kingsberg, 2000).

In contrast, there are psychosocial factors that negatively affect sexual interest, activity, and satisfaction. These factors include loss of a partner, changed living arrangements, retirement, and caring for aging parents.

Loss of a Partner

Loss of a partner can affect sexual interest and availability of sexual companionship. It has been documented that married males live longer than their single counterparts and happily married women have a one-year addition in life expectancy when compared with single women (Rowe & Kahn, 1998). Women and men tend to live with their partners in equal numbers when in their early fifties, but by age 65 and above, more than 75% of men and approximately 50% of women are living with their partners (Miret, 1995). From the 1900s to the late 1990s, the proportion of widows to widowers has multiplied more than twofold (U.S. Bureau of the Census, 2000).

Loss of a partner through death is a life crisis that many men and women will inevitably face. The loss and sense of bereavement may be so great for some that the surviving partner feels no need for or interest in a new relationship. However, some widows and widowers develop new relationships and remarry. More men than women remarry due in part because women have a longer life expectancy and as a result gradually outnumber men (Rossi, 1994). However, some men find that although they can become sexually aroused with a new partner, they experience problems achieving or maintaining an erection. This difficulty described as "widower's syndrome" could result from anxiety and guilt generated by having a sexual relationship with a woman other than his late wife (Rossi, 1994). A similar problem may be experienced by women who begin new sexual relationships after the loss of a partner.

Changed Living Arrangements

Increased frailty forces many persons into assisted living or nursing home facilities, or living with their offspring (Kellett, 2000). Although it is commonly assumed that physical or mental fragility eliminates sexual desire, this is not the case. As a result, many alternative living arrangements fail to address the sexual needs of older persons.

In many nursing homes, official and unofficial limits or restrictions about sexual behavior were often created for the comfort of the staff (Ehrenfeld, Bronner, Tabak, Alpert, & Bergman, 1999; McCartney, Izeman, Rogers, & Cohen, 1987). Sexual expression by nursing home residents may create anxiety for staff as well as relatives. Stiffl (1984) discusses the importance of encouraging sexuality and not separating it from other forms of relatedness as well as acceptance of masturbation and homosexual relationships for institutionalized aging persons.

Aging persons living with their offspring may also have limited privacy and options for sexual activity (Butler & Lewis, 1988). This problem is likely intensified in situations of role reversal, where the adult child becomes like a parent to the older person and expects that the person abide by limits and boundaries that he or she requires (Steege, 1986).

Retirement

Retirement may affect an intimate relationship in various ways. For some couples, the increased flexibility and freedom of retirement creates the opportunity to spend more time together and with family (Olson & DeFrain, 1994). However, for some couples, retirement creates stress. Like any significant life transition,

withdrawal from the workforce necessitates some degree of adjustment. Some retired people report "sleep difficulties, difficulty figuring out what to do with themselves, and sadness over not seeing work friends and colleagues regularly" (Olson & DeFrain, 1994, p. 449). This may impact an intimate relationship depending on the manner in which the individuals cope with this transition. Decreased sexual intimacy could result when couples fail to communicate effectively, develop adequate support networks, and remain pessimistic regarding their lifestyle changes.

Caring for Aging Parents

Many baby boomers (those who are currently considered middle-aged and typically born between 1946 and 1964) provide care for their children while also caring for aging parents as they deal with their own aging process. This affects their sexuality in a variety of ways. Multiple caretaking and financial demands often create additional stress that negatively impacts sexual desire. Increased medical and other care responsibilities for self or others may decrease energy, time, and access for sexual intimacy.

In addition, privacy issues may prevail when several generations—from teens to aging parents—reside in the same home. Couples may find themselves leaving their bedroom of many years to provide privacy and space for aging parent(s). This transition may prove considerably difficult and limit the separateness needed for sexual intimacy.

A couple's ability to communicate openly may also be impacted by lack of privacy. If an aging parent is primarily homebound, couples may find it difficult to have open and private discussions about intimacy or other relationship issues. It is well-documented that lack of communication about intimacy can lead to relationship stress and can even contribute to the termination of the relationship (Young & Long, 1998).

Consider the situation of Joellen and Leon, ages 52 and 63 respectively, who are in conflict over their needs as a couple and caretaking responsibilities for their 15-year-old daughter and Leon's ailing mother, aged 84. The couple has frequent disagreements about how they should divide the household, childcare, parent-care, and other responsibilities. Leon has also been considering retirement in two years and is concerned about the financial responsibilities of caring for his mother and their daughter's future college education. Joellen has agreed to decrease her work hours to manage the additional responsibility of caring for his mother, but she is upset with Leon because of his lack of support for periodic care relief. Leon is frustrated with Joellen because she seldom has the desire or energy for sexual intimacy. They agree that couple time is important to them and they have lost this time and the joy they have always experienced in their sexual relations. Their sexuality counselor helps them to understand how multiple demands and roles can easily overwhelm them. They are able to develop ways to manage the functions of parent, caregiver, and spouse and to get additional outside caregiver support so they can find ways to rebuild their sexual relationship.

Sexual Myths Versus Sexual Reality Related to Aging

There are multiple myths, negative stereotypes, and a double standard surrounding sexuality and aging. Often, aging has been associated with asexuality (Crooks & Baur, 2002; Kellett, 2000). Counselors should challenge their own biases, values, attitudes, beliefs, and stereotypes about aging as they may influence their ability to work effectively with this population. Staying current with literature that addresses aging issues and concerns is one method that will aid in preventing sexuality counselors from generalizing or making assumptions based on their experiences with older persons (Weinstein & Rosen, 1988). It is also important to seek consultation and supervision to increase sensitivity to aging issues and avoid potential prejudicial behavior.

Unfortunately, older persons are often treated as children by health-care providers and family members, the implication being that they are incapable of taking care of themselves. Sexuality counselors should be aware of subtleties in their own behavior, such as changes in posture or tone of voice, which may be interpreted as patronizing (Weinstein & Rosen, 1988). When counselors treat older couples as if they are immature or helpless, these clients are less likely to discuss sexual concerns (Weinstein & Rosen, 1988).

Sexual Double Standards, Media Messages, and Aging

Sexual standards for aging in the United States are considered restrained and are not representative of many other cultures and countries (Kellett, 2000). In their study of sexuality and aging persons in 106 cultures, Winn and Newton (1982) found that "many cultural groups have expectations for continued sexual activity

for older men" (p. 289). For females, they indicate that "older women frequently express strong sexual desires and interests, . . . engage in sexual activity in many instances until extreme old age, . . . and may form liaisons with much younger men" (p. 294). These findings suggest that sociocultural messages about aging and sexuality received by older adults can influence their beliefs about sexual activity.

Unlike many cultures, American society tends to focus on the vitality of youth and the importance of maintaining a youthful look as a primary determinant of sexual attractiveness. The idea of an "old face," sagging breasts, or a midsection with a "spare tire" is considered unsightly to our youth-oriented society. The media also tends to connect intimacy, passion, romance, and sexuality with the young (Levy, 1994).

Aging Women and Sexuality

Likewise, the societal picture of a sexually attractive and erotically appealing woman is typically one of youth and vitality (Crooks & Baur, 2002). The importance of remaining "forever young" is supported by cosmetics that promise to eliminate wrinkles, hair dyes that get rid of gray hair, and plastic surgery that attempts to eliminate crow's feet and other signs of aging. The implicit message is that as a woman ages, she becomes less and less physically and sexually appealing (Crooks & Baur, 2002).

An important and relatively new issue impacting women and sexuality is the controversial role of hormone replacement therapy (HRT). The social message attached to this treatment relates to the image of an older woman as "shriveled or dried up." Separate from the medical benefits or risks of HRT, the perceived social benefit of HRT is the perpetuation of sexual desirability and youth as a result of replacing hormones that are decreased or lost as a result of menopause. Aging and HRT will be discussed in more detail later in this chapter.

Aging Men and Sexuality

Media images for males regarding sexual attractiveness are somewhat different than images for females. Aging males are often considered "distinguished" in appearance and their sexual attractiveness is often considered improved with age (Crooks & Baur, 2002). It is also considered acceptable for an older man to be coupled with a younger woman, but there remains a double standard with regard to the pairing of an aging woman with a younger man. In general, it is fairly typical for male sexual appeal to be related to business or other accomplishments as well as financial and social status, both of which often increase as men grow older (Crooks & Baur, 2002).

In addition, media messages that publicize medical treatments such as Viagra and Cialis for erectile dysfunction typically depict aging males to promote product use. These images tend to send the message that erectile dysfunction is a part of aging. In spite of physical changes such as decreased testosterone levels in aging males, erectile dysfunction is not simply a function of getting older. Erectile dysfunction is often the result of disease (e.g., diabetes, vascular disease), surgery (e.g., radical prostate surgery), common medications (e.g., blood pressure drugs), as well as emotional factors such as anxiety and depression (Crooks & Baur, 2002).

Sexual Attitudes, Practices, and Aging

Faulty assumptions often negatively influence aging persons regarding their sexual attitudes, feelings, and practices. Younger persons, often family members of older adults, frequently ignore the sexual needs of aging persons and underestimate their sexual potential (Hodson & Skeen, 1994). For example, young adult children may have trouble accepting their parents' need for sexual expression (Walters, 1987).

Instead, older persons' attitudes toward sexuality are more open than is often assumed by societal stereotypes. Not only are the sexual attitudes of the aging more open than many believe, but actual sexual behavior is not as restricted or limited as is often assumed by many in Western society (Hodson & Skeen, 1994). The popular 1980s television comedy *The Golden Girls* portrayed four aging single women who sought intimate relationships and candidly acknowledged their sexuality. More recently, women, menopause, and sexuality have been humorously portrayed in the play, *Menopause The Musical*. Such notions of openness in sexual attitudes in older adults is supported by research on sexual behavior in the United States (Janus & Janus, 1993). Their work indicated that there was no evidence older adults were less open in their sexual attitudes compared with younger adults.

In addition to developing a knowledge base of the psychosocial factors associated with aging, sexuality counselors need to have an understanding of psychosocial factors related to health in order to effectively assess and treat those with aging or health-related concerns.

PHYSICAL CHANGES, AGING, AND SEXUALITY

There are physical changes that occur during the aging process for men and women that can impact their sexual functioning. Information about changes in sexual physiology can help eliminate faulty expectations and increase sexual satisfaction among aging couples. According to Stone (1987), "changes in physical capacity have their most significant effect when they change what may have been long-standing roles within the relationship" (p. 228). A reversal in a couple's roles as a result of decreased physical capacity can create significant stress on an intimate relationship. For example, a male who has been independent and the pursuer in sexual relations may experience significant difficulty coping when his partner is required to care for him and thus take on the sexual pursuer role. This role reversal may result in sexual distancing, separation, and decreased intimacy as partners attempt to make adjustments to their changing sexual and relational roles (Gilbert & Scher, 1999). Sexuality counselors must be alert to age-related physical changes that are a normal function of aging as well as medical conditions that may have a potential impact on couples' sexual relationships.

Medical Conditions and Sexuality

Aging couples may experience sexual difficulty as a result of medical conditions and the medications used to treat them. As couples age, physical ailments may interfere with myriad aspects of functioning, including sexuality (Dunn & Cutler, 2000). For example, a growing number of aging persons are being diagnosed with dementia, which impacts sexuality by creating libido changes in addition to creating difficulty with social interaction (Kellett, 2000). Diseases of the prostate, which are diagnosed more often in aging men, are also likely to affect sexual function (Kellett, 2000). Decreased libido is also an important symptom of depressed mood and the medications commonly prescribed to treat depression, such as selective serotonin reuptake inhibitors (SSRIs). SSRIs are a group of antidepressant drugs that include fluoxetine (Prozac), sertraline (Zoloft), paroxetine (Paxil), fluvoxamine (Luvox), and citalopram (Celexa). These drugs have been reported to exacerbate loss of sexual interest and to cause delayed ejaculation and absent or delayed orgasm in some individuals (Kellett, 2000; Rosen, Lane, &

Menza, 1999). It is important to note that although depression is not a normal part of aging, at least 15% to 20% of aging persons may experience depression (Kaplan & Sadock, 1998).

Physical Changes in Women Affecting Sexuality

Many of the physical changes in women that affect sexuality stem from decline in the production of estrogen around the time of menopause. Arousal tends to be the phase in the female sexual response cycle most affected by aging (Sharpe, 2004). During menopause, the vaginal walls lose some elasticity and grow paler and thinner. As a result, intercourse can become irritating and painful. In addition, the vagina also decreases in size and the labia majora, or large folds of skin along the sides of the vulva, lose many of their fatty deposits and become thin (Crooks & Baur, 2002). The vaginal opening becomes relatively constricted, and penetration can become difficult. On a positive note, however, the increased friction between the penis and vaginal walls could heighten sexual sensations (Rathus, Nevid, & Fichner- Rathus, 2000).

After menopause, the production of vaginal lubrication decreases, which can result in painful intercourse. The decrease in lubrication and thinning vaginal walls, all a normal part of aging, make it easier for microscopic tears to occur during intercourse, creating an entry point for bacteria and viruses to enter the body (Zeiss & Kasl-Godley, 2001). Consequently, older women may be at higher risk for contracting sexually transmitted infections. (See Chapter 8 for a detailed discussion of sexuality and sexually transmitted infections.)

One medical response to physical changes in women as a result of menopause is hormone replacement therapy (HRT), which "involves taking supplemental estrogen and progesterone to compensate for the decrease in natural hormone production during the female climacteric" (Crooks & Baur, 2002, p. 103). This therapy may alleviate some of the problems resulting from the significant reduction in estrogen after menopause.

Hormone replacement therapy is considered a controversial treatment, despite evidence that has linked it to possible health benefits such as protection against cardiovascular disease (Cutson & Meuleman, 2000) and osteoporosis (Crooks & Baur, 2002) as well as the maintenance of urethral and vaginal tissues, vaginal lubrication, clitoral sensitivity, orgasmic re-

sponse, and sexual interest (Walling, Ander, Johnson, 1990). However, hormone replacement therapy (estrogen only) has been associated with increases in the incidence of endometrial cancer (Schairer et al., 2000). It is common to combine progestin with estrogen to significantly decrease the risk of endometrial cancer. With growing concern about the use of hormone replacement therapy, some women are seeking alternative treatments to alleviate the symptoms of menopause and prevent postmenopausal cardiovascular disease and osteoporosis. Alternative treatments to treat symptoms of menopause such as night sweats and hot flashes include, but are not limited to, soy protein, aerobic exercise, antidepressant medication, evening primrose oil, black cohosh, dong quai (Morelli & Naquin, 2002), and Avlimil (a nonprescription daily supplement).

Current research suggests that menopausal women should weigh the potential benefits and risks of hormone replacement therapy against the symptoms of hormone deficiency (Morelli & Naquin, 2002). We recommend that women address these concerns with a physician who specializes in menopause and hormone replacement therapy.

Other age-related changes include decreases in breast swelling with sexual excitement, decrease in clitoral size, and fewer and less potent orgasms. However, the subjective experience of orgasm may be highly satisfying, despite the lessened intensity of muscular contractions (Rathus, Nevid, & Fichner-Rathus, 2000; Sharpe, 2004). A response to this change, as discussed in Chapter 6, is the use of Kegel exercises, which are often useful in cases where there is a decline in the intensity of contractions during orgasm and there is a decrease in satisfaction for the female. Figure 10.1 summarizes the physical changes that affect sexuality in women.

- Reduced estrogen, progesterone, and androgen levels
- Thinning of vaginal walls
- Decreased or delayed vaginal lubrication
- Reduced intensity of vaginal contractions
- Changes in the labia, which does not fully elevate to create funnellike entrance toward the vagina

---

FIGURE 10.1
Age-Related Physical Changes Impacting Sexuality in Females
Source: Adapted from Zeiss and Kasl-Godley (2001).

The case of Calvin, aged 62, and Julie, aged 52, illustrates the importance of having knowledge about age-related physical changes. Julie has been experiencing painful intercourse as a result of lubrication problems, and she has found herself resisting sexual advances from Calvin due to her discomfort. She has not discussed her "problem" with Calvin.

Calvin has become increasingly frustrated with Julie's rejection of his sexual advances. When he has attempted to discuss the problem with her, she says that she is "tired" to explain her lack of sexual desire. They agree they are frustrated with their relationship because sexual closeness has always been an important part of their intimate relationship.

Their sexuality counselor helps them to identify communication and age-related physical changes related to their sexual concerns and to develop a strategy for discussing sexual concerns more openly. They also receive information from Julie's gynecologist about changes in arousal and lubrication that frequently occur in postmenopausal women. Finally, they are able to devise ways to increase Julie's natural lubrication (e.g., more elaborate foreplay) and agree to invest in a commercial lubricant, if necessary.

Physical Changes in Men Affecting Sexuality

As men age, many of the changes that occur are related to the decreased production of testosterone. Hormone output slowly but steadily declines with age (Vermeulen & Kaufman, 1995), but it tends to stabilize around 60 years of age (Sharpe, 2004). In addition, a man may note a decrease in the size and firmness of his testicles and reduced sperm production (Sharpe, 2004). These factors may impact sexual functioning.

Changes in orgasmic and erectile function may also occur during the male aging process. After about age 50, men take progressively longer to have an erection (Crooks & Baur, 2002). Direct stimulation of the penis may be necessary to achieve an erection in older men. The refractory period, or period of time after an orgasm during which an individual is no longer responsive to sexual stimulation, increases with age (Crooks & Baur, 2002).

Erectile function may change as a result of aging, but erectile dysfunction is not inevitable with aging. Although men generally require more time to reach orgasm as they age, their partners may view delayed ejaculation as a positive part of sexual relations. In addition, older men produce less ejaculate, and it may flow slowly rather than rush out. This does not necessarily take away from orgasmic pleasure. In addition, an erection may subside more rapidly than it does in younger men. A study of sixty-five healthy men aged 45 to 74 showed an age-related decline in sexual desire, arousal, and activity. Yet there were no differences between younger and older men in level of sexual satisfaction or enjoyment (Rathus, Nevid, & Ficher-Rathus, 2000; Schiavi, Schreiner-Engel, Mandeli, Schanzer, & Cohen, 1990).

There are myriad reasons for problems with erectile function. "Although the incidence of erectile dysfunction increases with age, aging is not the cause" (Sharpe, 2004, p. 202). Instead medications, medical conditions, or emotional considerations are the likely cause (Beers & Berkow, 2000; Sharpe, 2004). When erectile difficulties occur in aging males, there are medical treatments available that may complement sexuality counseling. Viagra (sildenafil citrate) and Cialis (taladil) are oral medications designed to treat erectile problems.

Problems of the prostate and their treatments may contribute to a variety of problems in sexual functioning. For example, hormone treatments sometimes result in difficulty achieving an erection. Surgically removing portions of the prostate via the urethra can damage the bladder neck, which can result in retrograde ejaculation or ejaculate emptying into the bladder (Crooks & Baur, 2002). Figure 10.2 summarizes age-related physical changes in males.

Let's consider the case of Jean and Roger, who are seeking treatment because Roger, aged 68, has difficulty maintaining an erection. As a result Jean, aged 62, reports feeling sexually frustrated when Roger is unable to maintain his erection. They both describe

---

- Decreased testosterone levels
- Decreased firmness of erections
- Reduction in force and amount of ejaculate
- Longer refractory period
- The need for more direct stimulation of penis to help create longer duration for erection

FIGURE 10.2
Age-Related Physical Changes Impacting Sexuality in Males
Source: Adapted from Zeiss and Kasl-Godley (2001).

having fewer orgasms during intercourse since this difficulty began. They are frustrated because they have always had a very active sex life where they both had orgasms regularly and Jean enjoyed Roger's energetic thrusting. They find themselves arguing more frequently as their sexual frustration builds and they blame each other for their sexual problems. Trying to help them understand the physical changes associated with aging in order to minimize their blaming cycle, their sexuality counselor suggests that they try to develop ways to increase their repertoire of sexual behaviors so that they can increase their sexual satisfaction. They are also referred for a medical evaluation to determine if medical treatments such as Viagra or Cialis are appropriate.

THE PROCESS OF SEXUALITY COUNSELING FOR AGING COUPLES

Assessment of Aging Couples

Aging is an inevitable process that affects all of us. A familiarity with age-related concerns is thus required for sexuality counselors in order to make appropriate referrals and provide more effective treatment. A complete medical and sexual history is also critical to an accurate assessment. Collaboration with couples' physicians is an important part of the assessment and counseling process. Physicians can make a determination of biological causes for sexual problems as well as provide information on effects of medication and illness on sexuality. They can also provide information on normal age-related physiological changes.

Sexuality counselors must look for mental and physical changes that have occurred as a result of aging (Stone, 1987). These changes may be key indicators of sources of sexual distress. Although a comprehensive sexual assessment of couples is required at any age, Stone (1987) suggests four elements that should be included in the assessment process with aging couples: "responses to aging-related role changes, the personality styles of the two individuals, their expectations [of the relationship], and interactional style prior to aging" (p. 231). These factors can provide critical psychosocial information.

Overall, sexuality counselors are advised to examine individual and relational age-related changes during the assessment process. A significant goal of the assessment process is to determine how (if at all) the advancing years have been a variable in causing or exacerbating sexual distress. Aging couples who have been sexually active throughout their lives typically continue to maintain their sexual interest and responsiveness (Brecher, 1984; Capuzzi & Friel, 1990). According to Stone (1987), aging couples have more similarities than differences with younger couples, and unless aging is clearly a factor, these issues are not the focal point of the sexuality counseling process.

Questions to Consider

The following questions can be used by sexuality counselors to assess aging couples' concerns:

1. What changes have you noticed in your sexual relationship as you have aged?
2. Have you noticed any physical changes related to your sexuality? If so, what are they?
3. How has the aging process impacted your sexual functioning?
4. How do you and your partner deal with societal beliefs regarding aging and sexuality?
5. How have you adapted your sexual relationship to consider age-related changes?

A more detailed discussion of assessment and sexuality is presented in Chapter 3.

Issues Unique to Aging Couples

The need for sexuality counseling among older people is increasing as is our aging population. Despite such numbers, it is difficult for many older people to seek counseling services for sexual problems. As a result of this reluctance, it is important for medical practitioners to become alert to problems and to make referrals for sexuality counseling when appropriate. Issues about sexuality are often raised in the context of medical consultation or counseling about other issues (Weinstein & Rosen, 1988).

Disclosure Concerns

Although older couples may agree to counseling, they may experience discomfort in making full disclosure about sexual feelings to their sexuality counselor or in the presence of their partner (Stone, 1987). There may be a hesitance to work in the area of emotions or sexuality, possibly due to societal, cultural, or family messages. Couples may also have concerns about how disclosures related to feelings, behaviors, or attitudes will influence the counselor's perceptions or impact their partner's feelings.

Age-related Role Changes

Sexuality counselors working with aging couples should address phase-of-life issues and the influences of these issues on their attitudes, behavior, and values—in particular how they may influence gender roles. As couples age, there are often changes in traditional gender roles. For example, when John retired, he wanted to become more involved in the daily activities of running the household. However, his partner Lili found his "meddling" intrusive. The couple has been arguing more and becoming increasingly distant emotionally and sexually. In long-term relationships, such conflicts are a common cause of sexual problems (Trudel, Turgeon, & Piche, 2000). Sexuality counselors can work with couples on role flexibility after understanding how gender roles have been traditionally defined in older couples' relationships.

Sexual and Relational Style Prior to Aging

A couple's style of relating prior to older age provides a context for how they manage the physical and psychosocial effects of aging. Couples with relational and sexual problems when they were younger may find those concerns exacerbated as they age. In these instances, it is a mistake for sexuality counselors to assume that sexual and relational problems are the result of aging. Alternatively, couples who describe positive sexual relationships prior to aging may describe present sexual difficulties. Exploration of sexual and relational style during the assessment process is an important indicator of possible sources of current distress.

Adjustment to Inexorable Changes

There are important lifestyle, family, occupational, and physical changes that accompany aging. Older couples are often faced with losing a partner, occupational changes (e.g., retirement), decreased energy or mobility, and changes in family structure (e.g., caring for aging parents) (Kingsberg, 2000). Adjusting to these often unavoidable developmental changes can affect a couple's sexual intimacy. For example, the

needs of aging parents may draw emotional energy away from a couple. This type of situation not only puts a couple at risk to lose sexual desire for each other but also strains their emotional connection (Kingsberg, 2000).

Sexuality Counseling and Aging Couples

Sexuality counselors are encouraged to ask questions about age-related changes and how these changes have affected a couple's sexual functioning. At times, there may be differences in attitudes regarding sexuality due to aging (Leiblum & Segraves, 2000). The belief that penile penetration is necessary for sexual intimacy is held by many older males, and efforts to challenge that belief may prove to be fruitless (Leiblum & Segraves, 2000). It is often helpful if sexuality counselors provide aging couples psychoeducation about the natural processes of aging and the role of relational and psychosocial influences.

However, it is important to remember that reluctance to address sexual matters in sexuality counseling does not necessarily indicate there is sexual inhibition in an aging couple's relationship.

INTERVENTIONS FOR COUNSELING AGING COUPLES

There are myriad interventions for counseling aging couples with sexual concerns. Although many of the interventions discussed are appropriate for use with couples of all ages, we will highlight age-related considerations.

Challenging Maladaptive Beliefs

Sexuality counseling helps couples challenge maladaptive beliefs or distorted thinking that negatively affect their sexual functioning. Older persons may have beliefs about sexuality and advancing years that inhibit or deter sexual interest and activity. These beliefs may cause flawed ideas or impressions that negatively affect sexual functioning. Cognitive therapy for couples emphasizes how faulty thinking creates relational discord and is the cause of behavioral and emotional problems (Young & Long, 1998). This type of therapy can be particularly helpful when working with couples in which one or both partners are older because problematic ways of thinking and believing about aging and sexuality can be examined and addressed.

Communication Activities

Couples' communication skill building is also an important sexuality counseling intervention for use with aging persons. This population is subject to the same maladaptive communication problems that younger couples experience. However, aging partners may have unique communication issues about sexual desires and comfortable positions.

Many aging couples have patterns of communicating about sexuality that are entrenched and may or may not have functioned well for them in the past. Age-related changes may now be preventing effective interchange. Sexuality counselors can help aging couples increase effective communication by using interventions such as positive reframing, use of metaphor, perspective taking, use of "I" statements, and the speaker-listener technique.

Educational Skills Development

Although aging couples may confront sexual concerns as a function of age-related life changes, frequently the greatest challenge is lack of information about sexuality (Sharpe, 2004). Using psychoeducation or development of educational skills may be particularly appropriate with aging couples because it tends to be perceived as nonthreatening (Stone, 1987). Providing couples with information about age-related physical, social, and emotional changes as well as sexual alternatives may be accepted and integrated easily because it is tangible and concrete (Stone, 1987). Use of bibliotherapy may be an effective intervention for educating older clients about aging and sexuality (Capuzzi & Friel, 1990).

Sexuality counselors should provide couples with information about the strain created by role changes, normal sexual changes in functioning, and the fact that not all changes are organic in origin. They can also suggest possibilities for increased relatedness and intimacy (Sharpe, 2004; Trudel, Turgeon, & Piche, 2000).

Sensual and Sexual Exercises

Couples can increase their sexual repertoire through the use of sensual and sexual exercises to increase intimacy. These exercises serve to help aging couples increase awareness of physical sensations, develop openness, improve connectedness, and aid in understanding of partners' sexual desires and needs.

Alternatives to Intercourse

Adaptations or accommodations to effectively achieve sexual pleasure are often necessary for aging persons. Trying new sexual activities is a key element in the development of a satisfying sexual life (Farrow, 1990). With experimentation, sexual alternatives may arise. Sexuality counselors can help couples learn new methods of giving and receiving pleasure through their bodies. This requires the elimination of the emphasis on genitals as the only area of the body that can be excited sexually and on intercourse as the only means of sexual expression (Farrow, 1990). Cuddling, mutual massage, oral stimulation, attention to areas of the body such as neck, ears, lips, and inner arms can be highly pleasurable for both partners.

Use of Genograms

The sexual genogram is a valuable assessment intervention for all couples struggling with sexual concerns. However, sexuality counselors can work with couples to incorporate specific information and messages about aging into their genogram. This will help couples gain an understanding of the impact and role of these messages on their present sexual lives. This strategy has been described in detail in Chapter 3.

Developing a Support Network

Helping couples explore alternative avenues for social interactions and develop support networks that provide information about sexual health in aging can help couples improve sexual self-concept and increase feelings of social and sexual confidence and competence. The supportive involvement of partners, family members, and health-care professionals is also critical for achieving feelings of sexual acceptance and competence.

Writing New Sexual Scripts

Although the method of achieving intimacy may be different, sexual satisfaction may remain the same or improve. Helping couples to redefine sexual roles and rules and to develop new attitudes about sexual behaviors and practices can provide alternative ways of understanding and attaining sexual intimacy. Redefining prior problematic ways of relating offers an opportunity for couples to create new sexual scripts that provide alternative internal messages and external behaviors.

BOX 10.1

Interventions at a Glance

- Teach couples problem-solving skills in order to create alternatives to conventional sexual practices.
- Help couples challenge societal, historical, or family messages about sexuality that are detrimental to their sexual health.
- Provide bibliotherapy on a variety of topics related to aging and sexual well-being.
- Have couples practice alternatives to intercourse so that they may achieve effective sexual satisfaction.
- Create a sexual genogram that incorporates specific sexual messages about aging. Identify positive messages that may have passed from generation to generation.
- Teach couples to compliment each other and affirm their contributions to their sexual health as a couple.

Affirming Strengths

As couples age, they are often confronted with external messages that disaffirm their sexual needs, and their individual and relational abilities are often forgotten or ignored. Working with couples to recognize, utilize, and validate their strengths in a culture that emphasizes youth is important for finding solutions to sexual and relational problems. See Box 10.1 for sexuality counseling Interventions at a Glance for aging couples.

Case Example

Donahue, aged 75, and Rebecca, aged 58, have been in a relationship for eight months. Donahue's wife died two years ago, and Rebecca has been divorced for seven years from her ex-husband, who died four years ago. The couple met while Donahue's wife was hospitalized and Rebecca was a volunteer at the hospital. Since the illness and subsequent death of his wife, Donahue has been living with his daughter, son-in-law, and their four children. Recently retired, Rebecca is in good health and lives alone, but she is close to her three sons. She reports being quite lonely and desirous of companionship and intimacy.

Donahue and Rebecca would like to get married and live together in Rebecca's home. Both of their families are opposed to this union. Donahue describes feeling torn between his family and his new love. He reports that his daughter views him as a frail, childlike old man, rather than a mature, independent individual capable of making his own decisions. Donahue acknowledges he does not move or think as quickly as he did in the past, but he describes himself as "a lively old codger." He acknowledges concern about his ability to sexually satisfy Rebecca due to his occasional difficulty achieving and maintaining an erection. They have engaged in sexual relations several times and he believes they can find ways to mutually satisfy each other. Donahue does not feel particularly comfortable discussing sexual matters due to his upbringing, and he believes men should "know about such things." He is willing to attend counseling with Rebecca because he loves her but is quite uncomfortable sharing personal matters with "an outsider."

Rebecca also does not wish to alienate her three sons but is desirous of being involved in an intimate relationship once again. She reports that her sons' view of her as "only a mother" limits her freedom as a sexual being. She has met her sexual needs over the last several years through masturbation. She had two brief intimate relationships following her divorce but described those as unsatisfactory and as "rebound relationships." She states she loves Donahue and wants to share her life with him. She acknowledges some concern about the impact of Donahue's erectile difficulties on his sexual ability and how this will influence their relationship. She also describes being very limited in her own sexual repertoire and wants to ensure that she is able to meet his sexual needs. Rebecca feels less awkward discussing sexual issues and wants to openly address these concerns through counseling.

Application of the Integrative Couples' Model
Stage 1: Assessing the Problem
Donahue is concerned he will alienate his daughter if he continues his relationship with

Rebecca. He is also concerned he will not be able to satisfy Rebecca sexually and has fears about the impact on their relationship. He complains that Rebecca is somewhat limited in her sexual repertoire and that he requires direct oral or manual stimulation to achieve and maintain an erection. He does not feel comfortable communicating this need to her. Donahue expresses concern that Rebecca is pushing him to discuss things that he finds difficult and notices he tends to respond by withdrawing and becoming more silent. He does acknowledge that he is willing to try to discuss difficult issues but her impatience angers him.

Rebecca is concerned about distancing herself from her three sons when she marries Donahue. She reports that she has never had an orgasmic sexual relationship with a partner and does not know what to do about this matter. She is willing to discuss her sexual needs, but Donahue is from the "old school" and distances himself emotionally and sexually when she shares her sexual needs. She is concerned about her ability to satisfy him given her limited sexual repertoire. She reports she has initiated verbal fights with him to try to push him into discussing problems more openly.

Both feel considerable distress about the negative feedback they are receiving from their children about their relationship and recognize the need to find a way to communicate their feelings to them. They want to have a sexual relationship that is mutually satisfying and to develop techniques to pleasure each other more effectively. They also want to find ways to communicate more effectively with each other about their concerns and feelings prior to marriage.

During counseling sessions, their sexuality counselor helps Donahue and Rebecca recognize the ways problematic communication patterns and their lack of knowledge about each other's sexual desires are having a negative impact on their relationship. Information is obtained from Donahue's physician about potential medical causes for his erectile difficulties so that the couple can better incorporate techniques to improve sexual connectedness. The sexuality counselor is also able to help them develop skills to communicate with their children about their feelings.

Stage 2: Goal Setting

To improve their relationship, Donahue and Rebecca know that they will have to find a better way to communicate their feelings to each other (besides withdrawing into silence when frustrated or instigating an argument). They know that they will need to cue each other when communication is deteriorating. They will also have to investigate new sexual skills in order to improve their sexual relationship. Finally, they will have to work together on ways to communicate the importance of their independence to their families.

The sexuality counselor helps Donahue and Rebecca develop the following affective and behavioral goals:

1. By next week, we will talk about how we feel about our relationship with our children together and maintain a united front (behavioral) to feel increased autonomy and responsibility (affective) for our lives.
2. We will develop new ways to resolve conflicts and discuss difficult topics (behavioral) to feel increased competency and emotional connection (affective) as a couple.
3. We will explore new sexual techniques and strategies by reading sexual manuals and viewing sexual tapes (behavioral) in order to feel increased mutual sexual satisfaction (affective).
4. We will develop a specific strategy for our plans to marry and live together in one month (behavioral) in order to feel optimistic (affective) about the future.

Stage 3: Adopting New Perceptions and Behaviors

Donahue and Rebecca use their individual skills and strengths to implement their goals. Donahue has always been good at seeing the big picture and conceptualizing problems, and he possesses an adventurous spirit. Rebecca is very creative and articulate, and she enjoys exploring new interests and gathering information. Rebecca agrees to begin researching sexual methods and techniques they both can implement to please each other sexually. She will research and purchase sexual manuals and videos for this purpose.

Donahue and Rebecca plan to schedule time with each of their families to discuss their plans and communicate their feelings. They agree on a structure for their conversations about difficult issues, signaling each other when they need to take a break. Rebecca agrees to respect Donahue's need to process his feelings before discussing them; Donahue agrees to work harder to discuss issues he has traditionally avoided.

They both want to discuss and try a variety of new sexual techniques. They will use information gathered from Rebecca's research and begin communicating about sexual needs and identify activities they would like to try. Donahue and Rebecca both agree they will communicate with Donahue's physician about any questions and concerns they have about Donahue's erectile difficulties. Finally, they agree not to get into a blaming cycle should they encounter difficulty.

Stage 4: Maintaining Perceptions and Behaviors
Donahue and Rebecca realize they will need to move slowly in order to implement their plans most effectively. They acknowledge that continued conflict with family members will occur until they have taken the initiative and discussed their feelings openly and honestly. They also understand that in order for their relationship to progress in a positive manner, they must respect each other's boundaries and needs regarding communication and sexuality.

Donahue and Rebecca recognize they could easily get offtrack if they do not maintain the communication structure they have developed. To further aid in increasing intimate feelings, they have begun to discuss their feelings in a more constructive manner by using a system of agreed-upon signals. Donahue decides to wave his hand slowly when he needs space and Rebecca decides to tug her ear when she is distressed.

They also identify roadblocks and pitfalls that could sabotage their progress. Donahue knows he must monitor his tendency to withdraw when he finds conversation difficult as this will result in problematic communication. Rebecca knows that she must recognize when she is pushing so they can avoid old patterns. They both identify clues that indicate they are not feeling as close as they should. For example, they know that when they do not cuddle following sexual intimacy this is generally a sign of decreasing closeness. Lastly, they recognize they are both responsible for the solution and are willing to be responsive to feedback from the other to avoid potential pitfalls.

Stage 5: Validating New Perceptions and Behaviors
Donahue and Rebecca are enthusiastic and energized about the direction their relationship is now taking and encouraged by their ability to effectively communicate and solve problems with each other and their families. They support and encourage each other to continue to build trust, intimacy, respect, and connectedness in their relationship. They agree to confront each other in a respectful manner if one believes the other is falling off and returning to former patterns of relating. Also, they are able to continue to explore new ways of relating sexually and to communicate verbally and nonverbally about their desires and needs.

They enjoy spending time with each other and feel more relaxed and capable. Because of these connected and united feelings and their open and solution-focused communication, they feel able to move forward and plan for their marriage. Their success has helped them cope with relationship and family concerns because of their improved problem-solving skills. They are excited about their improved sexual intimacy and enjoy exploring new ways of pleasuring each other. They make a point of complimenting their successes and celebrating with bimonthly special dinners together. They recognize that as their relationship grows and changes, they will also have to adapt and change with it in a caring and nurturing manner.

SUMMARY

Aging persons are vital and important members of our society. As the number of persons over fifty continues to increase, so will the need for counseling interventions that address their unique needs. Many of the sexuality concerns of older couples are not different from those of younger couples. Problems related to sexual arousal, performance capabilities, time for intimacy, and partnering concerns are issues for people of all ages. Unfortunately, older couples are often viewed as not having sexual

CHAPTER 10   AGING AND SEXUALITY   193

interests or desires. Counselors will need to recognize that sexuality counseling with older persons often occurs in the context of counseling about other issues, which are often imbedded in grief, loss, retirement, or other psychosocial or developmental concerns.

Counselors cannot make assumptions about sexuality and aging or adopt negative stereotypes. Negative beliefs, values, and attitudes must be challenged to better serve an aging population. Counselors must also be willing to confront their feelings about their own aging process.

It is important for counselors to take the initiative to discuss the influence of aging with clients and consider the psychosocial, developmental, physiological, and cultural influences aging may have on their sexuality.

The integrative couples' model for sexuality counseling allows for many options so that sexuality counselors can work with older couples in a supportive, nonblaming, or shaming environment.

DISABILITIES, CHRONIC ILLNESS, AND SEXUALITY

KEY CONCEPTS

- Most people with disabilities or chronic illnesses have similar sexual needs, feelings, and desires as those of the nondisabled population.
- Chronic medical conditions encompass both disabilities and chronic illness, as both are marked by long duration or frequent recurrence.
- A disability may be acquired or congenital and include physical mobilities as well as developmental, psychiatric, cognitive, visual, and auditory disabilities.
- Chronic illness involves physical changes to the body resulting from a disease.
- There are unique psychosocial factors that sexuality counselors must consider when working with couples with disabilities and health-related issues.
- There are multiple sexual myths and negative stereotypes about those affected by chronic medical conditions.
- Sexuality counselors should be aware of their own values, attitudes, and beliefs about disability, chronic illness, and sexuality.
- There are often physical implications on sexuality related to having a chronic medical condition.
- A comprehensive assessment is important to providing meaningful sexuality counseling. This would include questions about sexuality before and after the disability or illness, family of origin messages about sexuality, and beliefs about sexuality.
- An integrative couples' model offers numerous treatment approaches for tackling the sexual questions and problems of those with chronic medical conditions.

When couples are faced with a chronic medical condition, the entire relationship is impacted. They must confront physical and psychosocial factors associated with medical conditions that may profoundly influence their sexual relationship. There may be a significant strain on intimacy as couples struggle to make adjustments in their sexual attitudes, values, and understanding of sexuality as it relates to chronic medical conditions and adaptations to sexual interactions. Sexuality counselors should be aware of the effect of chronic medical conditions on sexuality to better assist couples in managing the emotional and physiological adjustments necessary for maintaining a satisfying sexual relationship.

This chapter defines chronic medical conditions (disability and chronic illness), describes psychosocial factors associated with health-related concerns, and addresses myths and stereotypes associated with each. In addition, issues regarding physical implications of health on sexuality, information on assessment techniques, and counseling interventions are addressed. A case example illustrates how the integrative couples' model can help a couple facing a chronic medical condition.

DEFINITIONS OF HEALTH-RELATED ISSUES

Chronic Medical Conditions Defined

We use the term "chronic medical condition" to encompass both disabilities and chronic illnesses. This is due in part to the overlap of many of the issues that persons with disabilities and persons with chronic illnesses face. For example, persons with disabilities or chronic illnesses are often viewed by family, friends, and society as asexual (Lesh & Marshall, 1984), childlike, and having no need for sexual intimacy (Hanna & Rogovsky, 1991). Frequently, popular beliefs about sexuality are based on misconceptions about the sexual needs and sexual expression of this population.

Disability Defined

There are an estimated 50 million disabled persons in the United States, and this population has increased over the last 50 years (Sipski & Alexander, 1997). Some people are born with a disability and some acquire an impairment or suffer a loss of function or a disfiguring change in appearance during the course of their lifetime.

The term "physical disability" is often used to include a variety of disabilities. We have adopted the definition of physical disability given by Linton and Rousso (1988) because it is extensive and encompasses a wide range of disabilities: "body structure and function, including spinal cord injury, other mobility impairments, amputations, cerebral palsy, skeletal deformities and disfigurements, blindness, deafness, and speech impediments" (p. 114). These disabilities include a wide range of severity: "visible or invisible, and those that occur at birth, during childhood, or during adulthood" (p. 114).

There are additional specific categories or types of disabilities that include mobility disabilities, developmental disabilities, psychiatric disabilities, cognitive disabilities, visual disabilities, and auditory disabilities (Mackelprang & Salsgiver, 1999).

Mobility Disability.   There are two categories of mobility disabilities: "[those] acquired before, during, or immediately following birth, known as congenital disabilities, and . . . [those] acquired later in life" (Mackelprang & Salsgiver, 1999, p. 83). Cerebral palsy, muscular dystrophy, strokes, and rheumatoid arthritis are examples of mobility disabilities.

Developmental Disability.   Developmental disabilities are defined by the Developmental Disabilities Assistance and Bill of Rights Act as being attributed to either a mental or physical impairment, and are manifested before the age of 22. In addition, they are likely to continue throughout the person's life, create severe functional limitations in a person's capacity to handle major life activities, are severe and chronic in nature, and reflect the need for varied specialized or other services of extended duration (CESSI, 2003). Developmental disabilities include, but are not limited to, mental retardation, autism, and seizure disorders.

Psychiatric Disability.   A psychiatric disability is defined as the presence of severe and persistent mental illness. The U.S. federal government recognizes severe mental illness as a disability with regard to federal rights and benefits (Wedenoja, 1999). Bipolar disorder, schizophrenia, and other psychotic disorders are examples of psychiatric disabilities.

Cognitive Disability.   Cognitive disabilities are defined as conditions that significantly impact one's ability to understand what is seen and heard (Bruyere, 1994) or to process information. These disabilities include "learning disabilities, intellectual disabilities, traumatic brain injury, and Down syndrome" (Mackelprang & Salsgiver, 1999, pp. 191–192).

Visual Disability.   The National Federation of the Blind estimates that there are currently 1.3 million legally blind people in the United States. According to their guidelines, the generally accepted legal definition of blindness is a person who has "visual acuity of not greater than 20/200 in the better eye with correction or a field not subtending an angle greater than 20 degrees" (Jernigan, n.d.). When an individual's vision is 20/80 or less in the best eye with correction, then visual impairment is diagnosed (Mackelprang & Salsgiver, 1999).

Auditory Disability.   There are three types of hearing loss, any of which can result in auditory disabilities ranging from mild hearing loss to profound deafness (Mackelprang & Salsgiver, 1999). The National Institute on Deafness and Other Communication Disorders (NIDCD) estimates there are approximately 46 million people in the United States with auditory or communication impairments (NIDCD, n.d.).

Chronic Illness Defined

Chronic illness involves physiological changes to the body resulting from a disease. Chronic illnesses include diseases such as diabetes, cancer, heart disease,

Parkinson's disease, and acquired immunodeficiency syndrome (AIDS). The number of persons with chronic illness is increasing and it has been estimated that by 2030, approximately 150 million Americans will experience a chronic illness (Schmaling & Scher, 2000). More specific information on diabetes, cardiac and pulmonary conditions, and cancer will be discussed later in this chapter.

PSYCHOSOCIAL ASPECTS OF DISABILITIES, CHRONIC ILLNESS, AND SEXUALITY

The way that persons perceive themselves sexually impacts couples' psychological experience and is often informed by societal and cultural messages (Mona & Gardos, 2000). For men with chronic medical conditions, "issues of masculinity, sexual assertiveness, and/ or sexual competence often arise" (Mona & Gardos, 2000, pp. 312–313). The social and gender-affiliated messages that associate strength and virility with male sexuality are assumed to be incompatible with chronic medical conditions, particularly if a male's mobility or ability to obtain an erection is impacted by having a chronic illness or disability. For example, when Delroy's spinal cord injury affected his ability to maintain an erection, he experienced feelings of sexual incompetence and emasculation. Women with health-related issues may believe they do not meet social standards or norms of physical attractiveness and lack sexual appeal (Mona & Gardos, 2000). For example, Debra felt less physically attractive and experienced decreased sexual desire following her double mastectomy as a result of breast cancer. These societal messages often have a negative effect on the psychological experience of those with chronic medical conditions.

Psychosocial Factors and Disabilities

The age of onset and severity of a disability is considered to have an impact on sexual self-concept and sexual esteem (Mona & Gardos, 2000). Specifically, persons with congenital disabilities integrate their disability into their sexual development differently than persons with an acquired disability (Mona, Gardos, & Brown, 1994). However, when an acquired disability comes about later in life, there is interruption and potential alteration of gender and sexual roles that could result in problems due to family and social expectations of masculinity and femininity already ingrained

in the individual (S. Cole, 1988; T. Cole, 1975; Mona & Gardos, 2000).

When these problems are experienced by disabled persons, relational and sexual satisfaction are often more difficult to achieve. On the other hand, simply having a disability does not mean that sexual expression is not as important to disabled persons as it is to nondisabled persons.

Psychosocial Implications of Spinal Cord Injuries

Spinal cord injuries are generally categorized as acquired disabilities. Persons with such injuries often experience feelings of grief about the loss of their former nondisabled sexual selves and as a result may move into a state of asexuality (S. Cole, 1988). Changes in physical appearance and ability may affect the sexual self-definitions of persons with spinal cord injuries as well as influence the way in which others view them (Mona & Gardos, 2000).

Persons with spinal cord injuries often lose "physical sensation in the genitals and erogenous zones" (Mona & Gardos, 2000, p. 319). This has psychological implications such as feelings of anger, futility, or grief because there is no longer the ability to experience a physiological orgasm. Persons with spinal cord injuries are challenged with developing a different self and body image, as well as social persona (Mona & Gardos, 2000). In general, couples living with spinal cord injury are charged with adjusting to new ways of sexual and social relatedness.

Psychosocial Implications of Cerebral Palsy

Persons with cerebral palsy, a congenital disability, may experience "social rejection during adolescence and perceive themselves as unfit or unworthy of intimate sexual relationships, especially with people who are not disabled" (Rathus, Nevid, & Fichner-Rathus, 2000, p. 444). During childhood and adolescence, persons with cerebral palsy often learn to assume asexual roles (Rathus et al., 2000) and as a result may have difficulty establishing intimate relationships.

Psychosocial Implications of Rheumatoid Arthritis

Persons with rheumatoid arthritis, an acquired disability, often experience limits in many social, leisure, and professional activities. "These changes in activity level may occur not only because of physical limitations such as difficulties with mobility and severe pain but also because of experienced or feared stigmatization and rejection" (Danoff-Burg & Revenson, 2000, p. 108). This may result in persons with rheumatoid arthritis pulling away from others, perhaps their sexual partner. Often persons with rheumatoid arthritis have concerns about body image and fear of losing one's partner. Severity of the disability appears to play the most significant role in sexual satisfaction and sexual self-concept (Majerovitz & Revenson, 1994).

Psychosocial Implications of Amputation

Amputation can be either an acquired or congenital disability. When this disability is acquired, persons may experience feelings of grief over the loss of a limb, denial, fear of social rejection, and feelings of inadequacy (Tilton, 1997). Although amputees may not experience a direct physiological impact on sexuality (depending on the cause of amputation), the psychological impact of this disability may lead to feelings of sexual inadequacy.

Congenital amputees, persons who are born without a limb, may have similar psychological experiences as those persons with an acquired amputation regarding fears of social rejection and stigmatization depending on their overall social experience.

Psychosocial Implications of Stroke

Persons who have had a stroke or cerebrovascular accident, an acquired disability, may experience decreased self-esteem, fear, anxiety, concerns about a negative response from a partner, and problematic coping skills (Monga & Kerrigan, 1997). These emotional factors may significantly impact sexual functioning and the ability to achieve intimacy with one's partner.

Psychosocial Factors and Chronic Illness

The psychosocial factors affecting persons having a chronic illness are similar to those of persons with disabilities. Often a variety of emotions—self-worth, control of one's body, body image, and feelings of masculinity or femininity—are negatively affected (Danoff-Burg & Revenson, 2000; Halford, Scott, & Smythe, 2000). Issues of loss and dependence are also prevalent for some chronically ill persons. The manner in which these difficult feelings are managed are often predictors of sexual and relational competence and satisfaction (Krukofsky, 1988).

In addition, there is often the societal assumption that couples affected by chronic illnesses are or should be asexual, as it is assumed that sexuality is reserved for those who are physically healthy.

Psychosocial Implications of Diabetes

There are a number of psychosocial factors related to sexuality common in diabetic men. Sadness, anxiety, concerns about future health, and a poor body image have been found in this population (Jensen, 1985). For women, there is often hesitancy to engage in sexual intercourse which "may be influenced by culture, physical wellness, age, and psychological status" (Krukofsky, 1988, p. 266).

Psychosocial Implications of Cardiac and Pulmonary Conditions

Many people with cardiac conditions fear they may die if they engage in sexual activity, which may lead to psychological rather than physiological problems as well as inhibition in sexual activities (Mona & Gardos, 2000). In addition, there may be fear of a recurrence of the symptoms (e.g., angina), and persons with cardiac conditions will frequently interrupt sexual intercourse due to anxiety about possible sudden death (Krukofsky, 1988). Issues include anxiety, depression, avoidance, poor self-image, and mistaken beliefs about cardiac conditions.

Like persons with cardiac disease, individuals with chronic pulmonary conditions may experience shortness of breath, which often leads to diminished sexual activity. Poor sexual self-concept, anxiety about engaging in sexual activity with restricted breath, and fears about the ability to please one's partner also may result in an avoidance of sexual expression (Mona & Gardos, 2000).

Psychosocial Implications of Cancer

Common initial reactions to a diagnosis of cancer include feelings of disbelief, fear, depression, anger, anxiety, and emotional detachment (Derogatis et al., 1983; Mona & Gardos, 2000). These responses can have an important effect on sexual functioning. For example, women with gynecological cancers often have problems coping with body image and report feeling less sexually appealing (Andersen, Woods, & Copeland, 1997). In addition, redefining perceptions of intimate relationships and other family and social roles and goals can be a difficult and lengthy process (Mona & Gardos, 2000). As a result, many couples affected by cancer have decreased sexual intimacy.

Stereotypes Related to Disability and Chronic Illness

Persons with disabilities are often perceived as "ill" or "sick" and as objects of pity (Mona & Gardos, 2000). Disabled persons who are completely healthy are often expected to comply with ill or sick roles. People with mobility disabilities who require assisted care frequently are treated as unhealthy or incompetent. For example, when Jolie (who uses a wheelchair) is out with her partner (who does not have a mobility disability), questions or statements about Jolie's needs are directed to her partner instead of Jolie.

In addition to negative perceptions about disabled persons, their partners are often the objects of "pity" or viewed as "martyrs." The myths and stereotypes associated with disabilities have a negative impact on couples' sexual self-concept, competence, and satisfaction (Mona & Gardos, 2000).

Similar to reactions to disabilities, friends, family, and health professionals often view persons with chronic illnesses as incompetent, childlike, and incapable. As a result, questions and decisions about daily living or medical care are often directed to or made by family members rather than the chronically ill person. This behavior based on the myth of "incapability" devalues and diminishes the person with a chronic illness.

A common myth surrounding chronic illness involves fear of catching the disease. This fear may be manifested in a variety of ways. Avoidance of touching the ill person, breathing the same air, and sharing personal space, such as bathrooms, may be displayed. In addition, dodging contact such as not returning calls or outright abandonment may also result due to this fear of communicability.

The chronically ill may also be viewed as a drain on the social service system. Depending on the severity of the illness, chronically ill persons may be unable to work for periods of time and thus require disability income or other assistance. This may result in the belief that chronically ill persons are not doing their part and taxing the system.

Sexuality, Societal Myths, Disability, and Chronic Illness

Society does not readily recognize the sexuality and sexual potential of disabled and chronically ill people; rather they are frequently perceived by society as asexual (Hanna & Rogovsky, 1991). Although having a chronic medical condition requires some couples to modify their sexual practices, most couples with chronic medical conditions have the same sexual desires and emotions as persons without these conditions (Rathus et al., 2000).

Myths and stereotypes affect the sexuality of disabled or chronically ill couples in a variety of ways. To the extent that couples believe and internalize these stereotypes, there can be many negative emotional and relational consequences, including low self-esteem, negative body image, and limited social and sexual expectations for themselves. Any of these may inhibit their functioning in relational and sexual arenas. To help couples combat the consequences of negative social messages, sexuality counselors can provide education about sexual wellness.

Nosek et al. (1994) suggests five factors important for sexual wellness among disabled and chronically ill persons and their partners:

1. Positive sexual self-concept; appreciation of self as valuable sexually and as a person as well as freedom of sexual choice.
2. Knowledge about self-sexuality; information-seeking and application of sexual information and effects of chronic medical condition on sexuality.
3. Positive, productive relationships; satisfaction and stability in relationships.
4. Coping with barriers to sexuality (sexual, environmental, physical, social, and emotional).
5. Maintaining the best possible general and sexual health, given physical limitations; active in self-health promotion. (pp. 52–56)

The ability of disabled and chronically ill persons to express sexual feelings and needs depends on the physical limitations imposed by their medical conditions and their adjustment to these conditions.

Counselor Attitudes and Beliefs

When sexuality counselors are unaware of their own stereotypes and beliefs, their counseling behavior may unconsciously reflect many of the societal myths that disabled and chronically ill persons face.

Health-care professionals working with couples affected by chronic medical conditions may discount partners' sexual needs if sexual intimacy is not valued as essential for health and emotional responses contributing to sexual problems are ignored (Zilbergeld, 1979). Sexuality counselors can work with other health-care professionals to validate the importance of sexuality and its impact on quality of life for disabled and chronically ill individuals.

PHYSICAL CHANGES, DISABILITIES, CHRONIC ILLNESS, AND SEXUALITY

Sexuality is a multifaceted process made up of a range of biological systems (Phillips, 2000). Chronic medical conditions can be a frequent source of direct or indirect sexual difficulties. For example, vascular disease associated with diabetes might inhibit arousal. Heart disease may hinder sexual intimacy due to problematic respiration. In addition, difficulty with urination or pain from arthritis may cause discomfort or anxiety leading to a reduction in sexual intimacy or sexual dysfunction (Phillips, 2000). Finally, medications associated with depressive disorders may hinder sexual expression. (See Chapter 10 for a more detailed discussion of medical treatment for depression and its effect on sexuality.) Sexuality counselors must be aware of the specific physical implications of chronic medical conditions on couples' sexual relationships in order to provide effective treatment options.

Physical Implications of Disability Conditions

Disability conditions often result in persons having to achieve mobility through alternative means, to require adaptation or accommodations to maintain tasks and responsibilities of daily living, or to have need of attendant care (Mackelprang & Salsgiver, 1999). These differences may also affect the disabled person's ability to have a satisfying sexual relationship.

Physical Implications of Spinal Cord Injuries

In the United States, approximately 10,000 persons have spinal cord injuries (SCI) each year (Mackelprang & Salsgiver, 1999, p. 90). This kind of injury can result in total or partial paralysis, reduced motor control as well as loss of feeling depending on the level of damage to the spinal cord (Crooks & Baur, 2002). Damage to the spinal cord that occurs in the back (paraplegia) frequently results in paralysis to the lower portion of the body. Spinal injury to the neck results in quadriplegia (arm and leg or upper-body paralysis). With all types of SCI, bowel, bladder, and sexual functioning are impacted (Mackelprang & Salsgiver, 1999).

The level of injury to the spinal cord primarily determines the physiological impact of SCI on sexuality. The location of injury also determines a person's ability to feel his or her body becoming sexually aroused and to achieve a physiological orgasm.

The degree to which men with SCI experience neurologically based erectile dysfunction depends on the area of the spinal cord that has been injured and how completely the spinal cord has been damaged. Approximately 54% to 87% of males with SCI can achieve and maintain erections (Crooks & Baur, 2002). However, these erections are often not sufficient to sustain penile-vaginal penetration or to experience orgasm (Spark, 1991). Viagra has been found to increase psychological and physiological arousal for males and females with spinal cord injuries (Sipski, Rosen, Alexander, & Hamer, 2000).

There are conflicting reports on the physiological impact of SCIs on female sexuality. Overall, the major physical changes in the sexual functioning of women with SCI are a decrease or lack of vaginal lubrication, lack of the ability to perceive tactile stimulation (particularly genital), lack of motor function, and an inability to achieve physiological orgasm (Perduta-Fulginiti, 1992; Rathus et al., 2000).

Physical Implications of Cerebral Palsy

Cerebral palsy affects more than 700,000 Americans and is the result of "injury to the brain at birth or during fetal development before birth" (Mackelprang & Salsgiver, 1999, p. 83). Acquired cerebral palsy occurs after birth usually in the first months or years of life and most often is the result of meningitis, injuries to the head, and other types of cerebral damage (Crooks & Baur, 2002).

Cerebral palsy results in problems with motor control. The muscle spasticity and problems with motor control that result from cerebral palsy do not affect sexual desire, orgasmic capacity, genital sensation, or reproductive health (Reinisch, 1990). However, couples in which one or both partners has cerebral palsy may need to adjust sexual positioning or activities to adapt to problems with muscular control (Rathus et al., 2000).

Physical Implications of Rheumatoid Arthritis

Rheumatoid arthritis affects approximately 2.5 million people (Mackelprang & Salsgiver, 1999, p. 88) and 1% to 2% of adults in the United States (Danoff-Burg & Revenson, 2000). Rheumatoid arthritis is a systemic condition characterized by chronic joint inflammation and degenerative joint damage that results in severe pain (Danoff-Burg & Revenson, 2000). Body systems, including skin, blood vessels, nerves, eyes, and muscles are also often affected (Mackelprang & Salsgiver, 1999).

Although rheumatoid arthritis can interfere with sexual functioning, a number of studies have indicated there is little or no difference between the sexual desire, needs, and overall sexual contentment of couples affected and not affected by this disability (Danoff-Burg & Revenson, 2000; Majerovitz & Revenson, 1994). It has also been found that the severity of the disability is the greatest predictor of sexual satisfaction (Majerovitz & Revenson, 1994).

Physical Implications of Amputation

Persons without a limb or a significantly altered limb number more than 300,000 in the United States (Mackelprang & Salsgiver, 1999). This type of disability can be either congenital or acquired. Although amputation does not generally have physical implications for sexual functioning, low sexual desire or feelings of sexual inadequacy may result from issues regarding body image.

Physical Implications of Stroke

The degree of impairment from a stroke varies. Frequently, speech, mobility, emotional, sensory, and cognitive functioning are affected (Crooks & Baur, 2002).

Decreased sexual desire and orgasmic capacity, premature ejaculation, and lack of vaginal lubrication are difficulties frequently encountered after a stroke (Aloni, Ring, Rozenthul, & Schwartz, 1993; Monga & Kerrigan, 1997).

Sexual concerns that arise after a stroke are often the result of related medical conditions such as diabetes, hypertension, or psychological issues such as fear, anxiety, negative self-concept, and problematic coping (Mona & Gardos, 2000; Monga & Kerrigan, 1997).

Physical Implications of Chronic Illness on Sexuality

Chronic illnesses have varying degrees of impact on sexual functioning. The severity, duration, treatment, and nature of illness must be factored into the understanding of the impact of the illness on sexuality.

Physical Implications of Diabetes

Diabetes is a disease that affects approximately 16 million Americans (Tilton, 1997). This disease of the endocrine system occurs when the pancreas does not secrete sufficient insulin (Crooks & Baur, 2002).

Up to 50% of men with diabetes often experience problems with erectile dysfunction (Manecke & Mulhall, 1999; Tilton, 1997). Nerve damage, vascular difficulties, and hormonal abnormalities have also been cited as a cause of male sexual dysfunction (Jensen, 1981; Johannes, Araujo, & Feldman, 2000).

Women with diabetes often experience decreased sexual desire, vaginal dryness, and problems achieving an orgasm (Herter, 1998; Jensen, 1981). As a result of reduced blood flow to the vaginal region, women may experience painful intercourse and difficulty or inability to have an orgasm.

Physical Implications of Cardiac and Pulmonary Conditions

Cardiac conditions include, but are not limited to, congestive heart failure, cardiomyopathy, coronary artery disease, and myocardial infarction (Rankin-Esquer, Deeter, & Taylor, 2000; Stitik & Benevento, 1997). Congestive heart failure is a serious condition in which the heart loses its pumping efficiency. Cardiomyopathy occurs when the muscle of the heart is defective or damaged. Coronary artery disease has the greatest potential to negatively affect sexual function (Stitik & Benevento, 1997). A myocardial infarction, more commonly known as a heart attack, occurs when a blood clot blocks the flow in one or more coronary arteries.

Men with cardiac conditions often have problems with erectile dysfunction, premature ejaculation, orgasm, and sexual arousal (Scalzi, 1982). Physiological causes are rarely the origin of the development of sexual difficulties in persons with a cardiac condition (Krukofsky, 1988). Instead fears generated by misconceptions about exertion during sexual activity and lack of accurate health information can create sexual distress (Krukofsky, 1988; Stitik & Benevento, 1997). Less information is available on the impact of cardiac disease on sexual functioning in women. Despite the assertion in some literature that women may experience sexual pain, aversion, and orgasmic disorders (Stitik & Benevento, 1997), it is generally agreed that female cardiac patients are provided less information or education about sexuality than males (Krukofsky, 1988).

Physical factors resulting from cardiac conditions that have been found to impact sexual functioning include chest pressure during sexual activity, reduced cardiac capacity, and some heart medications (Hellerstein & Friedman, 1970).

Chronic obstructive pulmonary disease (COPD) refers to a number of chronic lung disorders that obstruct the airways (Schmaling & Afari, 2000). The most common form of COPD is a combination of chronic bronchitis and emphysema. Shortness of breath, limited lung capacity, and certain COPD medications often have negative effects on sexual functioning (Stitik & Benevento, 1997).

Physical Implications of Cancer

There are more than 200 types of cancer (Halford, Scott, & Smythe, 2000). Some cancers can affect one organ, others are more generalized. In any type of cancer, there is uncontrolled growth and spread of abnormal cells. Although any type of cancer can impact sexuality, we focus on breast and prostate cancers because of their high prevalence as well as their unique impact on sexual feelings and functioning.

Prostate cancer ranks third among the types of cancer that kill American men and is the cancer diagnosed most often for men (Mona & Gardos, 2000). Treatments for prostate cancer include surgical removal of the prostate, radiation therapy, and hormonal therapy (Halford et al., 2000; Mona & Gardos, 2000).

For breast cancer, surgery is typically the initial treatment and is often combined with radiation therapy, hormone therapy, and chemotherapy (Halford et al., 2000).

Following a diagnosis, sexual function is affected from both physical and psychological bases. The sexual organs may be harmed by the disease process and their neurovascular supply and treatment options (e.g., radiation, chemotherapy, surgery, and hormone changes) may affect sexual expression (Waldman & Eliasof, 1997).

In males, the removal of the prostate usually causes erectile dysfunction (Andersen & Lamb, 1995; Perez, Fair, & Ihde, 1989). There are newer forms of surgical prostatectomies that can protect some erectile function for many men (Brender & Walsh, 1992).

In females with breast cancer, patients who undergo mastectomy in an attempt to eradicate the disease may feel unattractive or less "like a woman" because breasts are associated with femininity and physical and sexual attractiveness. Breast cancer patients who have undergone mastectomy report more problems with sexuality than lumpectomy patients (Schain, d'Angelo, Dunn, Lichter, & Pierce, 1994).

Chemotherapy, another breast cancer treatment option, also causes hair loss that can affect feelings of sexual attractiveness. Women have often described loss of sexual desire and decreased sexual activity as a result of their cancer and treatment (Ganz, 1996). "For many women who receive chemotherapy, menstrual periods may cease and menopause will begin. As a result, a range of symptoms may occur, including hot flashes, vaginal lubrication problems, and lack of sexual desire" (Ganz, 1996, pp. 20–21).

Due to the psychological and physical implications of disabilities and chronic illnesses on sexuality, couples affected by chronic medical conditions have unique concerns that influence the process of sexuality counseling.

THE PROCESS OF SEXUALITY COUNSELING FOR COUPLES WITH HEALTH-RELATED CONCERNS

Assessing Disabilities and Chronic Illness

Sexuality counselors must assess the importance of a sexual relationship to a couple and how their sexual relationship has changed as a result of an acquired disability or chronic illness. They can initiate a discussion of how a couple defines sexuality with questions such as "how are you intimate with each other in ways other than sexual intercourse?" This may open the door to talk about the range of sexual expression couples can experience.

When working with couples in which one partner has a congenital disability, asking questions that address historical and family messages about disability and sexuality can provide valuable information. Suppose a disabled partner has been provided limited or inaccurate information about sexuality or has been treated as asexual by his or her family of origin. The nondisabled partner is frustrated because of the lack of sexual closeness in their relationship. The sheltered experience of the disabled person could be creating the problem of avoidance of sexual contact and limited sexual desire. In this example, the disability itself is not creating the obstacles to sexual satisfaction; instead it is the family and historical messages that the disabled client has internalized.

Sexuality counselors should also be prepared to gather information about the impact of societal myths and prejudices about disability and chronic illness in general as well as sexuality in particular. Obtaining information that addresses self-perceptions as well as feelings about prejudicial treatment from others opens a window on the couple's ideas, beliefs, and attitudes about their sexual relationship. Many disabled or chronically ill persons and their partners may internalize distorted ideas and images about sexuality and base their feelings and behaviors on those images, rather than on more positive and accurate self-images.

Finally, there are a number of tests and informal tools that sexuality counselors may employ in their work with disabled and chronically ill persons. For example, a detailed sexual history that includes specific information about the sexual relationship before and after the medical condition is critical to a comprehensive assessment. Figure 11.1 presents a list of selected inventories for couples affected by chronic medical conditions.

These various information-gathering methods allow counselors to work more effectively with couples to accurately identify the nature of the problem, develop appropriate goals, and subsequently achieve success in combating their mutually identified problem.

Questions to Consider

Sexuality counselors can ask the following questions when assessing the sexual concerns of couples affected by chronic medical conditions.

1. What changes have you noticed in your sexual relationship as a result of your condition?
2. Have you felt differently about yourself and your sexual relationship since becoming disabled or chronically ill?
3. How do you feel about sexual intimacy with each other in light of this disability or chronic illness?
4. How do societal attitudes affect your view of yourself as a sexual being?

Unique Issues for Couples Affected by Disability and Chronic Illness

Rolland (1994) identifies multiple issues that are important to consider when working with couples affected by illness and disability. We have chosen five of these issues to discuss.

Communication

It may be difficult for couples to discuss their feelings about chronic medical conditions. When a couple is affected by a chronic medical condition after partnering, the previous level of openness may become less functional and inadequate (Rolland, 1994).

Communication is often limited by fears about hurting one's partner, aggravating the health condition, or negatively impacting the relationship (Rolland, 1994). The consequences of restricting openness and avoiding discussions about the medical condition can interfere with emotional connectedness and sexual intimacy.

In addition, there are often specific concerns by couples. Often, the first question couples may have following an accident, surgery, or major illness is "Am I (or is my partner) going to be all right?" The next question (often unstated) may be "Am I (or is my partner) still going to be able to function sexually?" Helping couples discuss fears and concerns openly can alleviate anxiety and aid them in developing solutions to sexual problems.

My Problem Versus Our Problem

When a health condition influences a couple's relationship, there is the possibility of a "split" in the definition of "the problem." Specifically, if the problem is identified as the sole responsibility of the ill or disabled partner, this will negatively distort the

---

- *Millon Behavioral Health Inventory* (Millon, Green, & Meagher, 1982)
- *Psychosocial Adjustment to Illness Scales* (Derogatis, 1986)
- *Sexuality After Spinal Cord Injury Questionnaire* (Kettl, 1998)
- *Perception of Diabetes Mellitus Questionnaire* (Pieper, 1998)
- *Perceived Effect of an Ostomy* (Pieper & Mikols, 1998)
- *Asthma Quality of Life Questionnaire* (Marks, Dunn, & Woolcock, 1992)
- *Ways of Coping Questionnaire (Cancer Version)* (Dunkel-Schetter, Feinstein, Taylor, & Falke, 1992)
- *The West Haven-Yale Multidimensional Pain Inventory* (WHYMPI) (Kerns, Turk, & Rudy, 1985)
- *The Roland Disability Scale* (Roland & Morris, 1983)

FIGURE 11.1
Selected Inventories for Couples Affected by Chronic Medical Conditions

partnership (Rolland, 1994). The medical focus of health problems promotes the definition of the problem as one of the ill or disabled partner. However, a shared view of any problem that couples confront is a necessary ingredient to achieving mutually satisfying sexual and relational functioning. An integrative couples' model provides a way for couples to work collaboratively to move from a "split" in the view of health problems to a shared view.

Boundaries

It is important that a couple's relationship does not become consumed by the medical condition. There is the dangerous possibility that chronic medical issues will infiltrate even the healthiest of intimate relationships (Rolland, 1994). Consequently, couples' interactions become joined with the condition. The disorder is ever present and draining the emotional and sexual energy from a couple. Sexual desire problems are often the result.

Patient-Caregiver Roles

Similar to the understanding of roles in aging couples, cognizance of the roles defined in couples affected by medical conditions is also necessary. Long-term caregiving and dependency create inherent dilemmas concerning hierarchical structure and reciprocity in relationships (Scheinkman, 1988). Ambiguities and uncertainty about shifting roles create strain and confusion for couples (Rolland, 1994). For example, a physically disabled male may no longer be able to provide income equitably or manage physical tasks. Resentment regarding changes in ability, lack of professional assistance, and poor communication create schisms in sexual intimacy. Sexuality counselors can help couples develop a care plan that could involve professional assistance, establish healthy boundaries, and alter problematic communication styles to improve sexual relatedness.

Extramarital Relationships

When an enduring medical condition prevents a sexual relationship between partners, some couples develop an arrangement in which the well or nondisabled partner may engage in sexual intimacy outside of the previously monogamous relationship (Rolland, 1994). In these situations, the role of sexuality counselors is to facilitate discussion and help couples to understand the implications of their choices on their present relationship. It is also important for sexuality counselors to bear in mind it is the couples' choice how to negotiate this arrangement. This issue is highly sensitive and often creates considerable feelings of vulnerability for couples. If couples choose this type of arrangement, a strong commitment and responsibility to the primary partnership, as well as compassion and understanding regarding discretion, is required (Rolland, 1994).

On the other hand, there may be sexual relationships outside of the partnership that have not been discussed. In some cases of long-term illness, a sexual relationship outside the partnership may facilitate a well partner's ability to maintain the role of caregiver, especially when the medical condition develops early in the life of the couple (Rolland, 1994). It is important to note this approach does not support sexual relationships outside of committed partnerships. Instead, it illustrates the difficulties some couples face regarding sexual intimacy when the relationship has become exclusively patient-caregiver and shows that the standards applied to physically healthy couples may not fit for couples facing illness and disability given the long-term strains of these conditions (Rolland, 1994). Regardless of the origin of an affair, sexuality counselors can help partners work together to ease the pain and myriad concerns that arise when there is a sexual relationship outside of the primary relationship.

Sexuality Counseling for Couples Affected by Disabilities and Chronic Illness

The Sexuality Information and Education Council of the United States (SIECUS) suggests that sexuality counseling with couples affected by a disability or chronic illness should be based on a number of assumptions and goals. Couples affected by chronic medical conditions have the right to receive information and education about sexuality, health care that addresses sexuality, and opportunities for sexual intimacy. Medical professionals, family members, and other persons involved in the caregiving process should have education and training in accepting and advocating for the diverse sexual needs and behavior of couples affected by disability or chronic illness, and all sexuality counseling and other related services should be delivered without discrimination because of disability (SIECUS, 1992).

It is important for sexuality counselors to be aware of the different groupings and implications of congenital versus acquired disabilities. For example, for individuals having an acquired disability (e.g., rheumatoid arthritis), sexual adjustment following the disability is typically more dependent on their adjustment prior to the disability (including sexual beliefs, experiences, feelings, and attitudes) than on the actual disability (Mona & Gardos, 2000). In other words, it should not be assumed that sexual problems are the direct result of having a disability.

For persons with congenital disabilities such as cerebral palsy, the influence of being seen as ineffectual, asexual, and childlike should not be underestimated (DeLoach, 1994; Mona & Gardos, 2000). It is possible that disabled persons were not given the opportunity for age-appropriate sex play or were deprived of sources of early sexual information (Mona & Gardos, 2000). This would translate into adults having limited sexual expression opportunities as well as lacking any basic information beyond self-acquired knowledge about sexuality.

In addition, during discussions with medical professionals regarding their illness or condition, couples may have received little or no information about the topic of sexual functioning. Important information about sexual positioning, sexual difficulties as a result of chronic medical conditions, and alternative sexual practices may be unavailable (Mona & Gardos, 2000).

It is also important to recognize sexual practices other than penile-vaginal intercourse as valid sexual behaviors because "'traditional' sex may be painful, difficult, or even impossible" (Mona & Gardos, 2000, p. 339). There are personal assistance services available to aid couples affected by chronic medical conditions with daily living and other activities. However, assistance with sexual expression is not typically provided as a service. Consequently, it may be necessary for sexuality counselors to educate and work with personal assistance providers or to help disabled persons to talk about their sexual needs with assistance providers (Mona & Gardos, 2000).

In addition, it is important for sexuality counselors to understand the specific ways in which chronic illnesses impact sexuality. Knowledge about the direct physiological effects of the illness (e.g., diminished cardiac reserve) and treatment for the illness (e.g., removal of the prostate causes erectile dysfunction) on sexuality is important to understanding sexual functioning.

Sexuality counseling can provide couples experiencing chronic illness with some degree of relief from potential feelings of dismay, disappointment, and despair (Krukofsky, 1988). Developing intimacy and sharing sexual pleasure can enhance both partners' feelings of self-respect and improve sexual identity. It is necessary to view a person with a chronic illness as someone with a special problem, not someone without sexual feelings or needs. Sexuality counselors must be aware of ways in which the medical condition affects couples' relationships rather than adhering to preconceived notions about what is "normal" sexual functioning. Counseling tasks include support, acceptance, and assistance with sexual integration to alter the psychological impact that the illness can have on sexual functioning.

INTERVENTIONS FOR COUNSELING DISABLED AND CHRONICALLY ILL COUPLES

Interventions for counseling couples with a disability or a chronic illness overlap considerably. We will discuss interventions that apply to these groups collectively.

Problem-Solving Strategies

Helping disabled and chronically ill persons and their partners with creative problem solving is an important element of sexuality counseling. Problem solving must incorporate some potential "realities" of disability and chronic illness: "(1) there are realistic physical limitations and differences imposed by [medical conditions] that cannot be 'cured' by counseling, and (2) social options may be more limited, requiring some unique and creative 'solutions'" (Linton & Rousso, 1988, p. 129).

Creative problem solving can instead include inventive sexual options and alternatives that the couple feels comfortable with and that they are able to explore. For example, a woman with a mobility impairment enters sexuality counseling, stating that she and her husband are unable to have intercourse because she cannot assume a comfortable position. Helping the couple discover practical solutions is an important part of the counseling process. Many different alternatives can be explored. It is possible that using pillows or a water bed may make the physical act more comfortable. Perhaps new ways of achieving sexual intimacy that do not include intercourse can be explored. Critical to the success of interventions such as these are the clients' feelings, as it would also be true of sexuality counseling with nondisabled or chronically ill persons. What is unique in this situation is the nature of the solutions that are called for.

Social and psychological issues also call for creative problem solving. Helping clients explore alternative avenues for social interactions is helpful, as is helping them develop a support network. Providing such information about sexual health can help couples improve sexual self-concept and increase feelings of social and sexual confidence and competence.

Helping clients understand the sexual impact of myths and stereotypes also requires creativity in problem solving techniques. Reduction in desire for sexual intimacy is common in those living with chronic illness and can affect both ill and well partners. Reduced sexual desire in chronic medical conditions can be influenced by factors such as fatigue, changes in body image, concerns about fulfilling gender roles, fear, caregiving duties, sexual dysfunction, disease severity, and medical treatment. For example, sexuality counselors can facilitate a discussion of how chronic illness has affected both partners' feelings about changes in the ill partner's body. If the disease has caused changes in sensation, the ill partner can be encouraged to use touching exercises to relearn what feels good and which areas of the body are most sensitive. Learning what feels good in all areas of the body is the goal. Clients should also be encouraged to explore areas of the body that are not as sensitive to touch as they once were. Although these areas are often ignored, they are still part of the individual's body, and touching these areas can help incorporate these body parts back into the client's body image.

Testing and Changing Problematic Beliefs and Cognitions

Sexuality counseling helps couples test and confront problematic beliefs or distorted thinking that negatively affect their sexual functioning. Persons who have disabilities or chronic illnesses may have internalized societal, historical, or family messages about sexuality that are detrimental to their sexual health. These internalized messages may result in faulty thinking that subsequently impairs sexual functioning. Counseling that focuses on changing

distorted thinking helps couples move away from blaming themselves or others and facilitates proactive and positive relational communication (Young & Long, 1998). Cognitive therapy is helpful when working with couples in which one or both partners are disabled or chronically ill because it allows them to specifically address negative and destructive myths and stereotypes about sexuality and medical conditions.

For example, Eldon believes that he is sexually incompetent because he has cerebral palsy. As a result, he avoids sexual contact with his girlfriend, Terri. Terri is becoming increasingly frustrated and saddened by his lack of sexual response to her. When she feels rejected by Eldon, she believes she is unattractive and unlovable. Eldon and Terri describe feelings of frustration and sadness, and they report frequent arguments. The sexuality counselor working with Eldon and Terri helps them recognize their distorted thinking patterns, which often create feelings of anger and depression, as well as arguments between partners. By stopping automatic thoughts and introducing more reasonable interpretations, Eldon and Terri are able to alleviate negative symptoms and emotions and move toward a mutually satisfying sexual relationship.

Sex Education

An obstacle for disabled and chronically ill persons is that they may lack accurate information about sexuality in general or about their own sexual capabilities and needs (Linton & Rousso, 1988). Information about sexuality shapes people's perceptions and values, and therefore their behavior.

For example, when conducting sexuality counseling with couples in which one partner has a disability or a chronic illness, an issue may be that the nondisabled or well partner has little information about the condition itself, or sexual capability as it relates to the medical condition. It is important for sexuality counselors to investigate the reasons for this lack of information and how each partner feels about this information gap. This is true even when both clients are disabled or ill and may not understand or lack information about the other's medical condition or have little or no sexual information related to the condition. In either case, after the reasons and feelings surrounding the disparity in knowledge have been explored, it would be important to include appropriate sexual information and education and to provide resource assistance to clients seeking information about their medical condition as part of the counseling process.

Because of the significance of such information, sex education is often a critical component of sexuality counseling. Formal and informal sources of sex education may be limited for disabled and chronically ill persons. There are few sex education classes and limited literature available on sexuality disabilities or chronic illness that are geared toward couples. In addition, persons with chronic medical conditions often are protected and isolated by family from access to sexual information due to the family's fears that the chronically ill or disabled family member will experience rejection, abuse, or abandonment from nondisabled persons.

Sexuality counselors can be an important source of positive information for this population. Often, information that is available that addresses the sexuality of disabled and chronically ill persons emphasizes the limitations and problems of chronic medical conditions, rather than highlighting this population's capacity to give and experience sexual pleasure (Linton & Rousso, 1988). Sexuality counselors can help couples to understand that they have sexual options and to work with them to realize their sexual potential.

Communication Skills Building

Couples' communication skills building is also an important sexuality counseling intervention for use with disabled and chronically ill persons. These populations are subject to the same maladaptive communication problems that well or nondisabled couples experience. However, disabled and chronically ill partners may have unique communication issues about sexual desires and comfortable positions.

Although it may be better to discuss disability or chronic illness and sexuality-related matters prior to engaging in sexual activity, life circumstances do not always allow this. Therefore, sexuality counselors can help disabled persons practice what they plan to say in a given situation before it actually happens (rehearsal technique). This reduces anxiety when the actual time comes to engage in sexual activity. Partners of persons with disabilities sometimes fear that asking questions about potential sexuality activity may be offensive. Sexuality counselors can work with couples about ways to create an open and supportive environment in which to discuss sexual concerns.

Sensual and Sexual Exercises

Exercises to increase intimacy by creating pleasurable sensations are an effective tool for disabled or chronically ill couples. Sensual and sexual exercises increase awareness of physical sensations, develop openness, and expand a couple's repertoire of gratifying intimate activities. (See Chapters 6 and 7 for detailed descriptions of exercises such as sensate focus.)

Aids for Intercourse

Although sexual intercourse is not the only way to achieve sexual satisfaction, it is the most common. Sexuality counselors can help couples achieve penetration by suggesting various positions (e.g., quadriplegics may be more likely to have to be supine with their partner on top) and use of sex aids (e.g., vibrators, dildos). Sexuality counselors may also work with medical professionals on methods for achieving penetration. For example, penile implants or pumps are aids to achieving erection. Sexuality counselors can help couples to improve sexual functioning and satisfaction by helping them make adaptations to enhance sexual intimacy.

Use of Genograms

The sexual genogram is a valuable assessment intervention for all couples struggling with sexual concerns. However, sexuality counselors can work with couples to incorporate specific information and messages about disability or illness into their genogram. This will help couples gain an understanding of the impact and role of these messages on their present sexual lives. Genograms have been described in detail in Chapter 3.

Reframing Relationships and Roles

Helping couples to reframe sexual roles and rules and to develop new attitudes about sexual behaviors and practices can provide alternative ways of understanding and attaining sexual intimacy. Sexuality counselors can assist couples faced with chronic medical conditions to view problematic patterns of behaviors in a changed positive context that provides them with new ways of feeling and thinking about their sexual relationship (Young & Long, 1998). This contextual change allows couples to see their problems in a new manner. For example, Gaylene complains that Wilmer treats her as an "invalid" and tries to "do everything" following her recent loss of vision. Wilmer states that he is simply trying to be helpful and wants to "protect" Gaylene. As a result, Gaylene has withdrawn from Wilmer sexually and tends to view him as a "nursemaid." Their sexuality counselor might reframe Wilmer's caretaking behavior as his way of showing Gaylene that he loves her, even though Gaylene is a fully capable adult. The couple is able to reduce blame and frustration by creating a positive explanation for Wilmer's behavior. This enables them to determine how to better manage household and other responsibilities in a way that is comfortable for both. This changed interpretation of Wilmer's behavior helps the couple feel more connected emotionally and sexually.

Developing a Support Network

Developing and using a support network can be very helpful for couples coping with chronic medical conditions. A support network can provide couples with encouragement, empathy, information, and understanding regarding their unique social, relational, and sexual challenges. Such a network may be in the form of a group of friends, family members, spiritual connections, or support and counseling groups. Receiving encouragement and support from nonjudgmental others can help couples socially, relationally, and sexually. When couples can seek assistance external to the partner relationship, this helps them step outside of problematic relational issues and serves to provide relief during stressful times. It can also provide a place to freely discuss or receive information about sexuality so that couples feel decreased isolation and disconnection in their relationship.

Validating Strengths

As couples cope with the challenges of disabilities and chronic illnesses, they are often confronted with external messages that disaffirm their sexual needs, and their individual and relational abilities are often forgotten or ignored. Working with couples to recognize, utilize, and validate their strengths in a culture that emphasizes ability and health is important for finding solutions to sexual and relational problems. Box 11.1 describes sexuality counseling interventions for disabled and chronically ill couples.

BOX 11.1
Interventions at a Glance

- Teach couples problem-solving skills in order to create alternatives to conventional sexual practices.
- Help couples challenge societal, historical, or family messages about sexuality that are detrimental to their sexual health.
- Provide bibliotherapy on a variety of topics related to chronic medical conditions and sexual well-being.
- Ask partners to communicate with each other about their illness or disabilities and then identify what steps they can take to enhance their sexual pleasure.
- Have couples practice at home alternatives to intercourse so that they may effectively achieve sexual satisfaction.
- Ask couples to investigate sexual aids (e.g., vibrators, dildos) in order to improve sexual satisfaction.
- Create a sexual genogram that incorporates specific sexual messages about disability or chronic illness and discern positive messages that may have passed from generation to generation.
- Teach couples to compliment each other and affirm their contributions to their sexual health as a couple.
- Encourage couples to communicate their health concerns as they arise and elicit support from their partner during critical medical events.

Case Example

Enrique, aged 40, and Diandra, aged 35, had been married ten years when Diandra was in an automobile accident in which she received a spinal cord injury that left her paralyzed from the waist down. Following rehabilitation, Diandra was given a clean bill of health. In other words, she was told that she did not have any additional medical problems as a result of her injury. Following the accident and during rehabilitation, the couple received general information about physiology and sexuality after a spinal cord injury, but they were not given any information on psychological effects or sexual expression alternatives. Three years following the accident and after many unsuccessful attempts at reachieving a mutually satisfying sexual relationship, Enrique and Diandra decide to seek sexuality counseling to address their concerns about their sexual relationship.

Application of the Integrative Couples' Model
Stage 1: Assessing the Problem

Enrique and Diandra have differing views of the problem. Enrique describes feeling rejected because Diandra rebuffs his sexual advances approximately 70% of the time. He reports being sexually attracted to Diandra, but he is fearful about hurting her. Diandra reports that she has limited sexual desire because although she wants to be close to Enrique, she believes she is no longer sexually attractive and fears that she will be unable to satisfy Enrique. She reports that not having a physiological orgasm does not bother her, but it seems to bother Enrique even though he denies this. They both report that they had a positive sexual relationship prior to Diandra's accident.

The sexuality counselor helps them create a collaborative view of the problem and states the problem in interactive terms. "You have been feeling disconnected in your sexual relationship and neither of you is sure how to be intimate with each other following the accident." This shared view allows the couple to have a shared view of the problem and move away from guilt, shame, or blame.

Stage 2: Goal Setting

Enrique and Diandra develop the following behavioral and affective goals with their sexuality counselor:

1. We will develop ways to increase relational intimacy with each other starting with nonsexual contact (behavioral) in order to feel increased closeness and support (affective).
2. We will discuss our sexual feelings and fantasies and obtain information about alternative methods of sexual expression (behavioral) in order to feel more comfortable (affective) exploring our sexual options.

3. We will develop a support network (behavioral) that includes other couples in which one partner has a spinal cord injury to improve feelings of competence and acceptance (affective).

Stage 3: Adopting New Perceptions and Behaviors

Enrique and Diandra work with their sexuality counselor to identify individual and relational strengths that they can use to address their problem. Enrique has always been imaginative as well as nurturing. Diandra is excellent with developing and finding resources and information. When working together, they have always been able to solve problems effectively with nonsexual matters. These assets can be used to help them nurture, problem solve, and develop resources to help them with their sexual concerns.

Their sexuality counselor may ask the couple to talk about their attraction to each other and the things that they admire about their partner. This will help the couple adapt positive attributes from these stories for future possibilities and new outcomes. Emphasizing the positive aspects of the relationship encourages the couple and helps them identify how to use their strengths to make changes.

Their sexuality counselor may also design interventions that help Enrique and Diandra increase intimacy by helping them change negative attitudes about sexuality and disability. Helping the couple find support from a community of other couples facing similar problems will assist in facilitating change.

Specific techniques such as sensate focusing and massage may also be used to increase comfort with sexual expression. In this situation, sexual expression is inhibited as a result of psychological feelings about Diandra's spinal cord injury. Use of narrative techniques to restory and restructure the relationship could relieve some of the relational and sexual conflict.

Stage 4: Maintaining Perceptions and Behaviors

Diandra and Enrique work with their sexuality counselor so that they will not fall into past negative patterns. For example, when Enrique feels rejected, he becomes silent and distances himself emotionally from Diandra. Diandra reacts by distancing herself from her sexual feelings and feeling hurt and angry at Enrique's insensitivity. They work with their sexuality counselor to understand and recognize this pattern and interrupt it at any place in the cycle.

They focus on maintaining closeness and intimacy and commit to using their communication skills to talk out the problem rather than avoiding each other.

Stage 5: Validating New Perceptions and Behaviors Enrique and Diandra celebrate their success in conquering the problem and work with the sexuality counselor to use maintenance strategies to continue success. They commit to celebrating their new sexual intimacy by planning monthly romantic outings. They recognize that they will face difficulties, but they commit to support each other through these challenges.

SUMMARY

Persons with disabilities and chronic illnesses have sexual needs and concerns that are more similar than different from those of nondisabled and well people. One of the biggest barriers that persons with disabilities and chronic illnesses face is the negative myths and stereotypes about their condition as well as their sexuality. Sexuality counselors must be aware of their own attitudes and beliefs about medical conditions and sexuality so that they are able to be effective helpers to couples with chronic medical conditions.

Understanding physical and psychosocial implications of disabilities and chronic illnesses is also important to effective helping. Sexuality counselors must have a general knowledge about medical conditions

and treatment for these conditions. It is important to work with medical personnel to most adequately understand and help clients. In addition, sexuality counselors must recognize that their clients may experience sexual and social feelings of incompetence, fears related to recurrence of an illness, lack of sexual education about alternative means of sexual expression, and issues about sexual attractiveness that affect their ability to have a satisfying sexual relationship.

The integrative couples' model offers an encouraging and supportive environment and a diversity of intervention strategies for addressing the sexual questions and problems of couples affected by chronic medical conditions.

SEXUAL VARIATIONS AND ATYPICAL SEXUAL BEHAVIOR

KEY CONCEPTS

- Atypical sexual behavior includes paraphilias (PAs) and paraphilia-related disorders (PRDs).
- Paraphilias are uncommon expressions of sexual behaviors. They include exhibitionism, fetishism, frotteurism, pedophilia, sexual masochism, sexual sadism, transvestic fetishism, voyeurism, and paraphilias not otherwise specified. They range in degrees of severity from mild to criminal behavior.
- Paraphilia-related disorders are considered to be more common expressions of sexual behavior and include cybersex dependence, compulsive masturbation, pornography dependence, promiscuity, telephone sex dependence, and sexual desire incompatibility.
- There are multiple perspectives about the development of sexual variations (atypical sexual disorders) that stem from psychodynamic, behavioral, cognitive, biological, and developmental approaches.
- Assessment of atypical sexual behaviors may include a medical and sexual history, collaborative interviews, behavioral logs, questionnaires, and penile circumference measurements.
- Sexuality counselors help couples address sexual and relational problems that often result from atypical sexual practices.
- Treatment interventions for counseling couples engaging in variant forms of sexual behavior include strategies aimed at assisting couples to create mutually satisfying and healthy sexual relationships.
- Treatment interventions for individuals engaging in more problematic atypical behaviors (those causing harm to self, others, society) may include behavioral, cognitive, and biological approaches.
- An integrative couples' model offers a variety of theoretical intervention strategies for working with couples concerned with atypical sexual behavior.

Our sexuality begins with a slap on the behind and a cry of self-expression, which is quickly followed by "It's a girl" or "It's a boy." At that moment our sexual selves are defined by society, and we enter a world with preconceived expectations of who we should be and how we should behave as sexual beings. Society defines for us what type of sexual expression is acceptable, to what degree, and by whom.

As we enter the twenty-first century, sexual values are being challenged and redefined by our culture. A sense of uncertainty exists among people regarding which sexual expressions are acceptable and which are not. At no other time in history has sexual self-expression been so embraced by our culture as people seek to clarify their personal values and express their individuality. Research on sexual practices indicates that a person's sexual behavior is largely determined by religious practices, cultural meanings as well as the legal system in a particular culture (Feierman & Feierman, 2000; Laumann, Gagnon, Michael, & Michaels, 1994). However, when sexual activities and fantasies fall outside the range of what is generally accepted in society, they are considered atypical.

We use the term *atypical sexual behavior* to refer to sexual fantasies and behaviors that are not commonly practiced among most people and may produce adverse physical, emotional, and social consequences for themselves or for others (Schwartz, 1996; Southern, 1999). They include paraphilias (PAs) and paraphilia-related disorders (PRDs). These variant forms of sexual expression range from mild, occasional sexual behaviors (those that are [more common] more socially acceptable but excessive) to intense, recurrent behaviors that dominate a person's sexual practices (those that are [less common] less socially acceptable and produce more adverse consequences) (Crooks & Baur, 2002; Kafka & Hennen, 1999; Schwartz, 1996; Southern, 1999).

Paraphilias are defined by the *DSM-IV-TR* as "recurrent, intense, sexual urges, fantasies, or behaviors that involve unusual objects, activities, or situations" (APA, 2000, p. 535). The diagnosis is made only when the fantasies, urges, or sexual behavior lasts for a minimum of six months and cause significant distress or impairment in a person's ability to function in their job or social life. Paraphilias can be compulsive, long-standing, and distressing to some individuals. As defined by the *DSM-IV-TR* (APA, 2000) paraphiliac behaviors include exibitionism, fetishism, frotteurism, pedophilia, sexual masochism, sexual sadism, transvestic fetishism, voyeurism, and paraphilias not otherwise specified.

Paraphilia-related disorders involve normative sexual expressions, which increase in frequency or intensity and interfere with a person's sexual interactions and relationships (Kafka & Hennen, 1999). They are considered more socially acceptable although they share many of the same characteristics as paraphilias (Kafka, 1991; Kafka & Hennen, 1999). The most commonly reported disorders include cyber-sex dependence, compulsive masturbation, homosexual and heterosexual promiscuity, pornography dependence, telephone sex, and severe sexual desire incompatibility (Cooper, Scherer, Boies, & Gordon, 1999; Kafka & Hennen, 1999). Both paraphilias and PRDs

can interfere with couples' intimate sexual expression leading to sexual and relational problems.

In this chapter we describe various theoretical perspectives about the etiology of atypical sexual behavior and provide information on some common elements for assessment and intervention strategies. In addition, a case example demonstrates the use of an integrative couples' model for counseling those who engage in variant forms of sexual expression.

THE DEVELOPMENT OF ATYPICAL SEXUAL BEHAVIOR

Although many sexuality experts have proposed ideas about the development of atypical sexual behaviors, little is supported by research (Comer, 1998). It is recognized, however, that biological factors and learned behavior as well as early childhood experiences influence the development of variant sexual behavior (Comer, 1998; Davidson & Neale, 1998; Wincze, 2000). There are four theoretical perspectives to explain atypical sexual behavior.

Psychodynamic Perspective

From a psychodynamic perspective, variant forms of sexual expression originate as a defense mechanism that serves to protect the ego from repressed, distressed, or painful thoughts or memories (Davidson & Neale, 1998). Sexual expression thus enables people to avoid the anxiety of engaging in normal sexual and social relationships (Comer, 1998). Consequently, their sexual development is often immature (Davidson & Neale, 1998). For example, from this perspective, an exhibitionist's behavior is described as resulting from "a defense against castration anxiety, with the reaction of the female proving to the exhibitionist that his penis does exist" (Murphy, 1997, p. 32).

Behavioral and Cognitive Perspectives

From a behavioral perspective, atypical sexual behavior develops when a person's sexual responses become conditioned to stimuli that depart from normative sexual practices (Davidson & Neale, 1998). Consider, for example, that a 16-year-old boy masturbates to a videotape of a woman who is dancing provocatively and wearing a large velvet hat. He becomes sexually aroused and begins masturbating while watching the video on a daily basis. He begins to associate velvet hats with sexual arousal. Eventually, the sight of a velvet hat creates spontaneous sexual arousal resulting in the development of a fetish.

Another behavioral perspective is based on operant conditioning. From this perspective, paraphilias develop in childhood as a result of "inadequate social skills or unconventionality by parents or relatives" (Davidson & Neale, 1998, p. 374). For example, a young boy is applauded when he dresses in his mother's high heels and earrings. As he repeats these behaviors and enjoys his mother's approval and encouragement, his behavior becomes a common routine or excessive. As an adult he engages in cross-dressing.

From a cognitive viewpoint, people's belief systems are based on faulty assumptions, misperceptions, or self-serving interpretations and are the basis for variant forms of sexual behavior. In an extreme form, people's beliefs about their sexual selves influence the way they choose to behave. For example, a woman believes that in order to be successful and powerful, she must humiliate and dominate another person. She engages in sexual intimidation and sexually violent acts by whipping her partner and demeaning him with the use of obscene language and behavior. This supports her belief system that by diminishing her partner she is a more powerful person.

Developmental Perspective

Developmental conditions such as the occurrence of childhood sexual abuse, viewing pornography at an early age, or family psychopathology may influence the development of some atypical sexual behaviors such as the paraphilia-related disorders (Carnes, 1991; Coleman, 1995; Kafka, 2000). A child's psychosexual development can be hindered by environmental influences that interfere with normal growth. For example, a prepubescent boy may experience sexual arousal by fondling his mother's panties during masturbation. In the absence of opportunities for age-related sexual development (i.e., dating, sexual exploration, hooking-up), he associates sexual arousal and his mother's panties, which then become his norm for sexual arousal.

Biological Perspective

Wincze (2000) reviewed the work of Janssen (1997) and Bancroft (1998) who theorized that there may be neurophysiological differences between those who develop paraphilias and paraphilia-related behaviors regarding sexual inhibition and sexual risk-taking behaviors. These speculations infer that low sexual inhibition leads to higher risk-taking behaviors such as committing an infraction against the law or infringing on the rights of others. As such, these behaviors may be evident in those individuals exhibiting atypical sexual behaviors.

In addition, theories about the presence of androgen, the male hormone, and its function during fetal development suggest that hormones may be different in people exhibiting atypical sexual behaviors (Davidson & Neale, 1998). There has been no compelling evidence, however, to support this theory. In fact, there is no difference in the frequency of abnormal hormonal and genetic conditions for persons engaging in atypical forms of sexual behavior when compared with persons who engage in conventional sexual behaviors (Wincze, 1989).

Four-Stage Model

A four-stage model has been proposed by Abel (as cited in Wincze, 2000) to describe the development of atypical sexual behaviors and to explain "why some people may develop [immoderate] behavior and others experiencing the same event may not. . . . It all depends on how reinforcing or punishing a sexualized behavior was [over a period of time] to the individual" (p. 452). For example, a prepubescent boy hides in his mother's closet and watches her undress. One day she discovers him watching her and scolds him, calling him a "bad, dirty, boy." She then tells his father, who whips him with a belt. He does not repeat the behavior again.

In this case, the punishment was strong enough to deter further repetition of his behavior. In the next example, we demonstrate how atypical behaviors can develop through a pattern of positive reinforcement based on Abel's four-stage model. Obtaining this information by personal communication with Abel (1995), Wincze notes the following stages of development:

Stage 1: A child is exposed to sexual stimulation either by actual physical contact (directly) or by observing or hearing (indirectly).

Stage 2: A child rehearses what was experienced with imagined consequences (positive or negative).

Stage 3: A child experiments or tries out a behavior and directly experiences positive or negative consequences of the behavior.

Stage 4: Depending on the prior behavioral consequences, the behavior may be repeated or varied into different manifestations leading to greater reinforcement (adapted from Wincze, 2000, p. 452).

For example, a young boy observes his friend as he masturbates using a leather batting glove. He then thinks about engaging in the same behavior exhibited by his friend and fantasizes about how good it might feel. He mimics the technique while masturbating and enjoys the feeling he receives from his behavior. He begins to repeat the behavior but decides to vary his stimuli by using not only leather but also a silk robe, netting, a feather, and a cotton sheet. As he matures, he discovers that he becomes most aroused by using leather products. Pairing his sexual arousal with leather objects, he then begins to find that he may be unable to attain an erection in the absence of leather. This may lead to an ongoing sexual problem. Likewise, if his partner is unable to accept his wish to use leather during their sexual interactions, the couple may experience sexual difficulties. Furthermore, if the frequency of the use of leather interrupts his ability to function (e.g., if he is compelled to stop at a leather store once or twice a day to buy leather products) and the only way he can become sexually aroused is by using leather, he has developed a diagnosable fetish.

We do not know the exact origin of atypical sexual behaviors. What we do know, however, is that they are maintained because they satisfy individuals both physically and psychologically, in addition to reducing anxiety, managing pent-up anger, and in some cases occupying idle time (Wincze, 2000).

In the next section, we briefly describe the most common atypical sexual behaviors expressed in our society.

PARAPHILIAS

The word "paraphilia" means "beyond usual or typical love" (Crooks & Baur, 2002, p. 526) and includes sexual preferences and behaviors that may produce adverse physical, emotional, and social consequences (Schwartz, 1996; Southern, 1999). According to the *DSM-IV-TR*, these behaviors involve the following:

Recurrent, intense sexually arousing fantasies, sexual urges, or sexual behaviors generally involving (1) nonhuman objects, (2) the suffering or humiliation of oneself or one's partner, or (3) children or other nonconsenting persons that occur over a period of at least 6 months (Criterion A). (APA, 2000, p. 566)

The occurrence of "paraphiliac fantasies" for sexual arousal varies among individuals. Some require fantasies for arousal, whereas others fluctuate in their need for paraphiliac stimuli. The categories used by the *DSM-IV-TR* to describe paraphilias are exhibitionism, fetishism, frotteurism, pedophilia, sexual masochism, sexual sadism, transvestic fetishism, voyeurism, and paraphilia not otherwise specified. These variant forms of sexual expression are practiced in mild, moderate, and extreme forms.

Some variations are more commonly practiced among couples and contribute to a healthy and satisfying sexual relationship if both partners share common sexual expressions. However, when a sexual behavior is deemed harmful to self, others, or society, treatment focuses on decreasing or extinguishing the behavior.

Exhibitionism

Exhibitionism involves recurrent intense sexual arousal by the exposure of one's genitals (usually male) to an unwilling observer (most of the time, an adult woman or female child) (Comer, 1998; Crooks & Baur, 2002). Typically, exhibitionists make no attempt to initiate sexual activity with the persons to whom they expose themselves. They may, however, act on their sexual urges (APA, 2000) by masturbating during the time of exposure or engage in fantasizing about the exposure at a later time in order to achieve sexual arousal. Most exhibitionists want to "shock or embarrass the observer" (Davidson & Neale, 1998, p. 369).

Exhibitionists are usually male and initiate behavior prior to the age of 18 (APA, 2000). In general, they are not relating to the opposite sex in an age-appropriate manner and have difficulty with interpersonal relationships (Comer, 1998; Levine, 2000). In addition, they are often shy with others and feel inadequate about their masculinity (Crooks & Baur, 2002; Levine, 2000). More than half of exhibitionists are married; however, their sexual relationships with their spouses are reported as highly unsatisfactory (Comer, 1998; Mohr, Turner, & Jerry, 1964).

Many people engage in exhibiting within the boundaries of the law and their own comfort level.

For example, male and female strippers reveal their bodies and can be sexually stimulated by the act. This practice can lead to a desire to show oneself publicly to become sexually stimulated. This need often leads to relationship problems for those whose partners are not supportive.

Fetishism

Fetishism involves recurrent intense sexual arousal by the *exclusive* use of "an inanimate object" (Comer, 1998; Crooks & Baur, 2002; Davidson & Neale, 1998). Often, the person masturbates while touching, smelling, or rubbing the fetish object (APA, 2000; Comer, 1998). In some instances, individuals may ask their sexual partner to wear the object while engaging in sex. Popular fetish objects include women's lingerie; fur garments; gloves; toilet articles; shoes (especially high-heeled); boots; and a variety of leather, silk, and rubber goods (APA, 2000; Davidson & Neale, 1998). People may also have fetishes focusing on specific body parts, such as feet, buttocks, breasts, genitalia, or ears (Cautela, 1986).

The development of fetishes typically begins in adolescence, although some have been noted in early childhood (APA, 2000; Crooks & Baur, 2002). Most fetishes are harmless and do not offend others. People seek therapeutic intervention when they or their partner are troubled by their sexual interest or the social isolation that often goes along with it.

Frotteurism

Frotteurism refers to recurrent and intense sexual arousal that involves touching "and rubbing against a nonconsenting person" (Comer, 1998, p. 468). These behaviors typically occur in crowded public places such as subways, elevators, buses, or sidewalks (APA, 2000; Crooks & Baur, 2002). Most commonly, a man rubs his clothed penis against a woman's buttocks or legs (Crooks & Baur, 2002; Davidson & Neale, 1998). He may also touch her breasts or genitalia while fantasizing about an intimate relationship with a woman (APA, 2000; Crooks & Baur, 2002).

Most men who engage in frotteurism are between the ages of 15 and 25, after which the frequency of this behavior decreases (APA, 2000). They usually experience feelings of sexual and social inadequacy much like exhibitionists and find this type of sexual expression safe and nonthreatening.

Pedophilia

Pedophilia involves "obtaining sexual gratification by watching, touching, or engaging in simple or complex sexual acts with prepubescent children, usually those 13 years old or younger" (Comer, 1998, p. 469). It is the most serious and destructive manifestation of atypical sexual behaviors (Charlton, 1997) and typically falls within the legal description of a felony. Although pedophiles are interested in both males and females, most prefer engaging in inappropriate sexual behavior with females between the ages of 8 and 10 years old (APA, 2000; Charlton, 1997). Pedophiles who are attracted to males typically prefer them to be older than 10 years old and often repeat their offenses even after they have served time in jail or completed a treatment program (APA, 2000; Charlton, 1997).

The clinical description of pedophilia described in the *DSM-IV-TR* requires that an offender be at least "16 years [of age] or older and at least 5 years older than the [targeted] child" (APA, 2000, p. 571). Most often, pedophiles are immature, and their social and sexual skills are underdeveloped, resulting in anxiety about engaging in a normal sexual relationship (Comer, 1998; Groth & Birnbaum, 1978). Pedophiles are usually unsuccessful in their intimate relationships with adults; they are not good candidates for couples' sexuality counseling.

Stress can significantly impact a pedophile's acting-out behavior. For example, the loss of a job, the death of a loved one, or the accumulation of unmanaged day-to-day stressors may lead to the victimization of family members, close relatives, or children external to the family. The most disturbed pedophiles—classified as sexual sadists—gain sexual satisfaction by physically harming children. Those causing such bodily harm use varying degrees of force while penetrating them with a variety of objects (APA, 2000).

Sexual Masochism

Sexual masochism involves intense sexual arousal "by the act or thought of being humiliated, beaten, bound, or otherwise made to suffer" (Comer, 1998, p. 469). Although many people have masochistic fantasies such as being raped or bound by others during sexual intercourse or while masturbating, the diagnosis is only given to those who experience significant distress due to impairment by these fantasies or acts (APA, 2000; Comer, 1998). Some individuals engage in self-focused masochistic behavior by binding themselves, piercing themselves with needles, or mutilating themselves (APA, 2000; Comer, 1998). Others enlist their sexual partners to participate in acts of restraining, blindfolding, spanking, electrically shocking, pinning, and piercing. Still others seek to humiliate themselves by asking their partners to defecate or urinate on them or care for them as if they were infants (APA, 2000; Comer, 1998; Crooks & Baur, 2002). In the latter case, persons may engage in infantile behavior such as wanting their partner to dress them like a baby, change their diaper, or place them in a playpen.

A hazardous and sometimes fatal form of masochism known as "hypoxyphilia" involves decreasing oxygen to the brain in order to enhance erotic pleasure and orgasm (APA, 2000; Crooks & Baur, 2002). Such acts typically involve a noose, belt, or other device that puts pressure around the neck and restricts oxygen intake (by suffocating or hanging) (APA, 2000; Crooks & Baur, 2002). Sometimes a plastic bag or mask can be used to restrict oxygen as well. Performed individually or with another person, such acts lead to between 250 and 1,000 accidental deaths each year in the United States (Levine, 2000).

Sexual Sadism

Sexual sadism involves real acts of inflicting psychological or physical suffering on others in order to gain sexual excitement (APA, 2000). Some people like to fantasize about having complete power over their victims who await their sadistic acts. Others prefer acting on their sexual urges with nonconsenting individuals, thus committing a crime (APA, 2000).

The majority of sadists engage in sexual behaviors with consenting partners who are also masochists, thus deriving mutual sexual gratification. Moderate forms of sadistic activities include paddling, spanking, or whipping. More intense activities include mutilating, cutting, beating, raping, stabbing, strangulating, torturing, or even killing (APA, 2000; Comer, 1998).

Most individuals who engage in sexual sadism do so in early adulthood. The intensity of their behavior may increase over time, becoming problematic to themselves, to others, and to society (APA, 2000). People with severe forms of this behavior may be dangerous to others, injuring or killing their victims (APA, 2000; Dietz, Hazelwood, & Warren, 1990).

Transvestic Fetishism

Transvestic fetishism or transvestism pertains to cross-dressing (most often by males) in the clothes of a woman in order to attain sexual arousal (APA, 2000). Cross-dressing can begin in childhood, adolescence, or in adulthood (Comer, 1998). Transvestites are heterosexual males although some may engage in homosexual experiences (APA, 2000; Charlton, 1997). Many are married. Typically, their preferred sexual release is through masturbation while being stimulated by the female clothes they wear. Some wear a single female undergarment (such as panties or a bra) while otherwise appearing masculine in their demeanor, dress, and sexual preference. Others wear makeup and dress in women's clothing. Most often, cross-dressing is secretive, takes place in private, and occurs episodically rather than on a regular basis (Crooks & Baur, 2002). This can be most distressful to a couple when one partner discovers the other's transvestic behavior. In these instances, issues related to trust and intimacy must be addressed by sexuality counselors.

Voyeurism

Voyeurism (peeping) involves gaining sexual arousal by observing others, usually nonconsenting strangers, while they are undressing, unclothed, or engaged in sexual intercourse (APA, 2000; Comer, 1998). Voyeurs typically do not desire to have sex with the individual they observe (APA, 2000). Instead, they gain their excitement from the act of secretively watching, which usually leads to masturbation occurring during the incident or later as they fantasize about their memory (APA, 2000; Comer, 1998).

Sexual observation has become part of the norm for many adolescents as well as adults in our culture as they view the sexually explicit behavior and content offered in the entertainment world—from MTV and VH-1 to popular series and reality TV shows, as well as the talk shows hosted by Jerry Springer, Howard Stern, and others. A variety of X-rated and R-rated movies are also widely available in video stores or for viewing in hotel rooms. In addition, most people have access to Internet sites that provide them with an opportunity to view sexual pornography. These behaviors develop into atypical sexual acts when they become intense and are repeatedly chosen over engaging in sexual relations with another person, are consistently used to gain sexual arousal by posing a risk of being caught, or become the main focus of a person's sexual gratification (Charlton, 1997; Crooks & Baur, 2002).

Voyeurism usually begins before the age of 15 and tends to be chronic (APA, 2000). Much like exhibitionists, voyeurs are often young, single, and submissive, and they have fears about having direct sexual contact. "Peeping" allows them to feel powerful over the people they watch (Comer, 1998).

Other Atypical Sexual Behaviors

The most common forms of paraphilia that we have described here are by no means the only atypical sexual expressions that exist. There are more than 40 others that are described in the literature (Abel, 1989; Levine, 2000; Milner & Dopke, 1997; Money, 1984). They include but are not limited to zoophilia (sexual contact between humans and animals), necrophilia (viewing or having sexual intercourse with a dead body), klismaphilia (obtaining sexual pleasure from receiving enemas), coprophilia and urophilia (involving contact with feces and urine), and telephone

scatogia (obscene phone calls). These categories are included in the *DSM-IV-TR* and are listed under paraphilias that do not meet the criteria for any other paraphilia. Table 12.1 presents a more complete list.

PARAPHILIA-RELATED DISORDERS

Paraphilia-related disorders (PRDs), like the paraphilias, include "intense and sexually arousing sexual fantasies, urges, and [behaviors] and produce personal distress or significant psychosocial impairment" occurring for at least 6 months (Kafka, 2000, p. 478). The difference is that paraphilias are considered a *departure* from socially accepted sexual behaviors whereas PRDs are more socially accepted (Kafka & Hennen, 1999). The classification of PRDs is used to distinguish specific nonparaphilic hypersexual behaviors such as sexual compulsivity and addictions while acknowledging their similarities to paraphilias (Kafka, 2000).

TABLE 12.1

Paraphilia Not Otherwise Specified (NOS) Categories, Erotic Focus, and Possible Overlapping Paraphiliac Categories

PARAPHILIA NOS CATEGORIES	EROTIC FOCUS	POSSIBLE OVERLAPPING PARAPHILIA CATEGORIES
Nonhuman Objects		
Zoophilia (zooerasty, zoocrastia, bestiality, bestiosexuality)	Animals	
Formicophilia	Small creatures	Zoophilia
Klismaphilia	Enemas	
Olfactophilia (osmolagnia)	Odors	
Mysophilia	Filth	
Urophilia (urolagnia, urophagia, ondinisme reifleurism, undinism)	Urine	Fetishism, sexual masochism, sexual sadism
Coprophilia (coprolagnia)	Feces	
Vampirism	Blood	Sexual sadism
Suffering or Humiliation of Oneself or One's Partner		
Telephone scatophilia (telephone scatologia, telephonicphilia)	Obscenities over phone	Exhibitionism
Narratophilia	Obscene language with partner	
Chrematistophilia	Being charged or forced to pay	
Saliromania	Soiling/damaging clothing or body	Sexual sadism
Vomerophilia (erotic vomiting)	Vomiting	

TABLE 12.1   *(continued)*

PARAPHILIA NOS CATEGORIES	EROTIC FOCUS	POSSIBLE OVERLAPPING PARAPHILIA CATEGORIES
Children or Other Nonconsenting Persons		
Necrophilia	Corpses	
Somnophilia	Sleeping partner	
Symphorophilia	Stage-managed disaster	
Atypical Focus Involving Human Objects (Self and Others)		
Hypoxyphilia (asphyxiophilia, sexual asphyxia, autoerotic asphyxia, kotzwarrism)	Reduced oxygen intake	Sexual masochism
Urethral manipulation	Insertion of objects	Fetishism, sexual masochism
Morphophilia	One or more body characteristics of partner	Partialism
Partialism	Focus on a body part	Morphophilia
Stigmatophilia	Partner tattooed, scarified, or pierced for wearing jewelry	
Abasiophilia	Lame or crippled partner	Morphophilia, partialism
Acrotomophilia	Amputation in partner	Morphophilia, partialism
Apotemnophilia	Own amputation	Sexual masochism
Infantilism (autonepiophilia)	Impersonating or being treated as an infant	Sexual masochism
Adolescentilism (juvenilism)	Impersonating or being treated as an adolescent	Sexual masochism
Gerontophilia	Elderly partner	
Andromimetophilia	Andromimetic partner	
Gynemimetophilia	Gynemimetic partner	
Autogynephilia	Image of self as a woman	Transvestic fetishism
Gynandromorphophilia	Cross-dressed feminized male	
Scoptophilia (scophophilia, scoptolagnia)	Viewing sexual activity	Voyeurism
Mixoscopia	Viewing couple having intercourse	Voyeurism
Triolism (troilism)	Observing partner having sex	Voyeurism
Pictophilia	Pornographic pictures, movies, or videos	Voyeurism
Autagonistophilia	Being observed/being on stage	
Hybristophilia	Partner must have committed an outrageous act or crime	
Kleptophilia (kleptolagnia)	Stealing	

Source: From J. S. Milner and C. A. Dopke, "Paraphilia Not Otherwise Specified: Psychopathology and Theory," in *Sexual Deviance: Theory, Assessment, and Treatment* (p. 398), by D. R. Laws and W. O'Donohue, eds., 1997. New York: Guilford Press. Reprinted with permission.

TABLE 12.2
Paraphilia-Related Disorders: Nonparaphilic Hypersexuality

PARAPHILIA-RELATED DISORDER	OBJECTIVE FOR SEXUAL AROUSAL
Cybersex	A time-consuming dependence on Internet and Internet-related sexually oriented chat rooms, message boards, and so on, primarily for sexual arousal and activity.
Compulsive masturbation	Masturbation that occurs at least once a day and is a primary outlet even during a stable intimate relationship.
Prolonged promiscuity	A "persistent pattern of sexual conquests involving a succession of people who exist only as things to be used" (APA, 1980). This can include one-night stands, use of prostitutes, massage parlors, "cruising," brief or prolonged repetitive sex affairs, serial polygamy, escort services, and so on.
Pornography dependence	A persistent, repetitive pattern of dependence on visual pornographic materials (e.g., magazines, videos, Internet).
Telephone sex dependence	A persistent, repetitive dependence on telephone sex that is time-consuming and associated with significant cost.
Severe sexual desire incompatibility	An ongoing romantic affiliation in which excessive sexual desire in one partner produces sexual demands on the other partner that significantly interferes with the capacity to sustain the relationship.

Source: From M. P. Kafka, "The Paraphilia-Related Disorders: Nonparaphilic Hypersexuality and Sexual Compulsivity/Addiction," in *Principles and Practice of Sex Therapy,* 3rd ed. (p. 480), by S. R. Leiblum and R. C. Rosen, eds., 2000. New York: Guilford Press. Reprinted with permission.

Diagnosed as Paraphilias Not Otherwise Specified (NOS) in the *DSM-IV-TR,* PRDs include cybersex dependence, compulsive masturbation, homosexual and heterosexual promiscuity, pornography dependence, telephone sex dependence, and severe sexual desire incompatibility (Cooper et al., 1999; Kafka, 2000; Kafka & Hennen, 1999). The most commonly diagnosed PRDs are described in Table 12.2.

Cybersex

Cybersex involves an emotional dependency on Internet and Internet-related sexually oriented chat rooms, message boards, and pornography. It may include the use of sexual images or sound files that are used to stimulate sexual excitement and activity (Schnarch & Morehouse, 2002). In addition, individuals may engage in brief, noncommitted relationships that fulfill their social and sexual needs, leading to excessive Internet use (Cooper et al., 1999). Particularly vulnerable are individuals with ongoing sexual compulsive and addictive behavior as well as those who may be at risk for developing these behaviors (e.g., individuals who have experienced long-term sexual abuse or are members of sexually disenfranchised groups such as homosexuals and bisexuals) (Coleman, 1995; Cooper, Delmonico, & Burg, 2000; Kafka, 2000; Leiblum, 1997b). Some studies suggest that prolonged Internet usage contributes to the development of problematic sexual behavior as well as has a negative effect on one's life (Cooper et al., 1999; Greenfield, 1999).

Excessive Internet usage can affect a couple's relationship by serving as an ongoing emotional retreat or outlet for one partner, making it easy for that person to repeat the same behavior when encountering conflict in the relationship (Cooper et al., 1999). Typically there is no awareness that a partner is engaging in repetitive Internet activities until he or she is caught. Often the person involved in the activity feels ashamed, regretful, and guilty (Kafka, 2000). Some individuals may deny, minimize their problem, or even blame their partner for their compulsive behavior (Schneider, 2000).

Compulsive Masturbation

Compulsive masturbation involves the use of excessive self-stimulation as a primary sexual outlet, even for those who may be in a committed intimate relationship. In such cases, where individuals masturbate at least once per day, a couple's relationship will be affected, particularly if one partner discovers the practice and disapproves or shames the other partner. It also poses a problem if one partner wants to involve the other in the activity but that person is unwilling to participate.

Prolonged Promiscuity

Prolonged promiscuity refers to a consistent pattern of engaging in sexual activities as a way of attaining "sexual conquests." These patterns may include one-night stands, the frequent use of prostitutes and massage parlors, "cruising," brief or prolonged repetitive affairs, serial polygamy, and the use of escort services. Issues related to intimacy and betrayal of trust frequently emerge in relationships involving promiscuous behaviors.

Pornography Dependence

Pornography dependence involves a persistent, repetitive pattern of dependence on visual pornographic materials such as magazines, videos, and Internet pornography. Often, a partner discovers a dependence after it has been hidden from the other. In some cases a person participates in the use of pornographic materials in order to satisfy a partner. This pattern of behavior contributes to increased dependence on the pornography.

Telephone Sex Dependence

Telephone sex dependence involves a persistent, repetitive reliance on phone sex for sexual arousal. Time-consuming and expensive, phone sex generates issues related to trust, lying, and intimacy.

Sexual Desire Incompatibility

Sexual desire incompatibility refers to a difference between partners in their level of sexual desire. One partner typically places excessive demands on the other, causing that person to feel smothered by the other and unable to meet consistent demands for sex. This may lead to resentment and difficulties in sustaining a mutually satisfying relationship.

PROCESS OF SEXUALITY COUNSELING FOR COUPLES ENGAGING IN ATYPICAL SEXUAL BEHAVIORS

Treatment for couples with issues related to atypical sexual behavior is complex. Many people who engage in such behavior conceal their practices due to feelings of shame, self-blame, or insurmountable guilt associated with their sexual expressions. As a result, much time may elapse before they share their secret with their sexual partner or seek treatment (Kafka,

2000). In many cases they enter counseling because of legal charges brought against them, or in response to a neighbor, friend, or partner who has been affected by their sexual actions (Wincze, 2000). They may have no desire to give up their atypical behavior and their motivation for change may be limited. Others seek counseling because they are uncomfortable with their sexual behavior or how it is impacting their relationship with their partner. More often, people are motivated to change because of the severity of symptoms—including depression, anxiety, and relational conflict—that they are experiencing.

In general, it is important for sexuality counselors to be aware that most people engaging in variant forms of sexual behaviors are somewhat undecided about seeking counseling because it may entail disclosing their behavior to their sexual partner or relinquishing a sexual behavior that has served as "a powerful source of pleasure and/or psychological crutch" (Wincze, 2000, p. 453). Couples seeking counseling may feel uncomfortable or humiliated to disclose their own or their partner's sexual practices to a sexuality counselor, fearing judgment or disapproval; thus they remain secretive about their practices (Schneider & Schneider, 1996; Schwartz & Masters, 1983). This hesitancy prevents some couples from seeking treatment for their sexual and relational problems.

Counselor Qualifications

Although most licensed counselors are qualified to diagnose atypical sexual disorders, not all are trained or have the knowledge or comfort level to treat them. Sexuality counselors need to gain experience until they feel comfortable and competent to help couples resolve their issues surrounding variant forms of sexual expression. Some counselors are uneasy and inexperienced with asking detailed and probing questions (Charlton, 1997) such as "Have you ever dressed up in women's clothing or worn women's underwear under your outer garments?" or "Do you become aroused when someone urinates on you?" Their discomfort is the result of unexamined biases, values, or beliefs they learned in their upbringing or from society regarding uncommon sexual practices. In some cases, discomfort occurs because a counselor has experienced some form of sexual victimization (assault) that has resulted in an emotional reaction interfering with their ability to be objective (Charlton, 1997). In these instances, counselors are unable to effectively treat persons engaging in more severe atypical sexual behavior.

For example, a female counselor seeks supervision because she is having difficulty assessing a client who was referred to her because he was exposing himself to young girls. She reports feeling repulsed by his behavior and fearful that he may try to expose himself to her in session. She shares that when she was a young girl, two men exposed their genitals to her at a local park. She acknowledges that her reaction reflects her unresolved issues related to the incident and that she is unable to provide counseling services without bias. She decides to refer the case to another counselor "in the best interest" of the client. In this situation, the counselor recognizes her countertransference issues and acknowledges her inability to create a nonjudgmental environment in order to help her client.

Sexuality counselors must be willing to explore, understand, and accept couples' uncommon sexual practices and preferences in order to be effective. They must also understand and accept that not all couples are distressed or concerned by these practices. Additional training helps counselors to accurately assess, diagnose, and treat persons engaging in more severe forms of sexual behaviors. Counselors should be aware that many states require specific credentials for counselors to be able to treat sex offenders. Thus it is the counselor's ethical responsibility to refer to state guidelines when treating this population. The P-LI-SS-IT decision-making model (Annon, 1974, 1975) described in Chapter 1 assists sexuality counselors in determining which sexual disorders they are qualified to treat.

The P-LI-SS-IT model demonstrates that in less complex cases of atypical sexual problems or disorders (e.g., compulsive masturbation and pornography dependence), reassurance and education are integral components of treatment. Specific techniques such as keeping a diary of compulsive behaviors or practicing relaxation strategies might be suggested in order to address these sexual issues. However, in more complex cases (those causing significant distress to the individual and those involving harm to self or others), specific training and consultation are required.

For example, a man exhibiting masochistic behaviors such as wearing a leather collar and allowing his partner to tie him to the bed seeks sexuality counseling. He states that he and his partner are satisfied with their sexual practices; however, he has recently fantasized about wanting his partner to electrically stimulate his penis. He desires to explore the option of introducing electrical stimulation into their relationship and the effect it might have on his partner. According to the P-LI-SS-IT model (Annon, 1974, 1975), the sexuality counselor supports a couple's need to explore their sexual issues. The counselor provides limited information for the couple to read such as books or journal articles about human sexuality. This information includes variations in sexual expression and information about the sexual response cycle. In addition, the counselor refers the man to his urologist to answer any concerns about the effects of electrical stimulation to himself as well as his partner. More frequent, intense sexual behaviors require that sexuality counselors have advanced training or specific consultation in order to continue treatment with such couples.

Diagnosing Atypical Disorders and Problems

Determining if a person has a diagnosable paraphilia disorder or an atypical sexual problem has important implications for treatment. For example, a man with a certain fetish wears brassieres when he is at home in the evening. His partner discovers his secret and refuses to have sexual relations with him because she considers his actions to be perverse. In order to help this couple, a sexuality counselor must determine if the man is experiencing a sexual problem or a sexual disorder. This is determined by comprehensive assessment that takes into account the intensity and degree of the behavior. If he is experiencing a sexual problem, the focus of intervention will be on addressing his relationship with his partner and how his sexual expression affects his relationship. If it is determined that his behavior is a sexual disorder (producing more adverse physical, emotional, or social consequences), a sexuality counselor must assess the degree of severity of the behavior and the possibility of harm to self or others. A referral to a psychiatrist for medication evaluation, hospitalization, or a referral to a therapist specializing in a particular sexual variation may be in order.

In Chapters 6 and 7 we discussed the use of the specific criteria listed in the *DSM-IV-TR* for making a diagnosis of sexual disorders and dysfunctions. We must keep in mind that a sexual disorder is described by the *DSM-IV-TR* "as a clinically significant behavior or psychological syndrome or pattern that occurs in an individual" (APA, 2000, p. xxxi). In order for a problem to be classified as a diagnosable sexual disorder, it must cause "significant distress or impairment in social, occupational, or other important areas of functioning" (APA, 2000, p. 535). For example, if a man states that he likes to bathe nude in the privacy of his own courtyard, fantasizes about sunbathing at a nude beach, and is quite satisfied with this practice, he does not meet the *DSM-IV-TR* criteria for exhibitionism. However, if he states that he is distressed because he experiences a strong desire to expose himself to others in public and carries through with his desires, he, by definition, is exhibiting.

Questions to Consider

There are specific questions regarding atypical sexual behavior that sexuality counselors may ask to determine a diagnosis of atypical sexual disorder (both PAs and PRDs). Kafka (2000) has created a diagnostic screening questionnaire that can help sexuality counselors to elicit atypical (variant) sexual behaviors. He suggests that specific questions about the presence of atypical sexual behaviors should be pursued if a person responds positively to one or more of these questions. The screening questions are presented in Figure 12.1.

Once a sexuality counselor determines the possibility of atypical sexual behavior, more specific information can be elicited specific to the behavior. This information allows the sexuality counselor to best determine a treatment option.

Assessment Tools

A complete medical and sexual history is critical to an accurate assessment. In addition, due to the complexity of diagnosing severe forms of these disorders, other interventions—including collaborative interviews, behavioral logs, questionnaires, and penile circumference measurements—are often used by trained sexuality counselors and researchers in order to arrive at an accurate diagnosis (Schewe, 1997; Wincze, 2000). Multiple measures of assessment are encouraged when trying to diagnose these disorders. They provide sexuality counselors with a more comprehensive picture of a person's situation, helping them to select the most appropriate treatment intervention.

Collaborative Interviews

In many cases, persons engaging in atypical sexual behaviors that involve a sexual offense against another person will distort, minimize, or lie about their activities (Maletzky, 1997; Murphy, 1990). For this reason it is helpful to solicit the observations and opinions of family, friends, partners, or relatives to obtain other views of the situation. Other views may include court documents such as transcripts of court hearings and sentencing guidelines or an official police report.

---

1. Have you ever had persistent, repetitive trouble controlling your sexual behavior? (Carnes, 1989; Coleman, 1992; Kafka, 1997)
2. Has your sexual behavior ever caused you significant personal distress or caused significant consequences to you, such as loss of a relationship, legal problems, job-related problems, or medical problems including a sexually transmitted disease or unwanted pregnancy? (Carnes, 1989; Coleman, 1992; Kafka, 1997)
3. Have you ever had repetitive sexual activities that you felt needed to be kept secret or that you felt very ashamed of? (Carnes, 1989; Coleman, 1992).
4. Have you ever been troubled by feeling that you spend too much time engaging in sexual fantasy, masturbation, or other sexual behavior? (Carnes, 1989; Coleman, 1992; Kafka, 1997).
5. Have you ever felt that you have a high sex drive? For example, if we include both partnered sex and masturbation, have you ever been sexual seven or more times a week during at least a six-month period since adolescence? When was that? Did it last longer than six months? (Kafka, 1997)

FIGURE 12.1

Screening Questions for the Diagnosis of Paraphilia-Related Disorders

Source: From M. P. Kafka, "The Paraphilia-Related Disorders," in *Principles and Practice of Sex Therapy,* 3rd ed. (p. 481), by S. R. Leiblum and R. C. Rosen, eds., 2000. New York: Guilford Press. Reprinted by permission.

Behavioral Log

A behavioral log is used to help people track their sexual urges, fantasies, dreams, or actual sexual behaviors (Kafka, 2000). In addition, such logs offer clients an opportunity to record and review their progress toward their goals while also serving as a record of important information related to their thought processes (Kafka, 2000). As clients take time to record their thoughts, they invariably interrupt their thought process, which contributes to maintaining atypical behaviors. This interruption allows them to replace undesirable thoughts with more desirable ones, a first step in changing their behavior.

Sexual Questionnaires

Questionnaires serve as a way to acquire additional information about a person's sexual attitudes, relationships, practices, and sexual self. The Multiphasic Sex Inventory (MSI) prepared by Nicholes and Molinder (1984) and the Sex Fantasy Questionnaire (SFQ) by O'Donohue, Letourneau, and Dowling (1997) are comprehensive inventories that provide information pertaining to both typical and atypical forms of sexual expression. They include but are not limited to assessment of the paraphilias, sexual dysfunction, gender identity, and sexual and marital development (Schewe, 1997). In addition, The Abel Questionnaire for Men (Abel, 1996) covers all possible paraphiliac behaviors. An inclusive list of other questionnaires can be found in Prentky and Edmunds (1997), *Assessing Sexual Abuse: A Resource Guide for Practitioners.*

Penile Strain Gauge

The penile strain gauge is a physiological method of assessment that is used to determine male sexual arousal, most commonly in the assessment of sexual offenders (Maletzky, 1997; Schewe, 1997). The gauge is a device similar to a rubber band that is placed around the penis to measure changes in the circumference of the penis while the subject is being aroused by paraphilia-related visual and auditory stimuli (Maletzky, 1997).

Degrees of Variability

Sexuality counselors should be aware that there are degrees and variability related to atypical sexual behaviors (Charlton, 1997). Some atypical behaviors such as transvestic fetishism (cross-dressing) and excessive masturbation are considered harmless if the person acts out the behavior without potential to harm others. Other atypical behaviors such as sexual masochism and pedophilia involve others who can be seriously injured or killed (APA, 2000). It is therefore important for sexuality counselors to assess the probability of individuals to act out their sexual impulses, as well as to determine if they could harm themselves or another individual (Charlton, 1997; Kafka, 2000).

The Development of Sexual and Relational Problems

Sexual Problems and Dysfunctions

Couples engaging in variant sexual behavior may experience sexual problems or dysfunctions for some of the same reasons that couples practicing more conventional forms of sexual expression do. However, many times a variant form of sexual expression contributes to the development of, or helps sustain, a sexual problem or dysfunction. For instance, a woman who is disgusted by her partner's armpit fetish avoids sexual encounters by making excuses such as feeling too tired. Over time, this may lead to a sexual desire disorder due to her rejection of penis-to-armpit contact. Her partner may experience difficulty maintaining an erection based on her consistent rejection of his fetish.

Relational Problems

The discovery of variant sexual behavior in a partner can lead to issues of trust, commitment, and betrayal (Kafka, 2000; Schneider & Schneider, 1996). Some partners react to a disclosure with disgust and consider their partner perverted. Others may be understanding and willing to alter their sexual practices in order to accommodate their partner's sexual expression. Still others may choose to leave their relationship based on their partner's choice of sexual expression.

Relational issues also emerge due to differences in sexual practices. For example, Josh may be willing to engage in fulfilling his partner Sally's sadistic wishes by allowing her to tie him to the bedpost during sexual play. In return, Josh wants to be treated like an infant and dress in diapers having

Sally tend to him as if he were a baby. Sally rejects the idea, calling Josh weird and disgusting. This causes Josh to withdraw from the relationship due to feelings of humiliation and embarrassment. Their interaction results in a power struggle between the two.

Counseling Couples with Atypical Sexual Behaviors

Counseling couples for the treatment of atypical sexual behaviors often enhances a prognosis, particularly in the cases of paraphilia-related disorders. Often referred to as an "intimacy problem" (Carnes, 1991; Schneider & Schneider, 1991, 1996), some atypical behaviors are supported by sexual partners who engage in enabling behavior, shielding their partners from the consequences of inappropriate sexual practices (Carnes, 1991; Schneider & Schneider, 1991). This is particularly true for addictive sexual behaviors when a sexual partner displays codependent tendencies and is often unable to admit a partner's illness (Carnes, 1991). A 12-step program for couples as well as couples' counseling helps them address issues such as rebuilding trust, communicating clearly, and learning how to forgive oneself and each other (Schneider & Schneider, 1996).

Couples' counseling focuses on assessing the strength of commitment in the relationship along with exploring the effect of the PRD on sexual functioning. Success in couples' therapy is largely determined by "the quality of current sexual intimacy and interpersonal communication" (Kafka, 2000, p. 486).

The following goals may be used when treating couples who experience sexual and relational problems due to atypical sexual practice. These goals, based on mild to moderate forms of variant sexual expression, may be modified to address the individual needs of couples.

1. To increase a couple's knowledge of variant sexual practices and understand the development of the variant forms of sexual expression (behavior) in order to feel less fear about its occurrence or engaging in its practice (affect).
2. To develop a plan to identify and communicate feelings about current sexual practices and the impact these sexual expressions have on a couple's relationship (behavior) in order to increase feelings of trust and intimacy (affect).
3. To develop a plan to learn how to modify sexual practices (behavior) in order to enjoy sex and intimacy (affect).
4. To increase communication between partners about the practice of atypical behaviors (behavior) in order to increase feelings of trust and intimacy (affect).
5. To develop a plan to increase more mutually agreed upon sexual behavior (behavior) in order to establish a healthy sexual relationship and feel more emotionally intimate (affect).
6. To communicate each partner's sexual needs and desires to each other (behavior) in order to feel loved and understood (affect).
7. To establish emotional safety (behavior) in order to feel more connected to each other (affect).

Be aware that the above goals are not meant to address more problematic paraphilias that result in harm to self, others, or society. In these cases, treatment goals focus on decreasing atypical behavior, maintaining control over the behavior, and improving an individual's overall sense of well-being (Wincze, 2000).

The next section will focus on interventions that can be used with couples who engage in atypical sexual behavior.

INTERVENTIONS FOR TREATING COUPLES ENGAGING IN ATYPICAL SEXUAL BEHAVIORS

Disclosing Paraphiliac Behavior

Individuals who reveal their atypical behavior to their partner can expect life-changing consequences. Most times, the impact of disclosure leads to a relationship crisis, raising issues related to trust and betrayal (Kafka, 2000; Schneider & Schneider, 1996). Sexuality counselors guide individuals in determining if, and when, to disclose. Disclosure can lead to successful outcomes in cases of stable, committed relationships. However, if one partner is "too emotionally unstable to tolerate disclosure" (Kafka, 2000, p. 486), it must be considered in the overall therapeutic plan. Hence, sexuality counselors should jointly negotiate the precise timing of such disclosures in intimate partner relationships (Schneider & Schneider, 1991).

Psychoeducational Materials

Psychoeducational materials in the form of books, articles, and tapes are used to help couples understand variant forms of sexual expression and to identify what they know and do not know about their development and treatment. In most cases couples troubled by atypical behavior are able to normalize their experiences; in other cases they may determine that the behavior is excessive or more problematic. Psychoeducational materials also provide couples with information on alternative expressions of sexual intimacy and they can learn how to develop and maintain healthy intimate relationships.

Identifying Positive Assets

Sexuality counselors help couples identify their individual and relational assets that help them to resolve specific issues related to atypical sexual practices. They identify how they have managed sexual intimacy in the years they have been together and how they have created solutions.

Addressing Commitment in Relationships

Sexuality counselors help couples identify the strength of their commitment to their relationship by discussing examples of how they have demonstrated commitment to each other in the past. The strength of their commitment is highlighted as an ingredient for successful outcome in the treatment of their sexual concerns.

Addressing Enabling Behavior

When couples are addressing an atypical sexual behavior that is compulsive or addictive in nature (e.g., pornography dependence, telephone dependence, or cybersex), they may not be aware that they enable each other. Codependent behavior may involve buying one's partner a subscription to a pornographic magazine, upgrading the computer and software to accommodate more pornographic sites, or protecting a partner from the consequences of his or her behavior. Sexuality counselors help couples recognize and address enabling behaviors that contribute to their sexual problems or dysfunctions. Often, a referral to support groups for partners with sexual addictions is useful.

Examining Family of Origin

Sexuality counselors help individuals and their partners examine their family history for possible developmental trauma or conditions that could be identified as a risk factor in the development of a PRD (Kafka,

2000). This may include early exposure to sexually explicit adult behavior or pornography as well as the occurrence of sexual abuse or exploitation as a child (Kafka, 2000). This activity helps couples to gain a better understanding of possible origins of their personal or their partner's sexual expression, while at the same time engaging in effective communication about sexual behaviors.

Identifying and Exploring Feelings

Couples who are faced with an unexpected disclosure of an atypical sexual expression need an opportunity to explore their emotional reactions to the disclosure along with discussing the impact of a disclosure on the relationship. Sexuality counselors help couples identify and share the feelings commonly related to issues of shame, embarrassment, anger, trust, and betrayal.

Modifying Sexual Practices

Sexuality counselors help couples modify or control their sexual practices in order to create a more satisfying relationship for both partners. This requires couples to identify and understand sexual preferences and to create a plan to incorporate new sexual practices into their sexual play. Many couples find new expressions of sexual intimacy exciting and rewarding.

Managing Sexual Impulses

When one partner is having difficulty managing sexual impulses and it is threatening intimacy in the relationship, it can be helpful to involve both partners in the process of regulating sexual impulses. For couples, this may involve one partner helping the other discard pornography, cancel phone cards, hold or discontinue credit cards, or set up an Internet censor with a password controlled by the nonparticipating partner.

Interpersonal Communication Skills Development

It is important for couples to understand their variant sexual expressions and identify how these behaviors have impeded or contributed to their intimacy. It is also important for them to identify pitfalls that contribute to unsuccessful management. This may require practicing skills in assertiveness or communicating their desires to their partner.

Referral to Group Counseling as an Intervention

Group counseling for PRDs is effective for treating some individuals and their partners (Kafka, 2000). Such counseling offers therapeutic effects, including ventilation of feelings, support, validation, confrontation, expressions of empathy, and cohesiveness (Feierman & Feierman, 2000). Groups modeled after 12-step programs dealing with relapse prevention programs for sex offenders are commonly used in the treatment of paraphilia-related disorders. These would include Sexaholics Anonymous, Sex and Love Addicts Anonymous, Sex Addicts Anonymous, or Sexual Compulsives Anonymous (Carnes, 1989, 1991). Following the structure of the 12-step recovery programs, these self-help groups involve the use of sponsors and frequent meetings designed to help individuals to eliminate their acting-out behaviors (Cooper et al., 1999; Feierman & Feierman, 2000; Kafka, 2000). Couples' groups address topics related to negotiating financial decisions, rebuilding trust in the relationship, learning communication skills, and issues of forgiveness (Cooper et al., 1999; Schneider & Schneider, 1996). Individuals involved in group treatment can expect a recovery period lasting over several years (Carnes, 1991).

INTERVENTIONS FOR TREATING SEVERE ATYPICAL SEXUAL BEHAVIORS

As discussed earlier in this chapter, some paraphiliac behavior is harmful to oneself, to others, or to society. Certain behaviors may be practiced in such extremes that the individual is impaired in social, occupational, or other important areas of life functioning. Most of the individuals in these categories have difficulty establishing and maintaining stable relationships. If they do establish a relationship, they may come to counseling because their behavior has created significant conflict with their sexual partner or with society (Schneider & Schneider, 1996). Sexuality counselors should be familiar with treatment interventions aimed at reducing dangers, decreasing an atypical behavior, maintaining control over the atypical behavior, and improving the client's overall sense of well-being (Wincze, 1989, 2000). Interventions at a glance are provided in Box 12.1 and 12.2.

BOX 12.1
Interventions at a Glance

- Ask couples to communicate with each other about how the disclosure of an atypical sexual behavior has impacted their relationship.
- Ask couples to read literature pertaining to variant forms of sexual expression along with alternative expressions of sexual intimacy in order to develop and maintain a healthy and intimate sexual relationship.
- Ask couples to identify how they or their partner may be "enabling" the other to engage in undesirable forms of sexual expression.
- Assist couples in exploring their family history for possible events that may have contributed to the development of their sexual variation.
- Assist couples to discern how and if they desire to modify their sexual practices in order to create a more mutually satisfying sexual relationship.
- Ask couples to develop a plan involving their partner to help them regulate undesirable sexual expressions.

BOX 12.2
Interventions for More Severe Forms of Sexual Expression

- Assess the frequency and intensity of the sexual variation as it relates to harm to self, to others, or to society.
- Ask clients to keep a log of their sexual urges, fantasies, dreams, or sexual behaviors in order to assess the frequency and intensity of their sexual variations. If the client is involved in a committed relationship, ask their partner to record their feelings about their partner's behavior.
- Solicit observations from family, friends, and community partners regarding sexual behavior that involves a sexual offense against another person.
- Develop a plan to increase desired sexual behavior and decrease undesirable forms of sexual expression.

Reducing Danger

Sexuality counselors focus on reducing the harmfulness of individuals who are acting out their sexual impulses or intending to hurt themselves or others. This may entail the use of medication, cognitive-behavioral strategies, or admission to a psychiatric facility (Wincze, 2000). For example, one client states that since he disclosed his fetish of dressing up in women's underwear to his partner, she has decided to divorce him. He is disgusted with himself and feels as if he will never be able to have a normal relationship. He reports having symptoms of clinical depression and thoughts of wanting to hurt himself. He shares that he has a plan to lock himself in the garage, attach a hose to the exhaust pipe of his car, and feed it through the rear window. This way, he states, "It will be over quickly and painlessly." In this case, hospitalization is necessary to protect the client from hurting himself.

On the other hand, if a client presents a threat to others, as is often the case of child molesters, a sexuality counselor must take action to warn potential victims and ensure that the individual is not placed in a high-risk situation (Wincze, 2000). Sexuality counselors must refer to laws in specific states to determine their responsibility regarding duty to warn or protect the public from harm. For example, a pedophile working in a day care center with young children should be removed from that setting. It should be reported to the state abuse registry if abuse has been acted out or if suspected abuse of a child is in question.

When it has been established that an individual is not a danger to self or others and a clear statement of the problem has been determined, goals for treatment can be established.

Goals for Treatment

The following three goals have been suggested by Wincze (1989, 2000) when working with more severe atypical sexual behavior. We have modified these goals to include behavioral and affective components.

1. Develop a plan to increase more appropriate sexual behavior (behavior) in order to establish a healthy sexual relationship and feel more emotionally intimate (affect).
2. Develop a plan to learn how to manage the atypical behavior (behavior) in order to feel control over sexual urges and interactions (affect).

3. Develop a plan to improve the person's sense of well-being (e.g., self-esteem issues, coping skills, and interpersonal and intrapersonal conflicts) in order to establish an intimate relationship (behavior) and feel more connected to one's partner (affect).

We briefly describe some common behavioral, cognitive, and biological treatment approaches that can be used to meet the above goals. Again, by no means are the treatment approaches comprehensive. They vary depending on the specific disorder.

Behavioral Approaches

Aversive Techniques

Aversive techniques involve using stimuli to minimize or abolish an atypical behavior (Masters, Johnson, & Kolodny, 1995). In this way, the likelihood of an undesirable sexual response is reduced (Maletzky, 1997). Aversive techniques include the use of electric shock, foul odors (e.g., ammonia, rotting tissue), unpleasant tastes, or nausea-inducing drugs (Maletzky, 1980, 1991a). For example, electric shock may be given to a pedophile each time his penis begins to become erect while he is viewing child pornography. In this way, he pairs the shock with sexual urges for children. Aversion techniques have been criticized for producing mixed evidence in effectiveness for treating atypical sexual disorders, being intrusive to the client, and producing negative public reactions (Maletzky, 1997).

Another aversion technique, called *covert sensitization*, is often used as a substitute for physically aversive approaches. In this approach, a sexuality counselor asks the client to imagine a sequence of events leading up to the expression of the atypical sexual act. The client is then guided to imagine an adverse (painful or fearful) consequence based on personal experience (Travin & Protter, 1993). Each scene should include a gradual increase in the sexual arousal, an adverse consequence, and an escape scene linked to nonexposure (Maletzky, 1997). For example, an exhibitionist may be asked to visualize a common sequence of events leading to his genital exposure to young girls attending a summer camp. He typically exposes himself from his canoe on the lake. A counselor describes the setting: "It is late afternoon, and you are fishing in your canoe just offshore from a girls' summer camp. You notice a group of young girls laughing and talking on the dock. Their skin is smooth, and their hair is long and silky. You feel your enlarged penis press against your swimsuit. You approach the dock where the girls are sunbathing and pull up even with its edge. You observe the girls glancing at your enlarged but clothed penis. You begin to take your penis out of your shorts and accidentally get it caught in a fishhook. The hook penetrates your penis and you begin to bleed profusely. The girls are horrified and signal for their camp director by blowing a loud whistle and screaming for help." (At this point the counselor adds an escape scene that demonstrates nonoffending behavior): "You manage to remove the hook and stuff your flaccid penis back in your swimsuit. You canoe away from the dock and across the lake. You are far from the girls and able to calm yourself."

This technique can be used to construct several scenes in which the individual has the opportunity to practice self-control.

The goal of aversive techniques is to decrease or eliminate the atypical sexual behavior by associating negative consequences with its expression and then to generalize these feelings to real-life experiences (Travin & Protter, 1993). Aversive techniques are meant to pair pain, fear, or avoidance with an undesirable sexual behavior.

Masturbatory Satiation

This technique involves instructing a person to masturbate to orgasm while fantasizing about a sexually appropriate activity or object such as becoming sexually aroused by having one's partner stroke his penis or having sexual intercourse with an age-appropriate partner. The client is then instructed to shift to an atypical sexual preference such as having one's partner stroke his penis with a leather mitt, for example, and continue the activity for a lengthy period of time (30 to 60 minutes)(Laws & Marshall, 1991; Maletzky, 1998). The person is typically instructed to describe the scenes in detail and record them on audiotape to ensure compliance. The purpose of the procedure is to create a feeling of boredom that is then paired with the atypical sexual behavior (Travin & Protter, 1993).

Orgasmic Reconditioning

This technique involves instructing a person to masturbate to his atypical sexual fantasy to a point just before orgasm and then shift to a more appropriate fantasy at the moment of orgasm (Adshead, 1997; Crooks & Baur, 2002). A man with a silk panty fetish, for example, may be instructed to obtain an erection by imagining or viewing pictures of silk panties (holding or touching) and then to switch to an image of his partner in the nude (engaging in foreplay with his partner). As treatment progresses, he is asked to make the shift earlier in the sequence until he becomes aroused less to socially unacceptable sexual fantasies. This allows him to pair more socially acceptable sexual behavior with orgasm (Laws & Marshall, 1991).

Systematic Desensitization

This approach is designed to "neutralize the anxiety-producing aspects of [atypical] sexual situations and behavior by a process of gradual exposure" (Masters et al., 1995, p. 464). This is accomplished by assisting individuals to construct a hierarchy of situations or behaviors that provoke a progressive increase in inappropriate sexual arousal. They then practice a series of progressive muscle relaxation techniques as they learn to associate relaxation with each scene, beginning with the one that is least arousing. In this way clients learn to replace sexual arousal with relaxation.

Alternative Behavior Completion

This approach is based on desensitization techniques and has been used in the treatment of compulsive gamblers and a variety of sexual offenders (McConaghy, 1993). It involves having a person listen to detailed accounts of atypical sexual acts, including a sequence of events leading up to the expression of atypical sexual urges. These situations are based on the client's experiences and designed to begin with the least intense scenario and progress to more anxiety-producing scenes. As the person continues to listen to each scenario, he or she learns to successfully tolerate the urge to act out atypical sexual behavior by completing the sequence with an alternative behavior. A common scenario for an exhibitionist may unfold like this: "You are taking the subway home after attending a concert. You notice several attractive women standing in the back of the uncrowded train. You begin to feel aroused and think about exposing yourself to them. You realize your urge is no longer as strong as it has been in the past. You approach a seat in the back of the train in close proximity to the women and resist exposure. You begin to read the newspaper and enjoy the train ride home." In this case, the person was able to keep a relaxed composure and create a more socially acceptable behavior in place of exposing himself.

Social Skills Training

Social skills training can be used in the treatment of atypical sexual behaviors as an adjunct to other approaches. A particular focus when working with individuals includes providing guidelines for improvement of sexual communication between partners or initiating and sustaining a peer-appropriate sexual relationship (Levine, 2000). The purpose of this training is to help people learn how to form appropriate social relationships and thus engage in more appropriate sexual expression. For example, a man who "peeps" at women may be taught how to express affection and converse with women in a social setting along with learning how to conquer his anxiety of being rejected (Masters et al., 1995). Social skills training uses techniques such as role-playing, modeling, the assignment of homework (e.g., practicing new skills in real life, reading assignments), and behavioral rehearsal (practicing a desired behavior until it is performed the way a client wishes) (Travin & Protter, 1993). Social skills training is used in treating a variety of atypical behaviors, including exhibitionism, fetishism, and other paraphilias.

Cognitive Approaches

Cognitive Restructuring

This approach is commonly used to modify as well as control ongoing faulty belief patterns in persons expressing atypical sexual behaviors. Distorted thinking allows a person to justify atypical sexual behavior by denial, rationalization, or minimalization (Murphy, 1990; Travin & Protter, 1997). This approach requires that the sexuality counselor indirectly confront individuals in order to identify faulty beliefs and attitudes and explore the roles they play in order to maintain their atypical sexual behavior. Common assumptions and justifications used by sexual offenders include attributing blame to the victim, minimizing the consequences of their actions, and degrading the victim (Maletzky, 1997; Murphy, 1990). Sexuality counselors challenge clients' thinking by providing corrective feedback and appropriate information. Providing immediate and repetitive feedback helps clients learn how to incorporate automatic responses. Maletzky (1997) offers the following example to demonstrate this approach:

> A 15-year-old boy often exposed himself and masturbated in a parking structure when women were returning to their cars. He rationalized the behavior as justifiable:

> CLIENT: These women are older than me and, therefore, cannot be harmed.
> COUNSELOR: Women of any age can be traumatized by witnessing exposure.
> CLIENT: These women are enjoying it because they often smile.
> COUNSELOR: Sexual and emotional harm can occur to these victims, affecting some the rest of their lives. (p. 60)

Once distortions have been identified and confronted, counselors can assist clients in exploring the role they play in maintaining their atypical sexual behavior.

Relapse Prevention

Cognitive-behavioral approaches have been developed from relapse-prevention programs used in treating addictive behaviors such as substance abuse, nicotine dependence, compulsive overeating, and gambling (Travin & Protter, 1993). Adapted for use with sex offenders (Pithers, Marques, Gibat, & Marlatt, 1983), such programs are based on the assumption that atypical sexual disorders are forms of compulsive sexual behavior consisting of recurrent arousing fantasies, sexual urges, or activities (Travin & Protter, 1993). Relapse prevention programs help clients learn self-control by teaching them to (a) identify the atypical behavior they want to change, (b) identify thoughts, feelings, and behaviors leading up to an incident that contributes to a relapse, and (c) identify and implement a plan for coping with high-risk situations in order to prevent a relapse from occurring (Barbaree & Seto, 1997; Kafka, 2000). Techniques include, but are not limited to, interrupting the sequence of events or progression of thoughts leading to the expression of the atypical sexual behavior; identifying, avoiding, or learning to escape from high risk situations; and learning how to cope with urges (Pithers, 1990). In addition, offenders may receive training in anger management and stress management as well as social and sexual skills training (Krueger & Kaplan, 1997; Pithers, 1990).

Empathy Training

Empathy training involves the use of specific steps in helping sex offenders develop empathy for their victim (Murphy, 1990). It can be used in the initial phases of treatment or as part of a relapse prevention program. According to Maletzky (1997), the training is divided into five segments: "(1) identification of the victim, (2) identification of the victimizing act, (3) identification of the harm, (4) role reversal, and (5) development of empathy" (p. 62).

Biological Approaches

Hormonal Treatment

Medroxyprogesterone (MPA), also known as Depo-Provera, and cyproterone acetate (CPA) are two types of medications often used in combination with psychotherapy to treat male sexual offenders exhibiting extreme forms of atypical sexual behavior (Rosler & Witztum, 2000). These antiandrogens decrease the circulation of testosterone in normal male functioning either by completely reducing its secretion or by blocking cellular binding of normal circulating testosterone (Maletzky, 1997). Both hormonal medications reduce male sexual drive such as the frequency of erections, self-initiated behaviors, sexual fantasies, and desire. This also results in a decrease in masturbation. These medications are only effective in high doses and have a number of side effects, including weight gain, muscular cramps, and headaches (Maletzky, 1991b). At this time the Food and Drug Administration (FDA) has approved the use of MPA in the United States, but the use of CPA has not yet been approved (Maletzky, 1997). Most treatment centers use hormonal treatment simultaneously with cognitive and behavioral methods, tapering the hormone and providing close supervision to chart the person's progress (Knopp, Freeman-Longo, & Stevenson, 1992).

Most recently, a long-lasting antiandrogen, gonadotropin-releasing hormone (GnRH), has shown promising results, destroying testosterone in a reversible manner with few side effects (Rosler & Witztum, 2000). Along with psychotherapy, GnRH has demonstrated effective results in controlling selected paraphilias such as pedophilia, exhibitionism, and voyeurism (Rosler & Witztum, 2000).

Psychotropic Medication

Psychotropic medications, usually antidepressants, have also been used in the treatment of sexual offenders because they reduce sexual drive in the majority of people (Burnstein, 1983). Lithium carbonate, tricyclic antidepressants—clomipramine (Anafranil)—desipramine, antipsychotics—benperidol, thioridazine (Mellaril), haloperidol—and antiepileptics (carbamazpine) have been used intermittently over

the years to treat paraphilias and reduce deviant sexual arousal (Gijs & Gooren, 1996). Most recently, serotonin reuptake inhibitors (SSRIs)—namely, fluoxetine (Prozac)—have been used to reduce deviant sexual arousal with some case study success (Gijs & Gooren, 1996; Kafka, 1991). This suggests a possible relationship between paraphilias and obsessive-compulsive disorders (OCD). Rosler and Witztum (2000) concluded that psychotropic medication may be useful only in men with OCD components to their paraphiliac manifestations, making the use of psychotropic drugs highly argumentative.

When using the approaches described above, it is important to tailor specific interventions with the unique needs of the individual or couple. Not all interventions are appropriate for all individuals and their partners. Working with couples whose atypical behavior is interfering with healthy sexual functioning requires an array of interventions and clinical skills. An integrative couples' model allows a sexuality counselor to tailor interventions to the precise needs of individuals.

Case Example

Jarrod, aged 38, and Amalee, aged 37, have been married for 9 years and have two children, aged 1 and 3. Jarrod is an engineer who is hoping to make senior partner in the next year. Amalee is a stay-at-home mother who resigned her career as a magazine editor after the birth of their second child. Recently, Amalee observed her husband viewing a pornographic Web site, only to discover a history of such log-ons. In addition, she found more than 50 pornographic magazines and videotapes in his home office. Amalee is devastated and perplexed by her husband's secrecy.

Stage 1: Assessing and Obtaining an Interactional View of the Problem

Jarrod states that he has felt increasingly distant from Amalee since she became senior editor six years ago and even more so since the birth of their children. He states that he remembers using pornography as a young adult to relieve his anxiety about school performance although no one ever knew about it. He also states that he used to masturbate twice a day during that time. He admits that he is experiencing extreme anxiety about becoming a senior partner in the engineering firm he is working for and has felt helpless in communicating his sexual needs and concerns to Amalee. He feels guilty, ashamed, and angry with himself due to his compulsive sexual release. Amalee, on the other hand, states that Jarrod is spending too much time away from the family and is obsessing over this business partnership. She offers that over the last several years he has not made many attempts to get close to her and spends much of his time in his home office, including weekends, and working long hours. She reports feeling hurt, disgusted, angry, disappointed, and perplexed by his secretive behavior. After obtaining a historical view of the problem and a sexual and relational history, the sexuality counselor determines that Jarrod is exhibiting compulsive behavior involving masturbation, pornography, and cybersex dependence. Although his behavior does not meet *DSM-IV-TR* criteria, he is experiencing a significant atypical sexual problem that is affecting his relationship. The sexuality counselor helps them create a collaborative view based on their definition of the problem and explains the situation in interactive terms. "Both of you have experienced a lot of stress in your personal and professional lives and have managed it by distancing from each other. It sounds as if the two of you want to reestablish emotional safety and healthy ways of relating to each other in order to feel more intimate and connected."

Stage 2: Goal Setting
With the assistance of the sexuality counselor, three goals are set that include both behavioral and affective terms.

1. We would like to reestablish emotional safety in our relationship in order to feel more connected to each other.
2. We would like to communicate our sexual needs and desires to each other so we can feel loved and understood.
3. We would like to spend more time with each other in order to rekindle our passion for each other.

Stage 3: Adapting New Perceptions and Behaviors
During this stage, Jarrod's strengths—being bright and disciplined—are emphasized, as well

as his ability to design plans and follow through with them. Amalee's articulate communications skills are identified along with her ability to create a healthy balance in her life and make difficult personal decisions. As a couple, they discuss their renewed commitment to the relationship despite the hurdles of dual-career issues and managing young children. They also recognize the desire they both have to recapture the passion that was present in their earlier years.

The counselor next devises interventions that mobilize their assets and begin to change the relational system.

1. They will establish emotional safety by Jarrod agreeing to discontinue all pornography and cybersex. He will limit individual masturbation and increase mutual masturbation. Likewise, Amalee will stop "snooping" for evidence and will participate in their mutual masturbation.
2. They will learn to communicate about their sexuality and sexual needs through the use of social skills training (i.e., communication skill building) in order to enhance sexual intimacy.
3. They will take turns planning fun activities as a couple as a way of rekindling their passion.
4. Jarrod will attend a 12-step self-help program in order to better understand his compulsive behavior and the effect it has had on his relationship. Amalee will agree to read suggested literature about the nature of the 12-step program in an effort to support Jarrod and enhance her understanding of their relational dynamics.

Stage 4: Maintaining New Perceptions and Behaviors
During this stage, the sexuality counselor will help Jarrod and Amalee maintain the changes they have made in their sexual and intimate relationship and continue to focus on a healthy, satisfying relationship. They recognize that they could easily fall into old behavior patterns by withdrawing from the relationship (i.e., using pornography and excessive masturbation, snooping for evidence), keeping their feelings and concerns to themselves, and neglecting to make dates with each other in order to create

intimacy. Jarrod and Amalee's sexuality counselor might say, "What will you do when your realize that you are managing your stress and anxiety by distancing yourselves from each other?" This question can help the couple create a plan to help them remain successful.

Stage 5: Validating New Perceptions and Behaviors

Jarrod and Amalee congratulate each other on their continued commitment to the relationship and ability to confront a problem that might split up many couples. They celebrate their success by planning "get-away" weekends for just the two of them once every 8 weeks at a condominium on the beach. They agree to attend a "couple enhancement weekend" offered through their church once a year in order to keep their lines of communication open. They feel good about their relationship and see themselves as a strong, committed couple who has learned to grow closer as a result of examining the reality of their sexual relationship.

SUMMARY

Socially acceptable sexual expressions rest on the laws, religious practices, and cultural meanings in our changing times. When these sexual expressions fall out of this realm, they are termed "atypical." Atypical sexual behavior refers to the sexual fantasies and behaviors that are not commonly practiced among most people. They may produce adverse physical, emotional, and social consequences for themselves or for others. Atypical sexual expression exists on a continuum defined by the degree and intensity of the given sexual expression and includes paraphilias and paraphilia-related disorders. Although the development of these disorders is not well understood, theoretical perspectives stemming from psychoanalytic, behavioral, cognitive, and developmental models have been offered to help comprehend their etiology.

Paraphilias describe sexual interests that are associated with uncommon objects, partners, or activities. They encompass exhibitionism, fetishism, frotteurism, sexual sadism, sexual masochism, transvestic fetishism, voyeurism, and paraphilias not otherwise specified. Paraphilia-related disorders involve normative sexual expressions, which increase in frequency or intensity and interfere with a person's sexual interactions and relationships. They include cybersex dependence, compulsive masturbation and pornography, promiscuity, telephone dependence, and sexual desire incompatibility.

Diagnosis and assessment for atypical sexual behavior can be complex. In some cases, treatment may be brought about by legal charges. In other cases people seek intervention because they are uncomfortable with their sexual behavior or how their behavior is affecting their relationship with their partner. Couples seeking counseling may fear judgment or rejection based on their sexual practices.

Specific screening questions have been provided in this chapter to aid the sexuality counselor in determining atypical sexual behavior. Accurate assessment includes a complete medical history and sexual history. In addition, collaborative interviews, behavioral logs, sexual questionnaires, and a penile strain gauge may be used when assessing more severe forms of these behaviors.

Sexuality counselors can treat atypical sexual behaviors based on their level of training and expertise. AASECT standards require advanced information and training on all *DSM-IV-TR* disorders. In addition, many states require advanced credentials for treating individuals who have violated the law. The P-LI-SS-IT model can assist sexuality counselors in making this decision.

Interventions for treating couples engaged in mild to moderate variant forms of sexual expression may include helping them to tell their partner about the behavior, the use of educational materials, identifying individual and relational strengths, and addressing commitment in the relationship. In addition, couples may need to address enabling behavior in the relationship and explore their family history for evidence of developmental trauma. Finally, the sexuality counselor can intervene by helping couples to modify their sexual practices, explore ways to involve their partner in managing sexual impulses, and develop their interpersonal communication skills. Some individuals and couples may benefit from group counseling to help them maintain their desired sexual behavior or learn more about enabling behavior.

Atypical sexual behavior that is more severe (i.e., a problem to self, to others, or to society) may require behavioral, cognitive, or biological interventions. Behavioral approaches such as aversion techniques, masturbatory satiation, orgasmic reconditioning, systematic desensitization, alternative behavior completion, and social skills training are used. Cognitive approaches include cognitive restructuring, relapse prevention, and empathy training. Biological approaches include hormonal treatment and psychotropic medication.

An integrative couples' model assists those with atypical sexual problems to understand their sexual problems, set realistic goals as a couple, adapt new perceptions about each other and the issue, and work to maintain couple behaviors that promote healthy sexual relationships.

COUNSELING SURVIVORS OF RAPE AND THEIR PARTNERS

KEY CONCEPTS

- Rape is a traumatic event that often prevents survivors and their partners from progressing in their sexual relationships and their daily lives.
- Many experts believe that rape is a crime of violence rather than of sex.
- Culture influences the way society views and addresses issues of rape.
- At times, there are conflicting goals between the legal system and sexuality counselors.
- Sexual trauma can occur as a result of feared death or serious physical or emotional injury.
- Common reactions to rape trauma include physical, cognitive, emotional, and behavioral components.
- Acute stress disorder (ASD) and posttraumatic stress disorder (PTSD) may result from extreme reactions to a traumatic incident of sexual assault or sexual abuse.
- Sexual disorders related to PTSD are primarily disorders of desire, arousal, and orgasm.
- Relational problems are often a result of reactions to rape.
- Couples' counseling is a useful approach for addressing the concerns of survivors of rape and their partners.
- A broad range of interventions, including pharmacological treatment and cognitive and behavioral interventions as well as a variety of coping strategies can be used within the framework of an integrative couples' model.

Rape, or the threat of rape, is a reality that most women across all cultures are concerned about. In fact, one out of six women in this country has experienced rape or attempted rape. It does not occur uniformly or randomly. In a survey conducted in 2000, it was found that 302,100 women are raped in the United States each year (Vanderbilt University, 2000). Three-fourths of the women were assaulted by a current or former husband, a partner, or a date. In fact, two-thirds of the women between the ages of 18 and 29 who were attacked had a prior relationship with their attackers. Differences in power render some women more vulnerable to rape than others and are complicated by race, ethnicity, and class (Holzman, 1996). Women of all races are equally at risk for rape. Unfortunately, the number of police reports of completed rapes is low. Only 36% of the completed rapes were reported to the police between the years 1992 and 2000 (Victims' Rights, 2003).

Rape is described as a crime of violence rather than of sex with far-reaching physical, emotional, and sexual implications. According to Fox and Carey (1999) the intent of rapists is to

> terrorize, dominate, and humiliate [victims] and [to render them helpless]. Typically, victims do not experience rape as a sexual experience, rather, [as] a confrontation or brush with death. However, sexual problems often emerge much later in the form of post-traumatic stress when survivors attempt to negotiate a satisfying intimate relationship with a partner. (p. 187)

Rape ranges from violent attacks by a stranger to forced sexual intercourse following a planned, intimate evening with an acquaintance. All forms of rape involve disregard and disrespect for the feelings and welfare of the victim. The following forms of rape are typically identified by researchers (Ballard & Alessi, 2002).

- *Stranger rape:* A rape that occurs when the assailant is unknown to the victim. It is typically a surprise attack on a victim who is engaged in a daily routine or who is alone in a dangerous location.
- *Acquaintance or date rape:* A form of sexual assault that is committed by someone known to the victim (e.g., friend, acquaintance, co-worker). Acquaintance or date rape occurs during the time a victim is socializing with a friend or acquaintance.
- *Statutory rape:* A rape that involves sexual intercourse with a person under the age of consent for sexual intercourse. This age varies from state to state and usually ranges from ages 14 to 18. The apparent willingness or initiation of sexual behavior of the underage partner is not a factor in the definition of statutory rape (Crooks & Baur, 2002).
- *Marital rape:* A violent sexual act that is perpetrated by a spouse or a domestic partner. Any time there is lack of consent for sex, regardless of the legal status of partners, rape is committed. Husbands do not have any rights for sexual relations with their wives without their consent.
- *Rape of males:* A sexual act that is perpetrated on an unwilling male. It is unclear how many men have been victims of sexual assault. Accurate statistics are difficult to obtain because men are less likely than women to report that they have been violated. In addition, men often fear that they will be viewed as weak, passive, or helpless if they report sexual assault. The sexual victimization of males thus receives less attention in research, literature, and the media. Similar to rape of women, violence and imbalances of power are often associated with the rape of men. Regardless of the gender of the survivor, the aftereffects of rape are often devastating for individuals and their partners.

Couples affected by rape may experience sexual dysfunctions or problems, and other relational concerns that suggest a need for sexuality counseling. Sexuality counselors help couples cope more effectively with emotional, sexual, and relational challenges that occur as a result of rape. This chapter describes rape and common reactions to trauma for survivors of rape and their partners. We focus on the rape of women because the vast majority of rape victims are female.

We use the term "survivor" to describe individuals who have lived through a traumatic event and continue to cope with the aftermath of the event. There are various levels of survival—ranging on a continuum from individuals who are asymptomatic to those who suffer from cognitive, emotional, or behavioral impairments in their daily lives. More acute diagnoses related to rape trauma such as rape trauma syndrome and posttraumatic stress disorder are included in this chapter, in addition to intervention strategies to address trauma associated with rape.

HISTORICAL CONTEXT

Rape has long been a social problem in our culture. It is influenced by "warfare, genocide, or political repression" (Holzman, 1996, p. 48) that has been experienced or observed by survivors. For African American women, rape occurred in the social context of massive sexual exploitation under slavery—an exploitation, though less extreme, that continues in present times. The penalties for rape of African American women during slavery were nonexistent, and during recent times have been less frequently imposed than those for the rape of white women (Holzman, 1996).

Native American women have also been victims of colonization and genocide. In fact, Allen (1986) asserts that until Euro-American domination occurred in the United States, Native American women were accorded reverence and high status among their people. Throughout history, Native Americans have been falsely portrayed in the literature and in the media as patriarchal with men being viewed as cruel and violent toward women. The internalization of this portrayal by Native American people contributed to increased incidences of rape in their culture.

Female refugees from politically oppressive regimes or from war-torn countries have often experienced rape or other forms of sexual assault. In the 1960s, Vietnamese and Cambodian women were frequently raped while attempting to flee from their countries or while residing in refugee camps (Holzman, 1996). Other women have documented state-sponsored sexual torture in Latin America (Lykes, Brabeck, Ferns, & Radan, 1993).

Sexuality counselors must be aware of the historical and cultural narrative of survivors who seek help for sexual concerns, so that they are provided an appropriate context for the torture, exploitation, violence, and intimidation they have endured.

SOCIOCULTURAL CONTEXT

Many experts believe that rape not only is a consequence of oppression, but it is also used as a "tool of oppression, reinforcing subordination through intimidation and demoralization" (Holzman, 1996, p. 47). In fact, rapists often target their victims based on those "whom they perceive as the most vulnerable and who will be least likely to be taken seriously by the criminal justice system" (Holzman, 1996, p. 47).

Poverty and discrimination make it difficult for some women to avoid dangerous neighborhoods or occupations that in turn make them vulnerable to being raped (Holzman, 1996). In fact, women of low socioeconomic status have been identified as being at an extremely high risk for rape and are four times more likely to be raped as other women.

Likewise, homeless women are at exceptionally high risk for sexual assault. These women are more likely to be raped within one week after they lose their permanent housing. Illegal female immigrants are also targeted as potential victims by employers, work supervisors, or immigration officials who bring them into the United States (Holzman, 1996). Many of these immigrants do not report incidents to authorities.

Concepts of Rape

Rape is defined differently in various cultures and has been expanded in definition over time. Marital rape, for example, has only recently been included in the legal definition of rape in the United States. In addition, Latin American and Japanese women are less likely than European or American women to label an experience as a rape (Holzman, 1996). They often feel confused by their emotional reactions to their experience of rape and consequently they may not seek help from their own support network or from the criminal justice system (Holzman, 1996).

The Legal System and the Counseling Process

There are often inherent conflicts between the goals and values of the legal system and the psychological and therapeutic needs of survivors (Dorado, 1996). Often, being involved in the court system places survivors in a role of "victim." In fact, this role is some-times promoted by attorneys in hopes of putting a rapist behind bars, or of recovering economic remuneration for counseling, medical, and other services required as a direct result of the rape. Unfortunately, during legal proceedings a victim must continually define herself as a person without power (Dorado, 1996) and a person who is damaged beyond repair in order to get a conviction. This makes it very difficult to focus on her strengths and resilience in counseling.

Successful counseling includes helping survivors "confront, accept, and integrate" what has happened to them and strengthen their personal identity by addressing the traumatic event and moving beyond it (Dorado, 1996, p. 98). Too frequently, the truth and devastation of rape is denied by the perpetrator and by the legal defense team. On the other hand, in counseling, there is a vast difference between the "black and white" objective reality of the court system and the more complex, subjective reality of a survivor's experience. A traumatic experience such as rape is so overwhelming that it cannot be integrated into day-to-day experiences and cannot be fully explained to others because of the instinctive attempt each person makes to deny terrifying events. Denial serves as a mechanism to preserve self-esteem and to dissociate from the horror of the event.

The legal system in the United States is based on the notion that if two adversarial parties vigorously argue in favor of their position, the "Truth" will eventually be found. Unfortunately, harm often falls to victims in these matters and hinders their progress as survivors.

Sexuality counselors create a warm, supportive environment so that survivors can relate their experiences to trained professionals, make sense of their lives, and integrate the traumatic experiences into their personal narrative. At times, the disparate goal of the two systems (legal and therapeutic) influences counselors to avoid or remain ignorant of the legal system, focusing only on the therapeutic goals for the survivor. This avoidance is often harmful to women who need to confront their perpetrators in the legal system in order to feel more empowered and resilient. Experienced sexuality counselors provide clients with opportunities to examine assumptions about the process of the legal system and help survivors and their partners answer basic questions such as, "How will litigation help me move forward in my life?" "What do I hope to accomplish?" and "How will the legal process help me become stronger and more resilient as an individual and as a couple?" (Dorado, 1996).

In reality, both litigation and counseling are important aspects of healing for survivors. Sexuality counselors are responsible for being cognizant of the issues that may be in conflict as the two systems intersect. If the ethical principle of "do no harm" is applied, sexuality counselors can provide supportive interventions that parallel the legal process by helping their clients separate and remain clear about the goals of counseling and the goals of litigation. Awareness is the key to successful negotiations between the two processes so that clients are able to view themselves as strong and resilient and establish and maintain healthy relationships after the trauma.

Seeking Help Across Cultures

Many cultures assign much of the blame to survivors and offer little empathy or support for them or for their partners (Holzman, 1996). Often, blame is more intense if the perpetrator is a member of the same community as the survivor. In fact, many people may be reluctant to believe that a friend, neighbor, or family member is capable of committing a crime such as rape. In these cases, if a survivor attempts to report the crime to law enforcement officials, she may be ostracized or condemned and may experience isolation and rejection by her community.

Intense shame and feeling soiled or devalued are common themes associated with rape survivors. In some communities, loss of virginity as a result of rape demeans women and may deem them as being unmarriageable (Holzman, 1996). Families are then inclined to keep the rape a secret, or in some instances, urge the victim to marry the perpetrator.

Beliefs about seeking help vary from one culture to another. A need to appear strong and capable may influence African American women to think they can handle physical violations themselves (Holzman, 1996). Other cultures believe that male family members must avenge the honor of the family if a victim comes forward to admit she has been raped.

Although there are designated rape crisis centers and advocates who accompany women to the hospital, many survivors are reluctant to undergo medical examination in order to obtain the required evidence necessary to convict the perpetrator. Many women believe that if they are poor, uneducated, or of color, their issues will not be treated with the same respect as those of white, middle-class women. Likewise, undocumented immigrants may not speak or understand the language of the majority culture and fear their status will be discovered.

Every survivor, regardless of socioeconomic status, ethnicity, age, or gender has rights regarding disclosure, legal process, medical treatment, and mental health services, as shown in Figure 13.1.

Every survivor of sexual assault should have the following rights:

- To be treated with dignity and respect by institutional and legal personnel.
- To have as much credibility as a survivor of any other crime.
- To be considered a survivor of rape when any unwanted act of sex is forced on her through any type of coercion, violent or otherwise.
- To be asked only those questions that are relevant to a court case or to medical treatment.
- To choose whether to report the rape to the police.
- To receive medical and mental health treatment or participate in legal procedures only after giving her informed consent.
- To receive medical and mental health services at no cost, whether or not the rape is reported to the police.
- To not be exposed to prejudice against race, class, age, lifestyle, or occupation.
- To not be asked questions about prior sexual experience.
- To have access to support persons, such as advocates and peer counselors.
- To be provided with information about all possible options related to legal and medical procedures.
- To have her name kept out of the media.
- To be considered a survivor of rape regardless of the relationship with the assailant, including that of spouse.
- To have deterred an assailant by any means necessary. No woman should be criminally prosecuted for harming her assailant during or within a reasonable period of time after the rape or attempted rape.

FIGURE 13.1
Rights of Rape Survivors

REACTIONS TO TRAUMA FOR SURVIVORS OF RAPE AND THEIR PARTNERS

Definition of Trauma

Rosenbloom and Williams (1999) describe traumatic events such as rape as being different than common-place misfortunes and further define them as involving threats to life or confrontations with death. Many of the confrontations are violent in nature and result in feelings of fear and helplessness for victims of these encounters:

> There are two [primary] conditions [that make rape traumatic]. First, there is the nature of the event itself; it usually involves actual or feared death or serious physical or emotional injury. Second, there is what the event means to the survivor . . . Rape is likely to be traumatic for anyone, but [some] events are experienced as traumatic by one person, but not by another. (p. 17)

This definition emphasizes the uniqueness and variability of being raped and the wide range of reactions to the experience.

Reactions to Trauma

There is a wide range of reactions to trauma. Some people withdraw into silence or a flurry of individual activities, whereas others seek support from their family and friends and have a need to talk about what has happened. Some experience "obsessive review," or constant recounting of the events of the trauma. Others feel drained of all energy and sleep constantly, while others cannot sleep and are preoccupied with thinking about what they could have done differently to prevent the event. Many are filled with rage and anger at the injustice of the situation, or feel a deep sense of helplessness.

Rosenbloom and Williams (1999) assert that reactions to traumatic events are "shaped by each person's emotional makeup, personal, family and relationship history, age, . . . social and cultural relationships, previous coping strategies, and [the] availability of support before, during, and following the traumatic experience" (p. 18). Often traumatic events such as rape thwart or prevent survivors from developing positive self-esteem, developing healthy relationships with others, or from moving successfully from one life stage to another (Rosenbloom & Williams, 1999).

It is also important to remember that not all survivors are traumatized by rape. Some are able to use their personal resources and coping strategies in order to address their reactions to being raped and move beyond the event.

Reactions to trauma are conceptualized according to physical, cognitive, emotional, and behavioral symptoms. We have adapted the work of Rosenbloom and Williams (1999) in order to describe responses to rape in each of these domains:*

- *Physical reactions:* Women typically react to stressful situations by experiencing rapid heartbeat, muscle tension, nervousness, upset stomach, dizziness, teeth grinding, and lack of energy or fatigue. Some women may feel numb or out-of-touch with their bodies.

- *Cognitive reactions:* During the aftermath of a traumatic event, survivors make changes in the way they think about themselves or the way they think about the world and other people. They may also experience disruptions in their thoughts or they may not be able to stop replaying the event over and over. They may also become confused and be unable to remember the order of events, or they may experience difficulty concentrating on or remembering daily behaviors. Likewise, decision making may be difficult and there may be a tendency to disconnect from feelings in order to protect themselves. Everyone does this from time to time by "spacing out" or acting as if they are in a daze or are not paying attention. The extreme of this behavior is called *dissociation*—a reaction that makes it difficult to remember extended portions of life events, or present events are excluded from memory.

- *Emotional reactions:* Feelings of fear and lack of safety are common themes reported by rape survivors. Other feelings they commonly express include helplessness, emptiness, dullness, horror or dread, anger and rage, sadness, grief, irritability, depression, disconnection from others, or chaotic feelings that move from blunted to extreme emotion in a short period of time. There may also be feelings of loss, including loss of self-esteem and loss of self-trust or trust in others. There is no emotion that is the correct one to experience. Persons who have been traumatized may go through a wide array of emotions, many of them depending on the stage of grief they are in, or the reaction to resultant events that occur after the traumatic event.

---

*From *Life After Trauma* (pp. 18–22), by D. Rosenbloom and M. B. Williams, 1999. New York: Guilford Press. Adapted with permission.

- *Behavioral reactions:* Many people react to a traumatic event such as rape by becoming withdrawn or isolated from others. They may also experience a change in eating habits and drastically lose or gain weight in a short period of time. Others become restless or become confrontational or aggressive. It is also not unusual to experience a marked increase or decrease in sexual activity in response to acute traumatic stress.

All of these responses are normal reactions to stress and trauma. However, professional assistance is required for those extreme responses or those that extend for a period of time and interfere with a person's ability to continue a daily routine or maintain satisfying relationships. Sexuality counselors are trained to help survivors address these concerns and help them identify changes they can make in their lives in order to achieve a more intimate and satisfying emotional and sexual relationship with their partners.

THE PROCESS OF SEXUALITY COUNSELING FOR SURVIVORS AND THEIR PARTNERS

The process of sexuality counseling for survivors and their partners is challenging to both sexuality counselors and to couples. When couples enter counseling, the effects of a rape experience may not be recognized when discussing their initial concerns. Even when rape is the presenting problem, other issues such as depression, substance abuse, chronic self-destructiveness, or sexual dysfunction overshadow the rape itself (Briere, 1996). The counselor can help a couple determine which issues are rape-related and which issues are not. In this way, they can see that not all of the emotional or relational problems of survivors are associated with rape.

In order to be effective in working with survivors, sexuality counselors are confronted with examining their own biases. It is important that counselors do not blame victims by asking questions that imply that they are responsible for the rape. There is a common assumption that a woman is less powerful than a man and that during the rape, she was unable to defend herself. If the assumption is not made prior to counseling, sexuality counselors may contribute to a belief that a victim might have "asked for it" or participated in some way. The notion of a "guilty co-conspirator" does little to gain the trust of couples and contributes

to further abuse by the very system that is supposed to be part of the healing process.

Sexuality counseling for partners of survivors is challenging because partners often do not understand survivors' reactions to everyday events that impact their emotional, relational, and sexual relationships. These are all salient issues for counseling.

Once an issue of a sexual nature is discerned, sexuality counselors and couples agree about their goals for counseling. "Survivor" counseling emphasizes growth and resiliency of survivors and their partners. This means that attention is paid to healthy characteristics, learning new external and internal coping skills, desensitizing traumatic stress, and updating survival behaviors and perceptions, rather than focusing on weakness, victimization, and illness (Briere, 1996).

Counselor Qualities for Working with Survivors

Requisite personal qualities for counselors working with sexual assault survivors include emotional strength, empathy, understanding, caring, humor, and the ability to deal with rage, horror, and pain. It is important to embrace the terminology of "survivor" rather than "victim" early in treatment because clients have experienced a confrontation with death or betrayal in the most extreme sense and have survived. Survival is a strength that they have developed and should be validated by sexuality counselors. Similarly, survivors need to identify and embrace their strengths and positive assets rather than their weaknesses. This concept may be more accepted after some of the initial shock and denial have been addressed and cannot be forced prematurely on clients until they are ready to accept the terminology. Counselors must also respond proactively and must be knowledgeable about and have training on dynamics and treatment of rape. Counselors are cautioned to be aware of overidentifying with clients and to be aware of their own personal reactions to such trauma so that they remain objective and attend to the needs of their clients.

Assessing Survivors of Rape

Facilitative responding strategies are useful as methods to gather pertinent information and reactions to rape. By creating a safe, facilitative environment, couples feel more at ease to address their reactions to trauma and subsequently, to explore their sexual issues.

Reflective Listening Skills

Reflective listening skills promote a depth of understanding and help couples feel "heard" by communicating empathy, providing feedback through mirroring, stimulating exploration, and capturing significant components of the couples' story that might otherwise have remained hidden (Young, 1998). The following methods are suggested as a way to provide a level of understanding that supports and validates the survivor and her partner:

- Let her talk or cry or express her feelings in whatever way she wants to express herself. (Do not attempt to redefine the situation as being "more" or "less" critical than she sees it.)
- Let her know that you understand something "horrible" has happened to her (if that is the way she sees it) and that is helpful if she can express her feelings about the event.
- Let her know you are listening by reflecting back to her what feeling she is presenting and by summarizing what she is saying:

SURVIVOR: (crying) "I've hardly left the house since my remarriage and I have never met anyone in a bar before. I was just having a good time with my girlfriends. If my new husband finds out I was raped, I don't know what he'll do."

SEXUALITY COUNSELOR: "It seems like you have a lot of regrets for having met someone in a bar."

In this case, a counselor may sense that the survivor blames herself for what happened, and can help her recognize and cope with her feelings of self-blame. However, it is important to be careful not to plant the idea of guilt where it does not exist, nor to reinforce it. The above response lets the survivor know that you are really listening, and it gives her the opportunity to correct impressions if appropriate and to express more of her feelings.

In rare instances, a survivor's emotional state may begin to escalate to a degree that is extremely distressing. If this occurs it may be necessary to shift from a listening to a more active role.

Clinical Decision-Making/Clarifying Skills

Survivors and their partners are often confused and overwhelmed, and as a result they have difficulty identifying, clarifying, and prioritizing their problems. Sexuality counselors can facilitate this process by determining if a survivor needs help with clarifying whether she is extremely upset or feeling overwhelmed by what appear to be massive but ill-defined problems. If there are multiple problems, separating each from the other will help her see that the problems are specific and concrete. Differentiation and clarification of the problem is a first step toward helping her lower her anxiety level and feel control of her life.

SURVIVOR: "I can hardly walk and my children are going to be upset and my mother won't let . . . and my husband, my ex-husband, oh, I don't know why this had to happen or what to do . . . and even the landlord . . ."

SEXUALITY COUNSELOR: "You have quite a few separate issues that have arisen as a result of your situation. Let me see if I understand at least some of them. You're concerned about . . ."

At this point, or earlier, a survivor is likely to interrupt the conversation either to explain a concern or to express more of her feelings. It is important to allow her sufficient time to explore her feelings before she attempts to make a plan to move on.

In most situations sexuality counselors first determine if there is a physical problem that requires attention. If there is, this is a useful place to begin.

Referrals for Medical Treatment

Survivors of rape may require medical treatment. If a survivor decides to have a medical examination, it should be determined if there is a possibility that she intends to report the rape to the police. Many rape survivors do not want to report it at first, but in a day or so they change their minds. If there is any chance at all that they decide to report the incident, it is best to seek immediate medical attention so that evidence is obtained and documented for prosecution. It is also important to inform survivors that if there is a chance they will report it, they should not wash or douche. If they want to make a report, they should call 9-1-1.

Questions to Consider

A comprehensive sexual effects inventory devised by Maltz (2001) in *The Sexual Healing Journey* is presented in Figure 13.2. The inventory assesses sexual attitudes, reactions, behaviors, relational issues, and problems with sexual functioning. It can assist survivors with identifying the intensity of their reactions to sexual assault and can help survivors realize the impact the assault continues to have on their present lives. It also helps survivors to examine their sexuality and to

1. Attitudes About Sex

Sexual abuse generates negative, false attitudes about sex. These become hidden from your consciousness. You may have difficulty separating abusive sex from healthy sex. Offenders contaminate victims, imprinting them with an abusive way of thinking about sex, a sexual abuse mind-set. This mind-set can affect every aspect of a victim's sexuality: sexual drive, sexual expression, sex roles, intimate relationships, knowledge of sexual functioning, and sense of morality. How have you been affected by this sexual abuse mind-set?

Put a check mark in front of each statement you agree with and a question mark in front of each statement you sometimes or partially agree with. (Statements that don't fit either category should be left blank.)

____ I feel sex is a duty I must perform.
____ I feel sex is something I do to get something else.
____ In sex, one person wins and one person loses.
____ Sex feels dirty to me.
____ Sex feels bad to me.
____ Sex feels secretive to me.
____ I equate sex with sexual abuse.
____ Sexual energy seems uncontrollable.
____ Sex is hurtful to me.
____ I believe sex is something you either give or you get.
____ I feel sex is power to control another person.
____ I believe having sex is all that matters.
____ I think sex benefits men more than women.
____ I think people have no responsibility to each other during sex.
____ I think sexual desire makes people act crazy.
____ I think males have a right to demand sex from women.
____ Sex means danger to me.
____ I believe sex is a way to escape painful emotions.
____ Sex is humiliating to me or to others.
____ I feel sex is addictive.
____ I feel sex is a game.
____ I believe sex is a condition for receiving love.

2. Sexual Self-Concept

Sexual abuse, and its consequences, can unconsciously influence how you feel about yourself and about sex. You may now see yourself as sexually damaged, and suffering a poor sexual self-concept, or you may have developed a self-concept that is inflated, where you believe you're more powerful as a result of sex. Knowing how you view yourself as a sexual person is fundamental to eventually making changes in your sexual behavior.

Put a check mark in front of each statement you agree with and a question mark in front of each statement you sometimes or partially agree with.

____ I am an easy sexual target.
____ My sexuality is disgusting.
____ I hate my body.
____ There is something wrong with me sexually.
____ I am confused whether I'm gay or straight.
____ I feel I will lose control if I let myself go sexually.
____ I have no sense of being sexual at all.
____ I feel like a victim in sex.
____ I am sexually inadequate.
____ I don't like certain sexual parts of my body.
____ I want sex for all the wrong reasons.
____ I have to stay in control during sex.
____ I don't have a right to deny my body to any partner who wants it.
____ I can be loved only to the extent I can give sexually.
____ I am oversexed.
____ I have no right to control sexual interaction.
____ My primary value is in sexually serving a partner.
____ If I want sex, I'm as sick as a sexual offender.
____ I blame myself for past sexual abuse.
____ I deserve whatever I get sexually.
____ I wish I were the opposite sex.
____ I am inferior to other people because of my sexual past.
____ I am damaged goods.
____ I can easily be sexually dominated.
____ I'd be happiest in a world where sex didn't exist.
____ I couldn't live in a world without sex.
____ I am a sexual performer.
____ There are some things I have done sexually that I can never forgive myself for.
____ I am a sick person sexually.
____ I'm not lovable for who I am, only for what I do sexually.
____ I am a sexual object.
____ I feel bad about my gender.

FIGURE 13.2
Sexual Effects Inventory

Source: From *The Sexual Healing Journey: A Guide for Survivors of Sexual Abuse,* by Wendy Maltz, 2001a, New York: HarperCollins. Reprinted with permission.

3. Automatic Reactions to Touch and Sex

Sexual abuse can create a conditioned way of reacting to touch and sex. Some survivors get panicky, avoid sexual possibilities, and want to run the other way when sexually approached. Others freeze and feel helpless and unable to protect themselves. Still others get overexcited and may recklessly seek dangerous sexual encounters. You may experience spontaneous reactions to sex that cause you to numb sexual feelings, to divorce your mind from what is happening physically, or to become sexually aroused in inappropriate ways. Sexual settings and contact can bring back negative feelings associated with abuse. Flashbacks to sexual abuse may arise and interfere with sexual relating and satisfaction.

Put a check mark in front of each statement you agree with and a question mark in front of each statement you sometimes or partially agree with.

____ I am afraid of sex.
____ I have little interest in being sexual.
____ I am afraid of some sexual body parts.
____ I am preoccupied with sex.
____ I withdraw from sexual possibilities.
____ I am bothered by sexual thoughts I can't control.
____ When I get horny I feel extremely anxious.
____ I feel especially powerful when I'm having sex.
____ I get sexually excited at times when I shouldn't be.
____ I constantly look for sexual opportunities.
____ I believe that when a person touches me, he or she wants to have sex with me.
____ I lose all power to protect myself when sexually approached.
____ I have unhealthy sexual interests and desires.
____ I often have flashbacks to past sexual abuse during sex.
____ Unwanted fantasies intrude upon my sexual experiences.
____ I am sexually aroused by thoughts of hurtful sex.
____ I get panicky feelings when touched.
____ I feel emotionally distant during sex.
____ During sex my mind feels separate from my body.
____ I feel like I'm another person when I have sex.
____ I experience negative feelings such as fear, anger, shame, guilt, or nausea with sexual touch.
____ I get sexually aroused when I don't want to be.
____ I often feel emotionally pained after sex.
____ I am very sensitive to certain smells, sights, sounds, or sensations during sex.

4. Sexual Behavior

Sexual abuse can shatter our capacity for healthy sex. You may have been taught abusive patterns of sexual behavior and introduced to unhealthy, compulsive, abnormal sexual activities. Now as a reaction you may associate your sexual expression with secrecy and shame. Some survivors may withdraw from sex, preventing any fresh discovery of healthy sex. Other survivors may become preoccupied and driven by sex. Sometimes survivors reenact the abuse in an unconscious attempt to resolve deep-seated emotional conflict related to the original abuse. These reactions need to be identified so you can better understand your behavior and eventually work toward healthy changes.

Put a check mark in front of each statement you agree with and a question mark in front of each statement you sometimes or partially agree with.

____ I isolate myself from other people socially.
____ I am unable to initiate sex.
____ I avoid situations that could lead to sex.
____ I am unable to say no to sex.
____ I feel I have no physical boundaries when it comes to sex.
____ I need to be under the influence of alcohol or other drugs to really enjoy sex.
____ I spend money to have sex.
____ I feel confused about how and when to be sexual.
____ I engage in medically risky sexual behavior (using no protection against disease or pregnancy).
____ I engage in sex for economic gain.
____ I have had more sexual partners than was good for me to have.
____ I act out sexually in ways hurtful to others.
____ I manipulate others into having sex with me.
____ I engage in sadomasochistic sex.
____ I have more than one sexual partner at a time.
____ I become involved with sexual partners who are primarily involved with someone else.
____ I use fantasies of sexual abuse to increase sexual arousal.
____ I feel addictively drawn to certain sexual behaviors.
____ I feel compelled to masturbate frequently.
____ I engage in secretive sexual activities.
____ I engage in sexual behaviors that could harm me.
____ I engage in sexual behaviors that could have negative consequences for others.
____ I have sex when I really don't want to.

FIGURE 13.2
(*Continued*)

___ I am confused as to what is appropriate and inappropriate touch in dating.

___ I often rely on abusive pornography to turn me on.

___ I find it hard to say no to unwanted sexual touch.

___ My sexual behaviors have caused problems with my primary relationship, my work, or my health.

___ I use sex to help me feel better when I'm down.

5. Intimate Relationships

Sexual abuse influences a survivor's ability to establish and maintain healthy sexual relationships. Abuse can interfere with our ability to make good choices. Some survivors may have difficulty with selecting partners who are emotionally supportive. Other survivors may be unable to trust and feel safe with intimate partners who do care. Survivors may fear intimacy or have a limited capacity to experience closeness.

The sexual difficulties a survivor may have as a result of abuse often create emotional and sexual problems for the partner. Knowing where relationship difficulties lie, and how abuse has caused problems, can help you work with your partner to solve individual concerns and to build a more intimate relationship together.

Put a check mark in front of each statement you agree with and a question mark in front of each statement you sometimes or partially agree with.

___ I am drawn to partners who demand sex from me.

___ I am afraid of being emotionally vulnerable in relationships.

___ I am unable to attract the kind of partner that would be good for me to have.

___ I feel obligated to please my partner in sex.

___ My intimate relationships always fail.

___ I have difficulty being intimate and sexual at the same time.

___ I don't trust that a partner could really be faithful to me.

___ I hide my real feelings in an intimate relationship.

___ A partner would reject me if he or she knew all about my sexual past.

___ I experience difficulty initiating sexual contact with a partner.

___ My intimate partner is continually unhappy with our sex life.

___ Our relationship would end if we stopped having sex.

___ I want, but am unable, to remain faithful to one intimate partner.

___ My intimate partner reminds me of a sexual offender.

___ My intimate partner perceives me as sexually abusive.

___ I want to get away from my partner immediately after sex.

___ My partner feels sexually rejected by me.

___ My partner feels sexually pressured by me.

___ I have difficulty communicating my sexual wants and needs.

___ I am afraid to be emotionally close with my partner.

6. Sexual Functioning Problems

Sexual abuse can create specific problems with sexual functioning. Abuse may have taught you unhealthy patterns of responding to sexual stimulation. Stress and anxiety that originated with abuse may continue to shadow your sexual activity. Over time these sexual problems interfere with intimacy and long-term sexual satisfaction. As you identify problem areas in how you function sexually now, you are also identifying specific sexual concerns to work on in the healing process.

Put a check mark in front of each statement you agree with and a question mark in front of each statement you sometimes or partially agree with.

___ I find it difficult to become sexually aroused.

___ I have trouble experiencing sexual sensations.

___ I do not like to touch my genital area.

___ I have difficulty achieving orgasm when I stimulate myself.

___ I have difficulty having an orgasm with a partner.

___ I lack desire for sex.

___ I am hardly ever interested in sex.

___ I overcontrol sexual interactions.

___ My orgasms seem more related to relieving tension than to feeling pleasure.

___ My orgasms are not very pleasurable.

___ Sex in general is not very pleasurable.

___ I am limited in the types of sexual activity I feel comfortable with.

Men

___ I have difficulty getting or maintaining a firm erection.

___ I have difficulty ejaculating.

___ I ejaculate very fast.

Women

___ I do not like to touch my breasts.

___ I am unable to be vaginally penetrated.

___ I experience pain or discomfort with vaginal penetration.

___ I orgasm very fast.

FIGURE 13.2
(*Continued*)

determine what issues may be barriers to a more satis-fying sexual relationship. Through evaluation of their responses, women are able to focus on sexual issues they would like to address personally and in their inti-mate relationships. This information is valuable to survivors and to sexuality counselors who use the responses as a tool for assessing and treating women's sexual problems (Maltz, 2001).

As an adjunct to the sexual effects inventory, the following questions can be used by sexuality coun-selors to assess some of the concerns of individuals and their partners who have been affected by rape:

1. Whom have you told or who knows about the rape?
2. Who has been supportive to you since you dis-cussed the rape?
3. How has the incident impacted your feelings about yourself and your relationship?
4. How has the incident impacted your daily life?
5. How has the incident affected your sexual rela-tionship?
6. Since the occurrence of the rape, how do you create safety in your world?
7. What is your involvement with the legal process and how do you view law enforcement and social agencies? Has this incident impacted your view of law enforcement and other agencies?
8. Do you have physical symptoms resulting from being raped?
9. Have you had a medical examination?

Once the immediate issues are discerned through a series of questions, sexuality counselors can begin to examine the effects of the rape and can determine the extent of relational or sexual problems.

The Development of Sexual and Relational Problems

The effects of rape on survivors and their partners of-ten leads to the development of sexual and relational problems. Although there are commonalities between rape survivors, no two individuals experience the event in the same way or with the same degree of severity. Reactions that may occur immediately follow-ing the event include emotional blunting or numbness, disorientation, denial, loneliness and isolation, disbe-lief, and feelings of vulnerability. Somatic symptoms such as headaches, dizziness, fatigue, and sleep dis-turbances may also ensue (Calhoun & Wilson, 2000). These reactions may precede feelings of intense fear and anger as well as shame and guilt. After a period of

time long-term consequences may be evident. These include depression, fear and anxiety, low self-esteem, and sexual dysfunction. Posttraumatic stress disorder (PTSD) is not an uncommon occurrence and is char-acterized by nightmares, intrusive thoughts, irritability, and emotional distancing or avoiding partners, friends, family and co-workers (Calhoun & Wilson, 2000). Partners of women who have been raped may also ex-perience feelings of intense anger and guilt for not pro-tecting their partner, and they may blame their partner for not protecting herself. They may also experience intrusive thoughts, emotional distancing, and fears that the relationship will never recover.

When a woman is raped, she is confronted with an event for which she has no schema or which is incon-sistent with preexisting schemas. For example, if she believes that "bad things can never happen to careful people" she must either confront what has occurred or change her belief system. The world can become a scary place if she must adopt a worldview that includes negative events. Often, in an effort to deny the reality of a negative situation, she blames herself, thus keep-ing her positive worldview intact. Many survivors lament, "if only I had fought back," or "if I had just been smarter," or "if only I had screamed louder." These types of statements are self-defeating and unrealistic because women typically cannot outrun or outthink an assailant who has planned an assault. If a woman ac-cepts the notion that she is vulnerable to "bad events and people's bad behaviors," she must also accept her own vulnerability and competence to handle danger and may begin to experience fear and apprehension during many of her daily activities. Her belief system may change as dramatically as she starts thinking "no one can be trusted," "I will not allow myself to be vul-nerable," or "all men are not to be trusted and can be dangerous." These beliefs impact women's sexual and intimate relationships even in situations that have been positive prior to the rape. Often, lack of trust or an abil-ity to be intimate and vulnerable with a partner is an is-sue that brings couples to sexuality counseling (Briere, 1996; Calhoun & Wilson, 2000; Courtois, 1988).

The Development of Sexual Problems

Sexual problems and dysfunctions are among the most common responses to rape. Following a rape, women usually avoid all sexual contact for a period of time, ranging from a few weeks to several months. Partners may demonstrate concern and understanding during this initial stage of sexual avoidance. However, continued sexual avoidance with neither partner initiating or communicating about sexual desire frequently leads to anger, frustration, and resentment by one or both partners.

In contrast, partners may attempt to initiate sexual activity very soon after rape has occurred in order to negate the horrible memory of the incident. In these instances, they believe that they can replace the unpleasant memory with a pleasant one and that they can reconfirm their love of their partner or their femininity through sexual relations. In such circumstances, survivors are rarely able to accomplish their goal. In fact, they experience guilt, fear, or anger and they are less caring, and loving with their partners.

At this point partners may engage in a process called "spectatoring"—observing each other's responses and checking to see if the other is okay. Both partners may be anxious and tentative and may avoid certain sexual behaviors because of a concern that the behav-

ior is a reminder of the rape. This pattern of fear, anxiety, anger, resentment, self-observance, and spectatoring often leads to the development of many male or female sexual dysfunctions, although female dysfunctions are more common. For many survivors of rape, there is an awareness of sex that includes exploitation and trauma. This awareness often leads to women's increased vulnerability and fear of intimacy in their sexual relationships. Fear may lead not only to sexual dysfunction and powerful dissociative states during sexual contact but also to a general distrust of sexual partners and of men in general (Briere, 1996; Courtois, 1988).

It is important to continually assess a survivor's emotional reactions and mental status in order to differentiate between these normal reactions to trauma and more severe reactions such as acute stress disorder (ASD) and posttraumatic stress disorder (PTSD) (APA, 2000). The *DSM-IV-TR* diagnostic criteria for these disorders are presented in Figures 13.3 and 13.4. These

A. The person has been exposed to a traumatic event in which both of the following were present:
   (1) the person experienced, witnessed, or was confronted with an event or events that involved actual or threatened death or serious injury, or a threat to the physical integrity of self or others
   (2) the person's response involved intense fear, helplessness, or horror

B. Either while experiencing or after experiencing the distressing event, the individual has three (or more) of the following dissociative symptoms:
   (1) a subjective sense of numbing, detachment, or absence of emotional responsiveness
   (2) a reduction in awareness of his or her surroundings (e.g., "being in a daze")
   (3) derealization
   (4) depersonalization
   (5) dissociative amnesia (i.e., inability to recall an important aspect of the trauma)

C. The traumatic event is persistently reexperienced in at least one of the following ways: recurrent images, thoughts, dreams, illusions, flashback episodes, or a sense of

reliving the experience; or distress on exposure to reminders of the traumatic event.

D. Marked avoidance of stimuli that arouse recollections of the trauma (e.g., thoughts, feelings, conversations, activities, places, people).

E. Marked symptoms of anxiety or increased arousal (e.g., difficulty sleeping, irritability, poor concentration, hypervigilance, exaggerated startle response, motor restlessness).

F. The disturbance causes clinically significant distress or impairment in social, occupational, or other important areas of functioning or impairs the individual's ability to pursue some necessary task, such as obtaining necessary assistance or mobilizing personal resources by telling family members about the traumatic experience.

G. The disturbance lasts for a minimum of 2 days and a maximum of 4 weeks and occurs within 4 weeks of the traumatic event.

H. The disturbance is not due to the direct physiological effects of a substance (e.g., a drug of abuse, a medication) or a general medical condition, is not better accounted for by Brief Psychotic Disorder, and is not merely an exacerbation of a preexisting Axis I or Axis II disorder.

FIGURE 13.3

Diagnostic Criteria for 308.3 Acute Stress Disorder

Source: Reprinted with permission from the *Diagnostic and Statistical Manual of Mental Disorders,* Text Revision (pp. 471–472), Copyright 2000, American Psychiatric Association.

A. The person has been exposed to a traumatic event in which both of the following were present:
  (1) the person experienced, witnessed, or was confronted with an event or events that involved actual or threatened death or serious injury, or a threat to the physical integrity of self or others
  (2) the person's response involved intense fear, helplessness, or horror. **Note:** In children, this may be expressed instead by disorganized or agitated behavior.

B. The traumatic event is persistently reexperienced in one (or more) of the following ways:
  (1) recurrent and intrusive distressing recollections of the event, including images, thoughts, or perceptions. **Note:** In young children, repetitive play may occur in which themes or aspects of the trauma are expressed.
  (2) recurrent distressing dreams of the event. **Note:** In children, there may be frightening dreams without recognizable content.
  (3) acting or feeling as if the traumatic event were recurring (includes a sense of reliving the experience, illusions, hallucinations, and dissociative flashback episodes, including those that occur on awakening or when intoxicated). **Note:** In young children, trauma-specific reenactment may occur.
  (4) intense psychological distress at exposure to internal or external cues that symbolize or resemble an aspect of the traumatic event
  (5) physiological reactivity on exposure to internal or external cues that symbolize or resemble an aspect of the traumatic event

C. Persistent avoidance of stimuli associated with the trauma and numbing of general responsiveness

(not present before the trauma), as indicated by three (or more) of the following:
  (1) efforts to avoid thoughts, feelings, or conversations associated with the trauma
  (2) efforts to avoid activities, places, or people that arouse recollections of the trauma
  (3) inability to recall an important aspect of the trauma
  (4) markedly diminished interest or participation in significant activities
  (5) feeling of detachment or estrangement from others
  (6) restricted range of affect (e.g., unable to have loving feelings)
  (7) sense of a foreshortened future (e.g., does not expect to have a career, marriage, children, or a normal life span)

D. Persistent symptoms of increased arousal (not present before the trauma), as indicated by two (or more) of the following:
  (1) difficulty falling or staying asleep
  (2) irritability or outbursts of anger
  (3) difficulty concentrating
  (4) hypervigilance
  (5) exaggerated startle response

E. Duration of the disturbance (symptoms in Criteria B, C, and D) is more than 1 month.

F. The disturbance causes clinically significant distress or impairment in social, occupational, or other important areas of functioning.

Specify if:
Acute: if duration of symptoms is less than 3 months
Chronic: if duration of symptoms is 3 months or more

Specify if:
With Delayed Onset: if onset of symptoms is at least 6 months after the stressor

FIGURE 13.4
Diagnostic Criteria for 309.81 Posttraumatic Stress Disorder
Source: Reprinted with permission from the *Diagnostic and Statistical Manual of Mental Disorders,* Text Revision (pp. 467–468), Copyright 2000, American Psychiatric Association.

diagnoses may coexist with normal reactions to trauma exacerbating the development of sexual problems.

Ballard and Alessi (2002) describe the most severe reactions based on descriptions found in the *DSM-IV-TR:*

The symptoms of both ASD and PTSD are nearly identical, each being characterized by reexperiencing, avoidance, and increased arousal. The salient difference between the two disorders is the time of onset

and duration of symptoms. In order to confirm a diagnosis of ASD, the disturbance must occur within four weeks of the traumatic event. Conversely, PTSD symptoms must be present for more than one month, precluding this diagnosis until more than four weeks have passed following the trauma. (p. 312)

Acute Stress Disorder. The *DSM-IV-TR* describes acute stress disorder as reactions that occur when a person has been exposed to a traumatic event in which they experienced or were confronted with an event that involved threatened death or serious bodily harm (APA, 2000). Reactions to the event usually involve degrees of anxiety, fear, helplessness, or horror. According to the *DSM-IV-TR* a diagnosis of acute stress disorder can be made when the individual exhibits at least three of the following symptoms: "a subjective sense of numbing, detachment, or absence of emotional responsiveness; a reduction in awareness of his or her surroundings; derealization; depersonalization; or dissociative amnesia" (APA, 2000, pp. 471–472). These symptoms typically occur within 1 month after the event and according to the *DSM-IV-TR* involve persistent reexperiencing of the event by either recurrent "images, thoughts, dreams, illusions, flashback episodes, a sense of reliving the event, or distress on exposure to reminders of the event" (APA, 2000, p. 469). ASD has similar features to PTSD, the difference being that PTSD occurs over a longer period of time.

Posttraumatic Stress Disorder. Posttraumatic stress disorder (PTSD) as described by the *DSM-IV-TR* occurs following a trauma that involves threatened death or bodily harm. Like ASD, reactions include anxiety, fear, helplessness, and horror or may produce recurrent memories related to the event. These memories may occur immediately afterward or may be experienced as a delayed reaction to an event. This reaction is often referred to as a "flashback." In other words, the event is reexperienced through intrusive thoughts, perceptions, or dreams associated with the event or persistent feelings of anxiety that the event is recurring. Individuals who experience PTSD often avoid situations associated with the traumatic event and experience distress that includes disrupted sleep patterns, irritability, outbursts of anger, difficulty concentrating, exaggerated startle response or stress or impairment in social, occupational, or other important areas of functioning.

Once individuals feel overwhelmed by intrusions of the traumatic event, they begin to organize their lives around avoidance of reminders of the trauma and begin to view their world as an unmanageable place (Van Der Kolk, McFarlane, & Van Der Hart, 1996). These symptoms of PTSD are consistent with the experiences of many rape survivors, but they do not include various symptoms of sexual dysfunction that may occur. Desire disorders, arousal disorders, and orgasmic disorders are the most common symptoms and sexual disturbances found in most sexual assault survivors (Barnes, 1995). Distrust of others, poor self-concept, and other fears and phobias associated with terror and dissociation as well as "emotional blunting, loss of emotional and physical feeling, psychological and physical pain" (Talmadge & Wallace, 1991, p. 168) often accompany post–sexual assault difficulties. Talmadge and Wallace propose that these sexual difficulties are typically exacerbated by survivors' coping mechanisms that may include repression of emotions or dissociation from sexual interactions.

SEXUAL DISORDERS RELATED TO PTSD

Sexual adjustment and sexual satisfaction are two aspects of sexual life that are affected by rape. In fact, a significant number of survivors report fear of pain, loss of desire, thoughts of promiscuity, and confusion about sexual orientation based on their experiences of sexual assault. Women often report either a compulsive need for sex or abstention from sex and an inability to relax and enjoy themselves and their partners. They also seem to experience more sexual anxiety and guilt about participating in and enjoying sex.

Desire disorders are common problems for survivors of rape. One reason cited is an attempt to address unresolved issues of fear, vulnerability, and shame by denying one's sexuality (Barnes, 1995). However, Barnes cautions that partners tend to respond differently as they react to rape. For example, one partner might want to have sex often, as a way of "washing away" the experience of rape. Another partner might, as a result of the same experience, be disgusted with sex and view it as a "dirty" experience. In these situations couples maintain distance from each other and experience confusion about their sexual relationship and the role of the rape in their relationship. The more intensely one partner initiates sexual relations, the more the other resists it. They are maintaining the sexual problem based on their relational responses to each other and to the rape.

Arousal disorders are common reactions to rape trauma and are typically manifested by erectile difficulties in men and by lubrication difficulties in women. They may be physically or emotionally based, or both, and must be examined early in counseling prior to creating an effective treatment plan.

Orgasmic disorders are the most prevalent manifestations for rape survivors. Common symptoms include coital pain, dyspareunia, and vaginismus (Barnes, 1995; Sprei & Courtois, 1988).

DIAGNOSIS OF PTSD AND COUPLE FUNCTIONING

The relationship between a diagnosis of PTSD and relationship functioning cannot be ignored when assessing couples' sexual problems. Most couples experience some degree of conflict, anger, and fear as well as a desire to avoid threatening activities (Barnes, 1995). Many survivors report that their relationships with their partners are "superficial, empty, conflictual, or sexualized" (Sprei & Courtois, 1988, p. 276) In addition, feelings of distrust, guilt, and shame are not uncommon reactions to rape. Many times survivors experience negative feelings toward men and, consequently, their relationships are highly conflicted. In these cases, sexual issues and relationship issues emerge at the same time, resulting in further stress on survivors and their partners.

The Development of Relational Problems

Sexual dysfunction and sexual problems often do not initially emerge in couples' counseling because sexuality counselors are hesitant to address such intimate and private issues until couples express readiness to do so. Clients may have experienced a sexual trauma in the past but counselors are unsure about how much or when to confront the issue. Initially, survivors may not want to identify sexual issues as the presenting problem because the issues are associated with shame, guilt, and self-blame. Consequently, they may work on "safer topics" relating to their relationship. However, relationship issues, developmental concerns, and medical concerns mask serious concerns about sexual dysfunction or dissatisfaction (Barnes, 1995).

INTERVENTION STRATEGIES FOR SURVIVORS OF RAPE AND THEIR PARTNERS

A broad range of interventions, including pharmacological treatment and cognitive and behavioral interventions along with specific suggestions on how to talk with couples about their sexual issues, are discussed below. Box 13.1 provides additional suggestions.

Pharmacological Treatment for Survivors

The U.S. Food and Drug Administration (FDA) has approved the use of sertraline hydrochloride (Zoloft) for the treatment of posttraumatic stress disorder. Before this approval, Zoloft had been prescribed to treat depression, panic disorder, and obsessive-compulsive disorder (Nordenberg, 2000). Studies indicate positive effects for female patients, but not for males who experience the same trauma. Although Zoloft has been recommended by the FDA, there are other drugs that may be prescribed by physicians to accompany psychological treatment for survivors. These include some drugs in the same class as Zoloft, such as Paxil (paroxetine), Prozac (fluoxetine), Luvox (fluvoxamine), and Celexa (citalopram). Based on each individual's medical circumstances, other types of antidepressants or antianxiety medications may be used (Nordenberg, 2000). Sexuality counselors should determine if their clients are using any type of medication before proceeding with therapeutic treatment. A combination of psychotherapy and medication can often influence clients' success most efficiently and effectively.

Restructuring Thoughts

Restructuring thoughts help survivors and their partners begin to view themselves as survivors, rather than victims, of rape. Restructuring thoughts focus on a positive view of sexuality by helping survivors accept the reality that the event did occur and by helping them accept responsibility about how they will choose to express their sexuality. For partners, a similar process of cognitive restructuring must occur in relation to a survivors' reluctant sexual behavior, distrust, and lack of intimacy (Barnes, 1995).

Restructuring Behaviors

The goal of behavioral reconstruction is to restore a sense of well-being and sexual comfort, and restore feelings of personal power to control their sexual expressions in the future (McCarthy, 1986). In order to become intimately reconnected, survivors and their partners create experiences in risking and learning to trust in relationships. Usually, this process begins with behavioral exercises designed to increase

---

BOX 13.1
Interventions at a Glance

- Use reflective listening skills to demonstrate empathy and respect for the survivor as she tells her story.
- Address feelings of fear, betrayal, and guilt that she may feel.
- Coordinate with the legal system and law enforcement when necessary.
- Use crises intervention strategies that help your client feel safe:
    1. Recognize each situation as unique.
    2. Assess yourself as the sexuality counselor to make certain you remain objective.
    3. Show regard for your client's safety.
    4. Provide support and help develop a support system.
    5. Utilize client's coping strengths to help her get through the trauma and reduce stress.
    6. Attend to client's immediate needs to help her make a plan immediately following the counseling session.
    7. Assess for suicidal tendencies.
    8. Use referral resources.
    9. Help client commit to make it through her trauma and conquer the problem.
- Use a variety of relaxation strategies to help soothe client's fears. Deep-breathing activities and yoga may help clients feel more in control of themselves and their bodies.
- Help couple address fear of sexual expression and articulate what they are willing to do to meet each other's needs.
- Help survivor develop a safety plan with her partner.
- Help survivor develop trust of self and partner.
- Refer survivor for medical treatment.
- Help couple arrange for intimate time together. Identify what they are comfortable doing at the present. It may be taking walks, having quiet conversations, sexual touching or play, or initiating time away together.
- Teach survivor to conquer some flashbacks by the use of imagery techniques.
- Suggest the use of a personal journal in which to describe feelings and thoughts.

---

emotional contact and provide nondemanding sexual expression. Holding hands, taking a walk while holding hands, or massage are examples of activities couples can initiate early in treatment. Gradually, exercises become more intense sexually as partners become more comfortable. Sexuality counselors must be cautious about moving at a safe pace when treating couples at such a vulnerable stage in their relationship.

Identifying and Exploring Feelings

Addressing Guilt

A rape survivor's feelings of guilt are often as difficult to address in counseling as are the physical and legal problems. Many survivors blame themselves for having been raped, either for leading on their perpetrators or for not fighting harder to prevent the rape. No matter how strongly sexuality counselors stress that rape is not the survivor's fault, it is important to let a client express those feelings and then try to define in precise terms what she might have done differently. Survivors may need to talk about the incident a number of times before they are willing to consider possibilities that it was not their fault, that they were powerless over a rapist who had planned the assault, and that the rapist utilized an element of surprise in the attack. It may be true that a better safety plan could have been in place but that does not imply responsibility for the rape.

It is also important for sexuality counselors to ask survivors to identify friends or relatives who will support them. Building a support system is a critical part of self-care in the aftermath of rape and helps them feel emotionally safe during the healing process.

Addressing Fear

Fear is a very common reaction to rape. It is often quite rational because the rapist has threatened to kill the survivor. It is important to help survivors express and specify their fears. Sexuality counselors encourage clients to list all the things they can do to protect themselves, including actions that are unacceptable to them. These ideas range from triple-locking all doors and windows to never going out at night. They may determine that they will not walk on the same street where the rape occurred or more drastically, they will not go to work, the grocery store, or walk their children to school. All of these fears and beliefs must be expressed before survivors can make a plan and act upon their self-protective ideas. In addition, they may need to take specific actions: call a locksmith to change their locks, ask a friend or family member to stay with them for a while, or enlist neighborhood-watch help. In some instances they may decide to ask a coworker to travel to and from work with them, or ask a friend to shop with them until they feel safe. A survivor advocate may be helpful to them in order to assist with some of these choices.

The more steps survivors are able to take to empower themselves, the better they will respond as each independent action adds to their sense of well-being.

Decision Making Regarding Law Enforcement

Keep in mind that only a rape survivor lives with the guilt or fear that may be the result of deciding not to report the rape to the police. Sexuality counselors cannot make decisions for their clients, but they can provide them with information that will help them make a decision and then support them to follow through on their actions.

Sexuality counselors explain what is likely to happen in the legal system, given the particular circumstances of the rape. However, it is necessary that they point out that there are few guarantees. Although they can hypothesize about a survivor's chance in court and of the rapist being convicted, no one can be certain of the outcome.

For this reason, it is important for survivors to evaluate the support they might expect from their social environment (friends, family, co-workers), how prone they are to feelings of guilt, anxiety, anger, or fear, how stable their self-esteem is and how they will withstand pressure if they are required to testify in court and face their perpetrator.

Thinking About Coping Skills

One strategy that helps clients focus on their personal strengths is to have them make a list of coping skills they employ when faced with traumatic experiences. Then, together with their counselors, they examine the list they have created. It is important to explore the items on the list by asking open-ended questions because survivors are able to identify their skills and positive assets they have employed and generalize them to future situations. Rosenbloom and Williams (1999) suggest these questions:*

1. How does this coping strategy work?
2. If it works, does it have negative parts? What are the costs for this strategy? Are there less costly alternatives?
3. In which situations does the strategy work best?
4. What alternatives might we try to utilize to deal with the stress of the trauma?
5. How can we help each other try a new way of behaving or thinking about the situation?

Creating Safety in the Outside World

Couples can learn to reduce risk in the outside world through the use of a safety plan. They begin by identifying ways they can protect themselves, such as taking a new route home, meeting each other before going home, talking about fears, or identifying a safe place at home just to "be." Survivors can also describe activities that provide feelings of safety and reduce tension, such as physical sports, art projects, listening to music, or visiting friends or family (Rosenbloom & Williams, 1999). All of these activities help create a safer environment both emotionally and physically.

Learning Self-Regulation Skills

Self-regulation skills help survivors accept and control feelings or behaviors that have led them to

---

*From *Life After Trauma* (p. 41), by D. Rosenbloom and M. B. Williams, 1999. New York: Guilford Press. Adapted with permission.

avoid or dissociate from traumatic experiences in the past.

Vermilyea (2000) suggests four steps to assist counselors with offering survivors activities for self-regulation:*

1. *Experience:* Notice all of your feelings and observe them without judging them.
2. *Express:* Say something; tell yourself what you are noticing, write or draw your feelings, talk to a supportive person.
3. *Contain:* Postpone dealing with the overwhelming part of what you are experiencing, hold only what you can stand for a length of time, then put it aside; these will be stored in your pre-conscious rather than your conscious.
4. *Retrieve:* Later bring back a small part of what was stored and experienced and express only that part.

Maintaining Interpersonal Boundaries

Interpersonal boundaries help us know where we "end" and others "begin." Such boundaries give us the freedom to permit others to enter personal space (Rosenbloom & Williams, 1999). After experiencing sexual trauma, survivors may feel a loss of power or control over their boundaries and have fears that the incident could happen again. Survivors must thus learn to create new boundaries in order to feel safe as they continue to interact in their daily worlds. Withdrawal from daily life can interfere with addressing the issues necessary to rebuild trust and intimacy.

In order to establish appropriate boundaries, survivors must first recognize how it feels when a boundary has been crossed. They must then try out behaviors in order to reestablish what does feel comfortable to them. They may practice boundary maintenance by identifying situations that feel uncomfortable and then ask themselves relevant questions:

Would I like to respond differently? How will I respond?

Who can help me with this new response?

How will I address those who may not like my new response?

Feelings that occur when boundaries are protected as well as when they have been violated are explored. Positive feelings are linked to success

when boundaries are protected, while negative feelings that occur when personal space is violated are identified. Couples can practice setting boundaries by role-playing scenarios until they become more comfortable.

Building Trust

After trust has been violated by a traumatic event, it can be difficult to rebuild. Trauma disrupts a sense of trust in oneself as well as in others, which causes survivors to question their decisions and reactions to situations (Rosenbloom & Williams, 1999).

Building trust requires that a survivor learns to believe what people say and to open up again little by little. Because trust has been shattered, the decision to trust is based in part by examining the following questions:

How badly do I want to trust again?

What are the consequences if my trust in a person fails?

What are my past experiences in making decisions to trust people?

What have I learned about trust from my experience of being raped?

Do I feel safe to trust? Can I trust an individual or do I need to have others around for me to feel safe?

Survivors must first identify the people they trust. They can then review each individual's personal traits regarding trustworthiness. What is it that makes a person trustworthy? Which characteristics might be important in others when trust is attempted? Can those trusted people become a support system? Survivors and their partners identify areas in their relationship where trust is intact, and then determine where trust is damaged or does not exist. Finally, decisions about building and maintaining trusting relationships are made.

Feeling Positive About Self

Trauma can devastate self-esteem and affect how positively survivors feel about themselves and about others. When self-esteem has been shaken, it is important for survivors to take stock of themselves in order to determine how to best reestablish their confidence. Sexuality counselors help survivors describe themselves as complex and multifaceted people with many attributes, strengths, limitations, and gifts. Rosenbloom and

---

*From *Growing Beyond Survival* (pp. 28–29), by E. Vermilyea, 2000. Baltimore: Sidran Press. Reprinted with permission.

Williams (1999) suggest the following series of open-ended questions to help survivors:*

> What are the qualities you most like about yourself?
>
> How do you express your feelings?
>
> How do you take care of yourself emotionally?
>
> What activities do you enjoy doing for yourself?
>
> What types of activities do you enjoy having others do for you?
>
> What do you enjoy doing for others?
>
> What physical attributes do you feel good about?
>
> What aspects of your body's physical appearance do you like?
>
> In what ways do you take care of your body?
>
> How do you pleasure your body?

Exploring Intimacy

Sexuality counselors can help survivors relearn the important task of exploring intimacy. This includes paying attention to thoughts, feelings, behaviors, and beliefs—the first step for building intimacy with others. Rosenbloom and Williams (1999) suggest that sexuality counselors ask survivors and their partners to consider the following activities:†

> Writing in a journal
>
> Talking to someone who has had a similar experience
>
> Reading books about similar experiences
>
> Paying attention to feelings
>
> Listening to ideas without judging them
>
> Slowing down life in order to notice feelings
>
> Checking out physical reactions to feelings
>
> Making plans to allow time to relax (bath, walk, meditate, read, poetry)
>
> Spending time with friends
>
> Using touch with others appropriately, e.g., asking for a hug

Keeping a constant check on levels of intimacy will facilitate self-care and make it more difficult to revert back to negative recollections of being victimized.

---

*From *Life After Trauma* (pp. 238–238), by D. Rosenbloom and M. B. Williams, 1999. New York: Guilford Press. Adapted with permission.

†From *Life After Trauma* (p. 278), by D. Rosenbloom and M. B. Williams, 1999. New York: Guilford Press. Adapted with permission.

Relaxation Techniques

Relaxation techniques are useful to relieve stress and tension. Vermilyea (2000) offers the following activities for survivors to practice in order to feel less stressed:

1. Deep breathing exercises
2. Yoga or other low impact stretching
3. Therapeutic massage
4. Reading
5. Music
6. Warm shower or bubble bath
7. Movie (comedy)
8. Talk to a friend
9. Hobbies or sports
10. Laughter

These techniques can help reduce tension and can also increase energy to focus on other important areas in life. The goal is not to achieve total relaxation, rather, it is increased relaxation.

Journal Writing

Survivors can use journal writing to reflect on how they are feeling about themselves and others. As they write about current experiences, they may be able to determine connections with past as well as present events. Journal writing will not be useful during times when stress response reactions are high. If a journal is used to graphically describe the traumatic experience over and over, the survivor can become revictimized through feelings of helplessness and vulnerability (Vermilyea, 2000).

Imagery Techniques

Sometimes traumatic events emerge through unconscious images and through frightening thoughts called "flashbacks." Survivors can train their minds to fight these thoughts through the use of imagery techniques—a process that uses imagination to create scenarios that change negative thoughts or feelings into more positive ones. This strategy is used to help survivors to feel more calm and in control, to solve problems, and to visualize goals and possibilities for the future (Vermilyea, 2000).

A sexuality counselor might suggest the following activity to a survivor: "Imagine that you are in a safe place that comforts you, in safe surroundings. Close your eyes. Imagine yourself on the beach with the warm sand in your toes as you stroll along with someone you love. Touch the water with your toes and taste the salt air. Smell the fresh scent of the seaweed that has washed to shore. You can hear the gentle rolling of the waves. You can see a dolphin playing in the distance and the beginnings of a sunset. The sky is washed in hues of pink, blue, purple, and orange, as the sun appears to move across the sky. Appreciate the love you feel and the beauty of the setting you have created. Feel the support of the person who is walking beside you. Open your eyes and reflect on your images. How do you feel? What can you do to recall that feeling?"

Imagery techniques can thus help survivors train their minds to focus on a positive, safe place, rather than a scary or dangerous one, and to remain physically safe as well (Rosenbloom and Williams, 1999).

Eye Movement Desensitization and Reprocessing

Eye movement desensitization and reprocessing (EMDR) involves the use of rapid eye movements to eliminate painful memories. The technique takes the "emotional charge off a traumatic event from the past; also, the meaning of that earlier event changes, leading to new self-concepts and behaviors" (Quinn, n.d., p. 1). The sexuality counselor instructs the individual to "maintain an image of the original traumatic experience, and . . . simultaneously evoke the event and associated feelings while engaging in the eye movements" (Van Der Kolk, McFarlane, & Van Der Hart, 1996, p. 435). Because the recall of trauma occurs in the right hemisphere of the brain, talk therapy cannot adequately address the pain. EMDR can help individuals and their partners let go of the pain and begin to live life again without the negative memories or trepidation when placed in other uncomfortable situations that recall the original trauma. Specific training is required to use this treatment. Further information is available on the Internet at http://www.emdr.org.il/dls/1.html

Psychodrama

Psychodrama is a type of therapy that emphasizes enactment of situations past and present in order to help people gain insight and view a situation differently. Hudgins and Drucker (1998) suggest using the containing double, a technique that addresses the somatosensory, emotional, and cognitive aspects of the traumatic event. The containing double is a flexible psychological holding space where the counselor assumes the role of an inner voice that supports and reflects the survivor's strengths regardless of the degree of trauma experienced. The role is one of unconditional support that gently guides the survivor through the intense emotional flashback of the trauma. The counselor makes statements that mirror what the survivor may be feeling, such as "I am really terrified right now" or "I feel myself going back in time to that scary place." After the reflective statement, the containing double makes a containing statement that frames the feelings as manageable and then makes a statement that directs the survivor to the present where together the counselor and survivor (and partner if available) can make sense of the experience and process all the senses experienced in the here and now (Hudgins & Drucker, 1998). The role of the containing double can be taught to the survivor's partner in counseling sessions through the use of role reversal. This technique can be helpful because it promotes the partner's understanding of what the survivor is feeling.

Movement Expression: Dance, Martial Arts, and Theater

Sexuality counselors can suggest classes in all forms of movement expression—from dance and martial arts to participation in theater groups. These experiences should be processed in counseling in order to emphasize the personal power and related feelings that the survivor may experience. Martial arts classes also focus on learning self-protection skills that will make survivors feel safer in their various daily environments.

The use of meaningful physical experiences with survivors helps them process negative experiences in ways that promote "attention to the survivor's moods, physical sensations, and physical impulses within" (Wylie, 1998). Discovering positive experiences increases feelings of personal power and safety and provides an outlet for tension and stress (Centrum '45, n.d.). It also facilitates the integration of emotional, cognitive, and behavioral aspects of human experiences.

Music Therapy

Music therapy can be used as an adjunct to counseling sessions—for example, through participation in a musical group or choir—or it can actually be practiced and processed in counseling sessions. "Specific musical elements such as tempo, measure, rhythm, harmony, form, dynamics and sound color, are used for directed therapeutic interventions" (Centrum '45, n.d., p. 1). Music can help reduce tension, fear, and anxiety, and it can process and express emotions while promoting focus on the present and restoring self-confidence.

Art Therapy

Art therapy helps survivors express and explore feelings, thoughts, and behaviors through the use of artistic media. Drawing, painting, sculpting, modeling, and photography as well as quilting and other crafts are art forms that can be used to describe pain, joy, hopefulness, fear, and other emotions associated with the journey that survivors make as they attempt to move forward from a traumatic event. Art classes can help foster a supportive group experience in which the survivor is able to freely express emotions through artistic endeavors. Various types of art media can also be used in counseling sessions so that the survivor can process the emotional experience with immediate feedback from the counselor.

Case Example

Marnee, aged 33, was raped six months ago while walking home from work. She did not initially report the incident to the police, and in fact did not tell her partner until several days later. Since the time of the rape, Marnee has felt ashamed and does not want to admit that she knew her rapist. Her partner, Claudio, wants to go after the man but has been warned by the police to stay away from him and to let them do their jobs. At first, Marnee initiated sexual intercourse with Claudio and claimed that she wanted to rid herself of the bad memories and of the rapist's touch. Recently, however, she has not wanted to engage in sexual activity and has made excuses to avoid all sexual contact with Claudio. Initially, Claudio blamed Marnee for not being careful walking home at night and quizzed her about what she might have done to contribute to the situation by giving the man mixed messages. At this point, he is upset that Marnee refuses his sexual advances and wonders if she is no longer attracted to him. They come to sexuality counseling to work on the miscommunication in their relationship and to address their problems with intimacy and closeness. Claudio has threatened to "go out and have an affair with someone who is interested in him" if Marnee no longer finds him desirable.

Stage 1: Assessing and Obtaining an Interactional View of the Problem
Marnee and Claudio each have a different perspective on what is happening in their relationship. Claudio offers that he is frustrated that Marnee does not seem to want to be close to him in any way. He states that she is unwilling to engage in sexual activities and that she does not want to be close in any way—by talking, holding hands, or even snuggling on the sofa together while they watch television. Marnee, on the other hand, admits that she is angry with Claudio for initially blaming her in part for the rape. She reports that she just does not seem to have any sexual feelings and prefers not to be touched. She also acknowledges that she is less available to have long talks with Claudio as they used to do.

After taking a thorough sex history and constructing a sexual genogram, the sexuality counselor is able to offer a hypothesis. They both have survived a traumatic incident and have been unable to process that incident together and talk about what may need to be different in their relationship as a result. The counselor also explains that a lack of sexual desire is a common reaction to sexual assault and is not directed at Claudio to punish him. An interactive view of the problem is then offered to Marnee and Claudio by the sexuality counselor. "You have been unable to process the rape together and are motivated to do so. You would like to regain the closeness you once shared but have been pushing each other away because of your hurt and anger."

Stage 2: Goal Setting
Marnee and Claudio, with the sexuality counselor, construct the following behavioral and affective goals:

1. We will process the rape with each other and with our counselor so that we can understand it from each other's perspective and then move beyond (behavior) so that we can feel motivated (affect) to continue our relationship together.

2. We will begin to go out and have fun to-gether on weekends and spend time at home talking and enjoying each other's company (behavior) at least twice each week. These activities will help us feel re-connected to each other and will help to reestablish closeness (affect).

3. We will slowly engage in nonsexual touching (holding hands, massage, etc.) and when we are comfortable, we will begin to resume sexual activity. Marnee will serve as the guide in order to pace our intimate relationship (behavior). We want to feel united (affect) in our efforts to integrate the experience we had and go on with our lives.

Stage 3: Adopting New Perceptions and Behaviors

Marnee and Claudio work with their sexuality counselor to access their strengths in order to solve the problems they face. Marnee prides herself on her communication skills at work and realizes that she will have to initiate more con-versation with Claudio about her feelings and her hopes for their future. Claudio has been the creative one in their relationship and he will meet the challenge of finding new activities they can share during their couple time. He also commits to help Marnee with her fears and apologizes for his role in doubting her. Together they know that they will have to work slowly on rebuilding their sexual relationship, and understand that they must create a team effort in order to conquer the fears and trepidation Marnee experiences.

Stage 4: Maintaining New Perceptions and Behaviors

Both Marnee and Claudio acknowledge that they have worked hard to reestablish their relationship and know how easily they could slip into "old patterns." They have demonstrated their commitment to each other and to their counseling. The process thus far has required many months of intense work on their relation-ship and they know that they must constantly guard against relapse. They learn to be alert to triggers that may thwart their healthy cycle. They identify behaviors and feelings that can serve as signals that they must talk to each other, or return to counseling for a "tune up." Failure to initiate their dates together, lack of time to communicate and just be together at home, lack of sexual desire by either partner, dissociation by Marnee during lovemaking, or feelings by Claudio that he wants to explore sexual options outside the relationship are all signs that they must reassess their commitment to their relationship.

Stage 5: Validating New Perceptions and Behaviors

Both Marnee and Claudio are pleased with their ability to join forces against the trauma of rape and together fight to keep their relation-ship intact. They are confident that they can overcome any obstacles they may face and look back on their counseling as a positive step they made for each other and for their re-lationship. They are able to compliment each other on the hard work and want to celebrate their success periodically by taking some holi-day time together, perhaps a second honey-moon. Marnee offers that she thinks she is ready to consider having a family. Claudio is pleased, but proceeds slowly to ensure that Marnee is comfortable with this decision. They want to continue their new skills on a daily ba-sis but plan to return to counseling periodically for a "check up."

SUMMARY

Rape is a form of sexual assault that is underre-ported and can be defined as coerced sexual inter-course resulting from actual or threatened force. It is a traumatic event that often prevents survivors from progressing satisfactorily in their intimate re-lationships. Couples affected by rape may experi-ence sexual dysfunction or problems, and other re-lational concerns that suggest the need for sexual-ity counseling. Sexuality counselors help couples cope more effectively with the emotional, sexual, and relational challenges that occur as a result of rape.

There is a range of reactions to trauma resulting from rape. Some survivors withdraw into silence, some seek support from significant others, and some experience obsessive review—the need to constantly recount the traumatic event. Many are filled with rage and anger at the injustice of the situation or feel a deep sense of helplessness, fear, betrayal, or loss of control.

Physical reactions such as rapid heartbeat, muscle tension, nervousness, or an upset stomach are often experienced as well as cognitive reactions that disrupt the way survivors think about themselves, the world, and others. Emotional reactions include intense fear, emptiness, dullness, horror or dread, sadness, grief, irritability, anger, and depression. Some survivors react by losing or gaining weight, or by becoming withdrawn or isolated from others. Others may become confrontational or aggressive.

More intense reactions such as those associated with acute stress disorder and posttraumatic stress disorder are prevalent. Symptoms such as nightmares, intrusive thoughts, hyperarousal, irritability, emotional distancing, or avoidance of others may emerge.

Sexual problems and dysfunctions are common results of being raped. Desire disorders, arousal disorders, and orgasmic disorders are the most prevalent symptoms of sexual disturbances for survivors. In addition, sexual adjustment and sexual satisfaction are two aspects of sexual life that are also altered.

Survivors do not always present with sexual issues when seeking sexuality counseling. Instead, when they initially seek treatment they are apt to present with issues such as depression, substance abuse, or chronic self-destructiveness. Later, they may present with an array of sexual dysfunctions.

Sexuality counselors can enable survivors to experience growth and resiliency through the use of an integrative couples' model. After clients tell their stories in detail and receive acceptance and support from their partner, the sexuality counselor helps couples to set achievable goals and then to progress to a solution-focused approach for meeting their goals. Survivors integrate the truth of what happened into their personal narratives and then move beyond the incident toward healthier sexual functioning.

COUNSELING SURVIVORS OF CHILDHOOD SEXUAL ABUSE AND THEIR PARTNERS

KEY CONCEPTS

- Childhood sexual abuse and incest are traumatic events that often prevent survivors from achieving satisfying sexual relationships.
- Childhood sexual abuse and incest is a betrayal of intimacy.
- Culture influences the way society views and addresses issues of childhood sexual abuse.
- At times, there are conflicts between the goals and values of the legal process and the therapeutic process when addressing traumatic reactions to childhood sexual abuse.
- Survivors often present in sexuality counseling with issues of guilt, shame, anxiety, trust, and depression.
- Male survivors of childhood sexual abuse experience similar problems as women. However, there are differences in their reactions to these experiences.
- Common sexual problems that may result from childhood sexual abuse and incest are lack of sexual interest, difficulty becoming aroused and feeling sensation, difficulty experiencing orgasm, difficulty averting orgasm, and difficulty with sexual intercourse.
- Relational problems are often aftereffects of childhood sexual abuse.
- An integrative couples' model is a useful framework for counseling survivors of childhood sexual abuse.
- There are a number of intervention strategies used to treat survivors of childhood sexual abuse and their partners. These include addressing guilt, blame and shame, confronting the issue, clarifying responsibility, getting control over self, challenging myths, initiating and declining sex, learning to communicate openly, and creating a safe nest.

Over the last few decades childhood sexual abuse and incest have grown rapidly as mental health concerns. In fact, 28 to 33 percent of women and 12 to 18 percent of men have experienced incidences of sexual abuse during childhood or adolescence (Roland, 2002). Because more men and women are seeking help for sexual concerns related to past sexual abuse, sexuality counselors are required to recognize the effects of childhood abuse and incest on adult survivors and their partners. We focus primarily on adult women because of the higher incidence of women who report sexual abuse. Keep in mind that many incidences of sexual abuse, particularly among males, remain unreported. Although we focus on female survivors, both partners bring their sexual histories to their relationships and issues related to sexual abuse thus impact both of them. Often these issues concern current sexual and relational problems. In this chapter, we describe how sexual and relational problems develop and we outline strategies for treating these issues.

DEFINITION OF CHILDHOOD SEXUAL ABUSE AND INCEST

The term *sexual abuse* as used throughout this chapter incorporates features of the terms *childhood sexual abuse* and *incest*. Childhood sexual abuse is a sexual act imposed on a child who lacks emotional, maturational, and cognitive development. According to Sgroi, Bleck, and Porter (1982), the process of luring a child into a sexual relationship is based on the "all-powerful and dominant position of the adult . . . perpetrator, which is in sharp contrast to the child's age, dependency, and subordinate position. Authority and power enable the perpetrator, implicitly or directly, to coerce the child into sexual compliance" (p. 288).

The majority of incidents of childhood sexual abuse are committed by men against young girls. This dynamic reflects the disproportionate distribution of power for men and women in North American culture (Ogilvie & Daniluk, 1995; Reiss & Heppner, 1993). We refer primarily to father-daughter sexual abuse or incest because it is the dynamic most widely documented and is the most prevalent in the literature. Courtois (1988) posits that sexual abuse or incest

> involving members of the nuclear family, on average, seems to have the greatest potential for trauma. Parent-child incest, which in most cases means father/stepdaughter-daughter, is consistently reported as the most damaging type of incest, followed by sibling incest perpetrated by brothers. Many aspects of the nuclear family are potentially related to the greater traumatic impact: the degree of relatedness and contact between victim and perpetrator and therefore the degree of betrayal involved, along with the greater opportunity for contact and entrapment and its related opportunity for incest of longer duration, greater frequency, and greater severity. (p. 23)

Many argue that familial sexual abuse is a result of impaired intimacy of an adult perpetrator. In other words, fathers often approach their daughters because they fear intimacy with adult women or feel inadequate in their relationships with adult women. These feelings of fear and inadequacy contribute to a misuse of their power demonstrated by attempts of inappropriate closeness with their daughters. The results can be devastating to their daughters, although symptoms resulting from childhood sexual abuse may not emerge until women become adults and are involved in committed relationship themselves (Landis & Wyre, 1984).

HISTORICAL CONTEXT

Throughout the 1970s and 1980s, childhood sexual abuse was reported at alarming rates. Through extensive media coverage, such abuse was acknowledged as never before in human history. Research also documented the devastating personal, interpersonal, and societal consequences of sexual abuse prompting intervention initiatives and models for prevention and treatment for families and for adult survivors of childhood sexual abuse. Treatment models from the mid-1980s to the 1990s were implemented and comprised the first generation of treatment for past childhood sexual abuse. In general, these models were posttraumatic in perspective and emphasized sexual abuse as an important issue for treatment (Courtois, 1997). Spurred by increased data from research and clinical experience, more complex diagnostic formulations have been identified so that treatment for adult survivors of incest includes addressing characterological deformations and dissociative responses associated with chronic traumatization during childhood (Courtois, 1997). The integration of treatment for relational stress is included in these models for adult women and their partners.

SOCIOCULTURAL CONTEXT

The evolution of treatment for adult survivors of child sexual abuse has been shaped and influenced by a number of societal events and issues. Among these was the widespread publicity about childhood sexual abuse and other family dysfunctions during the 1980s and in some cases, the "tabloidization" of abuse (Courtois, 1997). Because these issues had remained in the closet until the 1980s, there were few skilled professionals who were trained in the dynamics and treatment of childhood sexual abuse and knew little about the long-term effects of sexual abuse on women and their relationships with others. Unfortunately, many counselors were forced to "learn while doing" in an effort to keep abreast of the increasing demand for mental health services. In addition, while learning about identifying and treating the wounds of incest there was increased interest in psychological dissociation; dissociative identity disorder (DID) often referred to as multiple personality disorder; and traumatic memory, which includes amnesia as well as delayed and repressed memory (Courtois, 1997).

There was also a rise in allegations of ritualistic forms of sexual abuse, particularly with clients who were diagnosed with multiple personality disorders (APA, 2000). These events paved the way for legislative changes in statutes of limitations for delayed identification of damage from past abuse and for reevaluation by the False Memory Syndrome Foundation. The foundation challenged the concept of recovered memories and charged that some counselors were creating false memories of sexual abuse through the use of suggestive techniques in order to receive financial gains (Courtois, 1997).

Because increasing numbers of adult survivors have attempted to sue their abusers in civil court, the legal system has been forced to determine a reasonable amount of time for a survivor to file a civil claim after reaching adulthood. In one state, the insanity clause exception to the standard statute of limitations allows adult incest survivors who have "repressed memories" of sexual abuse one year after the memory is revived to file a civil suit against a perpetrator (Dorado, 1996). Sexuality counselors are often called on to help women work through the issues that influence their individual lives and their emotional and sexual relationships with others.

With childhood sexual abuse or incest, there is trauma created usually by a loved one, which makes it more difficult for a survivor to understand or resolve. One example that illustrates this concept is a woman who discussed her prior sexual and physical abuse in a group counseling setting and described her feelings toward her father (the sexual abuser) as more positive than toward her mother (the physical abuser). The woman had warm feelings for her father because he did not physically hurt her during the sexual encounters, unlike the physical pain she endured at the hand of her mother. The broad range of differences in reactions to trauma reflects the normal differences among people of various groups and cultures and of individual differences in responding to traumatic events.

THE LEGAL SYSTEM AND THE COUNSELING PROCESS

There are a number of conflicts between the goals of the legal system and the emotional and therapeutic needs of survivors. Pursuing a case against a perpetrator through the court system requires that a survivor contend with these conflicts although that process may at times be detrimental to healing. Sexuality counselors need to be aware of the existence of potential conflicts in the two processes so that therapeutic progress is not thwarted (Dorado, 1996).

Most often, being involved with the court system places a survivor in the role of "victim." As a plaintiff, she must continually view herself as a person without power—an approach that is in direct conflict with her emotional need to focus on the strengths she possesses in order to initiate healing. She must convince the court how damaged she has been by her abuser. During this process, her story is vehemently questioned and confronted by a legal defense team. There is usually a radical difference between the legal system's black and white perception of "objective truth" and the truth as it is brought to bear by trauma survivors. For example, it may be true that a 16-year-old incest victim walked into her father's room, took off her jeans, and proceeded to have sexual relations with him. However, in context, over years of abuse, she learned that in order to go out with her friends she had to "take care of dad first." Is she responsible for the incestuous behavior? Certainly not—but at first glance it may seem so. At least that is what a defense attorney would have the court believe. After examining the relationship contextually, understanding the dynamics of father-daughter incest, and understanding the issues of control and power inherent in the relationship, it is apparent that she has been "set up" by her father to respond in that manner. Further, in order to have some semblance of a childhood, she "does her duty" and is rewarded afterward by being permitted to go out with her friends.

A defense attorney, however, may provide a scenario in court that points a finger at the victim and portrays her as the initiator and perpetrator of the sexual acts.

TREATMENT ISSUES FOR SURVIVORS OF CHILDHOOD SEXUAL ABUSE AND THEIR PARTNERS

Because sexuality is a developing process, children learn about their bodies and relationships over time. These sexual experiences should be associated with good feelings and with pleasure. Children who have been sexually abused have no control over this process and are thus prevented from developing their knowledge and sexual experience at their own pace. When instead they are introduced to sexual acts that are not appropriate for their age or level of development, they become confused and experience "traumatic sexualization," a process that brings about sexual images and feelings that are frightening or physically painful so that sex becomes associated with feelings of fear, shame, and dirtiness. Children who have been sexually abused also learn that sex can be exchanged for gifts, money, affection, or special favors (Ainscough & Toon, 2000).

Sometimes adult survivors report good feelings related to the sexual abuse and feel even more ashamed and responsible because they feel that way. Although certain aspects of sexual experiences may feel good to children, the results are negative. Survivors learn that although it is normal to say that the abuse may have involved some good feelings, they must recognize that they were subjected to sexual experiences that were too advanced for their ages and that they were experienced with inappropriate people. The acts were out of their control, and their freedom of choice was removed because they were children who were asked to behave sexually as adults (Ainscough & Toon, 2000).

Survivors of childhood sexual abuse typically present in counseling with issues related to self-image and self-esteem, both of which negatively influence their sexuality. They may also complain of relationship stress and an inability to freely express themselves sexually. The most basic needs that are usually resolved in sexual union between two people—including trust, openness, closeness, and intimacy—are often thwarted.

Basic issues of worthiness and entitlement are typically presented in sexuality counseling, often accompanied by intense feelings of shame, guilt, and self-consciousness. Adult survivors often strive to maintain control over their emotional and sexual feelings and expression by avoiding sexual acts because they are associated with unpleasant feelings, such as shame and guilt (Talmadge & Wallace, 1991). In other words, the shame of being violated creates an intense need to control emotions and sexual experiences. To "let go" and feel vulnerable with a male partner could recreate the feelings of helplessness that were experienced during the sexual abuse. Incest survivors differ notably from rape and sexual assault survivors. In the typical case, they know their abusers and have trusted them. This violation is a breach of intimacy, a crime that in many cases severely impairs trust in adult intimate relationships.

Reasons for Seeking Help

Rencken (2000) suggests that survivors of incest and childhood sexual abuse seek help for the following issues, all of which may impact sexual functioning:

- Depression: feelings of vulnerability, hopelessness, poor self-esteem.
- Anxiety, fears, and nightmares.
- Eating disorders: obesity, anorexia, bulimia, body image problems.
- Dissociative patterns: "spacing out," delusions, isolation, inaccessible memories.
- Somatic concerns: loss of feeling, chronic pain, gastrointestinal distress, gynecological concerns, chronic fatigue.
- Interpersonal problems: intimacy and closeness, social isolation, work or career instability. (p. 152)

Depression

Depression can be a frightening experience because it may appear to come from nowhere and can take over normal feelings, thoughts, and behaviors. Survivors may feel powerless to understand or control their feelings. They may also feel immobilized, so that they are unable to find pleasure in daily events (Ainscough & Toon, 2000). As sexually abused children, survivors have already had years of experience in thinking negatively about themselves. As a result, they tend to avoid others because they feel worthless and unacceptable and do not believe they have any value to offer.

Anxiety, Fears, and Nightmares

Survivors of childhood sexual abuse feel tense and anxious much of the time. Some do not like to be left alone, others have panic attacks. Anxiety and fear are common problems for those who suffered childhood abuse. Their traumatic childhood experiences caused such fear that as adults they still remain in a state of fear when confronted with their sexuality.

When people are anxious or fearful, they often have negative ideas about themselves and others. When survivors begin remembering or thinking about traumatic childhood events, the fears may be expressed as nightmares. "Nightmares often illustrate fears and memories that are too frightening or painful for survivors to face when they are conscious. [Unfortunately], nightmares are not necessarily accurate pictures of past events [and can further traumatize

Physical Symptoms
- Tension
- Palpitations (awareness of heartbeat)
- "Butterflies" in stomach
- Trembling, shaking
- Pins and needles
- Feeling short of breath
- Loss of appetite
- Poor sleep
- Sweating
- Chest pain

- Dry mouth
- Weak legs
- Aches and pains
- Vomiting
- Diarrhea
- Blurred vision
- Surroundings seem unreal
- Nausea
- Poor concentration
- Dizziness
- Churning stomach
- Headache

Behaviors
- Drinking too much
- Eating too much
- Eating too little
- Taking drugs (prescribed or illegal)
- Avoiding going places
- Escaping from places where you feel afraid
- Obsessive cleaning, counting, or checking

Negative Thoughts
- I'm going to have a heart attack.
- Everyone can tell what I'm really like.
- My children are going to have a bad accident.
- I'm cracking up.
- I'm going to end up in a mental hospital.
- Everyone is talking about me.
- People think I'm dirty.

FIGURE 14.1

Common Anxiety Symptoms

Source: From *Surviving Childhood Sexual Abuse* (p. 99) by C. Ainscough and K. Toon, 2000. Reprinted by permission of Perseus Books PLC, a member of Perseus Books, LLC.

survivors]" (Ainscough & Toon, 2000, p. 101). Figure 14.1 presents a list of common anxiety symptoms.

Eating Disorders

Eating binges may temporarily mask negative feelings, but they then often lead to feelings of guilt, self-hatred, and hopelessness. Interestingly, research studies of women with clinical eating disorders found that at least half of them had been sexually abused as children (Ainscough & Toon, 2000).

Survivors often dislike or hate the weight, size, or shape of their own bodies. They may dislike their entire body or just certain parts, such as the stomach, genitals, breasts, or hips. Survivors are often uncomfortable undressing in public areas because they are ashamed of their bodies and do not want others to view them. It is not surprising because most survivors have had their bodies violated or invaded during sexual abuse (Ainscough & Toon, 2000).

Dissociative Patterns

Sexual trauma inflicted by parents or familial friends is devastating on two levels. Assault by anyone is traumatic and painful but to be violated by the very adults who are supposed to be protective and nur-

turing is the ultimate betrayal. The innocence of childhood has been taken forever and a child's sense of safety and well-being has been shattered.

Children who are incest survivors are not able to develop a healthy sense of self because their needs and feelings are not encouraged or nurtured. In order to survive, such children may resort to defenses such as denial, distancing, splitting, avoiding, and projecting (Courtois, 1997).

In certain situations, survivors dissociate or remove themselves emotionally from their bodies and move to a safer place some distance away (e.g., a wall or ceiling). As children, they learned to protect themselves from pain by detaching from the situation. "Some children describe the experience of stepping outside their bodies and watching themselves being abused without experiencing any of the pain" (Ainscough & Toon, 2000, p. 91). They continue this pattern into their adult relationships when they perceive themselves to be unsafe.

Somatic Concerns

Some survivors exhibit somatic concerns such as fatigue or apathy or destructive behaviors in order to cope with feelings associated with abuse. Drinking alcohol, overeating, sleeping excessively, taking drugs, and self-injury are all ways of trying to erase or ignore negative thoughts and the feelings that accompany them (Ainscough & Toon, 2000; Courtois, 1988; Rencken, 2000).

Some gastrointestinal and respiratory problems may relate specifically to childhood sexual abuse. Nausea, vomiting, gagging, and choking reactions may be due to forced oral sex, or the swallowing of semen. Rectal discomfort, pain, hemorrhoids, constipation, and diarrhea are associated with anal intercourse, enemas, and analingus (Ainscough & Toon, 2000; Courtois, 1988; Rencken, 2000).

Interpersonal Problems

Adult survivors of childhood sexual abuse may experience difficulties in their intimate relationships, often in the area of trusting others. They may also experience familial problems, particularly as their daughters reach the age of onset of the survivor's own sexual abuse. In addition, they often experience difficulties in social situations and in their work settings, particularly regarding male authority figures. Feelings of shame, guilt, and helplessness often contribute to social isolation and impaired peer relationships.

PTSD and False Memory Syndrome

Posttraumatic stress disorder (PTSD) is frequently experienced by adult survivors of childhood sexual abuse. The connection between long-term PTSD symptoms and past childhood abuse in women is supported in the literature (Roland, 2002; Saunders, Villerponteaux, & Lipvsky, 1992). (See Chapter 13 for a detailed discussion of posttraumatic stress disorder as an aftereffect of a significant traumatic event.) Briere (1996) identifies false memory syndrome as an issue related to posttraumatic stress disorder. He describes the syndrome as a "label, applied to those who report recovered memories, of previously 'repressed' or dissociated memories of sexual abuse" (p. 47). Many of these claims were initiated by individuals who were accused of sexual abuse themselves by their now adult children. Briere (1997) suggests that from the False Memory Syndrome (FMS) perspective, such false reports usually arise from "psychologically vulnerable and suggestible women exposed to therapists who by virtue of malice, avarice, or incompetence directly or indirectly implant false memories of abuse" (p. 47). Defense teams often use the syndrome as an excuse or explanation for perpetrators of sexual abuse.

Loftus (2003) describes various ways that memory can be misinterpreted or distorted. In many cases, it is distorted as a result of the way that the questioner asks for information. Leading questions such as "Did you feel afraid when your father touched your vagina?" are inappropriate if the survivor has not yet documented that her father has, in fact, touched her vagina. Questioners can also help plant false memories with partners or other family members. This process is dubbed the "lost in the mall" technique because trusted family members provide vivid details about an event that never happened, and they continue to support the fictitious event until the individual actually believes that it happened. Loftus (2003) also refers to rich false memories as those that not only offer made up information, but also are expressed by the individual with confidence and with vivid details. These individuals can even express intense emotion about the event that never happened. Counselors who tell clients that they may not remember the sexual abuse, but they exhibit all the symptoms of an abused person are contributing to the creation of false memories. Law enforcement officers who interrogate a survivor may make suggestive statements or ask questions that promote a false memory. They may add events to an allegation of abuse that is founded or they may help an individual make up the story completely (Loftus, 2003). Counselors, attorneys, judges, jurors, law enforcement officers, and victim's rights advocates all need specific training on the issue of false memories, and they must learn how to support individuals and determine the facts of the event without providing false information or misleading the individual (Loftus, 2002).

Herman (1997) describes three stages of recovery from traumatic memories: (a) safety, (b) remembrance and mourning, and (c) reconnection. Prior to initiating the process in counseling, a trusting relationship with the counselor must be established. By developing a relationship with a human being in a safe and caring environment, survivors are empowered to begin to feel personal control of their bodies and respect for themselves. Because trauma has breached the traditional attachments to other human beings, the part of self that is viewed in relation to others is shattered. The first stage of recovery is safety, where survivors move from control of self to control of their environment. They must be in the presence of caring people and feel safe to develop a future safety plan. During the second stage, remembrance and mourning, survivors reconstruct their story. They provide a vivid narrative of the events of the abuse and then attempt to understand the meaning of the event in their lives. They are required to examine how the abuse has affected their sexuality and their capacity to connect intimately and physically with others. They also experience tremendous grief and loss for the normalcy they did not experience as children. In the third stage, reconnection, survivors have come to terms with their past and are ready to look to the future. They confront their fears and connect with themselves, their emotions, power over their bodies, and control of their actions. Then they are able to connect with others and their communities (Herman, 1997). It is during this stage that sexual and relational issues can be explored with their partners.

Survivors of Sibling Sexual Abuse

The effects of sibling sexual abuse on survivors are similar to the effects of parent-child sexual abuse. These effects include lower self-esteem, sexual dysfunction as adults, and difficulties with trust and intimacy in relationships (Rayment & Owen, 1999). In many cases the sibling perpetrator has had easier access to the survivor and may have a more lengthy offending history and may have "engaged in more invasive and covert sexual behavior" (Rayment & Owen, 1999). Sibling abuse may be ignored or minimized by the survivor's family, and in fact some families often protect perpetrators from the consequences of their actions. By minimizing the severity of such actions, young perpetrators often do not receive the help they need (Sasian, n.d.). Treatment for survivors of sibling sexual abuse requires the same types of interventions as for parent-child abuse. Some experts believe that the tendency to use mechanisms of denial, minimization, and repression of memory is more prevalent because over time the abuse may be remembered as child's play or normal exploration (United Way of Central New Mexico, 2004).

Male Survivors of Childhood Sexual Abuse

Although most adult survivors who come to counseling are women, many men have also been sexually abused as children by adult males, not necessarily by a father but instead by youth group leaders, extended family members, and members of the clergy. According to Rencken (2000), "a male survivor is like a 'stealth bomber,' invisible to radar, revealing itself only when totally safe and potentially explosive" (p. 155). Because men have been socialized not to show weakness, they are less likely to come forth with an accusation even if they know that, as children, they were smaller and less powerful than their perpetrators. This type of restriction of acceptable behaviors and feelings compromises creativity and flexibility to respond effectively to life situations.

Johanek (as cited in Rencken, 2000) identifies three myths that distort views of male victimization:

1. "Real men" would fight or resist the abuse.
2. Sexual response to abusive behaviors "shouldn't" happen.
3. Offenders are homosexual and forever "taint" the victim. (p. 155)

Although many of the issues faced by male survivors are similar to those faced by females, males tend to struggle more with issues of homophobia and vulnerability. Strong societal messages that men should be powerful, strong, and in control exacerbate the struggle. Many male survivors do not come forth to law enforcement to acknowledge their abuse because of the belief that men should be strong and in control of any situation, much less bring it to the attention of their partners, families, or friends.

Male survivors are more likely to direct rage and anger at others as a result of intense societal pressures to "behave like men" or engage in sexual "acting-out" behaviors. Although not all men who were sexually abused as children necessarily become sexual abusers themselves as adults, the majority of adult male offenders were themselves abused as children. Sexual addiction and compulsion are also aftereffects of abuse for males (Courtois, 1997; Rencken, 2000). For these reasons, it is important to help abused men to address their feelings when they feel safe to do so in order to resolve some of their issues of shame, vulnerability, and guilt. In addition, they must address the losses that manifest themselves in adult life—for example, the loss of childhood memories, loss of positive social contact, loss of opportunities to play, loss of opportunities to learn, loss of control over one's body, and loss of normal loving relationships. Once these men are able to acknowledge the abuse, address the emotional issues and mourn their losses, it is then possible to move forward to initiate satisfying relationships both emotionally and sexually, rather than use their unresolved feelings to perpetrate abuse on others.

THE DEVELOPMENT OF SEXUAL AND RELATIONAL PROBLEMS

Depression, anxiety, eating disorders, dissociative patterns, somatic concerns, and interpersonal problems all contribute to the development of sexual problems or dysfunctions. Most often, these issues manifest as "lack of sexual desire, addictive/compulsive patterns, anorgasmia or dystonic homosexuality" (Rencken, 2000, p. 151). According to Maltz (2001b), other issues can also manifest as sexual problems:*

> Avoiding or being afraid of sex;
>
> Approaching sex as an obligation;
>
> Feeling intense negative emotions when touched, such as fear, guilt, disgust, or nausea;
>
> Having difficulty becoming aroused or feeling sensation;
>
> Feeling emotionally distant or not present during sex;
>
> Having disturbed and intrusive sexual thoughts and fantasies;
>
> Engaging in compulsive, risky, or inappropriate sexual behaviors; and
>
> Having difficulty establishing or maintaining an intimate relationship.

Many survivors of childhood sexual abuse experience difficulties with sex and with their relationships in general as a result of their disturbing childhood sexual experiences. These problems often plague them over the course of many years. Once survivors have gained new understandings about the issues and aftereffects of their abuse, they are better able to understand the relationship between sex and sexual abuse and can develop new skills for relearning touch and sexual behaviors (Maltz, 2001a, p. 278).

Maltz (2001a) outlines five common sexual problems and symptoms that may result from childhood sexual abuse:†

> Lack of sexual interest: inhibited sexual desire, fear of sex

> Difficulty becoming aroused and feeling sensation: lack of lubrication in women, lack of erection in men
>
> Difficulty experiencing orgasm: lack of orgasm in women, inhibited ejaculation in men
>
> Difficulty averting orgasm: premature ejaculation in men, rapid orgasm in women
>
> Difficulty with intercourse for women survivors: muscle spasm, pain, discomfort, fear of penetration

According to Maltz (2001a), lack of sexual interest seems to be the most common specific sexual problem for survivors. It may be exacerbated because of fear of sex or fear of responses that may be triggered during sex. Sometimes survivors experience unresolved conflicts in their relationships, which are also tied to their past experiences. These conflicts also contribute to diminished sexual desire.

Desire is also affected when arousal is low. Women may notice a lack of vaginal secretions that normally lubricate the vagina. Sexual intercourse and other forms of penetration may be painful. Sexual abuse often inhibits a natural curiosity about genital sensations due to lack of self-exploration. Survivors typically have not explored their bodies because they feel dirty or ashamed of what happened to them. One of the first changes suggested during counseling may be to begin to spend time in self-discovery and genital pleasuring exercises (Maltz, 2001a). It is important to note that there is the risk of retraumatizing a survivor if sexuality counselors introduce sexual exercises too early in the treatment process. When a survivor is ready to address sexual concerns, the counselor may want to initially suggest relearning touch exercise. Counselors should demonstrate sensitivity when suggesting any exercise, recognizing that it may take some time before survivors are ready to tolerate sexual exercises (Maltz, 2001a).

Often, survivors have been given negative messages from their perpetrators and have come to believe that they are somehow physically or sexually inadequate. They must confront these negative beliefs and begin to view orgasm as a positive and pleasurable experience. Some survivors react by experiencing orgasm too quickly, their belief being that quick orgasms will help to relieve the painful feelings and shame felt during the abuse and to end the abuse more quickly. In these cases, sexual touch of any kind may trigger an early climax (Maltz, 2001a). Sometimes painful intercourse is the result of vaginismus or dyspareunia. (See Chapter 6 for more information on

---

*From Wendy Maltz, "Sex Therapy with Survivors of Sexual Abuse," in *New Directions in Sex Therapy: Innovations and Alterations* (p. 260), by P. Kleinplatz, 2001. Reproduced by permission of Routledge/Taylor & Francis Books, Inc.

†From Wendy Maltz, "Sex Therapy with Survivors of Sexual Abuse," in *New Directions in Sex Therapy: Innovations and Alterations* (p. 281), by P. Kleinplatz, 2001. Reproduced by permission of Routledge/Taylor & Francis Books, Inc.

- Dislike of touching or looking at oneself
- Dislike or avoidance of relationships
- Dislike or avoidance of sexual contact
- Dislike or avoidance of certain sexual activities
- Lack of physical pleasure in sex
- Dissociating or blocking off during sex
- Flashbacks
- Inability to have an orgasm
- Vaginismus (tightening spasms of the vaginal muscles)
- Not being able to say "no" to sex
- Having sex indiscriminately
- Prostitution
- Aggressive sexual behavior
- Sexual pleasure linked to pain
- Feeling guilty about sexual feelings
- Believing that sex is dirty or disgusting
- Confusion about sexual identity (male/female)
- Confusion about sexual orientation (heterosexual/homosexual)
- Lack of sexual knowledge
- Sexualizing relationships and situations
- Obsession with sex
- Obsession with masturbating

FIGURE 14.2
Sexual Difficulties and Responses to Sexual Abuse

these problems.) Figure 14.2 presents a summary of sexual difficulties.

The Development of Relational Problems

According to Courtois (1988), concerns related to satisfactory relationship functioning are manifested in four basic variations: "general relationship difficulties with both men and women; problems in intimate and/or committed relationships, problems with parents, family members, and authority figures; and problems in parenting" (p. 111).

Because of past betrayals, it is very difficult for survivors to trust others in intimate relationships. Trust and betrayal are often at the core of relationship problems. Survivors attempt to protect themselves by placing invisible barriers around themselves in order to remain safe. Many survivors characterize their relationships as guarded or superficial, which leads to mistrust or conflicted interactions with their partners (Courtois, 1988). These behaviors seem to be prevalent in committed relationships because the very nature of such relationships requires trust, vulnerability,

openness, and connectedness. Sexual relationships are particularly vulnerable to these feelings and consequently offer little satisfaction or intimacy for either partner.

When survivors become parents, they may have difficulty understanding appropriate parenting behaviors because of their unresolved abuse experiences and unresolved feelings for their own parents. In addition, they do not have role models of parents as trusted caretakers. These factors make it difficult for survivors to develop emotional and physical intimacy with their own children (Courtois, 1988).

The Process of Sexuality Counseling for Incest Survivors

The process of sexuality counseling with incest survivors and their partners requires counselors to possess specialized knowledge and skill regarding the dynamics and treatment of childhood sexual abuse and the ability to create a safe and supportive environment. Sexuality counselors are faced with helping clients sift through issues and deciding which ones are related to the abuse and which are not. It is important to assess a couples' current situation by inquiring about any occurrence of sexual abuse during childhood. Counselors can then draw on sound clinical judgment in order to evaluate which presenting symptoms are related to either partner's past sexual abuse (Briere, 1996).

Courtois (1997) presents a three-phase process for counseling adult survivors of incest and their partners: (a) alliance building, safety, and stabilization; (b) deconditioning, mourning, and resolution; and (c) self and relational development. We have adapted these phases here and have incorporated them with the integrative couples' model in these phases in order to demonstrate how couples progress through treatment.

During Stage 1 of the integrative couples' model, survivors are encouraged to provide a thorough history of their incest experiences as well as a history from their families of origin. Survivors, along with their partners, also describe their current relationship and identify each person's view of the issues that have been brought to counseling. A genogram is of particular importance to use with survivors because it can explicate the interplay of past sexual and relational patterns and provide insight into why the partners were attracted to each other. The incest history questionnaire presented in Figure 14.3 is also a useful tool for gaining information related to past sexual abuse.

Instructions

This 52-question Incest History Questionnaire is designed to assist you in describing your incest experience. It consists of five sections: (1) Family Description; (2) Pre-Incest Self-Description; (3) Description of the Incest; (4) Initial Aftereffects Rating Scale; and (5) Long-Term Aftereffects Rating Scale. The questionnaire can be completed in several ways: as a whole or in sections inside or outside of therapy. Discussions or responses with your therapist might be tape-recorded for later use.

The Incest History Questionnaire asks detailed questions. Respond according to your ability to answer and your degree of comfort. Do not rush yourself or put yourself under intense pressure. Respond in as much detail as you can remember and you are comfortable with. Another version of this questionnaire has been used in research. The survivors who completed it were unanimous in indicating that it asks direct questions pertinent to the family and the incest. They found it a helpful tool in disclosure and discussion. This revised version is designed to assist with information gathering for the therapy process. It will help you to analyze your family and its functioning, the incest and its aftermath, including direct and indirect aftereffects.

I. Your Family Description

1. Briefly describe what you know of your grandparents on both your mother's and your father's side. What were they like? How were your parents raised? Can you remember anything about what their relationship was like? Did they have any outstanding personal or family problems that you know about or have heard about? What was their socioeconomic level?

   a. mother's parents:

   b. father's parents:

   c. their relationship, parenting, family deficits or assets, etc.:

2. How many children were there in your parents' respective families?

   a. mother:
      number of siblings _____
      mother's birth order _____

   b. father:
      number of siblings _____
      father's birth order _____

3. Are you aware of any physical or sexual abuse in either of your parents' families? How about serious emotional problems or illness, alcoholism or drug abuse?

   a. mother:

   b. father:

4. Describe your parents as individuals. Note any particular personal strengths, weaknesses, and/or problems or assets they have.

   a. mother:

   b. father:

FIGURE 14.3
Incest History Questionnaire

Source: From *Healing the Incest Wound: Adult Survivors in Therapy* (Appendix A), by Christine A. Courtois. Copyright © 1988 by Christine A. Courtois. Used by permission of W. W. Norton & Company, Inc.

5. Describe your parents' relationship/marital history.

    a. How old were they when they met? When they married?

    b. Did they get together or marry under any special circumstances or strains (e.g., extreme economic hardship, "pregnancy")?

    c. Have they ever separated, or divorced and/or remarried? Please describe the circumstances.

    d. Describe your parents' relationship as best you can.

    e. Do you recall any major changes (good or bad) occurring in their relationship? When and of what type?

    f. Describe how your parents interacted with their extended family.

    g. Briefly describe as best you can the educational, occupational and work history of each of your parents.

        mother:

        father:

    h. Briefly describe how your parents and your family functioned in the community at large (e.g., Were they isolated? Did they have friends?).

    i. What was/is your parents' religion? How did religious traditions, beliefs influence family functioning?

    j. What was your family's ethnic or cultural background? How did traditions, beliefs influence family functioning?

6. How many children are in your family (include self and any half brothers/sisters and stepbrothers/sisters). List all according to birth and note their order, sex, and the number of years between them. Also note children who died and their birth order.

	Sex	Age Difference
_____	____	_____
_____	____	_____
_____	____	_____
_____	____	_____

7. Now describe as best you can the roles in your family, including any roles you think you held (e.g., older sister acted like a mother, brother was the family clown or scapegoat, mother was the "softy", father was the authoritarian).

    father:

    mother:

    siblings:

    self:

FIGURE 14.3
(*Continued*)

8. Describe as best you can what your household was like, how it functioned internally (e.g., mother was boss, father was quiet; father was domineering but mother was the power behind the throne; parents always did what the children wanted/always gave in).

   a. Do you recall any major changes in functioning in your family?
      Describe them and when they occurred.

9. Describe any family problems, trauma or upheavals you can think of that occurred before, during or after the incest (please note when). E.g., death in the family, divorce, alcoholism, severe illness or injury, desertion, child running away.)

10. Describe your relationship with your family and its members as you were growing up (e.g., warm, distant, conflicted).

   mother:

   father:

   siblings:

11. Describe your current relationship with family members and current interaction patterns (e.g., warm, distant, conflicted).

   mother:

   father:

   siblings:

II. Pre-Incest Self Description

12. If you can, describe what you can remember about yourself before the incest occurred.

13. Answer the next 4 questions on a scale of 1 to 5.

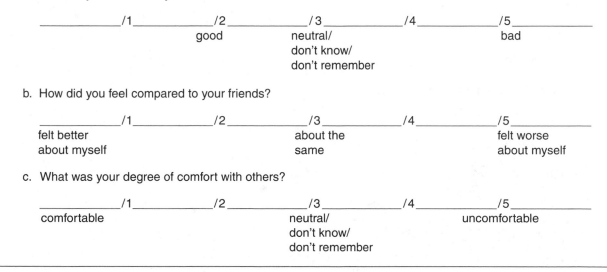

   a. How did you feel about yourself?

   _____/1_____/2_____/3_____/4_____/5_____
               good   neutral/   bad
                         don't know/
                         don't remember

   b. How did you feel compared to your friends?

   _____/1_____/2_____/3_____/4_____/5_____
   felt better   about the   felt worse
   about myself   same   about myself

   c. What was your degree of comfort with others?

   _____/1_____/2_____/3_____/4_____/5_____
   comfortable   neutral/   uncomfortable
                         don't know/
                         don't remember

FIGURE 14.3
(*Continued*)

d. How well did you relate to others?

_____/1_____/2_____/3_____/4_____/5_____
good   neutral/   bad
                                             don't know/
                                             don't remember

14. Indicate your general level of awareness of the following before the incest situation began. Using the following scale, please place the appropriate number next to the subject.

_____/1_____/2_____/3_____/4_____/5_____
very aware   somewhat aware   unaware

_____a.   sexuality, e.g., sexual behavior and functioning

_____b.   rape

_____c.   incest

_____d.   that strangers could be dangerous and that you should be cautious around them

_____e.   that family members could be dangerous and that you should be cautious around them

15. Did you experience any type of major disruption, crisis or trauma when you were young prior to the incest situation? Please describe (e.g., a family death, a separation from the family).

III. Description of the Incest
A. The Incest

16. Describe the incest situation in which you were involved as a child/adolescent.

   a. Please describe the type of sexual activity that took place.

   b. Describe if there was a progression of activity over time.

17. Onset of the incest.

   a. When did it begin?

   b. How did it begin?

   c. Do you have any idea why it started?

   d. Did you or anyone else do anything to stop it?

18. Termination of the incest.

   a. When did it stop? How old were you at the time?

   b. How did it stop?

   c. Do you have any idea why it stopped?

   d. Did you or anyone else do anything to stop it?

FIGURE 14.3
(*Continued*)

19. Duration. How long did the incest go on?

20. Frequency

    a. How often did the incest occur?

    b. Were there any patterns or particular circumstances surrounding the occurrence (e.g., drunkenness, violence, loneliness)?

21. Location. Where did the incest take place?

22. The Perpetrator

    a. Who was the perpetrator?

    b. What was his/her age when the incest began? When it ended?

    c. Can you remember anything about this person that would have caused him/her to engage in incest (e.g., loneliness, temper, drinking)?

    d. Please describe this individual as best you can.

23. Describe your relations with the perpetrator.

    a. prior to the incest:

    b. during the incest:

    c. after the incest:

24. Involvement

    a. Were you ever offered any favors or enticements for your participation?

    b. Did you ever refuse to participate? What happened when you did?

    c. Did you ever choose to participate? Please describe.

    d. Were you ever threatened if you didn't comply?

    e. Did you ever struggle? What happened when you did?

    f. Did you ever engage in any other type of behavior to get out of the situation (e.g., running away, getting married)?

25. Reactions at the time of the incest.

    a. What were your reactions to the incest?

    b. How do you think you coped with the incest? What did you do?

    c. What were your reactions to the perpetrator?

FIGURE 14.3
(*Continued*)

d. What were your reactions to yourself/within yourself?

e. What were your reactions to other family members?

26. Describe what you were like while the incest was ongoing.

27. How did you function at the time of the incest? Do you believe any aspects of your life suffered or improved at the time due to the incest (e.g., school, relations with others)?

28. Are you aware of any other incest in your family (nuclear or extended) (e.g., sister with father, brother and sister).

29. Were you ever sexually approached by or involved with any other family member?

_____ Yes   _____ No

B. The Issue of Disclosure

30. In your opinion, did anyone else besides you and the perpetrator know of the incest without a direct disclosure?

_____ No   _____ Yes

If yes, describe why you believe so.

31. Do you know if you had observable symptoms that would have cued someone to the incest?

32. Did the incest result in a pregnancy? If yes, what was the outcome?

33. If the situation was overt or became known, did the people who knew ever intervene?

_____ Yes   _____ No

a. What action did they take?

b. What reaction did you have?

34. Did you ever disclose the incest to anyone and/or seek help in any way?

_____ Yes   _____ No

If no, skip the rest of this section and continue to section IV.

a. To whom did you disclose?

b. When did your disclose the incest? How old were you then?

c. Describe your reasons for disclosure and any expectations and fears that you had.

d. What was your reaction after disclosure to this individual and to any action that was taken?

e. Did the perpetrator know of your disclosing to this person?
   What was his/her reaction?

FIGURE 14.3
(*Continued*)

C. Involvement of Social Agencies and Personnel

35. Was the incest ever reported outside the family to a social agency?

_____ Yes   _____ No

If no, go to section IV.

Which of the following agencies or personnel became involved?

a. police

b. medical services and personnel

_____ hospital

_____ clinic

_____ physician

_____ nurse

_____ other:

c. social service/mental health agency and personnel

_____ child protective agency

_____ community mental health center/family services

_____ psychiatrist

_____ counselor

_____ social worker

_____ other:

d. minister, priest or church member

e. legal agency and personnel

_____ the courts

_____ State Attorney's office

_____ private attorney

_____ other:

36. Go back and describe your involvement with and response from the agencies and personnel that you checked above.

FIGURE 14.3
(*Continued*)

37. Describe your reaction to these same involved agencies and personnel.

38. Describe your reaction to the perpetrator at this time.

39. Were you or the perpetrator ever removed from your home after reporting?

   _____ Yes   _____ No
   If no, go on to section IV.

   a. For what reason were you or the perpetrator removed?

   b. By whom?

   c. Where did you go if you were?

   d. What were your reactions?

   e. What was the experience like for you?

40. Have you ever received psychological counseling?

   _____ Yes   _____ No
   If no, go to section IV.

   a. If yes, reasons for seeking treatment.

   b. Did you disclose the incest experience in counseling?

   _____ Yes   _____ No

   c. If yes, how and why did you make the disclosure? How did the counselor deal with your disclosure?

   d. If no, why did you choose not to disclose it in counseling?

IV. The Initial Aftereffects

41. Describe any aftereffects you experienced in the following eight areas. These aftereffects are what you
   perceive were the immediate (rather than long term) effects of the incest. After describing each one, rate its
   effect on you using the following scale and explain your rating.
   A scale of from 1 to 7: 1 = strongly positive; 2 = moderately positive; 3 = somewhat positive; 4 = neutral;
   5 = somewhat negative; 6 = moderately negative; 7 = strongly negative

   a. social (e.g., feeling isolated, different from others, unable to interact, mistrustful of others).

   _____/1_____/2_____/3_____/4_____/5_____/6_____/7_____

   b. psychological/emotional (e.g., not being able to feel anything or having too many emotions. Please
   discuss specific emotions:

   _____/1_____/2_____/3_____/4_____/5_____/6_____/7_____

FIGURE 14.3
(*Continued*)

   c. physical (e.g., feeling sick at the mention of certain activities, pain, soreness, headaches).

   _____/1_____/2_____/3_____/4_____/5_____/6_____/7_____

   d. sexual (e.g., sexual confusion, sexual fears, wanting sex all the time or avoiding it, sexual preference).

   _____/1_____/2_____/3_____/4_____/5_____/6_____/7_____

   e. familial (within or with your family) (e.g., family members were estranged, got closer, parents got divorced).

   _____/1_____/2_____/3_____/4_____/5_____/6_____/7_____

   f. sense of self (e.g., powerful, ashamed, improved or lowered self-concept)

   _____/1_____/2_____/3_____/4_____/5_____/6_____/7_____

   g. relation to men (e.g., close, trusting, mistrusting, hostile)

   _____/1_____/2_____/3_____/4_____/5_____/6_____/7_____

   h. relation to women (e.g., close, trusting, mistrusting, hostile)

   _____/1_____/2_____/3_____/4_____/5_____/6_____/7_____

42. Please describe any other aftereffects and symptoms.

V. The Long-Term Aftereffects

43. Describe any aftereffects in the following eight areas that you experienced in the long-term aftermath of the incest. After describing each one, indicate how severe you believe the effect was on you on a scale of 1 to 7. 1 = strongly positive; 2 = moderately positive; 3 = somewhat positive; 4 = neutral; 5 = somewhat negative; 6 = moderately negative; 7 = strongly negative.

   a. social (e.g., feeling isolated, different from others, unable to interact, mistrustful of others).

   _____/1_____/2_____/3_____/4_____/5_____/6_____/7_____

   b. psychological/emotional? (e.g., not being able to feel anything or having too many emotions). Please discuss specific emotions.

   _____/1_____/2_____/3_____/4_____/5_____/6_____/7_____

   c. physical (e.g., feeling sick at the mention of certain activities, pain, soreness, headache).

   _____/1_____/2_____/3_____/4_____/5_____/6_____/7_____

   d. sexual

   _____/1_____/2_____/3_____/4_____/5_____/6_____/7_____

   e. familial

   _____/1_____/2_____/3_____/4_____/5_____/6_____/7_____

FIGURE 14.3
(*Continued*)

f. sense of self (e.g., powerful, ashamed, improved or lowered self-concept).

_____/1_____/2_____/3_____/4_____/5_____/6_____/7_____

g. relation to men (e.g., close, trusting, mistrusting, hostile).

_____/1_____/2_____/3_____/4_____/5_____/6_____/7_____

h. relation to women (e.g., close, trusting, mistrusting, hostile).

_____/1_____/2_____/3_____/4_____/5_____/6_____/7_____

44. Please describe any other aftereffects and symptoms.

45. Using the scale provided, indicate what type of effect the incest had on your life.

_____/1_____/2_____/3_____/4_____/5_____/6_____/7_____

a. Please discuss why you think this.

46. Describe your current feelings about the perpetrator.

47. Describe your current feelings about any other significant person(s) in your life.

48. Describe your current feelings about the incest. How do you understand your incest experience? Does it have any meaning to you?

49. Describe your current feelings about yourself.

50. Describe any difficulties or complaints you have concerning your present functioning or lifestyle (e.g., headaches, inability to concentrate, poor social skills).

51. Is there any other information you would like to add?

52. Do you have any immediate reactions to having discussed your incest experience in this way?

Courtois' First Phase: Alliance Building, Safety, and Stabilization

Courtois (1997) describes the tasks of the initial stage of treatment to include "the establishment of the parameters of treatment, the development of the therapeutic relationship and the working alliance, and the maintenance of safety and relative life stability" (p. 473). Although these tasks for survivors are very similar to those for nontraumatized women, they are more complex because of the sexual trauma they have suffered. Sexuality counselors may be perceived ambivalently—as another abusive authority figure or as a nurturing parental figure. Often, sexuality counselors are feared, challenged, or sexualized during counseling and they may not be trusted by survivors. Counselors are charged with the task of empowering clients by developing a collaborative approach to counseling, yet maintaining a high degree of structure, organization, and pace in order to move the therapeutic process in a positive direction.

The specific goals and tasks during this stage are determined "according to a couple's unique character structure, defensive and [protective] patterns, concerns, fears, symptoms, and personal resources, including motivation" (Courtois, 1997, p. 12). The work during this early phase is generally measured in terms of mastery of skills and personal resources, including the ability to develop a safety plan that includes physical and emotional elements and addresses specific steps for protection from further harm. The plan also includes information on how to address emotional reactions to fear and stress related to past sexual trauma. In addition, survivors identify significant others to help support them during these difficult times. It is not unusual to find that some partners offer little support. In fact, they often contribute to the problem by blaming or distancing from their partner. This issue is frequently a presenting issue for relationship counseling and is addressed throughout the counseling process. If a partner is unable to provide safety or is "re-abusing" the survivor, couples' counseling should be discontinued.

Survivors and their partners are taught relaxation skills and de-escalation skills early in treatment as part of a safety and stabilization plan. Because the lives of survivors at this stage may be chaotic and intensely emotional, crisis management skills must be part of the overall therapeutic plan. Life-threatening circumstances such as suicide attempts, self-mutilation, overmedication, and other forms of risk-taking and self-harm must also be addressed. At times, survivors may consider or begin to violate others, abuse drugs or alcohol, or engage in "obsessive review" of past childhood trauma (Courtois, 1997).

The early stage of treatment outlined by Courtois (1997) is a good fit with the integrative couples' model because it focuses early attention on safety issues and relaxation skills, and it encourages minimization of setbacks related to sexual trauma. Most of the interventions are cognitive and psychoeducational in format and are designed to focus on self-awareness and to provide information to partners about emotional and physical reactions to past abuse. Treatment interventions such as teaching relaxation techniques and relapse prevention strategies are usually addressed in later stages of counseling.

Prior to moving to Stage 2, a goal-setting stage, it is important that the sexuality counselor has listened to each partner's story about their current relational issues before providing a shared view of the problem. The shared view addresses the childhood incest but also focuses on how trauma currently affects their intimate relationship. The incest history questionnaire presented in Figure 14.3 provides specific information to help identify a shared view of the problem so that behavioral and affective goals can be set.

Courtois' Second Phase: Deconditioning, Mourning, and Resolution of Trauma

The primary goal of this phase is to face the trauma by examining the role that it plays in current life experiences. Survivors strive to achieve an emotional level that permits daily life (work, play, relationships, self-care) to progress at a normal pace (Courtois, 1997). This phase can be the most difficult because it meets trauma head-on and confronts critical issues associated with it. Sexuality counselors are cautioned not to allow survivors to get "stuck" by repeatedly recreating and focusing on every little detail of the abuse once it has been thoroughly explored in counseling. Avoidance, numbing, and denial of feelings and physical sensations should abate during this phase. Couples are encouraged to move beyond the trauma by developing appropriate coping strategies in order to negotiate everyday life.

Trauma resolution includes related issues such as seeking evidence for the legal system if action is being considered, determining appropriate disclosure of the trauma to selected friends or associates, exploring relationships with family members, and developing self-protective strategies for use in these relationships (Courtois, 1997).

Stage 3 of the integrative couples' model emphasizes the positive assets and strengths that couples can draw on to mobilize their resources in order to move beyond current issues related to sexual abuse. By focusing on their personal and relational strengths, couples are empowered and can better view themselves as survivors rather than victims.

Courtois' Third Phase: Self-Development and Relational Development

Gains achieved in earlier stages of treatment including self-care and improved intimate relationships with others are consolidated in this phase. According to Courtois (1997), "attention continues to be directed to personality issues, self and emotional development, mood stability, personal safety, self-care, and personal boundary management" (p. 477). Sexuality counseling centers on the establishment of secure emotional stability, regaining trust in personal relationships and extending these feelings to social relationships (Courtois, 1997). Sexual issues or dysfunctions begin to resolve during this stage and couples are free to focus on pleasure and emotional

BOX 14.1
Interventions at a Glance

- Ask the survivor to complete an incest history questionnaire (see Figure 14.3).
- Ask the couple to complete a thorough sexual genogram to ascertain the sexual messages each partner has been given; examine how these messages may cause conflict.
- Provide a safe setting for sexuality counseling; use relaxation techniques to help both partners feel comfortable.
- Ask the survivor what she is willing to discuss regarding the childhood abuse. She must give her consent before proceeding with exploration of past events.
- Help the survivor and her partner explore feelings and practice direct communication about her desires.
- Confront issues of shame, guilt, and self-respect.
- Address the responsibility issue. Help the survivor understand that the abuse is not her fault and that she could not prevent it at her young age.
- Suggest that partners use journaling to describe feelings and thoughts that affect sexual functioning.
- Suggest sensory exercises that will help a couple to get in touch with all pleasurable sensations.
- Suggest that partners practice initiating and declining sex.
- Use relaxation techniques that will help partners to overcome anxiety.
- Suggest that partners practice giving direct feedback about what they like and do not like sexually.
- Suggest that partners use sensate focus activities and masturbation training (see Chapter 6).
- Show survivors how to use physical exercise as a means to feel in control of their bodies.

bonding. Attention is paid to strategies that couples can use to maintain their positive changes and to prevent setbacks. Couples should be aware that setbacks are a normal part of the counseling process and some are to be expected. Survivors have often

lived with fears, guilt, shame, and self-doubt for many years so that the feelings and behaviors associated with them are deeply ingrained in their beliefs about themselves and their interactions with others. Termination of treatment and the therapeutic relationship is particularly significant because it may stir up feelings of abandonment, grief, and fear (Courtois, 1997). Care must be taken to provide sufficient time to explore these reactions. At times, their reactions contribute to backslides or revisiting intense traumatic reactions. During Stages 4 and 5 of the integrative couples' model, validation strategies are addressed by refocusing on positive, personal resources, which is particularly necessary with survivors of sexual trauma, and by helping them celebrate success. Specific interventions useful for all five stages of sexuality counseling are described in Box 14.1. Sexuality counselors make their clinical decisions about when to use interventions and how to implement them most effectively based on their consideration of responses to the following types of questions:

1. Who knows or whom have you told about your childhood incest experience?
2. Who supports you regarding your incest experience?
3. How has the incident affected your feelings about yourself and your relationship?
4. How has the incident affected your daily life?
5. How has the incident affected your sexual relationship?
6. How do you create safety in your world?
7. What was your involvement in the legal process and how do you view law enforcement?

INTERVENTION STRATEGIES FOR SURVIVORS OF CHILDHOOD SEXUAL ABUSE AND THEIR PARTNERS

Many of the interventions discussed in Chapter 13 can also be adapted to work with survivors of childhood sexual abuse and incest. In addition, many interventions already described in other chapters are useful with couples encountering childhood sexual trauma. Interventions should be selected only if they fit a particular situation and can be used to move a couple toward a more satisfying emotional and sexual relationship.

Dealing with Guilt, Blame, and Shame

Survivors often forget how small and powerless they were in comparison to their abusers. Counselors can suggest that survivors complete the following tasks and share them with their partner:

1. Find a photograph of yourself as you were near the time that the incest was occurring.
2. Find a photograph of your abuser.
3. Compare the two photographs. Be sure to note the differences in size and stature.
4. If photographs are not available, draw a picture of yourself and your abuser.

Often, adult survivors look at themselves as they are now when they tell themselves that they should have been able to say no. It is thus important for them to graphically illustrate the actual differences in age and size. They can then discuss these disparities with their partners and remember them in their mind's eye whenever they blame themselves or feel guilty about not being able to protect themselves. As this exercise clearly illustrates, they were manipulated and coerced by someone more physically powerful than they were.

Confronting the Issue

Once the initial story of abuse has been told, sexuality counselors can help survivors visualize the abuser through the use of the "empty chair technique." Survivors are asked to provide a photograph of the abuser or any articles that would serve as reminders of that person and as a target for their feelings. These items are then placed in an empty chair. Survivors are gently encouraged to express their feelings to the chair and then directly to the counselor. Decisions are then made about how, where, when, and with whom survivors should share their feelings. It is not always necessary or helpful to directly confront the perpetrator. All options should be discussed in depth during counseling.

Clarifying Responsibility

Sexuality counselors ask survivors to describe their lives as they were during the time of the abuse and to make a list of the rules about telling that were in effect during the time of the abuse. They are next asked to identify the consequences for breaking a family rule. Sexuality counselors explore with them some of their beliefs about what would have happened if they told anyone about their experiences. The counselor can remind them that because of their size and age,

they should realize that it was not their fault, that they were powerless over their abuser, and that they could not have prevented the sexual abuse from occurring.

Gaining Self-Control

Survivors are asked to become involved in physical activities that can help them feel more in control of their bodies and also serve as a healthy outlet for fears and anger. Tennis, dance, walking, running, squash, racquetball, aerobics, bodybuilding, and yoga are all positive ways to redirect feelings and gain control over their bodies.

Wilderness Therapy

Wilderness activities are often based on variations of Outward Bound programs where participants are required to negotiate a variety of challenges—from rope courses, overnight survival camps, and rock climbing to team-building activities—in order to build self-confidence, self-esteem, and trust (Courtois, 1988). By placing themselves in a position where they once again feel helpless, and then succeeding and accomplishing a series of required tasks, survivors are able to reexperience and rework their emotions and regain some of their personal efficacy and self-respect (Courtois, 1988, p. 210).

Keeping a Feelings Record

Because survivors have blocked their feelings for so long, it is important that they relearn what they are feeling. Sexuality counselors can help them in this process by suggesting that they keep a feelings record. Survivors are encouraged to check their feelings throughout the day and then to record them in a notebook so that they can refer to them later. They can discuss their feelings with their partners and elicit feedback from them about what they have said. The process of writing also helps release anxieties, fears, and memories so that they can be explored in a different light (Ainscough & Toon, 2000).

Challenging Myths

Sexuality counselors can help survivors challenge myths by asking them to write down all the messages that they received about sexuality from their abuser. They can then negate any messages that they find offensive or incorrect by reading books and talking to their partner. For example, an abuser says, "I am the best person to teach you about sex. Before you go out with young guys, you can learn from me and then you will know what to do." A survivor may respond, "I was too young to learn those things. Sex is supposed to be a part of a loving relationship with my partner, not with my father. You are wrong."

Initiating and Declining Sex

This is a role-play exercise developed by Maltz (2001a) in which partners take turns initiating and declining sexual activity. No sexual activity takes place as a result of this exercise. Sexuality counselors suggest that partners sit facing each other and assume the role of an initiator or a decliner. Each partner will have the opportunity to play both roles, but the survivor should be the first to choose the role she would like. The initiator expresses sexual interest for a brief time, perhaps saying "I am interested in having sex with you," "I would like you to touch me," or "I would like to touch you." The initiator should be clear and direct about what she likes and would like to do with her partner. The decliner expresses thanks to the initiator for the sexual interest, but declines the offer in a respectful manner, saying "I appreciate that you find me sexy, but I do not want to have sex with you right now." The two partners now reverse roles. At the end of this exercise, they process the experience with their partner, reflecting on which role was most comfortable and how they might have responded differently (Maltz, 2001a, p. 286).

Sensory Basket

In the sensory basket exercise, Maltz (2001a) suggests that sexuality counselors direct survivors in the following way:

> In a basket collect a variety of objects. Choose objects you think would be pleasurable to touch, smell, taste, or look at. For example, your basket might contain jewelry, stuffed animals, feathers, spices, fruit, and bells. Spend a few minutes interacting with each object. Practice relaxation and awareness by touching, smelling, and rubbing the objects. Arrange the objects in order beginning with your favorite and ending with your least favorite. Experiment, or make a design. Have your partner complete the same activity. Discuss your experience. How does the activity relate to what you like most sexually? Like least sexually? Continue your discussion. (p. 255)

This type of directed activity encourages survivors to examine pleasurable items so that they develop a frame of reference of positive responses on which they can rely when negative responses overwhelm them or intrude into their daily experiences.

Learning to Communicate Openly

Sexuality counselors ask survivors to make a list of five behaviors they would like to change in themselves. Next they are told to talk to their partner about each of them and to choose two that they would like to change. Each day they practice their new behaviors and tell their partner how successful they have been. They can ask their partner to complete the same activity. Next, when they are comfortable discussing positive changes, they describe two behaviors about the other they would like to see changed or modified in some manner. It is important to use "I messages" to describe the offensive behaviors. For example, "When you walk out of the room while I'm talking, I feel disrespected." Each time a partner uses an offending behavior it should be discussed. Practice saying, "I do not like it when_____," "When you_____, I feel_____," or "I am not comfortable when_____." This exercise helps initiate conversation about feelings and discussions about likes and dislikes. This was something that was not possible to accomplish as a child.

Creating a Safe Nest

Maltz (2001a) suggests that sexuality counselors use the following activity to help survivors create their own safe space when they are feeling insecure or vulnerable:

> Create a safe, warm environment in which you can be alone and relax. Include blankets, pillows and other nesting materials for your environment. Practice relaxation skills and breathing exercises. Invite your partner into your nest. Hug or embrace each other in a comfortable manner. Breathe deeply together and listen to each other's heartbeat. Hug your partner. Occasionally share your feelings with your partner, but remain still and calm. Later, after you have left your safe place, discuss the experience with your partner. How might this experience relate to your sexual relationship? What helps you feel safe and cared for? What can you each do to create this safe, warm environment in your bedroom? (p. 259)

Case Example

Gillian and Hans have been married for six years. Recently, their first child was born. Since the birth of their daughter, Gillian has been anxious and has not wanted Hans to be alone with the baby. In addition, she has not been comfortable engaging in any type of sexual touch or intercourse with her partner. She states that she is unable to feel close to him and is confused about her reaction to him.

Stage 1: Assessing and Obtaining an Interactional View of the Problem

During this stage, the sexuality counselor completes a genogram for each of them and upon inquiry learns that Gillian was sexually molested by her father from the time she was 2 years old until the age of 9. The counselor asks her to fill out an incest history questionnaire and asks the couple to describe their relationship over the last six years. Each partner is asked to describe the problems they are currently facing. Gillian states that she cannot feel intimate with Hans and she does not want to be approached sexually. She does not want to feel this way but cannot stop these feelings. Hans says that he feels frustrated and does not understand what is happening. "We have a beautiful baby girl and Gillian seems angry with me and doesn't want me to be near the baby." Gillian admits that the birth of their daughter has brought up some unpleasant memories from her childhood. The sexuality counselor explains to them that they are experiencing a very common problem for incest survivors. A critical event in their lives has triggered some of the old feelings from the abuse and it seems that she is feeling fearful about her daughter having close contact with Hans and wants to protect her so that a replication of the abuse cannot occur. In addition, she is remembering the feelings associated with sex that created feelings of vulnerability, powerlessness, and shame. Retreating from Hans's touch is a protective behavior she has initiated so that she can feel safe. Hans feels rejected and confused. The sexuality counselor provides a shared view of the problem that takes into account recurring memories from childhood sexual abuse. "It seems that the two of you would like to understand the recent reactions since the birth of your daughter and would like to learn how to be close again. It seems that you might also want to prevent the past from taking over your intimate relationship and put it back in perspective. Gillian, I know that you worked hard on this problem a few years ago, but your life has significantly changed with the birth of your daughter." The couple agrees that they want to solve their problem and recreate the intimacy they once shared.

Stage 2: Goal Setting

During the goal-setting stage, Gillian and Hans set the following goals:

1. We would like to revisit the issues Gillian experienced as a child and help her feel safe as a mother.
2. We would like to reconnect sexually, but begin slowly with touch and communication so that we feel close again.
3. We need to practice the two roles we now have as husband-wife and mother-father and feel comfortable with each other in those roles.

Stage 3: Adapting New Perceptions and Behaviors

During this stage, the strengths of each partner are emphasized. Gillian is very spontaneous and flexible and is the one who provides the spark in their relationship. Hans is the dependable one who provides the stability and structure. Both are willing to try new things. Hans has been the initiator of most sexual activity during their relationship. During counseling, they begin to experiment with the roles they have acquired and decide to take a parenting class together in order to learn more about caring for young children. In addition, they make time for themselves as a couple and initiate pleasurable activities on a weekly basis. They explore some of the feelings Gillian experiences related to her childhood abuse and use some cognitive restructuring techniques to change some of the thoughts she is having. They also begin slowly working on nonsexual touching exercises so that Gillian can feel more comfortable and progress to mutual touching and finally to intercourse. They utilize some of Gillian's spontaneity and fun-loving nature in order to create more playful sexual encounters in a safe environment. After several sessions, they are able to move in and out of the roles of mother-father and husband-wife freely and have been going out as a couple periodically. Gillian is leaving Hans with the baby for short periods of time but admits that she sometimes has feelings of anxiety. Finally, they have begun to feel more freedom in their sexual expression and have initiated much more touching, hand holding, and lying on the sofa and watching movies.

Stage 4: Maintaining New Perceptions and Behaviors

Gillian and Hans identify barriers that may impede their progress. Gillian understands that she must let Hans know when she has the feelings of doubt about him so that they can discuss them. Hans tries not to get angry, but instead reminds Gillian that he is trying to be the best father he can be and would not hurt their daughter. They agree to continue their dates with each other and vow not to let two weeks go by without a night out together. They will also work on their sexual relationship and try to be creative. Gillian agrees to take on the role of initiator at times so that she feels a sense of control over her body. They both know that they will need to continue to work on their issues, but they feel pleased with the progress they have made.

Stage 5: Validating New Perceptions and Behaviors

Gillian and Hans congratulate each other on their success and determine that they will have a weekly "counseling session" at home and review the issues they have addressed. They agree that they would like to return every three months for a progress report. They understand that they must talk about the issues as they arise and must confront fears and anxiety about parenting and sexuality head on. Their weekly counseling session at home will also serve as a forum for any problems that they may encounter.

SUMMARY

Reports of childhood sexual abuse and incest have grown rapidly over the last several decades. In fact, more women and men are seeking help for sexual and relational issues related to childhood sexual abuse. Childhood sexual abuse involves a sexual act forced on a child by an adult in a position of power or authority and with whom the child likely has a trusting relationship.

Because a trusted adult is supposed to love and protect them, survivors have a difficult time understanding why and how abuse occurred. Survivors typically come to counseling with issues of low self-esteem, guilt, shame, unresolved anger, trust issues, and anxiety. Sometimes they suffer from acute stress disorder (ASD), posttraumatic stress syndrome (PTSD), or depression. They may also exhibit dissociative patterns—"spacing out" or removing themselves emotionally from difficult situations. In some cases, they become delusional or are unable to access certain memories from the past.

Male survivors of childhood sexual abuse experience many of the same reactions as female survivors. However, they may also experience distorted thoughts related to male gender expectations, which would encompass notions such as "If I were a real man I could fight off abuse," "I should not have responded to the abuser sexually," or "I have been molested by a homosexual, therefore I am homosexual."

Many issues result in sexual problems, particularly lack of sexual desire, addictive or compulsive sexual patterns, and anorgasmia. Other sexual problems include lack of sexual interest, difficulty becoming aroused, difficulty experiencing orgasm, difficulty averting orgasm, and difficulty with intercourse. Relational issues typically manifest themselves as impairments of intimacy, problems with parents, family members, and authority figures, and problems in parenting.

An integrative couples' model is useful for treating survivors and their partners. Important features of the model for abuse survivors are to create a safe environment early in counseling and to complete a thorough incest history questionnaire. Survivors will proceed at their own rate and will inform sexuality counselors about the level of detail about their abuse that they can tolerate discussing. Couples' counseling is important because partners are often not certain how to respond when sexual and relational issues arise and they feel responsible for interactions they do not understand. Couples can explore the impact of past sexual abuse on their current relationship, and they can devise plans together for addressing issues as they surface.

REFERENCES

Abbey, A., Andrews, F. M., & Halman, L. J. (1991). Gender's role in responses to infertility. *Psychology of Women Quarterly, 15*, 295–316.

Abel, G. G. (1989). Paraphilias. In H. I. Kaplan & B. J. Sadock (Eds.), *Comprehensive textbook of psychiatry* (Vol. 1, pp. 1069–1085). Baltimore, MD: Williams & Wilkins.

Abel, G. G. (1996). *Abel Questionnaire for Men*. Distributed by Abel Screening, Inc., Atlanta GA.

Abel, G. G., & Roleau, J. L. (1995). Sexual abuses. *Psychiatric Clinics of North America, 18*, 139–154.

ACLU Fact Sheet. *Overview of lesbian and gay parenting, adoption, and foster care*. (n.d.). Retrieved July 12, 2004, from http://archive.aclu/issues/gay/parents.html

Addleston, J. (2000). *The use of narrative therapy with families of gay, lesbian, bisexual, and transgendered people*. Unpublished manuscript.

Adshead, G. (1997). Transvestic fetishism: Assessment and treatment. In D. R. Laws & W. O'Donohue (Eds.), *Sexual deviance: Assessment and treatment* (pp. 280–296). New York: Guilford.

Ainscough, C., & Toon, K. (2000). *Surviving childhood sexual abuse*. Tucson, AZ: Fisher Books.

Alan Guttmacher Institute. (2003). *Trends in abortion in the United States, 1973–2000*. Retrieved July 18, 2004, from http://www.agi-usa.org.

Allen, P. G. (1986). *The sacred hoop: Recovering the feminine in American Indian traditions*. Boston: Beacon.

Aloni, R., Ring, H., Rozenthul, N., & Schwartz, J. (1993). Sexual function in male patients after stroke: A follow-up study. *Sexuality and Disability, 11*(2), 121–128.

Althof, S. E. (2000). Erectile dysfunctions: Psychotherapy with men and couples. In S. R. Leiblum & R. C. Rosen (Eds.), *Principles and practice of sex therapy* (3rd ed., pp. 242–304). New York: Guilford.

Ambroziak, J., & Levy, J. A. (1999). Epidemiology, natural history, and pathogenesis of HIV infection. In K. K. Holmes, P. F. Sparling, P. Mardh, S. M. Lemon, W. E. Stamm, P. Piot, et al. (Eds.), *Sexually transmitted diseases* (3rd ed., pp. 251–258). New York: McGraw-Hill.

American Association of Sex Educators, Counselors, and Therapists. (1993). *Code of ethics*. Mount Vernon, IA: Author.

American Association of Sex Educators, Counselors, and Therapists. (2004, June 22). *About AASECT*. Retrieved June 28, 2004, from http://www.aasect.org/about.cfm

American Counseling Association (1995). *Code of ethics and standards of practice*. Alexandria, VA: Author.

American Psychiatric Association. (1980). *Diagnostic and statistical manual of mental disorders* (3rd ed.). Washington, DC: Author.

American Psychiatric Association. (2000). *Diagnostic and statistical manual of mental disorders* (4th ed., text revision). Washington, DC: Author.

Andersen, B. L., & Lamb, M. A. (1995). Sexuality and cancer. In G. P. Murphy, W. Lawrence, & R. E. Lenhard (Eds.), *American Cancer Society textbook of clinical oncology* (pp. 699–713). Atlanta, GA: American Cancer Society.

Andersen, B. L., Woods, X. A., & Copeland, L. J. (1997). Sexual self-schema and sexual morbidity among gynecologic cancer survivors. *Journal of Consulting and Clinical Psychology, 65*, 221–229.

Andersen, M. L. (2003). *Thinking about women: Sociological perspectives on sex and gender* (6th ed.). Boston, MA: Allyn & Bacon.

Anderson, C., & Stewart, S. (1983). *Mastering resistance: A practical guide to family therapy*. New York: Guilford.

Anderson, H. (1995). Collaborative language systems: Toward a postmodern therapy. In R. Miksell, D. D. Lusterman, & S. McDaniel (Eds.), *Integrating family therapy: Family psychology and systems theory* (pp. 27–44). Washington, DC: American Psychological Association.

Anderson, H. (1997). *Conversation, language and possibilities: A postmodern approach to therapy*. New York: Basic Books.

Anderson, H., Carleton, D., & Swim, S. (1999). A postmodern perspective on relational intimacy: A collaborative conversation and relationship with a couple. In J. Carlson & L. Sperry (Eds.), *The intimate couple* (pp. 208–226). Ann Arbor, MI: Brunner/Mazel.

Annon, J. S. (1974). *The behavioral treatment of sexual problems* (Vol. 1). *Brief therapy*. Honolulu: Enabling Systems.

Annon, J. S. (1975). *The behavioral treatment of sexual problems* (Vol. 2). *Intensive therapy*. Honolulu: Enabling Systems.

Aponte, J. F., & Johnson, L. R. (2000). The impact of culture and intervention and treatment of ethnic populations. In J. F. Aponte & J. Wohl (Eds.), *Psychological intervention and cultural diversity* (2nd ed., pp. 18–39). Needham Heights, MA: Allyn & Bacon.

Aral, S. O., & Holmes, K. K. (1999). Social and behavioral determinants of the epidemiology of STDs: Industrialized and developing countries. In K. K. Holmes, P. F. Sparling, P. Mardh, S. M. Lemon, W. E. Stamm, P. Piot, et al. (Eds.), *Sexually transmitted diseases* (3rd ed., pp. 39–76). New York: McGraw-Hill.

Arredondo, P., & Glauner, T. (1992). *Personal dimensions of identity model.* Boston: Empowerment Workshops.

Arredondo, P., Toporek, M. S., Brown, S., Jones, J., Locke, D. C., Sanchez, J., et al. (1996). *Operationalization of the multicultural counseling competencies.* Association for Multicultural Counseling and Development.

Atwood, J. D., & Dershowitz, S. (1992). Constructing a sex and marital therapy frame: Ways to help couples deconstruct sexual problems. *Journal of Sex and Marital Therapy, 18*(3), 196–218.

Avis, J. M. (1985). The politics of functional family therapy: A feminist critique. *Journal of Marital and Family Therapy, 11,* 127–138.

Axelson, J. A. (1999). *Counseling and development in a multicultural society* (3rd ed.). Pacific Grove, CA: Brooks/Cole.

Bagarozzi, D. A. (1997). Marital intimacy needs questionnaire: Preliminary report. *American Journal of Family Therapy, 25*(3), 285–291.

Ballard, M., & Allessi, H. (2002). Counseling sexual abuse and rape victims. In L. Burlew & D. Capuzzi (Eds.), *Sexuality counseling* (pp. 307–326). New York: Nova Science.

Bancroft, J. (1998, May). *Individual differences in sexual risk taking—A psycho-socio-biological theoretical approach.* Paper presented at a meeting of the Kinsey Institute, Bloomington, IN.

Bandura, A. (1969). *Principles of behavior modification.* New York: Holt, Rinehart and Winston.

Barbach, L. (2000). *For yourself: The fulfillment of female sexuality.* New York: Signet.

Barbach, L. (2001). *For each other: Sharing sexual intimacy.* New York: Signet.

Barbaree, H. E., & Seto, M. C. (1997). Frotteurism: Assessment and treatment. In D. R. Laws & W. O'Donohue (Eds.), *Sexual deviance: Assessment and treatment* (pp. 175–193). New York: Guilford.

Barnes, M. (1995). Sex therapy in the couples context: Therapy issues of victims of sexual trauma. *The American Journal of Family Therapy, 23*(4), 351–360.

Bartlik, B., & Goldberg, J. (2000). Female sexual arousal disorder. In S. R. Leiblum & R. C. Rosen, *Principles and practice of sex therapy* (3rd ed., pp. 85–117). New York: Guilford.

Baruth, L. G., & Manning, M. L. (2003). *Multicultural counseling and psychotherapy: A lifespan perspective* (3rd ed.). Upper Saddle River, NJ: Prentice Hall.

Bateson, G. (1951). Information and codification: A philosophical approach. In J. Ruesch & G. Bateson (Eds.), *Communication: The social matrix of psychiatry* (pp. 168–211). New York: Norton.

Bateson, G. (1978). The birth of a matrix or double-bind and epistemology. In M. M. Berger (Ed.), *Beyond the double-bind* (pp. 39–64). New York: Brunner/Mazel.

Bateson, G., Jackson, D. D., Haley, J., & Weakland, J. (1956). Toward a theory of schizophrenia. *Behavorial Science, 1,* 251–264.

Baumeister, R. (2000). Gender differences in erotic plasticity: The female sex drive as socially flexible and responsive. *Psychological Bulletin, 126,* 347–374.

Beavers, W. R., & Hampson, R. B. (1990). *Successful families assessment and intervention.* New York: Norton.

Beck, A. T. (1967). *Depression: Clinical, experimental, and theoretical aspects.* New York: Hoerber.

Beck, A. T. (1976). *Cognitive therapy and emotional disorders.* New York: Hoerber.

Beers, M. H., & Berkow, R. (2000). *Sexuality.* Retrieved June 28, 2004 from http://www.merck.com/mrkshared/mm_geriatrics/sex14/ch114.jsp

Beitchman, J. H., Zucker, K. J., Jood, J. E., daCosta, G. A., Akman, D., & Cassavia, E. (1992). A review of the long-term effects of child sexual abuse. *Child Abuse and Neglect, 16,* 101–118.

Bepko, C., & Johnson, T. (2000). Gay and lesbian couples in therapy: Perspective for the contemporary family therapist. *Journal of Marital and Family Therapy, 26*(4), 409–419.

Berg, I. K., & deShazer, S. (1993). Making numbers talk: Language in therapy. In S. Friedman (Ed.), *The new language of change: Constructive collaboration in psychotherapy* (pp. 5–24). New York: Guilford.

Berman, E. M., & Hof, L. (1987). The sexual genogram—Assessing family-of-origin factors in the treatment of sexual dysfunction. In G. R. Weeks & L. Hof (Eds.), *Integrating sex and marital therapy* (pp. 37–56). New York: Brunner/Mazel.

Bernstein, A. (2000). Straight therapists working with lesbian and gays in family therapy. *Journal of Marital and Family Therapy, 26*(4), 443–454.

Bertolino, B., & O'Hanlon, B. (2002). *Collaborative, competency-based counseling and therapy.* Needham Heights, MA: Allyn & Bacon.

Bewley, A. R. (1995). Re-Membering spirituality: Use of sacred ritual in psychotherapy. *Women and Therapy, 16,* 201–213.

Binik, Y. M., Bergeron, S., & Khalife, S. (2000). Dyspareunia. In S. R. Leiblum & R. C. Rosen (Eds.), *Principles and practice of sex therapy* (3rd ed., pp. 154–180). New York: Guilford.

Boen, D. L. (1988). A practitioner looks at assessment in marital counseling. *Journal of Counseling and Development, 66,* 484–486.

Bor, R., Miller, R., & Goldman, E. (1993). *Theory and practice of HIV counseling: A systemic approach.* New York: Brunner/Mazel.

Borelli, B., & Mermelstein, R. (1994). Goal setting and behavior change in a smoking cessation program. *Cognitive Therapy and Research, 18*, 69–83.

Boszormenyi-Nagy, I., & Spark, G. M. (1973). *Invisible loyalties: Reciprocity in intergenerational family therapy.* New York: Harper & Row.

Botwin, C. (1979, September 16). Is there sex after marriage? *The New York Times Magazine,* pp. 108–112.

Bourne, E. J. (2000). *The anxiety and phobia workbook* (Rev. 3rd ed.). Oakland, CA: New Harbinger.

Bowen, M. (1978). *Family therapy in clinical practice.* Northvale, NJ: Aronson.

Bowen, M. (1980). *Key to the genogram.* Washington, DC: Georgetown University Hospital.

Brandt, A. M., & Jones, D. S. (1999). Historical perspectives on sexually transmitted diseases: Challenges for prevention and control. In K. K. Holmes, P. F. Sparling, P. Mardh, S. M. Lemon, W. E. Stamm, P. Piot, et al. (Eds.), *Sexually transmitted diseases* (3rd ed., pp. 15–21). New York: McGraw-Hill.

Brecher, E. (1984). *Love, sex and aging: A consumer's union survey.* Boston: Little, Brown.

Brender, C., & Walsh, P. (1992). Prostate cancer: Evaluation and radio therapeutic management. *Cancer Journal for Clinicians, 42,* 223–240.

Briere, J. (1996). *Therapy for adults molested as children: Beyond survival.* New York: Springer.

Brown, J., & Brown, C. (2002). *Marital therapy: Concepts and skills for effective practice.* Pacific Grove, CA: Brooks/Cole.

Brown, L. (1995). Therapy with same-sex couples: An introduction. In N. S. Jacobson & A. S. Gurman (Eds.), *Clinical handbook of couple therapy* (pp. 274–291). New York: Guilford.

Brown, L. S., & Zimmer, D. (1986). An introduction to therapy issues of lesbian and gay male couples. In N. S. Jacobson & A. S. Gurman (Eds.), *Clinical handbook of marital therapy* (pp. 451–468). New York: Guilford.

Bruyere, S. M. (1994). *Working effectively with persons who have cognitive disabilities.* Ithaca, NY: Program on Employment and Disability, New York School of Industrial and Labor Relations, Cornell University.

Burke, C., & Ratelle, S. (1998). Sexually transmitted diseases. In The Boston Women's Health Book Collective, *Our bodies, ourselves: For the new century* (pp. 341–358). New York: Simon & Schuster.

Burlew, L. D., & Capuzzi, D. (2003). Sexuality counseling: Introduction, definitions, ethics, and professional issues. In L. D. Burlew & D. Capuzzi (Eds.), *Sexuality counseling* (pp. 3–16). New York: Nova Science.

Burnstein, J. G. (1983). *Handbook of drug therapy in psychiatry.* Boston: John Wright.

Butler, R., & Lewis, M. (1988). *Love and sex after 60.* San Francisco: Harper & Row.

Byrne, D., & Osland, J. A., (2000). Sexual fantasy and erotica/pornography: Internal and external imagery. In L. Szuchman & F. Muscarella (Eds.). *Psychological perspectives on human sexuality* (pp. 283–308). New York: Wiley.

Calhoun, K., & Wilson, A. (2000). *Rape and sexual aggression.* In L. T. Szuchman & F. Muscarella (Eds.), *Psychological perspectives on human sexuality* (pp. 573–602). New York: Wiley.

Capuzzi, D., & Friel, S. E. (1990). Current trends in sexuality and aging: An update for counselors. *Journal of Mental Health Counseling, 12,* 342–353.

Carl, D. (1990). *Therapy with same sex couples.* New York: Norton.

Carlson, J., Sperry, L., & Lewis, J. A. (1997). *Family therapy: Ensuring treatment efficacy.* Pacific Grove, CA: Brooks/Cole.

Carnes, P. (1989). *Contrary to love: Helping the sexual addict.* Minneapolis, MN: Comp Care.

Carnes, P. (1991). *Don't call it love: Recovery from sexual addiction.* New York: Bantam Books.

Carter, E., & McGoldrick, M. (1980). *The changing family life cycle: A framework for family therapy.* Needham Heights, MA: Allyn & Bacon.

Casas, J. M., & Pytluk, S. D. (1995). Hispanic identity development: Implications for research and practice. In J. G. Ponterotto, J. M. Casas, L. A. Suzuki, & C. M. Alexander (Eds.), *Handbook of multicultural counseling* (pp. 155–180). Thousand Oaks, CA: Sage.

Cass, V. C. (1979). Homosexuality identity formation: A theoretical model. *Journal of Homosexuality, 4,* 219–235.

Catania, J. A. (1998). Dyadic sexual communication scale. In C. M. Davis, W. L. Yarber, R. Bauserman, G. Schreer, & S. L. Davis (Eds.), *Handbook of sexuality-related measures* (pp. 129–131). Thousand Oaks, CA: Sage.

Cautela, J. E. (1986). Behavioral analysis of a fetish: First interview. *Journal of Behavior Therapy and Experimental Psychiatry, 17*(3), 161–165.

Centers for Disease Control and Prevention. Guidelines for Treatment of Sexually Transmitted Diseases. (1998). *Morbidity and Mortality Weekly Report 1998, 47*(RR-1), 1–118.

Centers for Disease Control and Prevention. Sexually Transmitted Diseases Treatment Guidelines. (2002). *Morbidity and Mortality Weekly Report 2002, 51* (RR-06), 1–80.

Centers for Disease Control and Prevention. (2004). *Sexually Transmitted Disease Surveillance, 2003.* Atlanta, GA: U.S. Department of Health and Human Services.

Centrum 45. (n.d.). *Nonverbal Therapy in Foundation Centrum 45.* Retrieved June 3, 2004, from http://www.centrum45.nl/ukindnom.htm.

Charlton, R. S. (1997). Treatment of paraphilias. In R. S. Charlton & I. D. Yalom, *Treating sexual disorders* (pp. 281–323). San Francisco: Jossey-Bass.

Charlton, R. S., & Brigel, F. W. (1997). Treatment of arousal and orgasmic disorders. In R. S. Charlton & I. D. Yalom, *Treating sexual disorders* (pp. 237–280). San Francisco: Jossey-Bass.

Cherry Engineering Support Services. (2003, July 1). *Federal statutory definitions of disability.* Retrieved February 14, 2004, from http://www.icdr.us/documents/definitions.htm

Coale, H. W. (1994). Therapeutic use of rituals with stepfamilies. *The Family Journal: Counseling and Therapy for Couples and Families, 2,* 2–10.

Cole, S. S. (1988). Women, sexuality and disabilities. *Women and Therapy, 7,* 277–294.

Cole, T. M. (1975). Sexuality and physical disabilities. *Archives of Sexual Behavior, 4,* 389–403.

Coleman, E. (1982). Developmental stages of the coming out process. *The Journal of Homosexuality, 7*(2/3), 31–43.

Coleman, E. (1985). Developmental stages of the coming out process. In J. Gonsiorek (Ed.), *A guide to psychotherapy with gay and lesbian clients* (pp. 31–43). New York: Harrington Park.

Coleman, E. (1992). Is your patient suffering from compulsive sexual behavior? *Psychiatric Annals, 22,* 320–325.

Coleman, E. (1995). Treatment of compulsive sexual behavior. In R. C. Rosen & S. R. Leiblum (Eds.), *Case studies in sex therapy* (pp. 333–349). New York: Guilford.

Coleman, E. (1998). Erectile dysfunction: A review of current medical treatments. *The Canadian Journal of Human Sexuality, 7*(3), 231–244.

Comer, R. J. (1998). *Abnormal psychology* (3rd ed.). New York: W. H. Freeman.

Comfort, A. (1991). *The new joy of sex: A gourmet guide to lovemaking for the nineties.* New York: Crown.

Cook, E. P. (1987). Characteristics of the biopsychosocial crisis of infertility. *Journal of Counseling and Development, 65,* 465–470.

Cooper, A. (1998). Sexuality on the Internet: Surfing in the new millennium. *CyberPsychology and Behavior, 1,* 181–187.

Cooper, N. (n.d.). *Making babies the gay way.* Retrieved June 2, 2004, from http://www.channel4.com/health

Cooper, N. (2004). *Making babies the gay way—The last taboo.* Retrieved February 22, 2005, from http://channel4.com/health/microsites

Cooper, A., Delmonico, D., & Burg, R. (2000). Cybersex users, abusers, and compulsives: New findings and implications. In A. Cooper (Ed.), *Cybersex: The dark side of the force* (pp. 5–29). Philadephia: Brunner Routledge.

Cooper, A., Scherer, C. R., Boies, S. C., & Gordon, B. L. (1999). Sexuality on the Internet: From sexual exploration to pathological expression. *Professional Psychology: Research and Practice, 30,* 1–24.

Cooper-Hilbert, B. (1998). *Infertility and involuntary childlessness: Helping couples cope.* New York: Norton.

Corey, G. (2001). *Theory and practice of counseling and psychotherapy.* Belmont, CA: Brooks/Cole.

Corey, G., Corey, M. S., & Callanan, P. (2003). *Issues and ethics in the helping professions* (6th ed.). Pacific Grove, CA: Brooks/Cole.

Corey, L., & Wald, A. (1999). Genital herpes. In K. K. Holmes, P. F. Sparling, P. Mardh, S. M. Lemon, W. E. Stamm, P. Piot, et al. (Eds.), *Sexually transmitted diseases* (3rd ed., pp. 285–312). New York: McGraw-Hill.

Corsini, R. J., & Wedding, D. (1995). *Current psychotherapies* (5th ed.). Itasca, IL: Peacock.

Corso, K. (1993). *Testing options for use in family therapy.* Unpublished manuscript.

Courtois, C. A. (1988). *Healing the incest wound: Adult survivors in therapy.* New York: Norton.

Courtois, C. A. (1997). Healing the incest wound: A treatment update with attention to recovered memory issues. *American Journal of Psychotherapy, 51*(4), 464–496.

Crooks, R., & Baur, K. (1990). *Our sexuality* (4th ed.). Redwood City, CA: Benjamin Cummings.

Crooks, R., & Baur, K. (1996). *Our sexuality* (5th ed.). Pacific Grove, CA: Brooks/Cole.

Crooks, R. & Baur, K. (2002). *Our sexuality* (8th ed.). Pacific Grove, CA: Wadsworth.

Crowe, M., & Norsigian, J. (1992). Sexually transmitted diseases. In The Boston Women's Health Book Collective, *The new our bodies, ourselves: A book by and for women* (pp. 308–326). New York: Simon & Schuster.

Cupach, W. R., & Comstock, J. (1990). Satisfaction with sexual communication in marriage: Links to sexual satisfaction and dyadic adjustment. *Journal of Social and Personal Relationships, 7,* 179–186.

Cutson, T., & Meuleman, E. (2000). Managing menopause. *American Family Physician, 61,* 1391–1400.

Daines, B. (1990). Sexual myths and sex therapy. *Journal of Sexual and Marital Therapy, 5,* 149–154.

Daniluk, J. C. (1997). Gender and infertility. In S. R. Leiblum (Ed.), *Infertility: Medical, ethical, and psychological perspectives* (pp. 103–125). New York: Wiley.

Danoff-Burg, S., & Revenson, T. A. (2000). Rheumatic illness and relationships: Coping as a joint venture. In K. B. Schmaling & T. Goldman Sher (Eds.), *The psychology of couples and illness: Theory, research and practice* (pp. 105–133). Washington, DC: American Psychological Association.

Dattilio, F. M., & Bevilacqua, L. J. (2000). A cognitive-behavioral approach. In F. M. Dattilio & L. J. Bevilacqua (Eds.), *Comparative treatments for relationship dysfunction* (pp. 137–159). New York: Springer.

Dattilio, F. M., Epstein, M. B., & Baucom, D. H. (1998). An introduction of cognitive-behavioral therapy with couples and families. In F. M. Dattilio (Ed.), *Case studies in couple and family therapy* (pp. 1–36). New York: Guilford.

Dattilio, F. M., & Padesky, C. A. (1990). *Cognitive therapy with couples.* Sarasota, FL: Professional Resource Exchange.

Davidson, G. C., & Neale, J. M. (1998). *Abnormal Psychology* (7th ed.). New York: Wiley.

Davis, C. M., Yarber, W. L., Bauserman, R., Schreer, F., & Davis, S. L. (Eds.). (1998). *Handbook of sexuality-related measures.* Thousand Oaks, CA: Sage.

Degges-White, S., Rice, B., & Myers, J. (2000). Revisiting Cass' theory of sexual identity formation: A study of lesbian development. *Journal of Mental Health Counseling, 22*(4), 318–333.

DeJong, P., & Berg, I. (1998). *Interviewing for solutions.* Pacific Grove, CA: Brooks/Cole.

DeJong, P., & Berg, I. K. (2002). *Interviewing for solutions* (2nd ed.). Pacific Grove, CA: Brooks/Cole.

DeJong, P., & Miller, S. D. (1995). How to interview for client strengths. *Social Work, 40,* 729–736.

DeLoach, C. P. (1994). Attitudes towards disability: Impact on sexual development and forging of intimate relationships. *Journal of Applied Rehabilitation Counseling, 25*(1), 18–25.

Derogatis, L. R. (1986). The psychosocial adjustment to illness scale. *Journal of Psychosomatic Research, 30,* 77–91.

Derogatis, L. R., & Melisaratos, N. (1979). The DSFI: A multidimensional measure of sexual functioning. *Journal of Sex and Marital Therapy, 5,* 244–281.

Derogatis, L. R., Morrow, G. R., Fetting, J., Penman, D., Piasetsky, S., Schmale, A. M., et al. (1983). The prevalence of psychiatric disorders among cancer patients. *Journal of the American Medical Association, 249,* 751–757.

deShazer, S. (1985). *Keys to solutions in brief therapy.* New York: Norton.

deShazer, S. (1988). *Clues: Investigating solutions in brief therapy.* New York: Norton.

deShazer, S. (1991). *Putting difference to work.* New York: Norton.

deShazer, S. (1994). *Words were originally magic.* New York: Norton.

Diamond, R., Kezur, D., Meyers, M., Scharf, C. N., & Weinshel, M. (1999). *Couple therapy for infertility.* New York: Guilford.

Dietz, P. E., Hazelwood, R. R., & Warren, J. (1990). The sexually sadistic criminal and his offenses. *Bulletin of the American Academy of Psychiatric Law, 17*(2), 163–178.

Diller, J. V. (2004). *Cultural diversity: A primer for the human services* (2nd ed.). Belmont, CA: Brooks/Cole.

Dorado, J. (1996). Legal and psychological approaches towards adult survivors of childhood incest: Irreconcilable differences? *Women and Therapy, 19*(1), 93–108.

Dove, N., & Wiederman, M. (2000). Cognitive distraction and women's sexual functioning. *Journal of Sex and Marital Therapy, 26,* 67–78.

Drescher, J. (1998). I'm your handyman: A history of reparative therapies. *Journal of Homosexuality, 36,* 19–42.

Drummond, R. J. (2000). *Appraisal procedures for counselors and helping professionals* (4th ed.). Upper Saddle River, NJ: Prentice Hall.

Duhl, B., & Duhl, F. (1981). Integrative family therapy. In A. Gurman and D. Kniskern (Eds.), *Handbook of family therapy* (pp. 483–513). New York: Brunner/Mazel.

Dunkel-Schetter, C., Feinstein, L. G., Taylor, S. E., & Falke, R. L. (1992). Patterns of coping with cancer. *Health Psychology, 11,* 79–87.

Dunn, M., & Cutler, N. (2000). Sexual issues in older adults. *AIDS Patient Care and STDs, 14,* 67–69.

Dwyer, T. F., & Niemann, S. H. (2002). Counseling and sexually transmitted diseases. In L. D. Burlew & D. Capuzzi (Eds.), *Sexuality counseling* (pp. 373–394). New York: Nova Science.

Ehrenfeld, M., Bronner, G., Tabak, N., Alpert, R., & Bergman, R. (1999). Sexuality among institutionalized elderly patients with dementia. *Nursing Ethics, 6,* 144–149.

Ellis, A. (1975). The rational-emotive approach to sex therapy. *Counseling Psychologist, 5,* 14–21.

Ellis, A., & Mitchell, R. (2000). Sexual orientation. In L. Szuchman & F. Muscarella (Eds.), *Psychological perspectives on human sexuality* (pp. 196–208). New York: Wiley.

Epperly, T. D., & Moore, K. E. (2000). Health issues in men: Part I. Common genitourinary disorders. *American Family Physician, 61*(12), 3657–3664.

Epstein, N. B., Baucom, D. H., & Daiuto, A. (1997). Cognitive-behavioral couples therapy. In W. K. Halford & H. J. Markman (Eds.), *Clinical handbook of marriage and couples interventions* (pp. 415–449). New York: Wiley.

Epston, D., & White, M. (1992). *Experience, contradiction, narrative, and imagination: Selected papers of David Epston and Michael White, 1989–1991.* Adelaide, South Australia: Dulwich Centre.

Erickson, E. H. (1963). *Childhood and society.* New York: Norton.

Erickson, M. H. (1944). The method employed to formulate a complex story for the induction of an experimental neurosis in a hypnotic subject. *Journal of General Psychology, 31,* 191–212.

Erickson, M. H. (1966). The interpersonal technique for symptom correction and pain control. *American Journal of Clinical Hypnosis, 3,* 198–209.

Erickson, M. H. (1973). A field investigation by hypnosis of sound loci importance in human behavior. *American Journal of Clinical Hypnosis, 16,* 92–109.

Eron, J. J., & Hirsch, M. S. (1999). Antiviral therapy for human immunodeficiency virus infection. In K. K. Holmes, P. F. Sparling, P. Mardh, S. M. Lemon, W. E. Stamm, P. Piot, et al. (Eds.), *Sexually transmitted diseases* (3rd ed., pp. 1009–1029). New York: McGraw-Hill.

Everaerd, W., Laan, E. T. M., Both, S., & Van Der Velde, J. (2000). Female sexuality. In L. T. Szuchman & F. Muscarella (Eds.), *Psychological perspectives on human sexuality* (pp. 101–143). New York: Wiley.

Everaerd, W., Laan, E. T. M., & Spiering, M. (2000). Male sexuality. In L. T. Szuchman & F. Muscarella (Eds.), *Psychological perspectives on human sexuality* (pp. 60–100). New York: Wiley.

Eyberg, S. M., Edwards, D., Boggs, S. R., & Foote, R. (1998). Maintaining the treatment effects of parent training: The role of booster sessions and other maintenance strategies. *Clinical Psychology: Science and Practice, 5,* 544–554.

Fairbairn, W. R. D. (1954). *An object-relations theory of personality.* New York: Basic Books.

Farrow, J. (1990). Sexuality counseling with clients who have spinal cord injuries. *Rehabilitation Counseling Bulletin, 33*(3), 251–259.

Feierman, J. R., & Feierman, L. A. (2000). Paraphilias. In L. T. Szuchman & F. Muscarella (Eds.), *Psychological perspectives on human sexuality* (pp. 480–518). New York: Wiley.

Feldman, L. (1990). Multi-dimensional family therapy. New York: Guilford.

Feldman, R. S. (2003). *Development across the life span* (3rd ed.). Upper Saddle River, NJ: Prentice Hall.

Finkelstein, L. (1987). Toward an object-relations approach in psychoanalytic marital therapy. *Journal of Family Therapy, 13,* 287–298.

Fisher, J. E., Swingen, D. N., & O'Donohue, W. (1997). Behavioral interventions for sexual dysfunction in the elderly. *Behavior Therapy, 28,* 65–82.

Fowers, B. J., & Olson, D. H. (1986). Predicting marital success with PREPARE: A predictive validity study. *Journal of Marital and Family Therapy, 12*(4), 403–413.

Fox, R., & Carey, L. (1999). Therapist's collusion with the resistance of rape survivors. *Clinical Social Work Journal, 27*(2), 185–201.

Freeman, J., Epston, D., & Lobovits, D. (1997). *Playful approaches to serious problems: Narrative therapy with children and their families.* New York: Norton.

Freud, S. (1910). The origin and development of psychoanalysis. *American Journal of Psychology, 21,* 181–218.

Freud, S. (1917). *A general introduction to psychoanalysis.* New York: Washington Press.

Friedman, E. H. (1991). Bowen theory and therapy. In A. S. Gurman & D. P. Kniskern (Eds.), *Handbook of Family Therapy* (Vol. 2, pp. 134–170). New York: Brunner/Mazel.

Frishman, R. (1996, October). Hormone replacement therapy for men. *Harvard Health Letter,* 6–8.

Fukuyama, M., & Ferguson, A. (2000). Lesbian, gay, and bisexual people of color: Understanding cultural complexity and managing multiple oppression. In R. Perez, K. DeBord, & K. Bieschke (Eds.), *Handbook of counseling and psychotherapy with gay, lesbian, and bisexual clients* (pp. 81–106). Washington, DC: American Psychological Association.

Furey, W. M., & Basili, L. A. (1988). Predicting consumer satisfaction in parent training for noncompliant children. *Behavior Therapy, 19,* 555–564.

Gagnon, J., Rosen, R., & Leiblum, S. (1982). Cognitive and social aspects of sexual dysfunction: Sexual scripts in sex therapy. *Journal of Sex and Marital Therapy, 8,* 44–56.

Gainor, K. (2000). Including transgender issues in lesbian, gay, and bisexual psychology implications for clinical practice and training. In B. Green & G. Croom (Eds.), *Education, research, and practices in lesbian, gay, bisexual, and transgendered psychology* (Vol. 5, pp. 131–160). Thousand Oaks, CA: Sage.

Ganz, P. (1996). Understanding cancer, its treatment, and the side effects of treatment. In B. Hoffman (Ed.), *A cancer survivor's almanac: Charting your journey* (pp. 3–30). Minneapolis: Chronimed.

Garippa, P. A. (1994). Case report: Anaesthetic ejaculation resolved in interactive sex therapy. *Journal of Sex and Marital Therapy, 20*(1), 56–60.

Garippa, P., & Sanders, N. (1997). Resolution of erectile dysfunction and inhibited male orgasm in a single homosexual male and transfer of inhibited male orgasm cure to his partner: A case report. *Journal of Sexual and Marital Therapy, 23*(2), 126–130.

Gibson, D. M., & Meyers, J. E. (2000). Gender and infertility: A relational approach to counseling women. *Journal of Counseling and Development, 78*(4), 400–410.

Gijs, L., & Gooren, L. (1996). Hormonal and psychopharmacological interventions in the treatment of paraphilias: An update. *Journal of Sex Research, 33*(4), 273–290.

Gilbert, L. A., & Scher, M. (1999). *Gender and sex in counseling and psychotherapy.* Needham Heights, MA: Allyn & Bacon.

Gilbert, M., & Shmukler, D. (1996). *Brief therapy with couples: An integrative approach.* New York: Wiley.

Gill, H. (1997). Medical evaluation of sexual function: Urological evaluation of erectile dysfunction. In R. S. Charlton & I. D. Yalom (Eds.), *Treating sexual disorders* (pp. 110–122). San Francisco: Jossey-Bass.

Gillan, P. (1987). *Sex therapy manual.* Chicago, IL: Year Book Medical.

Gilliand, B., & James, R. (1993). *Crisis intervention strategies.* Pacific Grove, CA: Brooks/Cole.

Gilligan, C. (1982). *In a different voice: Psychological theory in women's development.* Cambridge, MA: Harvard.

Gladding, S. T. (1998). *Family therapy: History, theory, and practice* (2nd ed.). Upper Saddle River, NJ: Prentice Hall.

Glazer, E. S. (1997). Miscarriage and its aftermath. In S. R. Leiblum, *Infertility: Psychological issues and counseling strategies* (pp. 230–245). New York: Wiley.

Gold, S. R., & Gold, R. G. (1993). Sexual aversions: A hidden disorder. In W. O'Donohue & J. H. Geer (Eds.), *Handbook of sexual dysfunctions: Assessment and treatment* (pp. 83–102). Needham Heights, MA: Allyn & Bacon.

Goldenberg, I., & Goldenberg, H. (2000). *Family therapy: An overview* (5th ed.). Pacific Grove, CA: Brooks/Cole.

Goldenberg, I., & Goldenberg, H. (2004). *Family therapy: An overview* (6th ed.). Pacific Grove, CA: Brooks/Cole.

Goldner, V. (1985). Feminism and family therapy. *Family Process, 24,* 13–47.

Goldsmith, L. (1988). Treatment of sexual dysfunction. In E. Weinstein & E. Rosen (Eds.), *Sexuality counseling: Issues & implications* (pp. 16–34). Belmont, CA: Brooks/Cole.

Golombok, S., Rust, J., & Pickard, C. (1984). Sexual problems encountered in general practice. *British Journal of Sexual Medicine, 11,* 65–72.

Green, A. H. (1993). Child sexual abuse: Immediate and long-term effects and intervention. *Journal of the American Academy of Child and Adolescent Psychiatry, 32,* 890–902.

Greene, B., & Boyd-Franklin, N. (1996). African American lesbian couples: Ethnic cultural considerations in psychotherapy. *Women and Therapy, 19*(3), 49–60.

Greenfield, D. N. (1999). *Virtual addiction: Help for netheads, cyberfreaks, and those who love them.* Oakland, CA: New Harbinger.

Grencavage, L. M., & Norcross, J. C. (1990). Where are the commonalities among the therapeutic common factors? *Professional Psychology: Research and Practice, 21,* 372–378.

Griffin, W. A., & Greene, S. M. (1999). *Models of family therapy: The essential guide.* Philadelphia: Brunner/Mazel.

Grotevant, H. D., & Carlson, C. I. (1989). *Family assessment: A guide to methods and measures.* New York: Guilford.

Groth, A. N., & Birnbaum, H. J. (1978). Adult sexual orientation and attraction to under-age person. *Archives of Sexual Behavior, 7,* 175–181.

Gurman, A. S. (1981). Integrative marital therapy: Toward the development of an interpersonal approach. In S. H. Budman (Ed.), *Forms of brief therapy* (pp. 415–462). New York: Guilford.

Hahleweg, K., Baucom, D. H., & Markman, H. (1988). Recent advances in behavioral and marital therapy and in preventing marital distress. In I. R. H. Falloon (Ed.), *Handbook of behavioral family therapy* (pp. 413–448). New York: Guilford.

Haley, J. (1963). *Strategies of psychotherapy.* New York: Grune & Stratton.

Haley, J. (1973). *Uncommon therapy: The psychiatric techniques of Milton H. Erickson, M.D.* New York: Norton.

Haley, J. (1976). *Problem-solving therapy.* San Francisco: Jossey-Bass.

Halford, W. K., Scott, J. L., & Smythe, J. (2000). Couples and coping with cancer: Helping each other through the night. In B. Schmaling & T. Goldman Sher (Eds.), *The psychology of couples and illness: Theory, research and practice* (pp. 135–170). Washington, DC: American Psychological Association.

Hall, M. (2001). Beyond forever after: Narrative therapy with lesbian couples. In P. Kleinplatz (Ed.), *New directions in sex therapy* (pp. 279–301). Philadelphia: Brunner Routledge.

Hall, C. S., Lindzey, G., & Campbell, J. B. (1998). *Theories of personality* (4th ed.). New York: Wiley.

Hamer, D., Hu, S., Magnuson, V., Hu, N., & Pattatucci, A. (1993). A linkage between DNA markers on the X chromosome and male sexual orientation. *Journal of Science, 26,* 321–327.

Hanna, W. J., & Rogovsky, E. (1991). Women with disabilities: Two handicaps plus. *Disability, Handicap, and Society, 6*(1), 49–62.

Hare-Mustin, R. T. (1978). A feminist approach to family therapy. *Family Process, 17,* 181–194.

Harrison, R. F., O'Moore, M., & O'Moore, R. (1986). The management of stress in infertility. In L. Dennerstein & J. Fraser (Eds.), *Hormones and behavior* (pp. 358–367). Amsterdam, Netherlands: Elsevier North-Holland.

Hatfield, E. (1988). Passionate and companionate love. In R. J. Sternberg & M. L. Barnes (Eds.), *The psychology of love* (pp. 191–217). New Haven, CT: Yale University Press.

Hedge, B. (1996). Counseling people with AIDS, their partners, family and friends. In J. Green & A. McCreaner (Eds.), *Counseling in HIV infection and AIDS* (2nd ed., pp. 66–82). Cambridge, MA: Blackwell Science.

Heiman, J. R. (2000). Orgasmic disorders in women. In S. R. Leiblum & R. C. Rosen, *Principles and practice of sex therapy* (3rd ed., pp. 118–153). New York: Guilford.

Heiman, J., LoPiccolo, L., & LoPiccolo, J. (1976). *Becoming orgasmic: A sexual growth program for women.* Upper Saddle River, NJ: Prentice Hall.

Heiman, J., LoPiccolo, L., & LoPiccolo, J. (1981). The treatment of sexual dysfunction. In A. S. Gurman & D. P. Kniskern (Eds.), *Clinical handbook of family therapy* (pp. 592–631). New York: Brunner/Mazel.

Heiman, J., LoPiccolo, L., & LoPiccolo, J. (1988). *Becoming orgasmic: A personal and sexual growth program for women* (Rev. ed.). Upper Saddle River, NJ: Prentice Hall.

Heiman, J., & Meston, M. (1997). Empirically validated treatment for sexual dysfunctions. *Annual Review of Sex Research, 8,* 148–194.

Heinen, J. R. (1985). A primer on psychological theory. *Journal of Psychology, 119,* 413–421.

Heitler, S. (1997). *The power of two: Secrets to a strong & loving marriage.* Oakland, CA: New Harbinger.

Heller, P. E., & Wood, B. (1998). The process of intimacy: Similarity, understanding and gender. *Journal of Marital and Family Therapy, 24,* 273–288.

Hellerstein, H. K., & Friedman, E. J. (1970). Sexual activity and the post coronary patient. *Archives of Internal Medicine, 125,* 987–999.

Helms, J. E., & Cook, D. A. (1999). *Using race and culture in counseling and psychotherapy, theory and process.* Needham Heights, MA: Allyn & Bacon.

Herlihy, B., & Corey, G. (Eds.). (1996). *ACA Ethical standards casebook* (5th ed.). Alexandria, VA: American Counseling Association.

Herman, J. (1997). *Trauma and recovery.* New York: Basic Books.

Herter, C. (1998). Sexual dysfunction in patients with diabetes. *Journal of the American Board of Family Practice, 11,* 327–330.

Hillier, S., & Holmes, K. K. (1999). Bacterial vaginosis. In K. K. Holmes, P. F. Sparling, P. Mardh, S. M. Lemon, W. E. Stamm, P. Piot, et al. (Eds.), *Sexually transmitted diseases* (3rd ed., pp. 563–586). New York: McGraw-Hill.

Hoagwood, K. (1990). Blame and adjustment among women sexually abused as children. *Women and Therapy, 9,* 89–110.

Hodson, D. S., & Skeen, P. (1994). Sexuality and aging: The hammerlock of myths. *Journal of Applied Gerontology, 13,* 219–235.

Hof, L. (1987). Evaluating the marital relationship of clients with sexual complaints. In G. R. Weeks & L. Hof (Eds.), *Integrating sex and marital therapy: A clinical guide* (pp. 5–22). New York: Brunner/Mazel.

Hof, L., & Berman, E. (1986). The sexual genogram. *Journal of Marital and Family Therapy, 12,* 39–47.

Hoffman, M. A. (1991). Counseling the HIV-infected client: A psychological model for assessment and intervention. *The Counseling Psychologist, 19,* 467–542.

Hogan, D. R. (1978). The effectiveness of sex therapy: A review of the literature. In J. LoPiccolo & L. LoPiccolo (Eds.), *Handbook of sex therapy* (pp. 58–84). New York: Plenum.

Holmes, K. K., Sparling, P. F., Mardh, P., Lemon, S. M., Stamm, W. E., Piot, P., et al. (1999). *Sexually transmitted diseases* (3rd ed.). New York: McGraw-Hill.

Holzman, C. (1996). Counseling adult women rape survivors: Issues of race, ethnicity and class. *Women and Therapy, 19,* 47–62.

Hook, E. W., & Handsfield, H. H. (1999). Gonococcal infections in the adult. In K. K. Holmes, P. F. Sparling, P. Mardh, S. M. Lemon, W. E. Stamm, P. Piot, et al. (Eds.), *Sexually transmitted diseases* (3rd ed., pp. 451–466). New York: McGraw-Hill.

Hovestadt, A., Anderson, W., Piercy, F., Cochran, S., & Fine, M. (1985). A family of origin scale. *Journal of Marriage and Family Therapy, 11,* 287–298.

Huber, C. H. (1996). Facilitating disclosure of HIV-positive status to family members. *The Family Journal:*

Counseling and Therapy for Couples and Families, 4(1), 53–55.

Hudgins, K., & Drucker, K. (1998). The containing double as part of the therapeutic spiral model for treating trauma survivors. *International Journal of Action Methods, 51*(2), 63–74.

Imber-Black, E. (1989). Rituals of stabilization and change in women's lives. In M. McGoldrick, C. M. Andersen, & F. Walsh (Eds.), *Women in families: A framework for family therapy* (pp. 451–469). New York: Norton.

Imber-Black, E., & Roberts, J. (1998). *Rituals for our times: Celebrating, healing, and changing our lives and our relationships.* New York: Aronson.

Imber-Black, E., Roberts, J., & Whiting, R. (1988). *Rituals in families and family therapy.* New York: Norton.

Jackson, D. D. (1957). The question of family homeostasis. *Psychiatric Quarterly Supplement, 31,* 79–90.

Jackson, D. D. (1965). Family rules: Marital quid pro quo. *Archives of General Psychiatry, 12,* 589–594.

Jacobson, E. (1974). *Progressive relaxation.* (Midway Reprint.) Chicago: University of Chicago Press.

Jacobson, N., & Christensen, A. (1996). *Integrative couple therapy.* New York: Norton.

Janssen, E. (1997). *Inhibitory mechanisms and sexual response.* Paper presented at 23rd Conference of the International Academy of Sex Research, Baton Rouge, LA.

Janus, S. S., & Janus, C. L. (1993). *The Janus report on sexual behavior.* New York: Wiley.

Jensen, S. B. (1981). Diabetic sexual dysfunction: A comparative study of 160 insulin treated diabetic men and women and an age-matched control. *Archives of Sexual Behavior, 10*(6), 493–504.

Jensen, S. B. (1985). Emotional aspects in diabetes mellitus: A study of somatopsychologic reactions in 51 couples in which one partner has insulin-treated diabetes. *Journal of Psychosomatic Research, 29,* 353–359.

Jernigan, K. (n.d.). *A definition of blindness.* Retrieved February 14, 2004, from www.nfb.org/definition.htm

Johannes, C., Araujo, A., & Feldman, H. (2000). Incidence of erectile dysfunction in men 40 to 69 years old: Longitudinal results from the Massachusetts male aging study. *The Journal of Urology, 163,* 460–463.

Kafka, M. P. (1991). Successful antiandrogen treatment of nonparaphilic sexual addictions and paraphilias in men. *Journal of Clinical Psychiatry, 52,* 60–65.

Kafka, M. P. (1997). Hypersexual desires in males: An operational definition and clinical implications for males with paraphilias and papaphilia-related disorders. *Archives of Sexual Behavior, 21,* 505–526.

Kafka, M. P. (2000). The paraphilia-related disorders: Non-paraphilic hypersexuality and sexual compulsivity/addiction. In S. R. Leiblum & R. C. Rosen (Eds.),

Principles and practice of sex therapy (3rd ed., pp. 471–503). New York: Guilford.

Kafka, M. P., & Hennen, J. (1999). The paraphilia-related disorders: An empirical investigation of nonparaphilic hypersexuality disorders in 206 outpatient males. *Journal of Sex and Marital Therapy, 25,* 305–320.

Kaplan, H. I., & Sadock, B. J. (1998). *Synopsis of psychiatry.* Philadelphia: Lippincott Williams & Wilkins.

Kaplan, H. S. (1974). *The new sex therapy.* New York: Brunner/Mazel.

Kaplan, H. S. (1979). *Disorders of sexual desire.* New York: Brunner/Mazel.

Kaplan, H. S. (1983). *The evaluation of sexual disorders: Psychological and medical aspects.* New York: Brunner/Mazel.

Kaplan, H. S. (1987). *The illustrated manual of sex therapy* (2nd ed.). New York: Brunner/Mazel.

Kaplan, H. S. (1989). *How to overcome premature ejaculation.* New York: Brunner/Mazel.

Kaplan, H. S. (1995). *The sexual desire disorders: The dysfunctional regulation of sexual motivation.* New York: Brunner/Mazel.

Karpel, M. A. (1994). *Evaluating couples: A handbook for practitioners.* New York: Norton.

Keen, S. (2002, July/August). The men's movement and beyond: Thoughts from Sam Keen. *Family Therapy Magazine,* 32–35.

Kellett, J. M. (2000). Older adult sexuality. In L. Szuchman & F. Muscarella (Eds.), *Psychological perspectives on human sexuality* (pp. 355–379). New York: Wiley.

Kelly, G. (1996). *Sexuality today: The human perspective* (5th ed.). Madison, WI: Brown and Benchmark.

Kelly, G. (2004). *Sexuality today: The human perspective* (7th ed.). New York: McGraw-Hill.

Kelly, K. R. (1991). Theoretical integration in the future for mental health counseling. *Journal of Mental Health Counseling, 13*(1), 106–111.

Kernberg, O. F. (1976). *Object-relations theory and clinical psychoanalysis.* New York: Aronson.

Kerns, R. D., Turk, D. C., & Rudy, T. E. (1985). The West Haven-Yale Multidimensional Pain Inventory (WHYMPI). *Pain, 23,* 345–356.

Kerr, M. E., & Bowen, M. (1988). *Family evaluation: An approach based on Bowen theory.* New York: Norton.

Kettl, P. A. (1998). Sexuality after spinal cord injury questionnaire. In C. M. Davis, W. L. Yarber, R. Bauserman, F. Schreer, & S. L. Davis (Eds.), *Handbook of sexuality-related measures* (pp. 179–182). Thousand Oaks, CA: Sage.

Kingsberg, S. A. (2000). The psychological impact of aging on sexuality and relationships. *Journal of Women's Health and Gender-Based Medicine, 9,* 33–38.

Kinsey, A. C., Pomeroy, W. B., Martin, C. E., & Gebhard, P. H. (1953). *Sexual behavior in the human female.* Philadelphia: Saunders.

Kitchener, K. S. (1984). Intuition, critical evaluation and ethical principles: The foundation for ethical decisions in counseling psychology. *The Counseling Psychologist, 12*(3), 43–55.

Klein, M. (1957). *Envy and gratitude.* New York: Basic Books.

Klein, M. (1975). *Love, guilt, and reparation and other works.* London: Hogarth.

Klein, M. (1997). Disorders of desire. In I. Yalom (Ed.), *Treating sexual disorders* (pp. 201–236). San Francisco: Jossey-Bass.

Knopp, F. H., Freeman-Longo, R. E., & Stevenson, W. E. (1992). *Nationwide survey of juvenile and adult sex offender treatment programs and models.* Orwell, VT: Safer Society.

Kohn, A. (1987, February). Shattered innocence. *Psychology Today,* 54–58.

Kohn, I., & Moffit, P. L. (1992). *A silent sorrow: Pregnancy loss.* New York: Bantam Doubleday Dell.

Kohut, H. (1971). *The analysis of self.* New York: International Universities.

Kohut, H. (1977). *The restoration of the self.* New York: International Universities.

Kolodny, R. C., Masters, W. H., & Johnson, V. E. (1979). *Textbook of sexual medicine.* Boston: Little, Brown.

Kottler, J. (1994). *Beyond blame.* New York: Jossey-Bass.

Koutsky, L. A., & Kiviat, N. B. (1999). Genital human papillomavirus. In K. K. Holmes, P. F. Sparling, P. Mardh, S. M. Lemon, W. E. Stamm, P. Piot, et al. (Eds.), *Sexually transmitted diseases* (3rd ed., pp. 347–359). New York: McGraw-Hill.

Krieger, J. N., & Alderete, J. F. (1999). *Trichomonas vaginalis* and trichomoniasis. In K. K. Holmes, P. F. Sparling, P. Mardh, S. M. Lemon, W. E. Stamm, P. Piot, et al. (Eds.), *Sexually transmitted diseases* (3rd ed., pp. 587–604). New York: McGraw-Hill.

Krueger, R. B., & Kaplan, M. S. (1997). Frotteurism: The theory of courtship disorder. In D. R. Laws & W. O'Donohue (Eds.), *Sexual deviance: Assessment and treatment* (pp. 131–151). New York: Guilford.

Krukofsky, B. (1988). Sexuality counseling of people with chronic illness. In E. Weinstein & E. Rosen (Eds.), *Sexuality counseling: Issues and implications* (pp. 259–273). Pacific Grove, CA: Brooks/Cole.

L'Abate, L., & Talmadge, W. C. (1987). Love, intimacy, and sex. In G. R. Weeks & L. Hof (Eds.), *Integrating sex and marital therapy: A clinical guide* (pp. 23–34). New York: Brunner/Mazel.

LaFromboise, T. D., Coleman, H. L. K., & Gerton, J. (1993). Psychological impact of biculturalism: Evidence and theory. *Psychological Bulletin, 114,* 388–397.

Laird, W., & Hartman, A. (1988). *Women, rituals, and family therapy.* New York: Haworth.

Landis, L., & Wyre, C. (1984). Mothers of incest victims: A step by step approach. *Journal of Counseling and Development, 63,* 2.

Landis, L. L., & Young, M. E. (1994). The reflecting team in counselor education. *Counseling Education and Supervision, 33,* 210–218.

LaSala, M. (2000). Lesbians, gay men, and their parents: Family therapy for the coming-out crisis. *Family Process, 39,* 67–81.

Laumann, E. O., Gagnon, J. H., Michael, R. T., & Michaels, S. (1994). *The social organization of sexuality: Sexual practices in the United States.* Chicago: University of Chicago Press.

Laws, D. R., & Marshall, L. W. (1991). Masturbatory reconditioning with sexual deviates: An evaluative review. *Advances in Behavior Research and Therapy, 13,* 13–25.

Lazarus, A. A. (1989). Dyspareunia: A multimodal psychotherapeutic perspective. In S. R. Leiblum & R. C. Rosen (Eds.), *Principles and practice of sex therapy: Update for the 1990s* (2nd ed., pp. 92–111). New York: Guilford.

Lebow, J. (1997). The integrative revolution in couple and family therapy. *Family Process, 30*(1), 1–17.

Leiblum, S. R. (1997a). *Infertility.* New York: Wiley.

Leiblum, S. R. (1997b). Sex and the net: clinical implications. *Journal of Sex Education and Therapy, 22*(1), 21–27.

Leiblum, S. R. (2000). Vaginismus: A most perplexing problem. In S. R. Leiblum & R. C. Rosen (Eds.), *Principles and practice of sex therapy* (3rd ed., pp. 181–202). New York: Guilford.

Leiblum, S., & Rosen, R. (1984). *Alcohol and human sexual response.* New York: Haworth.

Leiblum, S. R., & Rosen, R. C. (1982). *Guidelines for taking a sex history.* Handout by authors.

Leiblum, S. R., & Rosen, R. C. (Eds.). (2000). *Principles and practice of sex therapy* (3rd ed.). New York: Guilford.

Leiblum, S. R., & Segraves, R. T. (2000). Sex therapy with aging adults. In S. R. Leiblum & R. C. Rosen (Eds.), *Principles and practice of sex therapy* (3rd ed., pp. 423–448). New York: Guilford.

Lemon, S. M., & Alter, J. M. (1999). Viral hepatitis. In K. K. Holmes, P. F. Sparling, P. Mardh, S. M. Lemon, W. E. Stamm, P. Piot, et al. (Eds.), *Sexually transmitted diseases* (3rd ed., pp. 361–384). New York: McGraw-Hill.

Lesh, K., & Marshall, C. (1984). Rehabilitation: Focus on women with disabilities. *Journal of Applied Rehabilitation Counseling, 15*(1), 18–21.

Leslie, L. (1995). Psychotherapy: The evolving treatment of gender, ethnicity and sexual orientation in marital and family therapy. *Family Relations, 44*(4), 359.

Lever, J. (1976). Sex differences in the games children play. *Social Problems, 23,* 478–487.

Levine, H. (1997). A further exploration of the lesbian identity development process and its measurement. *Journal of Homosexuality, 34*(2), 67–78.

Levine, S. B. (2000). Paraphilias. In H. I. Kaplan & B. J. Saddock (Eds.), *Comprehensive textbook of psychiatry* (Vol. I, 7th ed., pp. 1631–1645). Philadelphia: Lippincott Williams & Wilkins.

Levy, J. A. (1994). Sex and sexuality in later life stages. In A. S. Rossi (Ed.), *Sexuality across the life course* (pp. 287–309). Chicago: University of Chicago Press.

Lightfoot-Klein, H., Chase, C., Hammond, T., & Goldman, R. (2000). In L. T. Szuchman & F. Muscarella, *Psychological perspectives on human sexuality* (pp. 440–479). New York: Wiley.

Lindemann, C. (1988). Counselling issues in disclosure of sexually transmitted disease. In M. Rodway & M. Wright (Eds.), *Sociopsychological aspects of sexually transmitted diseases* (pp. 55–70). New York: Hawthorn.

Linton, S., & Rousso, H. (1988). Sexuality counseling for people with disabilities. In E. Weinstein & E. Rosen (Eds.), *Sexuality counseling: Issues and implications* (pp. 114–134). Pacific Grove, CA: Brooks/Cole.

Litwin, M., Hays, R., Fink, A., Ganz, P., Leake, B., Leach, G., et al. (1995). Quality-of-life outcomes in men treated for localized prostate cancer. *Journal of the American Medical Association, 213,* 129–135.

Loftus, E. (2002). Memory faults and fixes. *Issues in Science and Technology,* Publication of the National Academies of Science.

Loftus, E. (2003). Our changeable memories. *Nature Review/Neuroscience, 4,* 232–234.

Loftus, E. (2003). Make-believe memories [Electronic version]. *American Psychologist, 58,* 11.

London, M., & Smither, J. W. (1995). Can multi-source feedback change perceptions of goal accomplishment, self-evaluations, and performance-related outcomes? Theory-based applications and directions for research. *Personnel Psychology, 48,* 803–840.

LoPiccolo, J. (1978). Direct treatment of sexual dysfunction. In J. LoPiccolo & L. LoPiccolo (Eds.), *Handbook of sex therapy* (pp. 1–17). New York: Plenum.

LoPiccolo, J., & Friedman, J. (1988). Broad-spectrum treatment of low sexual desire: Integration of cognitive, behavioral, and systemic therapy. In S. R. Leiblum & R. C. Rosen (Eds.), *Sexual desire disorders* (pp. 107–144). New York: Guilford.

LoPiccolo, J., & Heiman, J. (1978). Sexual assessment and history interview. In J. LoPiccolo & L. LoPiccolo (Eds.), *Handbook of sex therapy* (pp. 103–112). New York: Plenum.

LoPiccolo, J., & Lobitz, W. C. (1972). The role of masturbation in the treatment of orgasmic dysfunction. *Archives of Sexual Behavior, 2,* 163–172.

LoPiccolo, J., & Steger, J. C. (1974). The Sexual Interaction Inventory: A new instrument for the assessment of sexual dysfunction. *Archives of Sexual Behavior, 3,* 585–595.

LoPiccolo, J., & Stock, W. E. (1986). Treatment of sexual dysfunctions. *Journal of Consulting & Clinical Psychology, 54,* 158–167.

Loring, M. T., Clark, S., & Frost, C. (1994). A model of therapy for emotionally abused women. *Psychology, A Journal of Human Behavior, 31,* 9–16.

Ludgate, J. (1995). *Maximizing psychotherapeutic gains and preventing relapse in emotionally distressed clients.* Sarasota, FL: Professional Resource.

Lykes, M. B., Brabeck, M. M., Ferns, T., & Radan, A. (1993). Human rights and mental health among Latino American women in situations of state-sponsored violence: Bibliographic resources. *Psychology of Women Quarterly.*

Mackelprang, R., & Salsgiver, R. (1999). *Disability: A diversity model approach in human service practice.* Pacific Grove, CA: Brooks/Cole.

Madanes, C. (1991). Strategic family therapy. In A. S. Gurman & P. D. Kniskern (Eds.), *Handbook of family therapy,* (Vol. 2, pp. 396–416). New York: Brunner/Mazel.

Majerovitz, S. D., & Revenson, R. A. (1994). Sexuality and rheumatic disease: The significance of gender. *Arthritis Care and Research, 7,* 29–34.

Maletzky, B. M. (1980). Assisted covert sensitization. In D. J. Cox & R. J. Daitzman (Eds.), *Exhibitionism: Description, assessment and treatment* (pp. 187–251). New York: Garland.

Maletzky, B. M. (1991a). *Treating the sexual offender.* Newbury Park, CA: Sage.

Maletzky, B. M. (1991b). The use of medroxyprogesterone acetate to assist in the treatment of sexual offenders. *Annals of Sex Research, 4,* 117–129.

Maletzky, B. M. (1997). Exhibitionism: Psychopathology and theory. In D. R. Laws & W. O'Donohue (Eds.), *Sexual Deviance: Assessment and treatment* (pp. 40–74). New York: Guilford.

Maletzky, B. M. (1998). The paraphilias: Research & treatment. In P. Nathan & J. Gorman (Eds.), *A guide to treatments that work* (pp. 472–500). New York: Oxford University Press.

Maltz, W. (2001a). Sex therapy with survivors of sexual abuse. In P. Kleinplatz (Ed.), *New directions in sex therapy: Innovations and alterations* (pp. 258–278). Philadelphia: Brunner-Routledge.

Maltz, W. (2001b). *The sexual healing journey: A guide for survivors of sexual abuse.* New York: HarperCollins.

Manecke, R., & Mulhall, J. (1999). Medical treatment of erectile dysfunction. *Annals of Medicine, 31,* 388–398.

Markman, H. J. (1981). Prediction of marital distress: A 5-year follow-up. *Journal of Consulting & Clinical Psychology, 49,* 760–762.

Markowitz, L. (1993). Understanding the differences. *The Networker,* 50–59.

Marks, G. B., Dunn, S. M., & Woolcock, A. J. (1992). A scale for the measurement of quality of life in adults with asthma. *Journal of Clinical Epidemiology, 45,* 461–472.

Marlatt, G. A., & George, W. H. (1998). Relapse prevention and the maintenance of optimal health. In S. A.

Shumaker, E. B. Schron, & J. K. Ockene (Eds.), *The handbook of health behavior change* (2nd ed., pp. 33–58). New York: Springer.

Marmor, J. (1998). Homosexuality: Is etiology really important? *Journal of Gay and Lesbian Psychotherapy, 2*(4), 19–28.

Marr, L. (1998). *Sexually transmitted diseases.* Baltimore, MD: Johns Hopkins University Press.

Marrs, R., Bloch, L. F., & Silverman, L. L. (1997). *Dr. Richard Marrs fertility book.* New York: Dell.

Maslow, A. (1971). *The farther reaches of human nature.* New York: Viking.

Mason, M. J. (1991). Family therapy as the emerging context for sex therapy. In A. S. Gurman & D. P. Kniskern (Eds.), *Handbook of family therapy* (Vol. 2, pp. 479–507). New York: Brunner/Mazel.

Masters, W. H., & Johnson, V. E. (1966). *Human sexual response.* Boston: Little, Brown.

Masters, W. H., & Johnson, V. E. (1970). *Human sexual inadequacy.* London: Churchill.

Masters, W. H., Johnson, V. E., & Kolodny, R. C. (1986). *Masters and Johnson on sex and human loving.* Boston: Little, Brown.

Masters, W. H., Johnson, V. E., & Kolodny, R. C. (1995). *Human sexuality* (5th ed.). New York: HarperCollins.

McCabe, M. P., & Delaney, S. M. (1992). An evaluation of therapeutic programs for the treatment of secondary inorgasmia in women. *Archives of Sexual Behavior, 21*(1), 69–88.

McCarthy, B. W. (1986). A cognitive-behavioral approach to understanding and treating sexual trauma. *Journal of Sex and Marital Therapy, 17,* 163–182.

McCarthy, B. W. (1989). Cognitive-behavioral strategies and techniques in the treatment of early ejaculation. In S. R. Leiblum & R. C. Rosen, *Principles and practice of sex therapy: Update for the 1990s* (2nd ed., pp. 141–167). New York: Guilford.

McCarthy, B. W. (1993). Relapse prevention strategies and techniques in sex therapy. *Journal of Sex and Marital Therapy, 19*(2), 142–147.

McCarthy, B. W. (1994). Etiology and treatment of early ejaculation. *Journal of Sex and Marital Therapy, 20,* 5–6.

McCarthy, B. W. (1997). Chronic sexual dysfunction: Assessment, intervention, and realistic expectations. *Journal of Sex Education and Therapy, 22,* 51–56.

McCartney, J., Izeman, H., Rogers, D., & Cohen. N. (1987). Sexuality and the institutionalized elderly. *Journal of American Geriatrics Society, 35,* 331–333.

McCary, S. P., & McCary, J. L. (1984). *Human sexuality* (3rd ed.). Belmont, CA: Wadsworth.

McConaghy, N. (1993). *Sexual behavior: Problems and management.* New York: Plenum.

McGoldrick, M., Anderson, C., & Walsh, F. (1989). Women in families and in family therapy. In M. McGoldrick, C. Anderson, & F. Walsh (Eds.), *Women in families:*

A framework for family therapy (pp. 3–15). New York: Norton.

McGoldrick, M., & Gerson, R. (1985). *Genograms in family assessment*. New York: Guilford.

Meana, M., & Binik, Y. M. (1994). Painful coitus: A review of female dyspareunia. *Journal of Nervous and Mental Disease, 182*, 264–272.

Metzger, D. A. (1998). A physician's perspective. In B. Cooper-Hilbert (Ed.), *Infertility and involuntary childlessness: Helping couples cope* (pp. 1–21). New York: Norton.

Meyers, M., Diamond, R., Kezur, D., Scharf, C., Weinshel, M., & Rait, D. S. (1995). An infertility primer for family therapists: Medical, social, and psychological dimensions. *Family Process, 34*, 219–229.

Miller, R. M., Goldman, E., & Bor, R. (1994). Application of a family systems approach to working with people affected by HIV disease. In R. Bor & J. Elford (Eds.), *The family and HIV* (pp. 229–247). New York: Cassell.

Millon, T., Green, C. J., & Meagher, R. B. (1982). A new psychodiagnostic tool for clients in rehabilitation settings: The MBHI. *Rehabilitation Psychology, 27*(1), 23–35.

Milner, J. S., & Dopke, C. A. (1997). Paraphilia not otherwise specified: Psychopathology and theory. In D. R. Laws & W. O'Donohue (Eds.), *Sexual deviance: Theory, assessment, and treatment* (pp. 394–423). New York: Guilford.

Minuchin, S. (1974). *Families and family therapy*. Cambridge, MA: Harvard University Press.

Minuchin, S., & Fishman, H. C. (1981). *Family therapy techniques*. Cambridge, MA: Harvard University Press.

Miret, P. (1995, Autumn). Living together in Great Britain. *Population Trends, 37*–39.

Mohr, J. W., Turner, R. E., & Jerry, M. B. (1964). *Pedophilia and exhibitionism*. Toronto: University of Toronto.

Molica, R. F., & Son, L. (1989). Cultural dimensions in the evaluation and treatment of sexual trauma: An overview. *Psychiatric Clinics of North America, 12*(2), 363–379.

Mona, L. R., & Gardos, P. S. (2000). Disabled sexual partners. In L. T. Szuchman & F. Muscarella (Eds.), *Psychological perspectives on human sexuality* (pp. 309–354). New York: Wiley.

Mona, L. R., Gardos, P. S., & Brown, R. C. (1994). Sexual self-views of women with disabilities: The relationship among age-of-onset, nature of disability, and sexual self-esteem. *Sexuality and Disability, 12*(4), 261–277.

Money, J. (1984). Paraphilias: Phenomenology and classification. *American Journal of Psychotherapy, 38*(2), 154–179.

Monga, T. N., & Kerrigan, A. J. (1997). Cerebrovascular accidents. In M. A. Sipski & C. J. Alexander (Eds.), *Sexual function in people with disability and chronic illness: A health professional's guide* (pp. 189–219). Gaithersburg, MD: Aspen.

Morelli, V., & Naquin, C. (2002). Alternative therapies for traditional disease states: Menopause. *American Family Physicians, 66*, 129–134.

Murphy, W. D. (1990). Assessment and modification of cognitive distortions in sex offenders. In W. L. Marshall, D. R. Laws, & H. E. Barbaree (Eds.), *Handbook of sexual assault: Issues, theories, and treatment of the offender* (pp. 331–342). New York: Plenum.

Murphy, W. D. (1997). Exhibitionism: Psychopathology and theory. In D. R. Laws & W. O'Donohue, *Sexual deviance: Theory, assessment, and treatment* (pp. 22–39). New York: Guilford.

Musher, D. M. (1999). Early syphilis. In K. K. Holmes, P. F. Sparling, P. Mardh, S. M. Lemon, W. E. Stamm, P. Piot, et al. (Eds.), *Sexually transmitted diseases* (3rd ed., pp. 479–485). New York: McGraw-Hill.

National Institute of Allergy and Infectious Diseases. (2003). *Fact sheet: HIV infection and AIDS: An overview*. Retrieved March 2, 2005, from http://www.niaid.nih.gov/factsheets/hivinf.htm

National Institute on Deafness and Other Communication Disorders. (n.d.). *Mission*. Retrieved February 16, 2004, from www.nidch.nih.gov/about/learn/mission.asp.

Nelson, T., Fleuridas, C., & Rosenthal, D. (1986). The evolution of circular questioning: Training family therapists. *Journal of Marital and Family Therapy, 12*, 113–127.

Nichols, H. R., & Molinder, I. (1984). *Multiphasic Sex Inventory manual*. Tacoma, WA: Authors.

Nichols, M. (2000). Therapy with sexual minorities. In S. R. Leiblum & R. C. Rosen (Eds.), *Principles and practice of sex therapy* (3rd ed., pp. 335–365). New York: Guilford.

Nichols, M. P., & Schwartz, R. C. (1991). *Family therapy: Concepts and methods*. Boston, MA: Allyn & Bacon.

Nichols, M. P., & Schwartz, R. C. (2004). *Family therapy: Concepts & methods* (6th ed.). Needham Heights, MA: Allyn & Bacon.

Nichols, W. (1987). *Marital therapy: An integrative approach*. New York: Guilford.

Nichols, W. C. (1995). Treating people in families: An integrative framework. New York: Guilford.

Norcross, J. C., & Newman, C. F. (1992). Psychotherapy integration: Setting the context. In J. C. Norcross & M. R. Goldfried (Eds.), *Handbook of psychotherapy integration* (pp. 3–45). New York: Basic Books.

Nordenberg, J. (2000). Escaping the prison of a past trauma: New treatment for post-traumatic stress disorder. *FDA Consumer, 34*(3), 21–26.

Nosek, M. A., Howland, C. A., Young, M. E., Georgiou, D., Rintala, D. H., Foley, C. C., Bennett, J. L., et al. (1994). Wellness models and sexuality among women with physical disabilities. *Journal of Applied Rehabilitation Counseling, 21*, 50–58.

O'Donohue, W. T., Letourneau, E. J., & Dowling, H. (1997). Development and preliminary validation of a paraphilic sexual fantasy questionnaire. *Sexual Abuse: A Journal of Research and Treatment, 9,* 167–178.

Ogilvie, B., & Daniluk, J. (1995). Common themes in the experience of mother-daughter incest survivors: Implications for counseling. *Journal of Counseling and Development, 73*(6), 598.

O'Hanlon, W. H., & Weiner-Davis, M. (1989). *In search of solutions.* New York: Norton.

Okun, B. F., Fried, J., & Okun, M. L. (1999). *Understanding diversity, a learning-as-practice primer.* Pacific Grove, CA: Brooks/Cole.

O'Leary, K. D., Heyman, R. E., & Jongsma, A. E., Jr. (1998). *The couples psychotherapy treatment planner.* New York: Wiley.

Olson, D. H., & DeFrain, J. (1994). *Marriage and the family: Diversity and strengths.* Mountain View, CA: Mayfield.

Olson, D. J., Fournier, D. G., & Druckman, J. M. (1986). *Counselor's manual for PREPARE-ENRICH* (Rev. ed.). Minneapolis, MN: PREPARE-ENRICH.

Ossana, S. (2000). Relationships and couples counseling. In R. Perez, K. DeBord, & K. Bieschke (Eds.), *Handbook of counseling and psychotherapy with lesbians, gay, and bisexual clients* (pp. 375–402). Washington, DC: American Psychological Association.

Pattatucci, A. (1998). Molecular investigations into complex behavior: Lessons from sexual orientation studies. *Human Biology, 70*(2), 367–386.

Pattatucci, A., & Hamer, D. (1995). Development and familiarity of sexual orientation in females. *Behavioral Genetics, 25,* 407–420.

Pavlov, I. P. (1928). *Lectures on conditional reflexes* (W. H. Grant, Trans.). New York: International Publishers.

Pearlin, L. I. (1994). The study of the oldest-old: Some promises and puzzles. *International Journal of Aging and Human Development, 38,* 91–98.

Penner, C., & Penner, J. (1981). *The gift of sex: A guide to sexual fulfillment.* Nashville, TN: W Publishing.

Perduta-Fulginiti, P. S. (1992). Sexual functioning of women with complete SCI: Nursing implications. *Sexuality and Disability, 10,* 103–118.

Perez, C. A., Fair, W. R., & Ihde, D. C. (1989). Carcinoma of the prostate. In V. T. DeVita, S. Hellman, & S. Rosenburg (Eds.), *Cancer principles and practices in oncology* (3rd ed., pp. 1023–1058). Boston: Jones & Bartlett.

Perri, M. G., Sears, S. F., & Clark, J. E. (1993). Strategies for improving maintenance of weight loss: Toward a continuous care model of obesity management. *Diabetes Care, 14,* 200–209.

Perrin, E. (February, 2002). *Technical report: Co-parent or second-parent adoption by same-sex parents.* Retrieved June 3, 2004, from http://pediatrics.aa publication.org/cgi/content/full/109/2/341

Peterson, K. (2004, July). *Fifty-state rundown on gay marriage laws.* Retrieved July 12, 2004, from http://www.stateline.org

Phillips, N. A. (2000). Female sexual dysfunction: Evaluation and treatment. *American Family Physicians, 62,* 127–136.

Phinney, J. S., Chavira, V., & Williamson, L. (1992). Acculturation attitudes and self-esteem among high school and college students. *Youth and Society, 23,* 299–312.

Piaget, J. (1932). *The moral judgement of the child.* New York: Free Press.

Pieper, B. A. (1998). Perception of diabetes mellitus questionnaire. In C. M. Davis, W. L. Yarber, R. Bauserman, F. Schreer, & S. L. Davis (Eds.), *Handbook of sexuality-related measures* (pp. 176–179). Thousand Oaks, CA: Sage.

Pieper, B. A., & Mikols, C. (1998). Perceived effect of an ostomy. In C. M. Davis, W. L. Yarber, R. Bauserman, F. Schreer, & S. L. Davis (Eds.), *Handbook of sexuality-related measures* (pp. 491–494). Thousand Oaks, CA: Sage.

Piercy, P., & Sprenkle, D. H. (1986). *Family therapy sourcebook.* New York: Guilford.

Pinney, E. M., Gerrard, M., & Denney, N. W. (1987, May). The Pinney sexual satisfaction inventory. *The Journal of Sex Research, 23*(2), 233–251.

Pithers, W. D., Marques, J. K., Gibat, C. C., & Marlatt, G. A. (1983). Relapse prevention with sexual aggressives: A self-control model of treatment and maintenance of change. In J. G. Greer & I. R. Stuart (Eds.), *The sexual aggressor: Current perspectives on treatment* (pp. 214–239). New York: Von Nostrand Reinhold.

Pithers, W. E. (1990). Relapse prevention with sexual aggressors. A method for maintaining therapeutic gain and enhancing external supervision. In W. L. Marshall, D. R. Laws, & H. E. Barbaree (Eds.), *Handbook of sexual assault* (pp. 343–361). New York: Plenum.

Plummer, F. A., Coutinho, R. A., Ngugi, E. N., & Moses, S. (1999). Sex workers and their clients in the epidemiology and control of sexually transmitted diseases. In K. K. Holmes, P. F. Sparling, P. Mardh, S. M. Lemon, W. E. Stamm, P. Piot, et al. (Eds.), *Sexually transmitted diseases* (3rd ed., pp. 143–150). New York: McGraw-Hill.

Polonsky, D. C. (2000). Premature ejaculation. In S. R. Leiblum & R. C. Rosen (Eds.), *Principles and practice of sex therapy* (3rd ed., pp. 305–332). New York: Guilford.

Pope, M., & Barret, B. (2002). Counseling gay men toward an integrated sexuality. In L. Burlew & D. Capuzzi (Eds.), *Sexuality counseling* (pp. 149–175). New York: Nova Science.

Prentky, R., & Edmunds, S. B. (1997). *Assessing sexual abuse: A resource guide for practitioners.* Burlington, VT: Safer Society Press.

Pridal, C. G., & LoPiccolo, J. (2000). Multielement treatment of desire disorders: Integration of cognitive, behavioral, and systemic treatment. In S. R. Leiblum & R. C. Rosen (Eds.), *Principles and practice of sex therapy* (3rd ed., pp. 57–81). New York: Guilford.

Purnine, D. M., Carey, M. P., & Jorgensen, R. S. (1996). The inventory of dyadic heterosexual preferences: Development and psychometric evaluation. *Behaviour Research and Therapy, 34*(4), 375–387.

Quinn, S. (n.d.). *EMDR: A powerful new therapy for healing emotional pain.* Retrieved May 31, 2004, from http://www.selfgrowth.com/articles/quinn4.html

Rankin-Esquer, L. A., Deeter, A., & Taylor, C. B. (2000). Coronary heart disease and couples. In K. B. Schmaling & T. B. Sher (Eds.), *The psychology of couples and illness: Theory, research, and practice* (pp. 43–70). Washington, DC: American Psychological Association.

Rathus, S. A., Nevid, J. S., Fichner-Rathus, L. (2000). *Human sexuality in a world of diversity* (4th ed.). Boston, MA: Allyn & Bacon.

Rayment, S., & Owen, N. (1999, June 17–18). *Working with individuals and families where sibling incest has occurred: The dynamics, dilemmas and practice implications.* Paper presented at the Children and Crime: Victims and Offenders Conferences. Paper retrieved on June 6, 2004, from http://www.sexabuse/sibling.com

Reckler, J. M. (1983). The urologic evaluation of male dyspareunia. In H. S. Kaplan (Ed.), *The evaluation of sexual disorders: Psychological and medical aspects* (pp. 150–154). New York: Brunner/Mazel.

Reinisch, J. M. (1990). *The Kinsey Institute new report on sex: What you must know to be sexually literate.* New York: St. Martin's.

Reiss, S. D., & Heppner, P. P. (1993). Examination of coping resource and family adaptation in mothers and daughters of incestuous versus nonclinical families. *Journal of Counseling Psychology, 40*(1), 100–108.

Rencken, R. (2000). *Brief and extended interventions in sexual abuse.* Alexandria, VA: American Counseling Association.

Robinson, G. E., & Stewart, D. E. (1995). Infertility and new reproductive technologies. *American Psychiatric Press Review of Psychiatry, 14*, 283–306.

Roland, C. (2002). Counseling adult survivors of childhood sexual abuse. In L. Burlew & D. Capuzzi (Eds.), *Sexuality counseling* (pp. 285–306). New York: Nova Science.

Roland, M., & Morris, R. (1983). Development of a reliable and sensitive measure of disability in low back pain. *Spine, 8*, 141–144.

Rolland, J. S. (1994). In sickness and in health: The impact of illness on couples' relationship. *Journal of Marital and Family Therapy, 20*(4), 327–347.

Rosen, E., & Weinstein, E. (1988a). Introduction: Sexuality counseling. In E. Weinstein & E. Rosen (Eds.), *Sexuality counseling: Issues and implications* (pp. 1–15). Pacific Grove, CA: Brooks/Cole.

Rosen, E., & Weinstein, E. (1988b). Sexually transmitted disease counseling. In E. Weinstein & E. Rosen (Eds.), *Sexuality counseling: Issues and implications* (pp. 274–294). Pacific Grove, CA: Brooks/Cole.

Rosen, R. C., Lane, R. M., & Menza, M. (1999). Effects of SSRIs on sexual function: A critical review. *Journal of Clinical Psychopharmacology, 19*(1), 67–85.

Rosen, R. C., & Leiblum, S. R. (1989). Assessment and treatment of desire disorders. In S. R. Leiblum & R. C. Rosen (Eds.), *Principles and practice of sex therapy: Update for the 1990s* (2nd ed., pp. 19–47). New York: Guilford.

Rosenbloom, D., & Williams, M. B. (1999). *Life after trauma: A workbook for healing.* New York: Guilford.

Rosler, A., & Witztum, E. (2000). Pharmacotherapy of paraphilias in the next millennium. *Behavioral Sciences and the Law, 18*, 43–56.

Ross, M. W. (1999). Psychological perspectives on sexuality and sexually transmitted diseases. In K. K. Holmes, P. F. Sparling, P. Mardh, S. M. Lemon, W. E. Stamm, P. Piot, et al. (Eds.), *Sexually transmitted diseases* (3rd ed., pp. 107–113). New York: McGraw-Hill.

Rossi, A. S. (1994). A biopsychosocial approach to human sexuality and reproduction. In A. S. Rossi (Ed.), *Sexuality across the life course* (pp. 3–36). Chicago: University of Chicago Press.

Roughan, P., & Jenkins, A. (1990). A systems-developmental approach to counseling couples with sexual problems. *A.N.Z. Journal of Family Therapy, 2*, 129–139.

Rowe, J., & Kahn, R. (1998). *Successful aging.* New York: Pantheon.

Russell, L. (1990). Sex and couples therapy: A method of treatment to external physical and emotional intimacy. *Journal of Sex and Marital Therapy, 16*(2), 111–119.

Santrock, J. W. (1999). *Life-span development* (7th ed.). Boston, MA: McGraw-Hill.

Sasian—Sibling abuse survivors' information and advocacy network (n.d.). Retrieved June 3, 2004, from http://www.sasian.org

Satir, V. M. (1964). *Cojoint family therapy.* Palo Alto, CA: Science and Behavior Books.

Satir, V. M. (1972). *Peoplemaking.* Palo Alto, CA: Science and Behavior Books.

Satir, V. M. (1983). *Cojoint family therapy* (3rd ed.). Palo Alto, CA: Science and Behavior Books.

Satir, V. M. (1988). *The new peoplemaking.* Mountain View, CA: Science and Behavior Books.

Saunders, B. G., Villerponteaux, L. A., & Lipvsky, J. A. (1992). Child sexual assault as a risk factor for mental disorders among women: A community survey. *Journal of Interpersonal Violence, 7*, 189–204.

Scalzi, C. C. (1982). Sexual counseling and sex therapy for patients with myocardial infarction. *Cardiovascular Nursing, 18*, 13–17.

Schachter, J. (1999). Biology of *chlamydia trachomatis.* In K. K. Holmes, P. F. Sparling, P. Mardh, S. M. Lemon,

W. E. Stamm, P. Piot, et al. (Eds.), *Sexually transmitted diseases* (3rd ed., pp. 391–405). New York: McGraw-Hill.

Schaefer, M. T., & Olson, D. J. (1981). Assessing intimacy: The Pair Inventory. *Journal of Marital and Family Therapy, 7,* 47–60.

Schafran, L. H. (1995, August 26). Rape is still underreported. *The New York Times,* p. A19.

Schain, W. S., d'Angelo, T. M., Dunn, M. E., Lichter, A. S., & Pierce, C. J. (1994). Mastectomy versus conservative surgery and radiation therapy. *Cancer, 72,* 1221–1228.

Schairer, C., Lubin, J., Troisi, R., Sturgeon, S., Brinton, L., & Hoover, R. (2000). Menopausal estrogen and estrogen-progestin replacement therapy and breast cancer risk. *Journal of the American Medical Association, 283,* 485–491.

Scharf, C. N., & Weinshel, M. (2000). Infertility and late-life pregnancies. In P. Papp, *Couples on the fault line: New directions for therapists* (pp. 104–129). New York: Guilford.

Scharff, D. E., & Scharff, J. S. (1987). *Object relations theory and family therapy.* Northvale, NJ: Aronson.

Scharff, D. E., & Scharff, J. S. (1991*). Object relations couples therapy.* Northvale, NJ: Aronson.

Scharff, D. E., & Scharff, J. S. (1997). Object relations couple therapy. *American Journal of Psychotherapy, 51,* 141–173.

Scharff, J. S. (1989). *Foundations of object relations family therapy.* Northvale, NJ: Aronson.

Scharff, J. S. (1995). Psychoanalytic marital therapy. In N. S. Jacobson & A. S. Gurman (Eds.), *Clinical handbook of couple therapy* (pp. 164–193). New York: Guilford.

Scharff, J. S., & de Varela, Y. (2000). Object relations therapy. In F. M. Dattilio & L. J. Bevilacqua (Eds.), *Comparative treatments for relationship dysfunctions* (pp. 81–101). New York: Springer.

Scheinkman, M. (1988). Graduate student marriage: An organization/interactional view. *Family Process, 27,* 351–368.

Schewe, P. A. (1997). Paraphilia not otherwise specified: Assessment and treatment. In D. R. Laws & W. O'Donohue (Eds.), *Sexual deviance: Theory, assessment and treatment* (pp. 424–433). New York: Guilford.

Schiavi, R. C., Schreiner-Engel, P., Mandeli, J., Schanzer, H., & Cohen, E. (1990). Healthy aging and male sexual function. *American Journal of Psychiatry, 147,* 766–771.

Schmaling, K. B., & Afari, N. (2000). Couples coping with respiratory disorders. In K. B. Schmaling & T. B. Sher (Eds.), *The psychology of couples and illness: Theory, research, and practice* (pp. 71–104). Washington, DC: American Psychological Association.

Schmaling, K. B., & Scher, T. G. (2000). Introduction. In K. B. Schmaling & T. B. Sher (Eds.), *The psychology of couples and illness: Theory, research, and practice* (pp. 3–11). Washington, DC: American Psychological Association.

Schnarch, D. M. (1991). *Constructing the sexual crucible: An integration of sexual and marital therapy.* New York: Norton.

Schnarch, D. M. (1995). A family therapy approach to sex therapy and intimacy. In R. H. Mikesell, D. Lusterman, & S. H. McDaniel (Eds.), *Integrating family therapy: Handbook of family psychology and systems theory* (pp. 239–257). Washington, DC: American Psychological Association.

Schnarch, D. (1997). *Passionate marriage.* New York: Holt.

Schnarch, D. M. (2000). Desire problems: A systemic perspective. In S. R. Leiblum & R. C. Rosen (Eds.), *Principles and practice of sex therapy* (3rd ed., pp. 17–56). New York: Guilford.

Schnarch, D. (2002). *Resurrecting sex.* New York: HarperCollins.

Schnarch, D., & Morehouse, R. (2002, September/October). Online sex, dyadic crisis, and pitfalls for MFTs. *Family Therapy Magazine,* 15–19.

Schneider, J. P. (2000). Effects of cybersex addiction on the family: Results of a survey. In A. Cooper (Ed.), *Cybersex: The dark side of the force* (pp. 31–58). Philadelphia: Brunner Routledge.

Schneider, J. P., & Schneider, B. (1991, November). *Sex, lies and forgiveness: Couples speak out on the healing from sexual addiction.* Center City, MN: Hazelden Educational Materials.

Schneider, J. P., & Schneider, B. (1996). Couple recovery from sexual addiction/coaddiction: Results of a survey of 88 marriages. *Sexual Addiction and Compulsivity, 3,* 111–126.

Schover, L. R. (2000). Sexual problems in chronic illness. In S. R. Leiblum & R. C. Rosen (Eds.), *Principles and practice of sex therapy* (3rd ed., pp. 398–422). New York: Guilford.

Schrafan, L. H. (1995, August 1). Rape is still underreported. *The New York Times,* p. 19.

Schwartz, M. F. (1996). Reenactment related to bonding and hypersexuality. *Sexual Addiction and Compulsivity, 3,* 195–212.

Schwartz, M. F., & Masters, W. H. (1983). Conceptual factors in the treatment of paraphilias: A preliminary report. *Journal of Sex & Marital Therapy, 9*(1), 3–18.

Schwartz, R. (1994). *Internal family systems therapy.* New York: Guilford.

Schwartz, R. C. (1999). Narrative therapy expands and contracts family therapy's horizons. *Journal of Marital and Family Therapy, 25,* 263–266.

Schweibert, V. (2002). Counseling women considering abortion. In L. D. Burlew & D. Capuzzi (Eds.), *Sexuality counseling* (pp. 353–372). New York: Nova Science.

Selekman, M. D. (1993). Solution-oriented brief therapy with difficult adolescents. In S. Friedman (Ed.), *The new language of change: Constructive collaborations in psychotherapy* (pp. 138–157). New York: Guilford.

Selvini-Palazzoli, M. (1986). Towards a general model of psychotic games. *Journal of Marital and Family Therapy, 12,* 339–349.

Selvini-Palazzoli, M., Boscolo, L., Cecchin, G., & Prata, G. (1978). *Paradox and counterparadox.* New York: Aronson.

Semans, J. (1956). Premature ejaculation, a new approach. *Southern Medical Journal, 49,* 353–358.

Serovich, J. M. (2000). Helping HIV-positive persons to negotiate the disclosure process to partners, family members, and friends. *Journal of Marital and Family Therapy, 26*(3), 365–372.

Sexuality Information and Education Council of the United States. (1992). Sexuality and disability: A SIECUS annotated bibliography of available print materials. *SIECUS Report, 20*(6), 15–21.

Sgroi, S. M., Bleck, L. C., & Porter, F. S. (1982). A conceptual framework for child sexual abuse. In S. M. Sgroi (Ed.), *Handbook of clinical intervention in child sexual abuse* (pp. 9–38). Lexington, MA: Lexington Books.

Sharf, R. S. (2000). *Theories of psychotherapy & counseling* (2nd ed.). Pacific Grove, CA: Brooks/Cole.

Sharpe, T. H. (2004). Introduction to sexuality in late life. *The Family Journal: Counseling and Therapy for Couples and Families, 12*(2), 199–205.

Sherman, R. (2000). The intimacy genogram. In R. E. Watts & J. Carlson (Eds.), *Techniques in marriage and family counseling* (Vol. 1, pp. 81–84). Alexandria, VA: American Counseling Association.

Sherman, R., Oresky, P., & Rountree, Y. (1991). *Solving problems in couples and family therapy: Techniques and tactics.* New York: Brunner/Mazel.

Siegel, J. (1992). *Repairing intimacy in object relations approach to couples therapy.* Northvale, NJ: Aronson.

Sipski, M. L., & Alexander, C. J. (1997). *Sexual function in people with disability and chronic illness: A health professional's guide.* Gaithersburg, MD: Aspen.

Sipski, M. L., Rosen, R. C., Alexander, C. J., & Hamer, R. J. (2000). Sildenafil effects on cardiovascular responses in women with spinal cord injury. *Urology, 55,* 812–815.

Skinner, B. F. (1953). *Science and human behavior.* New York: Free Press.

Slipp, S. (1988). *The technique and practice of object relations family therapy.* Northvale, NJ: Aronson.

Smith, R. L. (2001). Integrative couple therapy: Beyond theory and practice. In L. Sperry & J. Carlson (Eds.), *Integrative and biopsychosocial therapy: Maximizing treatment outcomes with individuals and couples* (pp. 43–65). Alexandria, VA: American Counseling Association.

Snell, W. E., Jr. (1998). The multidimensional sexual approach questionnaire. In C. M. Davis, W. L. Yarber, R. Bauserman, G. Schreer, & S. L. Davis (Eds.), *Handbook of sexuality-related measures* (pp. 507–509). Thousand Oaks, CA: Sage.

Snyder, M., Simpson, J. A., & Gangestad, S. (1986). Personality and sexual relations. *Journal of Personality and Social Psychology, 51,* 181–190.

Southern, S. (1999). Facilitating sexual health: Intimacy enhancement techniques for sexual dysfunction. *Journal of Mental Health Counseling, 21,* 15–32.

Spanier, G. B., & Filsinger, E. E. (1983). The dyadic adjustment scale. In E. Filsinger (Ed.), *Marriage and family assessment: A sourcebook for family therapy* (pp. 155–169). Beverly Hills, CA: Sage.

Spark, R. F. (1991). *Male sexual health: A couple's guide.* Mount Vernon, NY: Consumer Reports Books.

Sparling, P. F. (1999). Natural history of syphilis. In K. K. Holmes, P. F. Sparling, P. Mardh, S. M. Lemon, W. E. Stamm, P. Piot, et al. (Eds.), *Sexually transmitted diseases* (3rd ed., pp. 473–478). New York: McGraw-Hill.

Spector, I. P., Carey, M. P., & Steinberg, L. (1996). The sexual desire inventory: Development, factor structure, and evidence of reliability. *Journal of Sexual and Marital Therapy, 22*(3), 175–190.

Speroff, L., Glass, R. H., & Kase, N. G. (1994). *Clinical gynecologic endocrinology and infertility* (5th ed). Baltimore: Lippincott Williams & Wilkins.

Sperry, L. (2001). Biopsychosocial therapy with individuals and couples: Integrative theory and interventions. In L. Sperry & J. Carlson (Eds.), *Integrative and biopsychosocial therapy: Maximizing treatment outcomes with individuals and couples* (pp. 67–99). Alexandria, VA: American Counseling Association.

Sperry, L., & Carlson, J. (1991). *Marital therapy: Integrating theory and technique.* Denver, CO: Love Publishing.

Sprecher, S., & Hatfield, E. (1996). Premarital sexual standards among U.S. college students: Comparison with Russian and Japanese college students. *Archives of Sexual Behavior, 25,* 261–288.

Sprecher, S., & McKinney, K. (1993). *Sexuality.* Thousand Oaks, CA: Sage.

Sprei, J., & Courtois, C. (1988). The treatment of women's sexual dysfunctions arising from sexual assault. In R. A. Brown & J. R. Fields (Eds.), *Treatment of sexual problems in individual and couples therapy.* Los Angeles, CA: PMA Publishing.

Stamm, L. V. (1999). Biology of *treponema pallidum.* In K. K. Holmes, P. F. Sparling, P. Mardh, S. M. Lemon, W. E. Stamm, P. Piot, et al. (Eds.), *Sexually transmitted diseases* (3rd ed., pp. 467–472). New York: McGraw-Hill.

Stamm, W. E. (1999). *Chlamydia trachomatis* infections of the adult. In K. K. Holmes, P. F. Sparling, P. Mardh, S. M. Lemon, W. E. Stamm, P. Piot, et al. (Eds.), *Sexually transmitted diseases* (3rd ed., pp. 407–422). New York: McGraw-Hill.

Standards of care for gender identity disorders (2004, May). Retrieved from http://encyclopedia.thefreedictionary.com/standards%20of%20care%20forgender)%201

Stanton, M. D. (1981). An integrated structural strategic approach to family therapy. *Journal of Marital and Family Therapy, 1*, 427–439.

Steege, J. F. (1986). Sexuality functioning in aging women. *Clinical Obstetrics and Gynecology, 29*, 462–469.

Sternberg, R. J. (1986). A triangular theory of love. *Psychological Review, 93*, 119–135.

Sternberg, R. J. (1988). Triangulating love. In R. J. Sternberg & M. L. Barnes (Eds.), *The psychology of love* (pp. 119–138). New Haven, CT: Yale University Press.

Stiffl, B. (1984). Sexuality and the aging. In B. Stiffl (Ed.), *Handbook of gerontological nursing* (pp. 450–464). New York: Von Nostrand Reinhold.

Stitik, T. P., & Benvento, B. T. (1997). Cardiac and pulmonary disease. In M. L. Sipski & C. J. Alexander (Eds.), *Sexual function in people with disability and chronic illness: A health professional's guide* (pp. 305–335). Gaithersburg, MD: Aspen.

Stone, J. D. (1987). Marital and sexual counseling of elderly couples. In G. R. Weeks & L. Hof (Eds.), *Integrating sex and marital therapy: A clinical guide* (pp. 221–244). New York: Brunner/Mazel.

Stone, K. M., Timyan, J., & Thomas, E. L. (1999). Barrier methods for the prevention of sexually transmitted diseases. In K. K. Holmes, P. F. Sparling, P. Mardh, S. M. Lemon, W. E. Stamm, P. Piot, et al. (Eds.), *Sexually transmitted diseases* (3rd ed., pp. 1307–1321). New York: McGraw-Hill.

Strong, B., & DeVault, C. (1994). *Human sexuality*. Mountain View, CA: Mayfield.

Strong, B., DeVault, C., Sayad, B. W., & Yarber, W. L. (2005). *Human sexuality: Diversity in contemporary America* (5th ed.). New York: McGraw-Hill.

Stuart, R. B. (1980). *Helping couples change: A social learning approach to marital therapy*. New York: Guilford.

Swenson, C. H., & Fiore, A. (1982). A scale of marriage problems. In P. A. Keller & L. G. Ritt (Eds.), *Innovations in clinical practice: A source book* (pp. 240–256). Sarasota, FL: Professional Resource Exchange.

Talmadge, L., & Wallace, S. (1991). Reclaiming sexuality in female incest survivors. *Journal of Sex and Marital Therapy, 17*(3), 163–182.

Tannen, D. (1994). *Gender and discourse*. Oxford, England: Oxford University Press.

Taylor, J. F., Rosen, R. C., & Leiblum, S. R. (1994). Self-report assessment of female sexual functioning: Psychometric evaluation of the Brief Index of Sexual Functioning for Women. *Archives of Sexual Behavior, 23*(6), 627–643.

Thompson, C. L., & Rudolph, L. B. (2000). *Counseling children* (5th ed.). Belmont, CA: Wadsworth.

Tilton, M. S. (1997). Diabetes and amputation. In M. L. Sipski & C. J. Alexander (Eds.), *Sexual functioning in people with disability or chronic illness: A health professional's guide* (pp. 279–302). Gaithersburg, MD: Aspen.

Trantham, P. (1996). The infertile couple. *American Family Physicians, 54*, 1001–1010.

Travin, S., & Protter, B. (1993). *Sexual perversion: Integrative treatment approaches for the clinician*. New York: Plenum.

Trudel, F., Turgeon, L., & Piche, L. (2000). Marital and sexual aspects of old age. *Sexual and Relationship Therapy, 15*(4), 381–406.

United Way of Central New Mexico. (2004). *Sibling abuse*. Retrieved June 4, 2004, from www.sasian.org

U.S. Bureau of the Census. (1996). *Statistical Abstract of the United States* (116th ed.). Washington, DC: U.S. Government Printing Office.

U.S. Bureau of the Census. (2000). *Statistical Abstract of the United States 2000*. Washington, DC: U.S. Government Printing Office.

Valentiner, D. P., Foa, E. B., Riggs, D. S., & Gershny, B. S. (1996). Coping strategies and posttraumatic stress disorder in female victims of sexual and non-sexual assault. *Journal of Abnormal Psychology, 105*, 455–458.

Valins, L. (1992). *When a woman's body says no to sex: Understanding and overcoming vaginismus*. New York: Penguin.

Van Der Kolk, B., McFarlane, A., & Van Der Hart, O. (1996). A general approach to treatment of posttraumatic stress disorder. In B. Van Der Kolk, A. McFarlane, & L. Weisaeth (Eds.), *Traumatic Stress* (pp. 417–440). New York: Guilford.

Vanderbilt University. Nashville, Tennessee. *ProjectSafe*. Retrieved May 30, 2004, from http://www.vanderbilt.edu/project/safe/statistic.html

Vaughan, S. M., & Kinnier, R. T. (1996). Psychological effects of a life review intervention for persons with HIV disease. *Journal of Counseling and Development, 75*, 115–123.

Vermeulen, A., & Kaufman, J. M. (1995). Aging of the hypothalamo-pituitary-testicular axis in men. *Hormone Research, 43*(1–3), 25–28.

Vermilyea, E. (2000). *Growing beyond survival*. Baltimore: Sidran Press.

Victims' Rights (n.d.). Retrieved May 30, 2004, from http://www.ojp.usdoj_gov/ovc/nevrw/2003/pg5m.html

Waldman, T. L., & Eliasof, B. (1997). Cancer. In M. L. Sipski & C. J. Alexander (Eds.), *Sexual function in people with disability and chronic illness: A health professional's guide* (pp. 337–354). Gaithersburg, MD: Aspen.

Walker, L. (1994). *Abused women and survivor therapy*. Washington, DC: American Psychological Association.

Walling, M., Andersen, B., & Johnson, S. (1990). Hormonal replacement therapy for postmenopausal women: A review of sexual outcomes and related gynecologic effects. *Archives of Sexual Behavior, 19*, 119–137.

Walters, L. (1987). The wall of silence: Sexuality and the aged. *Advice for Adults with Aging Parents or a Dependent Spouse, 2*, 5–7.

Walters, M., Carter, B., Papp, P., & Silverstein, O. (1989). *The invisible web: Gender patterns in family relationships.* New York: Guilford.

Waring, E. M. (1988). *Enhancing marital intimacy through facilitating cognitive self-disclosure.* New York: Brunner/Mazel.

Watson, J. H. (1914). *Behavior: An introduction to comparative psychology.* New York: Holt.

Watson, J. H. (1919). *Psychology from the standpoint of a behaviorist.* Philadelphia: Lippincott.

Watzlawick, P. A., Beavin, J. H., & Jackson, D. D. (1967). *Pragmatics of human communication.* New York: Norton.

Watzlawick, P. A., Weakland, J. H., & Fisch, R. (1974). *Change: Principles of problem formation and problem resolution.* New York: Norton.

Way, P. O., Schwartlander, B., & Piot, P. (1999). The global epidemiology of HIV and AIDS. In K. K. Holmes, P. F. Sparling, P. Mardh, S. M. Lemon, W. E. Stamm, P. Piot, et al. (Eds.), *Sexually transmitted diseases* (3rd ed., pp. 77–91). New York: McGraw-Hill.

Weakland, J. H. (1960). The "double-bind" hypothesis of schizophrenia and three-party interaction. In D. D. Jackson (Ed.), *The etiology of schizophrenia* (pp. 373–388). New York: Basic Books.

Webster's new collegiate dictionary (10th ed.). (2002). Springfield, MA: Merriam-Webster.

Wedenoja, M. (1999). Persons with psychiatric disabilities. In R. Mackelprang & R. Salsgiver (Eds.), *Disability: A diversity model approach in human service practice* (pp. 167–190). Pacific Grove, CA: Brooks/Cole.

Weeks, G., & Treat, S. (2001). *Couples in treatment: Techniques and approaches for effective practice* (2nd ed.). Philadelphia: Brunner Routledge.

Weingarten, K. (1991). The discourse of intimacy: Adding a social constructionist and feminist view. *Family Process, 30,* 285–305.

Weinstein, E., & Rosen, R. (1988). Sexuality and aging. In E. Weinstein & R. Rosen (Eds.), *Sexuality counseling: Issues and implications* (pp. 81–100). Belmont, CA: Brooks/Cole.

Westheimer, R. K. (2001). *Sex for dummies* (2nd ed.). New York: Hungry Minds.

Wheeler, A. M. (2003). *HIPAA FAQs for Counselors.* Unpublished manuscript.

White, M. (1989). *The externalizing of the problem and the re-authoring of lives and relationships.* Adelaide, Australia: Dulwich Center Publishers.

White, M., & Epston, D. (1990). *Narrative means to therapeutic ends.* New York: Norton.

Whitley, B. E. (1988). The relation of gender-role orientation to sexual experience among college students. *Sex Roles, 19,* 619–638.

Wile, D. (1993). *Couples therapy: A non-traditional approach.* New York: Wiley.

Wilson, J. (n.d.). *Male survivors of incest and sexual child abuse.* Retrieved June 3, 2004, from http://www.theviproom.com/visions/sex_abuse.htm

Wincze, J. P. (1989). Assessment and treatment of atypical sexual behavior. In S. R. Leiblum & R. C. Rosen (Eds.), *Principles and practice of sex therapy* (2nd ed., pp. 382–404). New York: Guilford.

Wincze, J. P. (2000). Assessment and treatment of atypical sexual behavior. In S. R. Leiblum & R. C. Rosen (Eds.), *Principles and practice of sex therapy* (3rd ed., pp. 449–470). New York: Guilford.

Wincze, J. P., & Carey, M. P. (2001). *Sexual dysfunction: A guide for assessment and treatment* (2nd ed.). New York: Guilford.

Winn, R., & Newton, N. (1982). Sexuality in aging: A study of 106 cultures. *Archives of Sexual Behavior, 11,* 282–298.

Wolpe, J. (1958). *Psychotherapy by reciprocal inhibition.* Stanford, CA: Stanford University Press.

Wolpe, J. (1969). *The practice of behavior therapy.* New York: Pergamon.

Worell, J., & Remer, P. (2003). *Feminist perspectives in therapy: Empowering diverse women* (2nd ed.). New York: Wiley.

Working Group on a New View of Women's Sexual Problems (2000, November 15). A new view of women's sexual problems. *Electronic Journal of Human Sexuality.* Retrieved July 6, 2004, from www.ejhs.org

Wylie, M. S. (1998). Secret Lives. *Family Networker, 22*(3), 63–78.

Yarhouse, M. A. (1999). Social cognitive research on the formation and maintenance of stereotypes: Applications to marriage and family therapy working with homosexual clients. *The American Journal of Family Therapy, 27*(2), 149–161.

Young, M. E. (1992). *Counseling methods and techniques: An eclectic approach.* New York: Macmillan.

Young, M. E. (1998). *Learning the art of helping: Building blocks and techniques.* Upper Saddle River, NJ: Prentice Hall.

Young, M. E. (2001). *Learning the art of helping: Building blocks and techniques* (2nd ed.). Upper Saddle River, NJ: Prentice Hall.

Young, M. E., & Long, L. L. (1998). *Counseling and therapy for couples.* Pacific Grove, CA: Brooks/Cole.

Zeiss, A. M., & Kasl-Godley, J. (2001). Sexuality in older adults' relationships. *Generations, 25*(2), 18–25.

Zilbergeld, B. (1979). Sex and serious illness. In C. A. Garfield (Ed.), *Stress and survival: The emotional realities of life-threatening illness* (pp. 236–242). St. Louis: C.F. Mosby.

Zilbergeld, B. (1999). *The new male sexuality: The truth about men, sex, and pleasure* (Rev. ed.). New York: Bantam.

Name Index

Subject Index